City College
NORWICH

Bolivia

written and researched by

James Read

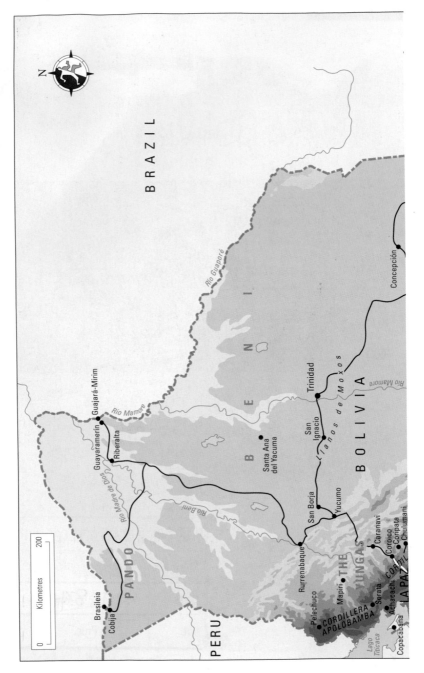

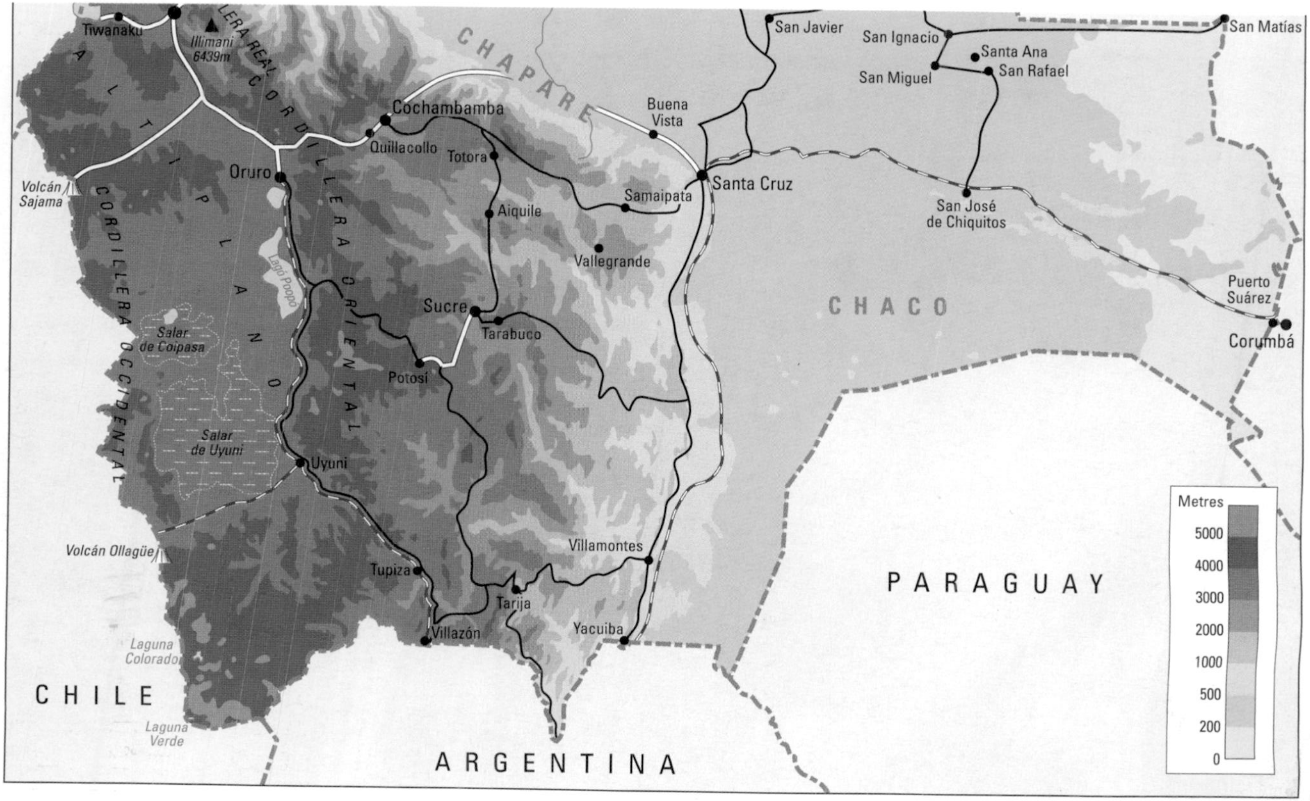
Tiwanaku
Illimani
6439m
CORDILLERA REAL
CHAPARE
Cochambamba
Quillacollo
Totora
Buena
Vista
San Javier
San Ignacio
Santa Ana
San Rafael
San Miguel
San Matías
Oruro
Volcán
Sajama
ALTIPLANO
CORDILLERA OCCIDENTAL
CORDILLERA ORIENTAL
Lagó Poopó
Aiquile
Samaipata
Santa Cruz
San José
de Chiquitos
Vallegrande
Sucre
Tarabuco
Salar
de Coipasa
Potosí
Salar
de Uyuni
Uyuni
CHACO
Puerto
Suárez
Corumbá
Volcán Ollagüe
Villamontes
Tupiza
Tarija
Villazón
Yacuiba
Laguna
Colorado
CHILE
Laguna
Verde
ARGENTINA
PARAGUAY
Metres
5000
4000
3000
2000
1000
500
200
0

Introduction to

Bolivia

Landlocked and isolated at the heart of South America, Bolivia encompasses everything that outsiders find most exotic and mysterious about that continent. Stretching from the majestic icebound peaks and bleak high-altitude deserts of the Andes to the exuberant rainforests and vast savannas of the Amazon basin, it embraces an astonishing range of landscapes and climates. The strangeness and variety of this natural environment are matched by the ethnic and cultural diversity of the country's population: the majority of Bolivians are of indigenous descent, and the strength of Amerindian culture here is perhaps greater than anywhere else in Latin America.

Indeed, to think of Bolivia as part of "Latin" America at all is something of a misconception. Though three centuries of Spanish colonial rule have left their mark on the nation's language, religion and architecture, this European influence is essentially no more than a thin veneer overlying indigenous cultural traditions that stretch back long before the conquest. Though superficially embracing the Catholic religion brought from Spain, many Bolivians are equally at home making offerings to the mountain gods of their ancestors or performing other

v

strange rites, such as blessing motor vehicles with libations of alcohol. And although Spanish is the language of business and government, the streets of the capital buzz with the very different cadences of Aymara, one of more than thirty indigenous languages spoken across the country.

Geographically, Bolivia is dominated by the mighty Andes, the great mountain range that marches through the west of the country in two parallel chains, each studded with snowcapped peaks which soar to heights of over 6000 metres; between these two chains stretches the Altiplano, a bleak and virtually treeless plateau that has historically been home to most of Bolivia's population, and whose barren and windswept expanses are perhaps the best-known image of the country. Northeast of the Altiplano, the Andes plunge abruptly down into the tropical rainforests and savannas of the Amazon lowlands, a seemingly endless wilderness crossed by a series of major rivers that flow north to the Brazilian border and beyond. East of the Altiplano, the Andes march down more gradually through a drier region of fertile highland valleys that give way eventually to the Eastern Lowlands, a vast and sparsely populated plain covered by a variety of ecosystems ranging from dense Amazonian rainforest in the north to the dry thornbrush and scrub of the Chaco to the south.

This immensely varied topography supports an extraordinary diversity of

> Following a diplomatic slight in the nineteenth century, Britain's Queen Victoria supposedly crossed its name from her map and declared, "Bolivia does not exist"

plant and animal life – the Parque Nacional Amboró, for example, is home to over 830 species of bird, more than the US and Canada combined – and new plant species continue to be identified every year. The country's underdevelopment and lack of infrastructure have been a blessing in disguise for the environment, allowing vast wilderness areas to survive in a near-pristine condition and serve as home to a variety of wildlife, ranging from the stately condors that glide above the high Andes to the pink freshwater dolphins that frolic in the rivers of Amazonia.

Though it covers an area the size of France and Spain combined, Bolivia is home to fewer than nine million people, most of whom live in a handful of cities founded by the Spanish. Some of these, such as Potosí and Sucre, were once amongst the most important settlements in the Americas, but are now half-forgotten backwaters, basking in the memory of past glories and graced by some of the finest colonial architecture on the continent. Others, like La Paz and Santa Cruz, have grown enormously in recent decades as a

Fact file

● Named after the South American independence leader **Simón Bolívar**, Bolivia became an independent republic in 1825, following nearly three centuries as a Spanish colony. Since independence, Bolivia has lost almost half its territory, including its Pacific Ocean coast, which was captured by Chile in a war in 1879 – a disaster which left the country entirely landlocked.

● Bolivia has a **population** of around 8.5 million, the great majority of whom are of indigenous descent. Over half speak an indigenous language, principally **Quechua**, the language of the Inca Empire, spoken by a third of the population, and **Aymara**, which is the mother tongue for about a quarter of Bolivia's inhabitants – another thirty or so indigenous languages are spoken by small minorities. Spanish, Quechua and Aymara are all official languages, though in practice **Spanish** remains the language of government.

● Bolivia has enjoyed relatively stable civilian rule, with democratic transitions between presidents since 1982. Historically, though, the country has been a byword for **political instability**. Between 1825 and 1982, Bolivia experienced 188 coups d'état – a statistic that won it a place in the *Guinness Book of Records*. The political and commercial centre of Bolivia is **La Paz**, which has been the seat of government and de facto capital since the end of the nineteenth century. Officially, though, **Sucre** remains the capital, at least in name, and is still home to the Supreme Court.

● Bolivia has long been one of the **poorest** and least developed countries in the western hemisphere. Historically, its economy has depended on mining exports, but these fell into sharp decline in the 1980s. Its main exports today are natural gas and soya.

Llamas and alpacas

Grazing herds of llamas and alpacas are an everyday sight throughout highland Bolivia, above all on the Altiplano. The only major domesticated animals in the Americas before Old World species were introduced, they still play a vital role in the lives of the indigenous communities of the Andes. Llamas, in particular, are able to survive at high altitudes on grasses too tough for sheep or cattle. High in protein and low in fat, the meat of both species is widely eaten, either fresh or in a dried form known as *charque* (the origin of the English word "jerky").

Alpacas produce fine wool that is used to make the warm clothing that is essential to survival in the harsh Andean climate; llama wool is tougher, being used mostly to make ropes and blankets. Llamas also serve as pack animals, though the large llama caravans that used to travel long distances across the Altiplano carrying salt and other goods are now fairly rare. Though similar in appearance, after a while you should find it easy to distinguish between the two species: alpacas have shorter legs, necks and snouts and a thicker, fluffier fleece.

In remote regions you can also see their wild relative, the graceful vicuña. Though population levels have recovered well in recent years, the vicuña is still a highly endangered species, driven to the verge of extinction by hunters seeking its highly prized wool – a wool so fine that in Inca times it was reputedly reserved for the emperor himself.

result of mass migration from the countryside, and are now bustling commercial cities where traditional indigenous cultures collide with modern urban environments.

Given all these attractions, it's perhaps surprising that Bolivia remains one of South America's least-visited countries. This is largely due to its very remoteness and inaccessibility: even from the capitals of neighbouring countries, Bolivia is a distant and peripheral land, cut off by towering mountain chains or endless expanses of forest and swamp. Ignorance, too, plays a part. Following a diplomatic slight in the nineteenth century, Britain's Queen Victoria is said to have ordered the Royal Navy to bombard Bolivia's capital; on learning the country was landlocked and the capital lay high in the mountains, she supposedly crossed its name from her map and declared, "Bolivia does not exist". Bolivians often cite this apocryphal anecdote to illustrate the outside world's lack of knowledge about their country, and not without reason – over a century later, Victoria's mistake was repeated by a US senator, who demanded an aircraft carrier be sent to Bolivia's coast to enforce compliance with the War on Drugs, only to be told that Bolivia didn't have a coastline. Amongst outsiders who have heard something of Bolivia, meanwhile, the country has a reputation for cocaine trafficking, military coups and chronic political instability. But though these clichéd images have some basis in reality, they obscure the fact that Bolivia is one of the safest countries in the region for travellers, and largely free of the violent crime that blights some of its neighbours. In addition, for those who make it here, the fact that Bolivia is not yet on the major tourist routes is an added advantage, since you're unlikely to find yourself sharing the experience with more than a handful of other foreign visitors, whilst local attitudes have yet to be jaded by the impact of mass tourism.

Where to go

ost visitors spend a few days in the fascinating city of **La Paz**, Bolivia's de facto capital, which combines a dramatic high-altitude setting with a compelling intermingling of traditional indigenous and modern urban cultures – this is a city where computer equipment and dried llama foetuses (used to make sacrifices to the mountain gods) are often sold on the same street. La Paz is also close to the magical **Lago Titicaca**, the massive high-altitude lake that straddles the border with Peru, as well as being a good base for trekking, climbing or mountain biking in the **Cordillera Real**, the magnificent range of Andean peaks that runs north of the city.

Just north of La Paz the Andes plunge precipitously down into the Amazon basin through the deep valleys of the **Yungas**, a region of dramatic scenery and sudden transformations in climate and vegetation. The Yungas towns of Coroico and Chulumani are perfect places to relax in relative warmth after the cold of the Altiplano, whilst Coroico also makes a good place to break the overland journey from La Paz to the **Bolivian Amazon**. The best base for visiting the Amazon is the town of Rurrenabaque, close to the near-pristine rainforests of the Parque Nacional Alto Madidi and the wildlife-rich Río Yacuma. More adventurous travellers can head east across the wild savannas of the Llanos de Mojos via the Reserva de la Bíosfera del Beni – another good place to observe wildlife – to the regional capital Trinidad, the start of exciting trips north along the Río Mamoré towards Brazil or south towards Cochabamba.

> The country's underdevelopment has been a blessing in disguise for the environment, allowing vast wilderness areas to survive in a near-pristine condition

South of La Paz, the **southern Altiplano** – the bleak, high plateau which stretches between the eastern and western chains of the Andes – is home to some of Bolivia's foremost attractions. The dour mining city of Oruro is unavoidable as a transport hub but unexciting outside carnival time, when it hosts one of the most colourful folkloric fiestas in all South America. The legendary and tragic city of Potosí, whose silver mines were the source of fabulous wealth and the scene of terrible cruelty in the colonial era, is worth visiting both for its treasure-trove of colonial architecture and for the

opportunity to experience at first hand life underground in the mines of Cerro Rico. Further south, Uyuni is the jumping-off point for expeditions into the astonishing landscapes of the Salar de Uyuni and the Reserva de Fauna Andina Eduardo Avaroa, a remote region of high-altitude deserts and half-frozen, mineral-stained lakes, populated by great flocks of pink flamingos and herds of vicuñas. Further southwest, towards the Argentine border, lie the cactus-strewn badlands and deep canyons around Tupiza and the isolated but welcoming southern city of Tarija.

A few hours north of Potosí by road, Bolivia's official capital, **Sucre**, boasts similarly fine colonial architecture, but is very different in character: a charming and refined city of students and lawyers set in a warm Andean valley in the midst of a region noted for its traditional weaving villages. The market city of **Cochabamba** has less obvious appeal, but enjoys a similar spring-like climate and a warm and friendly outlook that makes it a pleasant place to hang out. Northeast from here are the rainforests and coca fields of the Chapare region, but for most travellers Cochabamba is just somewhere to break the journey between La Paz

Coca: sacred leaf of the Andes

Nothing is more emblematic of Bolivia than coca, the controversial little leaf that has been cultivated for thousands of years in the foothills of the Andes. To ordinary Bolivians, coca is at once a useful stimulant, a medicine, and a sacred gift with magical powers. To the outside world, however, it is infamous as the raw material for the manufacture of cocaine – though few people realize it is also still thought to be a key ingredient of the world's most popular soft drink, Coca-Cola.

You'll find coca on sale in markets across Bolivia. Mixed with an alkaline reagent, it's a mild stimulant chewed throughout the highlands to combat hunger and tiredness; made into a herbal infusion, it's an effective natural remedy for altitude sickness; used in rituals and offerings, it's a key religious and cultural sacrament. Until recently Bolivia was the world's biggest source of the coca used to produce cocaine, and illegal exports were vital to the country's economy. In the last few years, though, under pressure from the US, the Bolivian government has eradicated much of the country's coca crop, despite vociferous protests by the thousands of indigenous farmers who depend on it for their livelihood.

and **Santa Cruz**, the country's eastern capital. Completely different in character to the introspective cities of the highlands, Santa Cruz is a brash, modern and lively tropical metropolis. Though it has little in the way of tourist attractions itself, it makes the best base for exploring the diverse attractions of the **Eastern Lowlands**, including the rainforests of the Parque Nacional Amboró and the idyllic town of Samaipata. Scattered across the forested lowlands east of Santa Cruz, the immaculately restored Jesuit missions of Chiquitos provide one of Bolivia's most unusual attractions, while a train line heads east to the Brazilian border and the wildlife-rich wetlands of the Pantanal. For those with the time or money to spare, Santa Cruz is also the jumping-off point for trips to the remote and beautiful Parque Nacional Noel Kempff Mercado, Bolivia's most spectacular protected area.

When to go

Generally speaking, climate varies much more as a result of altitude and topography – often over very short distances – than it does between different seasons. That said, there are clear-cut seasonal differences. As Bolivia is in the southern hemisphere, **winter** (*invierno*) runs between May and October. This is the **dry season**, and in many ways is the best time to visit Bolivia, though it's also the high season for tourism, so some prices will be higher and attractions busier. In the **highlands** it's noticeably colder at night, particularly in June and July, but though slightly shorter, the days are usually bright and sunny, and the skies crystal clear, making this the best time of year for trekking and climbing.

Generally speaking, climate varies much more as a result of altitude and topography than it does between different seasons

Winter is also the best time for visiting the hot and humid **lowlands**, when temperatures are generally slightly (but pleasantly) lower, although the dry season is less pronounced and rain remains a possibility all year

Average temperatures (°C) and rainfall

	Jan °C Max	Min	Rain Days	Mar °C Max	Min	Rain Days	May °C Max	Min	Rain Days	July °C Max	Min	Rain Days	Sept °C Max	Min	Rain Days	Nov °C Max	Min	Rain Days
La Paz	17	6	114	18	6	66	18	0	13	17	-1	10	18	0	28	19	6	48
Santa Cruz	29	21	180	29	21	130	25	18	94	25	17	58	28	19	62	31	21	135
Sucre	19	11	168	18	12	94	19	11	11	18	8	3	19	9	28	20	12	72

round. A few times a year, usually between July and August, the country is swept by cold fronts coming up from Patagonia, known as *surazos*, which can send temperatures plunging even in the Amazon. Towards the end of the dry season in late August and September, farmers set fire to cleared forest areas across much of Bolivia in a burning season known as the *chaqueo*; during this period heavy smoke can obscure views and cause respiratory problems.

Summer (*verano*) is the **rainy season**, which runs roughly from November to March and is much more pronounced in the lowlands. Rain affects the condition of roads throughout the country, making journey times much longer or blocking roads altogether. In much of the lowlands, particularly the Amazon, road transport becomes pretty much impossible, as huge areas are flooded and everything turns to mud – though, conversely, river transport becomes more frequent. Heat, humidity and mosquitoes are also much worse during the rainy season. In the highlands, particularly the Altiplano, it rains much less and travel is far less restricted, though delays and road closures still occur, while trekking trails get muddier and cloud often obscures views, particularly in the high mountains, where route-finding can become impossible. Despite this, the rainy season is also a very beautiful time in the Andes, as the parched Altiplano and mountainsides are briefly transformed into lush grassland and wild flowers proliferate as the earth comes to life.

things not to miss

It's not possible to see everything that Bolivia has to offer in one trip – and we don't suggest you try. What follows is a selective taste of the country's highlights: outstanding scenery, colourful fiestas, ancient sites and colonial buildings. They're arranged in five colour-coded categories, which you can browse through to find the very best things to see and experience. All highlights have a page reference to take you straight into the guide, where you can find out more.

01 **Oruro Carnival** Page **154** • One of the most colourful fiestas in South America, during which thousands of dancers in extravagant costumes parade through the streets, while revellers indulge in heavy drinking and indiscriminate water fighting.

02 **Mercado de Hechiceria** Page **74** • The most colourful of La Paz's street markets, the Mercado de Hechiceria (Witches' Market) offers a fascinating insight into the secretive world of Aymara mysticism and herbal medicine.

03 **La Paz**
Page **53**
Nestled in a deep canyon at an altitude of over 3500m above sea level, Bolivia's de facto capital is the highest in the world, and a fascinating melting-pot of modern urban and traditional Aymara cultures.

04 **Río Mamoré**
Page **325** • Taking a slow boat down this mighty wilderness river between Trinidad and the Brazilian frontier is the ideal way to experience the lazy pace of life in the Amazon.

05 **Tiwanaku** Page **351** • One of the cradles of Andean civilization, and once the centre of a massive empire, Tiwanaku is now among the most intriguing and monumental archeological sites in South America.

06 **Tinku** Page **189**
Of all the indigenous traditions practised in the Bolivian Andes, perhaps none is as strange – or as bloody – as this form of ritual hand-to-hand combat between rival indigenous communities.

07 **Cordillera Apolobamba**
Page **129** • The remote Cordillera Apolobamba offers some of the most spectacular scenery in Bolivia, and is also home to the Kallawayas – a secretive group of wandering herbalists whose healing abilities are famed throughout the Andes.

08 **Tupiza** Page **201** Explore the dramatic desert landscape of cactus-strewn badlands and canyons around Tupiza, following the trail of the infamous North American outlaws Butch Cassidy and the Sundance Kid.

09 **Chicha cochabambina** Page **238** • It may be an acquired taste, but no visit to the Cochabamba Valley is complete without a glass or two of *chicha*, the thick, tart and mildly alcoholic maize beer that was the sacred drink of the Incas.

10 **Dinosaur footprints** Page **233** • The world's biggest known collection of dinosaur footprints, recently discovered in a cement quarry just outside Sucre.

11 **Mountain climbing** Page **42** • With six peaks over 6000m high and many more over 5000m, Bolivia is a paradise for experienced mountaineers, while even complete novices can arrange a guided climb up the 6090-metre Huayna Potosí.

12 **Pink river dolphins** Page **340** Frolicking pink freshwater dolphins are a fairly common sight in the rivers of the Bolivian Amazon. You can even swim alongside them – if the piranhas and caimans don't put you off.

13 **Folk music and dance** Page **84** • Far more than just panpipes, Bolivian folk music and dance is as vibrant and varied as the country itself – you can catch performances in *peñas* in La Paz and other major cities, and in rural fiestas throughout the country.

14 Isla del Sol Page **115** • Set amidst the azure expanse of Lago Titicaca, the Isla del Sol is the spiritual centre of the Andean world, revered as the place where the Sun and Moon were created and the Inca dynasty was born.

15 Sorata Page **125** • Nestled in a deep valley in the heart of the Cordillera Real, the charming little town of Sorata is the perfect base for trekking in the surrounding mountains.

16 Salteñas Page **33** • Parcels of pastry filled with a rich stew of meat and vegetables, *salteñas* make the ideal mid-morning snack.

17 **Potosí** Page **168** • The highest city in the world, the legendary silver-mining centre of Potosí boasts some of the finest Spanish colonial architecture anywhere on the continent.

18 **Condors** Page **121** • With a wingspan of up to three metres, the mighty Andean condor is a magnificent sight as it glides on the thermal currents above the deep Andean valleys.

19 **Inca trails**
Page **122**
Perhaps the best of Bolivia's innumerable trekking routes, the Choro, Takesi and Yunga Cruz trails – the three so-called "Inca trails" – descend from amidst the icebound peaks of the Cordillera Real into the lush subtropical valleys of the Yungas.

20 **Aymara New Year** Page **92** & **108** • Celebrated at dozens of ancient sites throughout the highlands, the traditional religious ceremonies associated with the Aymara New Year vividly express the deeply seated pre-Christian beliefs still held by many Bolivians.

21 **Andean Textiles** Page **85** The traditional weavings of Bolivia's indigenous highland communities are amongst the finest expressions of Andean culture, with bright colours and intricate designs laden with symbolism.

22 **La Cha'lla** Page **110** • Known as *La Cha'lla*, the ritual blessing of cars and trucks with libations of alcohol, bright streamers and confetti is a bizarre and colourful spectacle, best seen outside the cathedral in Copacabana.

xxi

23 **Feria de Alasitas** Page **75** • Held in La Paz the last week of January, the Feria de Alasitas sees devotees offering miniature replicas of items such as cars, houses and wads of dollar bills to the household god Ekeko, in the hope of receiving the real thing back in exchange.

24 **The world's most dangerous road** Page **137** • Descending more than 3500m over a distance of just 64km, the perilous highway from La Paz to Coroico is amongst the most spectacular roads in the world, plunging from the frozen high Andes down into the lush valleys of the upper Amazon.

25 **Cerro Rico** Page **184** Once a source of fabled wealth, the mines of Cerro Rico now offer the chance to see the almost medieval working conditions endured by indigenous miners prospecting amongst the thousands of mineshafts that honeycomb the mountain.

26 Reserva de Fauna Andina Eduardo Avaroa Page 199

This remote region of high-altitude deserts, icebound volcanic peaks and half-frozen, mineral-stained lakes is home to a surprising array of wildlife, including great flocks of pink flamingos and herds of vicuñas.

27 The Jesuit Missions of Chiquitos Page 291 • The Jesuit mission churches of Chiquitos offer a splash of incongruous splendour in the midst of the wilderness, and a reminder of one of the more unusual episodes in Bolivia's colonial history.

28 Sucre Page 223

Known as the White City, Bolivia's official capital is a jewel of colonial architecture and a lively university city which combines serene dignity with an easy provincial charm.

29 **Salar de Uyuni** Page **193** • A vast, perfectly flat expanse of dazzling white surrounded by high mountain peaks, the Salar de Uyuni is the world's biggest salt lake and perhaps Bolivia's most extraordinary landscape – a truly surreal experience.

30 **Parque Nacional Noel Kempf Mercado** Page **303** • Perhaps Bolivia's finest national park, with abundant wildlife, exuberant Amazonian rainforest and magnificent waterfalls tumbling down from the plateau that inspired Sir Arthur Conan Doyle's *The Lost World*.

contents

Using the Rough Guide

We've tried to make this Rough Guide a good read and easy to use. The book is divided into six main sections, and you should be able to find whatever you want in one of them.

colour section

The front colour section offers a quick tour of Bolivia. The **introduction** aims to give you a feel for the place, with suggestions on where to go. We also tell you what the weather is like and include a basic country fact file. Next, our author rounds up his favourite aspects of Bolivia in the **things not to miss** section – whether it's great scenery, amazing wildlife or a special fiesta. Right after this comes a full **contents** list.

basics

The Basics section covers all the **pre-departure** nitty-gritty to help you plan your trip. This is where to find out which airlines fly to your destination, what paperwork you'll need, what to do about money and insurance, about internet access, food, security, public transport, car rental – in fact just about every piece of **general practical information** you might need.

guide

This is the heart of the Rough Guide, divided into user-friendly chapters, each of which covers a specific region. Every chapter starts with a list of **highlights** and an **introduction** that helps you to decide where to go, depending on your time and budget. Likewise, introductions to the various towns and smaller regions within each chapter should help you plan your itinerary. We start most town accounts with information on arrival and accommodation, followed by a tour of the sights, and finally reviews of places to eat and drink, and details of nightlife. Longer accounts also have a directory of practical listings. Each chapter concludes with **public transport** details for that region.

contexts

Read Contexts to get a deeper understanding of what makes Bolivia tick. We include introductions to Bolivia's history and music, plus a further-reading section that reviews dozens of **books** relating to the country.

language

The **language** section gives useful guidance for speaking Spanish, Bolivian-style, and pulls together all the vocabulary you might need on your trip, including a comprehensive menu reader. Here you'll also find a glossary of words and terms peculiar to the country.

index + small print

Apart from a **full index**, which includes maps as well as places, this section covers publishing information, credits and acknowledgements, and also has our contact details in case you want to send in updates and corrections to the book – or suggestions as to how we might improve it.

Chapter list and map

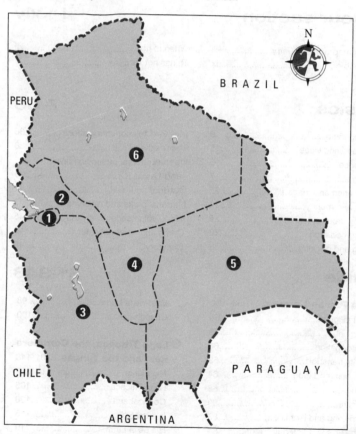

ntents

contents

Chapter list and map

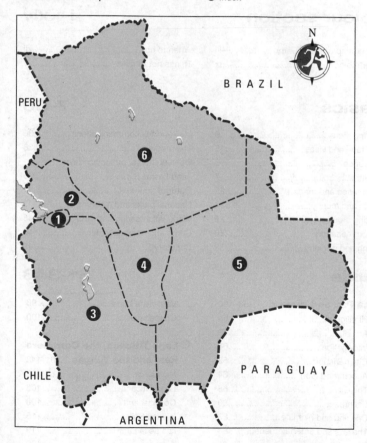

contents

Using the Rough Guide

We've tried to make this Rough Guide a good read and easy to use. The book is divided into six main sections, and you should be able to find whatever you want in one of them.

colour section

The front colour section offers a quick tour of Bolivia. The **introduction** aims to give you a feel for the place, with suggestions on where to go. We also tell you what the weather is like and include a basic country fact file. Next, our author rounds up his favourite aspects of Bolivia in the **things not to miss** section – whether it's great scenery, amazing wildlife or a special fiesta. Right after this comes a full **contents** list.

basics

The Basics section covers all the **pre-departure** nitty-gritty to help you plan your trip. This is where to find out which airlines fly to your destination, what paperwork you'll need, what to do about money and insurance, about internet access, food, security, public transport, car rental – in fact just about every piece of **general practical information** you might need.

guide

This is the heart of the Rough Guide, divided into user-friendly chapters, each of which covers a specific region. Every chapter starts with a list of **highlights** and an **introduction** that helps you to decide where to go, depending on your time and budget. Likewise, introductions to the various towns and smaller regions within each chapter should help you plan your

itinerary. We start most town accounts with information on arrival and accommodation, followed by a tour of the sights, and finally reviews of places to eat and drink, and details of nightlife. Longer accounts also have a directory of practical listings. Each chapter concludes with **public transport** details for that region.

contexts

Read Contexts to get a deeper understanding of what makes Bolivia tick. We include introductions to Bolivia's history and music, plus a further-reading section that reviews dozens of **books** relating to the country.

language

The **language** section gives useful guidance for speaking Spanish, Bolivian-style, and pulls together all the vocabulary you might need on your trip, including a comprehensive menu reader. Here you'll also find a glossary of words and terms peculiar to the country.

index + small print

Apart from a **full index**, which includes maps as well as places, this section covers publishing information, credits and acknowledgements, and also has our contact details in case you want to send in updates and corrections to the book – or suggestions as to how we might improve it.

contexts

350–380

language

381–389

index + small print

391–400

map symbols

maps are listed in the full index using coloured text

▬▬▬	International border		∴	Ruins
▬ ▬ ▬	Chapter division boundary		⊙	Statue
═══	Paved road		∩	Arch
▬▬▬	Unpaved roads		✕	Airport
·············	4WD only roads		★	Transport stop
- - - - -	Footpath		🛖	Lodge
⊪⊪⊪⊪⊪	Steps		🛆	Campground
▬╫▬	Railway		ⓘ	Information office
⊪⊪⊪⊪⊪	Cable car		ⓒ	Telephone
— — -	Ferry route		⊠	Post office
▬▬▬	River		@	Internet access
⧫	General point of interest		▪	Building
▲	Peak		✚	Church
⁄⊪	Volcano		⁺⁺⁺	Cemetery
⁑	Mirador		▨	Park
�	Lighthouse		▭	Marsh
⁂	Hot spring		▭	Salt pan

basics

basics

Getting there

There are relatively few flights to Bolivia. At present, the only direct services to the country depart from Miami in the US and from neighbouring South American countries – the most frequent connections are from São Paulo in Brazil, Buenos Aires in Argentina and Lima in Peru. In Bolivia itself there are just two international airports, one in the capital La Paz and the other in Santa Cruz. The only alternative to flying is to make your way to South America and travel overland – a full rundown of land routes into Boliva is given on p.14.

Airfares to Bolivia reflect the lack of competition, and are comparatively high. Prices depend on the season: high season runs from July to August and during Christmas and Easter; fares drop during the shoulder seasons (May–June & Oct) and even more during low season (Jan–March & Nov to late Dec). Note also that flying at weekends ordinarily adds £12–25/US$20–40 to the round-trip fare; price ranges quoted below assume midweek travel.

You can often cut costs by going through a **specialist flight agent** – either a consolidator, who buys up blocks of tickets from the airlines and sells them at a discount, or a discount agent, who in addition to dealing with discounted flights may also offer special student and youth fares and a range of other travel-related services such as travel insurance and tours. If Bolivia is only one stop on a longer journey, you might want to consider buying a **round-the-world (RTW)** ticket. Some travel agents can sell you an "off-the-shelf" RTW ticket with stopovers in half a dozen cities (unfortunately La Paz isn't on many itineraries, although Lima, São Paulo and Buenos Aires are); others will have to assemble one for you, which can be tailored to your needs, though this is likely to be more expensive. Reckon on around £1500/US$2300 for a RTW ticket including Bolivia or a neighbouring country.

Booking flights online

The websites of many airlines and discount travel agents allow you to book your tickets **online**, cutting out the costs of agents and middlemen. Good deals can often be found through discount or auction sites, as well as through the airlines' own websites.

Online booking agents and general travel sites

Ⓦ **www.cheapflights.com** Flight deals, plus links to travel agents and other travel sites.

Ⓦ **www.cheaptickets.com** Discount flight specialists.

Ⓦ **www.deckchair.com** Bob Geldof's online venture, drawing on a wide range of airlines.

Ⓦ **www.etn.nl/discount.htm** A hub of consolidator and discount agent web links, maintained by the nonprofit European Travel Network.

Ⓦ **www.expedia.com** Discount airfares, all-airline search engine and daily deals.

Ⓦ **www.flyaow.com** Online air travel info and reservations site.

Ⓦ **www.hotwire.com** Bookings from the US only. Last-minute savings of up to forty percent on regular published fares. Travellers must be at least 18 and there are no refunds, transfers or changes allowed. Log-in required.

Ⓦ **www.lastminute.com** Good last-minute holiday package and flight-only deals.

Ⓦ **www.priceline.com** Bookings from the US only. Name-your-own-price website that has deals at around forty percent off standard fares. You cannot specify flight times (although you can specify dates) and tickets are non-refundable, non-transferable and non-changeable.

Ⓦ **www.princeton.edu/Main/air800.html** Extensive list of airline toll-free numbers and websites.

Ⓦ **www.skyauction.com** Bookings from the US only. Auctions tickets and travel packages using a "second bid" scheme. The best strategy is to bid the maximum you're willing to pay, since if you win you'll pay just enough to beat the runner-up regardless of your maximum bid.

Ⓦ **www.smilinjack.com/airlines.htm** Up-to-date airline website addresses

Ⓦ www.travelocity.com Discounted web fares and cheap car hire, accommodation & lodging. Provides access to SABRE, the most comprehensive central reservations system in the US.

Ⓦ www.travelshop.com.au Australian website offering discounted flights, packages, insurance and online bookings.

Ⓦ www.uniquetravel.com.au Australian site with a good range of packages and good-value flights.

Flights from the UK and Ireland

There are no direct flights from Britain or Ireland to Bolivia. The three most direct routes go **via Miami** in the US, via **Buenos Aires** in Argentina or via **São Paulo** in Brazil. Both British Airways and American Airlines fly from London Heathrow to Miami daily – the most convenient routing is with British Airways to Miami (8hr 45min), then with American Airlines to La Paz (6hr 20min). The return fare from London to La Paz starts at £650 in low season, rising to over £800 in high season. There are also daily flights from Miami to La Paz via Santa Cruz on Bolivia's national carrier, Lloyd Aereo Boliviano (LAB).

Flying via a neighbouring country in South America is more expensive. The fastest routings are with Varig or British Airways from Heathrow to La Paz **via São Paulo**; the flight takes around twelve hours, plus a three-hour stopover in São Paulo. British Airways also fly daily to **Buenos Aires**, though at present you'll have to wait eight hours for a connecting LAB flight to Bolivia. Aerolineas Argentinas fly daily to Santa Cruz from Heathrow, although flights go via Madrid and Buenos Aires, a total journey of around 21 hours. It's also possible to fly to Bolivia via Madrid and **Lima or Santiago** with the Spanish airline Iberia and then pick up an onward LAB flight to La Paz or Santa Cruz. All flights via South America cost £600–800 in low season; £700–900 in high season.

If you're coming **from Manchester or Glasgow**, you can get a free transfer to London Heathrow on American Airlines to connect with their daily flight to Miami; flying with British Airways will add £30–50 to the fare. Alternatively, you can fly from Manchester to Miami via Washington with British Midland, or from Glasgow to Miami via Newark with Continental, though both these routes take around thirteen hours.

The most convenient routings **from Ireland** all entail flying back to London. **From Dublin** you can fly to Miami via London Heathrow with American Airlines, or to Miami via London Gatwick with Continental. **From Belfast**, British Midland services to London Heathrow connect with British Airways and American Airlines flights to Miami. Fares from Ireland are around £40–100 more than from London.

Airlines

Aerolineas Argentinas UK ☎020/7494 1001, Ⓦ www.aerolineas.com.ar
American Airlines UK ☎0845/778 9789, Ⓦ www.aa.com
British Airways UK ☎0845/773 3377, Republic of Ireland ☎0141/222 2345, Ⓦ www.britishairways.com
British Midland UK ☎0870/607 0555, Northern Ireland ☎0345/554554, Republic of Ireland ☎01/283 8833, Ⓦ www.flybmi.com
Continental UK ☎0800/776464, Republic of Ireland ☎01/814 5311, Ⓦ www.flycontinental.com
Iberia UK ☎0845/601 2854, Republic of Ireland ☎01/407 3017, Ⓦ www.iberiaairlines.co.uk
Lloyd Aereo Boliviano UK ☎020/7370 7453, Ⓦ www.labairlines.com
Varig ☎0845/603 7601, Ⓦ www.varig.com

Flight and travel agents

Apex Travel Republic of Ireland ☎01/671 5933, Ⓦ www.apextravel.ie. Specialists in flights to the US.
CIE Tours International Republic of Ireland ☎01/703 1888, Ⓦ www.cietours.ie. General flight and tour agent.
Co-op Travel Care Northern Ireland ☎028/9047 1717, Ⓕ028/471 339. Flights and holidays around the world.
Destination Group UK ☎020/7400 7000, Ⓦ www.destination-group.com. Good discount airfares.
Flightbookers UK ☎020/7757 2444, Ⓦ www.ebookers.com. Low fares on an extensive selection of scheduled flights.
Flynow UK ☎020/7835 2000, Ⓦ www.flynow.com. Large range of discounted tickets.
Joe Walsh Tours Republic of Ireland ☎01/872 2555 or 676 3053, Ⓦ www.joewalshtours.ie. General budget fares agent.
Liffey Travel Republic of Ireland ☎01/878 8322 or 878 8063. Package tour specialists.
London Flight Centre UK ☎020/7244 6411, Ⓦ www.topdecktravel.co.uk.

Long-established discount flight agent.

North South Travel UK ☎ 01245/608291, ⓦ www.northsouthtravel.co.uk. Friendly and competitive travel agency offering discounted fares worldwide – profits are used to support projects in the developing world, especially the promotion of sustainable tourism.

Quest Worldwide UK ☎ 020/8547 3322, ⓦ www.questtravel.com. Specialists in RTW discount fares.

STA Travel UK ☎ 0870/160 6070, ⓦ www.statravel.co.uk. Worldwide specialists in low-cost flights and tours for students and under-26s, though other customers are welcome.

Trailfinders UK ☎ 020/7628 7628, Republic of Ireland ☎ 01/677 7888, ⓦ www.trailfinders.com. One of the best-informed and most efficient agents for independent travellers; they also produce a very useful quarterly magazine worth scrutinizing for RTW routes.

Travel Cuts UK ☎ 020/7255 2082, ⓦ www.travelcuts.co.uk. Canadian company specializing in budget, student and youth travel and RTW tickets.

USIT Now Northern Ireland ☎ 028/9032 7111, Republic of Ireland ☎ 01/602 1777 or 677 8117, ⓦ www.usitnow.ie. Student and youth specialists for flights and trains.

Tour operators

Audley Latin America ☎ 01869/276210, ⓦ www.audleytravel.com. Classy tailor-made trips including two- and three-week tours of Bolivia, visiting La Paz, Potosí, Sucre, Santa Cruz and the Salar de Uyuni.

Austral Tours Ltd ☎ 020/7233 5384, ⓦ www.latinamerica.co.uk. Tailor-made tours to South America, plus bird-watching, photography and trekking trips.

Condor Journeys and Adventures ☎ 01422/822068, ⓦ www.condorjourneys-adventures.com. Imaginative ecotourism company with twelve different themed tours, ranging from two to eighteen days and covering most parts of the country.

Exodus ☎ 020/8675 5550, ⓦ www.exodus.co.uk. Adventure-tour operators taking small groups on walking, biking, overland, adventure and cultural trips. Bolivia is included as part of trips in combination with Peru or Chile, or longer South American circuits.

Explore Worldwide ☎ 01252/760000, ⓦ www.exploreworldwide.com. Big range of small-group tours, treks, expeditions and safaris on all continents, staying mostly in small local hotels. The eighteen-day tour of Bolivia includes

both Altiplano and jungle.

Guerba ☎ 01373/858956, ⓦ www.guerba.com. Leading adventure tour agency, with Latin American trips including a week's trekking (with llamas) in the Cordillera Real and a two-week trip through the Inca highlands from La Paz to Lima.

Journey Latin America ☎ 020/8747 3108, ⓦ www.journeylatinamerica.co.uk. Long-established specialists in flights, packages and tailor-made trips to Latin America.

Kumaka Expeditions ☎ 020/7937 8855, ⓦ www.kumaka.com. Tours and overland expeditions using local transport, with Bolivia featured as part of wider South American trips.

Magic of Bolivia ☎ 020/7221 7310, ⓦ www.magicofbolivia.com. Small, friendly company specializing in Bolivia and offering three-week escorted tours and tailor-made trips.

Sherpa Expeditions ☎ 020/8577 2717, ⓦ www.sherpa-walking-holidays.co.uk. Worldwide escorted or self-guided walking and cycling holidays. Their 21-day trip to Bolivia includes a 4WD tour across the Altiplano and Salar de Uyuni, plus six days' trekking in the Cordillera Real.

South American Experience ☎ 020/7976 5511, ⓦ www.southamericanexperience.co.uk. Escorted tours either in combination with Peru or as part of a 21-day "South American Experience" package.

South American Safaris ☎ 020/8767 9136, ⓦ www.southamericansafaris.com. Budget camping trips (3–14 weeks) in purpose-built trucks. Bolivia is included in combination with Peru and other Andean countries.

Travelbag Adventures ☎ 01420/541007, ⓦ www.travelbag-adventures.com. Offer a two-week 4WD trip with trekking to the Bolivian Andes and Chile.

Trips Worldwide ☎ 0117/311 4400, ⓦ www.tripsworldwide.co.uk. Tailor-made trips and escorted two-week highlights tour of Bolivia with car and driver.

Tucan Travel ☎ 020/8742 8612, ⓦ www.tucantravel.com. Latin America specialists with three-week adventure tours and overland camping expeditions to Bolivia and Peru.

Veloso Tours ☎ 020/8762 0616, ⓦ www.veloso.com. Escorted group and individual tours with varying levels of luxury and special interest themes, including two-week Bolivian trips.

Flights from the USA and Canada

Travelling to Bolivia **from the US**, there are direct flights **from Miami** with American Airlines to La Paz and with the national

Bolivian airline Lloyd Aereo Boliviano to Santa Cruz. Both flights take approximately seven hours and cost around US$850 return. There are regular daily flights to Miami from all major US cities. Full-time students and anyone under 26 can take advantage of the excellent deals offered by the student/youth travel agencies, such as Council Travel and STA Travel, listed below; tickets are valid for up to a year. You also qualify for discounted tickets if you're planning to study Spanish in Bolivia, even if you're not a full-time student.

Alternatively, it's possible to fly from other US cities to a South American gateway and then transfer onto a flight to La Paz. United Airlines and Delta fly direct to **São Paulo** from Chicago (10hr) and Atlanta (9hr) respectively. Delta also fly from Atlanta to **Santiago** (9hr 30min), while American Airlines go to Santiago from Dallas (9hr 30min). Continental and LanChile fly to **Lima** from Houston (6hr 30min) and Los Angeles (8hr 30min) respectively, while **Buenos Aires** can be reached from Chicago with United Airlines (11hr 25min); from Atlanta with LAPA (10hr); from Los Angeles with American Airlines (13hr); or from New York with American Airlines (10hr 30min). Tickets to all these destinations cost around US$1000.

Passengers **from Canada** will have to fly via the US and connect with a flight to South America. There are direct flights to to Miami **from Toronto** (3hr 30min) with Air Canada and American Airlines; from any other part of Canada you'll have to change planes at least once in Toronto or the US to reach Miami.

Airlines

Aerolineas Argentinas ☎ 1-800/333-0276, Ⓦ www.aerolineas.com.ar
Air Canada ☎ 1-888/247-2262, Ⓦ www.aircanada.ca
American Airlines ☎ 1-800/433-7300, Ⓦ www.aa.com
British Airways ☎ 1-800/247-9297, Ⓦ www.british-airways.com
Continental domestic ☎ 1-800/523-3273, international ☎ 1-800/231-0856, Ⓦ www.continental.com
Delta domestic ☎ 1-800/221-1212, international ☎ 1-800/241-4141, Ⓦ www.delta.com
LanChile ☎ 1-800/735-5526, Ⓦ www.lanchile.com
LAPA ☎ 0810/777-7274, Ⓦ www.lapa.com

Lloyd Aereo Boliviano ☎ 1800/337-0918, Ⓦ www.labairlines.com
United Airlines domestic ☎ 1-800/241-6522, international ☎ 1-800/538-2929, Ⓦ www.ual.com
Varig ☎ 1-800/468-2744 or 212/682-3100, Ⓦ www.varig.com

Discount travel companies

Air Brokers International ☎ 1-800/883-3273 or 415/397-1383, Ⓦ www.airbrokers.com. Consolidator and specialist in RTW tickets.
Airtech ☎ 212/219-7000, Ⓦ www.airtech.com. Standby seat broker; also deals in consolidator fares.
Council Travel ☎ 1-800/226 8624 or 617/528 2091, Ⓦ www.counciltravel.com. Nationwide organization mostly – but by no means exclusively – specializing in student and budget travel.
Educational Travel Center ☎ 1-800/747-5551 or 608/256 5551, Ⓦ www.edtrav.com. Student/youth discount agent.
High Adventure Travel ☎ 1-800/350-0612 or 415/912-5600, Ⓦ www.airtreks.com. Specialist in RTW tickets; their website features an interactive database that lets you build and price your own itinerary.
Skylink US ☎ 1-800/AIR-ONLY or 212/573-8980, Canada ☎ 1-800/SKY-LINK. Consolidator.
STA Travel ☎ 1-800/777-0112 or 1-800/781-4040, Ⓦ www.sta-travel.com. Worldwide specialists in independent travel; also sell student ID, travel insurance, car rental and rail passes.
TFI Tours International ☎ 1-800/745-8000 or 212/736-1140. Consolidator.
Travac ☎ 1-800/872-8800, Ⓦ www.thetravelsite.com. Consolidator and charter broker.
Travel Avenue ☎ 1-800/333-3335, Ⓦ www.travelavenue.com. Discount travel agent.
Travel Cuts Canada ☎ 1-800/667-2887, US ☎ 416/979-2406. Canadian student-travel organization.
Travelers Advantage Cendant Membership Services, Inc ☎ 1-877/259-2691, Ⓦ www.travelersadvantage.com. Discount travel club; three months' trial membership costs US$1.
Worldtek Travel ☎ 1-800/243-1723, Ⓦ www.worldtek.com. Discount travel agency for worldwide travel.
Worldwide Discount Travel Club ☎ 305/534-2642. Discount travel club.

Tour operators

Abercrombie & Kent ☎ 1-800/323-7308 or 630/954-2944, Ⓦ www.abercrombiekent.com.

Upmarket travel agent offering a twelve-day trip travelling from La Paz to Lima via Lago Titicaca and Cusco.

Adventure Center ☎ 1-800/228-8747 or 510/654-1879, ⓦ www.adventurecenter.com. Hiking and "soft-adventure" specialists with a range of reasonably priced 4WD tours of various lengths visiting Bolivia either on its own or in combination with neighbouring countries.

Adventure Life ☎ 800/344-6118, ⓦ www.adventure-life.com. Small, personal organization with a community focus. Trips include an eleven-day tour of Sucre, Potosí and the Salar de Uyuni, and seven days in the Amazon staying at the Albergue Ecológico Chalalán.

American Adventures/Roadrunner Worldwide Hosteling Treks ☎ 1-800/873-5872, ⓦ www.americanadventures.com. Budget adventure tours with camping or hostel accommodation. Trips include an eleven-day tour from Lima to La Paz or the southern Altiplano.

Andean Treks ☎ 800/683-8148, ⓦ www.andeantreks.com. Camping and trekking tours to Bolivia in conjunction with Peru or Chile, plus a fourteen-day llama-trekking trip through the Cordillera Real.

Elderhostel ☎ 877/426-8056, ⓦ www.elderhostel.org. Non-profit organization specializing in educational and activity programmes for senior travellers (55+). Tours include trips to the Altiplano and Santa Cruz Jesuit missions, with lectures on history and culture, and birdwatching trips.

Explore Bolivia ☎ 877/708-8810, ⓦ www.explorebolivia.com. Bolivian travel experts with an extensive range of activity and nature trips – including white-water rafting on the Río Tuichi, kayaking and mountain biking – with an emphasis on remote places.

Himalayan Travel ☎ 800/225-2380, ⓦ www.himalayantravelinc.com. Adventure trips to Peru and Bolivia with a focus on mountainous landscapes and including imaginative overland tours (from three weeks to two months) along the Andes.

Kon-Tiki Tours ☎ 1-877/566-8454, ⓦ www.kontikitours.com. South American tour operator offering one basic ten-day package of Bolivian highlights, including La Paz, Lago Titicaca, Potosí and Sucre, plus thirty different add-ons, including the Amazon and Salar de Uyuni, as well as mountain biking and mountaineering excursions.

Myths and Mountains ☎ 800/670-6984, www.mythsandmountains.com. Socially responsible cultural tours, including explorations of the medicinal heritage of the Andes and visits to community projects.

Worldwide Adventures ☎ 1-800/387-1483, ⓦ www.worldwidequest.com. Challenging mountain climbing and trekking expeditions in the Cordillera Real.

Flights from Australia and New Zealand

The fastest way to reach South America **from Australasia** is to fly with either Qantas or Aerolineas Argentina from Sydney or Auckland **to Buenos Aires**, from where there are onward services to La Paz (see p.10 for details). The journey takes around sixteen hours and tickets cost approximately A$2000. It's also possible to fly **to Santiago** via Tahiti and Easter Island with Quantas/Lan Chile, but the flight takes 23 hours, with lengthy stopovers.

Flying **from Australia via the US**, the quickest route is from either Sydney or Melbourne via Los Angeles and Miami. The American Airlines' service flies daily, arriving in Miami in time to connect with the American Airlines flight to La Paz. Fares are approximately A$2500. From **New Zealand**, United Airlines fly from Auckland to Los Angeles daily, from where you can pick up a connecting flight to Miami, which arrives in time to connect with the American Airlines' flight to Bolivia.

Airlines

Aerolineas Argentinas Australia ☎ 02/9252 5150 or 1800/222 215, New Zealand ☎ 09/379 3675, ⓦ www.aerolineas.com.au

American Airlines Australia ☎ 1300/650747, New Zealand ☎ 09/309 0735 or 0800/887997, ⓦ www.aa.com

Continental Airlines Australia ☎ 02/9244 2242, New Zealand ☎ 09/308 3350, ⓦ www.flycontinental.com

Lan Chile Australia ☎ 02/9321 9333, New Zealand ☎ 09/912 7435, ⓦ www.lanchile.cl

Qantas Australia ☎ 13/1313, New Zealand ☎ 09/357 8900 or ☎ 0800/808767, ⓦ www.qantas.com.au

United Airlines Australia ☎ 13/1777, New Zealand ☎ 09/379 3800, ⓦ www.ual.com

Travel agents

Anywhere Travel Australia ☎ 02/9663 0411 or 018/401014, ⓔ anywhere@ozemail.com.au

Budget Travel New Zealand ☎09/366 0061 or 0800/808040

Destinations Unlimited New Zealand ☎09/373 4033

Flight Centres Australia ☎02/9235 3522 (for your nearest branch call ☎13/1600), New Zealand ☎09/358 4310, ⓦwww.flightcentre.com.au

Northern Gateway Australia ☎08/8941 1394, ⓔoztravel@norgate.com.au

STA Travel Australia ☎13/1776 or ☎1300/360960, New Zealand ☎09/309 0458 or ☎09/366 6673, ⓦwww.statravel.com.au

Student Uni Travel Australia ☎02/9232 8444, ⓔAustralia@backpackers.net

Thomas Cook Australia ☎13/1771 or ☎1800/801002, New Zealand ☎09/379 3920, ⓦwww.thomascook.com.au

Trailfinders Australia ☎02/9247 7666, ⓦwww.trailfinders.com.au

Usit Beyond New Zealand ☎09/379 4224 or ☎0800/788 336, ⓦwww.usitbeyond.co.nz

Specialist agents

Adventure Associates Australia ☎02/9389 7466 or 1800/222141, ⓦwww.adventureassociates.com. Three-to-five-day tours of Sucre, Potosí and Cochabamba.

Adventure World, Australia ☎02/9956 7766 or 1300/363055, New Zealand ☎09/524 5118, ⓦwww.adventureworld.com.au. Agents for a vast array of international adventure travel companies that operate trips to every continent. Bolivian trips include a nine-day tour (with Peru), with stops in La Paz, Copacabana and the Isla del Sol.

Austral Tours Australia ☎03/9600 1733, ⓦwww.australtours.com. Central and South American specialist with catamaran trips on Lago Titicaca and three-day tours around the Salar de Uyuni.

Australian Andean Adventures Australia ☎02/9235 1889, ⓦwww.andeanadventures.com.au. Trekking specialist, with beginner's mountaineering courses in Bolivia and Peru.

South America Travel Centre Australia ☎1800/655051 or 03/9642 5353, ⓦwww.satc.com.au. Short tours to the Salar de Uyuni, the Yungas and Tarabuco.

Travelling overland from neighbouring countries

You can enter Bolivia **by land** from all five of the countries with which it shares a border. The most widely used and easiest route is

from Puno in **Peru** on the west shore of Lago Titicaca, via the Yunguyo–Kasani border crossing near Copacabana, or via Desaguadero, south of the lake (see p.113); both these crossings are an easy bus ride (3–4hr) from La Paz. It's also possible to enter Bolivia from Puerto Maldonado in Peru, travelling by boat along the Río Madre de Dios, crossing the border at the remote frontier post of Puerto Heath (see p.348). You'll need to get clearance from the authorities in Puerto Maldonado first, and you may get stuck for several days in Puerto Heath, as boats downriver to Riberalta are infrequent.

From **Brazil**, the main entrance point is at Quijjaro (see p.309), in the far east of Bolivia close to the Brazilian city of Corumbá, which is the main base for visiting the Pantanal wetlands and is well connected to the rest of the country. From Quijjaro you can travel to Santa Cruz by train, a journey of around 24 hours. There's another minor land crossing from Brazil in the far east of Bolivia at San Matías, a day's journey by bus from the town of San Ignacio in Chiquitania (see p.299). You can also enter Bolivia from Brazil at several points along the northern border in Amazonia, most notably from Brasiléia to Cobija (see p.347) and Guajarámerim to Guayaramerín.

From **Chile** there are three main routes, all of them passing through spectacular Andean scenery. You can travel to La Paz by bus along the well-paved road from Arica on the Pacific Coast via the border crossing of Tambo Quemado (see p.155); take the twice weekly train from Calama in Chile to Uyuni (see p.193); or cross the border at Laguna Verde in the far south of the Reserva Eduardo Avaroa on a jeep tour organized from the Chilean town of San Pedro de Atacama, a route which will bring you to Uyuni (see p.193).

From **Argentina** there are two straightforward crossings: from La Quiaca in Argentina to Villazón in the southern Altiplano (see p.208), from where there are road and rail connections north to Tupiza, Uyuni and Oruro; and from Pocitos in Argentina to Yacuiba in the Chaco (see p.312), from where you can travel by road and rail north to Santa Cruz or by road west to Tarija. There's also a minor crossing at Bermejo, south of Tarija.

From **Paraguay**, in the dry season (May–Sept) at least, you can enter Bolivia on the arduous two-to-three-day bus journey from Asunción to Santa Cruz along the rough Chaco road (see p.310), which crosses the great wilderness of thornbrush and scrub that separates the two countries.

Red tape and visas

Most visitors to Bolivia do not need a visa, although the situation does change periodically, so always check with your local embassy or consulate a few weeks before travelling. Note, however, that citizens of the Republic of Ireland do need to acquire a visa in advance. This currently costs US$20 (prices vary for other nationalities) and should take two to three working days to process through a Bolivian embassy in a third country.

On arrival, you'll be issued with a **tourist card** (*tarjeta de turismo*) valid for up to ninety days' stay for citizens of the US and most EU countries, and up to thirty days for citizens of Australia, Canada and New Zealand; your passport will also be stamped. Make sure you ask for the full ninety days if you need it and are eligible, as border officials sometimes give only thirty days, particularly at remote border crossings. A thirty-day tourist card can be extended to ninety days at the **migraciones** (immigration offices) in La Paz, Santa Cruz and other major cities; this is free, but usually takes 24 hours. Border officials may ask for evidence that you have enough money to support yourself during your stay, so be prepared to show a credit card or a wad of travellers' cheques; keep cash out of sight, as officials have been known to angle for bribes. Tourist cards, as well as entry and exit stamps, are free of charge.

If you want to **stay on** in Bolivia beyond the ninety-day limit it's best to leave the country overland and return the next day, when you'll be issued with a new tourist card. If you lose your tourist card, go to a *migración* office to get a new one before you try to leave the country – this involves a lengthy bureaucratic procedure, so it's best not to lose your card in the first place. If you overstay, you'll be charged a small fine for each extra day, payable at a *migración* before you try to leave the country. If you're leaving Bolivia by a particularly remote border crossing, you may need to get an exit stamp in advance from the *migración* in the nearest major town. **Under-18s** travelling to Bolivia without their parents need written parental consent authorized by a Bolivian embassy.

Officially you must carry your **passport** with you at all times in Bolivia, but away from border areas it's enough in practice to carry a photocopy of the main page, tourist card and entry stamps to show police or other officials when necessary.

Bolivian embassies and consulates

Australia Level 6, 74 Pitt St, Sydney, NSW 2000 ☎02/9235 1858.
Canada Suite 416, 130 Albert St, Ottawa, Ontario KIP SG4 ☎613/236-5730, ℻613/236-8237.
UK 106 Eaton Square, London SW1W 9AD ☎020/7235 4248 or 6235 2257, ℻020/7235 1286.

US 3014 Massachusetts Ave NW, Washington, DC 20008 ☎202/483-4410 or 483-4411, ℻202/328-3712; Suite 702, 211 East 43rd St, New York, NY 10017 ☎212/499-7401 or 687-0530, ℻212/687-0532, ⊛www.bolivia-usa.org.

Insurance

It's essential to take out an insurance policy before travelling to cover against theft, loss, illness or injury. Before paying for a policy, however, it's worth checking whether you are already covered: some all-risks home insurance policies may cover your possessions when overseas, and many private medical schemes include cover when abroad. In Canada, provincial health plans usually provide partial cover for medical mishaps overseas, while holders of official student/teacher/youth cards in Canada and the US are entitled to meagre accident coverage and hospital in-patient benefits. Students will often find that their student health coverage extends during the vacations and for one term beyond the date of last enrollment.

After exhausting the possibilities above, you might want to contact a specialist travel insurance company, or consider the travel insurance deal offered by Rough Guides (see box). A **typical policy** usually provides cover for the loss of baggage, tickets and – up to a certain limit – cash or cheques, as well as cancellation or curtailment of your journey. Most of them exclude so-called **dangerous sports** unless an extra premium is paid: in Bolivia this can mean white-water rafting, trekking and mountaineering, though probably not kayaking or jeep safaris. Many policies can be chopped and changed to exclude coverage you don't need – for example, sickness and accident benefits can often be excluded or included at will. If you do take **medical coverage**, check whether benefits will be paid as treatment proceeds or only after you return home, and whether there is a 24-hour medical emergency number. When securing **baggage cover**, make sure that the per-article limit – typically under £500 – will cover your most valuable possession. If you need to make a claim, you should keep receipts for medicines and medical treatment; in the event you have anything stolen, you must obtain an official statement (*denuncia*) from the police.

Rough Guides travel insurance

Rough Guides offers its own travel insurance, customized for our readers by a leading UK broker and backed by a Lloyd's underwriter. It's available to anyone, of any nationality and any age, travelling anywhere in the world.

There are two main Rough Guide insurance plans: **Essential**, for basic, no-frills cover; and **Premier** – with more generous and extensive benefits. Alternatively, you can take out **annual multi-trip insurance**, which covers you for any number of trips throughout the year (with a maximum of 60 days for any one trip). Unlike many policies, the Rough Guides schemes are calculated by the day, so if you're travelling for 27 days rather than a month, that's all you pay for. If you intend to be away for the whole year, the Adventurer policy will cover you for 365 days. Each plan can be supplemented with a "Hazardous Activities Premium" if you plan to indulge in sports considered dangerous, such as skiing, scuba-diving or trekking.

For a policy quote, call the Rough Guide Insurance Line on UK freefone ☏0800/015 09 06; US freefone ☏1-866/220 5588 or, if you're calling from elsewhere, ☏+44 1243/621 046. Alternatively, get an online quote or buy online at ⊛ www.roughguides.com/insurance.

Health

Although Bolivia is home to some very unpleasant tropical diseases, you shouldn't get too paranoid about contracting them: most are rare and pose more of a threat to poor locals with limited access to healthcare and clean water. Most serious illnesses can be avoided if you take the necessary precautions and make sure you have the right vaccinations before you go.

If you're planning a long trip it's worth consulting your doctor before you leave, as well as having a dental check up before you go. Take an adequate supply of any prescription medicines you normally use and, if you wear glasses or contact lenses, carry a spare pair and a copy of your prescription.

It's currently recommended that visitors to Bolivia have **immunizations** for hepatitis A, typhoid and yellow fever. Advice can change, however, so check with your doctor or a travel clinic at least two months before travelling so that there's time to have any courses of injections you might need. You should also make sure your polio and tetanus vaccinations and boosters are up to date. In the case of yellow fever, make sure you get an international vaccination certificate: you may have to show this when entering an infected area or arriving in the Bolivian Amazon from Brazil or Peru, and a certificate is always required when travelling overland to Brazil from Bolivia. If you don't have the certificate, you'll have to have an inoculation there and then.

Water and food

Though the **tap water** in some cities and towns is chlorinated, in general it's best to avoid drinking it entirely whilst in Bolivia. **Bottled water**, both mineral and purified, is sold throughout the country, though rarely consumed by Bolivians themselves: check the seals on all bottles are intact, as refilling is not unknown. Soft drinks, tea and coffee are also perfectly safe to drink, and more widely available.

There are several ways of **purifying water** while travelling, whether your source is tap water or a spring or stream. Boiling water for at least ten minutes is effective, though at high altitude water boils at below 100°C, so

you should let it boil for twice as long. Chemical purification with **iodine** (*yodo*) tablets or tincture (available in camping shops at home and at pharmacies in Bolivia) is easier, and generally effective, though not all microbes are eliminated and the resulting taste leaves much to be desired (although you can buy neutralizing powder that improves the taste somewhat, and a squeeze of lemon is also effective). Note that pregnant women, babies and people with thyroid complaints shouldn't use iodine. Portable **water filters** give the most complete treatment, but are fiddly, expensive and relatively heavy to carry.

Almost any kind of **food** served in any kind of restaurant can make you sick – even if the food is clean, the waiters' hands may not be – but you can reduce your chances of contracting a stomach bug by avoiding certain things. Be wary of anything bought from street stalls, and avoid salads, unpasteurized milk and cheese, undercooked or reheated fish or chicken, and anything that's been left lying around where flies can get at it.

However careful you are, the chances are that sooner or later you'll suffer a bout of **diarrhoea**, sometimes accompanied by vomiting and stomach cramps. This is usually caused by contaminated food or water, and there's not much you can do about it except drink plenty of liquid (but not alcohol or caffeine). Herbal teas like coca and camomile (*manzanilla*) can help with stomach cramps, and you should also replace salts either by taking oral rehydration salts or by mixing a teaspoon of salt and eight of sugar in a litre of purified water. "Blocking" drugs like loperimide (Imodium, Lomotil) are useful if you have to keep travelling when suffering from diarrhoea, but they only alleviate the symptoms temporarily and can actually make things worse if you have dysentery. Once you're holding down liquid, eat bland food like rice, soup, and crackers, but avoid spicy, fatty and fried food, dairy products, raw fruit and alcohol until you've recovered.

You should seek medical advice if your diarrhoea contains blood; if it continues for more than five days; if it's accompanied by a high fever (over 39°C); if abdominal pain becomes constant; or if the symptoms continue for more than five days. If your diarrhoea contains blood or mucus, the cause may be either amoebic dysentery, bacterial dysentery or giardia. With a fever, it could be caused by **bacterial dysentery**, which may clear up without treatment. If it doesn't, a course of antibiotics such as ciprofloxacin, tetracycline or ampicillin (consider taking a course of one of these with you if you're going off the beaten track for a while) should do the trick, though they will reduce your natural resistance to future bouts.

Similar symptoms to bacterial dysentery persisting or recurring over a period of weeks could indicate **amoebic dysentery**, which can have serious long-term effects such as liver damage. This can be treated with a course of metronidazole (Flagyl) or tinidazole (Fasigyn), antibiotics that should not be taken with alcohol. Sudden, watery and bad-smelling diarrhoea, accompanied by rotten-egg belches and flatulence is probably **giardia**, which is also treated with metronidazole or tinidazole. You should only take these drugs without consultation if there's no possibility of seeing a doctor. The only sure way to tell what is causing your diarrhoea is to have a **stool test**, which can be arranged by doctors in most towns.

The sun

The sun can be strong in Bolivia, and serious sunburn and sunstroke are real risks. This is particularly true at high altitudes (where the temperature is not that hot but the thin air amplifies the harm done by ultraviolet rays), or when travelling by boat on rivers or lakes (where cool breezes disguise the effects of the sun as it is reflected off the water). Exposure to the sun can also increase your chances of developing skin cancer. Long sleeves and trousers protect your skin from the sun and reduce fluid loss, and you should use a wide-brimmed hat, decent sunglasses to protect your eyes, and a high-factor sunscreen (fifteen or above) on all exposed skin. Sunblock and suntan lotion are available in pharmacies in the main cities, but they're generally expensive, so it's better to bring a supply with you from home. Sunscreen lip-balm is also worth using, particularly in the highlands. Drink plenty of liquid, particularly if you're exercising, to prevent dehydration, and consider adding extra salt to your food to compensate for the effects of excessive sweating.

Altitude sickness

Altitude sickness – known as **soroche** in Bolivia – is a serious and potentially life-threatening illness caused by reduced atmospheric pressure and correspondingly lower oxygen levels at high altitudes. It can affect anyone who normally lives at low altitude and ascends above about 2500m, and thus is a danger across much of Bolivia, including most major cities. You're most likely to be affected if you fly into La Paz from near sea level – the airport is at over 4000m, and almost everyone feels at least a touch of breathlessness. Mild symptoms can include headache, insomnia, breathlessness, nausea, dizziness, loss of appetite, tiredness, rapid heartbeat and vomiting. The best way to avoid this is to ascend slowly, if at all possible, and allow yourself time to acclimatize. Avoiding alcohol and physical exertion and drinking plenty of liquid also help. Bolivians swear by **coca tea** (*mate de coca*) as a remedy, and this is available throughout the country; the prescription-only drug acetazolamide (Diamox) can also help with acclimatization. Normal advice is to ascend no more than 300m a day once over 3000m, so far as possible.

The symptoms of **serious altitude sickness**, also known as **acute mountain sickness**, are usually experienced only over 4000m. In this condition, fluid can build up in the lungs or brain, causing high-altitude pulmonary or cerebral oedema respectively; left untreated, severely affected sufferers can lapse into unconsciousness and die within hours. Symptoms include loss of balance, confusion, intense headache, difficulty breathing and coughing up frothy, blood-stained sputum. Prompt and rapid descent is the only treatment, and you should seek immediate medical help.

Malaria and other insect-borne diseases

Malaria is fairly common in lowland regions of Bolivia, particularly the Amazon, and you should take anti-malaria tablets if you'll be going anywhere below 2500m – the altitude limit of the mosquito that spreads the disease (though it's uncommon over 1500m). Prophylactic treatment usually consists of chloroquine (Avloclor or Nivaquine) combined with proguanil (Paludrine); mefloquine (Lariam) is an alternative, particularly as chloroquine-resistant strains of malaria exist in Bolivia, but some nasty side effects have been reported. Consult your doctor on which drugs to take, and begin the course a week before you leave (two weeks for mefloquine) to ensure effective protection and see if you suffer any allergic reactions. With both treatments, it's crucial that you keep taking the tablets for four weeks after leaving malarial areas. Malaria symptoms include fever, joint pains, loss of appetite and vomiting; if you suspect you've caught the disease, see a doctor and get a blood test. For more information, visit ⓦwww.cdc.gov/travel/regionalmalaria.

The best way to avoid malaria, yellow fever and other diseases spread by mosquitoes is not to get bitten in the first place. Try to wear long sleeves, trousers and socks, and sleep in a screened room or under mosquito netting, preferably treated with a repellent chemical. It's a good idea to put repellent on your skin: make sure it has at least 35 per cent DEET content. It's best to bring this with you from home, as it's hard to come by, expensive and usually of poor quality in Bolivia.

Another insect-borne danger is American trypanosomiasis, better known as **Chagas' disease**. This is spread by the bite of the *vinchuca*, also known as the assassin bug, a small flying beetle found mainly in thatched roofs and adobe walls in rural areas of the Cochabamba, Chuquisaca and Tarija departments up to elevations of about 3000m. The disease is fatal, though usually only after a number of years, and in some rural areas up to 90 percent of the human population are thought to be infected. The bite is usually painful and infection can be detected by a blood test; though the disease does respond to some drug treatments, the best defence is to try to avoid being bitten – if you do have to sleep under a thatched roof in affected regions, use a mosquito net.

Leishmaniasis is a gruesome protozoan disease spread by the bite of the sandfly, common throughout the Bolivian lowlands. The bites enlarge and ulcerate, causing large lesions that over months or years can spread to other parts of the body and eat the cartilage around the nose and mouth. Treatment involves a course of antimony injections, available in some Bolivian hospitals; the only prevention is to avoid getting bitten. Less serious but still unpleasant is the **human botfly**, or *boro*, which lays its eggs on damp clothes or on the proboscis of a mosquito, which then transfers them to human flesh. When the eggs hatch, the larvae burrow under the skin, producing a painful lump as they grow. To remove them, cover with oil or Vaseline to cut off the air supply, then squeeze the larvae out.

Other health hazards

HIV and AIDS (SIDA in Spanish) are not as widespread in Bolivia as in some neighbouring countries such as Brazil, but they are on the increase. Although hospitals and clinics are supposed to use only sterilized equipment, many travellers prefer to take their own sealed hypodermic syringes in case of emergencies. It goes without saying that you should take the same kind of precautions as you would in your own country when having sex. **Condoms** (*condones* or *preservativos*) are available from pharmacies in cities and large towns, but they tend to be expensive and of poor quality, so it's best to bring your own supply. The contraceptive pill is also sold over the counter, but you're unlikely to be able to find the brand you usually take, so again, bring all you need from home.

Bolivia is home to a wide range of **venomous snakes** (*viboras*), some of which can be lethal. Most are more concerned with getting away from you than attacking and, even if they do strike, there's a good chance they won't inject any venom. Wearing boots, watching where you step and put your hands, and making a lot of noise when walking through vegetation all reduce the chances of getting bitten. In the event of a snakebite, keep the victim still and get medical help as quickly as possible. If possible, kill the snake for identification. **Stings and bites** from other creatures such as spiders and scorpions are uncommon but can be very painful or even fatal. It's a good idea to shake out your shoes and clothes before putting them on, and to check your bedclothes and under lavatory seats.

Rabies still exists in Bolivia and people do die from it. If you'll be spending time in remote areas or in contact with animals, it's worth having the vaccine, though all this does is buy you extra time to seek medical treatment. If you do get bitten by a dog, vampire bat or other wild animal, thoroughly clean the wound with soap and water followed by alcohol or iodine and seek urgent medical attention. The only treatment is a series of injections in the stomach, which must be administered as soon as possible; these are available in most Bolivian hospitals.

Hospitals and pharmacies

Generally speaking, the larger the city or town, the better the medical care available is likely to be. In La Paz and Santa Cruz, English-speaking doctors trained overseas are fairly easy to find. Standards decrease rapidly the further you go from the cities, and in rural areas medical facilities are poor to non-existent. If you have a choice, private hospitals and clinics are better staffed and equipped that public ones. Make sure you have adequate health insurance before you leave home, as costs can mount rapidly, and remember to obtain itemized receipts of your treatment so that you can recover your costs.

A traveller's first-aid kit

The following list covers some of the items you might want to carry with you, especially if you're going trekking or travelling in remote rural and wilderness areas.
• Antiseptic cream
• Anti-fungal powder
• Insect repellent
• Sticking plasters
• Anti-blister moleskin (Compeed)
• Lint. sealed bandages and surgical tape
• A course of ciprofloxacin and Fasigyn
• Imodium diarrhoea medicine
• Oral rehydration salts
• Paracetamol or aspirin
• Water-sterilization tablets or iodine tincture
• Sunscreen, lipsalve, sunglasses
• Multivitamins

You'll find **pharmacies** (*farmacias*) in most Bolivian towns; in larger places they operate a rota system, with at least one staying open 24 hours a day. These sell a wide range of familiar drugs and medicines without prescription, so for minor ailments you can usually buy what you need over the counter. For any serious illness, you should go to a doctor or hospital; these are detailed throughout the guide in the relevant city listings. Many Bolivians are too poor to afford modern medical attention, and most make frequent recourse to traditional herbalists, known as *curanderos* – the most famous are the Kallawayas from the Cordillera Apolobamba (see p.131). In addition, the market of every town has a section selling curative plants, herbs and charms for the most common ailments.

Medical resources for travellers

Websites

ⓦ **www.cdc.gov** Comprehensive website publishing outbreak warnings, suggested inoculations and precautions, plus other background information for travellers.

ⓦ **www.fitfortravel.scot.nhs.uk** UK NHS website carrying information about travel-related diseases and how to avoid them.

ⓦ **http://health.yahoo.com** Information on specific diseases and conditions, drugs and herbal remedies, plus advice from health experts.

ⓦ **www.istm.org** The website of the International Society for Travel Medicine, with a full list of clinics specializing in international travel health.

ⓦ **www.medicineplanet.com** Information on immunizations, diseases and risks, plus customized personal travel health recommendations.

ⓦ **www.tmvc.com.au** Contains a list of all Travellers' Medical and Vaccination Centres throughout Australia, New Zealand and Southeast Asia, plus general information on travel health.

ⓦ **www.tripprep.com** Provides a comprehensive database of vaccinations needed for most countries, as well as destination and medical service-provider information.

In the UK and Ireland

British Airways Travel Clinics 28 regional clinics (call ☎01276/685040 for your nearest branch, or visit ⓦwww.britishairways.com), with several in London, including 156 Regent St, London W1 (Mon–Fri 9.30am–5.15pm, Sat 10am–4pm; ☎020/7439 9584; no appointment necessary). All clinics offer vaccinations, tailored advice from an online database and a complete range of travel healthcare products.

Hospital for Tropical Diseases Travel Clinic 2nd floor, Mortimer Market Centre, off Capper St, London WC1E 6AU (Mon–Fri 9am–5pm, by appointment only; ☎020/7388 9600; a consultation costs £15, though this is waived if you have your injections here). A recorded health line (☎09061/337733; 50p per minute) gives hints on hygiene and illness prevention, as well as listing appropriate immunizations.

Malaria Helpline 24-hour recorded message (☎0891/600350; 60p per minute).

MASTA (Medical Advisory Service for Travellers Abroad) Operates prerecorded 24-hour travellers' health lines giving written information tailored to your journey by return of post. UK ☎0906/822 4100 (60p per minute); Republic of Ireland ☎01560/147000 (75p per minute).

Trailfinders Immunization Clinics (no appointment necessary) at 194 Kensington High St, London (Mon–Fri 9am–5pm, Thurs until 6pm, Sat 9.30am–4pm; ☎020/7938 3999). On-the-spot immunizations.

Travel Health Centre, Dept of International Health and Tropical Medicine, Royal College of Surgeons in Ireland, Mercers Medical Centre, Stephen's St Lower, Dublin ☎01/402 2337. Expert pre-trip advice and inoculations.

Travel Medicine Services, PO Box 254, 16 College St, Belfast 1 ☎028/9031 5220. Offers medical advice before a trip and help afterwards in the event of a tropical disease.

In the US and Canada

Canadian Society for International Health Canada ☎613/241-5785, ⊛www.csih.org. Distributes a free pamphlet, *Health Information for*

Canadian Travellers, containing an extensive list of travel health centres in Canada.

Centers for Disease Control US ☎1-877/FYI-TRIP, ⊛www.cdc.gov. Publishes outbreak warnings, suggested inoculations, precautions and other background information for travellers.

International Association for Medical Assistance to Travellers (IAMAT) US ☎716/754-4883, ⊛www.sentex.net/~iamat. A non-profit organization supported by donations, IAMAT can provide a list of English-speaking doctors in Bolivia along with climate charts and leaflets on various diseases and inoculations.

International SOS Assistance US ☎1-800/523-8930, ⊛www.intsos.com. Members receive pre-trip medical referral info, as well as overseas emergency services designed to complement travel insurance coverage.

Travel Medicine US ☎1-800/872-8633, ⊛www.travmed.com. Sells first-aid kits, mosquito netting, water filters, reference books and other health-related travel products.

Travelers Medical Center US ☎212/982-1600. Consultation service on immunizations and treatment of diseases for people travelling to developing countries.

In Australia and New Zealand

Travellers' Medical and Vaccination Centres 27–29 Gilbert Place, Adelaide ☎08/8212 7522; 1/170 Queen St, Auckland ☎09/373 3531; 5/247 Adelaide St, Brisbane ☎07/3221 9066; 147 Armagh St, Christchurch ☎03/379 4000; 270 Sandy Bay Rd, Sandy Bay, Hobart ☎03/6223 7577; 2/393 Little Bourke St, Melbourne ☎03/9602 5788; 5 Mill St, Perth ☎08/9321 1977; 7/428 George St, Sydney ☎02/9221 7133; Shop 15, Grand Arcade, 14–16 Willis St, Wellington ☎04/473 0991.

Information and maps

Bolivia has no official tourist offices abroad, and though you can sometimes get limited tourist information from some of the country's embassies, you'll probably find that tour companies who run trips to Bolivia are a better bet. The internet is another good source of information, and a growing number of websites offer everything on the country from hard facts to trivia and travellers' tales. It's also worth buying a good map of the country to take with you, as these are rarely available in Bolivia itself.

Tourist information

Bolivia has no national tourist offices either abroad or in the country itself. However, most major cities have a **regional tourism office**, either run by the city municipality or by the departmental prefecture. Most of these (La Paz, Oruro, Potosí, Sucre, Cochabamba) are fairly helpful, handing out free leaflets and doing their best to answer questions (though rarely in English). Others (notably Tarija) offer a much more limited service, though you should at least be able to get a plan of the city from them. Local Bolivian **tour operators** are generally a good source of information, and many are happy to answer queries, often in English, though obviously their main aim is to sell you one of their tours. Finally, the best source of information is often **word of mouth** from fellow travellers: recommendations and warnings from people who've just come from where you're heading can be like gold dust.

Maps

No two **maps** of Bolivia are identical, and none is absolutely correct. Most errors are made in the mapping of dirt roads and tracks: some maps mark them incorrectly as proper roads; some miss them out altogether; and many mark roads quite clearly in areas where they have never existed except in the dreams of planners.

That said, you can usually pick up a reasonably good national **road map**, entitled *Bolivia Highlights*, from the municipal tourist office in La Paz (see p.63), and from bookshops and tour agencies in La Paz and other major cities. The best **general map** of Bolivia is the *Travel Map of Bolivia* (1:2,200,000), produced by the US company O'Brien

Cartographics, which you should be able to find at any good map outlet in your home country; you can also buy it online at ⓦ www.boliviaweb.com/maps/travmap.htm. Most good map outlets also sell sectional maps of South America that cover Bolivia reasonably well.

If you're planning to do any **trekking** or **climbing** in the Cordillera Real, O'Brien Cartographics produce an excellent map of that range which you should try to get hold of before you travel. In addition, the Bolivian Instituto Geográfico Militar (IGM) produces maps at a scale of 1:50,000 and 1:250,000 that cover about three-quarters of the country. These are very useful for trekkers or anyone planning to explore more remote areas, and can be bought from the IGM office (Mon–Fri 8am–4pm) in the military headquarters (Estado Mayor) on Avenida Saavedra in the Miraflores district of La Paz. They also sell some good smaller-scale maps covering the whole country.

Map outlets

In the UK and Ireland

Easons Bookshop 40 O'Connell St, Dublin 1 ⓣ 01/873 3811, ⓦ www.eason.ie.
John Smith and Sons 26 Colquhoun Ave, Glasgow G52 4PJ ⓣ 0141/552 3377, ⓦ www.johnsmith.co.uk.
National Map Centre 22–24 Caxton St, London SW1H 0QU ⓣ 020/7222 2466, ⓦ www.mapsnmc.co.uk.
Newcastle Map Centre 55 Grey St, Newcastle upon Tyne NE1 6EF ⓣ 0191/261 5622, ⓦ www.traveller.ltd.uk.
Stanfords (ⓦ www.stanfords.co.uk) 12–14 Long Acre, London WC2E 9LP ⓣ 020/7836 132; c/o British Airways, 156 Regent St, London W1R 5TA

☎020/7434 4744; 29 Corn St, Bristol BS1 1HT ☎0117/929 9966. Maps can be ordered by phone or via @ sales@stanfords.co.uk.
The Travel Bookshop 13–15 Blenheim Crescent, London W11 2EE ☎020/7229 5260, @ www.thetravelbookshop.co.uk.

In the US and Canada

Elliot Bay Book Company, 101 S Main St, Seattle, WA 98104 ☎206/624-6600 or 1-800/962-5311, @ www.elliotbaybook.com.
GORP Adventure Library online only ☎1-800/754-8229, @ www2.gorp.com.
Rand McNally 444 N Michigan Ave, Chicago, IL 60611 ☎312/321-1751; 150 E 52nd St, New York, NY 10022 ☎212/758-7488; 595 Market St, San Francisco, CA 94105 ☎415/777-3131; plus around thirty stores across the US (call ☎1-800/333-0136 ext 2111 or check @ www.randmcnally.com for your nearest store).

Travel Books & Language Center 4437 Wisconsin Ave, Washington, DC 20016 ☎1-800/220-2665, @ www.bookweb.org/bookstore/travellers.
World Wide Books and Maps 1247 Granville St, Vancouver V6Z 1G3 ☎604/687-3320, @ www.worldofmaps.com.

In Australia and New Zealand

The Map Shop 6 Peel St, Adelaide ☎08/8231 2033, @ www.mapshop.net.au.
Mapland 372 Little Bourke St, Melbourne ☎03/9670 4383, @ www.mapland.com.au.
Mapworld 173 Gloucester St, Christchurch ☎03/374 5399, ℱ03/374 5633, @ www.mapworld.co.nz.
Perth Map Centre 1/884 Hay St, Perth ☎08/9322 5733, @ www.perthmap.com.au.
Specialty Maps 46 Albert St, Auckland ☎09/307 2217, @ www.ubd-online.co.nz/maps.

Useful websites

Boliviaweb
@ www.boliviaweb.com. Good general Bolivian site with links to many other Bolivia-related web pages and general background information on subjects such as Bolivian art, history and food.

British Foreign and Commonwealth Office
@ www.fco.gov.uk. Constantly updated advice for travellers on the safety situation in Bolivia, along with some 130 other countries.

Latin America Network Information Center
@ http://lanic.utexas.edu/la/sa/bolivia. An excellent resource, with links to a massive range of Bolivia-related sites divided into themes including art and culture, environment,

government, indigenous peoples and news, as well as other portals, directories and search sites.

South American Explorers Club
@ www.saexplorers.org. Site of the long-established non-profit organization which provides services for scientists, explorers and travellers in South America, with travel advice and warnings, online book and map sales, travellers' bulletin boards, links to other sites, and a range of membership services.

US State Department Travel Advisories
@ http://travel.state.gov/travel_warnings.html. US government website detailing the dangers of travelling in most countries of the world.

Costs and money

The Bolivian currency is the peso boliviano, referred to as both the peso and the boliviano. It's usually written "B/." and is subdivided into 100 centavos. The boliviano has been relatively stable in recent years, devaluing only gradually against the US dollar, though because of the weakness of the Bolivian economy it still remains extremely vulnerable to devaluation, and many businesses in Bolivia effectively operate in US dollars. Tour operators and many hotels quote their prices in US dollars rather than bolivianos, accepting payment in either currency. Otherwise, it's usual to pay for everything in bolivianos – indeed most places won't accept anything else.

Notes come in denominations of 200, 100, 50, 20, 10 and 5 bolivianos; coins in denominations of 1 and 2 bolivianos (these look very similar), and of 5, 10, 20 and 50 centavos. Because of the likelihood of devaluation, prices in this book are quoted in US dollars. At time of writing the exchange rate was roughly B/.6.8 = US$1 (you can check current exchange rates in any Bolivian newspaper).

Costs

Bolivia is one of the least expensive countries in South America, and considerably cheaper than neighbouring Chile, Brazil and Argentina. Imported goods are expensive, but food, accommodation and transport are all relatively cheap, and travellers on a tight budget should be able to get around on US$15–20 per day, staying in basic hotels and eating set meals in local restaurants. For US$30–40 per day you can enjoy more comfortable hotels and good food, take taxis when necessary and go on the occasional guided tour.

The simplest double room with a shared bathroom usually costs about US$5, while more comfortable rooms with private bath go for US$10 and upwards a night. Food costs are also low. The simplest set lunches and evening meals go for about US$1 in cheaper local restaurants and markets; a more substantial set meal in a better quality restaurant might cost US$2–3, and for US$5 or so you can a very good meal almost anywhere in the country.

Public transport is very good value given the distances involved, particularly on busy routes where several different bus companies are competing for passengers – the seven-hour bus journey between La Paz and Cochabamba, for example, costs just US$4–5. The most popular guided tours – into the rainforest or pampas from Rurrenabaque, or around the Salar de Uyuni and Reserva Eduardo Avaroa – cost about US$30 per person per day; good value when you think this includes food, basic accommodation, guide and transport over long distances.

Things are a bit more expensive in larger cities, especially Santa Cruz, and in isolated regions where goods have to be brought in over long distances. Goods and services aimed specifically at foreign tourists tend to be more expensive, and there is sometimes a tendency to slightly overcharge foreigners – if in doubt, always agree a price in advance before accepting a service. Prices in shops and restaurants tend to be fixed, but there is some room for bargaining in markets, when looking for a hotel room or buying a bus ticket – try asking for a reduction (rebaja). There's a limit to this, though. Bolivians don't generally enjoy bargaining for its own sake, and there are few sights more ridiculous than a wealthy gringo haggling vociferously for a tiny discount on an already inexpensive item being sold by a very poor market trader.

Credit cards, travellers' cheques and cash

The best way to carry money in Bolivia is to have your funds in several different formats – a credit card, some travellers' cheques, some cash dollars hidden away for emergencies – so that if one lets you down you can turn to another. The easiest way to access funds is using **plastic**. Banks in all major cities and larger towns are connected to the nationwide Enlace network of **ATMs**, from which you can withdraw cash in US dollars or bolivianos using a credit or debit card – Enlace machines accept both Visa and Mastercard. Other than in the most expensive shops and restaurants (and in some hotels and tour agencies), credit and debit cards can rarely be used to pay for services directly – where they are, Visa is the most widely accepted, followed by Mastercard; American Express cards are rarely used. Be sure to carry the international number to cancel your card in case it's lost or stolen.

Travellers' cheques are a less convenient but very safe way to carry funds. They can be changed in banks and exchange bureaux (casas de cambio) in cities and larger towns, and are also sometimes accepted as payment by hotels and tour companies, though you'll usually be charged a commission of up to five percent. Travellers' cheques should be denominated in US dollars, as no other currency is likely to be accepted, and should be issued by a globally recognized company such as American Express. Make sure you keep the purchase agreement, contact details of the issuing company and a record of the cheques' serial numbers safe and separate from the cheques themselves, so they can be replaced if lost or stolen. Most companies claim to be able to do this within 24 hours.

Outside cities and larger towns, debit and credit cards and travellers' cheques are pretty much useless, so it's important to carry plenty of **cash** with you when you head to rural areas. US dollars can be changed into bolivianos at banks and by street money-changers almost everywhere in the country, and are a good way of carrying emergency back-up funds – even if there are no official money-changers around, you can usually find someone to change dollars at a reasonable rate by asking around in shops or hotels.

Small change is in chronic short supply in Bolivia and people are often reluctant to accept larger-denomination bills, so it's best to break them at every opportunity – in big shops, hotels and bus company offices. You should also be wary of forged notes – dollars and bolivianos – particularly if changing money on the streets.

Wiring money

In emergencies, you can get money **wired** to you from home to a Bolivian bank, though this can take several days and involve a substantial fee. Your home bank will need the address of the bank where you want to pick up the money and the address and telex number of the head office, which will act as the clearing house. In La Paz and Santa Cruz, Western Union (@ www.westernunion .com) can arrange almost simultaneous transfers, though they're not cheap.

Getting around

Bolivia's topography, size and lack of basic infrastructure mean that getting around is often a challenge. Only about five percent of Bolivia's road network is paved – most highways are in a very poor condition and are kept open only through constant labour against floods, landslides and mud, and by the determination, skill and sheer bloody-mindedness of bus and lorry drivers. Despite the difficulties, however, travelling through the country's varied and stunning landscapes is also one of the most enjoyable aspects of a visit to Bolivia, and the pleasure of many places lies as much in the getting there as in the destination itself.

Most Bolivians travel around the country by **bus**, as these go pretty much everywhere

and are extremely good value. When there are no buses, they travel on **camiones** (lorries), which are slower, much less comfortable and only slightly cheaper, but often go to places no other transport reaches. The much-reduced **train** network covers only a small fraction of the country, but offers a generally more comfortable and sedate (though not necessarily faster or more reliable) service. In parts of the Amazon lowlands **river boats** are still the main means of getting around, but only in areas the road network has not reached: moving people and goods by bus or lorry is a lot cheaper than by motorized canoe. Though few Bolivians can afford it, **air travel** is a great way of saving a day or two of arduous cross-country travel, and most of the major cities are served by regular internal flights. The approximate journey times and frequencies of all services are listed in the Travel Details at the end of each chapter, but these should be treated with caution to say the least: the idea of a fixed timetable would strike most Bolivians as rather ridiculous. Buying or hiring a **car** is a possibility, but given the state of the roads in many areas and the long distances between towns, it's an adventurous way to travel and doesn't guarantee you'll reach your destination any faster. For details about **trekking** in Bolivia, see "Outdoor activities", p.41.

By bus

Known as *buses* or *flotas*, Bolivia's **buses** are run by a variety of private companies and ply all the main routes in the country, moving passengers at low cost over great distances despite often appalling road conditions.

Cities and larger towns have **bus terminals** – known as *terminales terrestres* or *terminales de buses* – from which buses to most (but often not all) destinations leave. Departing passengers usually have to pay a small fee for the use of the terminal; you either buy a ticket from a kiosk on the terminal floor or pay an official as you get on the bus.

The terminals usually have some kind of **information** office, but even so the number of different companies operating the same route can make it difficult at times to work out departure times and frequencies. If in doubt, taxi drivers usually have a good grasp of the timing of buses to different destinations and where they depart from. For less

frequently used routes it's worth buying a **ticket** in advance, but there's no need on busier routes: ticket touts will usually hustle you onto the next departing bus or point you in the direction of the company that serves your destination. If you're trying to catch a bus which has started from somewhere else, it's best to flag down and get on anything that's moving in the right direction. Unfortunately, buses on many longer-distance routes travel only at night so Bolivian travellers can visit other cities without paying for accommodation, but it means you miss out on the scenery.

The major long-distance intercity routes are served by more modern and comfortable buses, often equipped with reclining seats and televisions showing Hollywood blockbusters. Fierce competition between companies on these routes keeps prices very low, and last-minute discounts are often available. Some routes are also served by comparatively luxurious overnight **sleeper buses** (*bus-camas*), which have extra legroom and seats that recline to the horizontal. These cost about fifty percent more, but are well worth it.

Most buses, however, are much older and in poor condition, with broken windows, bald tyres and dodgy engines. Where there are several different companies it's worth having a look at their vehicles and going with whichever one appears to have the most modern models. Breakdowns are frequent, but fortunately many drivers are masters of mechanical improvisation. More local routes are served by smaller buses and minibuses known as **micros**; on some you also have the choice of travelling in **collective taxis**, which charge slightly more but are faster, more comfortable and depart with greater frequency. Other than sleeper-buses and some more upmarket long-distance services, Bolivian buses stop anywhere for anyone, even if they're only travelling a few miles, until every available crack of space has been filled with people, luggage and livestock – and even then the driver's assistant will insist there's still room for one more passenger.

Because of the poor conditions of most roads and many vehicles, **journey times** are unpredictable, and you should always be prepared for major delays. In the rainy season, buses can arrive days rather than hours late, and travelling with a tight schedule is a recipe for disappointment. Most buses stop for regular meal breaks (often with infuriating frequency), and food and drink sellers offer their wares at the roadside at every opportunity, but given the unpredictability of travel it's worth carrying some food and drink with you. When travelling in the highlands, you should have warm clothing to hand: even if it's hot at the start of your journey, you may climb over high passes where temperatures are much lower. If travelling by night, keep a blanket or sleeping bag and woollen hat to hand, as it can get bitterly cold and heated buses are virtually unheard of. If you can, avoid sitting at the back of the bus, as on bumpy roads (which is virtually all of them) this is where you'll get bounced around the most.

Unless it's small enough to keep with you inside the bus, your **luggage** will be put on the roof, at the back or in a locked compartment underneath the vehicle. This is usually pretty safe, but it's still worth keeping an eye out at each stop to make sure your bag isn't carried off, whether by accident or design. With better-organized companies you may be given a ticket with which to reclaim your luggage at the end of the journey, which also entitles you to minor compensation if your bags are lost or carried off by another passenger. Some travellers like to chain their bags to the roof, and you shouldn't be shy about climbing up to check yours if you're feeling nervous about its security. Even if it's under a tarpaulin on the roof or in a luggage compartment, it's a good idea to cover your luggage with a nylon sack (which you can pick up in any market) to protect it from dust, rain, engine oil and the prying fingers of other travellers.

By lorry

The heavy-goods **lorries** (*camiones*) are the other mainstay of Bolivian land transport, and sometimes the only option in remote or little visited regions. Most carry passengers to supplement their income from carrying goods, and some passengers actually prefer them because they're cheaper and have room for lots of luggage. On a good day, travelling in the back of an open-top truck with the wind in your face and 360° views is a fantastic experience – for the first hour at least. After that the dust, hard wooden seats (when there are any seats at all), exposure to

the elements and extremely bumpy ride start to take their toll. Lorries are also slower and generally more dangerous than buses, and stop more frequently. Still, travelling by lorry is a quintessential Bolivian experience.

The best place to find a lorry is around any town's market areas or at the police checkpoints (*trancas*) at the edge of town; most also stop for passengers who flag them down at the side of the road. This is the closest you'll get to **hitching** in Bolivia, and you will always be expected to pay something for the ride; private cars are few and far between outside towns and rarely pick up hitchers, and in any case hitching a lift in them is risky. For shorter journeys in remote areas, smaller pick-up trucks, known as **camionetas**, also carry passengers; these share the same drawbacks and pleasures as *camiones*, but are slightly faster and less bumpy.

By taxi, moto-taxi and micro

Taxis can be found anywhere at any time in almost any town and offer a cheap and safe way to get around. In Bolivia, anyone can turn their car into a taxi just by sticking a sign in the window, and many people in cities work as part-time taxi drivers to supplement their incomes. There are also **radio-taxis**, which are marked as such and can be called by phone; they tend to cost a little more.

Fares tend to be fixed in each city or town. A trip within any city centre will rarely cost more than US$1, though there's an occasional tendency to overcharge foreigners, so it's best to agree a price before you set off. Often, fares are charged per passenger rather than for the vehicle as a whole, and it's not unusual to share a taxi with strangers heading in the same general direction. You can also hire taxis by the day or half-day to go sightseeing; with a little bargaining this can actually be an inexpensive way of seeing a lot in a short time, especially if the cost is shared between several passengers.

As the name suggests, **moto-taxis** are motorcycles used as taxis, and are most frequently found in remote cities and towns in the lowlands. In cities like Trinidad, they're by far the most common form of transport. As a passenger you ride pillion on the back, with your backpack on or sitting in front of the driver on the gas tank. Travelling this way is cheap, fast and only slightly frightening. Most moto-taxi drivers are happy to rent their machines out for about US$1.50 an hour if you leave your passport as a deposit.

Micros are small Japanese-made minibuses that have almost completely replaced larger buses as the main form of urban public transport in Bolivia. A trip in a micro costs a boliviano or less, and they run with great frequency along fixed routes with their major destinations written on placards on the windscreen and shouted out by the driver's assistant – usually a small child. With extra seats fitted in their already small interiors, they're pretty cramped; if you need extra leg room, try to sit in the front seat next to the driver. Large estate cars – referred to as **trufis** or **colectivos** –are sometimes used in place of *micros*.

By train

Once a proud symbol of the country's tin-fuelled march to modernity, Bolivia's **railway** network, like the mining industry that spawned it, is now a shadow of its former self. There's occasional talk of reopening the line from La Paz to Oruro and to Arica on the Pacific coast of Chile, and also of reviving the Sucre to Potosí line, but for the moment only two networks still function, each run by a different private company. The **Ferrocarril Occidental** runs passenger trains from Oruro south across the Altiplano via Uyuni and Tupiza to Villazón on the Argentine border (see p.207). From Uyuni, another line, served once a week, runs southeast to Calama in Chile. The scenery on both these Altiplano routes is magnificent.

The **Ferrocarril Oriental** runs two lines: one from Santa Cruz east to the Brazilian border at Quijjaro; the other from Santa Cruz south to Yacuiba in the Chaco on the Argentine border. Trains on both these long routes are slow and unreliable, and the lowlands scenery is monotonous: the Santa Cruz to Quijarro route is known as the "Train of Death", not because it's dangerous but because it's such a boring ride.

By plane

Flying in Bolivia is a good way of avoiding exhausting overland journeys and saving

time; it's also relatively inexpensive, with most internal flights costing US$40–100, and offers splendid bird's-eye views of the high Andes or the endless green expanse of the Amazon. La Paz, Santa Cruz, Sucre and Cochabamba are all connected by daily flights, and there are also frequent services to Tarija, Trinidad, and a number of remote towns in the Amazon and the eastern lowlands, some of which are inaccessible by road for much of the year.

There are two main commercial carriers, **Lloyd Aéreo Boliviano** (🌐www.labairlines .com) and **AeroSur** (🌐www.aerosur.com). The Bolivian air force also operates passenger services under its commercial arm **Transportes Aereo Militar** (TAM). TAM is almost as reliable and somewhat cheaper than the two commercial airlines, and flies to some out-of-the-way places not served by the others (including, crucially, Rurrenabaque), as well as between most of the main cities. All three airlines have offices in the cities they serve, though you can also buy tickets from almost any travel agency for only a small extra charge, which is often faster and more convenient (especially in La Paz). The busier routes should be booked at least several days in advance, and it's important to reconfirm a couple of days before departure, as overbooking is not uncommon. Flights are often cancelled or delayed, and sometimes even leave earlier than scheduled, especially in the Amazon, where the weather can be a problem. If passengers haven't shown up twenty minutes or so before departure, their seats can be given to someone else, so it's important to turn up on time. Baggage allowance on internal flights is usually 15kg, with an additional charge payable on any excess.

Some particularly remote regions, such as the Parque Nacional Noel Kempff Mercado, are also served by light aircraft, such as five-seater Cessnas, which are an expensive but exciting way to travel.

By boat

Although Bolivia is a landlocked country, there are still several regions – particularly Lago Titicaca and the Amazon – where water is still the best way if getting around. There are no longer any scheduled passenger services between Bolivia and Peru on **Lago Titicaca**, but several upmarket tour agencies run hydrofoil and catamaran cruises on the lake, and smaller passenger launches run between Copacabana and the Isla del Sol.

River boats were for a long time the only means of transport in the Bolivian **Amazon**, but their use has declined rapidly with the expansion of the road network in the region. There are still plenty of river trips you can make, though, and travelling by boat is the ideal way to experience the rainforest. There are two main forms of river transport. **Dugout canoes** powered by outboard motors are still the workhorses of the back country river network and the only real way to get deep enough into the jungle to see the wildlife. Tour agencies use these to take groups into protected areas like the Parque Nacional Madidi and irregular passenger services operate along some rivers. Alternatively you can hire a canoe and its boatman for a few days – this means searching around the riverbank and negotiating, and the high fuel consumption of outboard motors means it won't be cheap.

The second (and much more economic) form of riverine transport are the larger **cargo boats** that ply the two main water routes not yet supplanted by roads: the Río Mamoré, between Trinidad and Guayaramerin on the Brazilian frontier, and the Río Ichilo, between Trinidad and Puerto Villaroel in the Chapare. Though generally far from comfortable, these slow-moving vessels allow passengers to hitch hammocks above the deck for a small fee and are a great way to see the Amazon if you're not in a hurry.

By car

If you're short on time or want to get to some really out of way destinations, **renting a car** is a possibility, though it's often easier and not much more expensive to hire a taxi or *camioneta* to drive you around for a day or longer.

Outside towns, most roads are unpaved and in very poor condition, so **four-wheel drive** (4WD) is essential. **Petrol** (gasoline) stations are few and far between and breakdown services even scarcer, so you should fill your tank whenever you can, carry extra fuel, and take food, drink and warm clothing in case you get stuck. **Spare parts** are hard to come by, but Bolivian mechanics are

masters of improvisation, and drivers tend to help each other out on the roads. Always carry your passport, driving licence and the registration documents of the vehicle when driving, as **police checks** are frequent, and any infringement will usually result in an on-the-spot fine, whether official or not. Small **tolls** are also charged on most roads. **Speed limits** are irregularly posted, but the speed is usually dictated by the state of the road. Most Bolivians regularly ignore traffic lights and don't indicate when turning, and many drive at night without lights. As a rule vehicles drive on the right, though this rule is obviated on some mountain roads when the vehicle going uphill drives on the right and has priority.

Virtually none of the major international **car rental companies** are represented in Bolivia, but you'll find local rental companies in all the major cities: see the relevant listings section in each city account for details. Rental costs vary but are generally a bit less than in Europe and the US. You pay a flat fee of US$25–40 per day, plus about US$0.50 extra for each kilometre you drive; 4WDs cost about double. You'll need to be over 25 to rent a car, and to leave a major credit card or large cash deposit as security; you'll also require some kind of insurance – most rental agencies can arrange this, though read the small print carefully.

In several lowland towns, such as Trinidad, Guayarámerin and Riberalta, it's also possible to hire **mopeds** and **motorbikes** by the hour or by the day, leaving your passport as a deposit – a good way of heading off into the back country for a day. Bikes typically cost about US$1.50 an hour.

By bicycle

Outside La Paz, **bicycles** are rarely available to rent, and those that are aren't usually suitable for extended riding. For proper touring, you'll need to bring you own bike from home; airlines are usually happy to carry them if they're packed in bike boxes with the pedals removed. Given the state of the roads, a mountain bike is better than a conventional touring bike. Bring a comprehensive tool kit and a selection of essential spares.

The roads of the Bolivian Andes are ideal for **downhill mountain biking**, and the country is home to some of the world's best downhill rides, including descents of over 3500 metres in one day. Several agencies in La Paz (see p.88) lead guided mountain bike trips in which you're taken to a high pass by bus and picked up at the bottom after riding downhill all day. See p.88 for more details.

Organized tours

Although relatively expensive, **organized tours** offer a quick and effortless way to see some of Bolivia's popular attractions; they're also a good way of visiting remote sites that are otherwise difficult to reach. In addition, many adventure tour companies both in Bolivia and abroad offer excellent and increasingly exciting itineraries, ranging from

mountain climbing, trekking, mountain biking and wildlife safaris to less strenuous city tours and countryside excursions. Tours tend to cost US$30–50 per person per day, depending on the nature of the trip, the degree of comfort and the number of people going along.

Most **tour agencies** are based in La Paz (see p.88), where you can arrange almost any trip in the country, but for the more popular wilderness excursions it's easier and cheaper to arrange things with local operators: in Uyuni for the Salar de Uyuni and Reserva Eduardo Avaroa, for example, and in Rurrenabaque for the Pampas del Yacuma and Parque Nacional Madidi. Relevant agencies are listed in the guide under each destination.

Accommodation

Accomodation in Bolivia is generally good value, but the standard is not particularly high. In the larger cities you'll find a broad range of places to stay, up to and including luxurious international hotels charging well over US$100 a night. In smaller towns, however, there's not much choice, particularly in the mid and upper price ranges, though there are usually plenty of decent but totally unexceptional budget places.

Room rates generally represent excellent value for money: budget travellers will almost always be able to find a double room, often with a private bathroom, in a clean and reasonably comfortable hotel for around US$10, while in the mid-range you'll find some very nice hotels for a fraction of the price a similar place would cost in Europe or the US. Room rates vary according to **season**: in areas popular with tourists, room rates rise during the May-to-September high season, and prices in any town can double or treble during a major fiesta. In addition, room rates in resort towns popular with Bolivians increase at the weekend. (These are also the only circumstances in which **reserving a room** in advance is really necessary.) Prices also vary by **region**: accommodation in big cities tends to cost more (Santa Cruz is particularly expensive), whereas smaller towns that see a lot of budget travellers – Coroico, Copacabana,

Rurrenabaque – tend to have a good range of inexpensive places to stay.

Accommodation names – *hotel*, *hostal*, *residencial* and *alojamiento* – mean relatively little in Bolivia. Virtually all upmarket accommodation will call itself a **hotel**, but then many basic places do so as well. Smaller and cheaper hotels – also known as **hostales**, **alojamientos** or **residenciales** – tend to offer basic rooms with shared bathrooms only, with rates charged per person rather than per room, but they still vary widely in price, cleanliness and comfort. **Cabañas** are self-contained cabins or bungalows, sometimes with their own kitchenettes, usually found away from big cities, particularly in resort towns popular with Bolivians. Note that a **motel** is not an inexpensive roadside hotel, but a place where unmarried couples go to have sex, while a **pension** is a cheap place to eat, rather than somewhere to stay.

Accommodation price codes

Unless otherwise indicated, accommodation in this book is coded according to the categories below, based on the price of a **double room in high season**.

❶ under US$5
❷ US$5–10
❸ US$10–15
❹ US$15–25
❺ US$25–40
❻ US$40–60
❼ US$60–80
❽ US$80–100
❾ US$100 and over

Hotels

The **cheapest** places to stay tend to be found around bus terminals. At their most basic they offer nothing more than bare, box-like rooms with a bed and shared bathroom, and can be far from clean, though for around US$10 you should expect a clean and reasonably comfortable double room. Many budget places offer a choice between private and shared bathroom – taking the latter can be a good way to save money. Some also have their own restaurant or cafeteria and include breakfast in the price, though this is by no means universal.

Mid-range accommodation (US$15 and upwards for a double room) should offer greater comfort, pleasant décor, efficient hot water, towels and soap, and extras like television. For US$25 or so you'll find some very pleasant hotels indeed, though you'll need to choose carefully – more expensive doesn't necessarily mean better, and some places are simply characterless and overpriced business hotels. At the **top end** of the scale (US$50 and upwards) there are some beautiful old colonial mansions which have been converted into delightful hotels, as well as more staid modern places aimed primarily at business people.

There's no standard or widely used **rating system**, so other than the information given in this book, the only way to tell whether a place is suitable or not is to have a look around – most proprietors don't mind if you do this. Even if you like the look of the place it's usually worth asking to see a few different rooms and choosing one you like rather than just accepting the first you're offered, as owners generally try to rent out the less attractive rooms first. There's usually some flexibility in all price ranges, so a little haggling is always worth a try, especially when

the hotel seems fairly empty or if you're in a group: the phrase *"Tiene un cuarto más barato?"* ("Do you have a cheaper room?") is useful. The cheapest places often charge per person, but otherwise **single rooms** tend to costs as much as or only slightly less than double rooms. Rooms with double beds (*cama matrimonial*) usually cost less than those with two beds.

Even in the coldest highland cities, **heating** is a luxury found only in the more expensive hotels. Try to get a room that receives some direct sunlight during the day, as this can really warm things up, and don't hesitate to ask for extra blankets if you're cold at night. In the lowlands, heat rather than cold is often a problem. All but the cheapest rooms are equipped with a fan, and many places offer the option of air-conditioning, though this costs considerably more and older systems can be very noisy. In the lowlands, you should also check whether the windows of your room are screened against mosquitoes or if the bed is equipped with a net.

All but the cheapest places have **hot water**, but the reliability and effectiveness of water-heating systems varies considerably. Most common are the individual electric heaters that you'll find attached to the tops of showers; some of these work well, but most don't: don't touch the apparatus while the water is running unless you want an electric shock. These electric heaters work in inverse proportion to the amount of water flowing – the less water, the warmer it is – and so require a delicate balance to get right. The gas-heated systems (known as *calefóns*) found in more upmarket places are usually better, though the hot water can run out if the tanks are too small.

Many hotels have a **strong box** where you can lock up your valuables – this is usually safer than carrying them on the street at night, though you should count cash carefully before handing it in, and ask for a receipt. Many places will also store luggage for you for days or even weeks while you go off around the country, often free of charge or for just a small fee.

Camping

With so few designated campsites in the country and budget accommodation so inexpensive, few travellers bother **camping** in Bolivia, unless they're exploring the country's wilderness areas. Outside cities and towns, however, you can camp almost everywhere, usually for free. Be aware, though, that in the highlands it gets extremely cold at night, while in the lowlands, mosquitoes can be a real problem if your tent isn't screened. In the rainforest, a hammock combined with a fitted mosquito net and a tarpaulin to keep off the rain allows you to camp out comfortably pretty much anywhere.

When looking for a **place to camp**, It's usually okay to set up your tent in fields beyond the outskirts of settlements, but you should ask permission from the nearest house first. In wilderness areas where there's no one around to ask, you can camp freely. On the more popular trekking routes you may be asked for a small fee of a dollar or two by local villagers; though not official, refusing this can lead to problems and disputes, and it's not unreasonable for the locals to expect to make something from wealthy foreigners camping on their land – if you don't want to pay you could try offering a gift of leftover supplies, or just camp away

from the village. Though **attacks** on trekkers are rare, you're obviously vulnerable if camping out alone: it's best to camp with at least one other person, and women shouldn't camp unless accompanied by men.

In some **national parks** and other protected wilderness areas you'll find shelters – called *albergues* or *refugios* – where you can stay for a small fee, often in the *campamentos* used by the park guards. These range from relatively comfortable rooms with beds, mosquito nets and bathrooms, to very basic huts where you can stretch out your sleeping bag or string a hammock. Rudimentary cooking facilities and running water are usually available.

Specialist **camping equipment** is expensive and difficult to come by in Bolivia, being sold only in a few shops in La Paz and Santa Cruz, so you should bring all you need from home. If you do need to buy stuff, the best place to look is often from other travellers wanting to get rid of equipment they no longer need – check out the notice boards in popular budget hotels in La Paz.

Eating and drinking

The style of eating and drinking varies considerably between Bolivia's three main geographical regions: the Altiplano, the highland valleys and the tropical lowlands. These differences reflect both the different produce commonly available in each region and the different cultural traditions of their inhabitants. Though the differences are fading with the growth of migration and commerce, every region has *comidas típicas* (traditional dishes), which include some of the highlights of Bolivian cuisine.

Restaurants

All larger towns in Bolivia have a fair selection of **restaurants** (spelt the same way as in English, without the extra "e" at the end used in most Spanish-speaking countries). Almost all offer a set lunch, or **almuerzo**, consisting of a substantial soup (*sopa*) and a main course (*segundo*), usually made up of rice, potatoes, some form of meat or chicken, and a little bit of salad. Sometimes all this will be preceded by a small savoury appetiser and followed by a sweet desert, and cof-

fee, teas or a soft drink may also be included. Usually costing between US$1 and US$3, these set lunches are enormously filling and represent great value for money. Many restaurants also offer a set dinner, or **cena**, in the evening. In addition, most have a range of à la carte main dishes (*platos extras*) available throughout the day – these are usually substantial meat dishes like steak, and rarely cost more than US$3–4. In smaller towns the choice is much more limited, and often the simple set almuerzo and cena will be the only meal on offer.

In more upmarket restaurants, you may find yourself paying US$5 for a main course, but for this you should expect a very good meal, and even in the best restaurants in La Paz or Santa Cruz few dishes cost more than about US$10. **Tipping** is not generally expected, but is always welcome, particularly in the more expensive restaurants, where a small service charge may anyway be added to your bill. In regular restaurants a tip of just a few Bolivianos is likely to make the waiter very happy. No additional tax is charged on meals, but there is often a cover charge in restaurants with live music performances, known as **peñas**, though they may not tell you this until you ask for the bill.

Ordinary restaurants rarely offer much in the way of **vegetarian food**; in out-of-the-way places, vegetarians may find themselves eating rather a lot of fried eggs – often the only alternative to meat that chefs can think of. The situation changes a great deal in popular travellers' haunts, where international food is more and more common, and salads and vegetarian dishes are widely available. Although as a landlocked country Bolivia is obviously not the place to come for seafood, **fish** features regularly on menus. Lago Titicaca produces an abundant harvest of succulent *trucha* (trout) and *pejerrey* (kingfish), while native fish are abundant in the rivers of the lowlands: the tastiest is the juicy white fish known as *surubí*.

Most cities have at least one **Chinese restaurant**, which usually offers a far wider range of vegetarian dishes as well as some welcome variety if you're bored with Bolivian food. **Pizzerias** are also fairly widespread and very popular with Bolivians, though they're relatively expensive. Another reliable option throughout Bolivia are the cheap **chicken restaurants** known as *pollos spiedo*, *pollos broaster* or *pollos a la brasa*, where you can get a quarter of spit-roasted chicken with fried potatoes and other trimmings for about US$1.

Few restaurants open much before 8am for **breakfast** (*desayuno*) – Bolivians tend either to make do with a hot drink and a bread roll or, if they want something more substantial, to head to the market for soup or rice and meat. In tourist-oriented places, though, you'll find continental and American breakfasts, along with fruit juices and travellers' favourites like banana pancakes and fruit salads.

Markets

Wherever you are in Bolivia, the cheapest place to eat is invariably the **market**. Here you'll find rows of stalls selling cheap and filling soups, snacks and meals that can satisfy most appetites for less than US$1, and they're also often the best places to try out regional specialities. You'll also find rows of **juice stalls**, where you can order any combination of the delicious fruits grown in Bolivia, blended with milk or boiled water in front of your eyes and costing about US$0.25 for a glass and a half. In addition, markets open far earlier than most restaurants and cafés. From around 6am you can find stalls selling coffee and tea with bread, sandwiches and pastries, and – more popular with the locals – *api*, a hot, sweet, thick maize drink flavoured with cloves and cinnamon and served with deep-fried pancakes known as *buñuelos*.

The standard of **hygiene** in market stalls is often not the highest, however, and you should probably avoid eating at them until your stomach has adjusted to local bacteria. In general, food cooked in front of your eyes is probably safe; food that's been left sitting around for a while may not be.

Markets are also the place to go to stock up for a trek, a picnic, or if just feel the urge to **prepare your own food**. For vegetarians, in particular, this may be a godsend, as many of the best fruits and vegetables – avocados, for instance – rarely make it onto restaurant menus outside tourist areas.

Snacks

The most popular snack throughout Bolivia is the **salteña**, a pasty filled with a spicy, juicy stew of meat or chicken with chopped vegetables, olives and hard-boiled egg. Named after the city of Salta in Argentina, *salteñas* are sold from street stalls and eaten in the mid-morning accompanied by a cold drink and a spoonful or two of chilli sauce if desired; eating them by hand without spilling the rich gravy all over your clothes is an acquired skill. The best *salteñas* are found in Sucre, where they're also sold in specialist cafés called *salteñerias*, which open only in the mid-morning and serve nothing else. *Salteñas potosinas*, made in Potosí, are less juicy (easier to eat down the mines) and are more likely to be meat-free.

Similar to *salteñas*, but deep-fried and with a higher potato content, are **tucumanas**, also named after a city (Tucumán) in Argentina. Also commonly available are **empanadas**, simpler pasties filled with meat, chicken or cheese and either baked or (particularly in the lowlands, where the humidity makes baking difficult) fried. Another snack typical of Santa Cruz is the **cuñape**, a tasty pastry made from cheese and yuca flour. Familiar international snacks are also common in Bolivia, including **hamburgers** (*hamburguesas*) and **hot-dogs** (*choripan*), sold from street stalls and in cafés and restaurants.

Comida típica

In the Altiplano, **traditional Aymara cuisine** is dominated by the **potato** in all its manifold guises, often served alongside rice as one of two or three different carbohydrates on the same plate. The Andes are the original home of the potato, and over two hundred different varieties are grown in Bolivia. As well as being boiled, baked, mashed and fried, they are also freeze-dried using ancient techniques involving repeated exposure to sunshine and frost. Known as *chuño* and *tunta*, these dehydrated potatoes have an unusual texture and a distinctive, nutty flavour that takes some getting used to. They're often boiled and served instead of (or as well as) fresh potatoes, but they're best appreciated in the many different **soups** that are a feature of Altiplano cuisine. These are thick, hearty affairs laden with potatoes, vegetables and whatever meat is to hand – one of the most typical and widely available is *chairo*, typical of La Paz. Another standard soup ingredient is **quinoa**, a native Andean grain that grows in poor soils and at high altitudes and has a distinctively nutty flavour and a remarkably high nutritional value.

The most common **meat** in the Altiplano is mutton, closely followed by llama, which is lean and tasty. Llama meat is often eaten in a dried form known as *charque* (the origin of the English word jerky). Other Altiplano mainstays include *sajta*, a spicy dish of chicken cooked with dried yellow chilli, potatoes, *tunta*, onions and parsley; and the *plato paceño,* a mixed plate of meat, cheese, potatoes, broad beans and maize which is typical of La Paz. If you like your food with a kick, all these dishes can be

doused in **llajua** – a hot sauce made from tomatoes, small chilli peppers (*locotos*) and herbs – which is served as a condiment throughout the country.

The *comida típica* of the **valley regions** around Sucre, Cochabamba and Tarija shares many ingredients with the traditional cuisines of the Altiplano, but combines them with a wider range of fresh fruit and vegetables and tends to be spicier. Maize features strongly, either ground into a flour and used as the basis for thick soups known as *laguas*, or boiled on the cob and served with fresh white cheese – a classic combination known as *choclo con queso*. Meat and chicken are often cooked in spicy sauces known as *picantes*. Pork also features strongly: deliciously deep-fried as *chicharrón*, roasted as *lechón*, or made into *chorizos chuquisaceños*, the spicy sausages that are Sucre's best known contribution to the national cuisine. A popular valley mainstay served throughout Bolivia is *pique a lo macho*, a massive plate of chopped beef and sausage fried together with potatoes, onions, tomatoes and chillies.

In the **tropical lowlands** of the Amazon and Santa Cruz, plantain and yucca (a starchy, fibrous root similar to a yam) generally take the place of potatoes alongside rice as the mainstay sources of carbohydrate. One classic staple eaten for breakfast is *masaco*: mashed plantain or yucca mixed with shredded *charque* and fried. The lowlands are cattle-ranching regions, so **beef** features strongly – the quality is good and the price relatively low. This is usually barbequed or fried as steak, or cooked on skewers in massive kebabs known as *pacumutus*. Another classic lowland dish is *locro de gallina*, a rich chicken soup that's a meal in itself. **Game** or bushmeat is also common in the lowlands: *jochi* (agouti), *tatú* (armadillo), *saino* (peccary), and *venado* (venison) all frequently appear on menus, though for conservation reasons it's better not to eat them.

Drinking

Known as **refrescos**, bottled fizzy drinks can be found all over Bolivia, including international brands like Coca-Cola and a wide range of nationally produced beverages, all of them brightly coloured and sickly sweet. Bottled processed **fruit juice** from the Cochabamba region, sold under the name

"Jugos del Valle", is a good alternative. Glass bottles can't usually be taken away without leaving a deposit, and though disposable cans and plastic bottles are becoming more widespread, they're also more expensive. The word *refresco* is also used to denote home-made soft drinks, usually fruit-based, served from street stalls. **Mineral water**, both sparkling (*agua mineral con gas*) and still (*sin gas*) is fairly widely available in large plastic bottles, as is less expensive purified water labelled "Naturagua" – a good thing, as it's best not to the drink tap water. Make sure the seals on all bottles are intact when you buy them.

The delicious variety of tropical fruits grown in Bolivia are available as **juices** (*jugos*) from market stalls throughout the country, and freshly squeezed orange and grapefruit juice is also sold on the streets from handcarts for about US$0.15 a glass. **Tea** (*té*) and **Coffee** (*café*) are available almost everywhere, though the latter is rarely prepared to the strength favoured by most Europeans, and sometimes comes with sugar already added – a shame, as Bolivia produces some excellent coffee. **Café con leche** is a big glass of hot milk flavoured with coffee. Many Bolivians prefer herbal teas, known as **mates**. *Mate de coca* is the best known, and a good remedy for altitude sickness, but many others are usually available, including *anis* and *manzanilla* (camomile). **Hot chocolate** is usually very good, and is usually made by grating blocks of the real thing and heating it with milk.

Locally produced **alcoholic drinks** are widely available in Bolivia, and drinking is a serious pasttime. When Bolivians get together to drink, the aim is generally to get drunk, and they usually pursue this end relentlessly until they run out of drink, money or consciousness. Drinking with locals can be great fun, but shouldn't be entered into lightly, as slipping away after a couple is easier said than done. Remember, too, that until you become acclimatized, high altitude magnifies both the effects of alcohol and the resulting hangover.

Beer (*cerveza*) is available in shops, restaurants and bars almost everywhere and Bolivians consume it in large quantities, especially at fiestas. All the major cities have their own breweries, producing German lager-style beers of reasonable quality with a strength of around five percent. These are usually sold cold when refrigeration is available, but drunk with equal gusto when it's not. Most beer still comes in returnable bottles, though cans are becoming more widespread; a large 750ml bottle costs about a dollar. Paceña, produced in La Paz, is the most popular and widely available, followed by Huari, made by the same company but with a slightly saltier taste. Taquiña from Cochabamba is also good, while Potosina, from Potosí, has a stronger malt flavour; Ducal from Santa Cruz and Sureña from Sucre are less well thought of. Most breweries also produce a dark, rather sweet, stout-like beer known as **malta**. On some beer labels you'll see the word **tropicalizada** – this means it has been produced in the highlands but is more highly pressurized for consumption at lower altitudes where the air pressure is higher: if opened at altitude it will spray all over the place. **Imported beers** are available only in larger cities and cost considerably more than local ones.

Although not widely consumed, Bolivia also produces a growing variety of **wines** (*vinos*). Production is centred in the Tarija valley, home to the highest vineyards in the world, and quality is improving all the time – the best labels are Concepción, Kohlberg and Aranjuez. Costing between US$2 and US$5 a bottle, wine is sold in shops and markets in most large towns and available in better restaurants. Imported wines from Chile and Argentina are also widely available and often cheaper, as they're frequently smuggled across the border to avoid tax and duty.

When Bolivians really want to get drunk they turn to spirits, in particular a white grape brandy called **singani**, produced in the Tarija valley. The more expensive high-grade *singanis* are very good, but most are pretty rough. It's usually drunk mixed with Sprite or Seven-Up, a fast-acting combination known as **Chufflay** (the cocktail was apparently invented by British mining engineers and named by Bolivian bartenders after they'd heard the engineers shooing flies away from their glasses). Those who can't afford *singani* (which includes most campesinos and miners) turn to virtually pure industrial **alcohol potable**, sold in large metal cans. Consumed at rural fiestas and used to make offerings to mountain spirits and other supernatural beings, this is fearsome stuff, and you drink it at your peril.

Finally, no visit to the Cochabamba is complete without a taste of **Chicha Cochabambina**, a thick, mildly alcoholic beer made of fermented maize which is available throughout the region wherever you see a white flag or bunch of flowers raised on a pole outside a house. Considered sacred by the Incas, its tart, yeasty flavour is definitely an acquired taste, and it can play havoc with the digestion.

Mail and telecommunications

All cities and most towns in Bolivia have telephone and post offices, so it's fairly easy to keep in touch with home. The postal service is generally reliable, as is the telephone system, though international calls are relatively expensive. By far the easiest and cheapest way to send and receive news is by email, and internet access is growing all the time, with most cities and towns now boasting at least one internet café.

Mail

Letters and postcards sent by airmail (*por avión*) to Europe and North America tend to take between one and two weeks to arrive; the rest of the world outside the Americas and Europe takes longer. Letters cost about US$1 to Europe, a little less to the US and Canada, and about US$1.20 to Australia and New Zealand. For a small extra charge, you can send letters **certified** (*certificado*), which is more reliable, but even then it's not a good idea to send anything you can't afford to lose.

Parcels up to 2kg can be airmailed from major post offices; this costs about US$15 per kilo to Europe and about half that to North America; the contents must be checked by a customs officer in a post office before being sealed. There's no point sending anything from small town post offices, as you'll almost certainly reach the nearest city or large town before your letter or package does. If you have to send anything particularly important or urgent internationally, it's worth splashing out and using one of the internationally recognized **courier services**: Federal Express and DHL have offices in major cities.

If you wish to **receive mail** in Bolivia, you can do so through the **poste restante** service available in most post offices – it's best to use those in major towns or cities. Have mail sent to "Lista de Correos, Correo Central, the town concerned, Bolivia", and make sure your surname is written in capitals and as obviously as possible, as your post will be filed under whatever the clerk thinks your surname is; if you suspect something sent to you has gone astray, ask them to check under your first name too. Mail is usually held for about three months, and you'll need your passport to collect it.

Telephones

Substantial funds have been invested in modernizing the Bolivian phone system in recent years, and it's now fairly efficient. The Bolivian national telephone company, **ENTEL**, has offices in all cities and most towns where you can make local, national and international calls. ENTEL offices are usually open daily from around 8am to 8pm, sometimes longer. Local calls are very cheap, and long-distance national calls are moderately priced, but international calls are relatively expensive: it costs about US$1.50 per minute to North America, about US$2 per minute to Europe, and even more to anywhere else in the world outside the Americas.

There are two ways of making calls. You can either get the clerk in an ENTEL office to dial the number, take the call in a booth (where there's often a digital display of the mounting charges) and then pay at the end. Alternatively, you can use a **cardphone**, which are found both in ENTEL offices and on the streets of most towns. The cost of either method is the same. Confusingly, there are two different kinds of **phone card** (*tarjeta telefonica*) – magnetic and chip – which each work only in some phone booths. Cards come in denominations of 10, 20 and 50 bolivianos, so the largest is good for a short international call. Phone cards are sold at ENTEL offices and in shops and street stalls throughout Bolivia. You'll also find a small number of **coin-operated phones** in most towns. Most departments also have their own **regional telephone cooperatives** – for example COTEL in La Paz – that have their own networks of cardphones. These are sometimes cheaper for local calls, though no good for international or national long-distance calls. Many shops and kiosks also have phones from which you can make short local calls for a small fee.

Telephone numbers have changed several times recently in Bolivia, and though the new system is supposed to be definitive, things could change again. If a number you call doesn't work, call ☎104 to check if it's changed and get the new number. All telephone numbers in Bolivia now have seven digits, plus a two-digit regional area code (see box below), which you must use if dialling from a different region or (minus the zero) internationally.

Collect calls and charge cards

If your home phone operator has an arrangement with ENTEL, you can phone home collect using a **telephone charge card**. This enables you to make calls from most public and private phones in Bolivia by dialling an international operator. The calls are charged to your own account back home. It's worth having one of these cards, if only for emergencies. To get a card and PIN, and to find out rates, contact your domestic operator before you leave (see the box below for a list).

The internet and email

Like almost everywhere else in the world, Bolivia has seen a huge growth in internet use in recent years and, because few Bolivians have their own computers, this has meant an explosion of **internet cafés**, especially in places where there are large student populations. Internet cafés tend to charge

---

Telephone codes and useful numbers

To phone abroad from Bolivia
Dial the international access code (00) + country code (see below) + area code (minus initial zero) + subscriber number

Australia	☎00 61	New Zealand	☎00 64
Canada	☎00 1	UK	☎00 44
Ireland	☎00 353	USA	☎00 1

To phone Bolivia from abroad
Dial the international access code followed by the Bolivian country code (☎591) and the relevant area code (see below), minus the initial zero, followed by the subscriber number.

Regional area codes

La Paz, Oruro and Potosí	☎02	Chuquisaca and Tarija	☎04
Beni, Pando and Santa Cruz	☎03		

Collect-call and calling-card access numbers

BT Direct (UK and Ireland)	☎0800/0044	USA MCI	☎0800/2222
Canada Direct	☎0800/0102	USA Sprint	☎0800/3333
USA AT&T	☎0800/112		

Useful numbers in Bolivia

Directory enquiries	☎118	Operator	☎101
Emergency services	☎110	Changed-number information	☎104

about US$1 an hour, though this can double or even treble in remote areas where competition is thin on the ground. The speed of machines and servers usually isn't very fast, but with a little patience you'll get a connection eventually.

Some of the better-equipped internet cafés also offer a **net phone** service, which allows you to make calls to the US via the internet for the same price as if you were just surfing the net – by far the cheapest way of calling home.

 # The media

The press

Newspapers in Bolivia are divided between a number of fairly good quality broadsheets offering news, current affairs, sport and features; and trashy tabloids like *Extra*, which feature lurid tales of sex, crime and violence – or if possible all three in the same story at once. In La Paz, the main quality dailies are *La Prensa*, which has good foreign coverage, the politically conservative *El Diario*, and the less reliable *La Razón*. The main provincial cities all have their own newspapers, which have a strongly regional outlook: *Los Tiempos* in Cochabamba is particularly good. The best of the Santa Cruz papers is *El Deber*, though its regional outlook is so strong that a stranger reading it could be forgiven for thinking La Paz was a minor province of some faraway country, so little attention does it pay to events in the de facto capital. In many provincial cities and towns the daily newspapers from La Paz or Santa Cruz don't arrive until late in the evening or early the next day, though people are still generally happy to read them when they do. Most Bolivian newspapers now have their own websites, which you can access through links on the Latin American Network Information Center website (see p.23), or via Ⓦwww.prensalatina.com. For serious analysis of political, social and economic developments, Bolivians turn to the weekly news magazine *Pulso*; the fortnightly *Juguete Rabioso* is also good, combining a provocative and irreverent take on Bolivian politics with good articles on literature and culture.

Bolivia's one **English-language newspaper** is the weekly *Bolivian Times*, published in La Paz and available in most major cities. Though the quality of writing varies, it's a good way to keep abreast of what's going on in Bolivia if you don't read Spanish, with interesting travel features and information on cultural background, plus good entertainment listings. It also has a classified ads column that's useful for finding private Spanish teachers and rented accommodation with other expatriates. **International newspapers and magazines** are quite hard to come by, though *Time*, *Newsweek* and *The Economist* are sold in the city centres and expensive hotels in La Paz and Santa Cruz. If you want to read daily newspapers from home, you're better off doing it over the internet.

Television

Bolivians watch a growing amount of television, although many homes are still without a set. Two government and five private **terrestrial channels** serve up an uninspired cocktail of football, news and imported soap operas. The state-run Canal 4 is worth watching for the shameless propaganda of its evening news bulletin, which begins each night with an editorial from the minister for information and reports nothing but good news for the government.

More serious Bolivian news channels are now available on **cable TV**, often available in rooms in better hotels – the best is Periodistas Asociados Televisión (PAT), which presents hard-hitting current affairs programmes. In La Paz and Santa Cruz, cable TV should give you access to international channels like CNN and BBC World, though in smaller cities local cable networks offer a far more limited selection.

Radio

Radio is the most democratic of Bolivia's media, and the only one that adequately reflects the country's cultural diversity, with many of the country's hundreds of different stations broadcasting in indigenous languages. For rural Bolivians, radio is the main source of news and a window on the world. The leading national news radio station is Radio Fides, which is owned by the Catholic Church and broadcast on different FM frequencies in all the major cities.

There's also no shortage of music stations, as a flick through the FM dial will quickly reveal. Other than the internet, carrying a short wave radio is about the best way of keeping in touch with events back home and in the rest of the world. You can pick up the BBC World Service in English in most of Bolivia (though not in La Paz, where the surrounding mountains block the signal – check ⓦ www.bbc.co.uk/worldservice for frequencies), as well other international broadcasters.

Opening hours, public holidays and fiestas

Shops, businesses and public offices in Bolivia generally open Monday to Saturday from around 8.30pm or 9.30am. They mostly close for a long lunch break between about noon and 2pm (longer in some regions), and then open again until around 5.30pm to 7pm. Some offices, however, have adopted a new system, known as _hora corrida_, whereby they work straight though from 8.30am to 4pm without closing for lunch.

Banks' opening hours are generally Monday to Friday from 8.30am to noon and 2.30pm to 5pm, and on Saturdays in the morning. ENTEL **telephone offices** usually open daily from around 8am to 8pm, sometimes later. Public **museums** usually open on Sundays for at least half the day, and close instead on Mondays. All these times are approximate, though: Bolivians aren't noted for their **punctuality**, and public offices in particular often open later and close earlier than they are supposed to; conversely, private businesses, particularly those connected with tourism, often work longer hours and open on Sundays. If you're arranging to meet a Bolivian, make it somewhere you don't mind waiting around, as they're unlikely to turn up on time. Note that during **public holidays** and **local fiestas** pretty much everything closes down.

Fiestas

Bolivians welcome any excuse for a party, and the country enjoys a huge number of national, regional and local **fiestas**. These are taken very seriously, often involving lengthy preparation and substantial expense, while the largest feature thousands of costumed dancers, massed brass bands and plenty of food and drink – for poor Bolivians, fiestas are often the only time they can eat and drink to their hearts' content. You should definitely try to catch a fiesta at some point during your visit, as they are amongst the most vibrant and colourful spectacles Bolivia has to offer, and at the heart of the country's culture.

Most national fiestas mark famous events in Bolivia's post-conquest history and the standard festivals of the Catholic Church, but many of the latter coincide with far older indigenous celebrations related to the sun, stars and agricultural cycle. **Carnival** time (late Feb or early March), is marked by fiestas and celebrations throughout the country (the most famous being in Oruro), and involves indiscriminate water-fighting – don't be surprised if you're hit by a water-filled balloon at any time during February; and don't be afraid of striking back.

In addition to the major national and regional celebrations, almost every town and village has its own annual **local fiesta** (some have several), usually held on the day of its patron saint. These celebrations can be much more fun to visit than major events in larger towns and cities, and often stretch out over a whole week, with religious processions, masked and costumed folkloric dances, traditional music, and eating and drinking. In indigenous communities these fiestas are often important ritual events associated with religious beliefs and agricultural cycles – it's believed that if they're not celebrated with due extravagance, the Catholic saints or mountain gods (or both) may be displeased, and the fortunes of the community will suffer as a result. Fiestas also play an important role in maintaining social cohesion, and are usually financed under a system known as **prestes**, whereby wealthier members of the community (often people who have migrated to the city but maintain close links with their home village) spend large amounts of money on food, drink and musicians, gaining enhanced status and respect in return.

The occasional visitor will usually be warmly welcomed to local fiestas, but these are often fairly private affairs, and crowds of camera-wielding tourists may provoke a hostile reaction – sensitivity is the key. The dates listed below are only for established events that are already on the tourist map, or for those that take place nationwide.

Calendar of major fiestas and public holidays

January to April

January 1 New Year's Day (public holiday).
January 6 Reyes Magos. The arrival of the three kings is celebrated with processions in various towns in the Beni.
January 24 Feria de Alasitas in La Paz. Large areas of the city are taken over by market stalls selling miniature items used as offerings to Ekeko, the household god of abundance (see p.75).
February 2 Fiesta de la Virgen de la Candelaria in Copacabana.
February 10 Public holiday in Oruro department.
February/March Carnaval. Celebrated throughout the country in the week before Lent. The Oruro carnival (see p.156) is the most famous, but Santa Cruz and Tarija also stage massive fiestas.
March 12 Pujllay. Thousands of indigenous revellers descend on the market town of Tarabuco,

near Sucre, to celebrate a local victory over Spanish troops during the Independence War.
March/April Semana Santa (Easter) is celebrated with religious processions throughout Bolivia. Good Friday is a public holiday.
April 15 Public holiday in Tarija department.

May to July

May 1 Labour Day (public holiday).
May 3 Día de la Cruz. *Tinku* ritual combats (see p.189) are staged in some communities in the northern Potosí region. The date marks the reappearance in the night sky of a constellation known as La Cruz, though celebrations often have a Christian veneer.
May 25 Public holiday in Chuquisaca department.
May/June Corpus Christi (public holiday). La Paz stages the Señor del Gran Poder (see p.58), its biggest and most colourful folkloric dance parade.
June 21–22 The winter solstice and Aymara New Year are celebrated with overnight vigils and religious ceremonies at Tiwanaku, Copacabana, Samaipata and other ancient sites throughout the country.
June 24 San Juan. Christian version of the winter solstice and Aymara New Year, marked with bonfires and fireworks.
June Santísima Trinidad. Major religious fiesta in Trinidad in honour of the Holy Trinity.
July 16 Virgen del Carmen. Processions and dances in honour of the Virgen del Carmen, the patron saint of many towns and villages across Bolivia. Public holiday in the department of La Paz.
July 31 San Ignacio de Mojos hosts the largest and most colourful folkloric fiesta in the Bolivian Amazon.

August to December

August 6 Independence Day (public holiday). Parades and parties throughout the country.
August 15 Virgen de Urkupiña. Pilgrims descend on the market town of Quillacollo, just outside Cochabamba, for the region's biggest religious fiesta.
August 24 San Bartolomé (also known as Ch'utillos). Potosí's biggest annual fiesta, a three-day celebration with pre-Christian roots, marked by folkloric dances and religious processions.
September 14 Public holiday in Cochabamba department.
October 1 Public holiday in Pando department.
November 1–2 All Saints and Day of the Dead (public holiday). Remembrance parties are held in cemeteries throughout the highlands.
November 10 Public holiday in Potosí department.
November 18 Public holiday in Beni department.
December 25 Christmas Day (public holiday).

Outdoor activities

Dominated by the dramatic high mountain scenery of the Andes and home to some of the most pristine wilderness areas in South America, Bolivia has the potential to become one of the world's top destinations for outdoor enthusiasts. As yet, though, its enormous potential has scarcely been tapped, and organized facilities are few and far between. To the true outdoor enthusiast, however, this should simply add to the appeal.

For climbers, trekkers and mountain bikers, Bolivia's possibilities are virtually limitless, with the added advantage that you're unlikely to find yourself sharing the wilderness with more than a handful of other adventurers. The best **season** for all these activities is between May and September, during the southern hemisphere winter – the most pleasant and reliable weather is between June and August. During the rainy season between December and March or April, rain turns paths and roads to mud and streams to impassable torrents, while cloud covers the high passes and blocks many of the best views.

Trekking

Whether you want to stroll for half a day or take a hardcore hike for two weeks over high passes and down into remote Amazonian valleys, Bolivia is a paradise for **trekking**. The most popular trekking region is the **Cordillera Real**, which is blessed with spectacular high Andean scenery and is easily accessible from La Paz. The mountains here are crisscrossed by paths and mule trains used by local people that make excellent trekking routes – the best of these are ancient stone paved highways built by the Incas and earlier Andean societies. Starting near La Paz, three of Bolivia's most popular treks – the **Choro** (see p.136), **Takesi** (see p.123) and **Yunga Cruz** (see p.124) – follow these Inca trails across the Cordillera Real before plunging down into the humid tropical valleys of the Yungas. Another good base for exploring the Cordillera Real is the town of **Sorata**, north of La Paz, where many good trekking routes begin and where the locals are well organized in terms of providing guides and mules.

The shores of **Lago Titicaca** and the Isla del Sol are also excellent for hiking, combining awesome scenery with gentle gradients. People looking for more seclusion should head for the remote and beautiful **Cordillera Apolobamba**, which is traversed by one of Bolivia's finest trekking routes, the **Trans-Apolobamba Trek** (see p.133). Elsewhere, the mountains around **Sucre** offer further excellent trekking possibilities, while the **Reserva Biológica del Sama**, above Tarija, is also home to a beautiful Inca trail (see p.216).

You should always be well **equipped** when walking, even if it's just a half-day hike. Weather can change quickly in the mountains and it gets very cold at night. You'll need strong hiking boots; warm layers such as a fleece or down jacket; a waterproof top layer; hat and gloves; an adequate first aid kit (see p.20); water bottle and water purifiers; and sunscreen, sun hat and sunglasses. For camping out you'll need a decent tent; a sleeping bag which will keep you warm in temperatures as low as at least –5°C; an insulating sleeping mat; and a cooking stove (ideally a multi-fuel stove capable of burning gasoline and kerosene – white gas is difficult to find, and gas canisters are expensive and available only in La Paz).

The easiest way to go trekking is on an **organized trip** with a local tour operator. There are dozens of these in La Paz and in several other cities. An organized trek takes all the hassle out of route-finding and means you don't need to supply your own equipment. You'll also have all your meals cooked for you and transport to and from trailheads arranged. If you pay a little more, you can also have your gear carried for you by a porter or pack animal. Trekking this way costs between US$20 and US$40 per person per day, depending on what's included and how many people are in the group.

Things are much cheaper if you have all your own equipment, organize the logistics yourself, and just hire a **guide**. In rural towns and villages you can usually find local campesinos who know all the trails and will act as a guide for a relatively small fee (on treks of more than one day you'll also need to provide them with food and possibly a tent). If you're hiring pack animals (see below) to carry some or all of your gear, then the mule handlers double-up as guides anyway. As well as making sure you don't get lost, a local guide can help avoid any possible misunderstandings with the communities you pass through – it's also a good way to ensure local people see a little economic benefit from tourism, something that can only improve their attitude to outsiders.

In the highlands it's often a good idea to hire a **pack animal** to carry your gear. The most common are mules, which cost about US$6–8 a day and can carry over 100kg with relative ease. Donkeys carry about half that, while llamas carry no more than around 30kg, and also move slowly; both should be proportionally cheaper to hire. You'll also need to pay for the *arriero* who handles the animals, and who can usually double as an effective guide.

If you plan to go trekking over longer distances without a guide, you should be competent at route-finding and map-reading, carry a compass and/or Global Positioning System, and equip yourself with the relevant topographical maps, where available. Most areas are covered by 1:50,000 scale maps produced by the Bolivian military and available in La Paz (see p.85). Really, though, it's much better to trek with a guide. Getting lost in remote mountain or forested regions is easy and can be very dangerous, and rescue services are pretty much nonexistent. In addition, you should always let someone in town (at your hotel, for instance) know your plans before you head off on a long walk. It's especially important **not to trek alone** – if you sprain an ankle that could be the last anyone ever sees of you.

Climbing

With hundreds of peaks over 5000m and a dozen over 6000m, Bolivia has plenty of types of **mountain climbing**, and many new routes still to explore. As with trekking, the most popular region is the dramatic **Cordillera Real**, which is blessed with numerous high peaks, easy access from La Paz, and fairly stable weather conditions during the dry season. In addition, the volcanic peaks of the **Cordillera Occidental**, particularly Sajama (see p.153), offer some excellent climbs, while the more remote **Cordillera Apolobamba** and **Cordillera Quimsa Cruz**, also offer a wealth of possibilities. Several of the higher peaks are well within the reach of climbers with only limited experience, while **Huayna Potosí** (6090m), in the Cordillera Real, is one of the few 6000m-plus peaks in South America that can be climbed by people with no mountaineering experience at all.

Though some **equipment** is available for hire in La Paz, you should really bring your own equipment from home if you're planning on doing any serious independent climbing. You should also take care to acclimatize properly and be aware of the dangers of altitude sickness (see p.18) and extreme cold. A number of agencies in La Paz (see p.98) offer guided ascents of the most popular peaks, though you should check carefully that the guide they provide is qualified and the equipment reliable – if in doubt, go with a more reputable and expensive agency. You can get good advice and find fully qualified mountaineering guides through the **Club Andino Boliviano** (☎02/2312875), in La Paz at Calle Mexico 1638, just up from Plaza Estudiante.

Mountain biking

Bolivia is home to some of the finest **mountain bike** routes in the world, and travelling by bike is one of the best ways to experience the Andes. In recent years a number of tour companies in La Paz (see p.88) have set up **downhill mountain biking** trips. These involve being driven up to a high pass, put on a bike, and then riding downhill at your own pace, accompanied by a guide and followed by a support vehicle in case you get a puncture or want to stop for any reason. As with climbing, this is not an activity where you should try to save money by going with a cheap operator – look for a company with experienced guides, well-maintained and high-quality bikes, and adequate safety equipment; Gravity Assisted Mountain Biking (see p.89) has the best reputation.

The most popular route by far is down the road from La Paz to Coroico in the Yungas (see p.137), a stunning 3500m descent which many travellers rate as one of the highlights of South America, never mind Bolivia. You don't need any previous mountain-biking experience to do this ride, which is easy to organize as a day-trip from La Paz. Other popular routes include Chacaltaya (see p.100) to La Paz, and down the Zongo valley into the Yungas from Chacaltaya, while hardcore mountain bikers can try their luck on the Takesi Trail (see p.123). As with trekking and climbing, though, the possibilities are pretty much endless, especially if you have your own bike.

For advice on new routes or mountain biking in general, talk to Bolivian mountain-bike pioneer and guru Alistair Matthew, of Gravity Assisted Mountain Biking – he can also help organize specialist guided tours.

Other activities

Though the many rivers that rush down from the Andes into the valleys of the Upper Amazon offer massive potential for **kayaking**

and **white-water rafting**, these activities have so far scarcely been developed in Bolivia. One or two companies in La Paz, such as Explore Bolivia (see p.89), do offer rafting trips, however, and some overseas specialist agencies, such as the US-based Explore Bolivia (not to be confused with its Bolivian namesake) occasionally make rafting and kayaking expeditions. The most easily accessible and popular river is the **Río Coroico**, in the Yungas, which offers rapids from grade II to IV (and sometimes higher) and Is accessible on daytrips from Coroico. The most challenging trip is down the **Río Tuichi**, which runs from the high Andes down into the rainforest of the Parque Nacional Madidi (see p.336). Organizing this two-week expedition will take time and involve considerable expense, and you'll need to hire 4WDs to access to the upper reaches of the river.

Skiing is possible at Chacaltaya (see p.100), the highest developed ski slope in the world at over 5000m. The run there is poor, however, and really worth skiing only for the novelty value. With the glaciers of the tropical Andes retreating, new slopes are unlikely to be developed.

National parks and reserves

Bolivia's system of protected areas currently covers some fifteen percent of the country, comprising eleven national parks (*parques nacionales*), seven national reserves (*reservas nacionales*) and three "natural areas" (*areas naturales de manejo integrado*). These protected areas encompass the full range of different terrains and ecosystems in Bolivia, from the tropical forests of the Amazon lowlands to the frozen peaks and high-altitude deserts of the Andes. They include many of Bolivia's most outstanding scenic attractions, but their principal aim is to to protect native flora and fauna, and facilities for tourism are virtually nonexistent. Though in some parks you can find primitive accommodation, in general visiting these areas involves a wilderness expedition, which is usually possible only with the help of a tour operator.

The country's national parks and reserves are administered by the **Servicio Nacional de Areas Protegidas** (SERNAP), based in La Paz at Avenida 20 de Octubre 2659 (☎02/22430881), though this office offers little in the way of information. In cases where you need **permission** to visit a park or

reserve, you can do so in the local or regional SERNAP offices. In the rare cases where you need to pay a small **admission fee**, this is also done locally. Details about permission and entrance fees for individual parks and reserves are given in the guide.

Protected areas range in size from the vast

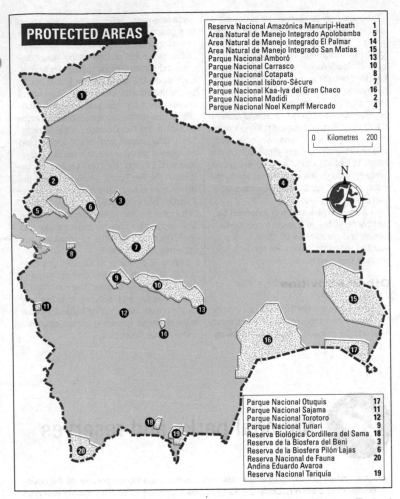

PROTECTED AREAS

Reserva Nacional Amazónica Manuripi-Heath	1
Area Natural de Manejo Integrado Apolobamba	5
Area Natural de Manejo Integrado El Palmar	14
Area Natural de Manejo Integrado San Matías	15
Parque Nacional Amboró	13
Parque Nacional Carrasco	10
Parque Nacional Cotapata	8
Parque Nacional Isiboro-Sécure	7
Parque Nacional Kaa-Iya del Gran Chaco	16
Parque Nacional Madidi	2
Parque Nacional Noel Kempff Mercado	4

0   Kilometres   200

N

Parque Nacional Otuquis	17
Parque Nacional Sajama	11
Parque Nacional Torotoro	12
Parque Nacional Tunari	9
Reserva Biológica Cordillera del Sama	18
Reserva de la Biosfera del Beni	3
Reserva de la Biosfera Pilón Lajas	6
Reserva Nacional de Fauna Andina Eduardo Avaroa	20
Reserva Nacional Tariquía	19

34,411-square-kilometre Parque Nacional Kaa-Iya del Gran Chaco, the largest in South America, to the relatively small 164-square-kilometre Parque Nacional Toro Toro. There are several different categories of protected area, each enjoying slightly different legal status and degrees of protection due to Bolivia's complex and sometimes contradictory laws. **Parques nacionales** are generally large areas of unspoilt wilderness, usually incorporating particularly fragile and important ecosystems and high levels of biodiversity. **Reservas nacionales** have a lesser degree of protection, while in **areas naturales de manejo integrado**, nature conservation measures are limited by the rights of long-established local populations. The legal status of some protected areas is further complicated by the fact that they overlap with indigenous territories (*territorios indígenas*, also known as *tierras comunitarias de origen* – areas over which Indigenous peoples enjoy territorial rights and a broad degree of autonomy).

Many of Bolivia's protected areas were established only recently in response to pressure and incentives from powerful international conservation groups. Some, including the Parque Nacional Madidi, were set up through **debt-for-nature swaps**, whereby international groups bought up large amounts of the country's international debt at discounted rates, then cancelled the debts in return for Bolivia agreeing to establish protected areas and invest money in their conservation. More recently, the Parque Nacional Noel Kempff Mercado has been expanded as part of a pioneer **carbon-trading** scheme, under which US energy corporations finance the protection of forest areas in Bolivia in return for being allowed to claim credits for the carbon dioxide the forests absorb from the atmosphere in meeting their own emissions targets (see p.303).

Despite such schemes, many national parks and other protected areas are under intense pressure from poor landless peasants, mostly migrants from the highlands looking for new areas of forest to clear and cultivate. Small teams of park guards with almost no resources struggle to protect thousands of square kilometres of wilderness from incursions by hunters, logging and mining companies, cattle ranchers and peasant colonizers, who are often better organized, financed and equipped. In addition, though many Bolivians are aware of the enormous value of their remaining wilderness areas and support conservation measures, there is also widespread opposition to the national parks system. Peasant federations in particular view the protected areas as a form of imperialism whereby natural resources that are rightfully theirs are handed over to international conservation groups intent, they believe, on stealing Bolivia's biodiversity and patenting any scientifically valuable species discovered.

Work, volunteering and study

There are several options available to people looking to work or study in Bolivia. Several cities have language schools where you can study Spanish, Quechua or Aymara, and those with initiative and enthusiasm shouldn't have much trouble finding voluntary work with one of the large number of non-government organizations operating in Bolivia, though this is usually done on an informal basis. Paid work is more difficult to come by, and getting formal permission to work even more so, but opportunities do exist, particularly for those with valuable skills to offer.

Work

Unless you have arranged something in advance with an international company or non-government organization, your chances of finding paid work in Bolivia are slim. The best bet is **teaching English** in La Paz, Cochabamba or Santa Cruz, though pay is low unless you get work with the British Council or a similar international agency – this is best arranged in advance. Obviously, work as a teacher is easier to find If you have a formal TEFL qualification. Even if you do find paid employment, getting an official work permit is a costly and long-drawn out bureaucratic nightmare – contact the *Migración* in La Paz or any other major city for details.

Aspiring journalists can often find work writing for the English-language *Bolivian Times* (see p.38), though they pay little or nothing – again, it's worth contacting the paper in advance if you're interested in doing this.

Volunteering

Some opportunities exist for **volunteering** in Bolivia, though most require you to pay for your own food and accommodation and to stay for at least a month. This is rarely organized by formal networks or agencies – the best way to find volunteer work is by word of mouth. Asking around in main cities like La Paz, Sucre or Cochabamba you're likely to find something worthwhile to do if you're prepared to work for free, especially if you have useful skills to offer – try contacting NGOs working locally. You'll need reasonable Spanish If you want to do any kind of volunteer work with local communities, while for research work you'll need the relevant scientific background.

One place that does take volunteers on a regular basis is the **Parque Machía Inti Wara Yassi** animal refuge in Villa Tunari in the Chapare region, east of Cochabamba (see p.258). Volunteers do everything from maintain trails and look after rescued animals to clean toilets and guide schoolchildren. You'll need to stay for at least fifteen days. Volunteers pay a small fee for dormitory accommodation and cook and eat together.

Studying Spanish

Bolivia is a good place to **study Spanish** lessons: Bolivian pronunciation is slow and clear, making the language easier to pick up, and tuition costs are lower than in neighbouring countries. Spending one or several weeks on an intensive course is a good way

of immersing yourself in Bolivian culture and getting to know a particular city in more detail, and can provide a good reason for living in Bolivia for a while without being a tourist.

La Paz, Sucre and Cochabamba are the most popular places for studying Spanish – **language schools** are detailed in the listings section for each of these cities in the guide. You'll also find individual Spanish language teachers offering their services on a one-to-one basis in these cities and in smaller towns around Bolivia. These can be very good, though it's worth trying a lesson or two before you commit to a course with a particular teacher. More adventurous linguists can also study **Quechua** (in Cochabamba) or **Aymara** (in La Paz); even a small grasp of either opens up a whole new world, and is worth acquiring just for the gasps of astonishment and amusement you'll get from many indigenous Bolivians when they are greeted by a gringo in their own language.

Crime and personal safety

Despite being amongst the poorest countries in the region, Bolivia has long enjoyed a reputation as one of the safest destinations in South America for travellers, with far lower levels of theft and violent crime than in neighbouring Peru and Brazil. In recent years crime levels have risen, however, partly in response to the country's worsening economic situation. This is to the dismay of most ordinary Bolivians, who are shocked and outraged by stories of theft or assault, and in general the threat of crime is no greater in Bolivian cities than in North America or Europe.

The difference is that whereas back home you blend in and can spot potential danger signs much more easily, in Bolivia you stand out like a sore thumb – an extremely wealthy sore thumb, moreover, at least in the eyes of most Bolivians. There's no need to be paranoid, though: the vast majority of crime against tourists is opportunistic theft, and violence is extremely rare. By using common sense, keeping alert and taking some simple precautions, you can greatly reduce the chances of becoming a victim and help ensure you join the most majority of foreign

visitors who visit the country without experiencing any trouble at all.

Theft

Petty theft is the most common crime that tourists face, and more often than not it's simply the result of carelessness. The first rule is, if you really don't want to lose something, don't bring it with you in the first place: wearing jewellery or expensive watches is asking for trouble. Secondly, make sure you have adequate **travel insurance** before you go (see p.16), and check what the insurance company's requirements are in the event that you need to make a claim – almost all will need a police report of any theft.

To reduce the problems of a potential theft, make a careful note of airline ticket numbers, hotline phone numbers if you need to cancel a credit card, travellers' cheque numbers (always keep the receipt separately) and insurance details; in addition, copy the important pages of your passport and travel documents and keep all these details separate from your valuables. You should also keep an emergency stash of **cash** hidden somewhere about your person. If you're staying in Bolivia for a while, consider registering with your embassy: this can save lots of time if you have to replace a lost or stolen passport.

Always carry your valuables – passport, money, travellers' cheques, credit cards, airline tickets – out of sight and under your clothing next to your skin; and keep them on you at all times. **Money belts** are good for this, but you can also get secure holders that hang under your shirt or from a loop on your belt under your trousers; a false pocket sewn inside your clothing, a leg pouch, or a belt with a secret zip for cash are even more difficult for thieves to find. It's also a good idea to keep your petty cash separate from your main stash of valuables, so your hidden money belt is not revealed every time you spend a few bolivianos. Better hotels will have a **safe** (*caja fuerte*) at reception where you can deposit your valuables if you trust the staff – this is usually safe, though it's better to leave stuff in a tamper-proof holder or a signed and sealed envelope, get an itemized receipt for what you leave, and count cash carefully before and after. Never leave cameras or other valuables lying around in your hotel room, and be cautious if sharing a room with people you don't know well, as other travellers can be thieves too. Officially, you're supposed to carry your passport with you at all times, but if asked by the police for ID it's usually sufficient to show them a photocopy of your passport and explain that the original is in your hotel.

You are at your most vulnerable, and have the most to lose, when you're on the move or arriving in a new town and have all your luggage with you. **Bus stations** are a favourite hunting ground of thieves the world over, and Bolivia is no exception: try not to arrive after dark, keep a close eye and hand on your bags

at all times, and consider taking a taxi from the bus terminal to your hotel as a security precaution. Unless you travel very light, when travelling by bus or train you'll often have to put your backpack into a luggage compartment or on the roof. This is usually safe, and some bus companies will give you a baggage reclaim ticket in return, but it's still worth keeping an eye out when the vehicle stops to make sure no one carries your bag off either by mistake or on purpose. It's also worth covering your backpack with a **sack** (which you can buy in any market) to make it less conspicuous and protect it from dust, dirt and rain – though mark it so you can distinguish it from others. Some travellers like to chain their bags together or onto an immovable object when waiting around, and onto the roof of the bus or train luggage rack when travelling. You can also buy lockable lightweight metal meshes to fit over your pack for extra security – though this seems a little excessive. As well as transport terminals, markets, city centres, fiestas and other crowded public places where tourists congregate are favoured by pickpockets and thieves. If you're carrying a daypack or small pack, keep it in front of you where you can see it to avoid having it slashed; when you stop and sit down, loop a strap around your leg to make it more difficult for someone to grab.

Mugging and **violent robbery** are much less common, but do occur, usually at night, so try to avoid having to walk down empty streets in the early hours, particularly alone. ATMs are an obvious target for robbers, so don't use them at night, if possible. If the robbers are armed, do not under any circumstances resist. Though usually safer than walking, **taxis** also carry an element of risk. If travelling alone, don't sit in the front seat, lock passenger doors to stop people jumping in beside you, and be wary of cabs driving away with your bags – if your luggage is in the boot, wait for the driver to get out first. Radio taxis called by phone are safer than unmarked cabs, and you can always refuse to share a cab with strangers if it makes you uncomfortable. Robbery is rare in **rural areas**, though campsites are sometimes targeted on some of more popular trekking routes – keep all your possessions inside your tent at night, and avoid camping near villages where possible.

As well as opportunistic theft, there are several **scams** used by teams of professional thieves that you should be aware of. One classic technique is distraction: your bag or clothing is mysteriously sprayed with mustard or the like, a friendly passer-by points this out and helps you clean it – while their accomplice picks your pocket or makes off with your coat or bag. Another involves something valuable – cash, a credit card – being dropped at your feet. A passer-by spots it and asks you to check your wallet to see if it is yours, or offers to share it with you. The story ends with your own money disappearing by sleight of hand, or you being accused of theft, so walk away as quickly as possible and ignore anything dropped at your feet. A third scam, usually used at bus terminals, involves thieves posing as plainclothes police officers, complete with fake documents, asking to see your money to check for counterfeit notes or something similar. Often, an accomplice (usually a taxi driver) will already have engaged you in conversation and will vouch for this being normal procedure. It isn't. If approached by people claiming to be undercover police, don't get in a car with them or show them your documents or valuables, and insist on the presence of a uniformed officer – you can call one yourself on ☎110.

The police

With any luck, most of your contact with the **police** will at frontiers and road checkpoints. Sometimes, particularly near borders and in remote regions, you may have to register with them, so carry your passport with you at all times (though a photocopy may be enough if you're not travelling far). Generally the police rarely trouble tourists, but in any dealings with them it's important to be polite and respectful, as they can make problems for you if you're not. A smart, clean appearance is a good way of staying out of trouble; if you're scruffy or look anything like what they might call a hippy, you'll attract attention. Anyone claiming to be an undercover policeman is probably a thief or confidence trickster (see above); don't get in a car with them or show them your documents or valuables, and insist on the presence of a uniformed officer.

If you are the victim of theft, you'll probably need to go to the police to make a report (*denuncia*) and get a written report for insurance purposes – this is rarely a problem,

though it may take some time. In La Paz you should go to the **tourist police** if you are the victim of any crime – their office (open 24hr; ☎02/2225016) is at Edificio Olimpia 1314, Plaza Tejada Sorzano, opposite the stadium in Miraflores.

Occasionally, the police may search your bags. If they do, watch carefully, and ideally get a witness to watch with you, to make sure nothing is planted or stolen – a rare but not impossible occurrence. Possession of (never mind trafficking in) **drugs** is a serious offence in Bolivia, usually leading to a long jail sentence. There are a fair number of foreigners languishing in Bolivian jails on drugs charges, and many wait a long time before they come to trial. It's not unusual to be offered an opportunity to **bribe** a policeman (or any other official for that matter), even if you've done nothing wrong. Often they're just trying it on, and there's no need to pay. But in some circumstances it can work to the advantage of both parties. In South America bribery is an age-old custom, and paying a bribe is certainly preferable to going to jail. Finally, bear in mind that all police are armed, and may well shoot you if you run away.

Other risks

The main **cocaine**-producing region of the Chapare in Cochabamba department is the scene of ongoing, sometimes violent, confrontations between the security forces and coca-growers opposed to the eradication of their crops. Towns on the main Chapare road are generally safe to visit, but you should be wary of going off the beaten track in this region, as you may be mistaken for a drug trafficker or undercover CIA or drug-enforcement agent. Watch the media for developments, as roadblocks by protesters are common; the same goes for the Yungas region north of La Paz if forced eradication is implemented there.

In recent years, **road blockades** have become a feature of Bolivian political life, particularly in the Altiplano, where radical Aymara peasants often block the roads between La Paz and Peru. Generally, this is an inconvenience that travellers have to put up with, and you should follow events in the media if you're worried you may get cut off. If you get caught up in the blockades, keep your head down and get out of the area, and don't try running the blockades unless you really have to. The army has killed several protesters in recent years, and tempers can run high, with blockade-breaking buses sometimes getting stoned or torched. **Political unrest** is a constant in Bolivia, and demonstrations are a regular event in La Paz and other major cities. These are usually fairly peaceful events and interesting to watch, but you should keep your distance and get out of the area if the tear gas grenades start to fly.

Directory

ADDRESSES Addresses are usually written with just the street name (and often just the surname if the street is named after a person), followed by the number – for example, "Paredes 704" rather than "Calle Max Paredes 704". Often, however, numbers are not used, and the nearest intersection is given instead – for example, "Illampu con Comercio". Note also that street numbers in Bolivia do not always run consecutively: number 6 could easily be between number 2 and 4.

AIRPORT TAX Passengers departing on international flights must pay a US$25 airport tax in cash dollars or bolivianos, payable at a separate kiosk after checking-in. If you can't pay you won't be allowed to board your plane, so make sure you set money aside for this. The departure tax on domestic flights is about US$1.50, payable in bolivianos.

DISABLED TRAVELLERS Very little provision is made in Bolivia for the disabled. Public transport, hotels and public places such as museums are seldom equipped with ramps, widened doorways or disabled toilets, and pavements, where they exist at all, are often narrow and covered with dangerous potholes and other obstructions.

ELECTRICITY The electricity supply In most of Bolivia is 220V/50Hz; in La Paz, however, there are both 110V and 220V supplies, often in the same house, so check carefully before plugging in equipment. Plugs are two pronged with round pins, but US-style flat-pinned plugs can also usually be used.

GAY AND LESBIAN TRAVELLERS Most Bolivians do not have a very liberal attitude to homosexuality: though legal, it is frowned upon and kept under wraps. Though gay travellers are unlikely to suffer any direct abuse, it's best to be discreet and avoid public displays of affection. Larger cities have a handful of gay bars, but these tend to be fairly clandestine to avoid harassment.

LAUNDRY In cities and larger towns you'll find laundries (*lavanderías*) where you can have your clothes machine-washed for a dollar or two per kilo; upmarket hotels can arrange this for you. Otherwise, most hotels can find someone to wash your clothes by hand if you ask. Some budget hotels have facilities for hand-washing your own clothes.

PHOTOGRAPHY The light in Bolivia is very bright, particularly at high altitudes, so use fast (100 ASA) film and a UV polarizing filter. In the highlands, the best times to take photos are early in the morning and late in the afternoon, when the sunlight is not too harsh. Under the forest canopy in the lowlands, on the other hand, light is poor, so you need to use slow film. Taking photos of people without permission can offend, particularly in rural areas. It's best to ask politely ("*Puedo sacar una fotito?*" – "Can I take a little photo?"); most people react favourably to this approach, though some may refuse outright or ask for a small fee.

TIME Bolivia is four hours behind Greenwich Mean Time, an hour ahead of US Eastern Standard Time.

TOILETS You'll find public toilets (*baños* or *servicios higenicos*) in most markets and bus terminals; there's usually a small charge for their use, in return for which you'll get a wad of toilet paper (*papel higénico*). Bars and restaurants will usually let non-customers use their toilets if you ask politely, though they're rarely pleasant and you'll need your own paper. Travelling long-distance by bus, you'll often have to do as the Bolivians do, and go alfresco. Throughout Bolivia, used toilet paper must be put in the bin or bucket beside the toilet, as if flushed down the toilet it can block the drains.

WOMEN TRAVELLERS The sexism and machismo characteristic of Latin American countries is arguably less prevalent in Bolivia than in many other countries, but it can still present an annoyance for foreign women, particularly those travelling alone or accompanied only by other women. Generally speaking, everyday sexual harassment is less of a problem in high-altitude cities like La Paz, where indigenous cultures predominate, and worse in lower, warmer cities like Santa Cruz, where Latino culture has more of a hold. Harassment usually takes the form of whistling and lewd cat-calling in the street: most Bolivian women just walk on and ignore this, and you'll probably find it easiest to do likewise. Many women find this problem increases in February and March in the run up to Carnaval, when the usually good-natured custom of water fighting is used by some men as an excuse to harass women with water bombs. Sexual assault and rape are not common in Bolivia, but there have been a number of incidents reported by female travellers. It's best to exercise at least the same degree of caution as you would at home: don't walk alone down dark streets at night; avoid hiking and camping alone or in small groups; try to avoid taking taxis alone at night (and, if you must, phone a radio-taxi and note the name of the company); and report any serious incident immediately to the local police and contact your embassy in La Paz for support and advice.

guide

guide

La Paz and around

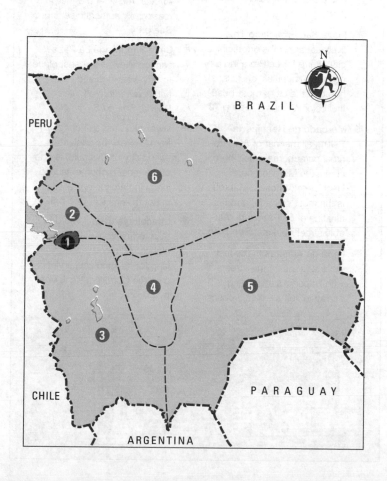

CHAPTER 1 # Highlights

* **Fiesta del Gran Poder** La Paz's biggest religious fiesta, during which thousands of extravagantly costumed Aymara dancers parade through the streets accompanied by massed brass bands and exuberant revellers. **See p.58**

* **Plaza San Francisco** This lively square is the unofficial city centre for La Paz's indigenous communities, and also home to the city's most beautiful colonial church. **See p.73**

* **Mercado de Hechicería** Selling all manner of Aymara ritual paraphernalia and herbal cures, the Mercado de Hechicería (Witches' Market) is the most colourful and fascinating of La Paz's innumerable street markets. **See p.75**

* **Feria de Alasitas** In the last week of January the streets fill with colourful stalls selling miniature items – cars, houses, dollar bills – which are bought and sold in a ritual commercial exchange thought to bring prosperity. **See p.75**

* **Peñas** La Paz's many folk-music venues offer the chance to enjoy traditional Andean music and dance in a reasonably authentic setting. **See p.84**

* **Calle Sagárnaga** La Paz's "gringo alley" is the best place to buy weavings and other handicrafts from all over Bolivia. **See p.85**

* **Tiwanaku** Just an hour away from La Paz, the ancient ruined city of Tiwanaku is one of the most monumental and intriguing archeological sites in South America. **See p.92**

* **Chacaltaya** Even if you don't take to the slopes, the world's highest ski resort is worth visiting for its spectacular views over the Cordillera Real. **See p.100**

La Paz and around

F ew cities in the world have a setting as spectacular as **LA PAZ**. Situated at over 3500m above sea level, the city cowers in a narrow canyon gouged from the high Altiplano, the cluster of church spires and office blocks at its centre dwarfed by the magnificent icebound peak of Mount Illimani, which rises imperiously to the southeast. On either side, the steep slopes of the valley are covered by the ramshackle homes of the city's poorer inhabitants, which cling precariously to even the harshest gradients.

With a population of just over a million, La Paz is the political and commercial hub of Bolivia and the capital in all but name (technically, that honour belongs to Sucre). But for all that it retains the feel of a provincial city, protected from the tides of globalization by its isolation and unique cultural make-up. Founded as a centre of Spanish power in the Andes, La Paz has always had a dual identity, with two very distinct societies, the indigenous and the European, coexisting in the same geographical space. Hi-tech international banks and government offices rub shoulders with vibrant street markets selling all manner of ritual paraphernalia for appeasing the spirits and mountain gods that still play a central role in the lives of the indigenous Aymara who make up the majority of the city's population. For them, life in the city they still refer to by the old indigenous name of Chuquiago Marka is conducted largely on the streets, and at times the whole place can feel like one massive, sprawling market. The exigencies of the high altitude make the pace of life quite slow, but there's an underlying bustle: everyone seems to be in a hurry, even though no one moves very fast. The warmth and vitality of La Paz is never more evident than during the **Fiesta del Gran Poder**, held in late May or early June, when young and old alike take to the streets in bizarre masks and outlandish costumes to dance in riotous celebration of the sacred and the profane.

Most visitors find La Paz's compelling street life and tremendous cultural vitality warrant spending a few days here. The city also makes an excellent base for trekking in the surrounding mountains and exploring the rest of the country. Lago Titicaca and the tropical valleys of the Yungas are within easy reach, and La Paz is also a good jumping-off point for trips to the southern Altiplano or down into the forests of the upper Amazon. Closer to hand are several good day-trips. To the west of the city the monumental ruins of **Tiwanaku** provide a reminder that great civilizations rose and fell in this region long before the arrival of the Spanish, and the dramatic mountain scenery that surrounds La Paz can be easily reached on excursions down the valley to the south or up to **Chacaltaya**, the highest ski resort in the world.

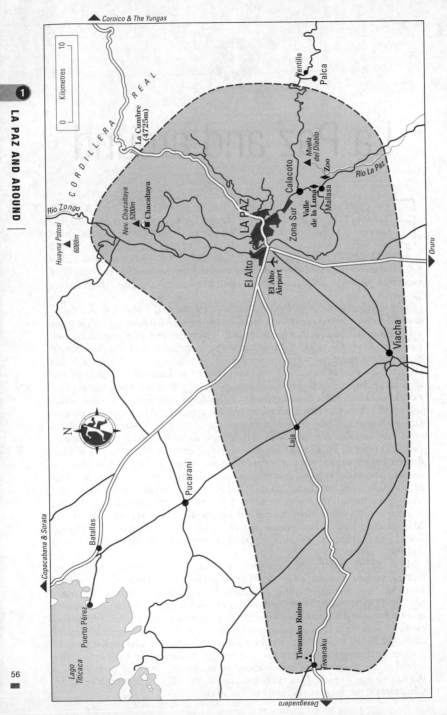

Some history

La Ciudad de Nuestra Señora de la Paz – the City of Our Lady of Peace – was founded in 1548 on the orders of Pedro de la Gasca, the supreme representative of the Spanish Emperor in Peru, to commemorate the end of almost ten years of bitter civil war between rival Spanish factions fighting over the spoils of conquest. Gasca ordered Captain **Alonso de Mendoza** to establish a new city midway between Cuzco and the recently discovered mineral wealth of Potosí, and on October 20, 1548, the new city's foundation ceremony was held outside the church at Laja, high on the Altiplano. Three days later the streets of the new settlement were traced out in the Choqueyapu valley, a short distance to the east. The site offered several advantages: the valley gave protection from the cold winds of the Altiplano and offered ample supplies of wood, water and indigenous labour from nearby settlements. It also had good agricultural lands nearby, and easy access to the products of several different ecological zones: meat and potatoes from the Altiplano; fish from Lago Titicaca; fruit, coca and other tropical crops from the valleys of the Yungas. Though some gold was found in the valley, this was quickly exhausted, and commerce rather than mining became the basis of the new city's economy.

The merchants of La Paz grew rich through the trade in coca from the Yungas to the mines of Potosí, and the city also prospered as a waystation on the route between the mines and the coast and between Lima and Buenos Aires, the two great centres of colonial rule in South America. The city also became an important centre for the spiritual conquest of the densely populated surrounding region, and before the end of the century the Dominican, Jesuit and Franciscan orders had all established bases from which missionaries were sent out to convert the indigenous population. By 1665 some five hundred Spaniards were living in La Paz, while a much larger indigenous population was housed in the three parishes that sprang up on the other side of the Río Choqueyapu, clearly separated from the Spanish city. When the king of Spain sought new officials to govern La Paz the appointment was evidently considered attractive: amongst the unsuccessful candidates was the writer **Miguel de Cervantes** – quite how the celebrated story of Don Quixote would have turned out had Cervantes come to live in La Paz is difficult to imagine.

La Paz's importance as a centre of colonial power made it an obvious target during the great rebellion that swept the Andes in 1780–81. In 1781 an indigenous army led by **Tupac Katari** twice laid siege to the city. The first siege lasted 109 days, during which perhaps a third of the defenders, led by **Sebastián de Segurola**, died of hunger or in bitter fighting before an army sent from Chuquisaca (Sucre) drove the rebels away. The relieving army was then drawn away to Oruro, however, and the siege resumed. This time the rebels employed a tactic they had used successfully against the town of Sorata, building a dyke to block the waters of the Río Choqueyapu above La Paz with the intention of releasing an apocalyptic flood to destroy the city. Fortunately for the desperate defenders, the dyke broke before sufficient waters had built up, and though the resulting torrent swept bridges and houses away, the city survived and held out until it was relieved by the army sent from Buenos Aires that finally crushed the rebellion.

The relative tranquillity that followed lasted only until 1809, when the leading citizens of La Paz – many of whom had fought against the uprising in 1781 – joined the revolutionary movement that was beginning to sweep the continent by making the first full declaration of independence from Spain. This initial revolt was quickly crushed, however, and La Paz suffered greatly during fourteen long years of civil war that followed, changing hands frequently as the fortunes of the royalist and pro-independence armies rose and fell. Its criollo citizens were generally supportive of the independence cause, but were deeply suspicious of the indigenous guerrilla armies that twice besieged the city.

By the time Bolivia's independence was finally secured in 1825, La Paz was the biggest city in the country, with a population of some 40,000. Though Sucre remained the **capital**, La Paz was increasingly the focus of the new republic's turbulent political life – a mixed blessing in a country where changes of government were frequent and often accompanied by bloodshed. In 1899 the growing rivalry between the two cities was resolved in a short but bloody **civil war** that left La Paz as the seat of government, home to the president and the congress, and the capital in all but name.

The first half of the twentieth century saw La Paz's population grow to over 300,000. In 1952 La Paz was the scene of the fierce street fighting which ushered in the **revolution** led by the MNR (see p.366). The sweeping changes that followed further fuelled the city's growth as the Aymara population of the Altiplano, released from servitude by the Agrarian reform (see p.366), migrated en masse to the metropolis. This migration from the countryside profoundly changed the character of La Paz, quadrupling its population to over a million and transforming it into a predominantly Aymara city. Certainly much of La Paz's

La Fiesta del Gran Poder

The defining cultural and social event of the year in La Paz is undoubtedly **La Fiesta del Gran Poder**, a dramatic religious fiesta held during late May or early June in homage to a miraculous image of Christ known as **Nuestro Señor del Gran Poder** (Our Lord of Great Power). The origins of the Gran Poder are surprisingly recent. It started little over half a century ago as a local celebration amongst Aymara migrants living and working in the market district around Avenida Buenos Aires, but since the beginning of the 1980s it has grown into an enormous festival that has taken over the centre of the city and is enjoyed by Paceños of all different classes. In part, this expansion has followed the growing wealth and influence of the Aymara merchants, but it also reflects a growing acceptance of Aymara culture and folklore amongst the city's white and mestizo residents.

Tens of thousands of costumed dancers belonging to over a hundred different folkloric fraternities take part in the *entrada* – the procession that marks the start of the fiesta – parading through the centre of La Paz to the cacophonous accompaniment of massed brass bands. The various dances performed during the *entrada* represent different themes from Aymara folklore and Catholic traditions from all over the department of La Paz and further afield. The sight of grown adults dressed in outrageous costumes drinking and dancing their way through the city may seem an odd form of religious devotion, but the participants and spectators see no contradiction in combining the sincere expression of religious belief with a riotous party – indeed the act of dancing non-stop for several hours at high altitude in a heavy costume can be seen as an exhausting form of devotional sacrifice, while the Señor del Gran Poder would doubtless be disappointed if the celebration of his fiesta were not accompanied by sufficient revelry.

The **cost** of the fiesta is enormous. Many dancers have to save for months to pay for the ever more elaborate costumes and masks – which are expected to change each year and can cost hundreds of dollars – and the dance troupes and their relatives must be provided with food, drink and musical accompaniment for about a week of non-stop revelry. These expenses are usually covered by sponsorship from wealthy individuals, whose prestige is thereby enhanced, and the different fraternities vie fiercely with each other for the title of best dance group, a competition that has led to ever more extravagant expenditure by fraternity sponsors.

European-descended elite has seen it in those terms, for as the poor indigenous neighbourhoods have crept up the steep slopes around the city and onto the Altiplano above (where the satellite settlement of **El Alto** is now recognized as a separate city), so the wealthier residents have retreated to the new residential suburbs of the Zona Sur, maintaining to some extent the city's old duality.

Arrival, information and city transport

Arriving in La Paz by **bus** or **plane** is a relatively painless experience: the city's small size makes it fairly easy to find your way around and there are inexpensive taxis and still cheaper public transport to hand, though the latter isn't always easy to travel in with big bags. Even if the high altitude doesn't take your breath away, your first sight of the city probably will. Unless you're arriving by bus from the Yungas to the north, you'll come in through El Alto, high on the Altiplano above La Paz, with panoramic views of the city nestled in the deep valley below and the magnificent peak of Illimani rising behind in the distance.

By air

International and domestic flights arrive at **El Alto airport** (flight information on ☎02/2810122), on the rim of the Altiplano about 10km away from – and almost 500m above – La Paz. At over 4000m above sea level, this is the highest international airport in the world, and it can feel as if planes have to climb rather than descend when they come in to land. Despite being an international airport serving Bolivia's de facto capital, the terminal has a very provincial feel. Its rather limited facilities include an **airport information desk** (erratic opening hours), a couple of **banks** where you can change US dollars and travellers' cheques (though not at the best rates), and an **ATM** where you can make cash withdrawals on Visa or MasterCard. There's also a café and restaurant, plus a few newsstands and souvenir shops.

The easiest way into town from here is by **taxi**, a half-hour ride that should cost about $6. Alternatively, an airport **shuttle minibus** (micro) runs down into the city and the length of the Prado to Plaza Isabella La Católica ($0.60 per person; Mon–Sat every 20min between about 8am and 6pm, hourly on Sun). If you're heading out to the airport, wait on the Prado and flag down any minibus marked "aeropuerto".

Internal flights with the military airline TAM arrive at the **military airport** (☎02/2841884), alongside the commercial airport on Avenida Juan Pablo II in El Alto. Taxis wait here for passengers, but the shuttle bus does not; to get down to La Paz by public transport you'll need to catch any micro heading west along Avenida Juan Pablo II to La Ceja, the district on the edge of the Altiplano above La Paz, and change there.

By bus

Buses from southern and eastern Bolivia and international buses arrive at the **Terminal Terrestre** on Plaza Antofagasta, about 1km northeast of Plaza San Francisco. From here, it's a short taxi ride or a twenty-minute walk down Avenida Montes to the main accommodation areas in the city centre. The terminal has snack bars, luggage storage, a post office, telephones and a bus **information office** (Mon–Sat 8am–8.30pm, Sun 9am–noon; ☎02/2280551), which has timetable information for lots of different bus companies. Departing passengers have to pay $0.30 to use the terminal – tickets are sold from a kiosk on the main concourse and checked when you get on the bus.

El Alto & Airport

LA PAZ

AUTOPISTA

See 'Central La Paz' map for detail

AV PERU

Bus Terminal

AV ARMENTIA

AV MANCO KAPAC

AV MONTES

PLAZA
ALONSO DE
MENDOZA

CEMETERY
DISTRICT

El Alto

★ **Buses to Charazani**

★ **Buses to Tiwanaku
& Desaguadero**

AV AMERICA

★
★ ★ **Buses to Tiwanaku**
Buses to Copacabana

KOLLASUYO

**Buses to
Huatajata
& Sorata**

PLAZA
TOMAS CATARI

AV BAPTISTA

AV BUENOS AIRES

MAX PAREDES

AV MARISCAL

SANTA CRUZ

ILLAMPU

SAGARNAGA

LINARES

MURILLO

PLAZA
SAN
FRANCISCO

Cementerio
General

MAX PAREDES

SAN PEDRO

AV BUENOS AIRES

0   Metres   400

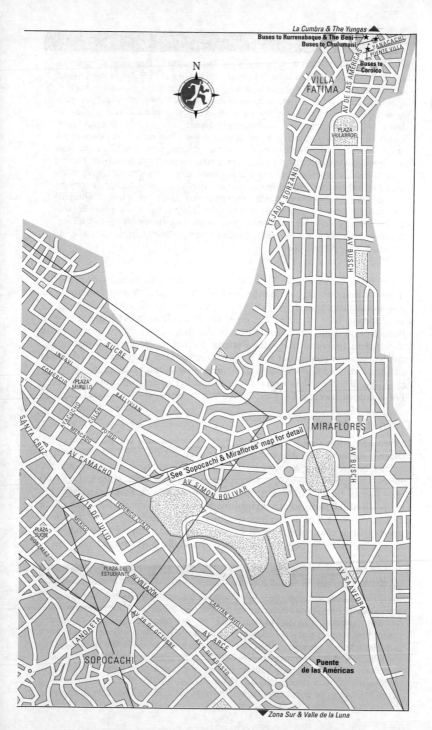

Buses from Copacabana, Tiwanaku, Sorata and Charazani arrive in the **cemetery district**, high up on the west side of the city. Plenty of micros head down to the city centre from here, but it's a pretty chaotic part of town, so it's a good idea to take a taxi ($1.20), especially if you have heavy luggage.

Buses from Coroico and Chulumani in the Yungas, and from Rurrenabaque and the Beni, arrive in the **Villa Fátima** district, in the far northeast of the city. The different companies all have offices around the intersection of Avenida de la Americas and Calle Yanacachi. Again, plenty of micros head down to the city centre from here, but a taxi ($1.20) is quicker, easier and more secure.

For details of **leaving La Paz**, see p.87.

Orientation

La Paz's geography makes it a difficult place to get lost in: if you do become disoriented, just head downhill and you'll eventually hit the city's main thoroughfare, the broad avenue known as the **Prado**. Running southeast along the course of the Río Choqueyapu, which is now entombed in concrete, the Prado neatly divides the city in two. At its top end is the **Plaza San Francisco**, the focal point of the **indigenous neighbourhoods** which climb the slopes of the valley to the west. This is the liveliest district of the city, an endless warren of markets that is also where much of the budget accommodation and other tourist services are found, centred above all on **Calle Sagárnaga**.

To the east of the Prado is the **colonial city centre**, still the main commercial district and home to most of the city's museums and surviving colonial churches. Heading southeast, the Prado's official name changes from Avenida Mariscal Santa Cruz to Avenida 16 de Julio as it passes the suburbs of **San Pedro** to the west and **Miraflores** to the east. The Prado ends on **Plaza del Estudiante**, south of which is the pleasant middle class suburb of **Sopocachi**.

Unlike most cities, in La Paz the richest neighbourhoods occupy the lowest altitudes, while the homes and markets of the poor are located high up on the steep slopes of the canyon. Many of the city's wealthiest residents now live in the upmarket suburbs that have sprung up down the valley in the **Zona Sur**, about 5km from the city centre, while recent Aymara rural migrants tend to live in the sprawling satellite city of **El Alto** on the rim of the Altiplano above La Paz.

Information

There's a small **tourist information office** (Mon–Fri 8.30am–7pm, Sat 9am–noon; ☏02/2371044) on Plaza Estudiante at the end of the Prado which has plenty of information on La Paz and the surrounding area, but not much on destinations further afield. The staff are helpful and there's usually someone who speaks a little English, plus they also sell good maps of the city and have flyers for most of the main **tour agencies**. These agencies – particularly concentrated on and around **Calle Sagárnaga**, off Plaza San Francisco – are the best places to go for information on the rest of the country, though obviously their main aim is to sell you a tour. There's also a reasonably helpful privately run **tourist information kiosk** (Mon–Fri 9am–6pm) on the ground floor of the *Café Angelo Colonial* at Linares 922, just off Sagárnaga. They can tell you about trekking and other organized tours around La Paz, but don't seem to push any particular agency.

City transport

You'll probably spend most of your time in the city centre, which is compact and easily **walkable** – it takes less than half an hour to get from one end of the Prado to the other on foot, and the traffic is so congested that walking is often the quickest way to get around, though at this altitude the steeper streets can be pretty exhausting to climb. That said, **taxis** are plentiful and relatively good value, and the city's **public transport** network, though slow and chaotic, is very cheap.

Taxis

Anyone with a car can work as a taxi driver just by putting a sign in their windscreen, and many Paceños do so part time to supplement their incomes – it's not unusual to find a university professor at the wheel of a cab. These **unlicensed taxis** charge about $0.50 per passenger for journeys anywhere in the centre of town – there are no meters and some drivers have a tendency to overcharge foreigners, so it's best to agree the fare at the beginning of the journey. If the cab isn't full it's not unusual for them to pick up other passengers who are heading in the same direction, though if you don't feel comfortable with this you can ask to have the cab to yourself. **Radio taxis**, which are marked as such and usually have a telephone number painted on the side, are more reliable. They charge a flat rate of about $1 for anywhere in the centre regardless of the number of passengers, which makes them good value for more than one person. Try Alfa (☏02/2412525) or Ideal (☏02/2222425). In both kinds of taxi fares increase for longer journeys, especially if they involve a steep climb, which consumes more fuel; a taxi to the Zona Sur should cost about $2.50. For trips outside the city there's a **long-distance taxi** office (☎02/2358336) outside the *Radisson* hotel on Avenida Arce.

Buses, micros and trufis

There are two main forms of public transport in La Paz: **city buses**, ageing leviathans that belch fumes as they trundle slowly around the city, and privately owned minibuses, known as **micros**, which run along all the city's main thoroughfares and are one of the main causes of traffic congestion. Though quicker and much more numerous than the big buses, micros can be incredibly cramped and are slowed by the need to stop at every street corner to pick up passengers.

Getting the hang of the city's bus and micro **routes** can be difficult. Most main routes are served by a variety of different drivers' syndicates, each with a different route number, which can be very confusing. The trick is to look for the names of the micro's destinations, which are written on signs inside the windscreen and bellowed incessantly by the driver's assistants, who hang from the open doors in the hope of coaxing just one more passenger into the already packed vehicle. The micros you'll most likely want to use are those which run **up and down the Prado** between the bus terminal and Plaza San Francisco in the north and Avenida 6 de Agosto in Sopocachi to the south. To go anywhere else in the city, it's usually enough to wait by any major intersection until you hear the name of your destination shouted out; alternatively, ask a driver's assistant where to catch the relevant micro.

The city's third main form of transport are **trufis** – large estate cars which are used as collective taxis and follow fixed routes, mostly between Plaza del Estudiante and the wealthy suburbs of the Zona Sur. They're designated by route numbers and, like micros, have their principal destinations written on a sign inside the windscreen.

Trufis and micros charge a flat **fare** of about $0.25 in the city centre; city buses cost slightly less. All charge extra if your luggage fills a space that might otherwise be occupied by another passenger.

Accommodation

There's plenty of accommodation in La Paz to suit most budgets, though things get pretty busy in the peak tourist season from June to August, when prices tend to increase. Most places to stay are in the **city centre** within a few blocks of **Plaza San Francisco**, close to or in the midst of the colourful market district and within walking distance of most of the city's main attractions. This area is also where most tourist services are concentrated, so it's convenient for booking tours, changing money and sorting out other practicalities. The other option is to stay in one of the more upmarket places down the **Prado**, towards the middle-class suburb of Sopocachi, south of the city centre, which is where most of the city's better restaurants and nightspots are located.

Budget accommodation tends to be pretty spartan, with small, sparsely furnished rooms. Pay a little more – about $20 and upwards for a double room – and you can stay in a decent **mid-range hotel**, where rooms tend to be larger, with more comfortable beds, better décor, and extras like towels and cable television. Ask to see a few rooms before you check in and try to choose one that gets some sunlight, as this makes a big difference in temperature at this alti-

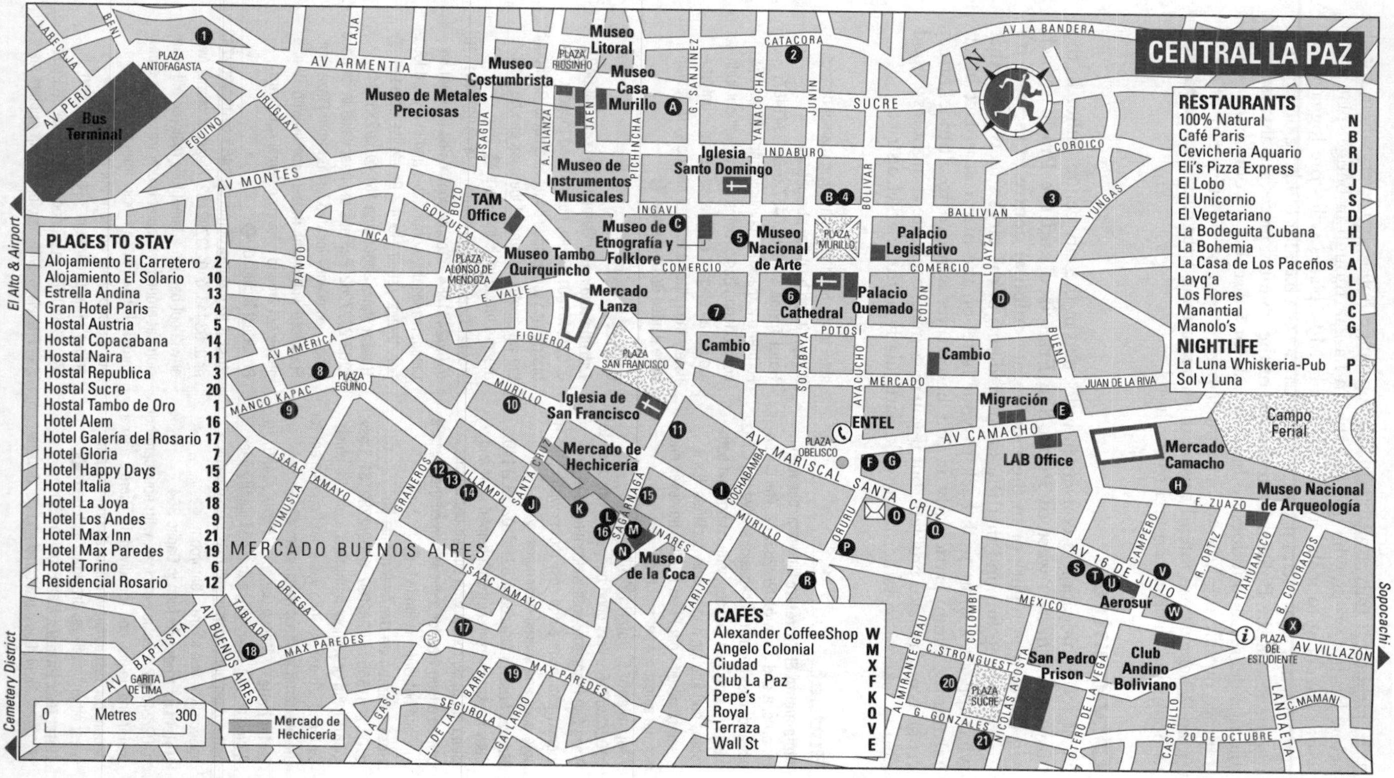

CENTRAL LA PAZ
RESTAURANTS
100% Natural N
Café Paris B
Cevicheria Aquario R
Eli's Pizza Express U
El Lobo J
El Unicornio S
El Vegetariano D
La Bodeguita Cubana H
La Bohemia T
La Casa de Los Paceños A
Layq'a L
Los Flores O
Manantial C
Manolo's G
NIGHTLIFE
La Luna Whiskeria-Pub P
Sol y Luna I
PLACES TO STAY
Alojamiento El Carretero 2
Alojamiento El Solario 10
Estrella Andina 13
Gran Hotel Paris 4
Hostal Austria 5
Hostal Copacabana 14
Hostal Naira 11
Hostal Republica 3
Hostal Sucre 20
Hostal Tambo de Oro 1
Hotel Alem 16
Hotel Galería del Rosario 17
Hotel Gloria 7
Hotel Happy Days 15
Hotel Italia 8
Hotel La Joya 18
Hotel Los Andes 9
Hotel Max Inn 21
Hotel Max Paredes 19
Hotel Torino 6
Residencial Rosario 12
CAFÉS
Alexander CoffeeShop W
Angelo Colonial M
Ciudad X
Club La Paz F
Pepe's K
Royal Q
Terraza V
Wall St E
0 Metres 300
Mercado de Hechicería
El Alto & Airport
Cemetery District
Sopocachi
Bus Terminal
Museo Litoral
Museo Costumbrista
Museo Casa Murillo
Museo de Metales Preciosas
Museo de Instrumentos Musicales
Iglesia Santo Domingo
TAM Office
Museo de Etnografía y Folklore
Museo Tambo Quirquincho
Museo Nacional de Arte
Palacio Legislativo
Palacio Quemado
Cathedral
Mercado Lanza
Cambio
Iglesia de San Francisco
Mercado de Hechicería
Museo de la Coca
MERCADO BUENOS AIRES
ENTEL
Migración
LAB Office
Mercado Camacho
Campo Ferial
Museo Nacional de Arqueología
Aerosur
San Pedro Prison
Club Andino Boliviano
PLAZA ANTOFAGASTA
PLAZA RIOSINHO
PLAZA ALONSO DE MENDOZA
PLAZA MURILLO
PLAZA SAN FRANCISCO
PLAZA EGUINO
PLAZA OBELISCO
PLAZA SUCRE
PLAZA DEL ESTUDIENTE
GARITA DE LIMA
AV ARMENTIA
AV MONTES
AV PERU
AV AMÉRICA
AV MARISCAL SANTA CRUZ
AV CAMACHO
AV 16 DE JULIO
AV VILLAZÓN
AV LA BANDERA
AV BUENOS AIRES
AV BAPTISTA
MANCO KAPAC
ISAAC TAMAYO
SAGARNAGA
ILLAMPU
COMERCIO
SUCRE
POTOSÍ
MERCADO
BALLIVIAN
YUNGAS
COROICO

tude. Heating is only available in the top-range hotels, but everywhere listed below has hot water, which is essential in La Paz, though in budget places it's worth checking to make sure it's working. Most places will store luggage for you, which is very useful if you're using La Paz as a base for trekking or exploring the rest of the Bolivia. As in the rest of the country, prices are always flexible to a degree, and it does no harm to ask for a discount – your chances will improve outside the June-to-September high season or if you're part of a big group. Wherever you intend to stay, if you're arriving after dark it's a good idea to book ahead and take a taxi to the hotel.

City centre

Most accommodation is conveniently located in the city centre, either in the busy market district **west of Plaza San Francisco and the Prado** (which can be noisy at night), or in the more sedate **colonial centre** to the east. It's worth bearing in mind that the steep gradients of the city's streets mean that what appears a short walk back to your hotel on the map can in fact be an exhausting climb, particularly if you haven't yet adjusted to altitude. Street crime is not a major problem, but if you're coming back late at night it's a good idea to take a taxi rather than walk, particularly in the market district.

Budget

Alojamiento El Carretero Catacora, between Yanacocha and Junín ☎02/2285272. The cheapest and most popular backpackers' dive in La Paz: basic, friendly and raucous, with communal bathrooms and kitchen and laundry facilities. It's a steep climb up from Plaza Murillo, however, and not the safest area at night. ➊

Alojamiento El Solario Murillo 776 ☎02/2367963. Very good budget option, close to Plaza San Francisco, with welcoming staff, a friendly atmosphere and cosy rooms with comfortable beds and shared bathrooms. ➋

Hostal Austria Yanacocha 531 ☎02/2351140. Busy backpackers' haunt with helpful staff and clean but basic rooms with shared bathrooms – it can be a long wait for a shower when the hostel's full, and hot water is limited. ➌

Hostal Tambo de Oro Av Armentia 367 ☎02/2281565 or 2282097, ℗02/2282181. Cosy rooms (with or without bath) fitted out with plush pink and red decor. Good value, and convenient for the bus terminal if not much else. ➌

Hotel Italia Av Manco Capac 303 ☎02/2456710. A gloomy, run-down place that has clearly seen better days but which is still reasonable value, especially if you share a bathroom. ➋

Hotel Los Andes Av Manco Capac 364 ☎02/2455327. Basic but clean, with abundant hot water and helpful and friendly staff. There's also a decent bar-restaurant which is a good place to meet other travellers. Breakfast included. ➌

Hotel Max Paredes Max Paredes 650 ☎02/2453634. Basic but clean and good-value hotel in the heart of the bustling market district, though it can be noisy at night. ➋

Hotel Torino Socabaya 457 ☎02/2341487. Former backpackers' favourite and still always busy, offering basic rooms with or without bath set around an elegant colonial courtyard – unfortunately the rather dour staff and noisy restaurant have dented its popularity. ➌

Moderate

Estrella Andina Av Illampu 716 ☎02/2456421, ℗02/2451401. Clean, modern and friendly, with bizarre neo-indigenous décor and cable TV, though the windowless rooms at the back can be cold. A meagre breakfast is included. ➍

Hostal Copacabana Illampu 734 ☎02/2451626, ℗02/2451684, ℮combicop@ceibo.entelnet.bo. Clean, reasonably comfortable and in a good location, though rather gloomy. Breakfast included. ➍

Hostal Naira Sagárnaga 161 ☎02/2355645, ℗02/2327262. Perhaps the best value in its price range, excellently located just up from Plaza San Francisco with bright, modern rooms with TV and phone set around a lovely colonial courtyard. Breakfast included. ➎

Hostal Republica Comercio 1455 ☎02/2202742 or 2203448, ℗02/2202782. Pleasant rooms (with or without bath) in a beautifully restored old mansion set around two quiet courtyards and a sunny garden. It's just three blocks from Plaza Murillo, but a steep climb up from the Prado. ➍

Hotel Alem Sagárnaga 334 ☎02/2367400, ℗02/2350579. In a good location just off Plaza San Francisco, with helpful and informative staff and small but comfortable and scrupulously clean rooms, with or without bath. Breakfast included. **❹**

Hotel del Rosario Santa Cruz 583 ☎02/2371565 or 2310618, ⓕ02/2316857, ⓦwww.hotgalvrosario .com.bo. Modern, stylish and good-value hotel: the glass roof lets in plenty of sunlight and there are lots of plants, creating a warm, tropical feel. Rooms are comfortable and well decorated, with cable TV and breakfast included, and heating and oxygen available if the altitude gets to you. It's a steep climb up from Plaza San Francisco. **❺**

Hotel Happy Days Sagárnaga 229 ☎02/2314759, ⓕ02/2355079, ⓔhappydays@zuper.net. Decent if slightly cramped rooms with cheerful bright yellow decor and a good central location. Cheaper rooms with communal bath are also available. **❹**

Hotel La Joya Max Paredes 541 ☎02/2453841, ⓕ02/2453496. Excellent-value mid-range hotel just off Calle Buenos Aires in the bustling market district. Rooms are bright and well furnished and come with cable TV and good views across the city. **❹–❺**

Expensive

Gran Hotel Paris Plaza Murillo ☎02/2319170, ⓕ02/2362547, ⓔparishot@ceibo.entelnet.bo. The oldest hotel in La Paz, built in 1911 in delightful belle époque style and recently refurbished. The spacious rooms come with period furniture and are set around a glass-roofed patio, while the suites with balconies looking out onto Plaza Murillo are well worth the extra cost. Heating, cable TV and a buffet breakfast included. Rooms **❻**, suites **❼**

Hotel Gloria Potosí 909 ☎02/2370010, ⓕ02/2391489, ⓔgloriat@datacom-bo.net. Uninspiring high-rise hotel offering comfortable modern rooms with telephone, cable TV, central heating and lurid psychedelic carpets – the upper rooms have great views across the city. There's also a good restaurant, and breakfast is included. **❻**

Residencial Rosario Illampu 704 ☎02/2451658 or 2451341, ⓕ02/2451991, ⓔturisbus@caoba.entelnet.bo. One of the longest-established tourist hotels in the city, always busy despite being a bit overpriced. Accommodation is in a warren of elegant heated rooms crammed in around a series of pretty, colonial-style courtyards. There's also a good restaurant, sauna, and two cafés. Breakfast included. **❻**

El Prado, San Pedro and Sopocachi

La Paz's more luxurious hotels are located **along the Prado** and in the prosperous suburb of **Sopocachi**, home to most of the city's more fashionable bars and restaurants, and a pleasant place to stroll around in the evening. There are also a couple of places to stay in **San Pedro**, a peaceful suburb midway between the city centre and Sopocachi, which offers a good compromise between the two. The San Pedro hotels are shown on the map on p.65.

El Rey Palace Hotel Av 20 de Octubre 1947, Sopocachi ☎02/2393016, ⓕ02/2367759, ⓔhotelrey@caoba.entelnet.bo. One of the best value upmarket options in La Paz, with big, comfortable and stylishly decorated rooms boasting the full range of facilities, including heating. Breakfast included. **❽**

Hostal Sucre Plaza San Pedro, San Pedro ☎02/2492038, ⓕ02/2486723. Friendly and well-located hostal, with basic rooms with or without bath set around a pleasant courtyard. There's also a kitchen and laundry for guests' use. **❹**

Hotel España Av 6 De Agosto 2074, Sopocachi ☎02/2442643 or 2441919, ⓕ02/2441329, ⓔhespana@ceibo.entelnet.bo. Clean, quiet and reasonably priced, with a good location just off Plaza del Estudiante in Sopocachi. The best rooms are those around the sunny garden at the back. Breakfast included. **❺**

Hotel Europa Tiahuanacu 64, Sopocachi ☎02/2315656, ⓕ02/8115656, ⓔunico@hotel-europa-bolivia.com. La Paz's most luxurious and expensive hotel, decorated in style and boasting all the features you could wish for, including heating and humidification, bars and restaurants, along with a swimming pool, sauna and gymnasium. **❾**

Hotel Max Inn Plaza San Pedro, San Pedro ☎02/2374391, ⓕ02/2341720. Bright, modern and well-decorated establishment, though slightly overpriced. The comfortable rooms all come with cable TV, and some also have balconies overlooking the plaza. **❻**

Hotel Radisson Plaza Av Arce 2177, Sopocachi ☎02/2316161, ⓕ02/2343391, ⓔradissonbolivia@usa.net. Luxurious high-rise landmark with all the facilities you would expect from a first-class international hotel. The fifteenth-floor restaurant has spectacular views. Breakfast included. **❾**

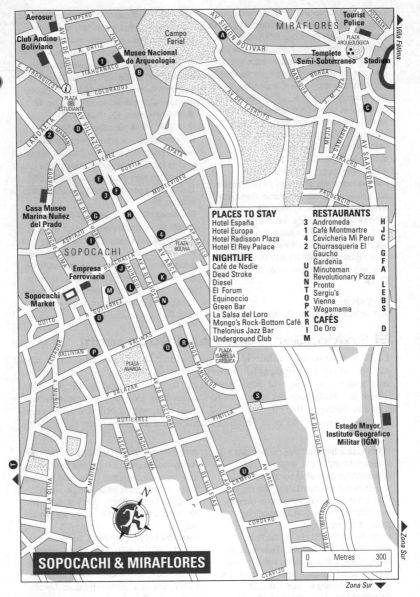

PLACES TO STAY
Hotel España — 3
Hotel Europa — 1
Hotel Radisson Plaza — 4
Hotel El Rey Palace — 2

NIGHTLIFE
Café de Nadie — U
Dead Stroke — Q
Diesel — N
El Forum — T
Equinoccio — O
Green Bar — P
La Salsa del Loro — K
Mongo's Rock-Bottom Café — R
Thelonius Jazz Bar — I
Underground Club — M

RESTAURANTS
Andromeda — H
Café Montmartre — J
Cevicheria Mi Peru — C
Churrasqueria El
Gaucho — G
Gardenia — F
Minuteman — A
Revolutionary Pizza — L
Pronto — E
Sergiu's — B
Vienna — S
Wagamama — S

CAFÉS
De Oro — D

SOPOCACHI & MIRAFLORES

The City

In terms of conventional tourist attractions La Paz's appeal is modest. There are still some fine **colonial palaces** and **churches** in the centre of town, but in general the city's architecture is drab and functional, while the city's few **museums** scarcely do justice to Bolivia's fascinating history and culture. But most visitors are enthralled by the energy of La Paz's **street life** and its rich cultural heritage, while the absence of green areas is more than redeemed by the sight of Illimani, the majestic mountain whose permanently snow-covered 6439-metre peak dominates the landscape, and which is still revered as a powerful tutelary deity by many of the city's inhabitants.

La Paz's main commercial thoroughfare, known as **El Prado**, runs southeast through the city, its official name changing from Avenida Mariscal Santa Cruz to Avenida 16 de Julio as it heads south. The boulevard is punctuated with statues of historical figures including Bolívar, Columbus, Isabel La Católica – the fact that not one of them is Bolivian says much about the cultural orientation of the European-descended elite that continues to dominate Bolivian politics. Lined with trees – a rarity in La Paz – and with a central promenade with pleasant gardens and benches, the Prado is one of the city's few flat and spacious areas, and a popular place for strolling and socializing, though the ceaseless traffic on either side and the modern high-rise buildings that now block out much of the sun have detracted somewhat from its original charm.

The Prado runs along the course of the **Río Choqueyapu**, whose heavily polluted waters are now entombed in concrete beneath the streets. During the colonial period the river formed the border between two different worlds, with the Spanish city centre on one side and the Aymara settlements on the other, a division which is still very much in evidence today. To the east of the Prado, the **colonial city centre** is still the main commercial and government district, dominated by banks, ministries and the men in grey suits who run them. To the west of the Prado, meanwhile, the main **indigenous neighbourhoods** sweep up the steep slopes of the valley, their narrow, winding streets filled with the colour and ceaseless bustle of seemingly endless street markets.

The colonial city centre

The well-ordered streets of the colonial city centre still preserve the neat grid pattern laid out by the city founders in accordance with Spanish laws governing the foundation of settlements in the Indies. At its centre stands the **Plaza Murillo**, home to both the Palacio Presidential and the parliament building, the Palacio Legislativo. A fair number of colonial buildings still survive, though most are in a poor state of repair, their crumbling facades and dilapidated balconies obscured by tangled phone lines and electric cables. The exceptions to this are concentrated on and around the Plaza Murillo and the nearby **Calle Jaen**, both of which are also home to several **museums**.

Plaza Murillo

Though it remains the epicentre of Bolivia's political life, the **Plaza Murillo** – the main square of the colonial city centre – has an endearingly provincial feel, busy with people feeding pigeons and eating ice cream in the shade. Known as the Plaza de Armas during the colonial era, the square was renamed after independence in honour of the independence martyr Pedro Domingo Murillo, who was hanged here in 1810 after leading a failed rebellion against the colonial authorities, one of several bloody scenes the square has witnessed during Bolivia's turbulent political past. A statue of Murillo now stands at the centre of the plaza.

The Cathedral

On the south side of the plaza stand two great symbols of political and spiritual power in Bolivia, the Cathedral and the Palacio Presidential. With its twin bell-towers and broad but rather plain Neoclassical facade, the **Cathedral** is remarkable more for the time in took to complete than for its aesthetic value. Begun in 1835 (when its colonial predecessor had to be demolished due to structural problems), it wasn't inaugurated until 1925, and was finally completed only in 1989 in a last-minute rush ahead of a visit by Pope John Paul II. The cool, vaulted interior is relatively unadorned, in contrast to La Paz's many Baroque churches; its most unusual feature is a stained-glass window depicting former presidents Mariscal Andrés de Santa Cruz and General José de Ballivián and their families receiving blessings from on high, a surprisingly explicit expression of the historic conflation in Bolivia of church, military and state. One of Bolivia's most revered former presidents, Santa Cruz (see p.360) was reburied in a small side chapel of the cathedral in 1965, a century after he died in exile in France.

In a crypt underneath the Cathedral – the entrance is just south of the plaza on Calle Socabaya – the **Museo de Arte Sacro de la Catedral** (Tues–Fri 9am–12.30pm & 3–7pm, Sat & Sun 9am–1pm; $0.45) houses a small collection of colonial religious art. As well as paintings, there's plenty of extravagant silverwork and sculpture, including the **Virgen de la Paz**, a fine wooden carving of the city's patron which was brought from Seville in the sixteenth century. The Virgin's devotional cult reached a peak during the siege in 1781, when she was widely credited with saving the city from indigenous rebels.

The Palacio Presidencial and Palacio Legislativo

Next door to the Cathedral stands the elegant Neoclassical **Palacio Presidencial** (Presidential Palace), its ceremonial guards in red nineteenth-century uniforms from the War of the Pacific discreetly backed up by military policemen with more modern equipment. The palace isn't open to the public, but the guards may let you have a look at the central courtyard when the president is not in residence. Completed in 1852, the palace is generally known as the **Palacio Quemado** – the "Burnt Palace" – after it was badly damaged by fire in 1875 during one of the more violent of Bolivia's many revolutionary episodes. Rebels opposed to the then president, Tomas Frias, set the palace alight after repeated attempts to storm it failed. The following morning the bodies of some 130 people killed in the fighting were strewn across the square and in nearby streets. In front of the cathedral a bust of former president, Gualberto Villaroel, provides a reminder of a more successful, if equally gruesome, revolutionary attempt which occurred in 1946, when Villaroel was thrown from a palace window by an angry mob and hanged from a lamppost. On the east side of the plaza is the **Palacio Legislativo**, the seat of the Bolivian parliament, was built in a similar Neoclassical style in the early twentieth century on the site previously occupied by the Jesuit headquarters until their expulsion from the Spanish Empire in 1767.

The Museo Nacional de Arte

On the southwest corner of the plaza the **Palacio de Los Condes de Arana**, one of La Paz's finest surviving colonial palaces, now houses the **Museo Nacional de Arte** (Tues–Sat 9.30am–noon & 3–7pm, Sun 10.30am–6.30pm; $0.85), well worth visiting for its comprehensive collection of works by major Bolivian painters. Completed in 1775, when La Paz was at the peak of its colonial prosperity, the palace (also known as the Palacio de Diez Medina – it's not clear exactly who had it built) is a magnificent example of Baroque architecture, with a grand portico opening onto a central patio overlooked by three floors of arched walkways, all elaborately carved from pink granite in a rococo style with stylised shells, flowers and feathers. The emphasis of the museum's art collection is firmly on colonial religious art. Amongst the highlights are several works by **Melchor Pérez de Holguín**, the great master of Andean colonial painting, and a magnificent eighteenth-century picture by an anonymous La Paz artist of an Archangel Arquebusero, an iconic image of an angel carrying a primitive firearm which neatly encapsulates the spiritual–military contradictions of the Spanish conquest.

Along Calle Ingavi

A block northeast from the plaza along Calle Ingavi, the **Iglesia Santo Domingo** boasts a richly detailed eighteenth-century facade in mestizo-Baroque style. Carved from soft white stone, the facade exemplifies the intimate combination of Spanish and indigenous symbolism which is characteristic of Andean colonial architecture, with delicately carved trees, grapes and pomegranates (typical Spanish Baroque devices representing the Eucharist) intermingled with New World fruits and parrots. The main body of the church dates from the mid-seventeenth century, when the Dominicans took a leading role in the evangelization of the Andes, while the interior was remodelled in the nineteenth century in rather anodyne Neoclassical style.

Set inside an elegant colonial mansion a little further down Calle Ingavi is the small but rewarding **Museo de Etnografía y Folklore** (Tues–Fri 9am–12.30pm & 3–7pm, Sat & Sun 9am–noon; free), housed in a seventeenth-century mansion built for the Marques de Villaverde, whose coat of arms looks down on the central patio from an exquisite mestizo-Baroque portico, complete with floral designs, parrots and feline figures. The mansion's street facade boasts the only surviving example of the elegant carved wooden balconies which were common in colonial La Paz.

Inside, the museum has exhibitions on two of Bolivia's most distinctive indigenous cultures. One room concentrates on the **Chipayas**, or Uros, a minority ethnic group which has been displaced from much of its territory by Aymara groups and now subsists on the watery margins of the great lakes of the southern Altiplano. The other focuses on the Quechua-speaking **Tarabucos** from the highlands east of Sucre, whose colourful striped ponchos and hats in the shape of the helmets of Spanish conquistadors are widely used to represent the "exoticism" of Bolivia to the outside world. Both rooms are well laid out, with good explanations and plenty of photos, models, weavings and other artefacts from the two groups' fascinating cultures. Given the phenomenal cultural diversity of Bolivia, though, it's a shame the museum isn't more extensive. For those interested in further research, there's also an extensive ethnographic **library**, which is open to the public.

Calle Jaen and the municipal museums

A short walk uphill along Calle Gerardo Sanjinez and then left along Calle Indaburo brings you to the foot of **Calle Jaen**, the best preserved colonial street in La Paz and home to no fewer than four **municipal museums** (all Tues–Fri 9.30am–12.30pm & 3pm–7pm, Sat & Sun 10am–3pm). A narrow cobbled street lined with whitewashed houses adorned with elegant wooden balconies, red tiled roofs and carved stone doorways opening onto quiet courtyards, Calle Jaen could almost be in a small town in Andalucia or Extremadura, so strong is the Spanish feel. Originally known as Cabracancha ("Goat Enclosure"), the street was renamed in honour of Apollinar Jaen, a co-conspirator of the independence leader Pedro Domingo Murillo. Both lived in this street, and the opulence of their homes makes you realize quite how much they had to lose when they launched their ill-fated rebellion against Spanish rule: that they were prepared to risk what must have been comfortable existences reflects well on the strength of their idealism.

The four municipal museums are all accessed on a single ticket ($0.5), which is sold at the **Museo Costumbrista Juan de Vargas**, at the top of the street (the

△ Market scene, La Paz

entrance is just around the corner on Calle Sucre). Set inside a renovated colonial mansion, this museum gives a good introduction to the folkloric customs of the Altiplano, in particular the traditional dances and processions that form a central part of the region's religious fiestas. Amongst the exhibits is a small collection of the elaborate costumes and grotesque masks worn in dances such as the *Waka-Waka*, which ridicules the Spanish by aping the antics of bullfighters, with one dancer dressed as a bull; and the *Morenos*, whose performers represent colonial-era African slaves, the bulging eyes and lolling tongues of their lurid black masks evidence of the strange exoticism such figures must have held to contemporary Andean eyes. Look out too for the monstrous *Danzante* mask, whose wearer used to be expected to dance until he literally dropped dead, thereby ensuring a drought- and disease-free year for his community. There is also a series of richly detailed ceramic dioramas of colonial scenes, ranging from comic scenes of drunken fiestas complete with traditional dance troupes through to the hanging of independence hero Domingo Murillo and the execution of the eighteenth-century Aymara revolutionary Tupac Katari, who was torn apart by four horses.

Housed in the same building but accessed from Calle Jaen, the **Museo Litoral** is dedicated to one of Bolivia's national obsessions: the loss of its coastline to Chile during the nineteenth century War of the Pacific (see p.361). Unless you share that obsession, however, the collection of old uniforms, photos of the lost ports, and maps justifying Bolivia's claim to the coast is not very inspiring. Next door, the **Museo de Metales Preciosas** has a small but impressive hoard of Inca and Tiwanaku gold ornaments, housed in a steel vault. Informative displays explain the techniques used by pre-Columbian goldsmiths, and the delicate skill evident in the work make it obvious why these indigenous artisans were so quickly enrolled into producing religious artwork by the Spanish. On the other side of the road, inside the sumptuous mansion which was once the home of the venerated independence martyr after whom it's now named, the **Museo Casa Murillo** houses an eclectic collection ranging from colonial religious art and portraits of former presidents to artefacts used in witchcraft and miniatures from past Alacitas fiestas (see p.75). Particularly interesting are a painting of La Paz during the siege of 1781, which gives a good idea of the size and layout of the colonial city, and a sixteenth-century version of the Roman Catholic creed, written in hieroglyphics on sheepskin, which was apparently used by missionaries in the conversion of indigenous people.

Set around yet another pretty colonial courtyard a little further down Calle Jaen, the delightful **Museo de Instrumentos Musicales** (daily 9.30am–12.30pm & 2.30–6.30pm; $0.85) is home to an astonishing variety of handmade musical instruments from all over Bolivia, some of which you can play. A collection of pre-Columbian pipes and drums is followed by a plethora of the stringed instruments – guitars, violins, mandolins and charangos – which were introduced by the Spanish and eagerly seized upon by the indigenous population, who quickly combined these two elements to create the distinctive Andean music of today.

Plaza San Francisco and the market district

At the north end of the Prado, **Plaza San Francisco** is the gateway to the main Aymara neighbourhoods of La Paz, which climb up the slopes of the valley to the west. Founded in the colonial era as the *parroquias de Indios* – the Indian parishes – these neighbourhoods were where the Aymara population from the surrounding countryside was encouraged to settle, living around churches built as part of the effort to convert them to Christianity; less idealistically, this separate indigenous quarter was also designed as a pool of cheap labour, neatly separated from the Spanish city by the Río Choqueyapu. Today the area retains a very strong Aymara identity and its narrow, winding and at times almost vertical streets are filled with the bustling markets that make it one of the most vibrant and distinctive parts of the city, nowhere more so than in the **Mercado de Hechicería** – without doubt one of the most extraordinary sights in La Paz.

Plaza San Francisco

Though the frenetic traffic running alongside detracts from its charm, the **Plaza San Francisco** is the focal point for the city's Aymara population and one of the liveliest plazas in La Paz, busy with people enjoying snacks and juices or crowding around the many comedians, story-tellers, magicians and sellers of miracle cures who come here to ply their trade. It's also the usual focus of the city's frequent **political protests**, and if you're in La Paz for more than a few days you're likely to witness a march by striking teachers, unemployed miners, indebted small traders or whichever social or political group has taken to the streets that week. Such marches are a constant feature of Bolivia's political life and very much part of the democratic process in a country that has only recently emerged from the shadow of military dictatorship. They're usually colourful pieces of political theatre, but they can sometimes provoke heavy-handed responses from the authorities, and clashes between police and demonstrators involving the fairly unrestrained use of tear gas are not uncommon.

On the west side of the plaza stands the **Iglesia de San Francisco**, the most beautiful colonial church in La Paz. First built in 1549 as the headquarters of the Franciscans' campaign to christianize Alto Peru, the original structure collapsed under a heavy snowfall early in the seventeenth century and most of what you see today was built between 1750 and 1784, financed by donations from mine owners. The richly decorated facade is a classic example of the mestizo-Baroque style, showing clear indigenous influence, with carved anthropomorphic figures reminiscent of pre-Columbian sculpture as well as more common birds and intertwined floral designs. Above the main door is a statue of St Francis himself, facing towards the old city with his arms held aloft. **Inside**, the walls of the church are lined with extravagantly carved altarpieces where smiling angels and abundant gold leaf frame gruesome depictions of the crucifixion or images of individual saints that are the principal objects of veneration for those who come here to pray. San Judas Tadeo, the patron saint of the poor and miserable, is particularly popular amongst indigenous supplicants. To the right of the altar, the neon halos on a figure of San Antonio carrying an infant Christ add a bizarre touch of modernity to the Baroque extravaganza.

To you right as you face the church, the plaza is overlooked by a bizarre modern statue known as the **Pucara**, crowned by abstract figures of huddled Aymara women and with a massive carving of the head of the Mariscal Andrés de Santa Cruz at its foot looking down the avenue that bears his name – its exact meaning (if any) remains obscure.

The Mercado de Hechicería and Museo de la Coca

To the left of the Iglesia San Francisco is **Calle Sagárnaga**, La Paz's main tourist street, crowded with hotels, tour agencies, restaurants, handicraft shops and stalls. It's sometimes referred to rather dismissively as "Gringo Alley", though to be fair, catering to travellers has always been Calle Sagárnaga's main function: in the colonial era, this was where wayfarers en route between Potosí and the Peruvian coast would be put up, and several of the buildings now occupied by hotels were actually built for that purpose in the eighteenth century.

Ekeko: the household god of abundance

One of Bolivia's most unusual fiestas is the **Feria de Alasitas**, held in La Paz in the last week of January, when large areas of the city are taken over by market stalls selling all manner of miniature items. At the centre of the festivities is a diminutive figure of a mustachioed man with rosy cheeks and a broad smile, dressed in a tiny suit and hat and laden with foodstuffs and material possessions. This is the **Ekeko**, the household god of abundance. A common sight in Paceño homes, the Ekeko is a demanding god who must be kept happy with regular supplies of alcohol, cigarettes and miniature gifts. In return, he watches over the household, ensuring happiness and prosperity and returning in kind any gift he receives. At the fair each year, people buy objects they desire in miniature to give to Ekeko, thereby ensuring that the real thing will be theirs before the year is out. Originally, gifts to the Ekeko would have been farm animals and foodstuffs, but in the modern urban context of La Paz, miniature cars, houses, electrical goods, wads of dollar bills and even airline tickets and university degrees are preferred to more traditional items.

Some anthropologists believe the Ekeko is a modern manifestation of **Thunupa**, an ancient Aymara deity who somehow survived the extirpation of idolatry through which the Spanish Inquisition sought to wipe out pre-Christian rituals. His new incarnation is thought to date from the siege of La Paz during the great indigenous rebellion of 1781. During the terrible famine suffered by the defenders, the Aymara maid of the wife of the governor of La Paz, Sebastián de Segurola, stayed alive thanks to food smuggled to her by her lover, who was serving in the rebel army. Seeing her mistress on the point of starvation, she took pity and shared some of the food with her. When he returned from a day's fighting in defence of the city walls, Segurola was amazed to find his wife still alive, and asked the maid how she had come by the food. Anxious to protect her lover, the maid told him it had been miraculously provided by the small statue of Thunupa she kept in her room. Convinced a miracle had occurred, when the siege finally ended Segurola decreed a celebratory fiesta on January 24 to give thanks to the Virgin of La Paz. Most Paceños, however, accepted the maid's story that her little idol had been responsible, and the buying and selling of miniature goods to give to idols (now suitably disguised as moustachioed gentlemen to hide their pagan origin) soon became an integral part of the festivities for Aymara, mestizos and whites alike.

Two blocks up Sagárnaga on Calle Linares is the **Mercado de Hechicería**, or Witches' Market, which provides a fascinating window on the usually secretive world of Aymara mysticism and herbal medicine. The stalls here are heavily laden with a colourful cornucopia of ritual and medicinal items, ranging from herbal cures for minor ailments like rheumatism or stomach pain to incense, coloured sweets, protective talismans and dried llama foetuses. These items are combined in packages known as *mesas* or *pagos* and burned or buried as offerings to placate the various tutelary spirits and magical beings that are believed to hold sway over all aspects of daily life. There's no clear border between the medicinal and magical here: the *Yatiris* and *Kallawayas* – indigenous traditional healers – who are the market's main customers adopt a holistic approach in which a herbal cure for a specific symptom is usually combined with magical efforts to address the imbalances in the supernatural world that may be responsible for the ailment. Most visitors just wander around the market ogling the bizarre variety of goods on offer, but to get some insight into the uses and meaning of it all, it's worth chatting with the stallholders and perhaps making a purchase or two. Spending a few bolivianos on, say, a magic charm to protect you during your travels will certainly make the stallholders

1

more talkative and amenable to having their photos taken, and could even prove to be a wise investment.

Also on Calle Linares, a block south of Sagárnaga, is the excellent **Museo de la Coca** (Mon–Fri 10am–1pm & 2–6pm; $1.15), dedicated to the small green leaf which is both the central religious and cultural sacrament of the Andes and the raw material for the manufacture of cocaine. Crammed into a couple of small rooms, the museum gives a good overview of the history, chemistry, cultivation and uses of this most controversial of plants, imaginatively illustrated and explained in English and Spanish. There are excellent photos showing the cultivation and processing of coca – along with military attemps to eradicate it – and of its manifold uses: as a herbal medicine and ritual sacrament by Andean campesinos; as a means of warding off hunger and exhaustion by Bolivian miners; and, transformed into cocaine, as a recreational stimulant by needle- and pipe-wielding Westerners.

Other exhibits include one of the massive wooden presses that were once used to compress the leaves for transport on the backs of mules, and a mock up of a clandestine laboratory complete with all the chemicals necessary to turn coca into cocaine. A good selection of the packaging of some of the many modern **medicines** derived from coca underlines its continuing industrial uses, despite the rhetoric of the war on drugs. There's also a fascinating and revealing collection of posters and other advertisements for the many non-medicinal cocaine-based products that were marketed worldwide before it was declared illegal. These include Vino Mariano, a cocaine-infused wine endorsed by a gold medal from Pope Leon XIII; and **Coca-Cola**, whose early adverts claimed it relieved exhaustion, which given the fact that it originally contained cocaine is entirely believeable. One of the more surprising revelations is that, despite US anti-drugs rhetoric, the world's most popular soft drink still contains coca extract – according to the museum, in 1995 the Coca-Cola corporation imported over 200 tons of the leaf.

The Mercado Buenos Aires

Three blocks further up Sagárnaga, a right turn along Calle Max Paredes takes you into the heart of the **Mercado Buenos Aires**, also known as the **Huyustus**, an old indigenous name for the district. Centred on the intersection of Max Paredes with Calle Buenos Aires, this is where La Paz's Aymara majority conduct their daily business, a vast open-air market sprawling over some thirty city blocks where anything and everything is bought and sold. Street after street is lined with stalls piled high with all manner of goods: sacks of sweet-smelling coca leaf and great mounds of brightly coloured tropical fruit from the Yungas; enormous heaps of potatoes from the Altiplano; piles of smelly, silver-scaled fish from Lago Titicaca; stacks of stereos and televisions smuggled across the border; endless racks laden with the latest imitation designer clothes. Behind almost every stall sits or stands a bowler-hatted Aymara woman, calling out her wares or counting out small change from the deep pockets of her apron, often with a baby strapped to her back or sleeping in a bundle nearby, oblivious to the cacophonous din of the market all around. Other stallholders sell the inexpensive drinks, meals and snacks that keep the market traders going through the day, ladling soup from steaming cauldrons, blending juices on wheeled trolleys, or hawking spicy *salteñas* from portable trays. Away from the main roads the streets are usually overrun with pedestrians, but every so often a taxi will nudge its way through, horn blaring, or the crowds will part to make room for yet another truck to unload the latest consignment of goods which flow into the city to meet the market's insatiable demands.

Highlights of the market include the numerous workshops above **Calle Buenos Aires** where the elaborate masks and costumes for dancers in the city's main fiestas are made, and the shops and stalls along **Calle Max Paredes** selling the bowler hats, knee-length laced boots and endless petticoats favoured by Aymara women. Though they are cheap and plentiful the quality of the goods available in the street is not particularly high, and it's not really a place to come looking for souvenirs. It's also worth keeping an eye open for thieves and pickpockets in this part of town, as gringos make attractive targets.

Museo Tambo Quirquincho

Just north of Plaza San Francisco is Plaza Alonso de Mendoza, a pleasant square named after the founder of La Paz, whose statue stands at its centre. On the southern side of the square, the **Museo Tambo Quirquincho** (Tues–Fri 9.30am–12.30pm & 3–7pm, Sat & Sun 10am–12.30pm; $0.20) is one of the most varied and interesting in La Paz, with an eclectic collection focusing on the city's culture and history. Exhibits include an extensive collection of grotesque yet beautiful folkloric masks; several rooms full of quaint old photos of La Paz, which give a good impression of life in the city in the late nineteenth and early twentieth century; and a room dedicated to the city's quintessential icon, the **chola** (see box below).

La chola paceña

One of the most striking images in La Paz is that of the ubiquitous **cholas paceñas**, the Aymara and mestiza women dressed in voluminous skirts and bowler hats who dominate much of the day-to-day business in the city's endless markets. The word *chola* (*cholo* for men) was originally a derogatory term used to refer to indigenous women who moved to the city and adopted the lifestyle of urban mestizos, but now refers more to women who were born in La Paz (*paceñas*) and are proud of their urban indigenous identity.

The distinctive dress of the *chola* is derived from seventeenth-century Spanish costumes, which indigenous women were obliged to copy under colonial rule. The crucial element of the outfit is the **pollera**, layered skirts made from lengths of material up to five metres long, which are wrapped around the waist and reinforced with numerous petticoats to emphasize the width of the wearer's hips. These skirts can make women appear almost as wide as they are tall, and represent a glorious celebration of a very distinct ideal of female beauty. The *pollera* is worn in combination with knee-high boots, an elaborate lacy blouse, a shawl wrapped around the shoulders and a felt bowler or derby hat. The **bowler hats** became common attire in the 1930s, though the origins of this fashion are somewhat mysterious. Some say the style was adopted from the hats worn by gringo mining and railway engineers; others that the trend was started by a businessman who erroneously imported a job lot of bowler hats from Europe and struck on the idea of marketing them as women's headgear.

The *chola* costume was originally confined to the wealthier mestiza women of La Paz, but has since become widespread amongst Aymara migrants in the city and across the Altiplano. Complete outfits can cost about a month's salary, and many women spend far more, opting for lavish materials, elaborate embroidery and extravagant jewellery in an outward show of pride in commercial success. The acceptability of the *chola* as one of the central icons of La Paz and an expression of pride in indigenous culture was confirmed in 1989, when **Remedios Loza** became the first woman to take a seat in the Bolivian Congress dressed in full *chola* regalia.

The museum is set inside a beautifully restored eighteenth-century **Tambo**, a compound which served during the colonial era both as accommodation and marketplace for Aymaras from the surrounding countryside when they came to the city to sell agricultural produce. The *tambo* was owned and under the protection of the *cacique* Quirquincho, and he was in turn under the protection of the king of Spain – hence the crown carved on the arch above the main entrance, a symbol Spaniards were not allowed to use. The ornate mestizo-Baroque arches around the main courtyard were recovered from the ruins of the Conceptionist nunnery on Calle Genaro Sanjines after it was torn down to build a cinema.

San Pedro, Miraflores and Sopocachi

South of Plaza San Francisco, the busy, tree-lined Prado passes between the peaceful suburb of **San Pedro** – whose **prison** now attracts travellers jaded with more traditional tourist attractions – and the more modern neighbourhood of **Miraflores**, before reaching the relatively wealthy suburb of **Sopocachi**, home to the modest **Museo Nacional de Arqueología**, as well as some of the city's best restaurants and a lively nightlife.

Plaza Sucre and the San Pedro Prison

Two blocks southwest of the Prado along Calle Colombia is **Plaza Sucre**, the centre of **San Pedro**, one of the city's oldest suburbs. Also known as the Plaza San Pedro, the square's peaceful and well-tended gardens surround a statue of Bolivia's first president, the Venezuelan General Antonio José de Sucre, and are popular with portrait photographers with ancient box-cameras. On the plaza's southeast side is the pretty **Iglesia de San Pedro**, built in the late eighteenth century after the original structure was burnt to the ground by rebels in 1781 during the siege of La Paz. Its most notable feature is a magnificent gilded Baroque altarpiece, which dates from 1714 and is thought to have been brought here from the Jesuit church of Loreto which used to stand on the Plaza Murillo.

On the southeast side of the square rises the formidable bulk of the **Cárcel de San Pedro**, which has become one of La Paz's most unusual attractions. Though visiting a jail full of hardened criminals, many of them sentenced for violent crimes, may seem a rather macabre idea, in fact a tour of the prison offers some surprising insights into Bolivian society. It's not really officially allowed, but if you turn up with your passport between nine and ten on weekday mornings the guards will usually let you in for a brief tour. For about $8, an English-speaking prisoner will show you around for about half an hour, accompanied by a couple of bodyguards. The inside of the prison is like a microcosm of Bolivian society: there are shops, restaurants and billiard halls, and prisoners with money can live quite well. Comfortable cells in the nicer areas change hands for thousands of dollars, and many inmates have cellphones and satellite televisions. Like the city on the other side of the walls, the prison is divided into rich and poor neighbourhoods, with the most luxurious area reserved for big-time drug traffickers, white-collar criminals and corrupt politicians: recent residents have included a former mayor of La Paz. Those without any income, however, sleep in the corridors and struggle to survive on the meagre official rations. Family visitors seem to come and go regularly, and some children live inside with their fathers. The presence of guards is minimal and drink and drugs seem to be widely available, though trying to take the latter out is the best way to make your stay last longer than you intended.

Sopocachi and around

Shortly before the Prado ends at Plaza del Estudiante, a left turn down the steps and two blocks along Calle Tiahuanaco brings you to the **Museo Nacional de Arqueología** (Mon–Fri 9am–12.30pm & 3–7pm, Sat 10am–12.30pm & 3–6.30pm, Sun 10am–1pm; $0.80). Set inside a bizarre neo-Tiwanaku building that was originally home to the naturalized Bolivian archeologist Arthur Posnansky, who led some of the first serious excavations at Tiwanaku, the museum has a reasonable collection of textiles, ceramics and stone sculptures from the Inca and Tiwanaku cultures, though the exhibits are poorly explained. Amongst the more eye-catching items are a collection of post-conquest Inca drinking cups, known as *kerus*, painted and carved with human faces, one of which is clearly chewing coca. Also interesting is a selection of drugs paraphernalia from the Tiwanaku era, including long wooden tubes used for snorting powerful hallucinogens.

There are a few more Tiwanaku sculptures on display outside the National Stadium over in the district of Miraflores, about 1km to the northeast, in a sunken open-air museum known as the **Templete Semi-Subterraneo** (open 24hr; free). The Templete is based on the identically named structure at Tiwanaku, and the sculptures here include the Bennett monolith, a seven-metre-high statue whose intricate carvings have been interpreted as a Tiwanaku solar and lunar calendar more exact than our own. Sadly, air pollution is taking its toll on the statues and the busy traffic intersection is hardly ideal for contemplation. Unless you really don't have time to make it to Tiwanaku itself (see p.92) it's scarcely worth the trouble.

To the south of the Plaza del Estudiante at the end of the Prado lies the middle-class suburb of **Sopocachi**, the city's most pleasant residential area and home to many of its more upmarket restaurants and nightlife spots – the centre is around the parallel Avenues 6 de Agosto and 20 de Octubre. A few blocks from Plaza Estudiante at Avenida Ecuador 2034, the **Casa Museo Marina Núñez de Prado** (Mon, Sat & Sun 9.30am–1pm, Tues–Fri 9.30am–1pm & 3–7pm; $1) is dedicated to the work of Bolivia's most famous modern artist, Marina Nuñez del Prado, whose abstract stone sculptures of indigenous women, condors and llamas, while clearly influenced by European sculptors like Henry Moore, nevertheless have an inspired, earthy quality which captures something of the austere beauty and the intimate relationship between humans and nature in the Andean World.

The outskirts: El Alto and the Zona Sur

With the dramatic growth of its population in recent decades, La Paz has grown to fill the immediate confines of the Choqueyapu valley and further expanded in two directions: down the canyon to the southeast, into a series of new suburbs collectively known as the **Zona Sur**, and up onto the Altiplano around the airport, where the settlement of **El Alto** is now recognized as a separate city. Separated by almost a thousand metres in altitude, the two areas represent the two extremes of Bolivian society.

The Zona Sur

From Plaza del Estudiante at the end of the Prado in Sopocachi, Avenida Villazon heads southeast, turning into Avenida Arce and then winding down into the **Zona Sur**, where the upmarket suburbs of **Calacoto**, **San Miguel** and **Cota Cota** are home to a growing number of La Paz's wealthiest residents, including politicians, senior military officers, and most of the foreign business and diplomatic community. Just five kilometres or so away from central La Paz but almost five hundred metres lower in altitude, the Zona Sur has a noticeably warmer climate and feels much closer in style to suburban USA than to the rest of La Paz, with little other than the surrounding mountains to remind you that you're in Bolivia, though the juxtaposition of luxury boutiques and villas with the harsh badlands landscape verges on the surreal, and the contrast with the rest of La Paz is striking. There's not much reason to come down here, but if you're passing through on the way to the Muela del Diablo or the Valle de la Luna, it's worth stopping for a drink in one of the many cafés just to get an impression of how the city's elite live. If you're in Cota Cota, the modest **Museo de Historia Natural** (Mon–Fri 8.30am–4pm, Sat & Sun 10am–noon & 2–6pm; $0.50), on Calle 26 a short walk up from the main square, is worth a brief visit for its giant fossilized bones of prehistoric mammals.

El Alto

At the opposite extreme in every sense from the Zona Sur is **El Alto**, the huge urban sprawl that has grown up over the last few decades around the airport on the rim of the Altiplano overlooking La Paz. At over 4000m above sea level, El Alto enjoys beautiful views along the length of the snowcapped Cordillera Real, and the views of La Paz from the rim of the Altiplano are spectacular, but these are the limits of its advantages. Populated largely by Aymara migrants from the surrounding Altiplano, when it was officially recognized as a separate municipality from La Paz in 1986, El Alto instantly became the fourth biggest, poorest and fastest growing city in Bolivia.

With a population estimated at over half a million, El Alto resembles a vast urban squatter camp, its endless stretches of tin-roofed adobe shacks broken only by the strangely minaret-like spires of churches and occasional shops and industrial warehouses. Much of the population has no access to running water or electricity, employment is scarce and freezing night-time temperatures make it a desperately harsh place to live. But migrants continue to arrive, and there's a growing sense of a separate identity amongst the residents of what was previously considered merely a satellite settlement of La Paz. Many Alteños maintain close links with the Altiplano communities they came from, often moving between the two according to the agricultural season, and this emerging urban–rural identity is combined with a growing pride in their Aymara culture and a recognition that moving to the city does not inevitably entail abandoning their traditions, sentiments that are well expressed by the municipal advertising hoardings which proclaim "we are a young city from a millenarian culture". Alteños take pride in their collective struggle against adversity and the challenges of urban life in what they refer to as the biggest indigenous city in the Americas, and denigrate La Paz, where many of them work, as *la hoyada* – the hole.

As the poorest city in the country El Alto is far from being a conventional tourist attraction, and you'll probably see enough to get an impression of the place travelling to and from the airport or by bus from La Paz to other parts of Bolivia. But if you do want to spend some time in this harsh but fascinating city, it's worth going up on a Thursday or Sunday, when a huge **market** is held in the streets around the **Plaza 16 de Julio**, in La Ceja.

Eating

La Paz has an excellent range of **restaurants**, **cafés** and **street stalls** to suit pretty much all tastes and budgets. For those whose stomachs have adjusted to basic local food, the cheapest places to eat are the city's **markets**, where you can get entire meals for less than $1, as well as hearty soups, snacks and large quantities of roast meat. Try Mercado Lanza, just up from Plaza San Francisco, or Mercado Camacho, at the end of Avenida Camacho. **Street food** is another good low-cost option: the ubiquitous *salteñas* and *tucumanes* – delicious pastries filled with meat or chicken with vegetables – make excellent mid-morning snacks, especially if washed down by the freshly squeezed orange and grapefruit juice which is sold from wheeled stalls all over the city.

Few places open for breakfast much before 8am, and Paceños treat lunch as the main meal of the day, eating lightly in the evening. Most restaurants serve set lunch menus known as **almuerzos**, which are generally extremely filling and very good value. The city also has a good range of **upmarket restaurants**, concentrated in the Sopocachi neighbouhood. Though quite expensive for Bolivia, you don't have to spend that much to get a very good meal, and the exotic range of cuisines on offer can be very tempting after a few weeks away from the city. We've given phone numbers for places where advance **reservations** are advisable or a delivery service is available.

Cafés

Alexander Coffee Shop Av 16 de Julio 1832. Very fashionable but expensive café conveniently located on the Prado, with extremely good coffee, juices, salads and sandwiches, and fantastic home-made cakes and cookies.

Angelo Colonial Linares, just off Sagárnaga. Popular gringo hangout set around a colonial courtyard and imaginatively decorated with masks and antiques. Serves reasonable sandwiches and drinks, as well as some more substantial meals, and also offers tourist information, a book exchange and plenty of internet terminals.

Ciudad Plaza del Estudiante. Lively and long-established café that's open 24 hours a day and is always busy, even though the coffee and food are hardly the best.

Club La Paz Av Camacho, just beyond the corner with the Prado. Atmospheric, smoke-filled café with wood-panelled walls and an old-world feel where the great and the good of La Paz – mostly old men in grey suits – come to discuss Bolivia's latest political crises. Once popular with escaped Nazis, it still has bratwurst on the menu, as well as

salteñas and good strong coffee.

De Oro Av Villazon 1964, just off Plaza del Estudiante. Cosy little place with a mellow atmosphere serving the best coffee in the city, as well as drinks and modest snacks. Closed Sun.

Pepe's Pasaje Jimenez 894, just off Linares between Sagárnaga and Santa Cruz. Friendly little café near the heart of the Mercado de Hechicería which serves good strong organic coffee and decent vegetarian food.

Royal corner of Av Santa Cruz and Grau. Bright, sunny corner café that's a great place to watch the world go by, with excellent espresso and cappuccino and spicy *salteñas*.

Terraza Av 6 de Agosto and Rosendo Gutierrez. Expensive and very chic café with excellent coffee, salads and sandwiches and the most incredible hot chocolate. There's another branch on Av 16 de Julio.

Wall St Av Camacho 1363. US-style diner popular with downtown office workers. Good but pricey coffee, breakfasts, sandwiches, hamburgers, pastries and Middle Eastern snacks. There's another branch in Sopacachi at Av Arce 2142.

Restaurants

The least expensive **restaurants** are no-nonsense places catering to hungry and impecunious workers and students. In these, you'll usually get a filling set almuerzo for about $1, while main dishes like steak will cost $2–3; fast food like pizza tends to cost about the same. In mid-range places catering mainly to tourists or wealthier Paceños you'll pay more like $4–5 for an à la carte main course, but many of these places also serve very good set almuerzos (often dubbed *almuerzo ejecutivo*) for $3–4 – not bad for five courses. At the top of the range there are some excellent places serving all kinds of international food, but even in these you'll rarely need to spend more than $20 a head to enjoy a really good meal; great value given the quality of food and service.

Cheap

Cevicheria Aquario on Rodriguez, a steep climb up from Mexico. One of several small, inexpensive restaurants in this area serving *ceviche*, a cold, spicy and delicious Peruvian dish of raw fish or seafood marinated in lime juice, chilli and onions.

Eli's Pizza Express Av 16 de Julio 1800 ☎02/2318171. No-nonsense fast-food outlet with reasonably good pizza and a wide range of inexpensive hot snacks. Good value, though the neon lighting and plastic décor don't encourage a lengthy stay.

El Vegetariano Loayza 420. Cubbyhole serving tasty, inexpensive vegetarian snacks, pizzas and juices, plus a good almuerzo for just over $1.

Gardenia Av 6 de Agosto 2135. US style-diner with bubblegum-pink booth seating and excellent breakfasts, a good range of snacks and a reasonable almuerzo.

La Bohemia Av 16 de Julio 1648. Cosy hideaway serving tasty and moderately priced Middle Eastern food, including doner kebabs (gyros), falafel in pitta bread with salad and good Turkish coffee. Open late.

Los Flores Av Mariscal Santa Cruz, on the same block as the post office. Cheap, cheerful and popular with locals, serving all the Bolivian mainstays, a hearty almuerzo for just over $1, and good *salteñas*.

Manolo's Av Camacho, just off the Prado. Spacious, moderately priced café-restaurant serving tasty sandwiches, snacks, ice cream and Bolivian beef and chicken mainstays. Open late for drinking to music from La Paz's largest and most eclectic record collection. Closed Mon.

Sergiu's Av 6 de Agosto 2040. Hole-in-the-wall snack bar serving tasty pizza by the slice, hotdogs and doner kebabs – it's good value and extremely popular with students from the nearby university. Daily 3.30–11pm.

Moderate

100% Natural Sagárnaga 345. Largely vegetarian health-food restaurant serving a good range of salads and fruit juices, plus main courses like trout and soya steaks.

Andromeda Av Arce 216. Classy little place popular with local office workers, who come for the excellent four-course set almuerzo. Also does good pastas, salad bar, European dishes and plenty of vegetarian options.

Café Montmartre Fernando Guachalla 399. Authentic French food and drink in a lively bistro atmosphere. Crepes and omelettes are particularly tasty and, at $4, the almuerzo is very good value. Live music Thurs–Sat evenings. Closed Sun.

Cevicheria Mi Peru Av Saavedra 1983, near the football stadium in Miraflores ☎02/2227578. Small, homely Peruvian restaurant serving excellent seafood dishes including *ceviche* and an exquisite *chupe de mariscos* – a traditional seafood soup.

El Lobo Av Illampu with Santa Cruz. The most popular hangout for Israelis in La Paz, with good vegetarian and Middle Eastern dishes as well as burgers, sandwiches, salads, pasta and pizza. Internet access available.

El Unicorno Av Mariscal Santa Cruz 1460. Popular lunch spot for local office workers and a good place to watch the world go by. The set almuerzo is excellent value at just over $2, and so large it's almost impossible to finish.

La Bodeguita Cubana Av Federico Zuazo 1665 ☎02/2310064. Lively Cuban restaurant with a graffiti-covered interior loosely modelled on one of Ernest Hemmingway's favourite haunts in Havana. Good chicken and meat dishes, excellent cocktails and pumping salsa. Open evenings only; closed Sun.

La Casa de los Paceños Av Sucre 856, a block from the museums on Calle Jaen. Inexpensive and filling set almuerzo and a great place to sample traditional La Paz dishes like *sajta* (a spicy chicken stew) or *chairo* (a hearty soup). Live piano music at weekends. Closed Sat, Sun and Mon evenings.

Layq'a On the first floor above the corner of Linares and Sagárnaga. Excellent place to try traditional Altiplano dishes, including llama steaks and *crema de chuño* – a delicious soup made from freeze-dried potatoes. There's also a good salad bar, and the set almuerzo is a challenge to even the biggest appetite.

Manantial inside the *Hotel Gloria* at Potosí 909. At around $2.50, the set almuerzo is probably the best vegetarian food in La Paz, with four excellent courses including a salad bar. In the evenings you can choose your own ingredients for Chinese stir-fry. Closed Sun.

Minuteman Revolutionary Pizza Av Simón Bolívar 1882 ☎02/2245995. The best US-style pizzas in La Paz, heavily laden with imaginative toppings, whole or by the slice. Evenings only; closed Sun. Delivery available.

Expensive

Café Paris Plaza Murillo, opposite the Palacio Presidential ☎02/2319170. Lavishly decorated, upmarket restaurant serving an imaginative mix of European and Bolivian food, along with an excellent but expensive almuerzo.

Churrasqueria El Gaucho Av 20 de Octubre 2041, near the corner with Aspiazu

☎02/2310440. First-class Argentine steak house with attentive service, good wine and excellent meat dishes – it's decorated with football memorabilia and quotations from Argentina's greatest. Closed Sun.

Pronto Jáuregui 2248 just off Fernando Guachalla ☎02/2441369. Classy Italian restaurant serving authentic pizza and delicious home-made pasta, with opulent decor, good service and a lively, upbeat atmosphere. Evenings only, closed Sun.

Vienna Federico Zuazo 1905 ☎02/2441660. Probably the best restaurant in La Paz, with exquisite Central European cuisine and immaculate service, though it's still surprisingly good value, with main courses from about $6. Closed Sat.

Wagamama Pasaje Pinilla 2557, just off Av Arce ☎02/2434911. Upmarket and authentic Japanese restaurant with a varied menu including sublime sushi and sashimi. Closed Mon.

Drinking and nightlife

La Paz is generally fairly quiet on weekday evenings, but explodes into life on **Friday** nights – known as *viernes de solteros* (bachelor Fridays) – when much of the city's male population goes out drinking. Saturday nights are not quite so frenetic, but still pretty lively. In the city centre – and above all in the market district along Max Paredes and Avenida Buenos Aires – there are countless rough and ready **whiskerías** and **karaoke bars** where hard-drinking, almost exclusively male crowds gather to drown their sorrows in beer and *chufflay*, a lethal mix of Singani and lemonade, while playing *cacho*, a popular dice game, or singing along to the latest Latin pop songs. Going out to these popular bars is certainly a very authentic Bolivian experience and can be great fun, but as a foreigner you should expect to attract a good deal of attention and be prepared to drink until you drop – refusing an invitation from a fellow drinker is considered rather rude. For women, such places are best avoided altogether.

With one or two exceptions, the more upmarket nightspots – where as a foreigner you'll probably feel more at home – are concentrated in the middle-class suburb of **Sopocachi**, particularly on and around Avenida 20 de Octubre. Here you'll find a good variety of **bars** and **nightclubs**, many of which have live music and dancing at the weekends. Generic Latin American pop and dance music tends to predominate, but you'll also find jazz, salsa, house and rock music. Details of live performances and special events are published each week in *Happening*, a free listings leaflet, and on the website ⓦwww.boliche-ando.com. For live music and at weekends you may have to pay a **cover charge**, though this will never be more than a few dollars.

Bars and nightclubs

Café Montmartre Fernando Guachalla 399. Bar-bistro with a lively and authentic French atmosphere, appropriately surly staff and live music Thurs–Sat evenings. Closed Sun.

Café de Nadie Campos 296. Arty but upmarket bar-café with good finger-food, expensive drinks and live jazz at the weekends. Closed Sun.

Dead Stroke Av 6 de Agosto 2460. Stylishly seedy US-owned late-night bar and pool hall with good tables and its fair share of hustlers.

Diesel Av 20 de Octubre with Rosendo Gutierrez. Lively and very stylish bar with an extraordinary post-apocalyptic design complete with aircraft engines hanging from the ceiling and bathrooms straight out of a science-fiction movie.

Equinoccio Sanchez Lima 2191. Popular dance club attracting an energetic young crowd with frequent and varied live rock and Latin music performances. Closed Mon.

El Forum Victor Sanjines 2908. High-tech, split-level disco where the city's rich young things come to flaunt their wealth and strut their stuff to Latin and international dance music.

Green Bar Av Salinas, just up from Plaza Avaroa. Informal little place which attracts a good blend of gringos and Paceños with its intimate, pub-like atmosphere and cold draught beer. One of several small bars in this part of Sopocachi. Closed Sun.

La Luna Whiskeria-Pub Oruro with Murillo. Atmospheric late-night drinking dive with a huge and eclectic music selection and good cocktails, conveniently close to the main budget accommodation area.

La Salsa del Loro Rosendo Gutierrez, just up the steps from Av 6 de Agosto. Lively salsa nightclub where serious *salseros* dance the night away to throbbing Latin beats. Open Thurs–Sat.

Mongo's Rock-Bottom Café Hermanos Manchego 2444. Lively and fashionable bar-restaurant where televised sports and decent food give way to serious drinking, loud music and raucous dancing as the evening wears on. Hugely popular with Bolivians, travellers and expats alike, and packed at weekends.

Sol y Luna Cochabamba with Murillo. Groovy bar-café serving strong coffee and cold beer in a mellow candlelit atmosphere. It's conveniently close to the main accommodation area and is a good place to meet other travellers.

Thelonious Jazz Bar Av 20 de Octubre 2172. The best jazz bar in town, with an intimate basement atmosphere and live music Wed–Sat. $3.50 cover charge. Closed Sun and Mon.

Underground Club Pasaje Medinacelli 2234, just off Av 20 de Octubre. Funky basement nightclub attracting a youngish crowd – on Friday and Saturday nights it's a heaving mass of sweaty bodies dancing the night away to pumping techno.

The arts and entertainment

Appreciation of the **performing arts** in La Paz is limited to a small minority, but there are a few places where you can catch theatre, classical music concerts, ballet and even opera. The **cinema** is more popular, though audiences have declined with the proliferation of backstreet video shows. The emphasis tends to be on Hollywood action blockbusters, almost always in English with Spanish subtitles; the one exception to this is the Cinemateca Boliviana. The best **entertainment listings** are in the weekly *Bolivian Times*, available from newsstands all over the city.

For more traditional entertainment you should head to one of the folk music venues known as **peñas**, where you'll see Andean folk dancing accompanied by traditional Andean music involving drums, *charangos*, guitars, *quenas* (notched flutes) and the inevitable *zampoñas* (panpipes). Though primarily aimed at tourists, *peñas* are also very popular with Bolivians and feature some of the best and most authentic folk dancing and music groups in the country. Most *peñas* also serve hearty meals cooked to traditional Bolivian recipes.

Theatres and cinemas

Casa Municipal de la Cultura Franz Tamayo Av Mariscal Santa Cruz, opposite Plaza San Francisco (☎02/2374668). Hosts a wide range of cultural events including theatre, folk music, art exhibitions and film screenings, and also has a café-bar popular with La Paz's intellectual types.

Cine 16 de Julio Av 16 de Julio just off Plaza del Estudiante ☎02/2376099. Comfortable up-market cinema showing the latest international releases.

Cinemateca Boliviana Pichincha with Indaburo

☎02/2325246. Run-down but charming old place that shows an eclectic selection of Bolivian and international films.

Cine Monje Campero Av 16 de Junio 1495 ☎02/2323333. Along with Cine 16 de Julio, the most modern cinema in the city, showing the latest Hollywood blockbusters.

Teatro Municipal Genaro Sanjines con Indaburo ☎02/2375275. Elegant Neoclassical building that is now the city's premier venue for theatre, classical music, opera and ballet.

Peñas

Los Escudos Av Santa Cruz with Camacho ☎02/2322028. Cavernous folk music venue popular with tour groups. $4 cover charge; closed Sun.

Peña Huari Sagárnaga 339 ☎02/2316225. Long-established *peña* with a reasonably authentic folk music show and good traditional Altiplano food. $3.50 cover charge; shows start around 9pm.

Peña Markatambo Jaen 710 ☎02/2280041.

Perhaps the most authentic traditional music and dance show in La Paz, with an ideal setting in an old colonial mansion, though the food is mediocre. $4 cover charge; shows start at 10.30pm.

Peña Naira Sagárnaga 161 ☎02/2325736. Good if slightly touristy folk music and dance performances with decent but expensive food. US$5 cover charge; shows start about 10pm.

Shopping

Given that the city can at times feel like one massive marketplace, it should come as no surprise that La Paz is a good place to go **shopping**. You'll find a wider range of **artesanía** (handicrafts) here than anywhere else in Bolivia, with goods from all over the country, which means you don't have to lug a sackful of souvenirs back with you from Sucre or Potosí. Most of what's on sale is good quality, too, and prices aren't much higher than at the point of manufacture.

Artesanía

The best place to shop for handicrafts and other souvenirs is on **Calle Sagárnaga** and the surrounding streets, where you'll find dozens of shops and street stalls; there's also a good handicrafts market in the gallery next to the church on Plaza San Francisco. Prices (though not necessarily quality) are generally lower on the street stalls than in the shops. It's worth shopping around and comparing prices before you buy, and there's room for a certain amount of bargaining, but don't expect prices to come down too much. Acting as if you're in an Oriental bazaar won't get you very far, and haggling with someone far poorer than you over a dollar or two will just make you look foolish and mean-spirited

Amongst the best stuff on offer are the **traditional textiles** from all over the highlands, including beautiful handmade ponchos, woven belts, blankets and womens' shawls than can make very nice wallhangings. Be warned, though, that a well-made poncho with an intricate design can cost well over $100. For a more moderately priced and practical souvenir, you can't beat the llama and alpaca wool **jumpers, socks** and **hats**. You can pick up a hat for just $1 and a warm sweater for as little as $8 on the street stalls, though you can pay several times that for a finely made and professionally designed one in some of the shops on Sagárnaga. **Leather** items are also pretty good value, especially the hard-wearing and very stylish belts and bags made of leather decorated with strips of traditional weavings. **Silver** jewellery is also abundant and very good value, though the silver content of the stuff sold on the streets isn't always as high as vendors claim it is. There are also several good **musical instrument** shops on Sagárnaga and Linares where you can pick up some beautiful handmade guitars, *charangos* and other stringed instruments, as well as cheaper *quena* flutes and *zampoñas* (panpipes), which make excellent gifts. Many of the different magic charms, bracelets and carved stone figures sold in the Mercado de Hechicería also make inexpensive souvenirs and outlandish gifts for people back home. Most of the **fossils** sold on the street are fake.

Books and maps

Los Amigos del Libro, at Mercado 1315 with Loayza in the city centre, is by far the best bookshop in La Paz, with a good selection of books in English and Spanish, including many of the various travel guides to Bolivia and other South American countries, some trekking and tourist maps, plenty of glossy coffeetable books, and international magazines like *Time* and *Newsweek*. They have another branch at the bottom end of the Prado near the university, where there are several other bookshops selling books (Spanish only) as well as stalls on the street selling bootleg copies of novels by Latin America's best-known authors. You can buy 1:50,000 and 1:250,000-scale topographical **maps** of most of Bolivia (some areas are yet to be surveyed) from the Instituto Geográfico Militar (IGM; Mon–Fri 8am–4pm), which is in the military headquarters (Estado Mayor) on Avenida Saavedra in Miraflores.

Food

If you want to buy **food** to prepare yourself, you'll find pretty much everything you need at La Paz's food markets. **Mercado Lanza**, just north of Plaza San Francisco, and **Mercado Camacho**, at the end of Avenida Camacho, sell a wide range of fresh fruit, vegetables, tinned and dried goods; Lanza also sells all kinds of imported wines and spirits, often for less than they cost in their countries of origins. **Mercado Sopocachi**, on Guachalla with Ecuador in Sopocachi, sells much the same range of stuff, with a wider selection of imported goods, though as you would expect of a wealthier suburb, things are a bit more expensive here. Less good for fresh food but better for dry stuff and luxury imports are the growing number of US-style **supermarkets** in Sopocachi: try Ketal on Avenida Arce just south of Plaza Isabella La Católica, or ZATT, on Sanchez Lima with Salinas.

Listings

Airlines For flights with the military airline TAM, it's easiest to book through a travel agent.
Aerocontinente, Av Camacho 1223 ☎02/2337533; Aerolineas Argentinas, Reyes Ortiz 73 ☎02/2351711; AeroMexico, Capitan Ravelo 2101 ☎02/2443306; Aero Sur, Av 16 de Julio 1607 ☎02/2369292 or 0800/3030; American Airlines, Plaza Venezuela 1440 ☎02/2351360; British Airways, Capitan Ravelo 2102 ☎02/2443306; Continental Airlines, Alto de Alianza 664 ☎02/2280232; Iberia, Ayacucho 378 ☎02/2324378; KLM, Plaza del Estudiante 1931 ☎02/2441595; LAN Chile, Av 16 de Julio 1566 ☎02/2358377; Lloyd Aéreo Boliviano (LAB), Av Camacho 1456–60 ☎0800/3001 or 02/371020; Lufthansa, Av 6 de Agosto 2512 ☎02/2431717; SAETA, Plaza del Estudiante 1931 ☎02/2441223; Transporte Aero Militar (TAM), Av Montes 728 ☎02/2443487 or 2379286; Varig, Av Mariscal Santa Cruz 1392 ☎02/2314040.
Airport Information ☎02/2810122 for flight enquiries, ☎02/2841884 for the military airport.
American Express The Amex representative is Magri Turismo, Capitán Ravelo 2101, though they don't change Amex travellers' cheques.
Banks and exchange There are plenty of banks with ATMs in the centre of town, especially on Av Camacho, and a growing number of freestanding ATMs, including one next to the *Hotel Alem* on Sagárnaga. If you lose your card, you can cancel Visa and Mastercard on ☎02/2314410. The best places to change cash and travellers' cheques are the many cambios on Av Camacho, the Prado and elsewhere in the city centre; a couple of good ones are Money Exchange International, Mercado 990 (Mon–Fri 8.30am–12.30pm & 2.30–7.30pm, Sat 8.30am–2pm), and Casa de Cambios, Colon 330 between Mercado and Potosí (Mon–Fri

9.30am–noon & 2.30–6.30pm). Street money-changers congregate on Av Camacho, the Prado and around Plaza del Estudiante. They offer a convenient way to get money at night or at weekends, but it's not a good idea to change large sums and you should check what you get carefully.
Car rental American, Av Camacho 1574 ☎02/2202933; Dollar ☎0800/9010; Imbex, Av Montes 522 ☎02/2316895; Oscar Crespo Maurice, Av Simón Bolívar 1865 ☎02/2220989.
Dentist Zulema Arias, C 9, Obrajes ☎02/2782292.
Doctor You can get a consultation for $10 at the Clinica 6 de Agosto, Av 6 de Agosto, Sopocachi. A good laboratory for stool tests is Dr Luis Valdivia, 2nd floor, Edifico Alameda, Av 16 de Julio 1655. If you get severe altitude sickness go to the High Altitude Pathology Clinic, Clinica IPPA, Av Saavedra 2302 ☎02/2245394.
Embassies and consulates Argentina, Av Sanchez Lima 497 ☎02/2417737; Australia, Av Arce Edificio Multicentro ☎02/2359357; Brazil, Capitán Ravelo 2334 Edificio Metrobol ☎02/2430303; Canada, Av 20 de Octubre 2475 ☎02/22431215; Colombia, C 9 Calacoto 7835 ☎02/2784491; Chile, Av Hernando Siles 5873 ☎02/2785275; Ecuador, Av 16 de Julio 1440 Edificio Hermann ☎02/2321208; Mexico, Sanchez Bustamante 509 Calacoto ☎02/2771824; Paraguay, Edificio Illimani, Av 6 de Agosto ☎02/2432201; Peru, Av 6 de Agosto 2190 Edificio Alianza ☎02/2352352; UK, Av Arce 2732 ☎02/2433424; US, Av Arce 2780 ☎02/2430251; Venezuela, Av Arce 2678 ☎02/2431365.
Emergencies Ambulance ☎118, police ☎110, tourist police ☎02/2225016.
Immigration For visa extensions go to the Oficina de Migración at Av Camacho 1433 (Mon–Fri

8am–4pm). It should be a same-day service, but don't count on it.

Internet access There are internet cafes all over the city and their number is growing very quickly. Most charge about $1 an hour. Try Amazon@s Net, Potosí 1320, near the corner with Colón (daily 9am–9.30pm); Fullinternet, Av Mariscal Santa Cruz, just south of the post office (daily 8.30am–10pm); or W@r@ Net, Santa Cruz 504, just up from the Plaza San Francisco (Mon–Sat 9am–8pm).

Language schools Instituto de la Lengua Española, C 14 with Aviador, in the Achumani neighbourhood of the Zona Sur ☎02/2796074 or 2799685, ✉ilebol@latinwide.com; Instituto de Lengua y Cultura Aymara (ILCA), Casilla 2681 ☎02/2396806, ✉ilca@mail.megalink.com. Private teachers offering one-to-one Spanish tuition often advertise in the *Bolivian Times*.

Laundry Most hotels have a laundry service, and there are plenty of *lavanderías* around town. Try Lavandería Laverap, Av Illampu 714, next to the *Hostal Estrella Andina*, or Lavandería Express, just off Sagárnaga at Linares 972.

Outdoor equipment Andean Summits and Bolivian Journeys, both on Sagárnaga, have a good selection of mountain equipment for sale or rental,

including tents, camping gas, stoves and boots.

Pharmacies There are plenty of pharmacies all over the city; they take it in turns to open late. Superdrugs, on Plaza Avaroa in Sopocachi (☎02/2434444), is open 24hr a day every day and can deliver.

Photo equipment and film There are photo developing labs all over the city centre and along the Prado; try El Punto del Color, 16 de Julio 1655. Foto Linares, at Loayza with Juan de la Riva, develops slide and black-and-white film, repairs cameras and sells a reasonable range of equipment.

Post office Correo Central, Av Mariscal Santa Cruz with Oruro (Mon–Sat 8am–9.30pm, Sun 9am–noon).

Telephones The main ENTEL office is at Ayacucho 267, just below the corner with Av Illimani (daily 7am–midnight). There are phone booths all over the city which accept cards available from any street stall – the most expensive card costs about $16, for which you can make a short international call. Directory enquiries are on ☎104.

Tourist police Edificio Olimpia 1314, Plaza Tejada Sorzano, opposite the stadium in Miraflores (open 24hr, ☎02/2225016). Come here to report thefts for insurance claims.

Moving on from La Paz

As the de facto capital of Bolivia it's no surprise that La Paz is the country's major transport hub, and many travellers use it as a base to which they return to collect or drop off luggage and equipment and rest up between forays into Bolivia's many different geographical and climatic regions.

Sadly, passenger **trains** no longer operate out of La Paz, but if you are heading down to Uyuni, Tupiza or the Argentine border at Villazon it's faster and more comfortable to get a bus to Oruro and catch a train from there. You can buy train tickets in advance from the Empresa Ferroviaria Andina office, Fernando Guachalla 494, on the corner with Sanchez Lima in Sopocachi (☎02/2416546).

By bus

The main means of moving on from La Paz is by **bus**. Most **long distance inter-departmental buses** – including those to Oruro, Potosí, Sucre, Cochabamba, Tarija and Santa Cruz – leave from the **Terminal Terrestre** on Plaza Antofagasta, a few blocks north of Plaza San Francisco. This is also the departure point for **international buses** to Chile and Argentina. Though there's usually no need for busier routes, it's not a bad idea to buy a ticket in advance when travelling long distance. The terminal's **information office** (Mon–Sat 8am–8.30pm, Sun 9am–noon; ☎02/2280551) has full details of all bus departures from the city, and can usually give you the number of the relevant company so you can reserve a seat over the phone. Departing passengers

Tour operators

La Paz is home to a growing number of **tour operators** offering everything from half- or one-day tours in and around the city to expeditions to remote parts of the country lasting several weeks. The standard day-trips offered by almost every company include a **city tour**, usually combined with a visit to either the Valle de la Luna and Muela del Diablo, plus Tiwanaku or Chacaltaya. More popular are the activity-focused outdoor adventure tours, particularly one-day **mountain biking** trips down to Coroico, and longer **mountaineering expeditions** and **treks** in the Cordillera Real. The most popular trekking routes are the Choro, Takesi, Takesi Alto and Yunga Cruz trails (see Chapter 2 for further details). Many travellers choose to do this kind of trip with an agency, as remote wilderness regions are otherwise difficult to reach without the necessary transport, equipment and a guide who knows the area.

Smaller agencies whose tours are aimed primarily at backpackers on a budget are concentrated on and around Calle Sagárnaga, while more established and upmarket operators tend to have offices on the Prado or down in Sopocachi. **Prices** vary considerably between different agencies, but depend above all on the number of people on the tour: the more of you there are, the cheaper it gets. With an average-sized group of four to six people, typical prices are about $10–15 per person for a full-day city tour and $25–30 per person per day for climbing or trekking with guides, food, transport and all equipment. Well-established agencies with good reputations who receive most of their bookings from outside Bolivia charge considerably more, but in return generally give a better and more reliable service. When comparing prices, always make sure you know exactly what is included, particularly equipment, food and accommodation. You may also want to check whether you'll get an **English-speaking guide** – most operators can arrange this, though it may cost more. For longer trips, see if you can meet the guide before signing up to the tour. When it comes to climbing, mountain biking and other **dangerous sports**, it's worth spending a bit extra to go with a more professional company, which can guarantee experienced guides and reliable equipment.

Most agencies sell internal **airline tickets** for a small commission, which can save time, particularly when it comes to the military airline, TAM. Whatever their speciality, most will also book pretty much any tour you want to do or pass you onto another company for a small commission if they can't run it themselves. Though at times this can save time, often you'll just end up paying more for the same service with no guarantee that the subcontractor will keep to their side of bargain, particularly if you're booking a trip that starts a long way from La Paz. Bear in mind that for popular trips like **rainforest and pampas excursions** from Rurrenabaque or tours on the **Salar de Uyuni**, it's easier, cheaper and usually more reliable to book the trip when you get to Rurrenabaque or Uyuni rather than from La Paz.

Akhamani Trek, Illampu 711 ☎02/2460372 or 2375680, ✉tourtrek@ceibo.entelnet.bo. Well-organized and moderately priced trekking agency with knowledgeable and enthusiastic English-speaking guides specializing in the Cordillera Apolobamba and the Choro, Takesi and Yunga Cruz trails. Also do city tours and excursions to Tiwanaku, Chacaltaya and Lago Titicaca.

America Tours, ground floor office 9, Edificio Avenida, Av 16 de Julio 1490 ☎02/2374204, ℻02/2328584, ⓦwww.america-ecotours.com. Efficient and reliable travel agency: they're the main booking agent for Chalalán Ecolodge in Parque Nacional Madidi, and are a good place to book internal flights, as well as trips to the Pampas del Yacuma and the Salar de Uyuni if you want the limited security

have to pay $0.30 for use of the terminal – tickets are sold from a kiosk on the main concourse and checked when you get on the bus.

Buses and micros to the **Lago Titicaca region**, the Peruvian border, Sorata of booking in advance.

Andean Summits Branches at Sagárnaga 189 and at Armaza 710, Sopocachi ℡ & ℻02/2422106, ⓦwww.andeansummits.com. Highly professional adventure-tour operator with an excellent reputation that runs mountaineering and trekking expeditions throughout Bolivia, led by experienced English-speaking guides. They also rent and sell outdoor equipment.

Bolivian Journeys, Sagárnaga 363 ℡02/2357848, ℻02/2233818, ⓔbolivian.journeys@mailexcite.com. Specialist mountaineering agency offering moderately priced climbing expeditions in the Cordillera Real as well as most of the popular treks. They also rent and sell outdoor equipment, though you should check it carefully before you take it away.

Crillon Tours, Av Camacho 1223 ℡02/2337533, ℻02/2116482, ⓦwww.titicaca.com. Luxury tour agency running hydrofoil cruises on Lago Titicaca. They also own the exclusive *Inca Utama Hotel and Spa* in Huatajata on the lake shore and the *Hostal Posada de los Incas* on the Isla del Sol.

Explore Bolivia Branches at Sagárnaga 399 and Av 16 de Julio 1806 ℡02/2391810 or 2312721, ⓦwww.andes-amazon.com. Adventure travel operator offering white-water rafting, all the most popular treks and mountain biking to Coroico and the Zongo Valley (with good bikes), plus city tours and excursions to Tiwanaku, Chacaltaya and Lago Titicaca. Not to be confused with the US-based operator of the same name.

Fremen, Pedro Salazar 537, Plaza Avaroa ℡02/2416336, ℻02/2417327, ⓦwww.andes-amazonia.com. La Paz branch of the excellent and highly respected Cochabamba-based agency offering a wide range of excellent tailor-made tours throughout Bolivia, including river trips on the Río Mamoré on

their own luxury floating hotel, the *Reina de Enín*.

Gravity Assisted Mountain Biking, ground floor office 9, Edificio Avenida, Av 16 de Julio 1490 ℡02/2374204, ⓦwww.gravitybolivia.com. The original and best downhill mountain-bike operator, offering daily trips to Coroico or the Zongo Valley with excellent US-made bikes and experienced and enthusiastic English-speaking guides. They also organize more extreme mountain-bike adventures for experienced riders, are a good source of free tourist advice and have a book exchange. They share the same office as America Tours (see above).

Huayna Potosí Travel Agency, Illampu 626 ℡02/2740045, ℻02/2456717, ⓔbolclimb@mail.megalink.com. Runs the *Refugio Huayna Potosí* mountain lodge at the foot of Mount Huayna Potosí and organizes climbing and trekking expeditions in the region.

Magriturismo, Capitán Ravelo 2101 ℡02/2442727, ℻02/2443060, ⓦwww.magri-amexpress.com.bo. Highly respected and long-established upmarket agency running the full range of tours throughout Bolivia, from La Paz city tours to trekking in the Andes and excursions in the Amazon rainforest.

Paititi, Av 6 de Agosto with Aspiazu ℡02/2336061 or 2440744, ℻02/2329625, ⓦwww.paitititravel.com. Upmarket adventure-tour operator with a good reputation for trekking with small groups and specialist trips to the more remote corners of Bolivia, as well as tours throughout the country. Can also organize car and light-aircraft rental.

Transturin, Av Santa Cruz 1295 ℡02/2310442, ℻02/2310647, ⓦwww.turismo-bolivia.com. Long-established upmarket operator offering luxury catamaran cruises on Lago Titicaca, including a visit to their exclusive Inti Watana cultural complex on the Isla del Sol.

and Charazani leave from several different streets close to the **cemetery district**, high up on the northwest side of La Paz. You can get here on public transport by catching any micro marked "Cementerio" running up Calle Santa

Cruz from Plaza San Francisco. Buses and micros to **Copacabana** leave from several different offices on Calle Aliaga, just off Avenida Baptista opposite the cemetery itself. If you want to **continue into Peru**, it's very easy to do so from Copacabana, where there are frequent cross-border micros; you can also book a more expensive tourist micro direct to Puno in Peru through any tour agency in La Paz.

Buses and micros to **Tiwanaku** and the Peruvian border at **Desaguadero** leave from offices stretched out along Calle Eyzaguirre between Calle Aliaga and Calle Asin in the cemetery district. Buses to **Sorata** depart from offices a block further east on Calle Bustillos, and those to **Charazani** in the **Cordillera Apolobamba** leave from Calle Reyes Cardona, another block further along. The once-weekly bus to **Pelechuco** in the Cordillera Apolobamba leaves on Wednesdays at about 7am from the Tranca Río Seco on the outskirts of El Alto; you can buy tickets in advance the day before from Cancha Tejar in El Alto. To find either of these places, you'll need to take a taxi, either from La Paz or once you arrive in El Alto by micro.

Buses and micros to the **Yungas** and on into the Amazon lowlands of the **Beni** leave from the **Villa Fátima** district in the far northeast of the city, which you can reach either by picking up any micro marked "Villa Fátima" heading east along J. J. Perez or south on Avenida 6 de Agosto. Buses and micros for **Coroico** leave from Calle Yanacachi, just off Avenida de las Américas, Villa Fátima's main thoroughfare; Flota Yungueña has the best reputation. Those going to **Chulumani** leave from offices a block further down the same street and around the corner on Calle San Borja. Buses to **Rurrenabaque**, **Riberalta**, **Guayaramerín** and elsewhere in the Beni and on to **Cobija** in the Pando depart from the offices of several different companies further along Avenida de Las Américas and just off it to the left on Calle Virgen del Carmen. Most *flotas* running these long-haul routes to the Beni and Pando depart in the evening; it's well worth coming up here and buying a ticket in advance.

Bus departures from La Paz

Destination	Frequency	Duration
Arica, Chile	2 daily	8hr
Charazani	1–2 daily	10hr
Chulumani	4–6 daily	4hr 30min
Cobija	1 weekly	48hr
Cochabamba	every 30min	7–8hr
Copacabana	every 30min	3hr 30min
Coroico	hourly	4hr 30min
Desaguadero	every 30min	1hr 30min
Guayaramerín	4–5 weekly	32hr
Oruro	every 30min	3hr 30min
Potosí	4–6 daily	11hr
Riberalta	1–2 daily	30hr
Rurrenabaque	1–2 daily	20hr
San Borja	1 daily	20hr
Santa Cruz	15–20 daily	16–18hr
Sorata	every 30min	4hr 30min
Sucre	4–5 daily	15hr
Tarija	2–3 daily	24hr
Tiwanaku	every 30min	1hr

By plane

Given the great distances involved and the generally poor condition of the country's roads, many travellers choose to travel on **internal flights** – indeed during the wet season this is sometimes the only way to reach certain destinations. The two main domestic operators, **Lloyd Aereo Boliviano** (℡0800/3001 or 02/2371020) and **AeroSur** (℡0800/3030, 02/2369292 or 02/2313233), have frequent flights from La Paz to all Bolivia's main cities. The military airline **TAM** (℡02/2443487 or 02/2379286) flies to some cities, as well as to more out-of-the-way destinations like Rurrenabaque. You can buy tickets from all three airlines from their own offices or, for a small commission, through any of the travel agents in La Paz. Phone ℡02/2810122 for flight enquiries (℡02/2841884 for the military airport). See the box below for a run-down of schedules.

Domestic flights from La Paz

Destination	Frequency	Duration	Airline
Cobija	1–2 daily	1hr 40min	AS/LAB/TAM
Cochabamba	3–5 daily	45min	AS/LAB/TAM
Guayaramerín	1–2 daily	1hr	AS/LAB/TAM
Puerto Suarez	5 weekly	2hr	AS/LAB/TAM
Riberalta	1–2 daily	1hr	AS/LAB/TAM
Rurrenabaque	5 weekly	40min	TAM
Santa Cruz	6–8 daily	1hr 30min	AS/LAB/TAM
Sucre	2–3 daily	1hr	AS/LAB/TAM
Tarija	4 weekly	1hr 20min	AS/LAB/TAM
Trinidad	1–3 daily	1hr	AS/LAB/TAM
Yacuiba	2–3 weekly	1hr 30min	TAM

Around La Paz

There are some worthwhile attractions within a few hours of La Paz, most notably the mysterious ruined city of **Tiwanaku**, Bolivia's most impressive archeological site. In addition, the spectacular high Andean scenery of the Cordillera Real can be easily reached on a day-trip to **Chacaltaya**, the highest developed ski slope in the world at over 5000m above sea level. Just south of the city the barren, moonlike landscape of the **Valle de la Luna** and the **Muela del Diablo** make a good day out if you want a little taste of the kind of dramatic mountain scenery that awaits you elsewhere in Bolivia.

La Paz to Tiwanaku

The road across the Altiplano to Tiwanaku from La Paz is well paved as part of a new strategic route linking Bolivia with the port of Ilo on the Pacific coast of Peru. About 35km out of El Alto it passes through the village of **LAJA**, where Alonso de Mendoza carried out the inauguration ceremony for the city of La Paz in 1548, a few days before the actual founding of the city in the Choqueyapu valley. The church here was one of the first established in the Altiplano, and has an attractive mestizo-Baroque façade remodelled in 1680 with carvings of monkeys and the double-headed eagle of the Habsburg emperors. Shortly after Laja the road rises to a summit from where there are spectacular views of the entire chain of the Cordillera Real.

The small market **town** of Tiwanaku is about ten minutes' walk west of the ruins. Buses going to the town pass by the the ruins first, so you don't need to come here on your way – just ask the bus driver to drop you off at the entrance to the site (ask for "*las ruinas*"). The town is the easiest place to get a bus back to La Paz, though, and is worth visiting for a look at the colonial **church**, built in the sixteenth century with stones taken from the ruins. Two Tiwanaku idols stand incongruously on either side of the entrance, and the façade is carved with dancing monkeys and topped by puma-faced gargoyles. The Aymara residents of the town and surrounding communities consider themselves the direct descendants of the builders of Tiwanaku, and have been known to occupy the site when they feel they are not getting a sufficient share of the ticket revenue.

Tiwanaku

Set on the Altiplano 71km west of La Paz, the ancient ruined city of **TIWANAKU** (also spelt **Tiahuanaco**) is one of the most monumental and intriguing archeological sites in South America. Founded some three millennia ago, Tiwanaku became the capital of a massive empire that lasted almost a thousand years, developing into a sophisticated urban-ceremonial complex that at its peak was home to some 50,000 people. The city was in many ways the cradle of Andean civilization, making an enormous cultural impact throughout the region and providing the fundamental inspiration for the better-known Inca empire. And though the society that built it disappeared many centuries before the first Europeans arrived in the Andes, Tiwanaku remains a place of exceptional symbolic meaning for the Aymara of the Altiplano, who still come here to make ceremonial offerings to the *achachilas* – the gods of the mountains. The most spectacular of these takes place on June 21, the winter solstice, when hundreds of *yatiris* (traditional priests) from all over the region congregate to watch the sun rise and celebrate the **Aymara New Year** with music, dancing, elaborate rituals and copious quantities of coca and alcohol.

Some history

Tiwanaku was first established around 1000 BC, with an economy based on potato cultivation and llama herding. By 100 BC it had become an important urban centre, and an organized state with distinct classes of priests, warriors, artisans and aristocrats is thought to have emerged. By 400 AD this state controlled the whole Titicaca basin and had begun extending its influence, while from around 700 AD Tiwanaku expanded rapidly to dominate an area comprising much of modern Bolivia, southern Peru, northeast Argentina and much of northern Chile.

The key to this expansion was a remarkable agricultural system of raised fields, known as **sukakullo**, which revolutionized food production along the shores of Lago Titicaca (see box below). Using this system, the plain surrounding the city – which today provides a marginal living for just over 7000 campesinos – was 1500 hundred years ago producing harvests big enough to feed over 100,000 people. The same intensive system was implemented in valleys all around the lake, creating a huge food surplus which offered security against poor harvests and freed vast amounts of labour for the construction of monumental temples and palaces. It also allowed trade with other societies and provided food for conquering armies.

Some experts think that the influence of Tiwanaku's **culture** spread as a result of trade and religious influence; others believe it was the result of military conquest. The truth probably lies somewhere in between. Like all Andean societies, Tiwanaku needed access to products from different ecological zones: potatoes and llamas from the Altiplano, maize and peppers from the temperate valleys, coca and hardwoods from the tropical lowlands. As their power grew, direct control of other regions through conquest or colonization probably came to replace trade with neighbouring kingdoms. What's certain is that Tiwanaku's influence spread to encompass a vast area, which was crisscrossed with paved roads along which caravans of hundreds of llamas carried all kinds of produce to the centre of the empire.

Sukakullos

The most impressive achievement of the Tiwanaku civilization was undoubtedly the intensification of agriculture along the shores of Lago Titicaca using a system of raised fields known in Aymara as **sukakullo**. This system enabled the inhabitants of Tiwanaku to overcome the problems of drought, floods, frost and soil exhaustion in the Altiplano, converting what is today a harsh and semi-barren region scarcely suitable for agriculture into a vast breadbasket which was able, it's estimated, to produce food for up to six million people. What's unquestionable is the enormous manpower it would have required to build the raised fields, many of which can still be seen around the fringes of the site and at other locations all around Lago Titicaca.

The platforms stand over a metre high, with planting surfaces up to 200m long and 15m wide, and each is carefully structured, with a base of stones followed by a layer of clay to prevent salination by the slightly brackish waters of Lago Titicaca. Above this is a layer of gravel, followed by one of sandy soil and finally a coating of a rich, organic topsoil. The raised fields run in parallel lines, with water-filled ditches running between them, providing irrigation during the dry season and preventing flooding when the level of the lake rose. By storing the heat of the sun during the day and releasing it at night, the water in the ditches also protected crops from frost, extending the growing season considerably. Algae flourished in the warmed water, providing food for fish and ducks, which formed an important part of the Tiwanaku diet. The nutrient-rich sludge of duck excrement, decaying algae and fish remains which accumulated at the bottom of the ditches provided a vital source of organic fertilizer which was periodically scraped up and deposited on the fields to further boost production. Whereas present-day farmers produce about three tons of potatoes per hectare, research suggests that the *sukakullo* produced astonishing yields of up to twenty tons a hectare. Experimental projects are now underway to help local campesinos reintroduce these techniques. Rather than expensive modern technology, it seems the ancient knowledge of their ancestors may yet provide the solution to the problems faced by Aymara farmers on the Altiplano.

Some time after 1000 AD, Tiwanaku fell into a rapid and irreversible **decline**. The fields were abandoned, the population dispersed and, within a period of about fifty years, the empire disappeared. Several theories have been put forward to explain this sudden collapse, including a cataclysmic earthquake or foreign invasion, though the most likely cause of Tiwanaku's downfall was climatic change: scientists studying ice cores from Andean glaciers have discovered that from about 1000 AD the region suffered a long-term decline in rainfall. Though the imperial storehouses could no doubt withstand a few lean years, this searing drought lasted for decades, even centuries. Unable to feed the hungry masses, Tiwanaku's civilization collapsed.

Most of the **destruction** of the remains of Tiwanaku occurred relatively recently. When the Spanish first came here many of the buildings were still standing, but the presence of gold meant that they quickly set about tearing them down. Licenses to loot the site were handed out by the Spanish crown in the same way as for mining, and many of the great stones were dragged away to build churches and houses. Still more were destroyed with dynamite at the beginning of the twentieth century to provide gravel for the foundations of the railway that passes nearby, while early archeological excavations varied little in nature from the looting of the Spaniards, stripping the site of its most beautiful statues to adorn the museums of Europe and the US. Despite the destruction, though, the sheer scale of Tiwanaku and the magnitude of the remaining structures remain deeply impressive, revealing a sophisticated and well-organized society that could call on almost limitless manpower.

The ruins

Though the city of Tiwanaku originally covered several square kilometres, only a fraction of the site has been excavated, and the main **ruins** (daily 9am–5pm; $2.50) occupy a fairly small area which can easily be visited in half a day – the only other major site that has been excavated is Puma Punku (see p.98), a pyramid complex a couple of kilometres to the north. A **museum** (see below) by the entrance houses many of the smaller archeological finds. The main ruins cover the area which was once the ceremonial centre of the city, a jumble of tumbled pyramids and ruined palaces and temples made from megalithic stone blocks, many of which weigh over a hundred tons. It requires a leap of the imagination to visualize Tiwanaku as it was at its peak: a thriving city of some 50,000 people whose great pyramids and opulent palaces were painted in bright colours and inlaid with gold, surrounded by extensive residential areas built largely from mud brick (of which little now remains) and set amid lush green fields, rather than the harsh, arid landscape you see today.

For all its political and economic power, Tiwanaku's transcendental importance was undoubtedly religious. The first Spanish chroniclers to visit the site were told its name was "Taipicala", the stone at the centre, where it was believed the universe was created and from whence the first humans set forth to colonize the world. The Incas themselves consciously sought to associate themselves with the spiritual legitimacy of Tiwanaku, claiming their own dynasty had also been brought into existence at Lago Titicaca. The US anthropologist Johan Reinhard has sought to explain the spiritual importance of Tiwanaku in terms of **sacred geography**, a system of beliefs related to mountain worship and fertility cults which is still prevalent in the Andes today. The high mountain peaks are considered powerful deities, known as *achachilas* in Aymara, who control meteorological phenomenon and the fertility of crops

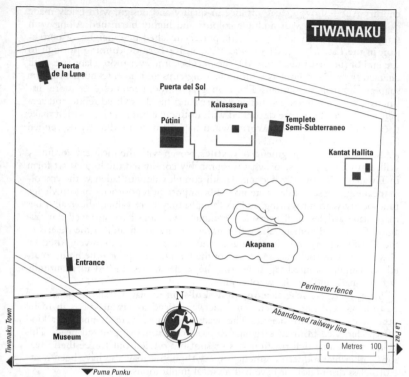

In the map:

TIWANAKU

Puerta de la Luna

Puerta del Sol

Kalasasaya

Pútini

Templete Semi-Subterraneo

Kantat Hallita

Akapana

Entrance

Perimeter fence

Tiwanaku Town

Abandoned railway line

La Paz

Museum

N

0   Metres   100

Puma Punku

and animals. Lago Titicaca, the biggest body of water in the Andes, also plays a dominant role. In terms of sacred geography, Tiwanaku's position could not be more propitious, set close to the lake with a view east to Illimani, the most important mountain god in the Altiplano, and aligned with Illampu and Sajama, the second and third most important peaks. Though it can't be proved, it seems likely that the builders of Tiwanaku chose the site with these concepts in mind, even though it meant they had to transport stones weighing hundreds of tons from across the lake.

The museum
The best place to start your visit in the modest **museum** (daily 9am–5pm; admission free with entrance to site) beside the entrance where tickets are sold. Though much of what archeologists have uncovered at the site is dispersed in museums all over the world, there's still enough on show here to give you some idea of the culture and daily life of the city. Some of the best **carved stone idols** and **friezes** are kept here, and there's a big collection of **ceramics** which are the main means used to distinguish between the different eras in Tiwanaku civilization. The earliest pottery, from between about 1000 and 300 BC – a period known as the Village Stage or Tiwanaku I – consists mainly of simple but well-made pots decorated with geometric incisions and designs painted in red, white and yellow on a chestnut brown background. Even at this stage, many of the most distinctive features of Tiwanaku decorative art are in evidence, including puma and bird motifs. Ceramics from the period known as the Urban Stage – Tiwanaku II, from about the first

century AD – show a clear advance in quality and design, with finely made pots richly painted with multiple colours and highly burnished. Along with sculpture, metallurgy and stonework, pottery reached new heights of perfection in the Late Urban, Classical and Expansive Periods, running through to the end of the first millenium AD. The pots become ever more elaborate, with characteristic flared goblets with undulating rims and incense-burners in the shape of animals or humans. The iconography, too, becomes ever more distinctive, with complex geometric patterns and highly stylised feline and serpentine figures. Some are decorated with distinctive human faces which make it easy to believe the local Aymara when they claim to be directly descended from the builders of Tiwanaku.

Also on display are fragments of **textiles**, woven with the most extraordinary skill, that offer a glimpse of what was probably considered the highest art form in Tiwanaku. Beautifully decorated with complex designs laden with symbolic meanings, these textiles were no doubt important repositories of knowledge in a society without writing, and it's thought they were valued above all other man-made articles. Sadly, very few complete weavings have survived the ravages of time and climate (those that have were mostly found in the deserts of the Pacific coast), but it's thought that textiles were extensively used in Tiwanaku, with the walls and floors of the temples and palaces being decorated with multicoloured tapestries and the stone statues dressed in beautifully woven alpaca and vicuña-wool clothes.

Finally, there are several **elongated skulls** on display, revealing the bizarre custom of trepanning which was widely practiced in Tiwanaku, as in many other ancient Andean societies. The heads of children were strapped in a kind of wooden vice from an early age to produce distinctive pointed heads. This deliberate cranial deformation was presumably carried out for aesthetic reasons, rather like modern cosmetic surgery, though it may also have been related to class distinction or have had mystical implications.

Akapana

As you enter the ruins, the big mound on your right is **Akapana**, a great earth pyramid with seven terraced platforms faced with stone. This was the biggest structure in the complex and is thought to have been the city's most important religious centre. From the west it now looks more like a hill than a man-made feature, but you can still make out the pyramid's seven tiers, and some of the huge stone blocks are still in evidence on the east side, many of them carved with a step motif characteristic of Tiwanaku.

Akapana is thought to have been constructed as an imitation of a sacred mountain, with a system of internal and external water channels and tanks inside the pyramid representing lakes and rivers. Measuring about 180m by 140m and some 18m tall, the structure is so huge that archeologists at first thought it had been built around a natural hill, but they now believe it was entirely man made, a monumental achievement which testifies to the empire's extraordinary organizational capacity and the importance of the city's religious and ceremonial functions. There are good views of the rest of the site from the summit, and local Aymaras still sometimes come here to make ritual offerings to the sacred snowcapped peak of Illimani, the most important of the mountain gods, which is clearly visible to the east.

Kalasasaya

Next to Akapana to the north is **Kalasasaya**, a walled temple compound that's thought to have been the sacred centre of Tiwanaku, where the ruling god-emperors were buried. The stone walls of the complex are amongst the most impressive masonry still standing at the site, made with colossal megaliths weighing up to 150 tons interspersed with smaller blocks and with carved stone drains that may also have been related to the ritual importance of water.

Just inside the entrance on the north side is the iconic **Puerta del Sol** – the Gateway of the Sun – an elaborately decorated portico carved from a single piece of rock weighing ten tons that has sadly been broken, probably when it was moved here from its original location, believed to have been Puma Punku. The **central figure** above the doorway is the best known image of Tiwanaku, probably the supreme creator god known to the Aymara as Thunupa and to the Incas as Viracocha. The twenty-four rays emanating from his head have led some to think of him as a sun god, but there's not much evidence to suggest such a cult existed before the Incas: it's more likely that they're just a stylised representation of hair. Some of the rays end in puma's heads, and the central figure is surrounded by winged human forms with the heads of condors. Elsewhere around the site there are several representations of serpents, and these three animals – condors, pumas and snakes – are all still revered through-out the Andes as messengers of the gods, representing the heavens, earth and underworld respectively. Several other features seem to confirm the central fig-ure's status as a supreme deity. In each hand he holds a staff very similar to those still used today in traditional Andean communities as symbols of authority, while the stylised tears that fall from his eyes are probably related to his role as a rainmaker. From his arms hang severed heads, probably trophies of war. These are no mere metaphors: sixteen headless bodies were found during excavations in the Akapana pyramid, and human sacrifices involving decapitation are still occasionally reported around the shores of Lago Titicaca.

Kalasasaya means standing stones in Aymara, a reference to the many **statues** that were found here. Two still remain: the most impressive stands on a raised platform in the centre of the complex, a three-metre-tall anthropomorphic fig-ure with an inscrutable face holding a ceremonial drinking cup in his hands. The platform is surrounded on three sides by another stone wall, on the northwest corner of which is a hole in one of the stones which amplifies sound if you put your ear to it. In front of the statue to the east, a massive doorway opens onto stairs carved from a great stone block that lead down to the Templete Semi-Subterraneo. The whole Kalasasaya complex is astronomically aligned so that at the spring and autumn equinoxes the sun appears in the centre of this doorway. The doorway is usually sealed off, however, so to reach the Templete Semi-Subterraneo you have to walk back out and around the Kalasasaya compound.

Just west of Kalasasaya, ongoing excavations have revealed the remains anoth-er extensive complex, known as **Putini**, which was probably a residential area for the city's ruling elite, or possibly a burial area. Several enormous stones cut with holes big enough to accommodate human bodies led early twentieth-century investigators, no doubt influenced by their contemporaries' fascination with Egyptology, to call it the "Palace of the Sarcophagi". You can make out the foundations of several buildings and a large central square, which was orig-inally paved with stone. A little to the north, the **Puerta de la Luna** – the Gateway of the Moon – is another gateway cut from a single piece of stone, though smaller and without the elaborate decoration of the Puerta del Sol.

Templete Semi-Subterraneo

The **Templete Semi-Subterraneo** – the Semi-Subterranean Temple – is a sunken rectangular patio about two metres deep whose walls are studded with almost two hundred carved stone heads, which jut out like keystones. These are thought to represent the gods of different ethnic groups conquered and absorbed into the expanding empire – they may even have been idols taken from these peoples and held as symbolic hostages to represent their submission to the supremacy of Tiwanaku. Three anthropomorphic stone statues stand in the centre of the patio: the largest – known as the **Estela Barbada** because it appears to be bearded – is one of the oldest at Tiwanaku, intricately carved from red sandstone, with images of serpents on either side and pumas at its feet. The much larger Bennett Monolith, now in the mock-up of the Templete outside the football stadium in La Paz (see p.79), was originally unearthed here. East of the Templete amongst a jumble of fallen stones known as **Kantat Hallita** are two worth examining: one is a huge, beautifully decorated lintel, the other a flat stone carved with what appears to be an architectural model of a building, possibly Kalasasaya.

Puma Punku

Set apart from the main complex, some two kilometres to the north (unless you've come on a tour or have your own vehicle, you'll have to walk) on the other side of the road and the abandoned railway, are the ruins of another major pyramid, **Puma Punko** – the Gateway of the Puma. Similar in style and function to Akapana, though slightly smaller, this pyramid is believed to have been built some two hundred years later, in around 700 AD. It's difficult to imagine what the building must have looked like when still standing, but the first Spanish chroniclers to come here described a great stone hall with windows. The skill and exactitude with which the massive stone blocks were carved is deeply impressive, particularly in a society without iron tools. The enormous floor slabs are cut with notches that provided a snug fit for the megalithic blocks, which were joined together perfectly to form the walls. Some of these were held together with copper cramps that were hammered into the T-shaped depressions you can see cut into adjacent sides of the blocks.

Practicalities

Minibuses to Tiwanaku depart from the corner of Aliaga and Eyzaguirre in the cemetery district in La Paz (every 30min; 1hr 30min; $1.10); on the way back they leave from the square in Tiwanaku town, though you can flag them down as they pass the entrance to the ruins. Most tour agencies in La Paz (see p.88) run one-day **tours** to the site for about $15 per person. You can hire a **guide** outside the museum to show you around the ruins for about $2 an hour, but if you want a guided tour you're better off coming with an agency from La Paz.

For most people a one-day visit to Tiwanaku is enough, but if you want to overnight, **accommodation** is available at the *Hotel Tiahuanaco* (T02/8132009; ③), a block from the main square towards the ruins, which also has a decent restaurant, or at one of the very basic *alojamientos* on the square. There are a couple of slightly overpriced **restaurants** next to the museum, and several more basic places to eat on the main square in Tiwanaku town. You can buy copies of Tiwanaku **sculpture and pottery** outside the entrance to the site.

Valle de la Luna, Mallasa and La Muela del Diablo

South of La Paz, just beyond the last suburbs of the ever-expanding Zona Sur, the harsh, arid landscape of the La Paz valley provides an easy escape from the city, and at less than 3500m is a good place to do some light walking if you're having trouble acclimatizing. Two particular areas here make reasonable places for short hikes: the **Valle de la Luna** and the **Muela del Diablo**. The former is also close to **Mallasa**, a pleasant outlying village popular with Paceños on weekend excursions and home to the La Paz **Zoo**. Both are easily reached by public transport from La Paz and can be combined to make a full day out; if you want to do this, you don't need to come all the way back to La Paz between the two: just get a micro back as far as the Zona Sur and set off again from there. Many of the La Paz tour agencies (see p.88) also offer excursions to the Valle de la Luna and Muela del Diablo, often either together or as part of a wider city tour. Going this way is quicker and a bit easier, but you won't have time to do much more than take a few photos.

The Valle de la Luna and Mallasa

From Calacoto, the southernmost suburb of the Zona Sur in La Paz, a road follows the course of the Río Choqueyapu about 5km southeast towards Mallasa, passing through a stretch of eerie, cactus-strewn badlands known as the **Valle de la Luna**. Scarred by deep canyons and strange formations of clay and rock carved by seasonal rains into pinnacles resembling church organ pipes, the valley is a popular excursion from the city and makes a pleasant area for a half-day walk, though if you're travelling in the Bolivian highlands for any length of time, you may find the scenery here rather tame by comparison. To reach the valley take any micro heading to Mallasa from Plaza del Estudiante in La Paz (these include numbers #11, #231 and #237) and get off shortly after the road passes through two tunnels. Just before a right turn leading to the Mallasa golf course (predictably dubbed the world's highest), you can walk down into the valley on a marginal path that leads off the road to the left.

If you're in the area it's worth continuing to **MALLASA** to have a drink or something to eat in one of the many restaurants and snack bars, and to visit the surprisingly good **La Paz Zoo** (daily 10am–6pm; $0.50) – though the big cats and the larger birds look pretty miserable, most of the animals have fairly spacious enclosures. Set in ample parkland and shaded by eucalyptus groves, the zoo is a good place to familiarize yourself with Bolivian wildlife, and home to a comprehensive collection of the nation's fauna, including the rare Andean spectacled bear, pumas, jaguars, llamas, vicuñas and all manner of birds.

La Muela del Diablo

Set amid a similar badlands landscape east of Calacoto, the volcanic outcrop known as **La Muela del Diablo** – the Devil's Molar – makes another good half-day trip out of the city. To get there, take a micro (number #207 or #288) from the Plaza del Estudiante in La Paz to the outlying village of Pedregal, a couple of kilometres beyond the spreading urbanization of the Zona Sur. From Pedregal, it's a good hour or so steeply uphill to the foot of the Muela – the trail starts behind the cemetery and is easy to follow. The jagged rock formation is impressive rather than spectacular, especially if you've already travelled elsewhere in the high Andes, but the views back across the desert-like landscape towards La Paz are a dramatic reminder of just what an inhospitable and unlikely place this was to build a major city. You can climb the Muela, though this is not advisable without experience and some basic equipment. Further trails lead around the back of the peak and down towards Mallasa, but there's no bridge at the moment and crossing the heavily polluted waters of the Choqueyapu isn't recommended: it's better to go back the way you came. Be sure to take plenty of water if you go hiking in this area.

Chacaltaya

About forty kilometres north of La Paz, **Chacaltaya** is Bolivia's only developed ski slope and, at over 5000m above sea level, the highest in the world. The skiing here isn't actually that great – the 200m slope is getting shorter by the year as the glacier retreats, and the primitive ski lift is a bit dodgy – but it's worth visiting just for the magnificent high-Andean scenery, though you need to be altitude-acclimatized first. From up here the massive icebound peak of Illimani seems close enough to touch, while La Paz and El Alto, far below in the Altiplano, look miniscule by comparison. You can also see the crystalline waters of Lago Titicaca to the west, with the mountains of Peru rising behind, and on clear days the volcanic cone of Sajama, Bolivia's highest mountain, is visible far across the Altiplano to the southwest. If you make the short climb up the peak of **Mount Chacaltaya** behind the ski refuge, the views open up still more, a truly breathtaking panorama. There can't be many places in the world where you can climb to such a high altitude – the peak is about 5500m above sea level – with so little effort. Just below the refuge, next to the lift machinery, there's a four-metre glass pyramid which is claimed (inevitably) to be the highest in the world, and which is supposedly built to the exact proportions of the Great Pyramid in Egypt.

Practicalities

Chacaltaya is managed by the **Club Andino Boliviano**, which has its offices at Calle Mexico 1638, just up from Plaza Estudiante (open Mon–Fri 9.30am–12.30pm & 3–7pm; ☎02/2312875). They run a **bus service** up to the ski lodge every Saturday and on weekdays if there are six or more passengers, leaving at 8am and returning in the afternoon ($10 per person). The journey takes about two hours, though you may have to walk the last few hundred metres if there has been a recent snowfall. Several tour agencies in La Paz (see p.88) also take groups up, but tend to charge a bit more. The ski refuge has a small **restaurant** where you can get basic meals and hot drinks: many consider coca tea essential at this altitude, though others favour the delicious hot chocolate with rum. The well-insulated refuge also offers basic overnight **accommodation** for $5 per person sleeping on the floor; more comfortable and expensive rooms are currently under construction. The ski season runs roughly from November to March. The slope is open from 10am to 5pm and a lift pass costs $7. You can hire skis or a snowboard for $10, though the equipment is not very good. Note that because of the danger of **altitude sickness** you shouldn't come up here unless you've already adjusted to the altitude of La Paz. Conversely, if you're planning some high-altitude climbing, Chacaltaya is a good place to acclimatize. Take plenty of warm clothing as well as sunscreen and sunglasses.

Lago Titicaca, the Cordillera Real and the Yungas

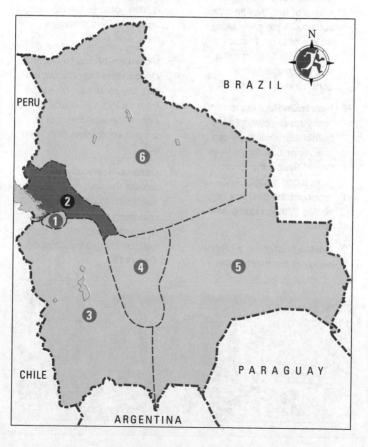

PERU

BRAZIL

N

CHILE

PARAGUAY

ARGENTINA

CHAPTER 2 # Highlights

* **Copacabana** Beautifully located on the shores of Lago Titicaca, this pretty town is also a major pilgrimage centre, and home to the Virgen de Copacabana, Bolivia's most revered religious image. See p.108

* **Isla del Sol** The spiritual centre of the Andean world, set amidst the deep blue waters of Lago Titicaca and dotted with ancient ruins and traditional Aymara communities. See p.115

* **Inca trails** Running from the high Andes down into the humid subtropical valleys of the Yungas, Bolivia's three "Inca" trails – the Choro, Takesi and Yunga Cruz – are amongst the best trekking routes in the country. See p.122

* **Sorata** Nestling in a deep valley at the heart of the Cordillera Real, the charming town of Sorata is the perfect base for trekking in the surrounding mountains. See p.125

* **Cordillera Apolobamba** This remote and beautiful mountain range offers some of the best trekking in Bolivia, and is also home to the mysterious Kallawaya medicine men. See p.129

* **Mountain-biking to Coroico** Descending over 3500m in a day, the mountain-bike trip from La Paz to Coroico is one of the world's most breathtaking rides. See p.137

* **Coroico** Scenically set amidst the lush subtropical valleys of the Yungas, this charming resort town offers the perfect antidote to the cold of the nearby Altiplano. See p.138

2

Lago Titicaca, the Cordillera Real and the Yungas

The region immediately around La Paz is sometimes known as "Little Bolivia", because the variety of landscapes it encompasses can seem like a microcosm of the entire country. The city itself lies in a canyon gouged out of the northern end of the **Altiplano**, the rolling, 3800-metre-high plateau that stretches between the eastern and western chains of the Andes – the Cordilleras Oriental and Occidental – as they march south through Bolivia. Some 75km northwest of La Paz lies **Lago Titicaca**, the vast, high-altitude lake that straddles the border with Peru and dominates the northern Altiplano, its deep waters a vivid blue against the parched grasslands which surround it. The best base from which to explore the Bolivian side of Lago Titicaca is **Copacabana**, a small town close to the Peruvian border which is the home of the country's most revered religious image and an important Catholic pilgrimage centre. It's also the jumping-off point for boat trips to the **Isla del Sol** and **Isla de la Luna**, two idyllic islands inhabited by deeply traditional peasant communities and dotted with the ruins of Inca temples and shrines which attest to the lake's position as the sacred centre of the Andean world.

Just east of Lago Titicaca is the **Cordillera Real**, the highest and most spectacular section of the Cordillera Oriental within Bolivia. Stretching some 160km along the edge of the Altiplano, from **Mount Illimani** (6439m), southeast of La Paz, to the **Illampu** massif (6370m), which towers over the eastern side of Lago Titicaca, the Cordillera Real can easily be explored from La Paz itself, and some of the best **treks** start close to the city. Alternatively, hikers can base themselves in the delightful colonial town of **Sorata**, at the northwestern end of the range. Further north, on the border with Peru, the isolated **Cordillera Apolobamba** (also part of the Cordillera Oriental) offers similar trekking and climbing opportunities in a far more remote setting.

Some of the most popular treks in the Cordillera Real – the **Choro**, **Takesi** and **Yunga Cruz** trails – actually go right across the range, following pre-Hispanic paved trails that connect the Altiplano with the **Yungas**, a series of deep

104

PERU

Juliaca

Puno

San Borja

RESERVA
DE LA BIÓSFERA
PILÓN LAJAS

PARQUE NACIONAL
MADIDI

PARQUE NACIONAL
MADIDI

Apolo

Pelechuco

Curva

Ulla Ulla

Charazani

CORDILLERA
APOLOBAMBA

AREA NATURAL
DE MANEJO INTEGRADO
NACIONAL APOLOBAMBA

Puerto Acosta

Escoma

Ancoraimes

Sorata

Consata

Santa Rosa

Mapiri

Guanay

Río Tipuani

Río Challana

Illampu
6427m

CORDILLERA

Achacachi

Isla de la Luna

Isla del Sol

Copacabana

Yunguyo

Tiquina

Huatajata

Huarina

Lago
Titicaca

Desaguadero

Guaqui

Tiwanaku

LA PAZ

Chacaltaya

Huayna
Potosí
6088m

PARQUE NACIONAL
COTAPATA

CHORO TRAIL

Río Zongo

Río Coroico

Caranavi

Coroico

Yolosa

Unduavi

Yanacachi

Puente
Villa

Chulumani

YUNGA
CRUZ
TRAIL

TAKESI TRAIL

Ventilla

Illimani
6439m

CORDILLERA REAL

Y U N G A S

Río La Paz

Rurrenabaque

Oruro

N

0   Kilometres   50

valleys where the northeastern slopes of the Andes plunge down into the Amazon lowlands. The Yungas' rugged, forest-covered mountains, rushing rivers and warm, fertile valleys offer the starkest possible contrast to the austere cordillera and arid Altiplano, both of which are just a few hours away by road. If you don't walk, the main route down to the Yungas from La Paz is along a hair-raising road, often described as the most dangerous in the world – it's so spectacular that many visitors choose to ride down it by mountain bike rather than take the bus. The most popular Yungas destination is **Coroico**, a pleasant resort town set amid beautiful scenery just off the Yungas road, though you could also base yourself in the less touristy town of **Chulumani**, which is reached by a less dramatic but still scenic road and is set amidst equally spectacular scenery.

Lago Titicaca

An immense, sapphire-blue lake sitting astride the border with Peru at the northern end of the Altiplano, **LAGO TITICACA** is one of the classic images of Bolivia, and few scenes are more evocative of the country than the sight of a poncho-clad fisherman paddling across its azure waters against the backdrop of snow-capped mountains. Set at an altitude of 3810m, and measuring some 190km by 80km, it's by far the biggest high-altitude body of water in the world – the remnant of an ancient inland sea which was formed as the Andes were thrust up from the ocean floor. The area around the lake is the heartland of the **Aymara**, whose distinct language and culture have survived centuries of domination, first by the Incas, then by the Spanish, and who continue to cultivate maize on ancient mountainside terraces around the lake, grow barley, quinoa and potatoes on the fertile plains, and raise herds of llamas, alpacas, cattle and sheep. The lake itself is rich in fish, and the water it contains stores the heat of the sun and then releases it overnight, raising average temperatures around its shores, extending the growing season and making the region one of the most productive in the high Andes. Lago Titicaca is fed by a number of rivers that carry rainfall down from the Cordillera Real and across the Altiplano, though none of its waters ever reach the sea, and almost ninety percent of the lake's water loss is through evaporation (the rest is drained by its only outlet, the Río Desaguadero, which flows south before disappearing in the salt lakes of Uru Uru and Poopó). Because of the large area it drains, the water level in the lake fluctuates sharply with slight variations in rainfall, and every few years the low plains around its shores are flooded.

Titicaca has always played a dominant role in Andean religious conceptions. As the single biggest body of water in this arid region, it's considered a powerful female deity that controls climate and rainfall, and the Incas believed that the creator god Viracocha rose from its waters, calling forth the sun and moon to light up the world. The Incas also claimed their own ancestors came into being here, and the remains of their shrines and temples can still be seen on the **Isla del Sol** (Island of the Sun) and the nearby **Isla de la Luna** (Island of the Moon), whose serene beauty and tranquillity is a highlight of any visit to the lake. Nor did Lago Titicaca lose its religious importance with the advent of Christianity: it's no coincidence that the Bolivia's most important Catholic shrine can be found in **Copacabana**, the lakeside town closest to the Isla del Sol.

Luxury cruises on Lago Titicaca

Two upmarket La Paz tour agencies offer **luxury cruises** on Lago Titicaca – they're also the only regular way to reach Peru from Bolivia by water. Transturin (Av Santa Cruz 1295 ☎02/2310442, ⊜02/2310647, ⊚www.turismo-bolivia.com) run one- and two-day sightseeing tours to Copacabana and the Isla del Sol, plus trips to Puno on the Peruvian side of the lake, in luxurious catamarans from their dock at Chúa, a few kilometres west of Huatajata. A two-day cruise with an overnight stay at their comfortable *Hotel Titicaca*, also in Chúa, costs about $180 per person. Crillon Tours (Av Camacho 1223 ☎02/2337533, ⊜02/8116481, ⊚www.titicaca.com) run a similar service, with faster luxury hydrofoils from Huatajata and overnight accommodation at either the classy *Inca Utama Hotel and Spa* in Huatajata or at the exclusive *Hostal Posada de los Incas* on the Isla del Sol. Their trips are similarly priced at a little under $100 per person per day.

La Paz to Copacabana

The main road to Lago Titicaca from La Paz runs northwest across the Altiplano, with the majestic peaks of the Cordillera Real rising imperiously to the north. Shortly after the lake first comes into view, about 75km from La Paz, the road forks at the small town of **Huarina**. One branch heads north towards the town of Achacachi (see p.120), from where you can continue to Sorata in the Cordillera Real (see p.121), or along the remote east coast of the lake and up into the Cordillera Apolobamba (see p.129). The other branch continues west towards Copacabana, running along the north shore of the smaller section of the lake, known as **Wiñay Marka** or Lago Menor, which is joined to the main body of the lake by the narrow straits of Tiquina.

Strung out along this road about 10km further west is **HAUTAJATA**, a lakeside resort village popular with Paceños, who come here to eat fresh trout and drink beer whilst enjoying the lake views from the dozen or so restaurants along the shore. Almost all these restaurants also run boat trips out to the nearby islands of Suriqui, Pariti and Kala Uta. About 45 minutes by motor boat from Huatajata, **Isla Suriqui** is home to a small fishing community that still uses traditional boats made from the totora reeds that grow all around the lake. In the 1970s the boatmakers of Suriqui put their ancient skills to work for the Norwegian explorer Thor Heyerdahl, helping him design and build the *Ra II*, a large reed boat in which he sailed from Africa to the Caribbean in an attempt to prove that transatlantic travel was possible using ancient technology. Partly as a result of the fame that followed this, Isla Suriqui is now rather over-touristed, but you still get a glimpse of a lakeside lifestyle that can have changed little over the centuries. Just to the south, the smaller **Isla Pariti** is home to another small Aymara fishing community, while close by, connected to the mainland by a narrow spit when the level of the lake is low, **Isla Kala Uta** has a series of stone tombs, known as *chullpas*, which were built by the Aymara-speaking tribes who dominated this area before the Inca conquest. Almost all the restaurants in Hautajata hire out boats to visit the islands: a motorboat should cost you about $30; a sail boat will cost less but take considerably longer – allow the best part of a day.

From Huatajata the road continues another 26km west to the **Estrecho de Tiquina**, the narrow stretch of water that joins Wiñay Marka with the main body of the lake, known as Lago Mayor, and separates the Copacabana peninsula from the rest of Bolivia. All motor vehicles heading to Copacabana cross the straits on barges. Passengers have to get off and cross on little launches

△ Cathedral, Copacabana

($0.20), a requirement introduced after a barge capsized, sending a bus and many of its passengers to the bottom of the lake. Outside the rivers of the Amazon lowlands, this is one of the few places where you'll see the Bolivian Navy. Deprived of access to the seas, Lago Titicaca is one of the few places they have to float a boat, though this doesn't stop them from appointing a full complement of admirals. Naval troops may ask to see your passport here, and hand out life jackets to wear on the ten-minute crossing. From San Pedro on the west side of the straits, it's another 40km or so to Copacabana.

Copacabana and around

The pleasant little town of **COPACABANA** overlooks the deep blue waters of Lago Titicaca just a few kilometres from the Peruvian border. As well as being a good base from which to explore the Bolivian side of the lake, the town is also the most important Catholic pilgrimage site in the country, being home to Bolivia's most revered image, the **Virgen de Copacabana**. Several times annually the town is overwhelmed by thousands of religious devotees who come to pay homage to the Virgin in colourful religious **fiestas**, while the rest of the year sees a steady stream of pilgrims arriving to seek the Virgin's blessing. Copacabana is also the jumping-off point for visits to the **Isla del Sol** and the **Isla de la Luna**, Titicaca's two sacred islands, while a series of mysterious **Inca ruins** within easy walking distance of the town show that this was a site of great spiritual importance long before Christianity reached the Andes.

Arrival, information and accommodation

Copacabana is a small town and it's easy to find your way around. **Buses** and **micros** from La Paz and Kasani at the Peruvian border arrive and depart from on and just off Plaza Sucre, midway between the lake shore and the central Plaza 2 de Febrero. There's no formal tourist **information** office in Copacabana, but the cluster of tour agencies on and around the Plaza Sucre can tell you all you need to know about how to get to the islands in the lake or on to Peru – the two main services they offer. If you're staying at the *Hostal La Cúpula* the staff there can give you good information and advice on Copacabana and the surrounding area; the owners even speak English.

> ### Fiestas in Copacabana
>
> Copacabana's main religious fiestas are the **Fiesta de la Virgen de la Candelaria** (Feb 2) and the **Coronación de la Virgen de Copacabana** (Aug 5), both of which attract thousands of pilgrims and revellers from all over Bolivia and southern Peru. The statue of the Virgin is paraded around town in processions accompanied by massed brass bands and numerous colourful folkloric dance troops. Several days of eating, drinking, dancing and fireworks culminate in chaotic bullfights held in the ring on the northern outskirts of town. **Semana Santa** (Easter) is an altogether more solemn occasion. Many pilgrims walk to Copacabana from as far away as La Paz in penance, and thousands more take part in a candlelit nocturnal procession up the slopes of Cerro Calvario, where they pray for the forgiveness of their sins and material success in the coming years. Far more mysterious and distinctly non-Christian ceremonies are staged on the night of June 21 to celebrate the winter solstice and **Aymara New Year**, when small crowds led by traditional Aymara religious leaders gather to perform ceremonies at the Horca del Inca and Intinkala – two ancient shrines on the outskirts of town.

COPACABANA

PLACES TO STAY					PLACES TO EAT	
Alojamiento Aroma	**2**	Hotel Gloria	**9**		Café Pacha	**E**
Alojamiento Oasis	**6**	Hotel Playa Azul	**5**		Chuquiago Marka	**B**
Hostal Emperador	**11**	Hotel Rosario del Lago	**10**		La Cúpula	**A**
Hostal La Cúpula	**1**	Residencial Aransaya	**7**		Puerta del Sol	**C**
Hostal La Luna	**8**				Snack 6 de Agosto	**F**
Hotel Ambassador	**3**				Sol y Luna	**G**
Hotel Brisas del Titicaca	**4**				Tatú Carreta	**D**

The Banco Cooperativa Multiactiva, next to the *Hotel Playa Azul* on Avenida 6 de Agosto, changes US dollars and **travellers' cheques**, as do several of the artesanía shops on Plaza 2 de Febrero; the Banco Unión on Avenida 6 de Agosto has an **ATM** for Visa and Mastercard withdrawals. There's **internet access** at @lfa-internet, just off Plaza Sucre on Avenida 6 de Agosto, while the **post office** is on Plaza 2 de Febrero, though if you're heading to La Paz you're better off posting letters when you get there. The **ENTEL** office is a block south of Plaza 2 de Febrero on Calle Murillo.

Accommodation

Due to its role as a pilgrimage centre, Copacabana has an enormous number of **places to stay**. Most are simple and very inexpensive *alojamientos* and *residenciales* catering mainly to Bolivian and Peruvian pilgrims, but there are several more comfortable upmarket places aimed specifically at foreign tourists. The abundance of accommodation doesn't mean it's easy to find a room during the main fiestas, however, when everything fills up fast and prices double or treble.

Alojamiento Aroma Jaúregui and Destacamento 211 (no phone). Ramshackle budget place with | basic rooms (shared bath only), plenty of hot water and a sunny roof terrace overlooking the lake. **①**

Alojamiento Oasis Pando and Av 6 de Agosto ℡02/8622037. Basic but inexpensive rooms with shared bath; the two on the rooftop enjoy sunshine and a partial view of the lake. ●

Hostal Emperador Murillo 235 ℡02/8622083. Good budget option, popular with backpackers, with clean, simple rooms (with or without bath) around a bright courtyard. Staff are helpful, there are kitchen and laundry facilities, and breakfast is available. ●–❷

Hostal La Cúpula Michel Pérez ℡02/8622029. Delightful European-owned hotel built in a neo-Moorish style on a hillside overlooking the town and lake, with pleasant rooms (with or without bath) and a nice garden with hammocks. Staff are helpful, and facilities include a kitchen and laundry, video and games room, and a good vegetarian restaurant. ❸–❹

Hostal La Luna José Mejía and J.J. Pérez ℡02/8622051. Friendly and good-value place, with basic but clean and bright rooms (with or without bath), plus laundry facilities and helpful staff. Breakfast available. ●–❷

Hotel Ambassador Jaúregui and Plaza Sucre ℡02/8622216. Large mid-range hotel with a variety of comfortable rooms, set around a sunny courtyard, and a rooftop restaurant with lake views. Heating is available, and breakfast is included. ❹

Hotel Brisas del Titicaca Av 6 de Agosto and Av Costanera ℡02/8622178. The only budget hotel on the waterfront, with small but clean and pleasant rooms; those without private bath have good views over the lake. ❷–❸

Hotel Gloria Av 16 de Julio ℡02/8622094. Grand hotel run by the same company as its namesakes in La Paz and Coroico, with spacious and comfortable rooms, some with excellent views over the lake. There's also a good restaurant, and breakfast is included. ❺

Hotel Playa Azul Av 6 de Agosto and Bolívar ℡02/8622283 or 8622227. Comfortable but charmless modern hotel popular with tour groups, with clean, carpeted rooms set on three levels around a central courtyard. Breakfast included. ❹

Hotel Rosario del Lago Rigoberto Paredes and Av Costanera (℡02/8622141). Plush modern waterfront hotel in a charming colonial-style building. Rooms are small but very comfortable and well furnished, and have excellent views over the lake. There's also a restaurant, and breakfast is included. ❻

Residencial Aransaya Av 6 de Agosto and Bolívar ℡02/8622229. Simple but clean rooms with shared bath (but limited hot water); rooms on the top floor are warmer. ●

The Town

Copacabana is a fairly untidy collection of red-tiled houses and modern concrete buildings nestled between two steep hills that provide some shelter from the winds that sometimes sweep across the lake. Though without the attractions of its more famous namesake in Brazil (which was named in honour of the shrine here), Copacabana **beach** is a pleasant place for a lakeside stroll. There are several restaurants and stalls where you can enjoy a beer and a plate of fried trout whilst looking out over the water, and you can rent pedalo boats and kayaks (about $3 an hour) – exciting stuff for the many Bolivian visitors who have never seen the sea. You can also rent motor launches ($10 an hour with boatman) and catch boats to the Isla del Sol and Isla de Luna from here.

The Cathedral

The focal point of Copacabana is the imposing **Cathedral** (daily 9am–noon & 1–5pm; free), set on the Plaza 2 de Febrero six blocks east of the waterfront. Known as the "Moorish Cathedral", it shows clear *mudéjar* influences in its design, with whitewashed stone walls and multiple domes decorated with deep blue *azulejo* tiles. Originally built between 1589 and 1669 by the Augustinian order to house the miraculous Virgen de Copacabana, it has since been extensively modified. Early construction work was funded partly by gold and silver offerings that were still being looted from pre-Christian shrines in the region. The **plaza** outside the cathedral is often occupied by cars, buses and trucks, decorated with brightly coloured streamers and rosettes. These are blessed with holy water by a priest and doused liberally in beer and liquor in a ritual known as *ch'alla*, thereby ensuring their future safety. Afterwards there's usually enough alcohol left over for the supplicants themselves to have a drink. At fiesta times, pilgrims bring models of cars, houses and other desirable objects to be blessed, in the belief that doing so ensures that the real thing will be theirs within a year – a modern version of traditional requests for sufficient rain, bountiful harvests or successful fishing.

Between the plaza and the cathedral is a broad walled **courtyard** with a minor chapel at each corner – a layout very similar to that of pre-conquest indigenous ceremonial centres. Inside the bright vaulted interior a door beside the massive gold altarpiece leads upstairs to a small chapel that houses the **Virgen de Copacabana** herself. A surprisingly slight image, with a brown, Andean face, the Virgin is dressed in lavish robes embroidered with gold and silver thread and crowned with a golden halo, while at her feet is a wide silver crescent moon – a symbol of female divinity in traditional Andean religion. Encased in glass, the statue is only taken out of the sanctuary during fiestas: locals believe moving her at any other time could trigger catastrophic floods. A small **museum** (Mon–Fri 11am–noon & 2–6pm, Sat 8am–noon & 2–6pm; $0.50) inside the compound houses a collection of colonial religious art and sculpture, but this is only open to groups of five or more. To the left of the Cathedral is the **Capilla de Velas**, a side chapel where supplicants come to light candles. A dark, narrow room with an image of the Virgin at one end, the chapel is black with soot, its walls covered with rough wax images of cars and houses stuck there by hopeful pilgrims.

The lady of the lake

The speed with which the Virgen de Copacabana emerged as the most revered religious image in the Altiplano after the Spanish conquest suggests that her cult was simply a continuation of previous, pre-Christian religious traditions associated with Lago Titicaca. Immediately after the conquest the Inca temples around the lake were looted by Spanish treasure-seekers, followed by priests who destroyed the remaining shrines and idols. These included, at Copacabana, a large female idol with a fish's tail – probably a representation of the lake as a goddess. The town was refounded in 1573 as the parish of Santa Ana de Copacabana, but a series of devastating early frosts swiftly ensued, ruining crops and convincing locals of the need for a new supernatural protector. Santa Ana was abandoned and the town was rededicated in honour of the **Virgen de la Candelaria**, one of the most popular representations of the Virgin Mary during the Spanish conquest of the Americas.

A locally born man, **Francisco Inca Yupanqui**, grandson of the Inca Huayna Capac, began fashioning an image of the Virgin. After his first crude efforts were rejected by the Spanish priests he went to Potosí to study sculpture, eventually returning with the brown-faced figure that graces the church today. The new image, called the **Virgen de Copacabana**, was immediately credited with a series of miracles, and the town quickly became the most important Catholic pilgrimage destination in the southern Andes, a position it still holds today. After independence, the Virgin was also proclaimed the religious patron of Bolivia.

Appropriately, the original Virgen de la Candelaria was also closely associated with water – and idolatory. The Spanish came across the image during their conquest of the Canary Islands in the late fifteenth century. Brown-faced and carrying a candlestick (hence "Candelaria"), it was being worshipped as an idol by the indigenous inhabitants of Tenerife, the pagan Guanches, who had found it washed up on the beach decades before. Once in Spanish hands the image was quickly deemed miraculous, and churches across the Americas were named in her honour (though it brought little luck for the Guanches, who were defeated and enslaved).

Cerro Calvario

Another interesting religious site is **Cerro Calvario**, the hill that rises steeply above the town to the north. It's a half-hour walk up to the top along a trail that begins beside the small church at the north end of Calle Bolívar, five or so blocks up from Plaza Sucre. The trail follows the stations of the cross – signs ask pilgrims not to dump stones on the summit, a reference to the distinctly pre-Christian Andean custom of carrying rocks up to high places out of respect for the mountain gods. The summit of the hill is marked by a cross from where there are splendid views over the town and across the lake, particularly at sunset. It's popular with pilgrims throughout the year, but particularly during Semana Santa (Easter), when thousands accompany the Virgen de Copacabana when she is carried up here in a candlelit procession. Several stalls sell the miniature cars and lorries, models of houses and wads of fake dollar bills that are used by pilgrims. As well as the formal Christian crosses at the top of the hill, the summit is dotted with ramshackle stone altars where pilgrims light candles, burn offerings and pour alcoholic libations to ensure their prayers are heard.

Eating and drinking

There's no shortage of **restaurants** in Copacabana, most of them catering to Bolivian and Peruvian pilgrims. Concentrated on Avenida 6 de Agosto and Calle Jáuregui, all offer unexciting set almuerzos and cenas for about $1.50, or big plates of the delicious Titicaca trout (*trucha*) cooked in a variety of different styles for about $4. You can find more varied (and expensive) fare at a handful of more upmarket restaurants aimed at foreign tourists; a couple of these also double as bars which are popular travellers' hang-outs in the evening. The **market** just off Plaza 2 de Febrero on Calle La Paz is a good place for really cheap local meals and fruit juices, and there are also several simple **foodstalls** on the waterfront where you can get inexpensive fried trout.

Moving on from Copacabana

Buses and **micros** to **La Paz** leave every half-hour or so from on and just off Plaza Sucre; tickets should be bought in advance either from the bus conductors on the plaza or from the offices of Flota 2 de Febrero and Flota Manco Capac on Plaza 2 de Febrero. If you want to get to **Sorata** without travelling via La Paz, take a La Paz-bound bus as far as Huarina, where you can flag down a bus to Sorata (3hr; every 30min).

Crossing the Peruvian border

Crossing **into Peru** from Copacabana is easy. Micros to the border at **Kasani**, fifteen minutes away, leave from Plaza Sucre every half-hour or so when full. At Kasani you can get your exit stamp at the passport control (8am–6pm) and then walk across the border. On the Peruvian side, micros and taxis wait beside the *migración* office to take passengers to the town of **Yunguyo**, a ten-minute ride away; they depart when full. From Yunguyo, regular buses head to **Puno** and on to **Cusco**, and there are several places to stay if you arrive too late to move on. Alternatively, you can catch one of the **tourist micros** which travel direct to Puno from Copacabana several times a day; these are run by one of three companies – Combi Tours, Diana Tours and Vicuña Tours – all of which have offices around Plaza Sucre, though this will cost you around $5 (about twice as much as on public transport) without saving much time.

Crossing to Peru via Desaguadero

You can also cross into Peru at **Desaguadero**, on the south side of the lake, a scenic route which is mainly used by lorry drivers heading to the Pacific cost at Ilo. The route is served by regular micros from La Paz, which leave from offices stretched out along Calle Eyzaguirre between Calle Aliaga and Calle Asin in the cemetery district. The frontier crossing is equally straightforward: get your exit stamp from the Bolivian passport control (8am–6pm), then walk across the bridge over the Río Desaguadero into Peru and get an entry stamp at the Peruvian *migración*. The scruffy Peruvian border town of Desaguadero has some basic places to stay, but again you're better off moving on immediately on one of the frequent buses to Puno (hourly; 3–4hr).

Café Pacha Av 6 de Agosto and Bolívar. Popular travellers' hideaway, with a warm candlelit atmosphere, serving decent pizzas for about $5, as well as good pasta and salads. Evenings only.
Chuquiago Marka Av Costanera and 6 de Agosto. One of several inexpensive beachfront restaurants serving up trout, beef and chicken, as well as decent breakfasts – a good place to hang out if you're waiting for a boat departure in the morning.
La Cúpula Inside the hotel of the same name on Michel Perez. Probably the best vegetarian food in town, with good breakfasts, salads and tasty meat-free main courses ($3–5), served up in a bright room with views over the lake. Closed Tues morning.
Puerta del Sol Av 6 de Agosto and Oruro.

Generous servings of standard Bolivian food, including an inexpensive set almuerzo and very good trout, dished up at indoor or outdoor seating.
Snack 6 de Agosto Av 6 de Agosto and Oruro. One of several places on this street serving straightforward, reasonably priced Bolivian food, including a good set almuerzo and very good trout.
Sol y Luna Beside the *Hotel Gloria* on Av 16 de Julio. Cosy candlelit bar-café serving the best coffee in town, as well as cold beer, cocktails and good but pricey meals and snacks. There's also a book exchange, and it's open late.
Tatú Carreta Oruro and 6 de Agosto. Lively Argentine-run pub serving good coffee, beer and cocktails as well as snacks and meat-based main meals every evening till late.

Around Copacabana

Before the Spanish conquest the Copacabana peninsula was covered with shrines and temples built by the Incas. Though many of these were systematically destroyed by the Spanish, the area is still scattered with enigmatic ruins and strange carved stones. Three of these mysterious remains – the **Horca del Inca**, **Intinkala** and **Kusijata** – are within easy walking distance of Copacabana; entry is with a single ticket ($1.60), usually on sale at each one.

From Copacabana you can also make the pleasant four-to-five-hour hike along the lakeshore, following the route taken by Inca pilgrims, to **Yampupata** at the trip of the peninsula, from where they took (and you can still take) a boat across to the Isla del Sol.

Horca del Inca, Intinkala and Kusijata

High on Cerro Sancollani, the hill that rises above Copacabana to the south, stands the **Horca del Inca**, a structure formed by two vertical crags of rock, their bases buried in the ground and topped by a stone lintel, creating a rock gateway. The name means "Gallows of the Incas", but in fact this structure was almost certainly used by Inca astronomer-priests to observe the sun, since a small hole carved in another rock crag about 20m to the northeast casts a well-defined point of light onto the centre of the lintel on the morning of June 22, the date of the winter solstice and Aymara New Year. Other stones on the same hill were probably also used for astronomical purposes, although the effects of five centuries of weather and human interference mean that their original function can't now be precisely reconstructed. To reach the Horca del Inca walk south to the end Calle Murillo, then follow the dirt path up the hill – the route is marked by arrows painted on rocks.

Just outside town to the southeast, opposite the cemetery about 300m along the road to La Paz, a path to the left leads to **Intinkala**, a collection of large boulders carved with niches, steps, channels and abstract designs. The name means "Seat of the Sun" in Aymara, and it's likely that this site was a religious shrine used for astronomical observations – according to local folk memory a large number of idols were destroyed here in the sixteenth century by Spanish priests as part of their drive to stamp out pagan beliefs. The biggest boulder is carved with a groove shaped like a serpent which was probably used to channel offerings of *chicha* (maize beer) or sacrificial blood – it's believed throughout the Andes that large rocks like these are the home of powerful spirits, like smaller versions of the mountain gods. Some are thought to be petrified members of an earlier race of humans, turned to stone when Viracocha created the sun on the Isla del Sol. Along with the Horca del Inca, Intinkala hosts a small gathering of Aymara *yatiris* (traditional priests) to celebrate the winter solstice on the night of June 21–22. Another 200m further along the road out of town in a field on the left are several other carved rocks: one is cut with deep, seat-like niches and known as the **Trono del Inca** (The Inca's Throne) – the niches were perhaps used as ceremonial seats for idols or the mummified remains of long-dead Incas.

About 3km outside town to the northeast is **Kusijata**, a small network of well-made Inca agricultural terraces and stone irrigation canals, one of which feeds a pool known as the **Baño del Inca** – possibly a ritual bath, as the name implies. There's also a little museum here with a small collection of ceramics which were excavated at the various Inca sites around Copacabana. Opening hours are very irregular: there's usually someone here at the weekend, but otherwise you may need to ask around the nearby houses to find whoever has the key. Even if you can't get in the museum, the pleasant walk out along the lakeside makes the trip worthwhile. To get there, follow Calle Junín out of town past the bullring, then take the path to the right that cuts across the football pitch; it then joins a track which climbs towards a eucalyptus grove on the hillside – a total walk of about thirty to forty minutes.

Copacabana to Yampupata

Instead of taking a boat direct from Copacabana to the Isla del Sol (see opposite), you can follow the trail formerly used by Inca pilgrims by hiking to the tip of the Copacabana peninsula at the village of Yampupata, the closest point on the mainland to the island, and then taking a boat from there. The walk to Yampupata takes about four to five hours, following an easy and very pleasant seventeen-kilometre trail around the shores of Lago Titicaca (for a map of the route, see opposite). Follow Calle Junín out of town to the bullring, then continue along the lakeside road round the shore to the north. The shoreline is usually busy with ducks and wading birds, and the flat, marshy land beside the lake is worked using the ancient system of raised fields called *sukakullos* (see p.93), which use the warmth of water taken from the lake to protect crops from frost and boost production.

After about an hour the road climbs into the hills overlooking the lake; after another hour you'll see a grotto-like cave on the hillside to your left; now occupied by a statue of the Virgin, it was doubtless also a pre-Christian shrine. The road then climbs gently to a pass before descending, reaching the lakeside hamlet of **Titicachi**, which stands on a perfect horseshoe bay, after about 45 minutes. Another half-hour's walk along the shore brings you to the village of **Sicuani**, where you can spend the night and get a basic meal at the simple

Alojamiento Inca Thaki (no phone; ❶). The owner, the venerable Señor Hilario Quispe, also takes visitors out onto the lake in his traditional totora reed boat for a small fee, and is a mine of information about local customs and beliefs. From Sicuani it's another hour or so to the village of **Yampupata**, where it shouldn't take long find a boat to take you across to **Yumani** (see p.119) on the Isla del Sol. In a rowing boat the trip takes 45 minutes and costs about $3; a motor boat (if you can find one) is obviously faster, but will cost around twice as much.

Isla del Sol

Just off the northern tip of the Copacabana peninsula about 12km northwest of Copacabana, the **Isla del Sol** (Island of the Sun) has been attracting visitors for many hundreds of years. Now a quiet rural backwater, in the sixteenth century the island was one of the most important religious sites in the Andean world, revered as the place where the sun and moon were created and the Inca dynasty was born, and covered in a complex of shrines and temples that attracted thousands of pilgrims. After the Spanish conquest the island became a looting ground for treasure hunters, and the cut stones of its temples were plundered to build churches on the mainland. But five centuries later it's still easy to see why it was (and still is) considered sacred. Surrounded by the azure expanse of Lago Titicaca, with the imperious peaks of the Cordillera Real rising above the shore on the mainland to the east, it's a place of great natural beauty and tranquillity – were it not for the snowy peaks rising beyond the shoreline, the lake could be mistaken for the Mediterranean.

Measuring 21km long and 8km across at its widest point, the Isla del Sol is the largest of the forty or so islands in Lago Titicaca and is home to several thousand Aymara campesinos, who still follow a largely traditional lifestyle based on fishing, herding llamas and cultivating the Inca agricultural terraces that contour the island's steep slopes. The three main settlements, **Yumani**, **Challa** and **Challapampa**, are all on the east coast. Scattered with enigmatic ancient ruins and populated by traditional Aymara communities, it's an excellent place to spend some time hiking and contemplating the magnificent scenery.

ISLA DEL SOL & ISLA DE LA LUNA

Visiting the island

You can visit the Isla del Sol (along with the nearby Isla de la Luna) on a day- or even half-day trip from Copacabana, but it's really worth spending at least one night on the island to fully appreciate its serene beauty. The best way to see it is to walk the length of the island from Challapampa in the north to Yumani in the south – a 21-kilometre hike (5–6hr). At Yumani, you can either catch a boat back to Copacabana immediately, spend the night and return the next morning, or get a boat across to the Isla de la Luna (see p.119) or to the mainland at Yampupata (see p.115), from where a seventeen-kilometre trail leads back to Copacabana. You could also do the walk across the Isla del Sol the other way around, starting in Yumani and heading north to Challapampa – or simply visit both locations by boat. Basic **accommodation** and food is available in Challapampa, Challa and above all in Yumani, and there are plenty of places to camp.

The Isla del Sol and the Incas

The remains of ritual offerings found by archeologists show that the Isla del Sol was an important local religious shrine long before the arrival of the Incas. When the island came under Tiwanaku control around 500 AD, larger ritual complexes were built and pilgrimages to the island began. Under **Inca rule**, though, the island was transformed into a religious centre of enormous importance, a pan-Andean pilgrimage destination which was visited every year by thousands of people from the length and breadth of the empire. The Incas believed that the creator god **Viracocha** rose from the waters of Lago Titicaca and called forth the sun and moon from a rock on the island. They also claimed the founding fathers of their own dynasty – **Manco Capac** and **Mama Ocllo** – were brought into being here by Viracocha before travelling north to establish the city of Cusco and spread civilization throughout the Andes. In fact, it's very unlikely the Incas originated on the shores of the lake. This dynastic myth was probably an attempt to add legitimacy to the Inca regime by associating them with Lago Titicaca and the birthplace of the sun – from which the Inca rulers claimed to be directly descended – as well as providing a link with the pre-existing Tiwanaku civilization that was based on the shores of the lake.

After conquering the region in the mid-fifteenth century, the Incas invested heavily in building roads, agricultural terraces, shrines and temples on the Isla del Sol, and establishing the town of **Copacabana** as a stop-off point for pilgrims. The entire Copacabana peninsula, as well as the sacred islands, was cleared of its indigenous Lupaqa and Colla population and turned into a restricted sacred area, its original populace being replaced by loyal settlers from elsewhere in the empire, who maintained the places of worship, attended the needs of the astronomer priests and visiting pilgrims, and cultivated maize for use in elaborate religious rituals. A wall was built across the neck of the peninsula at Yunguyo, with gates where guards controlled access to Copacabana (nearly five centuries later the peninsula is still separated from the rest of the mainland by the border between Peru and Bolivia, which follows almost exactly the same line). Pilgrims entering Copacabana would abstain from salt, meat and chilli and spend several days praying at the complex of shrines here before walking round to the tip of the peninsula at Yampupata, from where they would cross over the water to the Isla del Sol.

Part of the island's religious importance was no doubt related to the fertility of its fields. Insulated by the waters of the lake, the Isla del Sol enjoys slightly higher average temperatures than the mainland, as a result of which its terraced slopes produce more and better maize than anywhere else in the region. Maize was anyway a sacred crop for the Incas, but that grown on the Isla del Sol was especially important. Though most was used to make *chicha* (maize beer) for use in rituals on the island, grains of maize from the Isla del Sol were distributed across the Inca empire, carried by returning pilgrims who believed that a single grain placed in their stores would ensure bountiful harvests for ever more.

Full- and half-day boat **tours** to the Isla del Sol leave every morning from the beach at the end of Avenida Jaúregui in Copacabana – one boat usually departs at around 8am for a full day, another at around 10am for a half day. Full-day tours ($3–4) first visit Challa, then Challapampa and Yumani, before returning to Copacabana; the Isla de la Luna may also be included in your itinerary if enough passengers want to visit it. If you want to walk across the island, you can get off at Challapampa, walk to Yumani and be picked up in the afternoon or the next day by the same boat; your ticket will still be valid. Alternatively, you can buy a one-way ticket ($2) and pay the return fare to any available boat as and when you want to come back. Half-day tours only give you a brief glimpse of the southern end of the island, and aren't worth doing unless you're really short of time. Tours are run by **Titicaca Tours** (☎02/8622509) and **Inti Tours** (☎02/8622118), both of which have offices on Avenida 6 de Agosto and a kiosk on the beach where you can buy tickets in advance. Unless things are really busy you can just turn up in the morning and buy a ticket for that day; you're likely to end up on the same boat wherever you buy a ticket from.

Challapampa and the Santuario

The island's northernmost settlement, **CHALLAPAMPA** was founded by the Incas as a service centre for the nearby ceremonial complexes. Set on a narrow spit of land between two large bays on the east coast of the island, the pretty village has a small but interesting **museum** (daily 8am–noon & 2–5pm; $0.80) which houses artefacts found both on the island and offshore – underwater archeologists have discovered substantial sites off the coast of the Isla del Sol, where offerings were dropped into the water, and tales of lost underwater cities persist to this day. The collection includes some little bronze idols; plenty of carved stones from Inca buildings; Inca and Tiwanaku pottery (including some finely crafted incense-burners shaped like puma heads); and some miniature llama and human figures delicately carved from spondylus shells brought from the Pacific Ocean. You may have to hunt down the attendant to let you into the museum; the ticket also gives admission to the Santuario. There are a couple of simple but friendly **places to stay**: the *Hostal Wiñaycusi* (no phone; ❶) and the *Restaurant Chincana* (no phone; ❶), both of which will also prepare basic meals if you order in advance.

Kasapata and the Santuario

From Challapampa it's a twenty-minute walk northwest along an easy-to-follow path to the ruins of a substantial Inca site known as **Kasapata**. This was probably a *tambo* (waystation) where pilgrims stayed. It's mostly rubble now, but to the left of the path a large building still stands with five characteristically Incan trapezoidal doorways, while to the north is a large carved stone block that probably had ritual importance.

Another twenty minutes' further along the same path is the **Santuario** (8am–6pm; $0.80), the ruined Inca complex built around the sacred rock where the creator god Viracocha is believed to have created the sun and moon. At the height of Inca power the rock was the focal point of a ceremonial complex staffed by hundreds of priests and servants, and at certain times of year thousands of pilgrims, including the Inca himself, would come here to take part in elaborate rituals involving music, dance and sacrifices. Most pilgrims would not even be allowed near the rock, but worshipped from outside the sanctuary wall; those who entered the inner sanctum did so only after passing through a series of doorways where they would undergo cleansing rituals.

The **entrance** to the Santuario is marked by the remnants of a low wall which was probably as close to the sacred rock as most pilgrims were allowed to approach. About 100m beyond the entrance you can make out the rectangular foundations of a series of buildings that housed the priests and servants who attended the temple complex. The path then crosses a bare rock marked by two depressions shaped like giant footprints – dubbed the "Huellas del Sol" ("Footprints of the Sun") – before reaching the centre of the sanctuary. Here stands **Titikala**, the sacred rock from which the Incas believed the sun and moon first rose and after which Lago Titicaca was named, though there's little in the appearance of this large outcrop of weatherbeaten pink sandstone to suggest what an important religious site it once was. During Inca times gold, silver, coca, shells, birds' feathers and sacrificial animals (not to mention the occasional human) were all brought here as offerings to the sun god, Inti, while the rock itself would have been covered in fine cloth and silver and gold plates; in the open space on its southern side was a large stone basin where sacred libations of *chicha* were poured and an altar where sacrifices were made. The winter and summer solstices were probably amongst the most important religious celebrations; on the ridge to the northwest of the rock the point where the sun sets on the June solstice was marked by structures whose foundations can still be made out today. The nearby table made from a massive cut stone slab was recently put together with stones from other ruined buildings as a place for tourists to have picnics.

About 200m beyond Titikala to the northwest is a rambling complex of ruined buildings looking out west across the lake to the Peruvian shore. Known as **La Chincana** (The Labyrinth), this series of interlinked rooms, plazas and passageways with numerous trapezoidal niches and doorways is thought to have been both the storehouse for sacred maize grown on the island and the living quarters for the *mamaconas*, the so-called "Virgins of the Sun", women specially chosen for their beauty and purity who attended the shrine, making *chicha* and weaving cloth for use in rituals. If you have the energy, it's worth walking ten to fifteen minutes up to the peak at the far northern tip of the Isla del Sol for panoramic views of the island, the lake, and the majestic peaks of the Illampu massif to the east.

Challapampa to Yumani

Two different paths head from the Santuario towards Yumani at the other end of the island. The first runs directly southeast to Yumani along the bare, uninhabited ridge which bisects the centre of the island, with good views of the coast on both sides. The second returns to Challapampa, from where it continues southeast along the sheltered east coast of the island, passing scattered hamlets and neatly terraced hillsides where maize and potatoes grow. About an hour south of Challapampa on the coastal path you reach **Playa Challa**, a picturesque stretch of sand on a wide bay where you can stay at the basic *Posada del Inca* (no phone; ❶). Shortly beyond here the path climbs over a headland then drops down again to the village of **CHALLA**, which sits above another calm bay. Close to the waterfront beside the football pitch is a small **Museo Etnografico** (daily 9am–noon & 2–6pm; $0.80), set up by the local community to preserve and explain some of their cultural traditions. On display is a collection of intriguing dance costumes decorated with pink flamingo feathers and jaguar skins, as well as elaborate masks and handmade musical instruments. Most boats bringing tourists to Challapampa from Copacabana stop here to see the museum; when they do, the locals sometimes put on costumed folkloric dance performances.

Yumani

From Challa, it's about another two hours' walk southeast to **YUMANI**, the largest village on the island and home to most of its accommodation. Perched on a steep hillside above the lake, the tightly packed thatched houses are arranged in a labyrinthine street plan that's difficult to find your way around, particularly after dark. There are now perhaps a dozen very basic **alojamientos** in Yumani, all owned by local families. Most have no running water and some open only in December and January to cater for the large numbers of Argentines who visit the island at that time of year. The best of the bunch are the *Posada de las Ñustas* (no phone; ❶) and *Inti Wayra* (no phone; ❶), on the ridge above the village with excellent views, and the *Imperio del Sol* (no phone; ❶), about halfway down the hill near the small church. All three usually serve simple meals, and you can also get food at the *Restaurant Las Islas*, just above the church. A more comfortable option is the *Ecolodge La Estancia* (no phone; ❹–❺), which has delightful traditional-style cottages with solar electricity, heated water and fantastic views over the lake, as well as a decent restaurant; you can book in advance through Magri Tours in La Paz.

From Yumani a functional Inca stairway, the **Escalera del Inca**, runs steeply down to the lakeshore through a natural amphitheatre covered by some of the finest Inca agricultural terracing on the island, irrigated by bubbling stone canals. The canals are fed by a three-spouted natural spring that's the main source of fresh water for the village. Known as the **Fuente del Inca**, the spring is believed to have magic powers: drink from all three, the locals say, and you'll gain knowledge of the Spanish, Quechua and Aymara languages. At the bottom of the stairway by the beach are the remains of another Inca building, including an unremarkable wall with several niches. Boats from Copacabana dock here on their way to Challampampa and pick up passengers on their way back in the afternoon. There are also usually smaller boats available to take you over to the Isla de la Luna and back (about $10), or across to the mainland at Yampupata (see p.115), from where you can walk to Copacabana. A short walk around the coast to the south along a path raised on an Inca stone platform brings you to **Pilco Kayma** (8am–6pm; $0.80), the best-preserved Inca site on the island. Set on a cliff about 20m above the lake, the main structure is a large and fairly well-preserved two-storey stone building with classic Inca trapezoidal doorways facing east across the lake to the Isla de la Luna and the mountain peaks beyond – its original function remains obscure. Pilgrims travelling to the Titikala from the mainland would have passed through here after landing at the far southern tip of the island.

Isla de la Luna

About 8km west of the Isla del Sol, the far smaller **Isla de la Luna** (Island of the Moon) was another important pre-Columbian religious site. Made up of a single ridge 3km long and just over 1km across at its widest point, the island has limited agricultural land and is home to a small community of about forty people – for much of the twentieth century the island was used as a prison for political detainees. For the Incas, however, it was a site of great spiritual importance. Known as Coati ("Queen Island") it was associated with the moon, considered the female counterpart of the sun, and a powerful deity in her own right. Many pilgrims would continue here after their visit to the Santuario on the Isla del Sol.

The secrets of the stars

Anyone who sees the night sky from the Altiplano, away from major settlements when the weather is clear and before the moon has risen, can't fail to be impressed by the bright canopy of the southern sky, and it's no surprise that the Incas were fascinated by the stars, using their comparatively advanced astronomical understanding to forecast agricultural cycles and future climatic events. What is surprising, however, is that nearly five centuries after Inca civilization was destroyed by the Spanish conquest, their astronomical knowledge is still being used by Quechua and Aymara campesinos in the Andes of both Peru and Bolivia. In June of each year the campesinos observe the **Pleiades** – a group of stars sacred to the Incas. If the eleven-star cluster appears bright and clear in the pre-dawn sky, they anticipate early, abundant rains and a bountiful potato harvest. If the stars appear dim, however, they expect a poor harvest and delay planting to reduce the adverse effects of late and meagre rains. This practice was long considered simply a superstitious peasant tradition, at least until 1999, when a team of anthropologists and astronomers from the US discovered that using this method the campesinos were accurately forecasting the arrival of **El Niño**, a periodic change in Pacific Ocean currents that occurs every two to seven years, triggering changes in global weather patterns, including drought in the Andes. The scientists found that in El Niño years, high-altitude clouds form which are invisible to the naked eye but which are sufficient to decrease the brightness of the stars. Thus, by using a traditional folk technique, Andean campesinos accurately predict the onset of El Niño, a capability modern science achieved less than twenty years ago.

The main site on the island – and one of the best-preserved Inca complexes in Bolivia – is a temple on the east coast known as **Iñak Uyu** (8am–6pm; $0.80), the "Court of Women", which was probably a temple dedicated to the moon and staffed entirely by women; it takes about an hour to reach by boat from Yumani on the Isla del Sol. From the beach a series of broad Inca agricultural terraces lead up to the temple complex, a series of stone buildings facing inwards from three sides onto a broad central plaza. The façades of the buildings contain eleven massive external niches over 4m high and 1.5m deep, still covered in mud stucco, and is decorated with smaller niches with a stepped diamond motif more characteristic of the Tiwanaku Inca architectural style – the Inca builders may have incorporated this design to please local sensibilities. Colonial-era materials including finely made textiles have been found buried here, suggesting that ritual offerings were still being made long after the fall of the Incas.

Achacachi and the northern shore

From Huarina, on the road between La Paz and Copacabana, a side road heads northeast to the town of **ACHACACHI** and beyond, to the northeastern shore of the lake and the remote Cordillera Apolobamba (see p.129). The bustling market centre for a densely populated rural hinterland, Achacachi has long been infamous within Bolivia as a centre of Aymara discontent. Many non-Aymara Bolivians are afraid to come here, and though the lurid tales you may hear of anthropophagous Aymaras should be ignored, this is not place to linger long if you're an outsider – there have been serious outbreaks of violence here recently, and there's a good deal of animosity towards foreigners. The focus of major uprisings throughout the colonial and republican periods, in recent decades Achacachi and the surrounding province of Umasuyos have been at the centre of an increasingly radical Aymara nationalist movement. In 2000 and 2001 peasant leaders from the region were at the forefront of a campaign of road blockades in pursuit of a broad range of political demands, including land grants and farming credit, the abandonment of neo-liberal economic policies and coca-eradication, and the establishment of an independent Aymara Republic. The symbols of the Bolivian state have now been almost totally driven out from the town: there are no magistrates or banks, the police station is a burnt-out shell and the local government has been replaced by Aymara leaders. The only official presence now is the army, and even they rarely stray from their fortress-like barracks at the north end of town. There are a few simple places to stay here and some pretty good traditional restaurants on and around the main plaza, but really you should move through Achacachi as quickly as possible. Soldiers sometimes stop buses to check documents here, so have your passport with you if you're passing through.

From Achacachi the unpaved road northeast continues along the marshy fringes of Lago Titicaca through a series of small Aymara market towns and villages. At **Escoma**, 75km from Achacachi, there's a police post where your documents will be checked. Here the road forks. One branch climbs north towards the Cordillera Apolobamba, while the other continues 25km northeast to **Puerto Acosta**, the last town on the Bolivian side of the lake. To cross the border here you'll need to have got an exit stamp in La Paz first, and even then you may well have problems getting an entry stamp in Peru, not to mention finding transport round the remote northern fringe of the lake to Juliaca, the nearest major town on the Peruvian side.

The Cordillera Real and Cordillera Apolobamba

Stretching for about 160km along the northeastern edge of the Altiplano, the **Cordillera Real** – the "Royal Range" – is the loftiest and most dramatic section of the Cordillera Oriental in Bolivia. With six peaks over 6000m high and many more over 5000m, it forms a jagged wall of soaring, ice-bound peaks that separates the Altiplano from the tropical lowlands of the Amazon basin. Easily accessible from La Paz, the mountains are perfect for climbing and trekking – indeed spending a few days walking above the treeline amongst the lofty peaks or down the steep eastern slopes into the tropical valleys of the Yungas (see p.135) is the only way to really appreciate the overwhelming splendour of the Andean landscape. Populated by isolated Aymara communities who cultivate the lower slopes and valleys and raise llamas and alpacas on the high pastures, the cordillera is a largely pristine natural environment. The mighty Andean condor is still a common sight, circling on thermal currents above deep ravines or nesting amongst lonely mountain spires, and other birds like eagles, caracaras and hawks are also frequently seen. Though rarely spotted, pumas still prowl the upper reaches, while the elusive Andean spectacled bear roams the high cloud–forest that fringes the mountains' upper eastern slopes.

Trekking and climbing in the Cordillera Real

The easiest base from which to explore the Cordillera Real is **La Paz**. Many of the best and most popular treks start close to the city, including the three so-called "Inca trails" which cross the cordillera, connecting the Altiplano with the warm, forested valleys of the Yungas (see p.135). Two of these ancient paved routes – the **Choro Trail** (see p.136) and the **Takesi Trail** (see opposite) – are relatively easy to follow without a guide; the third, the **Yunga Cruz Trail** (see p.124), is more difficult. You can do all three of these treks, as well as many other more challenging routes, with any of the adventure tour agencies based in La Paz (see p.88).

The other major base for trekking is the small town of **Sorata**, nestled in a valley at the north end of the range at the foot of the mighty Illampu massif. From here, numerous trekking routes take you high up amongst the glacial peaks, while others plunge down into the remote forested valleys of the Yungas. Local campesinos in Sorata have organized a cooperative which provides trekking guides, mules and porters, making organizing your own trip easier and cheaper than going with a La Paz tour operator. Further afield, the remote and beautiful **Cordillera Apolobamba**, a separate range of the Cordillera Oriental north of Lago Titicaca with almost no tourist infrastructure, also offers excellent trekking possibilities for the more adventurous traveller.

Unless you're going on a fully organized trip with a tour agency you'll need all your own **camping equipment**, including tent, sleeping bag, warm and waterproof clothing, cooking stove and fuel. If you're an experienced hiker, able to communicate effectively with local campesinos in Spanish (though many locals speak only Aymara) and have maps, detailed directions and a compass and/or GPS, you can try doing some of these treks without a guide. The books *Trekking in Boliva: a Traveller's Guide*, by Yossi Brain, and *Peru and Bolivia: Backpacking and Trekking*, by Hilary Bradt, both have detailed descriptions of many of the trekking routes and are usually available in La Paz bookshops, as well as in the UK and US. Most of the routes are also covered in the excellent *Cordillera Real Recreation Map*, published in the US by O'Brien Cartographics, while the Instituto de Geográfico Militar in La Paz (see p.85) sells larger-scale maps that cover some of the routes.

Really, though, it's much better to go with a **local guide**. Getting lost in this remote region is easy and can be very dangerous, and rescue services are pretty much non-existent. As well as making sure you don't get lost, a local guide can help avoid any possible misunderstandings with the communities you pass through. Hiring a guide is also a good way to ensure local people see some economic benefit from tourism. You may also want to hire a mule to carry your pack, either for your entire trip or for that first gruelling ascent to a high pass. Whatever you do, don't go trekking in these mountains alone, as the consequences of a minor fall or a twisted ankle can quickly prove disastrous if there's no one around to help.

With so many high peaks, the Cordillera Real is obviously an excellent place for **mountain climbing**. While serious climbers should bring all their own equipment from home, inexperienced climbers can also scale some of these high peaks with help from specialist agencies in La Paz (see p.88). **Huayna Potosí** (6090m), near La Paz, is one of the few peaks in South America over 6000m that can be climbed by people with no mountaineering experience. Agencies in La Paz will take you up it for not much over $100 per person, though you should check carefully that the guide they provide is qualified and experienced and the equipment adequate – if in doubt, go with a more reputable and expensive agency.

To locals, the high mountain peaks are more than just breathtaking natural phenomena. Known as *achachilas* in Aymara and *apus* in Quechua, they're also considered living beings inhabited by powerful spirits that exert a strong influence over human affairs. As controllers of weather and the source of vital irrigation water, these mountain gods must be appeased with constant offerings and worship, since if angered they're liable to send hailstorms, frost or drought to destroy crops. At almost every high pass you'll see stone cairns known as **apachetas**. As well as marking the pass on the horizon to make it easier for travellers to find, these *apachetas* are also shrines to the mountain gods. Travellers carry stones up to the pass to add to the *apacheta*, thereby securing the good will of the *achachilas* and leaving the burden of their worries behind. Offerings of coca and alcohol are also made at these shrines, which vary in size and form from jumbled heaps of rocks to neatly built piles topped by a cross, depending on the importance of the route and the relative power and visibility of the nearby peaks.

The Takesi Trail

One of the best and most popular treks in Bolivia is the **Takesi Trail**, a fantastic two- to three-day hike starting near La Paz that crosses the Cordillera Real and plunges down into the steamy forested valleys of the Yungas, emerging at the village of Yanacachi, west of Chulumani on the road from La Paz. Also known as the Camino del Inca – the Inca Trail – the Takesi is one of the finest remaining pre-Columbian paved roads in Bolivia, and passes through an amazing variety of scenery. Relatively easy to follow and not too strenuous, it's an ideal hike for less experienced trekkers and can be done without a guide; it's also and the fastest and easiest way to descend from the highlands to the Yungas on foot.

The Takesi Trail starts at **Ventilla**, a small village set at an altitude of 3200m some 20km east of La Paz. A bus to Ventilla (3hr) departs every morning at about 5.30am from the corner of Max Paredes with Rodriguez in La Paz; alternatively, a long-distance taxi should cost around $15. From Ventilla, turn left off the main road and follow the clearly signposted track that winds up the valley northeast to the village of **Choquequta**, ninety minutes away. Here you can usually hire mules for the ascent to the pass or the entire length of the trek. Follow the track uphill for another ninety minutes until you reach a crumbling wall with a map of the route painted on it. Turn off the road to the right along a broad path which winds steeply uphill, with fine pre-Columbian paving soon evident along its length. After ninety minutes or so you reach the highest point on the trail, a 4600-metre pass marked by a stone *apacheta* from where there are fantastic views of the looming glacial peak of Mururata (5868m) to the east. From the pass, the trail continues about ninety minutes northeast down a broad valley through llama pastures to the herding hamlet of **Estancia Takesi**, passing an abundance of good camping spots along the way.

Below Estancia Takesi, the path crosses the Río Takesi onto the right bank, where it winds along steep slopes high above a thundering gorge. The air gets warmer and more humid by the minute as the trail drops below 3000m, and the sides of the valley are soon covered in lush vegetation. After two to three hours you'll reach the village of **Kakapi**, after which the path again crosses a river, now heading east. Continue uphill for half an hour to **Chojila**, a small and friendly settlement where enterprising locals have terraced some ground to create a campsite with gorgeous views over the lush subtropical valleys below. It's still over three hours from here to Yanacachi, so if you're not in a hurry, it's the perfect place to stay overnight.

From Chojila, descend for 45 minutes until you reach a concrete bridge; cross it and turn to the right. After a while, you'll reach an aqueduct, which leads straight to a road. Be careful if you're following the aqueduct in the dark – there are holes in the concrete slabs underfoot. When you reach the road, follow it around the bend and take the left, uphill fork. Soon, the road passes the unpleasant sulphur mining camp of **Chojlla**. Unless you get a lift from a passing vehicle, you'll have to follow the road another two hours to get to the tranquil village of **Yanacachi**, just off the La Paz–Chulumani road, which is a pleasant spot to rest after the trek, and has several basic *alojamientos* and places to eat. A bus leaves for La Paz early each morning; buy a ticket from the driver the night before to be sure of getting a seat. Otherwise, you can walk to the main road in about an hour, and then flag down buses travelling in either direction between Chulumani and La Paz (4–6 daily).

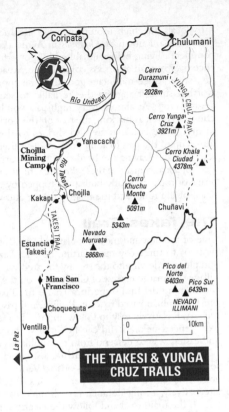

THE TAKESI & YUNGA CRUZ TRAILS

The Yunga Cruz Trail

Connecting Chuñavi, at the foot of the mighty Mount Illimani, with Chulumani in the Yungas (see p.135), the **Yunga Cruz Trail** (3–4 days) is at once the toughest, most scenic and most pristine of the three Inca trails which link the Altiplano with the tropical valleys. Instead of following a river, like most Bolivian trails, the path leads along the spine of a giant ridge nearly all the way, giving trekkers a condor's eye view of the dramatic landscape. Water is scarce along much of the route and the weather unpredictable, with heavy rain a possibility even during the dry season: carry at least two one-litre water bottles per person and take waterproof clothing. Route-finding is fairly difficult, so ideally go with a guide, and take a machete, as stretches of the trail may be overgrown. The trail starts **Chuñavi**, a small village on the northeast slopes of Mount Illimani, six hours by road from La Paz – a micro leaves at around 8am most days from Calle Burgoa in the San Pedro neighbourhood in La Paz. Take a taxi to be sure off finding the right micro, and turn up early to ensure you get a ticket.

From Chuñavi a path heads east to a small lake about ninety minutes away, before curving left along a broad ridge with plenty of decent places to camp, but no good source of water. The path then continues for about two hours along the ridge and around the side of the 4378m **Cerro Khala Ciudad** (Stone City Mountain) – look out for the condors that nest amidst its soaring towers. After a sharp turn to the right, the Inca stonework suddenly stops and

Illimani disappears from view. Look out for the faded white arrow painted on the rock and turn uphill – after a few big steps, you should be climbing an impressive stone staircase. Another two hours further on, the path curves to the right, leading along the top of a broad green valley. Half an hour later, a stream crosses the path. Fill up enough water for the night and continue for another hour until you reach a soggy campsite, just below the summit of Cerro Yunga Cruz, the last place to pitch a tent for several hours.

Soon after leaving the campsite, the trail is crossed by a stream which is the last reliable water source before Chulumani. From here, the trail descends some 2000m through dense cloudforest. After two hours, the trail splits in two; take the right fork. Half an hour later, you'll reach a clearing. Go to the end of it, then turn right, leaving the peak of Cerro Duraznuni behind you to the left. **Chulumani** should be visible in the distance to the northeast, perched on the edge of the ridge across the valley on your left. From here it's another three to four hours to the main road just southeast of Chulumani, past deforested hillsides patchworked with bright green coca plantations.

Sorata and around

Some 55km north of Achacachi, **SORATA** is a peaceful and enchanting little town that's now the most popular base for trekking and climbing in the Cordillera Real. Enclosed in a deep, fertile valley, patchworked with green fields at the foot of the mighty 6400m Illampu massif, Sorata has perhaps the most beautiful setting of any town in Bolivia. Hemmed in on all sides by steep mountain slopes and often shrouded in cloud, it has a real Shangri-la feel – the contrast with the harsh Altiplano is so striking that early Spanish explorers compared the valley to the Garden of Eden. Set at an altitude of 2695m, it also enjoys a significantly warmer climate than La Paz, but is still cool and fresh at night compared to the Yungas.

During the colonial era Sorata was an important trade and gold-mining centre with a large Spanish population. In 1781, during the Great Rebellion, it was successfully besieged by supporters of the neo-Inca rebel Tupac Amaru, who dammed rivers above Sorata and then released a torrent that swept the town away. During the republican era Sorata enjoyed considerable prosperity as one of the main routes into the Yungas from the Altiplano: travellers heading towards the Amazon from La Paz would pass through here before descending along the tortuous trails down to Mapiri in the Yungas, from where they would continue down to Rurrenabaque and beyond by canoe. Mule trains loaded with precious cargoes of quinine, coca and rubber flowed the other way, generating fortunes for the German merchants who dominated the town in the nineteenth century. Though you can still travel down to Mapiri on foot or by road (see p.145), Sorata was bypassed as a major route into the lowlands in the 1930s with the construction of the Yungas road from La Paz. Today, the town's fortunes depend more and more on its growing popularity with Bolivians and foreigners alike as a base for exploring the beautiful mountain scenery of the Cordillera Real.

Arrival, information and accommodation

Buses from La Paz pull up in front of the two bus company offices, Trans Sorata and Trans Larecaja, on the Plaza Enrique Peñaranda, the main square. **Wagonetas** arriving from Santa Rosa in the Yungas (see p.145) also stop in the plaza on their way through to La Paz, usually in the early hours of the morning. Sorata has no formal tourist office, but there are several different places where you can get good **information** and advice on trekking in the surrounding mountains. The Sorata Guides and Porters Association, just off the plaza on Calle Sucre, and the Club Sorata trekking agency, inside the *Hotel Copacabana*, are both helpful, though obviously with a view to selling you their services, while the manager of the *Residencial Sorata*, Louis Demers, is an expert on the region and can usually be persuaded to share some of his knowledge and experience.

Almost all the other facilities you'll need are concentrated on or near Plaza Enrique Peñaranda: the **post office** is on the plaza itself, while the **ENTEL** office is just south on Calle 14 de Septiembre; you can also make long-distance

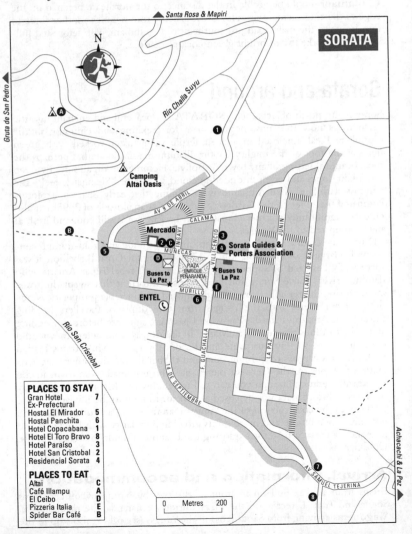

PLACES TO STAY
Gran Hotel Ex-Prefectural	7
Hostal El Mirador	5
Hostal Panchita	6
Hotel Copacabana	1
Hotel El Toro Bravo	8
Hotel Paraíso	3
Hotel San Cristobal	2
Residencial Sorata	4

PLACES TO EAT
Altai	C
Café Illampu	A
El Ceibo	D
Pizzeria Italia	E
Spider Bar Café	B

Metres   0   200

calls from booths inside the *Hostal Panchita* on the plaza. **Internet** access is so far limited to one machine at the *Residencial Sorata*, on the plaza, and connections are erratic. There are no **banks** in Sorata and changing money can be a problem: try the *Hotel Copacabana* or *Residencial Sorata*, or ask in the Artesanía Sorata shop on the plaza, where you can also buy good local weavings and other handicrafts.

Moving on from Sorata, buses to La Paz leave every half-hour or so from the offices of Trans Sorata and Trans Larecaja, both on Plaza Enrique Peñaranda. Wagonetas (passenger jeeps) making the tough ten-to-twelve-hour trip down to Santa Rosa in the Yungas (see p.145) pass through the plaza twice a week or so, usually late in the evening.

Accommodation

There's a good choice of inexpensive **places to stay** in Sorata, as well as a couple of mid-range options with creature comforts that grow more alluring the longer you've spent climbing or trekking in the surrounding mountains. There are also two good **campsites** outside town (about $1 per person per night): the campsite at the *Café Illampu* is fifteen to twenty minutes' walk across the valley on the road leading to the Gruta de San Pedro; *Camping Altai Oasis* is slightly closer to town, down by the river (the owners run the *Restaurant Altai* on the plaza if you want to check whether there's space before heading down to the campsite). Both are well equipped with hot showers, cafés, fireplaces and hammocks.

Gran Hotel Ex-Prefectural Av Samuel Tejerina ☎02/8117378. Grandiose but slightly dilapidated hotel popular with Bolivians, with large rooms (with or without bath), a bar, restaurant, billiards table, a large garden and swimming pool, and a disco at weekends. ❸–❹

Hostal El Mirador Calle Muñecas (no phone). The best budget place in town, with small but clean rooms with or without bath, a pleasant terrace and unbeatable views across the valley. ❷

Hostal Panchita Plaza Enrique Peñaranda ☎02/8115038. Friendly and good-value establishment, with small, clean but unexceptional rooms (with or without bath) around a small courtyard. ❷

Hotel Copacabana Av 9 de Abril, below the football pitch on the edge of town ☎02/8115042, ⓦwww.khainata.com/sorata. Comfortable German-owned hotel with big, well-equipped rooms offering good views across the valley, a nice garden, video lounge, upmarket restaurant and Jacuzzi. They also rent out two fully equipped cabins on the other side of the valley with room for six and fourteen people (around $40 and $90 per day respectively). ❹

Hotel El Toro Bravo Av Samuel Tejerina (no phone). Modern concrete hotel popular with Bolivian families, with spacious, comfortable rooms giving good views of Illampu. Breakfast included. ❹

Hotel Paraíso Calle Villavicencio ☎02/8115043. Small, modern hotel with a rooftop terrace and clean, comfortable rooms with private bath. Breakfast available. ❸

Hotel San Cristóbal Calle Muñecas (no phone). Very basic and inexpensive lodging (shared bath only). ❶

Residencial Sorata Plaza Enrique Peñaranda ☎02/8115044, ⒻFax02/8115218, Ⓔresorata@ceibo.entelnet.bo. Set in the delightful, rambling nineteenth-century Casa Gunther, with metre-thick walls and pleasant, moderately priced rooms (with or without bath) set around a series of flower-filled courtyards that buzz with hummingbirds. There's also a restaurant, video lounge, and internet access, and the helpful French-Canadian manager Louis Demers is a good source of trekking information. ❷–❸

The Town

Though there's not a lot to do in Sorata itself, it's a great place to hang out and relax while preparing for or recovering from some hard trekking or climbing, as well as a good base for less strenuous walks in the surrounding countryside. Built on a steep hillside, the town's narrow, cobbled streets are lined with crumbling old houses with red-tiled roofs and overhanging balconies. The heart of town is the ample **Plaza General Enrique Peñaranda**, shaded by massive palm trees and with good views of Mount Illampu, the looming glacial peak that dominates the town to the southeast – the square is named after the former military president whose statue stands at its centre. Inside the municipal offices on the west side of the square is a one-room **museum** (Wed–Sun 9.30am–noon & 2.30–5pm; free), with a rather paltry collection of pre-Columbian pots from nearby burial sites and some ornate old dance costumes. The most interesting building is the **Casa Gunther**, on the plaza's northeast corner, a massive, rambling nineteenth-century mansion that was once home to a family of powerful German merchants, and which now houses the *Residencial Sorata*.

Eating and drinking

Sorata's popularity with foreign trekkers and climbers is beginning to be reflected in the range of **food** on offer. As well as standard and inexpensive Bolivian eateries, there are also one or two very good places, catering mainly to tourists, where you can find exotic dishes like pizza and vegetarian food. For early breakfasts, fresh fruit juices and cheap soups, try the **market** just off the plaza on Muñecas.

Altai Plaza Enrique Peñaranda. By far the best place to eat in Sorata, with excellent vegetarian food (including a different set almuerzo every day), goulash and a few other well-prepared meat dishes for carnivores, as well as a wide range of breakfast choices, all served in a warm and welcoming atmosphere.

Café Illampu On the road to the Gruta San Pedro, a fifteen-to-twenty-minute walk out of town. Friendly open-air café on the mountainside looking back across to Sorata, serving beer, coffee, juices, good sandwiches, snacks, and delicious homemade cakes in a laid-back atmosphere. Closed Tues.

El Ceibo Calle Muñecas. First-floor restaurant serving standard Bolivian fare at moderate prices, including filling set almuerzos and cenas for $1.

Pizzeria Italia Plaza Enrique Peñaranda. The best of three restaurants on the southeast corner of the plaza with near-identical names and similar menus. This one has reasonably good pizza and pasta from about $3, as well as juices, cold beer and wine by the glass. Also does decent breakfasts.

Residencial Sorata Plaza Enrique Peñaranda. The restaurant inside the *residencial* serves a good American breakfast in the morning and good-value and filling set almuerzos at lunchtime.

Spider Bar Café Down the steps at the bottom of Muñecas. Cosy little gringo bar with a mellow atmosphere serving coffee, cocktails and cold beer from early evening until late at night. It's a handy place to meet other travellers over a drink or two, and also has games and a book exchange.

Gruta de San Pedro

There are numerous half- and one-day walks from Sorata – simply follow any trail out of town – but the best is the hike down the San Cristóbal valley to the **Gruta de San Pedro**, a large cave about 12km away (4–6hr round trip). Follow Avenida 9 de Agosto out of town past the *Hotel Copacabana*, then take the left turn, signposted to the *gruta*, about fifteen minutes outside town, which leads you along the opposite side of the valley, past the *Café Illampu* (alternatively, you can cut straight across the valley from town). The road continues down the narrow ravine of the Río San Cristóbal, with good views of Illampu looming above. After about 11km you'll reach the small village of **San Pedro**; the Gruta de San Pedro (daily 8am–5pm; $1) is just above the road on the right, about 1km further on. The cave is long, narrow and about 12m high, with plenty of bats – you can go about 150m inside before your way is blocked by an underground lake. A guardian will turn on the lights in the cave in return for the admission fee.

For most visitors, the main attraction of Sorata is the chance to walk some of the spectacular **trails** that run through the surrounding mountains. As well as numerous half- and one-day hikes immediately around Sorata (the most popular of which is to the Gruta de San Pedro, described opposite), some excellent longer treks start near the town. These take you through remote traditional communities and memorable high Andean scenery, up amongst the glacial peaks of Mount Illampu or even across the spine of the cordillera and down into the steamy tropical valleys of the Yungas.

Local guides, porters and mule handlers in Sorata have formed an organization known as **Sorata Guides and Porters**, whose office, opposite the *Residencial Sorata*, just off the plaza on Calle Sucre (☎02/811544, ℻02/8115218), is a good place to meet up with other people if you want to form a group to share costs. They can arrange guides for all the main trekking routes around Sorata for about $10 a day plus food, and also organize the hire of **mules**, which can carry up to about 20kg and cost about $8 a day plus food for the handler. They also have a limited amount of camping equipment available for rent, including tents, stoves and sleeping bags, though don't count on what you need being available. There will also usually be guides available who know the routes up to the main base camps for climbing Illampu, though they're not qualified climbing guides. The long-established **Club Sorata** travel agency (☎02/8115042, ⓦwww.khainata.com/sorata), based in the *Hotel Copacabana*, also organize treks along the main routes – these cost twice as much but include food, mules, tents and other equipment, plus the services of an experienced guide. They can also organize climbing expeditions with experienced and qualified guides, though you'll need to book these in advance. Otherwise, if you want a climbing guide you should hire one through a climbing agency in La Paz (see p.88).

The treks

One of the most popular high-altitude treks from Sorata is the four-day **Lagunas Glaciar and Chillata Trek**. This takes you high up the western side of the Illampu massif to two lakes set at over 5000m, from where there are beautiful views of the glaciers and back down into the San Cristóbal Valley. Longer, tougher and even more spectacular is the **Illampu Circuit** (6–7 days), which takes you right round the Illampu massif over several passes between 4500m and 5000m. There are also two long treks that head from Sorata down into the tropical valleys of the Yungas. The **Mapiri Trail** (7–8 days) is a tough descent to the mining town of Mapiri in the Yungas (see p.145), from where you can continue by motorized canoe and road to Coroico or down to Rurrenabaque. Built in the nineteenth century as a route for bringing quinine up from the Amazon lowlands, the Mapiri Trail runs through a beautiful and remote region of forest-covered mountains. The trail is frequently overgrown with vegetation or blocked by fallen trees, so carry a machete, as well as plenty of water containers during the dry season, as water is scarce along much of the trail. The **Camino de Oro** (Goldminers' Trail; 5–7 days) also runs down to the Yungas, taking you through dramatic changes in landscape and vegetation. Dating back to pre-Columbian times, the trail connects the Altiplano with the alluvial goldfields of the Yungas, and impressive remnants of Inca stonework can still be seen along its length, though the lower stretches pass through areas badly deforested by mining activity. The trail emerges at the gold-mining camps along the Río Tipuani, from where transport is available downriver to Guanay (see p.144).

The Cordillera Apolobamba

North of Lago Titicaca flush with the Peruvian border rises the **Cordillera Apolobamba**, the remote northern extension of the Cordillera Oriental. The splendour of the high mountain scenery in this isolated range equals or even exceeds that of the Cordillera Real, and the environment is more pristine. The region is now protected by the recently established **Area Natural de Manejo Integrado Nacional Apolobamba**, which covers nearly 5000 square kilometres and is home to a small number of mostly Quechua- and Aymara-speaking farmers and herders. The range is still rich in Andean wildlife which is only rarely seen elsewhere: condors, caracaras and other big birds are frequently seen; pumas and spectacled bears still roam the most isolated regions; and large herds of vicuña can be seen from the road which crosses the plain of **Ulla Ulla**, a high plateau that runs along the western side of the range. The Cordillera Apolobamba is also home to Bolivia's most mysterious indigenous culture, the **Kallawayas**, itinerant herbalists, famous throughout the Andes, who preserve secret healing techniques handed down over generations and still speak an arcane language that may have come to them from the Incas.

During the colonial era the Cordillera Apolobamba was an important goldmining centre, and the mining settlements established by the Spanish also served as bases for conquistadors and missionaries to launch expeditions down into the Amazon lowlands, though these were never brought under effective Spanish control. During the Great Rebellion of 1781 many of the colonial mines in the region were abandoned, and rumours persist of a mother lode of gold concealed in a long-abandoned mine, still waiting to be discovered.

Tourist infrastructure is virtually nonexistent in this isolated region, but for the adventurous it offers perhaps the best high-mountain trekking in Bolivia. The only real towns in the Cordillera Apolobamba are **Pelechuco** and **Charazani**, both of which can be reached by tough but spectacular bus journeys from La Paz. Between the two runs the fabulous four- or five-day **Trans-Apolobamba Trek**, which takes you through the heart of the range, past glacier-covered peaks and through traditional indigenous villages. Some tour operators in La Paz take groups on this trek; alternatively you can organize local guides and mules in either Charazani or Pelechuco.

Charazani, Curva and Lagunillas

From **Escoma** (see p.121), on the remote northeastern shore of Lago Titicaca, a rough road heads north into the Cordillera Apolobamba, climbing to over 4500m. After about 50km it forks, one branch heading north along the western edge of the cordillera and the Peruvian frontier to Ulla Ulla and Pelechuco (see p.133), the other dropping down to the town of **CHARAZANI**, about 260km by road from La Paz. Perched at about 3200m on the side of a deep valley, Charazani is the market centre for the Kallawaya communities of the surrounding area, and the nearest town to the Trans-Apolobamba Trek north across the heart of the Cordillera Apolobamba to Pelechuco (see p.133 for details). The town itself dates back to colonial times, but the area was settled long before the arrival of the Spanish; the steep valley slopes all around are sculpted into pre-Hispanic terraces, built to increase the area of land available for maize cultivation in this vital ecological niche.

A few crumbling colonial houses still survive, but most of the town's buildings are cheap modern constructions of adobe or cement. The **central plaza** is lined with shops selling basic supplies to the campesinos from surrounding communities. Daily **buses** to and from La Paz (8–10hr) terminate outside the two transport company offices on the plaza, where you'll also find a couple of basic *pensiones* where you can get simple meals. The best **place to stay** is the *Hotel Akhamani* (no phone; ❷), a block south of the plaza, which has clean rooms with shared bathroom; the helpful owner, Egberto Alvarez, can help organize mules and guides for the trek to Pelechuco. About ten minutes' walk east of town along the road to Curva and then down a steep path to the valley floor are the **aguas termales** (daily 8am–6pm; free), natural hot springs

The Kallawayas: medicine men of the Andes

The Cordillera Apolobamba is home to Bolivia's smallest and most mysterious ethnic group: the **Kallawayas**. Inhabiting just half a dozen villages in the Upper Charazani Valley, the Kallawayas are a secretive caste of traditional herbal medicine practitioners, thought to number just a few hundred, who are famous throughout the Andes for their healing powers. The enormous ecological diversity of the Cordillera Apolobamba means the Kallawayas have a vast natural pharmacy of plants to draw on, while the region's proximity to the tropical lowlands has also given them access to the vast medicinal resources of Amazonian shamanism. Individual Kallawayas may know the medical properties of over 900 different plant species – an encyclopedic herbal knowledge which is passed from father to son. Some historical sources credit the Kallawayas with being the first to use the dried bark of the Cinchona tree, the source of quinine, to prevent and cure malaria; taken to Europe by the Jesuits, quinine remains to this day the basis for most treatments of the disease. More recently, scientists from the University of California have been studying chemicals derived from herbs used by the Kallawayas as possible treatments for the HIV virus.

For many centuries the Kallawayas have wandered through the Andes collecting herbs and bringing their specialist medical skills to local people. Individual healers roamed huge distances, often on foot, travelling to Peru, Chile, Argentina and as far as Panamá during the construction of the canal, as well as the length and breadth of Bolivia. Most Kallawayas are also powerful ritual specialists, combining their skills as herbalists with the supposed ability to predict the future and diagnose illness by reading coca leaves. Their holistic cures involve tackling the spiritual causes of sickness too, and they are experts at placating the mountain gods and other natural spirits through ritual offerings, as well as being able to make highly prized protective amulets. The most enigmatic thing about the Kallawayas, however, is their language. Although the main language spoken in their communities is Quechua, and many also speak some Aymara or Spanish, the Kallawaya medicine men famously speak a secret tongue known as **Machaj Juyay**, which is used only in healing rituals and other ceremonies. This language has provoked intense speculation: some researchers believe that Machaj Juyay is related to the secret language spoken in private by the Inca ruling elite, distinct from Quechua, which was the lingua franca of their empire. Certainly, the earliest post-conquest chroniclers linked the Kallawayas to the Incas. One wrote that the Kallawayas were brought to the imperial city of Cusco to act as herbalists and carry out important religious ceremonies and divination rituals for the Inca rulers; another claimed they had been charged with carrying the litter of the Inca himself. Other evidence suggests that the Kallawayas date back far into Andean prehistory: in 1970 archeologists uncovered a skeleton in the Charazani valley which had been buried with recognisable Kallawaya paraphernalia – this was carbondated to between 800 and 1000 BC, two thousand years before the rise of the Inca Empire.

These days the Kallawayas no longer wander as far and wide as they used to, and their numbers are thought to be dwindling, as fewer sons acquire their fathers' knowledge. However, a growing number are now resident in La Paz, where their skills remain in high demand – up to eighty percent of Bolivians are thought to have called on a natural healer at some point in their lives, and nearly half use only traditional medicine.

channelled into an open-air concrete swimming pool which offer an excellent way to soothe tired muscles after a long trek.

Every other day or so, one of the buses from La Paz to Charazani continues up the valley to the village of **CURVA**. Curva is the centre of Kallawaya culture (see box on p.131) and the starting or ending point of the Trans-Apolobamba Trek. If there's no bus you can walk up to Curva from Charazani in about four hours, following the footpath that starts near the hotsprings and cuts across the valley floor, before climbing up the other side to Curva (the road itself contours round and takes much longer to walk). Even if you're not planning to trek to Pelechuco, the walk up to Curva is very rewarding: the valley is very beautiful, its steep sides sculpted by ancient terraces, and the path takes you through several Kallawaya farming villages.

Perched at about 3780m on a narrow ridge above the valley, with the snows of Akhamani, the sacred mountain of the Kallawayas, rising above, Curva itself is a deeply traditional community and the effective capital of Kallawaya culture. With thatched stone houses and cobbled streets it's a picturesque village, but people here are quite wary of outsiders, and if you're staying the night you're better off in **LAGUNILLAS**, the modern settlement beside the lake a fifteen-minute walk below Curva. The protected areas agency SERNAP has opened a **refugio** (no phone; **❷**) for trekkers here, with warm dormitories boasting bunks and solar-heated showers, and you can also **camp** beside the lake, which is usually busy with ducks, *huallata* geese and other wildfowl. The lake is actually artificial, having been built as a reservoir to feed a series of pools nearby which are used to prepare freeze-dried potatoes known as *tunta*, a food-preservation technique dating back to the Incas and before. The rangers at the *refugio* can help find guides and mules to take you on the trek to Pelechuco, and you should register with them before proceeding further into the mountains. Ask around here and you should be able to arrange a consultation with a **Kallawaya medicine man**, who'll read your future in coca leaves for a few Bolivianos and may even be able to treat any ailments you might be suffering from.

Ulla Ulla

From the junction where the side road to Charazani branches off, the road running north along the Peruvian frontier towards Pelechuco (see opposite) climbs onto a high and windswept plateau, known as **Ulla Ulla**, which runs along the western side of the Cordillera Apolobamba. Covering some 2000 square kilometres at an average altitude of 4300m, Ulla Ulla's broad expanse of green pasture and marshland, set against a dramatic backdrop of snow-capped peaks, supports great herds of alpacas and llamas, as well as smaller groups of vicuñas, their delicate wild cousins. The plateau has been a protected area since 1972, when the **Reserva Nacional de Fauna Ulla Ulla** was established to protect the highly endangered vicuña population – it's made an astonishing recovery since then, and just driving across the plateau you'll see dozens of vicuñas and many hundreds of alpacas, as well as a wide variety of birds including flamingos, ibises and *huallata* geese. The only signs of human habitation are the occasional herders' hamlets, lonely clusters of stone houses and animal corrals surrounded by pointed adobe structures known as *putucos* – they look a bit like Buddhist stupas, but are in fact used to store llama and alpaca dung, the only fuel available on this treeless plain. The biggest settlement is **Ulla Ulla village**, though it has no facilities of any kind. If you want to spend the night here and explore areas away from the road you'll need to camp. If you've got your own transport, there are some good natural **hot springs** an hour's drive or so further north of Ulla Ulla village, just off the road at **Putina**.

Pelechuco

Beyond Ulla Ulla the road climbs up from the plateau and over a 4860-metre pass between glittering glacial peaks before dropping down to the town of **PELECHUCO**, set in a deep valley which is often shrouded in cloud (its name is derived from the Quechua expression *puyu kuchu*, meaning place of clouds). This is the end of the road for vehicles but the starting (or ending) point of the **Trans-Apolobamba Trek** (see below). Pelechuco was founded by the Spanish in 1560 as a gold-mining outpost, and limited mining activity continues in the region, but otherwise the town serves mainly as a market centre for the Quechua-speaking farming and herding communities of the surrounding mountains.

Some buildings survive from the colonial era, notably the simple adobe **church** with its stone belltower (currently under restoration), but the rough stone houses with thatched roofs are gradually being replaced by ugly modern zinc-roofed brick and concrete structures. The steep valley slopes around the town are still covered in dense cloudforest, including large numbers of the rare queñua (*polylepis*) tree, a gnarled shrub that can survive at very high altitudes. On some of the hillsides above the town you can make out the remains of pre-Hispanic agricultural terracing, as well as occasional stone look-out posts, known as *pucaras*, which were probably built in Inca or pre-Inca times to guard the approach to the pass against raiding tribes coming up the valley from the Amazon lowlands.

Buses to Pelecucho from La Paz (15–18 hours) leave on Wednesdays and return on Friday, Saturday and Sunday. They usually depart from Calle Reyes Cardoso in the cemetery district of La Paz, though they sometimes only leave from the Tranca Rio Seco on the outskirts of El Alto, where you can buy tickets in advance from a kiosk: you'll need to take a taxi to find it. The best **place to stay** is the basic *Hotel Llajtaymanta* (✆02/8137283; ❷), on the central plaza, where you can also get simple meals. The helpful owner, Reynaldo Vasquez, can help you find mules and guides for the Trans-Apolobamba Trek, and also sells bus tickets to La Paz.

The Trans-Apolobamba Trek

The tough four- or five-day **Trans-Apolobamba Trek** between Pelechuco and Curva takes you through the heart of the Cordillera Apolobamba and some of the most magnificent high-Andean scenery in Bolivia. It also passes through the homeland of the Kallawayas (see box on p.131), and around the peak of their sacred mountain, Akhamani. Crossing several high passes, including one over 5100m, this is a hard trek, and shouldn't really be attempted without a guide. There are no reliable maps of the region (the last survey was conducted by the British Royal Geographical Society in 1911–13), and even if you have good directions it's easy to get lost, particularly if you're over 4000m high and the clouds close in.

You can walk the trek either from Pelechuco south to Curva or vice versa, though it's best to start in Pelechuco, where guides and mules can be more easily arranged, and finish in Curva, close to Charazani, from where transport out is much more reliable – end your trek in Pelechuco and you could wait five days for the next bus. **Guides and mules** can be organized in Curva (through the rangers at Lagunillas), Pelechuco (ask at the *Hotel Llajtaymanta*) and Charazani (ask at the *Hotel Akhamani*), or you can arrange to do the trek with a tour operator in La Paz (see p.88). Guides, mules and mule handlers should cost about $6 per day each. You can buy basic foodstuffs (pasta, potatoes, tinned fish) in both towns, but you'll need to bring all other equipment and supplies with you from La Paz.

The route

From **Pelechuco**, the route heads steeply out of town to the southeast, climbing to a high pass at 4800m (4–5hr). Beyond the pass, the path zigzags down a steep scree slope to the head of a glacial valley about 300m below (30min). You can camp here, or continue down the valley to the village of **Ilo-Ilo** (30min), where you can buy basic supplies. From Ilo-Ilo the path climbs southeast towards the 5100m **Sunchuli Pass**, passing through the small village of Piedra Grande. A mining road runs up to the pass, but you should take the more direct path that branches off it to the left after the village. In all it's a five-to-six-hour climb from Ilo-Ilo to the pass. Don't attempt to clear the pass after about 4pm, as cloud can close in quickly and completely, reducing visibility and making route-finding impossible. There's a good but cold camping site on a green meadow about ninety minutes before the pass, where you should overnight if you can't clear the pass before mid-afternoon.

On the other side of the pass, follow the mining road down for about fifteen minutes to the top of a green valley; there are good camping spots a little further down beside a stream in the valley. Otherwise, when the road contours round to the left, cut across to the right-hand side until you hit a narrow irrigation canal, then take the path running above it to the east. After about 45 minutes the path climbs over the shoulder of the mountain to the east, opening up fantastic views to the south of the last cloud-covered ridges of the Andes marching down into the Amazon lowlands, with the distant peaks of the Cordillera Real rising behind. It then drops steeply down to the abandoned mining village of **Viscachani**, then contours round to the south, past a lake and up over another ridge. Above the lake to the right rises the peak of **Akhamani** (5700m), the sacred mountain of the Kallawayas.

From the ridge you can see the next pass, marked by two stone *apachetas* to the southwest. From there, take the path down to the southeast, which soon descends a hair-raisingly steep switchback path known as *mil curvas* ("a thousand bends") carved out of a loose scree slope. This descends from 4650m to 4150m in just an hour or two, bringing you out beside a small stream. Across the stream you'll find **Incachani**, a collection of ancient (and presumably Inca) ruined buildings at the top of a green valley which is an excellent place to camp.

From here the path climbs southwest to a 4700-metre pass below the peak of Akhamani before dropping down and contouring southwest to another pass, again marked by stone *apachetas*. From here, the path heads south down a deep valley to **Jatun Pampa**, an alpaca-herding hamlet set on the grassy valley floor where you can camp. From Jatun Pampa it's another two to three hours to Curva. Continue down and across the river then climb diagonally up to the left on the opposite slope. Descend again and cross another river, then pick up a path climbing to the left to another mountain spur. From here you can see **Curva** a short distance below to the left, and **Lagunillas** (see p.132) by the lake a little further down to the right.

The Yungas

East of La Paz, the Cordillera Real drops precipitously into the Amazon low-lands, plunging down through a region of rugged, forest-covered mountains and deep subtropical valleys known as **the Yungas**. Blessed with fertile alluvial soils and watered by the plentiful rains which are formed when hot air from the Amazon basin hits the Andes, the warm valleys of the Yungas produce abundant crops of coffee, tropical fruit and coca for the markets of La Paz and the rest of the Altiplano – indeed long before the Spanish conquest the peoples of the Andes maintained agricultural colonies here to supply the Altiplano with coca and other subtropical products, linking these outposts to the main population centres by well-built stone roads. Three of these so-called "Inca" trails (though they were probably earlier routes which were used and modified by Incas) – the **Takesi**, **Choro** and **Yunga Cruz trails** – are still in good condition, and make excellent three- to four-day hikes from La Paz. The Choro Trail also passes through the pristine cloudforests of the **Parque Nacional Cotapata**, one of the few areas where the natural Yungas vegetation is still well preserved. Even if you don't hike, the journey down to the Yungas from the Altiplano is truly spectacular. The **road from La Paz to Coroico** is widely considered the most dangerous in the world, hugging the forest-covered mountain slopes as it winds above fearsome precipices. It's also amongst the most scenic, and so dramatic that many travellers now tackle it on mountain bike, an unforgettable descent of over 3500m in just over 60km.

The most frequently visited Yungas town is the idyllic resort of **Coroico**, set amidst spectacular scenery and exuberant tropical vegetation and boasting a warm climate that provides the perfect antidote to the bleak Altiplano. From Coroico, the road continues north towards Rurrenabaque and the Bolivian Amazon (covered in chapter 6), passing the run-of-the-mill town of **Caranavi**, from where an exciting journey by road and river leads through the gold-mining region of the Yungas and back up to Sorata. Alternatively, you can avoid Coroico and head

Coca in the Yungas

The Yungas is one of Bolivia's major **coca**-producing regions, a role it has fulfilled since the colonial era, when the Spanish established coca plantations here to meet the massive demand for the leaf in the mines of Potosí. Considered sweeter and better for chewing than that produced in the Chapare region near Cochabamba, coca grown in the Yungas still dominates the markets of the Andes, and remains legal for traditional use. Despite this, the US government is convinced that much of the region's production ends up being processed into cocaine, and the Bolivian authorities have come under pressure to extend the coca-eradication programme applied in the Chapare to the Yungas. In 2001 a large Bolivian army contingent was sent to Chulumani to commence operations. Days later it was forced to return ignominiously to La Paz after local peasant communities rose in revolt and blocked all roads, cutting the troops off from their supplies. The project has subsequently been shelved, though it could easily be revived in the future, and it's worth checking what the coca-eradication situation is before travelling anywhere off the beaten track in the Yungas. If US-backed eradication efforts begin again, the region could quickly become embroiled in conflict, and strange gringos wandering around the back-country might easily be misidentified as undercover US drug-enforcement agents.

instead to **Chulumani**, a less-touristed Yungas market town that's the centre of the equally scenic but less frequently visited **South Yungas**.

Parque Nacional Cotapata

Around 20km north of La Paz, some 400 square kilometres of the north face of the Cordillera Real are protected by the **Parque Nacional y Area Natural de Manejo Integrado Cotapata**. Ranging in elevation from 1000m to 6000m, Cotapata embraces many of the astonishing range of different ecosystems and climatic zones formed as the Andes plunge down into the valleys of the upper Amazon Basin. Within a remarkably short distance high mountain peaks, snowfields and puna grasslands give way to dense cloudforest, which in turn gradually blends into the humid montane forest that covers the lower slopes of the Andes in a thick green blanket. The **cloudforest** – also known as the *ceja de selva*, or "jungle's eyebrows" – is particularly striking, made up of low, gnarled trees covered in lichens and epiphytes which absorb moisture from the clouds which are formed when warm air from the Amazon lowlands hits the cold ridges of the Andes. It's also home to many unique bird species, as well as elusive mammals like the puma and spectacled bear.

The Choro Trail

The only way to visit Cotapata properly is by walking through the park along the pre-Hispanic **Choro Trail**. Running almost entirely downhill, the trail is easy to follow and can be walked in three to four days. Most trekking agencies in La Paz run tours along this route, but if you have your own camping equipment, a compass and (ideally) a map, it's relatively simple to do without a guide.

To reach the trail, take any bus heading to the Yungas from Villa Fátima in La Paz and get off at **La Cumbre**, the high pass 22km north of the city. From the lakes just before La Cumbre, head north-northwest to another pass, **Abra Chukura** (4860m), which is marked by a stone cairn (*apacheta*). This 45-minute walk is the only part of the route which is difficult to follow – if in doubt stick to the rough track that winds up to the pass. From the *apacheta*, a well-paved Inca or pre-Inca stone path (up to 4m wide in places) plunges down the left side of the deep valley of the Río Phajchiri, passing the ruins of an Inca waystation, or *tambo*, after an hour or so. After another two to three hours you'll reach the small village of **Chukura**.

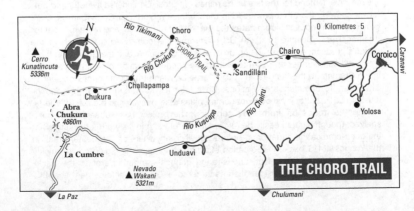

Below Chukura the cloudforest begins, the vegetation gradually thickening as you descend. After another hour you reach **Challapampa**, a small village with a shop that sells soft drinks, beer and basic foodstuffs. There's a good camping spot by the stream here, though the locals will expect you to pay a dollar or two. The next campsite is another three hours down the valley, just before the village of **Choro**. At Choro the path crosses over the river on a bridge and climbs east along the right-hand side of a deep, densely forested valley – the track is still largely paved and is supported by a well-preserved stone platform in places. The next available water and camping spot is another two hours or so away where a stream crosses the path; about three hours beyond that you reach **Sandillani**, where you can camp in the beautifully tended garden of a venerable Japanese man; there's also a small shop here. From Sandillani it's another two hours down the valley to the end of the trail at the village of **Chairo**, where you can camp and buy supplies.

From Chairo it's about 11km to the main road and another 4km to **Yolosa** (see p.138), from where there's regular transport on to Coroico and back to La Paz. If you're lucky you'll find a *camioneta* from Chairo to Yolosa (about $2 per person), though it's more likely you'll either have to walk or hire a driver to take you there, which should cost about $20 for the vehicle and driver.

La Paz to Coroico

Few highways in the world have as intimidating a reputation as the road linking La Paz with Coroico in the North Yungas. A rough, narrow track chiselled out of near-vertical mountainsides that descends more than 3500m over a distance of just 64km, it's widely referred to as the **world's most dangerous road**, a title bestowed on it by the Inter-American Development Bank. Statistically, the sobriquet is difficult to dispute: every year dozens of vehicles go off the road, and with vertical drops of up to 1000m over the edge, annual fatalities often reach into the hundreds. Even in the context of the heavy traffic it receives – it's the main link between the Altiplano and the Amazon, and between Brazil and the Pacific coast – this is worrying stuff. For a while the road was declared one-way on alternate days and accidents were much reduced as a result, but two-way traffic was reintroduced after lorry drivers complained that their incomes were being affected. A new $120 million bypass around the most perilous stretch is currently under construction, but with a long tunnel still to be excavated and the money already spent it may be years before it's completed.

What the statistics don't tell you, however, is that this is also amongst the most beautiful roads in the world. Starting amidst the icebound peaks of the Cordillera Real, it plunges down through the clouds into the humid valleys of the Yungas, winding along deep, narrow gorges where dense cloudforest clings to even the steepest slopes. So spectacular is the descent that travelling the Yungas road by **mountain bike** is fast becoming one of Bolivia's most popular tourist attractions, an exhilarating ride that's easy to organize as a day-trip with tour companies in La Paz (Gravity Assisted Mountain Biking – see p.89 – have the best reputation). Though cycling down the most dangerous road in the world may sound like a crazy proposition, in fact it's arguably safer than travelling by public transport if you go with a reputable tour company which has good guides and well-maintained bikes. Of course biking the road is not entirely without risk, and people have been hurt during the descent, but at least on a bicycle you're in control of your own speed, and you'll also avoid head-on collisions (the guide goes first) with oncoming trucks and catastrophic brake failure – two problems that cause many of the motor-vehicle accidents. Going by bike also means you can stop and enjoy the unforgettable views whenever you want.

Nor, indeed, should you think of **public transport** as overly dangerous. Most accidents that happen on the road involve heavy lorries, which are often poorly maintained and driven by tired, drunk or simply inexperienced drivers. The micros that are the main public passenger carriers on this route are much safer, and are driven by highly experienced drivers who are just as keen to get home in one piece as you are – most of the foreign travellers who have died on this route were in vehicles driven by other foreigners.

In total, the journey from La Paz to Coroico takes about four and a half hours. From Villa Fátima in La Paz, the road to the Yungas first climbs northeast to **La Cumbre**, a 4800-metre pass over the Cordillera Real. From here it descends to **Unduavi**, a roadside hamlet with a police checkpoint where vehicles are searched for unauthorized coca on the way out of the Yungas, precursor chemicals for cocaine manufacture (such as hydrochloric acid and acetone) and cocaine itself. At Unduavi the road forks, one branch descending southeast towards Chulumani in the South Yungas (see p.145), the other descending northeast towards Coroico and the Amazon lowlands beyond.

Shortly beyond Unduavi on the Coroico branch the tarmac ends – the next 40km from here are the most perilous and spectacular of the entire route. For the most hair-raising views, sit on the left of your vehicle. At times the road is only 3m wide, and trucks and buses appear to lean out over precipices more than a kilometre deep. To make matters worse, the road is often swathed in cloud, and in places waterfalls crash down onto its surface. At one particularly perilous blind corner, you'll see a solitary figure with a red flag who signals to oncoming vehicles to let them know whether the road ahead is safe or not. This is not some half-hearted official safety initiative. The man with the flag lost his entire family when a bus went over the edge in 1988. Ever since, he's lived where they died, warning traffic by day and sleeping in a small hut, surviving on food donated by sympathetic drivers.

About 86km from La Paz, the road reaches **YOLOSA**, a hamlet set at about 1200m. Here, a side road climbs up to Coroico, 11km away, while the main road continues 74km north to Caranavi and beyond to Rurrenabaque. If you're not on a direct bus to Coroico you can change here and catch one of the regular pick-up trucks (*camionetas*) that carry passengers up to Coroico from the police checkpoint. You can also get transport further north along the main road towards Caranavi and Rurrenabaque.

Coroico and around

The peaceful little town of **COROICO** is rightly considered one of the most beautiful spots in the Yungas, perched on a steep mountain slope 600m or so above the river of the same name, with panoramic views across the forest-covered Andean foothills to the icy peaks of the Cordillera Real beyond. Founded in the colonial era as a gold-mining outpost, the town is still an important market centre for the surrounding agricultural communities, and in recent years has also become a popular destination for Paceños looking to escape the cold of the Altiplano. Set at an altitude of 1760m, it enjoys a warm and pleasantly humid climate, and this, combined with the dramatic scenery and good facilities, makes it an excellent place to relax and recuperate. Indeed, most travellers find they need a little time in Coroico just to recover from reaching the town in the first place – but whether you make the short but hair-raising journey down from the Altiplano by micro, follow the same route by mountain bike or make the slower trek on foot down the Choro Trail, Coroico is worth visiting just for the sheer thrill of getting there. It also makes a great stop-off if you're attempting the tough overland journey from La Paz to Rurrenabaque or elsewhere in the Amazon lowlands, and if you're heading in the opposite direction it's a good place to begin acclimatizing to the higher altitude.

It's hardly surprising, then, that most visitors spend much of their time in Coroico lounging by a swimming pool, sipping a cold drink and enjoying the fantastic views. For those with a bit more energy, however, there are some pleasant walks through the surrounding countryside, whose forested mountain slopes are covered in a lush patchwork of coffee and coca plantations and banana and orange groves. Coroico gets very busy at **weekends** and during Bolivian public holidays, when it's transformed by large numbers of Paceños on vacation. This certainly makes things livelier, especially where nightlife is concerned, but if you want to relax in peace – and avoid hiked-up hotel rates – it's best to visit during the week.

Around October 20 each year, Coroico celebrates its biggest annual **fiesta** with several days of drinking, processions and costumed dances. The fiesta commemorates the day in 1811 when the statue of the Virgin in the church – brought here from Barcelona in 1680, when Coroico was founded – supposedly summoned a ghost army to drive off a force of indigenous rebels that were besieging the town.

Arrival and information

Buses and micros from La Paz drop passengers off outside the offices of the two bus companies, either right in the centre of town on Plaza Principal or just off it on Calle Sagárnaga, the road that leads up to Coroico from Yolosa. If you're coming to Coroico from anywhere else, you'll have to catch a pick-up truck for the fifteen-minute ride up from the main road at Yolosa – these drop passengers off outside the Mercado Municipal, also on Sagárnaga.

Coroico's a small town and almost everything is within easy walking distance of the plaza, where you can also usually find a taxi to take you to the more outlying hotels. There's a small **tourist office** on the plaza (Tues–Sun 9am–noon & 2–7pm; mobile ☏71597319), which usually has a selection of fliers and maps of the town and can give limited advice in Spanish on accommodation and the attractions of Coroico and the surrounding area. You can usually get more useful information – often in English – at your hotel.

Accommodation

For a small town Coroico has a good range of **places to stay**, aimed primarily at visitors from La Paz. At weekends and on public holidays everywhere gets very full and prices go up, so it's worth booking in advance. Conversely, things are pretty quiet midweek, when prices are much more reasonable. Even if you're on a tight budget, it's worth spending a little more to stay somewhere comfortable with a swimming pool, as you may end up spending a lot of your time lounging around it.

Hostal Kory Linares ☏71564050. Long-standing backpackers' favourite, with plenty of small but clean rooms (with or without bath) around a series of terraces and a large swimming pool, with fantastic views across the valley. There's also a reasonable restaurant, and laundry facilities are available. ❸

Hostal Sol y Luna Just under 1km outside town

COROICO

Santa Rosa & Mapiri

2 & Coripata
Waterfalls
Cerro Uchumachi
Yolosa & La Paz

Vagantes Eco-Aventuras

ENTEL

PLAZA PRINCIPAL

Buses & Micros to La Paz

Football Pitch

Swimming Pool

Mercado Municipal

El Calvario

0 Metres 100

PLACES TO STAY		PLACES TO EAT AND DRINK	
Hostal Kory	6	Back-Stube	E
Hostal Sol y Luna	9	Pasteleria Alemana	A
Hotel Don Quijote	2	Bamboo's Café	A
Hotel Esmeralda	8	Comedor popular	B
Hotel Gloria Coroico	4	El Cafetal	H
Hotel Lluvia de Oro	1	Esmeralda	F
Residencial La Casa	5	La Casa	D
Residencial Las Peñas	7	La Taberna	C
Residencial Las Torres	3	La Tropicana	G

uphill on Julio Zuazo Cuenca, beyond the *Hotel Esmeralda* ☎71561626. Peaceful and secluded hideaway with six delightful rustic cabins spread out in a beautiful hillside forest garden with hammocks, firepits and two small plunge pools. There are also several simple, inexpensive rooms (❷), and camping space is available. Staff are friendly and welcoming, and there's a small restaurant. ❸

Hotel Don Quijote About 1km outside town on the road to Coripata ☎02/8116007. Very good value chalet-style hotel, popular with Bolivian weekenders and foreign tour groups alike, with clean, modern rooms, good views, bar, restaurant and a spacious swimming pool. ❸

Hotel Esmeralda 400m above town up Julio Zuazo Cuenca ☎02/8116434, ℗02/8116017, ⓦwww.latinwide.com/esmeralda. Large but peaceful German-owned hotel with good views across the valley, an attractive garden and swimming pool, and a reasonable restaurant. The more expensive rooms have private baths and good views; the cheaper ones have neither and are rather cramped. ❹–❺

Hotel Gloria Coroico Linares ☎02/8116020,

ⓦwww.gloria-tours-bolivia.com. Rather grand, formerly state-run hotel popular with Bolivian families, with a slightly holiday-camp feel. Rooms are fairly pleasant, and the more expensive ones are en suite (though cheaper ones are gloomy and share too few bathrooms). There are good views too, a big swimming pool, billiard tables, and a bar and restaurant. ❷–❸

Hotel Lluvia de Oro Reyes Ortiz ☎02/8116005. Rather run down, with simple rooms with or without bath around a colonial-style courtyard and a greenish swimming pool. ❷

Residencial La Casa Linares ☎02/8116024, ℮lacasa@ceibo.entelnet.bo. Efficient, European-run place with small but comfortable and reasonably priced rooms with or without bath, plus a small swimming pool and a very good restaurant. ❷

Residencial Las Peñas Sagárnaga ☎71924615. Friendly place offering very basic rooms with shared bath – good value, but strictly for those on a tight budget. ❶

Residencial Las Torres Julio Zuazo Cuenca (no phone). Simple but clean rooms with shared bath, set around a central courtyard. ❷

Eating and drinking

There's no lack of variety when it comes to **places to eat**, including some good European-owned places where you can find everything from pizza and Mexican food to quality French cuisine, German pastries and even Swiss fondue. There are also plenty of places around the plaza serving inexpensive standard Bolivian food. As always the best-value places are the food stalls in the **Mercado Municipal**, a block south of the main plaza on Sagárnaga; there's also a cheap **comedor popular** a block north of the plaza on Tomás Monje. During the week, **nightlife** tends to involve drinking beer in the town's bar-restaurants or poolside in the better hotels. At weekends, however, several bars and a disco – *La Tropicana*, on the edge of town on the road down to Yolosa – cater for the many young visiting Paceños, who also fill the plaza, drinking on the streets accompanied by the blaring stereos of their 4WDs.

Back-Stube Pasteleria Alemana Plaza Principal. German café-bakery serving excellent soups, snacks, sandwiches and salads, and deliciously decadent home-made cakes. Closed Tues.

Bamboo's Café Iturralde. Candlelit hideaway open in the evenings for reasonable Mexican food like burritos and enchiladas at about $4 a plate, as well as ice-cold beers and mean margaritas. It's open late, and there's live music at weekends.

El Cafetal Beside the hospital about 10min walk southeast of the town centre. Small French-run restaurant with panoramic views and delicious snacks and meals, including excellent pasta and crêpes.

Esmeralda In the hotel of the same name, 400m from the plaza up Julio Zuazo Cuenca. Efficient restaurant with indoor and outdoor seating and great views. Food includes good breakfasts, a wide range of meat, fish and vegetarian main courses, plus a salad bar, a filling set almuerzo and decent pizza on Tuesday and Friday nights.

La Casa In *Residencial La Casa*, Linares. Swiss-run restaurant serving authentic cheese, meat or chocolate fondues for a minimum of two people at about $5 each. They also offer other European dishes like raclette and goulash, as well as a filling set almuerzo.

Moving on from Coroico

Micros to **La Paz** leave at least once an hour from the offices of Turbus Totai, on the plaza, and Flota Yungeña, half a block away on Sagárnaga. It's worth buying a ticket in advance, especially at weekends, and also worth travelling by day, both for safety and to enjoy the spectacular views. If you're heading north into the Amazon, you can buy a ticket on a through bus to **Rurrenabaque** from La Paz with Turbus Totai, which passes through Yolosa on the main road every day – you'll have to pay the full fare from La Paz, but in return you get a guaranteed seat for the arduous ride, which takes at least fifteen hours. Alternatively, you can flag down any through bus (1–2 daily) or truck at the police checkpoint (*tranca*) in Yolosa, though there's no guarantee you'll find a seat on a bus, while travelling by truck makes for an even longer and rougher ride. Getting a ride on a bus (hourly; 2–3hr) or truck to **Caranavi** from Yolosa is easier, as they pass by more regularly. To get to **Yolosa** from Coroico, jump on one of the pick-up trucks that leave from outside the market on Sagárnaga when full – usually every fifteen minutes or so.

If you want to go to **Chulumani** from Coroico by public transport you'll need to head back to **Unduavi**, where the roads to the north and south Yungas divide, and catch a through bus from La Paz to Chulumani. This is a shame, as the more direct route via the town of **Coripata** passes through a beautiful valley that is the coca-growing heartland of the Yungas. Unfortunately, the Coroico–Coripata road is currently in such poor condition that it isn't served by regular public transport, though if you ask around in Coroico you may find a truck or *camioneta* covering part of the 30km or so route to Coripata. If you're feeling adventurous, and are equipped to camp if necessary, you could then walk the rest of the way. Basic accommodation and meals are available in Coripata, from where there's regular transport back to La Paz and on to Chulumani.

La Taberna Plaza Principal. Cosy corner café with good music and a laid-back atmosphere, serving good breakfasts (including pancakes), plus juices, coffee and snacks throughout the day, and cocktails and cold beer in the evenings, when videos are shown.

Listings

Banks and exchange The Banco Mercantil, on Sagárnaga, changes US dollars cash and gives advances on Visa and Mastercard. Several hotels will change travellers' cheques: try the *Esmeralda* or *Kory*.

Horses You can hire horses for about $5 an hour from El Relincho (☎71923814), about 10min walk beyond the *Hotel Esmeralda* on the road to the *Hostal Sol y Luna*.

Hospital, about 10min walk southeast of the town centre along Pacheco.

Internet access A few hotels offer internet access, but Coroico's poor telephone connections mean they are uniformly slow, expensive and unreliable – the best place is the *Residencial La Casa*.

Post Office The post office is on Plaza Principal, though it's only open irregularly and you're better off sending letters when you get back to La Paz.

Swimming pools If your hotel doesn't have one, you can cool off in the Piscina Municipal (daily 10am–7pm; $1), south of the plaza on Tomás Monje.

Telephone office The ENTEL office is on Plaza Principal, where there are also several phone booths.

Tour operators Vagantes Eco-Aventuras, just off the plaza on Julio Zuazo Cuenca (☎71912981), run guided half-day and full-day hikes up Cerro Uchumani above the town and down to the Río Vagantes in the valley below. They can also organize excursions by 4WD to Afro-Yungueño villages like Tocaña and further afield, plus visits to coca, coffee and orange plantations. The La Paz-based agency Explore Bolivia run white-water rafting trips on the Río Coroico – contact them in advance in La Paz (see p.89) or ask at the tourist information office on the plaza.

Around Coroico

There are some excellent hikes in the countryside around Coroico, the most popular being the climb up to the summit of **Cerro Uchumachi**, the hill that rises above the town, which takes about two hours there and back. To reach the summit, continue uphill beyond the *Hotel Esmeralda* along the clear path, marked by the stations of the cross, that leads to the small chapel of El Calvario. From the red and white antenna behind the chapel an easy-to-follow path climbs through low, dense vegetation to the summit, which is marked by three wooden crosses. With excellent views over the town and across the valley to the jagged peaks of the Cordillera Real, it's no surprise that this is the preferred spot for locals to pay homage to the *achachilas* (mountain gods), and you'll see signs of alcohol libations and burnt offerings all around the summit. When the weather closes in the whole peak quickly becomes shrouded in cloud and the views disappear. Each year on June 21 a lot of people camp on Cerro Uchumachi, celebrating the Aymara New Year and winter solstice by watching the sun rise over the mountain peaks to the west.

Another good hike is to the **waterfalls** (*cascadas*) that are Coroico's main water source – a three-to-four-hour walk there and back. From El Calvario chapel, follow the path to your left as you face uphill; this leads around the hillside to the *cascadas*. More difficult to follow but equally rewarding is the path that heads down into the valley to the **Río Coroico** from beside the football pitch. After about an hour's walk downhill the path hits the main road to Caranavi; turn right and you'll soon reach **Puente Mururata**, a bridge over the stream of the same name, upstream of which there are some pools where you can swim in the cool, clear waters. From the other side of Puente Mururata a path climbs to the left of the road to the peaceful Afro-Yungueño village of **Tocaña**, about a twenty-minute walk away.

Isolated in a handful of villages in the Yungas valleys is perhaps the most forgotten ethnic group in Bolivia: the **Afro-Bolivianos**. Now numbering about 8000, the Afro-Bolivianos are the descendants of African slaves brought to the Andes by the Spanish during the colonial era to work in the mines of Potosí. When silver-mining declined they were moved to the Yungas to work on coca and other plantations – their higher natural resistance to malaria meant they were more resilient workers than Aymara migrants from the Altiplano. Though slavery was officially abolished with independence from Spain in 1825, Bolivia's black population remained in bondage to landowners until after the Revolution and Agrarian Reform of 1952–53, when they finally gained control of their own lands and freedom from servitude. Most subsequently remained in the Yungas, cultivating coca, fruit and coffee on small farms.

Living in small communities in the midst of a far larger Aymara population, the Afro-Bolivianos have been heavily influenced by their indigenous neighbours: most speak Aymara as well as Spanish, and many Afro-Bolivian women dress in the bowler hats and pollera skirts favoured by the Aymara. But they also maintain a distinctive cultural identity – indeed until recently they even elected their own king. The most powerful reminder of their African cultural roots is undoubtedly to be found in their music and dance, such as the intricate and compelling drum-driven rhythms of musical styles like the *saya*. Incorporated into dances like the *Morenada*, seen at the Oruro Carnaval and fiestas throughout the Andes, these rhythms are also reminders of the cultural influence this small group has had on mainstream Bolivian society, despite a tendency by the authorities to ignore their existence.

Caranavi to Santa Rosa: the gold-mining loop

From the dusty town of **Caranavi**, an adventurous journey by road and river leads through the main alluvial **gold-mining region** of the Yungas back up into the highlands at Sorata. This tough but exciting two-to-three-day trip by road and river via the mining settlements of **Guanay**, **Mapiri** and **Santa Rosa** takes you through a ruggedly beautiful region of fast-flowing rivers that rush through the forest-covered foothills of the Andes, where hardy independent miners make a living extracting gold from the sediments washed down from the high mountains. Many of the miners came to the Yungas after being made redundant when the big state-owned mines of the Altiplano closed down in the late 1980s. Migrants from all over the Bolivian highlands, they share a pioneer optimism and camaraderie, determined to snatch from nature the living their home communities could not provide.

Caranavi

Beyond Yolosa (see p.138), the road from La Paz continues north towards the Amazon lowlands along the deep, narrow gorge of the Río Coroico, which widens as it approaches the hot and dusty market town of **CARANAVI**, a scruffy settlement about 160km from La Paz which lies at the centre of a populous region producing coca, coffee and fruit. Beyond Caranavi the main road continues north through the heavily settled **Alto Beni** region to Yacumo, about 160km away, from where one road heads east across the Llanos de Mojos towards Trinidad, and another heads northwest to Rurrenabaque (all of which are covered in chapter 6).

Buses to La Paz (6–7hr) leave every hour or so from the terminal at one end of Caranavi's main street, where you can also pick up through buses to Rurrenabaque and elsewhere in the Amazon lowlands. Buses and micros to Guanay (see below) leave from beside the market, at the other end of the main street about ten minutes' walk from the terminal. The main street is lined with cheap **restaurants** and roast-chicken joints, as well as several **places to stay** – if you get stuck here for the night try the basic *Residencial Norte Paceño* (no phone; ❶), or splash out on the much more upmarket *Hotel Landivar* (☎02/8116234; ❷–❸), which has a swimming pool and air-conditioning.

Guanay

From Caranavi, regular buses (6 daily; 3–4hr) make the seventy-kilometre journey northwest along the banks of the fast-flowing Río Coroico to **GUANAY**, a small gold-mining settlement with a real frontier feel. Little more than a collection of tin-roofed wooden houses and stores selling dried foodstuffs, mining equipment and other supplies, Guanay stands at the confluence of several rivers that rush down through the Andean foothills, bringing with them a rich cargo of alluvial gold. The town serves as a supply base for the isolated mining camps strung out along these rivers, which are reached by dugout canoes equipped with powerful outboard motors. Guanay is not as busy as it once was. The fall in world gold prices and the exhaustion of nearby deposits, along with damage caused by a flood which swept through the town in 2001, have together conspired to give it rather a mournful, post-boomtown feel. But it still comes to life at weekends, when gold miners come into town from outlying camps to sell gold, buy supplies and blow much of the change in the many rough-and-ready bars.

In terms of mining activity, the busiest river is currently the **Río Tipuani**, and you should be able to find a boatman happy to take you up it if you want to check out the prospecting operations. Otherwise, you'll see some mining activity from one of the regular **passenger canoes** that go up the **Río Mapiri** to the town of Mapiri (see below), the next step on the loop round to Sorata. The various rivers combine near Guanay to form the **Río Guanay**, or Kaka, which in turn flows north to join the **Río Beni**. River traffic downstream to Rurrenabaque along the Beni is rare these days, as moving people and cargo by road is more economical. If you want to make this exciting jungle river journey through the sparsely populated wilderness of the Alto Beni you'll have to rent a canoe yourself, which is likely to cost several hundred dollars – ask around at the river bank and be prepared to negotiate hard and wait around a day or two.

Buses and **micros** from Caranavi and La Paz arrive and depart from the main plaza, around which you'll also find several basic **places to stay**: the *Hotel Pahuichi* and *Alojamiento Mexico* (no phones; both ❶) are both adequate, though noisy at weekends. The *Pahuichi* also has a reasonably good **restaurant**, one of several around the plaza, and there are also a couple of *heladerías* where you can cool off with an ice cream or a cool drink. In addition, there are several snack bars down by the riverbank where you can find early-morning coffee and breakfasts of fried beef and rice. From the river bank a boat departs almost every morning upriver to **Mapiri**, a five-hour journey. In the dry season (May–Sept) jeeps make the same journey along a rough road, but the river trip is much more scenic.

Mapiri and Santa Rosa

As you speed between the steep forested banks of the Río Mapiri you'll pass occasional impromptu mining camps made from plastic sheeting stretched over rough wooden frames, where Aymara migrants pan for gold in the shallows or use water pumps to wash sand and gravel through sluices to extract the precious dust. Every so often you'll pass the semi-submerged hulk of an abandoned dredging barge, which used powerful pumps to suck up mud and sand from the river bank to wash it for gold. The river was largely worked out in the 1990s, and most major mining operations have since moved on. Though the forest on either side is largely pristine, there's little life in the river. Its waters are contaminated by the highly toxic mercury used to separate gold dust from mud and sand, so fish and water birds are rare.

The town of **MAPIRI** is a smaller version of Guanay. You could spend the night at the *Alojamiento Plaza* (no phone; ❶) on the small square, where there are also a couple of basic restaurants, but there's really no reason to stop here. From Mapiri, several *camionetas* leave daily for the scruffy, tin-roofed mining settlement of **SANTA ROSA**, a one- to two-hour trip along a rough road. In Santa Rosa you can stay at the friendly *Hotel Judith* (no phone; ❶), which has a small swimming pool and a good restaurant. Toyota Landcruisers with passenger seats – called *wagonetas* – make the trip up to Sorata (10–12hr) two or three times a week, depending on demand; let the transport office on the plaza know you want to travel as soon as you arrive to avoid missing a departure. This is a boneshaking journey on a rough track that climbs up into the Andes through beautiful scenery, but unfortunately the locals tend to travel by night.

Chulumani and the South Yungas

From Unduavi on the road from La Paz to the Yungas, a side road heads east off the main highway towards the provincial capital of **CHULUMANI**, providing a dramatic ride as it plunges down from the high Andes into the lush vegetation of the Yungas, though it's neither as spectacular nor as dangerous as the road to Coroico. Chulumani itself is far less frequently visited than Coroico, though its setting – amidst beautiful countryside at an elevation of 1640m, on a steep hillside overlooking a broad river valley – is equally scenic. Today Chulumani is a friendly and very tranquil little town where life is taken at an easy pace, and though some locals have attempted to turn it into a resort like Coroico, it's never really caught on as a retreat for wealthy Paceños, and even at weekends it doesn't get particularly busy. With its palm-shaded plaza and steep and narrow cobbled streets, lined with neat houses with red-tiled roofs, Chulumani is a typical Yungas town, and makes a perfect base for exploring the surrounding countryside. It's now the capital of the Sur Yungas province and the market centre for an extensive rural hinterland, though in the 1950s it was notorious as a hideout for fugitive Nazi war criminals, such as Klaus Barbie, the "Butcher of Lyon", who some people say once sold fruit juices on the plaza.

Buses from La Paz arrive outside the bus offices on Plaza Libertad, the main square. There's no tourist information office, but Javier Sarabia, owner of the *Hostal Country House*, can give useful advice on hikes from Chulumani; he also runs guided excursions and camping trips on foot or by jeep and can arrange bicycle and motorbike rental.

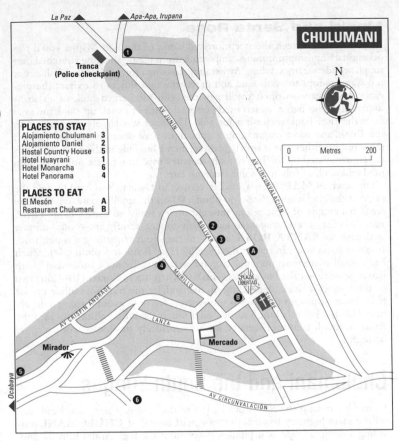

Practicalities

The selection of **places to eat** in Chulumani is disappointing, and the better places are usually open only at weekends. The most reliable restaurants are in the *Monarcha* and *Panorama* hotels, which serve decent set almuerzos and standard main courses including fresh local trout. Less expensive set almuerzos and cenas are available at *El Mesón* and *Restaurant Chulumani*, on Plaza Libertad. There are also a couple of **snack bars** on the plaza where you can get cold drinks, sandwiches, fried chicken and ice cream. Just east of the plaza on Calle Lanza the **market** offers the usual fruit juices and simple meals, and there's also a series of unexciting food stalls by the *tranca* on the road out of town to the north.

Accommodation options are also rather limited. Apart from the *Hostal Country House*, it comes down to a choice between budget *alojamientos* and rather overpriced hotels with swimming pools aimed at weekenders from La Paz. You can also stay outside town at the delightful Bosque Ecológico Apa Apa (see opposite).

Alojamiento Chulumani Uphill from the plaza on Bolívar (no phone). Basic but clean rooms with shared bath set around a peaceful courtyard. **2**

Alojamiento Daniel Uphill from the plaza on Bolívar ☎02/8116359. Simple but clean rooms

with shared bath; those upstairs have balconies and good views. **2**

Hostal Country House 1km southeast of town beyond the mirador (no phone). Quirky little guesthouse with a welcoming, homely feel and comfortable rooms (with private bath) around a lovely garden with a small swimming pool. The helpful English-speaking owner Javier Sarabia is a mine of information, and also organizes guided excursions. Breakfast is included, and snacks and drinks are available. **❸**

Hotel Huayrani Near the police *tranca* on Av Junín (no phone; for reservations in La Paz call ☎02/332294). Family-oriented hotel with nicely furnished suites for up to four people (about $10 per person) and a decent swimming pool. Breakfast included. **❹**

Hotel Monarcha Below the town on Av Circumvalación ☎02/8116121. Reasonably priced holiday camp-style hotel with clean, comfortable chalets (with fans and private bathrooms) looking out onto a huge and sparkling swimming pool surrounded by fruit trees – it gets busy at weekends. There's also a bar and a good restaurant. Breakfast included. **❹**

Hotel Panorama Murillo ☎02/8116109. Pleasant rooms set around a flower-filled garden and small swimming pool. Staff are friendly, there's a reasonable restaurant and breakfast is included. **❸**

Around Chulumani

The main attraction of Chulumani is the opportunity to explore the peaceful hamlets, splendid scenery and exuberant tropical vegetation of the surrounding countryside. Many of the steep surrounding mountain slopes have been sculpted over centuries into neat terraces covered in bright-green coca bushes, while the fertile valley floor is a patchwork of coffee and orange groves where flowers and hummingbirds abound. The best day-trip is to the Bosque Ecológico Apa Apa (see below), but almost any path leading out of town makes for a good hike: try following the path that climbs up the ridge behind the town – the views get better the higher you ascend. Alternatively, follow the path that runs from the mirador a few blocks east of the plaza down to the village of **Ocabaya** on the valley floor; a three-to-four-hour walk.

From Chulumani, a road runs northeast, past the Bosque Ecológico Apa Apa, before curving south to reach the picturesque colonial village of **Irupana**, 15km away on the other side of the valley, which is served by occasional *camionetas* from Chulumani (as well as micros from La Paz). From Irupana you can visit **Pasto Grande**, an area of extensive but largely overgrown Inca agricultural terracing a couple of hours' walk away. Further afield you can reach the coca-growing centre of **Coripata**, about 35km north of Chulumani, by heading back along the road to La Paz as far as the turn-off at Puente Villa, where you can pick up through traffic. There's basic food and accommodation available in Coripata, and you may be able to find a *camioneta* travelling along the scenic but very rough road to Coroico, 30km away.

Bosque Ecológico Apa Apa

Comprising some five square kilometres of the dense and humid montane forest that once covered most of the Yungas, the **Bosque Ecológico Apa Apa** (☎02/8116106), 9km from Chulumani on the road to Irupana, is a private nature reserve whose dense vegetation stands in stark contrast to the deforested slopes of the surrounding mountainsides. The family that owns the reserve runs **tours** ($5 per person; minimum of five people) led by informative English-speaking guides along trails running into the forest. Tours last three to four hours and you're likely to see a great variety of bird life including hummingbirds and flocks of parrots; if you're lucky you may even spot deer or monkeys, while pumas and spectacled bears are known to inhabit the higher reaches. The family also rents out clean, comfortable **rooms** (**❸**) in the delightful old hacienda that is their home and the centre of a working farm, and prepare very good meals for guests. There's also a fully equipped but expensive **campsite** (**❷**) complete with hot showers and cooking facilities. The owners will pick you up from Chulumani if you contact them in advance; otherwise, to get to the reserve you'll need to walk or catch a lift with a passing vehicle.

It's 9km along the road leading out of Chulumani to the northeast, then another 2km or so up the marked turn-off to the left to reach the hacienda.

Travel details

Bus and micro

Caranavi to: Guanay (6 daily; 3–4hr); La Paz (hourly; 6–7hr).

Charazani to: La Paz (1–2 daily; 10hr).

Chulumani to: La Paz (4–6 daily; 4hr 30min).

Copacabana to: La Paz (every 30min; 3hr 30min).

Coroico to: La Paz (hourly; 4hr 30min).

Desaguadero to: La Paz (every 30min; 3hr).

Guanay to: Caranavi (6 daily; 3hr).

La Paz to: Caranavi (every hour; 6–7hr); Charazani (1–2 daily; 10hr); Chulumani (4–6 daily; 4hr 30min); Copacabana (every 30min; 3hr 30min); Coroico (hourly; 4hr 30min); Desaguadero (every 30min; 3hr); Pelechuco (2–3 weekly; 15–18hr); Sorata (every 30min, 4hr 30 min).

Pelechuco to La Paz: (2–3 weekly; 15–18hr).

Sorata to: La Paz (every 30min; 4hr 30 min).

Camionetas and Wagonetas

Mapiri to: Santa Rosa (5–6 daily; 1–2hr).

Santa Rosa to: Mapiri (5–6 daily; 1–2hr); Sorata

(2–3 weekly; 10–12hr).

Sorata to: Santa Rosa (2–3 weekly; 10–12hr).

Boat

Guanay to: Mapiri (1 daily; 5hr).

Mapiri to: Guanay (1 daily; 5hr).

3

The southern Altiplano

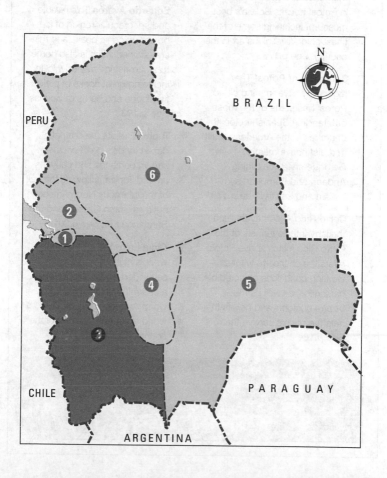

CHAPTER 3

Highlights

✳ **Oruro Carnaval** One of the most colourful and uproarious folkloric fiestas in all South America, featuring thousands of dancers in extravagant devil costumes. **See p.156**

✳ **Casa Real de la Moneda** The monumental former royal mint in Potosí houses Bolivia's best museum, including some of the finest colonial religious art in the country. **See p.176**

✳ **Churches of Potosí** The legendary silver-mining city of Potosí has some of the most outstanding Spanish colonial churches in the Americas, built in a distinctive mestizo-Baroque style combining Andean and European symbolism and artistry. **See p.179**

✳ **Cerro Rico** A journey through the labyrinthine tunnels of the Cerro Rico mines above Potosí offers the chance to witness working conditions of incredible harshness, as well as the bizarre customs and beliefs that help the miners survive them. **See p.184**

✳ **Salar de Uyuni** Perhaps Bolivia's most extraordinary landscape, featuring the world's biggest salt lake – a vast expanse of dazzling white surrounded by high mountain peaks. **See p.193**

✳ **Reserva de Fauna Andina Eduardo Avaroa** This remote and spectacular region of ice-bound volcanic peaks and mineral-stained lakes is also home to a surprising array of wildlife, including great flocks of pink flamingos and herds of vicuñas. **See p.193**

✳ **Tupiza** Explore the dramatic desert landscape of cactus-strewn badlands and canyons around Tupiza, following the trail of the infamous North American outlaws Butch Cassidy and the Sundance Kid. **See p.201**

✳ **Tarija** Enjoy the wine from the world's highest vineyards in the self-styled Andalucía of Bolivia, a charming colonial town in a warm Andean valley that feels a world apart from the rest of the country. **See p.208**

The southern Altiplano

S outh of La Paz, the **southern Altiplano** – the high plateau that lies between the eastern and western chains of the Andes – stretches 800km to the Chilean and Argentine borders, a bleak, rolling plain, swept by unforgiving winds and illuminated by a harsh sunshine that seems to leach all colour from the earth without warming the rarefied air. Set at an aver-age altitude of around 3700m, this starkly beautiful landscape is the image most frequently associated with Bolivia: a barren and treeless expanse whose arid steppes stretch to the horizon, where snow-capped mountains shimmer under deep-blue skies. With scant rainfall and infertile soils, the southern Altiplano supports only a sparse rural population: traversing its lonely expanse you'll see occasional clusters of huts in the distance whose adobe walls seem to merge into the brown earth. These are home to hardy Aymara communities, which scrape a marginal living by growing tubers and grains and herding llamas and alpacas, using survival techniques that have served them for centuries.

The Altiplano was formed millions of years ago by sediments washed down from the mountains to fill the deep valley that formed between the two Andean chains – the cordilleras Oriental and Occidental – as they were pushed up from the sea bed. Hemmed in on both sides by these high mountain ranges, the Altiplano is actually a closed basin: what little rain falls here never reaches the sea; instead, it collects in shallow lakes and salt pans where it slowly evap-orates. Since the Spanish conquest, the Altiplano's prime importance has lain in the rich **mineral deposits** found in the Cordillera Oriental, the mountain range on its eastern edge. Mines established here to exploit first silver and then tin were for centuries the basis of the Bolivian economy, and the two biggest cities in the region are both formerly rich mining centres fallen on hard times.

The unavoidable transport nexus of the Altiplano is the unattractive tin-min-ing city of **Oruro**, 230km south of La Paz, a grim monument to industrial decline – its spectacular Carnaval celebrations are now the only reminder of its former wealth and power. West of Oruro, a chain of snow-capped volcanic peaks – the Cordillera Occidental – marks the border with Chile and the edge of the Altiplano. One of these peaks, **Sajama**, is the tallest mountain in Bolivia and centre of the country's oldest national park, which is easily visited from La Paz. Some 310km further southeast of Oruro is the legendary silver-mining city of **Potosí**. Once the richest jewel in the Spanish empire, it's now a city of

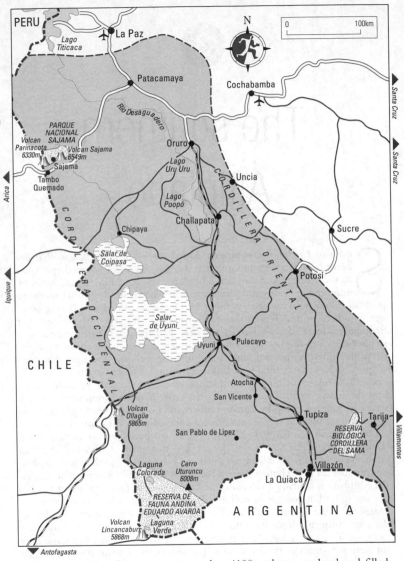

sublime colonial architecture, marooned at 4100m above sea level and filled with monuments to a glorious but tragic past.

The Altiplano grows more desolate still as it stretches south towards the Argentine border. From the forlorn railway town of **Uyuni**, 323km due south of Oruro by road and rail, you can venture into the dazzling white **Salar de Uyuni**, the world's biggest salt lake, whose otherworldly beauty has made it one of Bolivia's best-known scenic attractions. Beyond the Salar in the far southwestern corner of the country is the **Reserva de Fauna Andina Eduardo Avaroa**, a nature reserve that encompasses a landscape of such unremitting bleakness that at times it's difficult to believe it could support any life at all. Despite appearances, however, this remote region of high-altitude deserts, surreal wind-blasted rock formations, icebound volcanic peaks and half-frozen mineral-stained lakes is home to a surprising array of wildlife, including great flocks of pink flamingos and herds of vicuñas.

Southwest of Uyuni the Altiplano changes character. The pleasant little mining town of **Tupiza** is surrounded by arid red mountains and cactus-strewn badlands eroded into deep gullies and rock pinnacles, a region which many travellers compare to the deserts of the southwest US. Different again is the provincial capital of **Tarija**, in the far south of the country, a remote and welcoming city set in a deep and fertile valley that enjoys a much warmer climate than the Altiplano, and which is known as the Andalucía of Bolivia for its many similarities to southern Spain.

The region is bitterly **cold** at night, with temperatures often falling well below zero, particularly between May and July. Even during the day temperatures can drop sharply when the sun slips behind a cloud, and the wind chill makes things colder still – although you'll also need to protect yourself from the fierce, high-altitude sunshine. In addition to the harshness of the natural environment, **travel** around the region is painfully slow, given that none of the roads south of Oruro are paved, although the trains which run between Oruro and Villazón on the Argentine border offer a faster and more comfortable alternative.

Parque Nacional Sajama

Southwest of La Paz, the road to Chile passes through some of the Altiplano's starkest scenery, a desert plain almost totally devoid of vegetation from the middle of which rises the perfect snow-capped cone of **Volcán Sajama**. At 6542m, Sajama is the highest mountain in Bolivia, and the first in a chain of icebound volcanic peaks known as the Cordillera Occidental that straddle the Chilean border and mark the edge of the Altiplano – although Sajama stands alone, separated by some distance from the rest of the range. Sajama is also the centre of Bolivia's oldest national park, the **PARQUE NACIONAL SAJAMA**, which was established in 1939 to protect the local population of **vicuñas**, a wild Andean relative of the llama which has been hunted to the verge of extinction for its highly prized wool. The park covers roughly one thousand square kilometres, encompassing the entire mountain as well as a large area of the surrounding desert, where pumas, rare Andean deer and flightless, ostrich-like rheas are also found – though rarely seen. The slopes of Sajama also support the highest forest in the world, a patch of hardy **queñua** trees that survive up to an amazing 5200m. The records don't stop there: in 2001 the highest football match in the world was played in the crater at the top of Sajama – the game, between local villagers and mountain guides from La Paz, ended in a draw.

Most of the visitors who come to Sajama are **mountain climbers**, drawn by the chance to ascend a peak of over 6000m which requires little technical expertise. But the beauty of the region is such that you don't need to be a climber to enjoy a visit: the lower slopes of the mountain make for excellent **hiking**, and there are bubbling geysers and hot springs to be explored in the plain of volcanic ash that surrounds the peak. West of the park on the Chilean border, the two volcanic peaks of **Parinacota** (6132m) and **Pomerata** (6222m) provide a stunning backdrop. Known as the *payachatas*, or twins, and considered the female consorts of Sajama, these mountains can also be climbed.

At over 4200m, the desert of grey volcanic ash that surrounds the volcano is simply too dry, cold and infertile to allow agriculture, and the hardy Aymara communities that live here have traditionally depended for survival on herding llamas and alpacas, which graze on the tough grasses that grow in patches on the plain and the volcano's lower slopes. These days, the region is dotted with semi-abandoned hamlets and crumbling adobe churches, as the young turn their back on the harsh lifestyle of their parents and head to the city in search of education, modernity and an easier life, though with the emergence of a primitive tourist industry based in Sajama village at the foot of the volcano, the local economy is beginning to recover.

Visiting the park

The administrative centre of the park is **SAJAMA VILLAGE**, a cluster of simple adobe houses and a crumbling whitewashed colonial church huddled at the foot of the volcano in a setting at once desperately bleak and stunningly beautiful. Home to just a few hundred people, the village is the place to find food, accommodation, guides and information, and you can also hire a jeep and driver to take you around if you don't want to hike.

The routes to attractions close to the village are marked with signposts and are reasonably easy to follow. One of the best hikes (3–4hr each way) is up to the **Sajama base camp** on the volcano's lower slopes, a well-marked trek that offers fantastic views of the chain of volcanoes along the Chilean border. If you want to camp here – or anywhere else in the park – you need to be prepared for very low temperatures. The **highest forest in the world** is about thirty minutes' walk up from Sajama village but, statistics aside, the stunted, slow-growing queñua trees are not overwhelmingly impressive. The **geyser field** 8km or so west of the village in the foothills of the *payachatas* is another good excursion. An easy walk (1hr 30min–2hr) along a well-defined trail, the geyser field is made up of 87 different pools of boiling water which vary in shape, size, colour and temperature. Some bubble furiously like cauldrons, and the mixture of mineral salts and algae that thrive in the warm waters creates bizarre colours, including blood reds, shiny greens and sulphurous yellows. On no account should you bathe in any of the geysers, as temperatures can change rapidly. If you do fancy a soak, there are some **aguas termales** (hot springs) about 4km north of the village, again along an easy-to-follow trail. The natural hot water is fed into an open-air pool, making it a fantastic place to wallow and relax while enjoying the matchless scenery, and an excellent way to ease aching limbs. The park's **vicuña** population has made a dramatic recovery since the park was established, though you'll have to travel some distance to actually see them – large herds can be found grazing 25km or so north of the village at the area known as Patoca.

Mountain climbing is only allowed between April and October, when the ice is sufficiently frozen. To climb Sajama or any of the surrounding peaks you

Crossing the Chilean border

The **Chilean border** is 9km west of the turn-off to Sajama at **Tambo Quemado**. Crossing into Chile is straightforward: there's a *migración* where you get your exit stamp and a couple of restaurants catering mainly to truck drivers. If you're coming from La Paz the bus will take you all the way through to Arica on Chile's Pacific coast, though you may want to stop off at the **Parque Nacional Lauca**, which encompasses similar scenery to the Parque Nacional Sajama. If you're heading to Chile from Sajama, you can get to the border on the 7am micro to Patacamaya, which comes to Tambo Quemado to pick up passengers, then walk across the frontier and pick up transport on the Chilean side.

must first register with the park administration in Sajama village (see below). They can help arrange guides, mules and porters, but you'll need to bring your own equipment and supplies from outside. **Volcán Parinacota**, to the west of the park on the Chilean border, is also considered a technically simple climb and, as you can drive to the base camp, is particularly popular with climbers eager to conquer a 6000-metre peak.

Practicalities

There are two ways to reach Sajama by **public transport** from La Paz. The first is to take any Oruro-bound bus as far as the crossroads town of **Patacamaya** (every 30 min; 1hr 30min), from where a micro goes direct to Sajama village (3hr 30min) every day at about 1pm, returning to Patacamaya at 7am the next day. The other way of reaching the park is to get on a bus from La Paz (2 daily; 3hr 30min–4hr) headed for Arica in Chile and alight at the turn-off to Sajama on the main road. Jeeps from the village usually wait at the turn-off to collect passengers arriving from La Paz – they charge about $6 per vehicle for the twelve-kilometre drive back to the village. Alternatively, you could walk to the village in two-and-a-half to three hours.

On arrival in Sajama village you must register at the **park office** (daily 8am–noon & 2.30–7pm; ☎0811/5260) and pay the $1.50 entrance fee. The usually helpful park rangers can answer most questions about the reserve and will help you arrange **accommodation**. Several people in the village have basic *alojamientos* (❶): these are uniformly simple, with cold, bare rooms with blankets on straw mattresses and outdoor toilets. In keeping with the egalitarian traditions of the Altiplano, guests are shared out, so you'll simply be allocated to one of the *alojamientos* by the park office. There are also several **places to eat** in the village, where you can get simple and inexpensive set almuerzos, cenas and breakfasts for about $1, though it's best to order a few hours in advance. Most of these places double as shops where you can choose from a limited range of beer, soft drinks, and basic foodstuffs.

The rangers at the park office can also arrange **porters**, **mules** and **guides** for people wanting to climb Sajama or one of the other volcanoes; once again, these will be allocated to you on a rota basis and charge a set price: mules, mule-handlers (*arrieros*), guides and porters each cost about $10 per day. You can also rent a **jeep** with driver if you want transport to any of the park's attractions or back to the main road to catch a bus. The drivers double as guides and charge according to a more-or-less fixed tariff for the whole vehicle regardless of the number of passengers: expect to pay about $6 to the *aguas termales* and $10 to the geysers.

Oruro

Huddled on the bleak Altiplano some 230km south of La Paz, the grim mining city of **ORURO** was the economic powerhouse of Bolivia for much of the twentieth century, centre of the country's richest **tin-mining** region and the hub of its now much-reduced railway network. Oruro owed its fortunes to the enormous mineral wealth found in the rugged, ochre-coloured mountains that rise to the east of the city. Tin mines established here in the late nineteenth century turned Oruro into a thriving modern industrial city and generated such huge fortunes for the mining magnates who owned them that they effectively ran the country. The same mines formed the crucible from which

Dancing with the Devil: the Oruro Carnaval

A moveable feast celebrated a week before Lent each year – usually late February or early March – the **Oruro Carnaval** attracts tens of thousands of visitors who come to enjoy what is by far the most raucous and spectacular fiesta in Bolivia. During the week-long party thousands of costumed dancers parade through the streets in a vibrant and bizarre celebration of the sacred and profane that combines Christian beliefs with Andean folklore, with a good deal of heavy drinking and chaotic water-fighting thrown in for good measure. Preparations for the fiesta begin several months before Carnaval. On the first Sunday of November a special mass is held in the Santuario del Socavón church, where dancers swear to dance at the Carnaval for three consecutive years – dancing is considered a serious religious duty. Thereafter, rehearsals are held every Sunday leading up to Carnaval itself, so even if you miss the main event, if you're passing through Oruro on a Sunday in the preceding months you can see what all the fuss is about.

The Carnaval's main event is the **Entrada** on the Saturday before Ash Wednesday, a massive procession through the streets of the city involving more than fifty different troops of costumed dancers, each accompanied by four or five brass bands. The parade is led by a motorcade of cars and trucks festooned with silver, cheap jewellery, old coins, food and drink. Known as **cargamentos**, these floats are offerings for the Virgen del Socavón (see p.163), in whose honour the Carnaval is held. Behind them comes the dance that is the Carnaval's central feature: the **Diablada**, or Dance of the Devils. This is led by two lavishly costumed dancers representing Lucifer and St Michael, followed by hundreds of devil dancers who leap and prance through the streets in brightly embroidered, multicoloured costumes, while massive brass bands pump out a thunderous, hypnotic rhythm. The dancers wear intricate masks festooned with bulging light-bulb eyes, long twisted horns, tangled hair and leering mouths, and decorated with bright mirrors and writhing with serpents and lizards. Amongst them dance smaller groups of she-devils known as *China Supay*, carnal temptresses in lascivious masks with long eyelashes and red mouths, dressed in tight costumes with short skirts and revolvers tucked into their belts. The origins and meaning of the Diablada are multiple. On one hand, the dance in its modern format is a clear morality play in which the Archangel Michael triumphs over the Devil of Christian belief. But the dance is also a celebration of the devil as an incarnation of **Huari**, the pre-Columbian god of the underworld (closely related to El Tío – see p.186) who is the owner of the mineral wealth of the mines and the jealous patron of the miners who dance in his honour.

emerged the militant miners' trade union that was one of the dominant political forces in the country after the mines were nationalized in 1952. Since the fall of world tin prices in 1985, however, Oruro's fortunes have plummeted, and though it's still the biggest city in the Altiplano after La Paz and El Alto, with a population of about 170,000, more than fifteen years of economic decline have turned it into a shadow of its former self.

Situated 3709m above sea level, swept by the bitter Altiplano winds and often coated in dust from its few still-functioning mines, Oruro is a cold and rather sombre place, with the melancholic air of a city forever looking back on a golden age that is unlikely to return. This dour demeanour is deceptive, however. Every year in late February or early March Oruro explodes into life, celebrating its **Carnaval** (see box above) in what is without doubt one of the most spectacular cultural events in all South America. If you're anywhere near Oruro at Carnaval time, this is a fiesta that should not be missed. At any other time of year, though, there's not much reason to stop here, though given its importance as a transport hub you're almost certain to pass through the city at some stage during

Behind the Diablada follow a bewildering variety of other costumed dance troupes, each with its own folk history and mythology, and each trying to be noisier and more spectacular than the last. Amongst them are the **Incas**, who re-enact the Spanish conquest in a burlesque satire; the **Tobas**, whose painted faces and feathered head-dresses represent the wild tribes of the Amazon lowlands; the **Doctorcitos**, whose tailcoats and top hats with glasses and long noses are a clear satire of gringo mine owners and capitalists; and the **Morenadas**, who represent African slaves brought here during the colonial era, their tongues lolling and eyes bulging with exhaustion, shaking rattles which replicate the clanking of manacles, and dressed in great finery to represent the wealth of their masters. The procession continues well into Sunday morning, with each troupe taking its turn to dance in the plaza in front of the Santuario del Socavón in honour of the Virgin. Dancing and drinking continues for much of the following week. On Ash Wednesday, dancers and townsfolk visit a series of rocks on the outskirts of Oruro to make ch'alla offerings of alcohol, coca and coloured streamers to what are claimed to be the petrified remains of the giant frog, serpent and other fearsome beasts defeated by the Virgin to save the town. Finally, on Thursday, the different troupes conduct their **despedida fiestas** in private houses, saying their farewells until the following year.

Carnaval practicalities

Even though the number of Bolivian and foreign visitors coming to Oruro increases every year, you can still turn up a day or two before the Saturday Entrada and find somewhere to sleep and a seat on the route of the procession. Though all the hotels in the city fill up well in advance and charge up to five times their normal rates, you should be able to find a bed in a private home – ask at the tourist information kiosk. The route of the main procession is lined with raised banks of benches which are rented out by the day, either by the shop or house in front of which they stand or by the Caseta de Información on the Plaza Manuel Castro de Padilla. Prices vary between about $3 and $10; the most expensive seats are on the Plaza de Armas and outside the Santuario del Socavón, where the dancers perform their most complicated routines. Even if you turn up the day before you should be able to find a seat – if it's in front of a shop that sells beer and will let you use their toilet and a tap for filling water bombs, so much the better. Other than the dancers no one is immune from water-bomb attack, and gringos are amongst the most popular targets, so be prepared to get utterly soaked – and to strike back.

your travels in Bolivia. If you do decide to break a journey here, there's enough in the city and the surrounding countryside to keep you busy for a day or two.

Some history

Named the Villa Imperial de Don Felipe de Austria in honour of the reigning Spanish king, Felipe III, the city of Oruro was **founded** on November 1, 1606, a decade after the discovery of rich silver deposits in the nearby Pie de Gallo mountain. Though its mines never rivalled those of Potosí in terms of production, Oruro grew quickly, and by the 1670s was the second biggest city in Alto Peru, with a population of about 80,000. Unlike Potosí, Oruro was denied the royal provision of forced labour through the *mita* system, and the mine owners had to rely on free labourers. The relatively high wages they paid raised production costs but also attracted great numbers of free indigenous workers and encouraged more permanent settlement than in Potosí. Oruro quickly became the largest free mine labour centre in Alto Peru, a disorderly and sometimes violent society with a thriving mestizo population.

Oruro was the biggest Spanish city to be captured during the **Great Rebellion** of 1780–81, when the city's mestizos and criollos joined the indigenous uprising led by Tupac Amaru, massacring the Spanish-born population. This unusual multi-class alliance did not last long, though: the rebel army raised from the *ayllus* of the surrounding Altiplano made little distinction between Spanish and American-born whites, and soon turned on the criollo instigators of the uprising, looting and burning their houses and killing their leader, Sebastián Pagador, before meeting the same fate themselves at the hands of the royalist army when it eventually retook the city.

Oruro changed hands several times during the long years of the **Independence War**. With many mines and smelters destroyed and the economy severely disrupted, the population fell below 5000 in the post-war period. This gradually recovered as silver production grew again, aided by foreign capital, improved industrial technology and the completion of a railway linking Oruro with the Pacific coast in 1892. The rail link meant Oruro was perfectly placed to exploit the growing world demand for **tin**, which was found in great abundance in the surrounding mountains. Tin production quickly became Bolivia's primary industry, and Oruro prospered.

The three Bolivian mining entrepreneurs who controlled most of the mines of Oruro – Aramayo, Hochschild and Patiño – soon came to dominate the national political scene, but in their treatment of the miners they sowed the seeds of their own downfall. The radical FSTMB mineworker's union that emerged from the mining camps around Oruro played a key role in the 1952 revolution that led to the nationalization of themines. But nationalization couldn't protect Bolivia from global economic forces. When the price of tin crashed in 1985, the mining industry collapsed; with it went the power of the miners' union and the economic fortunes of Oruro. The corrupt and inefficient state mining corporation was broken up, most of the mines were closed and thousands lost their jobs. Though new operations like the Inti Raymi gold mine have since opened – along with some of the tin mines, which have reopened as cooperatives – Oruro has never recovered from the collapse of tin mining and remains a shadow of its former self.

Arrival and information

Almost all long-distance **buses** pull in at the Terminal Terrestre, ten blocks northeast of the city centre on Avenida Raika Bacovick. A **taxi** into town from here should cost $0.50 per person, the flat rate for journeys within the city; alternatively, take any micro heading south along Avenida 6 de Agosto. There's a reasonably helpful **bus information office** (daily 8am–10pm; ☎02/5279535) on the first floor of the terminal. The only long-distance buses that don't arrive at the terminal are those passing through from Tarija on their way to La Paz, which will drop you off on Avenida Ejército on the eastern outskirts of the city. The **train station** is a short walk east of the city centre on Avenida Galvarro.

Surprisingly, there are two tourist information offices in Oruro. The most helpful is the **Caseta de Información** (Mon–Fri 8am–noon & 2–6pm; ☎052/57881) kiosk on Plaza Manuel Castro de Padilla, whose young and enthusiastic staff do their best to answer questions (in Spanish only) and can help you find somewhere to stay if you can't find a hotel room during Carnaval; they also usually have a free map and other leaflets to dish out. The **Unidad de Turismo Prefectural** (Mon–Fri 8am–noon & 2–6pm; ☎052/50114), on the west side of Plaza 10 de Febrero, is less informative, and really only worth visiting if the kiosk is closed.

ORURO

0   Metres   200

SANTA CRUZ
AYACUCHO
SOTOMAYOR
JUNIN
LIRA
A
WASHINGTON
PDTE MONTES
LA PLATA
B   Cathedral
S GALVARRO
Banco
Unión   C
A. MIER
OBLITAS
VILLARROEL
AV 6 DE AGOSTO   Bus Terminal
Migración
i
PLAZA
10 DE FEBRERO
PLAZA
MANUEL CASTRO
DE PADILLA
1
2
3
Police
ENTEL
i
AROMA
D
Banco
de Crédito
E   BOLIVAR
F
4
RODRIGUEZ
SUCRE
LEON
5
AV LA PAZ
1 DE NOVEMBRE
N
HERRERA
Faro de
Conchupata
MONTECINOS
CARO
HT Viajeros
del Tiempo
AV DEL FOLKLORE
COCHABAMBA
Casa de Cultura
Simón I. Patiño
6
Santuario
del Socavón
PLAZA DEL
FOLKLORE
TARAPACA
PETOT
CAMACHO
WASHINGTON
PDTE MONTES
LA PLATA
S GALVARRO
B DE OCTUBRE
POTOSI
PAGADUR
V GALVARRO
JUNIN
H BAKOVIC
BRASIL
AYACUCHO
G
7   H
Mercado
Campero
A. MIER
BOLIVAR
8
9   SUCRE
See Inset
Train Station
MURGUIA
I   10
ALDANA
BALLIVIÁN
SAN FELIPE
ARCE

PLACES TO STAY
Alojamiento 15 de Octubre   5
Alojamiento San Salvador   10
Hotel Bernal   1
Hotel Gran Sucre   8
Hotel Hidalgo   7
Hotel Lipton   4
Hotel Monarcha   6
Hotel Repostero   9
International Park Hotel   2
Residencial Bonaventure   3

PLACES TO EAT
Bar Huari   G
Club Social Croata   A
Confitería Center   C
Confitería SUM   E
El Fogón   D
El Hornito   F
Govinda   H
Nayjama   I
Unicornio   B

Museo Antropológico Eduardo López Rivas & Museo de Mineralógia ▼

Accommodation

There's a fairly good range of places **to stay** in Oruro. Those around the bus terminal are obviously more convenient if you're just passing through; otherwise it's better to stay in the city centre. Everything fills up during Carnaval, when prices go up by as much as five times, and most places will only rent rooms to those who take them for the Friday, Saturday and Sunday night of the Carnaval weekend. If you can, it's best to book well in advance, but even if you arrive the day before the festivities begin you should be able to find a place to sleep in a private home – ask at the Caseta de Información.

Alojamiento 15 de Octubre Av 6 de Agosto and Av Herrera ☎02/5276012. Excellent budget rooms (with shared bathrooms) midway between the bus terminal and the city centre, with cramped but cosy rooms and a homely feel. Cooking and laundry facilities available. ❶

Alojamiento San Salvador Av Galvarro 6325 ☎02/5276771. The best of several inexpensive places to stay near the train station, with box-like and gloomy but clean rooms with or without bath. ❷

Hotel Bernal Av Brasil 701, opposite the bus terminal ☎02/5279468. A bit run-down but very good value, with decent beds, abundant hot water, internet access and helpful, English-speaking management. ❷

Hotel Gran Sucre Sucre 510 ☎02/5276800 or 5276320, ℱ02/5254110. Characterful hotel that preserves some of the grandeur of Oruro's heyday, with elegant wood-panelled corridors and a glass-roofed ballroom where breakfast is now served. The hotel offers a range of accommodation to suit most budgets, with a choice between simple but adequate rooms with shared bath or spacious, well-appointed modern rooms with private bath. ❸–❺

Hotel Hidalgo Av 6 de Octubre 1616 ☎02/5257516. Modern but gloomy place with big comfortable beds in carpeted but rather cramped rooms with or without bath and cable TV. Breakfast

included. ❸–❹

Hotel Lipton Av 6 de Agosto and Rodriguez ☎02/5276583. Uninspiring but convenient, with small but adequate rooms (with or without bath) and plentiful hot water. ❷–❸

Hotel Monarca Av 6 de Agosto and Av Ejército Nacional ☎02/5254300 or 5254222, ℱ02/5250006. Modern high-rise hotel with bright, well-furnished rooms (but rather chintzy décor); some rooms have good views over the city. Breakfast in the top-floor restaurant included. ❹

Hotel Repostero Sucre 370 ☎02/5258001 or 5258002. A once elegant nineteenth-century building now crumbling and rather run-down, though rooms, overlooking a sunny central courtyard, are bright and warm, with comfortable beds and cable TV. Breakfast included. ❸

International Park Hotel Rajka Bakovick ☎02/5276277 or 5277247, ℱ02/5275187. Directly above the bus terminal in a modern but rather anodyne high-rise, and so convenient if you're just overnighting in Oruro. The comfortable rooms have heating and cable TV, and there's also a restaurant, bar and sauna. Breakfast included. ❻

Residencial Bonaventure Av Brasil, opposite the bus terminal ☎02/5279412. The best of several basic places near the terminal, with small but warm and clean rooms. ❷

The City

There's relatively little in Oruro to remind you that this was once the industrial centre of Bolivia, a booming city with a sophisticated middle class and a sizeable international community. A few buildings that date from Oruro's heyday in the late nineteenth and early twentieth century are still in evidence around the centre, built from large stone blocks with arched doorways and wrought-iron balconies overhanging the street. Otherwise, though, the city is dominated by the unlovely, functional architecture you'd expect to find in a mining town at the wrong end of half a century of decline. Architecture aside, the **Museo Antropológico Eduardo López Rivas**, in the southern outskirts of the city, is one of Bolivia's better provincial museums, with a good archeological collection and a display of Carnaval masks and costumes. It's also definitely worth checking out the **Santuario del Socavón**, the focus of the Carnaval celebrations, which sits on top of an abandoned mineshaft now occupied by the unusual **Museo Etnográfico Minero**.

Around the Plaza 10 de Febrero

At the centre of the city is the **Plaza 10 de Febrero**, named for the date the people of Oruro joined the Great Rebellion of 1781. It's a pleasant enough square, shaded by cypress trees, with an over-elaborate fountain decorated with bronze animals in the centre and a statue of Aniceto Arce, the conservative president who oversaw the construction of the vital first railway link between Oruro and the coast in 1892. On and around the square are a few buildings which hint at the prosperity the city enjoyed in that era, most notably the **Palais Concert Theatre** on the southeast corner, with its lavish stucco facade, and the grandiose **post office** a block north on Avenida Montes.

Two blocks west and three blocks north of the plaza on Soria Galvarro, the **Casa de Cultura Simón I. Patiño** (Mon–Fri 9am–noon & 2–6pm; $2) is the city's best reminder of the great wealth that the mines of Oruro once produced, as well as of the unequal way in which it was distributed. Designed by French architects in the first years of the twentieth century, this elegant Neoclassical palace was built as a town house for the great tin baron Simón Patiño, though by the time it was completed he no longer lived in Bolivia. Seized by the state after the 1952 revolution, the house is now administered by the city's university, but many of the rooms have been maintained in their original state. Set around a beautifully tiled, glass-roofed central patio are the astonishingly opulent living quarters of Patiño and his family, with chandeliers of Venetian crystal, Louis XV furniture from France, fine Persian carpets and lashings of marble and gold leaf. Certain features suggest that Patiño's taste never quite lived up to his wealth: witness the countless portraits of him and his wife, or the cigar-toting angels painted on the roof of the smoking room. Other interesting items include the massive mechanical organ made in Holland, and the steel safe which was blown open with dynamite by revolutionaries in 1952.

Three blocks further up Sonia Galvarro, a left turn takes you up a steep hill to the **Faro de Conchupata**, a lighthouse monument built to commemorate the first raising of the current Bolivian national flag, which took place on this site in 1851. The lighthouse serves no practical purpose but – municipal budget permitting – it still lights up every evening and sweeps the night sky. There are good views foot of the lighthouse over the urban sprawl of Oruro, across the Altiplano to Lago Uru Uru to the south and the Vinto ore-processing plant to the southeast. In the colonial era the rocky promontory on which the lighthouse stands marked the boundary between the Spanish city to the south and the clearly segregated indigenous miners' settlements to the north.

This part of town is where most of the Carnaval costumes and masks are made, in dozens of workshops concentrated along the length of **Calle La Paz**, which runs northwards parallel to Soria Galvarro. Most of the workshops have shopfronts where the masks and costumes are on display, and if you're not in Oruro for Carnaval it's worth strolling along this street to have a look at their intricate and beautiful craftsmanship. The Carnaval celebrations are now so big that they support an entire industry which works year round to produce the ever more elaborate outfits worn by the dancers. Most of the artisans rightly take pride in their work and are usually happy to show you their wares even if you're not looking to buy anything. As well as being very expensive, most of the masks are too bulky and delicate to make good souvenirs, though some shops sell pocket-sized copies, which are affordable and easy to get home in one piece.

The King of Tin: Simón Patiño

Few individuals played a greater role in shaping modern Bolivia than the tin baron **Simón Patiño**, who rose from humble mestizo origins to become one of the richest men in the world, popularly known as the Rockefeller of the Andes and the King of Tin. Born in 1860 to a poor family in a small town in the Cochabamba valley, Patiño moved to Oruro in 1894 to begin work as a clerk in a mining supply store. A year later he bought his first share in the La Salvadora mine, southeast of Oruro, and in 1897 bought out his partner to control what turned out to be one of the biggest deposits of high-grade tin in the world. Legend has it that at first he and his wife Albina dug out the precious ore with their own hands and carried it downhill in wheelbarrows and then across country by llama train. But in 1900 Patiño struck one of the richest veins of ore ever found in Bolivia, the mother lode that was to make his fortune. Many put his success down to a pact with the devil, and he certainly always participated in the ritual offerings made by miners to El Tío, the horned god of the underworld.

By 1905, La Salvadora was the most productive mine in the country, operated by foreign technicians using the most modern equipment. Patiño used the wealth it generated to buy up all the surrounding mines and to link them all by rail to the main railway line to the coast. By the early 1920s he controlled about half Bolivia's tin output, was the country's most important private banker, and enjoyed an income far greater than the government, which he effectively controlled. This wealth came at the expense of the many thousands of miners he employed, however, who suffered low pay and appalling conditions, as well as severe oppression at the hands of the military garrisons in the mining camps, which received extra pay from Patiño.

Not content with his Bolivian holdings alone, Patiño also expanded his commercial empire internationally, creating a powerful multinational corporation by buying up mining interests in Asia and Africa and foundries in Germany, the USA and Britain. This corporation controlled the entire production process for about a quarter of the world's tin and played an important role in setting international prices. Rumoured to have Nazi sympathies, he was said to have played a large part in financing General Franco's victory in the Spanish Civil War. Described by one contemporary as "seam-faced, short and swarthy with a long, twisting, tight mouth that opens seldom and says little when it does open", by the early 1920s his fortune was estimated at $100 million, making him one of the five richest men in the world. But for all his riches, Patiño never really overcame the prejudices of Bolivia's white elite, and from 1924 lived permanently abroad after being snubbed by the Cochabamba aristocracy. In 1925 he moved his corporate base to the USA to avoid increased Bolivian taxes, but he spent most of his time in London, Paris and the French Riviera, where he became known as a bon viveur. He died in Buenos Aires in 1947, and thus never lived to see the nationalization of his Bolivian mine holdings, an event which no doubt had him turning in his grave.

The Santuario del Socavón

Five blocks east of the Plaza 10 de Febrero at the foot of the Pie de Gallo mountain stands the **Santuario del Socavón** (Sanctuary of the Mineshaft), home to the image of the Virgin del Socavón, the patron saint of miners, in whose honour the Carnaval celebrations are staged. The sanctuary was first built around 1781 to shelter the image, and was expanded and rebuilt in the 1990s. It's now a rather haphazard construction, with a modern brick and reinforced concrete shell, a stone belltower that survived from the nineteenth-century building, and an elegant sixteenth-century portico – the latter was rescued from the rubble of the Iglesia de la Compañía de Jesús more than ten years after it was demolished to make way for the modern cathedral on the

Plaza 10 de Febrero. Inside, the high, arched ceiling is painted with bright frescoes of the Virgin del Socavón, flaming sword in hand, defending Oruro from the various supernatural menaces that have threatened it in the mythical past, including a giant serpent, an enormous frog and a dragon.

Painstakingly restored in the 1990s, the image of the **Virgin del Socavón** stands behind the altar, painted on an adobe wall. A simple picture of the Virgin Mary in a blue robe being crowned by two cherubs, the image is said to have appeared miraculously in the late eighteenth century inside the abandoned mineshaft which the church is built on top of. This mineshaft was used as a hideout by **Chiru-Chiru**, a bandit with a reputation for stealing from the rich and giving to the poor. As he lay mortally wounded in the mine after a shoot-out with the authorities, Chiru-Chiru repented of his crimes before a vision of the Virgin; after his death, her image was discovered painted on the wall beside his body. Chiru-Chiru's deathbed scene is depicted in one of the stained-glass windows of the church; other windows feature images of miners and their families in the mining camps.

In front of the church is the **Plaza del Folklor**, a broad paved square where the climax of the Carnaval procession takes place. At the south end of the square stands a modern **statue** commemorating the revolutionary role played by the mineworkers in Bolivia's recent political history. It depicts four miners working in a mineshaft while a fifth strikes a classic revolutionary pose outside, rifle held triumphantly above his head and broken manacles dangling from his wrist; at the entrance to the shaft a bowler-hatted Aymara woman sits breaking rocks, a reminder of the important role played by the miners' wives in both the day-to-day battle to survive in the mining communities and in their wider political struggles.

The abandoned mineshaft beneath the church is now home to the **Museo Etnográfico Minero** (Mon–Sat 7.30am–noon & 3–6pm, Sun 7.30am–noon & 4–6pm; $0.50), which looks at the history of mining from the miners' perspective and is well worth a visit, not least because of its unusual underground location. After buying a ticket from the nuns in the *secretaria* next to the church, you enter the museum by going down the steps into the mine at the back of the church. On your way down, you'll see a lifesized statue of the outlaw hero Chiru-Chiru, who bled to death here in his underground hideout. At the bottom of the shaft the mine gallery stretching left and right is lined with a collection of **mining equipment** ranging from leather spoilbags from the colonial era to more modern helmets, electric headlamps and powerdrills, accompanied by photos of miners at work. Particularly interesting are the various pouches and slings used by the miners to conceal lumps of ore beneath their clothes so they could be smuggled out of the mine and sold behind the mineowner's back. At one end of the shaft stand two statues of **El Tío**, the devil-like figure worshipped by Bolivian miners as the king of the underworld and owner of all minerals. With fearsome horned masks and cigars clenched between their teeth, the two Tíos are draped in paper streamers and surrounded by offerings of coca, alcohol and tobacco brought by the miners to ensure their success and safety underground (for more on El Tío see p.186).

The Museo Antropológico Eduardo López Rivas

On Avenida España in the southern outskirts of the city, best reached by taxi or micro #7, #101 or #102 heading south from Plaza 10 de Febrero, the worthwhile **Museo Antropológico Eduardo López Rivas** (Mon–Fri 8am–noon & 2–6pm, Sat & Sun 10am–noon & 3–6pm; $0.50) is home to an extensive collection of archeological and ethnographic artefacts from the

Oruro region, ranging from ancient stone axes and arrowheads to modern Carnaval masks and costumes. Sadly, though, most of the items on display are poorly explained, with little background information on the cultures that produced them.

Many of the archeological finds are from the **Aymara** or **Colla** kingdoms that dominated the Altiplano between the fall of Tiwanaku and the Inca conquest of the region in the fifteenth century. These include various objects taken from the many stone tombs, or *chullpas*, found throughout the Altiplano, among them some beautifully carved decorative stone puma and llama heads; bronze tools and weapons; fragments of finely woven textiles; and several shrivelled mummies and elongated skulls deliberately deformed through trepanning.

One section of the museum is dedicated to the **Chipayas**, or Urus, the ethnic group which was probably the first to inhabit the Altiplano, arriving from the Pacific coast in around 2500 BC – the Chipayas are now confined to a small territory in the desolate region around the Salar de Coipasa, west of Oruro. The display of everyday artefacts from contemporary Chipaya life gives some idea of how they manage to survive in this unforgiving environment, including examples of the distinctive woven costumes which most Chipayas still wear; a full-sized example of one of their circular huts, with doors made from cactus and roofs thatched with aquatic reeds; and examples of the nets and throwing bolas (a type of weighted lassoo) they use to catch the fish and aquatic birds that form a major part of their diet.

A beautiful collection of **Carnaval masks** complements the archeological displays well, showing how the distinctive culture of the Andean peoples has survived almost five centuries of cultural oppression. Brightly painted and intricately made, with gleaming metal teeth and twisted horns decorated with mirrors and writhing with serpents and lizards, the splendidly grotesque Diablada masks are true works of art, and it's a pleasure to be able to examine them at such close range.

Museo de Mineralógia

A few kilometres north of the city – take any micro marked "Ciudad Universitaria" from outside the train station or hop in a taxi (about $1) – the **Museo de Mineralógia** (Mon–Fri 9.30am–noon & 2–5pm; $1) has one of the biggest collections of minerals in South America, comprising about four thousand different pieces. The mineral collection is all there is, though, and unless you have a specialist knowledge of geology or mineralogy there's only so much you can get out of gazing at a load of rocks, though the bewildering variety of shapes and colours is impressive.

Eating, drinking and nightlife

Oruro has a fairly varied selection of **places to eat**, including several restaurants serving up the hearty local cuisine based on meat and potatoes, including delicious roast-lamb dishes like *mecheado* or *brazuelo*. Most places don't open until mid-morning, so for an early **breakfast** your best bet is to head for the Mercado Campero, where you'll find hot drinks, snacks, juices and filling soups throughout the day. There are plenty of cheap roast-chicken **restaurants and snack bars** on Calle 6 de Octubre, where late on Friday and Saturday night stalls serve the local speciality *rostro asado*, roasted sheep's head, from which the face is peeled off and served along with the eyeballs. Some say the reason it's served late at night is because you have to be drunk to eat it, and there's usually no shortage of takers among the drinkers who frequent the motley collection of rough-and-ready bars, clubs and karaokes in the city centre that are the mainstay of Oruro's low-key **nightlife**; the liveliest of these is *Brujas*, on Calle Junín and Avenida 6 de Agosto, where dancing and drinking continues into the night on the weekends.

Restaurants, bars and cafés

Bar Huari Junín and Galvarro. Once the most fashionable bar in Oruro, but now sadly run-down, though it preserves a certain dilapidated charm and is still a lively place for a beer and a bite to eat at weekends. Legend has it that Bolivia's national cocktail, the *chufflay* (a mixture of *singani* and Seven-Up), was invented here by British mining engineers.

Club Social Croata Junín and Montes. The grandiose wood-panelled dining room on the first floor now houses a simple restaurant serving good-value set almuerzos and cenas. The name is about all that remains of Oruro's once thriving Croatian community.

Confitería Center Plaza 10 de Febrero and Meier. Mellow little bar-café attracting an older, arty and intellectual crowd with good coffee, juices and snacks, giving way to beers and spirits in the evening.

Confitería SUM Bolívar 615. Spacious student hang-out serving coffee, juices, snacks and ice cream, as well as a reasonable set almuerzo and more expensive meat and chicken main courses.

El Fogón San Felipe and Brasil. The best restaurant near the bus terminal, specializing in pork dishes like *lechón* and *chicharrón*, accompanied by

wa'tya – potatoes cooked in a traditional earth oven.

El Hornito Galvarro with Bolívar. No-nonsense *salteñería* serving tasty meat and chicken *salteñas* from mid-morning to mid-afternoon. There's another branch on Junin with Montes as well as several foodcarts that roam the city centre serving up *salteñas*.

Govinda 6 de Octubre and Bolívar. Peaceful vegetarian restaurant run by Hare Krishna devotees providing healthy, tasty and inexpensive alternatives to the meat-based Orureño cuisine, including muesli and yoghurt, samosas, pastas and a filling set almuerzo. Closed Sun.

Nayjama Pagador and Aldana. By far the best restaurant in town, serving huge portions of deliciously cooked local food for $4–5 a plate. Specialities include sublime roast lamb, a substantial vegetarian plate, and a mixed grill dish known as *El Intendente* after the visiting government official who devised it. The *criadillos* – prairie oysters – are not for the faint-hearted.

Unicornio La Plata and Meier. Popular and good-value restaurant with a broad choice of well-prepared meat and chicken dishes and a filling set almuerzo for $1.50. Sit upstairs if you don't want to watch big-screen TV while you eat.

Listings

Banks and exchange The Banco de Crédito, Montes and Bolívar, and Banco Union, at Mier and La Plata, both change cash and travellers' cheques and have ATMs.
Bus information ☎02/5279535.
Hospital Hospital General (☎02/5277408), 6 de

Octubre and San Felipe.
Internet access Plenty of places in the city centre, especially on 6 de Octubre – try Café Internet, 6 de Octubre with Junín, or Full internet, 6 de Octubre and Mier (both 9am–10pm; $0.60 per hour).
Laundry Lavandería, Washington and Cochabamba.

Moving on from Oruro

Oruro is the main transport hub of the Altiplano. All buses heading south or west from La Paz pass through here, and it's also at the centre of what's left of Bolivia's once-proud railway network. Almost all **long-distance buses** depart from the Terminal Terrestre. Ticket sales are upstairs, where there's also a small restaurant and a reasonably helpful **information office** (daily 8am–10pm; ☎052/79535). You board buses from the ground floor, where you have to pay the $0.30 fee for using the terminal. The only long-distance buses that don't use the terminal are those for Tarija, which depart from a stop on Avenida Ejército on the eastern outskirts of the city.

Trains heading south to Tupiza or Villazón on the Argentine border via Uyuni depart four times a week from the train station (☎052/74605) on Avenida Galvarro. See the box on p.166 for full details.

Post Office Half a block north of the Plaza 10 de Febrero on Av Montes.

Telephone office The ENTEL office is on Plaza Manuel Castro de Padilla, at Bolívar with Soria Galvarro.

Tour operators HT Viajeros del Tiempo, at Soria Galvarro 1232 (☎02/5271166, ☎02/5277339), offer half-day city tours, day-trips to various attractions just outside the city, and longer jeep excursions to the Chipaya and Salar de Coipasa.

Train information ☎052/74605.

Train travel in the Altiplano

Bolivia's last surviving railway line, running between Oruro and Villazón via Uyuni and Tupiza, offers a faster and more comfortable alternative to travelling across the Altiplano by bus. There are two trains: the faster and more luxurious **Expreso del Sur** – with heated carriages, a fully functioning bar and dining car complete with waiters in bow ties – and the slower but less expensive **Wara Wara del Sur**; each has three different classes of carriage of varying cost and comfort. The full timetable is given below, but schedules are liable to change. If possible, you should buy tickets in advance, but there's usually space for last-minute passengers. You can also buy tickets in La Paz from the office on the corner of Fernando Guachalla and Sanchez Lima.

Expreso del Sur

	Mon	Fri
Oruro	11am	3pm
Uyuni	5.15–5.20pm	9.15–9.25pm
Tupiza	10.05pm	2.15–2.25am
Villazón	–	5.20am

	Tues	Sat
Villazón	–	3.30pm
Tupiza	7am	6.10–6.20pm
Uyuni	12.05–12.15pm	11.25–11.30pm
Oruro	6.40pm	6pm

Wara Wara del Sur

	Sun–Mon	Wed–Thurs
Oruro	7pm	7pm
Uyuni	2–2.35am	2–2.35am
Tupiza	8.05–8.40am	8.05–8.40am
Villazón	11.40am	11.40am

	Mon–Tues	Thurs–Fri
Villazón	3.30pm	3.30pm
Tupiza	6.30–7pm	6.30–7pm
Uyuni	1–1.35am	1–1.35am
Oruro	8.35am	8.35am

Around Oruro

There are a couple of worthwhile half-day excursions **around Oruro**. To the northeast of the city, about 25km away on a turn-off from the road to Cochabamba, the **aguas termales** (thermal baths) at Obrajes (daily 7am–6pm; $1.50) are a good place to relax and soak away the chill of the Altiplano. The recently remodelled baths are fed by natural hot springs with reputedly curative powers, and there are also more expensive private baths for rent, as well as a place to buy drinks and snacks. Micros heading to Obrajes leave every half-hour or so from the corner of Avenida 6 de Agosto and Caro.

About 12km southeast of the city, meanwhile, begin the marshy margins of **Lago Uru Uru** (say it quickly and you'll see where Oruro got its name), a shallow, brackish lake fed by the Río Desaguadero, which drains the overflow from Lago Titicaca to the north. When water levels are high during the rainy season between January and March (later if it has been a wet year) you may see hundreds of flamingos in the shallow waters of the lake, as well as many ducks and other wading birds. The fringes of Lago Uru Uru have long been home to small communities of **Urus**, the oldest ethnic group of the Altiplano. The Urus traditionally scrape a marginal existence by fishing and hunting water fowl, as well as by herding llamas and cultivating quinua and other crops, though the salination of the land around the lake as the water level has fallen, together with mining pollution, pressure from Aymara farmers and the lure of the city, has seen population levels decline over the last few decades.

A rough road heads southeast to the **Chilean border** at Pisiga, 228km from Oruro, cutting across the northern fringes of the lake along a raised causeway, the **Puente Español**, built in the colonial era to allow the year-round passage of mule trains taking silver down to the coast and returning with mercury for processing the metal. Despite a recent crackdown, this route is popular with smugglers bringing cars and other goods from Chile, and there's a police checkpoint at the start of the causeway, about thirty minutes' drive from Oruro. From the checkpoint, a thirty-minute walk around the lakeshore to the northwest takes you to **CHUSAQUERI**, an all but abandoned farming hamlet overlooked by about a dozen pre-Columbian tombs known as **chullpas**, in varying states of repair. These carefully built adobe structures are around two metres high and sit on solid stone platforms, their roofs tiled with flat stones and with narrow doorways looking out across the lake to the west. It's thought they were built by the Wankarani culture, which dominated this region in the period preceeding the arrival of the Incas. Some of the artefacts found here are on display in the Museo Antropológico Eduardo López Rivas in Oruro (see p.160).

The Chipayas

About 180km southwest of Oruro across the Altiplano, the remote village of Chipaya is home to the **Chipayas**, an ethnic group that is culturally and linguistically distinct from both the Aymara and Quechua. Now confined to a small territory in this desolate region, the Chipayas are thought to be descended from the **Urus**, an ancient people who are considered to be the oldest inhabitants of the Altiplano, having arrived from the Pacific coast in around 2500 BC. Driven into the unforgiving environment of this remote corner of the Altiplano over several centuries under population pressure from the Aymara, the Chipayas eke out a marginal living by growing quinua in the saline soils and by catching fish and aquatic birds, though even this has become more difficult in recent years because of mining pollution. Despite the desperate poverty and external pressures they face, the Chipayas have maintained their unique language, culture and religious beliefs, which are a source of continuing fascination to anthropologists, and though modern concrete buildings are beginning to make their presence felt, many of the buildings in the village are still the distinctive circular huts with doors made from cactus and roofs thatched with aquatic reeds. Given the difficulty of getting here and the lack of accommodation, if you're interested in observing something of the Chipayas's daily life, it's best to do it in a 4WD – the Oruro tour agency HT Viajeros del Tiempo can organize this, and have guides who know the region.

South from Oruro a road and railway line run 118km across the Altiplano to the small town of **CHALLAPATA**, an important market centre for the Aymara and Quechua *ayllus* who inhabit the rugged mountain chain to the east. On the way south you pass the shallow and brackish waters of **Lago Poopó**, the final destination for the overflow water which is drained from Lago Titicaca by the Río Desaguadero. You can see the lake shimmering in the distance from the road and can sometimes spot flamingos and other waterfowl, though mining pollution has greatly reduced the number of birds that once flocked there. At Challapata, the road forks: one branch continues (together with the railway) due south across the ever more arid and inhospitable Altiplano to Uyuni (see p.190), just over 200km away. The other branch climbs into the sparsely populated mountains to the southeast, passing through a series of high plains where hundreds of llamas graze, then dropping into a deep but relatively fertile valley before climbing again to reach the city of Potosí (see below), 201km from Challapata.

Potosí

I am rich Potosí, treasure of the world, king of the mountains, envy of kings.
Legend on the coat of arms of Potosí

Set on a desolate, windswept plain amid barren mountains at almost 4100m above sea level, **POTOSÍ** is the highest city in the world, and at once the most fascinating and tragic place in Bolivia. Given its remote and inhospitable location, at first glance it's difficult to see why it was ever built here at all. The answer lies in **Cerro Rico** ("Rich Mountain"), the conical peak that rises imperiously above the city to the south. Cerro Rico was, quite simply, the richest source of silver the world had ever seen – one seventeenth-century chronicler described it as a "singular work of the power of God, unique miracle of nature, perfect and permanent wonder of the world, happiness of mortals, emperor of summits, king of the mountains, prince of all the minerals". The silver extracted from this mountain turned Potosí into the richest jewel in the Spanish emperors' crown, and one of the wealthiest and largest cities in the world – in the early seventeenth century it was home to about 160,000 people, far bigger than contemporary Madrid, and equal in size to London. In its heyday the city was so famous for its riches that the expression "*eso vale un Potosí*" ("this is worth a Potosí") was used in colloquial Spanish to describe anything priceless. However, this wealth was achieved at the expense of the millions of indigenous Andean forced labourers and African slaves who died working in the mines and silver foundries. Though it was said that you could build a bridge stretching from Potosí to Spain with the silver of Cerro Rico, others have pointed out that two such bridges could have been built with the bones of those who died mining it.

Today, Potosí's legacy reflects both the magnificence and the horror of its colonial past. The city is a treasure trove of **colonial art and architecture**, with hundreds of well-preserved buildings, including some of the finest churches in Bolivia. But its tragic history weighs heavily on the shoulders of the living and is evident both in the sense of sadness that seems to haunt its narrow streets and in the appalling conditions still endured by those who work the mines of Cerro Rico, for though the silver veins were almost all exhausted centuries ago, the labyrinthine tunnels that perforate the scarred mountain are still worked for tin and other metals by thousands of indigenous miners

Fiestas in Potosí

Potosí is known within Bolivia as the *ciudad de los costumbres* (the city of customs) because of the great importance its inhabitants attach to traditional religious rituals and celebrations. The city's fiestas combine the veneration of Catholic saints with ceremonies associated with traditional Andean beliefs, and are usually marked by processions, folkloric dances and copious eating and drinking.

The Circumcision of Christ (Jan 1). Procession and folkloric dances in the San Benito neighbourhood.

Día de los Compadres (Feb, two weeks before Carnaval). The miners carry the crosses which stand at the entrances to the mines, known as *Tata Ckacchas*, down from Cerro Rico in a procession accompanied by brass bands, costumed dancers and dynamite explosions.

Carnaval (February/March). Carnaval is celebrated with waterfights and costumed dances, and is also the occasion for *ch'allas* – the blessing of cars, buildings and other property with ritual libations of alcohol, coloured streamers and llama or sheep blood.

San Juan de Dios (March 8). Procession of the image of San Juan de Dios which is kept in San Lorenzo de Carangas, accompanied by folkloric dances.

Semana Santa (April). Easter is marked by a series of Masses and processions of different saints and celebrated with the preparation of a special meal, available on steets and made up of seven different meat-free meals.

Pentecostés (May or June). Llama sacrifices – accompanied by eating, drinking, coca-chewing, music and dance – are performed in all the mines on the seventh Sunday after Easter in honour of Pachamama, the earth goddess, to ensure safety and success in finding minerals.

San Bartolomé or **Ch'utillos** (Aug 24–26). Potosí's biggest annual fiesta, centred on the re-enactment of an ancient legend by unmarried young men (known as *Ch'utillos*) mounted on horseback and dressed in their finest traditional costumes. Accompanied by dancers and musicians, the *Ch'utillos* ride to and from the Cueva del Diablo (Devil's Cave) near the village of La Puerta, where according to legend an evil spirit was exorcized by Jesuit priests using a statue of San Bartolomé.

Señor de la Vera Cruz (Sept 14). Religious procession in honour of Potosí's miraculous patron saint, whose statue is housed in San Francisco.

using techniques little changed from a century or more ago. A visit to these mines has become as essential a part of a visit to Potosí as any of its museums or churches, and is fascinating for the insight it affords into both the working lives of the miners and the customs and beliefs that help them survive. Perhaps as a consequence of its woeful past, Potosí and the surrounding rural hinterland are famous within Bolivia for their carefully preserved traditional customs and folkloric **fiestas**.

Some history

The discovery of the silver mountain of is shrouded in myth. Legend has it that the **Incas** were on the point of mining here in 1462 when a thunderous supernatural voice warned them off, saying the gods were saving the silver for others who would come from afar. When the Inca Huayna Capac was told of this, he declared the mountain sacrosanct and named it *Ppotojsi*, a Quechua word meaning "thunder" or "burst". The silver was apparently rediscovered in 1545 by a llama herder named **Diego Huallpa**. Caught out after dark whilst pursuing stray llamas on the slopes of Cerro Rico, Huallpa started a fire to keep warm, and was amazed to see a trickle of molten silver run out from the blaze. News of this discovery soon reached the ears of the Spaniards, and a silver rush was quickly underway. Within a year and a half the disorderly new mining camp that had sprung up – grandiosely named the Villa Imperial de Carlos V de Potosí – was home to over 14,000 people. Over the next twenty years Potosí became the richest single source of silver in the world, and its population mushroomed to over 100,000, making it easily the biggest city in the Americas.

This growth was based on the extraction of surface deposits with high ore contents, which were easily processed by the indigenous miners using primitive smelting techniques. As these surface deposits ran out and shaft mining developed, the purity of the ore declined and production costs rose; in addition, labour became increasingly scarce, as workers became aware of the appalling conditions in the mines. This crisis was overcome by the energetic **Viceroy Francisco de Toledo**, who arrived in Potosí in 1572 determined to modernize the silver industry and revive a vital source of imperial revenue. Toledo persuaded the leading mine owners to invest in the construction of a massive system of dams, artificial lakes and aqueducts in the mountains above the city to provide a constant supply of water to power the water wheels that crushed the ore for processing. Toledo also introduced the newly discovered amalgam process for refining silver using mercury; established the first royal mint, where all silver mined in Potosí had to be turned into coins or ingots; and introduced a basic mining code to regulate property rights, reducing violent disputes between mine owners. Most importantly, Toledo tackled the acute labour shortage in the mines by adapting the Inca system of labour service known as the *mita*. Under this regime, an area stretching from Cuzco to northern Argentina was divided into sixteen districts, each of which was obliged to send one-seventh of its male population to the mines each year. This provided an annual workforce of about 13,500 men – known as *mitayos* – at almost no cost to the mine owners. The *mitayos* were housed in fourteen *parroquias de Indios* (Indian parishes), clearly separated from the Spanish city centre, whose chaotic street layout Toledo ordered redrawn to conform to royal ordinances governing town planning.

These reforms greatly boosted silver production, and Potosí entered a boom that lasted almost a century and generated fabulous riches. By the beginning of the seventeenth century Potosí was home to more than 160,000 people and boasted dozens of magnificent churches, as well as theatres, gambling-houses, brothels and dancehalls – for the Corpus Cristi celebrations of 1658 the streets of the city were literally paved with silver bars. The silver also had a global impact, funding the wars of Spain, fuelling long-term inflation and economic growth in Europe, and financing emerging trade relations between Europe and Asia.

For the **indigenous workers and African slaves** who produced this wealth, however, the consequences were catastrophic. Conditions inside the mines were truly appalling. Staying deep underground for up to a week at a time and forced to meet ever more outrageous quotas, the *mitayos* and other labourers died at a terrible rate; outside, the highly toxic mercury used in processing the silver posed an equal threat to those working in the *ingenios*, the large foundries in which the ore was processed. In 1626, four thousand people were killed when the restraining dyke of an artificial lake collapsed and flood waters swept away entire blocks of the city. Even contemporary observers were shocked by the horrors of Potosí: one sixteenth-century writer described the mines as a ravening beast that swallowed men alive. In all, it's thought that seven of every ten men who went to Potosí to work under the *mita* never returned. Estimates of the total number who died over three centuries of colonial mining in Potosí run as high as nine million, making the mines of Potosí a central factor in the demographic collapse that swept the Andes under Spanish rule.

Like all such booms, the silver bonanza at Potosí eventually cooled. From about 1650 silver production entered a century-long decline that saw the population of Potosí dwindle to just 30,000, as people abandoned the city to seek economic opportunity elsewhere. The Spanish monarchy helped recovery by reducing the tax rate on silver production to ten percent, creating a mineral-purchasing bank, establishing an academy of metallurgy and building a new royal mint, but Potosí never recovered its economic predominance. It remained a rich enough prize to be hotly disputed during the **Independence War**, however, changing hands frequently between royalist and Argentine armies, both of whom looted the city. By the time independence was won in 1825, Potosí's population was just nine thousand.

Silver mining recovered somewhat in the following decades, but from the end of the nineteenth century Potosí came to rely more and more on the mining of **tin** – another metal found in abundance in Cerro Rico, but previously ignored. Even this was just a temporary reprieve, however. Government efforts to support the industry culminated in the construction of the modern tin-smelting plant at Karachipampa, on the road to Sucre, a white elephant of epic proportions which was completed shortly before the price of tin collapsed in 1985 and never operated. The state-owned mines closed down or were privatized, despite the best efforts of the powerful miners union. Though co-operative miners continue to scrape a living by working the tired old veins of Cerro Rico for tin and other metals, Potosí never recovered from the decline of silver production, much less the tin crash. Today the city's many fine churches are all that remains of the immense wealth that once flowed from its mines.

Arrival and information

All **buses** (except those from Uyuni) arrive at the Terminal de Buses on Avenida Universitario, on the way out of town towards Oruro. Buses from Uyuni pull in at the various bus company offices on the corner of Avenida Universitario and Sevilla, two blocks up from the terminal. The Terminal de Buses has a restaurant, phone boxes, post office, luggage storage and a small **bus information office** (daily 7am–noon & 2–8pm; ☎02/6227354). From the terminal, a **taxi** into the city centre costs $0.50 per person (the basic rate for journeys throughout the city), or you can catch **micro** "A" heading up Avenida Universitario, which will take you to Plaza 10 de Noviembre, the central square. On foot, it's a steep twenty- to thirty-minute walk up to the city centre – not much fun at this altitude. If you're arriving from the valleys of Sucre or Tarija it's a good idea to take things easy for the first day or so while you get used to the higher altitude.

The best place for information is the **Oficina de Turismo Municipal** (Mon–Fri 8am–noon & 2–6pm; ☎062/29185 or 26916) in the striking modern mirrored building through the arch of Torre de la Compañía on Calle Ayacucho, a block west of Plaza 10 de Noviembre. The generally helpful staff do their best to answer enquiries (though in Spanish only) and can give advice on visiting the co-operative mines and other attractions outside the city; they also have various maps and books about Potosí in both English and Spanish for sale. It's also worth reporting any problems you might have with tour agencies or hotels here. Exhibitions of weavings and other handicrafts are sometimes held on the ground floor, and you have to pass through the building to climb to the top of the church tower (see p.178). There's a second tourist office in the **Caseta de Información** (Mon–Fri 8am–noon & 2–6pm), at the west end of Plaza 6 de Agosto, where you can get much the same information, but the opening hours are less reliable.

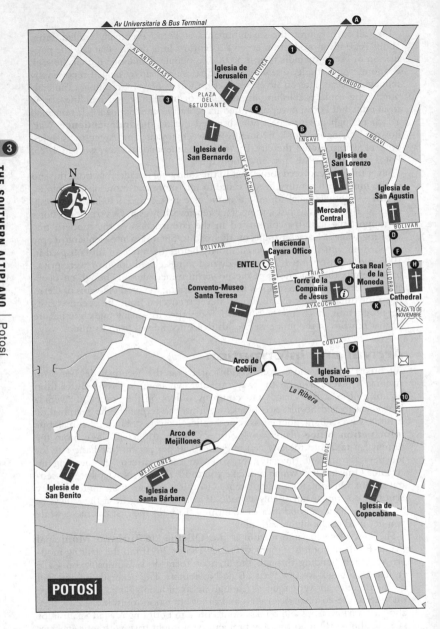

Av Universitaria & Bus Terminal

Iglesia de Jerusalén

PLAZA DEL ESTUDIANTE

Iglesia de San Bernardo

AV ANTOFAGASTA

AV CIVICA

AV SERRUDO

INGAVI

INGAVI

Iglesia de San Lorenzo

CHAXITA

BUSTILLOS

Iglesia de San Agustín

ORURO

AV CAMACHO

Mercado Central

BOLIVAR

N

BOLIVAR

Hacienda Cayara Office

ENTEL

COCHABAMBA

FRIAS

Casa Real de la Moneda

QUILLORBO

Convento-Museo Santa Teresa

Torre de la Compañia de Jesus

AYACUCHO

Cathedral

PLAZA 10 DE NOVIEMBRE

COBIJA

Arco de Cobija

La Ribera

Iglesia de Santo Domingo

LANZA

Arco de Mejillones

MEJILLONES

VILLARROEL

Iglesia de San Benito

Iglesia de Santa Bárbara

Iglesia de Copacabana

POTOSÍ

Accommodation

With night-time temperatures often falling below zero, the main consideration when choosing where to stay in Potosí is warmth. A couple of the more upmarket places have central heating, but otherwise try to find a room that gets some sun during the day, and don't hesitate to ask for extra blankets if you need them. There's a fairly good range of budget places to stay, but only a limited

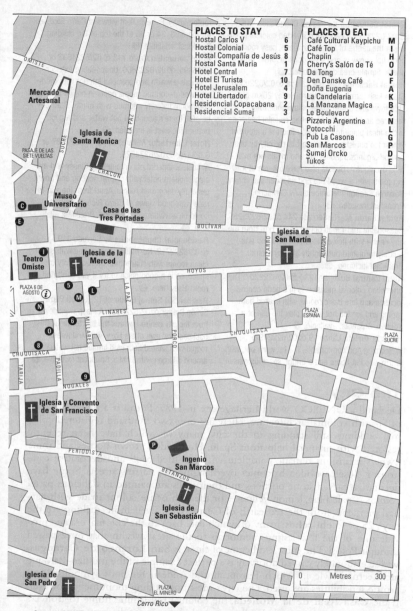

PLACES TO STAY

Hostal Carlos V	6
Hostal Colonial	5
Hostal Compañía de Jesús	8
Hostal Santa Maria	1
Hotel Central	7
Hotel El Turista	10
Hotel Jerusalem	4
Hotel Libertador	9
Residencial Copacabana	2
Residencial Sumaj	3

PLACES TO EAT

Café Cultural Kaypichu	M
Café Top	I
Chaplin	H
Cherry's Salón de Té	O
Da Tong	J
Den Danske Café	F
Doña Eugenia	A
La Candelaria	K
La Manzana Magica	B
Le Boulevard	C
Pizzeria Argentina	N
Potocchi	L
Pub La Casona	G
San Marcos	P
Sumaj Orcko	D
Tukos	E

selection of mid-range hotels – if you want to stay in one of these, it's not a bad idea to book in advance, especially between June and August.

Hostal Carlos V Linares 42 ☎02/6225121. Charming converted colonial house with simple but clean rooms looking out onto a glass-roofed central patio. Breakfast available. ❷
Hostal Colonial Hoyos 8 ☎02/6224265 or

6224809, ℱ02/6227146. Beautifully restored colonial mansion with a centrally heated modern interior and comfortable, well-furnished rooms set around two peaceful tiled courtyards with fountains. ❻

Hostal Compañía de Jesœs Chuquisaca 445 ℡02/6223173. Delightful converted colonial building in the centre of town with clean, cosy rooms, good hot showers and a welcoming family atmosphere. Simple breakfast included. ❸

Hostal Hacienda Caraya Caraya ℡02/6226380. Set in lush farmland in a warm valley 20km outside town and 500m lower, this wonderfully restored and opulently furnished colonial hacienda is the ideal place to stay if you find the altitude of Potosí too punishing. Transport to the city by taxi can be organized (about $8) and meals are available on request. Guests also have full use of a living room with a wood fire and an extensive library. Reserve through the office on Av Camacho. Breakfast included. ❻

Hostal Santa Maria Serrudo 244 ℡02/6223255. Reasonable mid-range option about 1km from the city centre with flower-filled corridors and adequately furnished but slightly gloomy rooms. Breakfast included. ❹

Hotel Central Bustillos 1230 ℡02/6222207. This crumbling colonial mansion is in a good central location and has basic rooms with shared bathrooms and limited hot water, plus the use of a kitchen. Breakfast available. ❷

Hotel El Turista Lanza 19 ℡02/6222492. Welcoming and comfortable, if a bit worn out, with warm wooden floors and a bright, spacious glass-roofed lobby. For excellent views of Cerro Rico, ask for room 33, 34 or 35 at the top of the building. Breakfast available. ❸

Hotel Jerusalén Oruro 143 ℡02/6224633 or 6226095, ℻02/6222600. Unappealing exterior conceals a warm and peaceful interior with modern, well-decorated rooms opening onto a bright, communal balcony adorned with plants. Staff are helpful, there's abundant hot water and a good buffet breakfast is included. ❺

Hotel Libertador Millares 58 ℡02/6227887 or 6223470, ℻02/6224629, ✉hostalib@cedro.pts.entelnet.bo. Classy and efficient modern hotel with central heating and bright, tastefully decorated rooms. Apart from the sun terrace with good views of Cerro Rico, though, it could be anywhere in the world. Breakfast available. ❺

Residencial Copacabana Av Serrudo 319 ℡02/6222712. No-frills budget option with small, clean rooms with shared bath. It has plenty of space, so is a good place to try if you can't find a room elsewhere. ❷

Residencial Sumaj F. Gumiel 12, just off Plaza Simón Bolívar ℡02/6223336. A steep walk down from the city centre towards the bus terminal, this backpackers' dive offers boxy and windowless rooms with shared bath (and limited hot water) around a large central patio. Breakfast available. ❷

The City

Declared a UNESCO world heritage site in 1987, Potosí is a living museum of Spanish colonial architecture. There are over two thousand registered colonial buildings still standing in the city, many of which have been recently restored with financial help from Spain. Hundreds of town houses and mine owners' mansions remain, complete with red-tiled roofs and decorative cast-iron or closed wooden balconies overhanging the narrow streets. Some have decorative carved stone porticos and their walls are painted in delicious pastel colours – pale blue, lemon yellow – or the rich ochre colour made with natural pigments from the red earth of Cerro Rico. Even more striking are the city's 25 or so **churches**, many of which date back to the colonial era and provide one of the few lasting memorials to the great wealth that once passed through Potosí. The most exuberant of these is **San Lorenzo de Carangas**, whose elaborately carved doorway is a perfect example of the mestizo-Baroque architectural style in which European and Andean religious symbolism and artistic sensibilities are fused. The city's most outstanding monument, however, is the **Casa Real de la Moneda**, the colonial royal mint, home to Bolivia's finest museum, whose varied collection includes some of the best colonial religious art in the country.

Plaza 10 de Noviembre

The centre of the city is the **Plaza 10 de Noviembre**, a pleasant square shaded by trees, with a broken fountain and a small copy of the Statue of Liberty, erected in 1926 to commemorate Bolivian independence. The heart of Spanish

Organized tours

There are a growing number of **tour operators** in Potosí, all of which offer half-day trips to the mines of **Cerro Rico** (see p.184). These are fairly standard and are supposed to cost a fixed $10 per person. Make sure your guide is licensed and that the company provides you with a helmet, jacket or overalls, boots and a headlamp, as well as transport to and from the mines; an English-speaking guide can be arranged at no extra cost. Most companies also run half- or one-day **city tours**, and some also organize hiking trips in the **Cordillera Kari-Kari** and excursions to other attractions outside Potosí. You can also organize tours of the **Salar de Uyuni** from here, though this costs more than if you arrange the trip in Uyuni itself.

Andes Braulio Expeditions Plaza Alonso de Ibañez and Padilla ☎02/6225175. Long-established operator with a good reputation offering the usual mine and city tours as well as trips outside Potosí and excursions to the Salar de Uyuni.

Hidalgo Tours Bolívar with Junín ☎02/6225186, ℉02/6222707, ⓦwww.salar-uyuni.com. Upmarket operator offering the usual mine tours as well as guided tours of the city and expensive but relatively luxurious trips to the Salar de Uyuni.

Koala Tours Ayacucho 5 ☎02/6222092, ℮wgarnica@hotmail.com. Experienced and reliable operators with good English-speaking mine guides and a

small mining museum inside a mine reserved exclusively for their groups. They also run hiking trips around the Kari Kari lakes (see p.188) with accommodation in mountain huts (2–3 days; $20 per person per day), and special trips to the Tinku in Macha (see p.189) in the first week of May, as well as other special events in the region. Mountain bike excursions and rental are also planned.

Sumaj Tours Oruro 143, inside the *Hotel Jerusalén* ☎062/24633 or 22495, ℉062/22600, ℮hoteljer@cedro.pts .entelnet.bo. Friendly and well-organized company running tours of the mines with good English-speaking guides as well as city tours and excursions.

colonial power in Potosí, the square was formerly surrounded by the city's principal church, the *cabildo* (town hall) and the first royal mint, which stood here from 1572 to 1767, though sadly none of these has survived. On the north side of the square, the site of the original church (which collapsed in 1807) is now occupied by the twin-towered **Cathedral**, completed in Neoclassical style in 1836. It's open most mornings and afternoons, and the bright, well-lit interior with a high ceiling supported by gilded pillars is worth a look, not least for the striking wooden images of Christ carved in the sixteenth century by the renowned sculptor Gaspar de la Cueva, who was responsible for many of the city's other religious statues. The site of the *cabildo* is now occupied by the departmental **Prefectura**, a nineteenth-century administrative building whose simple carved stone portico is all that remains of the colonial town hall; the site of the first Casa Real de la Moneda is occupied by the late nineteenth-century **Palacio de Justicia**.

To the east, the plaza adjoins another open space, the **Plaza 6 de Agosto**, at the centre of which is a column commemorating the Battle of Ayacucho, which secured Bolivian independence in 1824. From the north side it's overlooked by the **Teatro Omiste**, a former church, hospital and convent completed in 1753, with a recessed mestizo-Baroque facade under its one central arch. During the Independence War the church was used as a headquarters and bastion by royalist forces, who demolished its twin towers to make room for rooftop artillery emplacements (another church which stood in the plaza was completely demolished to clear a field of fire). It was converted into a theatre in 1850. Along the east side of the plaza runs **El Boulevard**, the bustling pedestrianized street which is the favourite meeting point for Potosinos young and old.

Casa Real de la Moneda

Half a block west of the Plaza 10 de Noviembre on Calle Ayacucho stands the unmissable **Casa Real de la Moneda**, or Royal Mint (Tues–Fri 9.30am–noon & 2–6.30pm, Sat & Sun 9am–1pm; visits by guided tour only; $3, cameras $1.50), one of the most outstanding examples of colonial civil architecture in all South America and now home to the best museum in Bolivia. The vast and eclectic collection includes the original machinery used in the various stages of the minting process; some of Bolivia's finest colonial religious art; militaria; archeological artefacts; and a vast collection of coins and banknotes. Visits are by **guided tour** only: these are included in the entrance price and conducted in Spanish, English or French depending on demand. There are only two tours daily, usually beginning each morning and afternoon shortly after opening, so it's worth turning up on time; tours last about two hours. Be warned that even when the sun is shining outside it's very cold inside the complex, so wrap up warm.

Built over three decades between 1759 and 1773 to replace the earlier royal mint, La Moneda is a truly formidable construction, built as part of a concerted effort by the Spanish crown to reform the economic and financial machinery of the empire in order to increase its revenues. Along with Lima and Mexico City, Potosí was one of only three cities in Spanish America authorized to produce coins. The construction costs were so high – over a million pesos de oro – that emperor Carlos III is said to have asked if the new mint had been built entirely of silver. Occupying an entire city block – over 7,500 square metres – La Moneda is enclosed by stout stone walls over a metre thick with only a few barred windows looking out onto the street, giving it the appearance of a fortress. Inside is a rambling two-storey complex of about two hundred rooms set round five internal courtyards, all finely built with cut stone blocks and neat brickwork, with soaring roofs supported by massive hardwood beams. As well as housing all the heavy machinery and equipment needed to produce coins – much of which is well preserved and on display – La Moneda also housed troops, workers, African slaves and the senior royal officials responsible for overseeing operations and ensuring the Spanish crown received its ten percent cut of all silver produced in the mines of Cerro Rico. A vital nerve centre of Spanish imperial power in the Andes, it also served as a prison, treasury and near-impregnable stronghold in times of disorder.

The main **entrance** on Calle Ayacucho is an ornate Baroque portal with mighty double doors four metres high. The coat of arms above the door, bearing the lion and castle of the Spanish kingdoms of Castille and Léon, and the doorknockers in the form of the double-headed eagle of the Habsburg dynasty leave little doubt as to whom this building belonged. From the doorway, a corridor leads through into the first interior patio, built in classic Spanish style with twelve stone arches supporting a second floor with a covered balcony running around the top and with a stone fountain in the centre. Overlooking the courtyard from above one of the arches is a large plaster mask of a smiling face crowned by a garland of leaves and grapes. Known as **El Mascarón**, this leering caricature has become one of the best-known symbols of Potosí, even though neither its origin or meaning are clear. The most likely story is that it was made by Eugenio Mulón, a Frenchman working in the mint in the mid-nineteenth century – it's variously thought to represent Bacchus, the Roman god of plenty; Diego Huallpa, the llama-herder who discovered the silver of Cerro Rico; a parody of either President Belzu or of the director of the mint; or a veiled caricature of avarice. It has also been suggested that the mysterious mask was created during the Independence War to cover a royal coat of arms in mockery of Spanish rule.

Colonial religious art

The guided tour of the museum begins in a room full of **colonial paintings**, including a series depicting eighteenth-century battles between Spain and the Turks – one of the many wars funded by the silver of Potosí. There's also a good portrait of the Spanish emperor, Carlos III, on horseback, and portraits of several leading Potosí mine owners from the same period. The next room is exclusively dedicated to colonial paintings of the Virgin Mary, many of them painted by unnamed indigenous artists in the highly distinctive mestizo-Baroque style. Of these, the most outstanding is the **Virgen del Cerro**, one of the most important paintings ever produced in Bolivia and a supreme expression of Andean religious syncretism. Painted sometime in the eighteenth century by an anonymous but presumably indigenous artist, it depicts the Virgin Mary in the form of the Cerro Rico, fusing the Catholic Mother of God with Pachamama, the bountiful Andean earth goddess. From the heavens above the Virgin-Mountain, the Christian trinity of Father, Son and Holy Ghost (depicted as a white dove) reach down from amidst an escort of archangels and cherubim to place a crown on her head. On the earth below, the coronation is witnessed by the earthly spiritual hierarchy of pope, archbishop and priest (bottom left), and the temporal hierarchy of emperor, town councillor and knight of Santiago (bottom right). In the sky to the left and right of the Virgin, the sun and the moon, central figures in Inca religion, look on from the distance like exiled deities. The slopes of the mountain itself are richly detailed. Diego Huallpa sits by the fire that first revealed the existence of silver; miners work in search of the precious metal; a lordly Spaniard arrives, preceded by a priest on horseback; llamas graze on the lower slopes; and at the foot of the mountain stands the Inca Huayna Capac, no doubt issuing his legendary prohibition on extracting the silver, his presence a subtle reminder, perhaps, of the people to whom these lands once belonged.

The next room is filled entirely with paintings by **Melchor Pérez de Holguín**, the Cochabamba-born artist who was perhaps the finest exponent of the Andean Baroque style. Known as *La Brocha de Oro* – the Golden Brush – Holguín was the outstanding painter of the Potosí school and produced works at an extraordinary rate. His religious paintings found their way into all the major churches and convents of the city as well as further afield, and his style was widely imitated. The paintings on display here form the single biggest collection of his work anywhere, and range from his earliest efforts to the series of portraits of the evangelists he produced shortly before his death in about 1730. Holguín's distinctive style is most evident in these delicate portraits: the more mystical evangelists are portrayed with soft faces and bright, shining eyes; aesthetes are depicted with hard, drawn faces beneath which muscles and veins are visible as in an anatomical drawing.

Coins, minting machinery and the smelting rooms

The tour then returns to the ground floor and the massive halls with high vaulted ceilings in which silver was processed and coins minted. The **Numismatic Room** is filled with coins of all different sizes and denominations minted in Potosí over a period of four hundred years, right through the colonial period and into the republic. The earliest silver coins – known as *macuquinas*, from the Quechua *makaicuna*, meaning "beaten things" – were crudely made using hammers and primitive die stamps. Later coins, produced with more advanced machinery, have regular edges and clearer detail. More interesting, however, are the massive wooden **laminadoras**, or rolling mills, which were used to press the silver into thin sheets from which the coins were punched. Made by Spanish craftsmen from European oak, then shipped to the Americas and carried across the Andes on the backs of mules, these huge, intricate and perfectly preserved machines are the only examples of Spanish engineering of their type and era still in existence. They were powered by mules or African slaves, who were tied to driveshafts on the floor below that in which the silver was rolled.

After this the tour continues into the **smelting rooms**, where the silver was melted down before rolling – one of these has been preserved intact, complete with furnaces and crucibles, its high ceiling stained with the soot of a thousand fires. Other smelting rooms now house a haphazard collection of carved wooden retablos from some of Potosí's churches, plus other displays including a collection of arms and uniforms from Bolivia's three disastrous wars with its neighbours; a modest archeological collection featuring pre-Columbian ceramics and stone idols, as well as some rather macabre mummified Spanish babies found in the walls of San Bernardo church in 1980; and a selection of silverwork ranging from religious paraphernalia to plates and sugar bowls.

La Compañia and Santa Teresa

A block further east along Calle Ayacucho from the Casa Real de la Moneda stands **La Torre de la Compañia** (Mon–Fri 8am–noon & 2–6pm; $0.80), the bell tower which is all that now remains of a Jesuit church originally founded in 1581. Completed in 1707 and recently restored, the grandiose tower is one of the finest eighteenth-century religious monuments in Bolivia and a sublime example of the mestizo-Baroque style, built with a triumphal arch underneath and 32 columns carved with decorative flowers and grape-laden vines. You can climb to the top of the tower, from where there are excellent panoramic **views** of the city and Cerro Rico. To get in, go up the stairs inside the municipal tourism building, whose sloping mirror-glass front reflects the tower perfectly from behind, a rare case in Bolivia of modern architecture complementing rather than detracting from the beauty of an older monument.

Walk a block further east down Ayacucho and then turn left to reach the **Convento-Museo Santa Teresa** (daily 9am–noon & 3–6pm; $2, cameras $2; the ticket is also valid for the Iglesia de Jerusalén – see p.183), a beautiful colonial church and convent worth visiting both for its fine collection of colonial religious painting and sculpture, and for a somewhat disturbing insight into the bizarre lifestyle of nuns in the colonial era. Visits are by guided tour only, so you need to get here at least an hour before closing. The tours can last for over two hours, which is more than enough for most people – if you want a shorter tour or the sheer quantity of gold leaf and religious images gets a bit much, just let the guide know. Built between 1686 and 1691 by the order of Carmelitas Descalzadas shortly after it was founded, the convent thrived on donations from rich mine owners, and once sprawled over several city blocks. It's now greatly reduced in size, and much of what is left has been converted into the museum, though some areas are still reserved for the small surviving community of nuns – after the tour you can buy some of the delicious marzipan and other sweets they make following centuries-old recipes.

Double meanings: the churches of Potosí

The most striking reminder of Potosí's incredible former wealth is to be found in its magnificent **churches and convents**. With beautifully carved porticos and interiors dripping with gold leaf, they're amongst the finest examples of the Andean mestizo-Baroque style, in which Christian European and pre-Christian Andean symbolism are combined in a unique and distinctive synthesis. The churches were of course built partly as a straightforward expression of religious faith, but gratitude for the wealth of Potosí also played a part: whereas Catholic churches almost always face west, those of Potosí face due south towards Cerro Rico, so the silver mines could be blessed from the altar through their open doors. The churches also formed part of a determined effort to **convert the indigenous population** to Christianity. Spreading the Catholic faith was considered both a religious duty and a moral justification for conquest, as well an offering a powerful means of maintaining control over the new empire. Religious architecture and art therefore took on enormous importance: magnificent churches were built partly to impress the indigenous population, while paintings and sculptures provided new symbols and objects of worship to replace their now forbidden idols. This Catholic proselytism took on a special significance in Potosí. With hundreds of thousands of indigenous people from different ethnic groups spending time in the city as workers under the *mita* system, Potosí offered a perfect opportunity for inculcating the Catholic faith in the newly conquered peoples. As well as the many churches and convents built for their own use, the Spaniards built fourteen parish churches for exclusive use by the indigenous *mitayos*, each one the centre for a settlement of one or two particular ethnic groups.

With time, Christianity gained widespread acceptance amongst the indigenous population, at least on the surface. But as responsibility for building and decorating the churches in Potosí was handed over to locally trained indigenous and mestizo craftsmen and artists, a very distinct religious vision began to emerge. From the second half of the sixteenth century onwards the religious art and architecture of Potosí began incorporating more and more indigenous religious motifs in a style that became known as **mestizo-Baroque**. Using this style, local craftsmen brought the facades of the city's churches alive with tropical vegetation and fruits, inhabited by exotic birds and animals, bare-breasted caryatids and strange, idol-like figures. The sun, moon, stars – all central objects of worship in pre-Christian religion throughout the Andes – appear alongside images of Christ and the saints, and the same indigenous iconography appears in wood carvings, silverwork and oil paintings, with the Virgin Mary represented in triangular form like a mountain, clearly conflated with the Andean earth goddess Pachamama.

These developments did not pass unnoticed by the Spanish authorities. Viceroy Toledo complained that the indigenous population were constantly returning to their idols, and at one stage issued a ordinance banning depictions of the sun, moon and stars. The Dominicans felt the same way about the apparent pagan iconography, but both had to cede before the force of indigenous culture, which expressed itself within the unrestricted decorative liberty of the Baroque. To some extent, no doubt, the religious authorities were happy to turn a blind eye to this. Religious syncretism works both ways, and incorporating a little Andean religious imagery into the decoration of churches may have seemed a small price to pay for getting the indigenous population to accept Christianity, albeit superficially.

Despite their beauty, however, these churches were the product of indigenous slave labour, and for all their gilded opulence they could scarcely conceal the contradiction between the avowed Christian beliefs of the Spanish mine owners who funded them and the brutal reality of the mining regime which these same men controlled. With some reason it was said that though God ruled in Potosí's 34 churches, the Devil laughed in his 6000 mines.

During the **colonial era**, young women who entered the convent as nuns renounced the material world in order to dedicate themselves to matters spiritual, a choice no doubt made more attractive by the horrors of the mines outside. These women were mostly drawn from the families of wealthy Spanish aristocrats and mine owners, each of whom handed over a fortune in gold or property in return for their daughters' acceptance into the convent. Once inside, girls submitted to a rigid regime of prayer, work and abstinence. They were able to talk to each other for just two hours a day and were forbidden to see or be seen by outsiders – even parental visits were received behind screens. Nor was there any escape in death: nuns were buried beneath the floorboards in the lower choir, where the body of one of the founders of the order is said to be miraculously preserved, though (not surprisingly) you can't verify this for yourself.

The simple but elegant **facade** of carved pink stone, decorated with the coats of arms of the order and its two biggest funders, is the oldest example of mestizo-Baroque architecture in Potosí, dating back to 1691. Inside, the convent is a peaceful complex of interconnected courtyards, gardens and cloisters leading to rooms now filled with an exhaustive (and exhausting) collection of colonial religious art. There are more than two hundred beautifully preserved **paintings** here, including outstanding works by Melchor Pérez de Holguín and Gaspar Miguel de Berrio. Particularly interesting are the paintings of Biblical scenes by Juan Luis Willca, a student of Holguín's, which feature flamingos, hummingbirds and other Andean birds; and a painting of the Last Supper in which the traditional Andean delicacy of guinea pig is served. The convent **church** features a lavish carved wooden Baroque retablo smothered in gold leaf, along with a beautiful panelled wooden roof painted in Mudéjar style, a clear indication of the Moorish influence brought by Spanish craftsmen from Andalucía.

From Santa Teresa to San Francisco

Heading south from Santa Teresa and following the street down and round to the left brings you to the **Arco de Cobija**, a colonial stone gateway that formerly marked the entrance to the Spanish city centre from the Indian Parishes to the south. A block east of here along Calle Cobija stands the – by Potosí's standards – unexceptional **Iglesia de Santo Domingo**, which dates back to 1620 but was extensively remodelled in the nineteenth century in Neoclassical style. It's rarely open to the public, but if you do manage to get in on a Sunday morning it's worth checking out the carved wooden statue of the Virgen del Rosario, which was brought over from Spain in the sixteenth century and used as a model by Tupac Yupanqui when he carved the Virgen de Copacabana in 1582 (see p.111). Almost nothing remains of the once substantial Dominican monastery which was founded here in 1553 – its buildings were confiscated by the government in 1826 and served briefly as a public jail before being demolished.

A right turn down the alley beside the church brings you to the foot of **Calle Chuquisaca**, on and around which are some of Potosí's best preserved and most luxurious **colonial town houses**, their carved stone doorways decorated with the coats of arms of the Spanish noblemen who owned them. A couple of blocks south of Chuquisaca down Calle Tarija is the church and convento of **San Francisco** (Mon–Fri 9.30am–noon & 2.30–5pm, Sat 9.30am–noon; $1.50, cameras $1.50), now a museum and worth visiting for the views from its roof, as well as for its collection of colonial religious art – if you haven't seen enough of this already. The original church, the first to be built in Potosí, was created when the Franciscan monastery was founded in 1547, but was demolished in 1707 and replaced by the bulky structure you see today, with its multiple-domed roof and tall, square bell-tower. Amongst the **paintings** on display inside are two big canvases by Holguín, one a luridly detailed Day of Judgement, with saints, priests and monks ascending to heaven while sinners burn or are eaten by ravening beasts in hell.

The Baroque retablos that once adorned the church were removed in the early nineteenth century, and the rather dreary interior's main point of interest nowadays is the reputedly miraculous statue of the **Señor de la Vera Cruz**, the deeply venerated patron saint of Potosí, which stands behind the altar. According to legend this statue of a crucified Christ appeared in front of the church one morning in 1550 and was adopted by the Franciscans. Christ's beard is made of real human hair and is said to need regular trimming, while the cross is also thought to grow a little each year – some believe the world will end when it reaches the floor of the church. The climb up onto the roof of the church is well worth it for the panoramic **views** of Cerro Rico and the rooftops of Potosí. You can also visit the **crypts** underneath the church, where the skulls of the monks and wealthy citizens buried here lie in heaps.

Ingenio San Marcos

Three blocks east of San Francisco along Nogales and a block south down Calle La Paz is the **Ingenio San Marcos** (Mon–Sat 2.30–6.30pm; $0.70), Potosí's only colonial-era silver foundry to have survived in a reasonable state of preservation. The *ingenio* has recently been restored and converted into a museum which provides a fascinating insight into what was, in the sixteenth and seventeenth centuries, the biggest industrial mining complex in the world. The *ingenio* was one of eighty or so foundries built in the late sixteenth century as part of the modernization programme introduced by Viceroy Toledo to improve silver production. Previously, ore had been smelted on Cerro Rico itself by the indigenous miners in small ovens known as *huayras* (Quechua for wind).

Though the surrounding area is still covered by rubble and the ruins of other defunct industrial installations, much of the colonial machinery in San Marcos is still intact. You can see the raised stone canal that carried water from the lakes and reservoirs in the mountains above the city – the water was used to power the huge waterwheel and heavy stone hammers which crushed the ore for processing – as well as the nineteenth-century furnaces used to cook the mineral ore to remove impurities before processing. Far more machinery from the age of steel and steam – including pistons to crush ore, water turbines and huge machines that used vibrations to separate different kinds of ore – is on display inside the old Republican-era plant. This also houses the *San Marcos* **restaurant** (see p.187), so if you come here to eat outside the official opening hours you can still have a look around the museum, though without the benefit of the knowledgeable guides who otherwise accompany visitors.

La Merced to San Martín

Back in the centre of town, a block east of Plaza 6 de Agosto along Calle Hoyos, stands the **Iglesia de la Merced**, completed in 1687 alongside a Mercedarian monastery dating back to 1555, with a two-level carved stone facade featuring the coat of arms of the Mercedarian order. From here, a 400-metre walk east up Calle Hoyos brings you to the much more impressive **Iglesia de San Martín**, an adobe church with a simple stone portico whose plain exterior belies a beautiful interior. The church was built in 1592 as the parish church for *mita* labourers from the Lupaca tribe, on the shores of Lago Titicaca. Inside, the walls are covered in colonial-era paintings, including individual portraits of all the archangels, whilst behind the altar stands a fabulous wooden retablo smothered in gold leaf and decorated in mestizo-Baroque style with delicately carved and painted flowers and fruit.

Along Calle Bolívar

Returning to La Merced then walking two blocks north brings you to **Calle Bolívar**, a narrow street that bustles with commercial activity as it runs down towards the Mercado Central. As you walk west you'll pass the **Casa de las Tres Portadas**, an eighteenth-century colonial house with wooden balconies hanging over the street and three highly ornate doorways imaginatively decorated with designs including the sun and moon, angels, floral patterns and gargoyle-like faces. The doorways are made of brick covered in plaster rather than carved stone, a reflection of the economic decline Potosí was undergoing by the time they were built.

A short distance further down Bolívar a narrow alley, Calle Chacon, leads off north to the unexceptional **Iglesia de Santa Monica**, originally built in the mid-seventeenth century but remodelled several times since, most recently in the nineteenth century, when the elegant ochre Neoclassical belltower was added. A block further down Bolívar inside a courtyard on the right is the quirky **Museo Universitario** (Mon–Fri 9am–noon & 2–6pm; $0.80), which has a rather haphazard and poorly explained collection of local archeological finds, including the usual deliberately deformed skulls (see p.96), ceramics, arrowheads and Mastodon teeth.

At the end of the same block Bolívar crosses Calle Junín. A short distance off to the left is the **Casa de los Marqueses de Otavi**, a colonial mansion (now occupied by the Banco Nacional de Bolivia) with a strikingly carved mestizo-Baroque stone facade – unusual in a non-religious building – featuring two lions with near-human faces holding aloft a coat of arms, flanked by images of the sun and moon. If you turn right down Calle Junín and then right again you'll reach the narrow, twisting alley known as **El Pasaje de las Siete Vueltas** ("Seven-turn Passage"), the only remnant in the Spanish city centre of the disorderly street plan which existed before Viceroy Toledo ordered it relaid.

Just east of the intersection with Junín on the right-hand side is the seventeenth-century **Iglesia de San Agustín**, which was the church used by Potosí's substantial Basque community in the colonial era. Only the simple but elegant Renaissance portico survives from the original structure, and the bare interior is rarely open.

San Lorenzo de Carangas

Another block down Bolívar is the bustling **Mercado Central**, Potosí's lively covered central market – some of the stallholders here still wear the tall, wide-rimmed stove-pipe hats that are the traditional attire of Potosina women. Behind the market on the corner of Bustillos and Heroes del Chaco stands the spectacular **Iglesia de San Lorenzo de Carangas**, whose splendid carved stone portal is perhaps the defining example of the mestizo-Baroque architectural style in Potosí. One of the first churches in Potosí when it was built in the mid-sixteenth century, it was initially called La Anunciación and used only by the Spanish, but was renamed a few decades later when it became the parish church for *mitayos* belonging to the Carangas tribe from the Lago Poopó region.

The richly decorated **doorway** was created by indigenous craftsmen in the eighteenth century, when the church was thoroughly remodelled. It features fantastically intricate floral patterns intertwined with twisting vines laden with grapes and angels' faces, while the inner arch on either side of the door is supported by bizarre carved figures of bare-breasted women. Stranger still are the mermaids who strum guitars above the doorway. Surrounded by a carved sun, moon and stars – classic Andean religious iconography – these sirens are thought to represent creatures who figure in legends of the powerful mountain god Thunupa, a volcano on the Altiplano south of Oruro. The central niche above the doorway is occupied by a winged archangel dressed in contemporary Spanish costume and armed with sword and shield – a suggestion, perhaps, that the indigenous artists were well aware of the contradiction between the ideals of Christianity and the harsh military reality which underwrote Spanish power and the presence of the Catholic Church in the Andes.

San Bernardo and Jerusalén

From the Mercado Central, Calle Oruro runs northwest down to the university and the **Plaza del Estudiante**, which is flanked by two colonial churches. On the south side stands the bulky **Iglesia de San Bernardo**, built from uncut stone blocks and completed in 1731. It now houses the workshops used in the ongoing restoration of Potosí's churches and other historic buildings, and though it's not officially open to the public, you can usually have a peep inside at the stone and wood carvings which are taken there for restoration. On the north side of the plaza, the small, late seventeenth-century **Iglesia de Jerusalén** (Mon–Fri 3–7pm, Sat 9am–noon; $1, or free with tickets for Santa Teresa – see p.178) has been converted into a museum featuring yet more colonial religious art. There's some good stuff here, including an extravagant eighteenth-century mestizo-Baroque retablo smothered in gold leaf, and an ornate carved pulpit decorated with tiny pictures painted on bronze by Melchor Peréz de Holguín. Of the many paintings of religious scenes, the most unusual is a portrait of **Francisco de Aguirre**, a wealthy mine owner who turned his back on worldly goods to become a priest, and is now buried in the walls of the church. In the picture (to the right as you face the altar) Aguirre holds his heart in his hand to surrender to Christ, whilst stepping on a prostrate Cupid (in rejection of his womanizing past) and ignoring the calls of his erstwhile friends, who are attempting to inveigle him back to a life of vice.

The southern outskirts

South of the city centre, the lower slopes of Cerro Rico were formerly the site of ten of the fourteen *parroquias de Indios* (Indian parishes), which were established to house the many thousands of indigenous labourers who came here to work in the mines under the *mita* system. The Indian parishes were divided from the Spanish city centre by **La Ribera**, an artificial river built to provide water for the foundries (*ingenios*) in which ore was processed, and though the waters of the river now run underground, the difference between the two halves of the city is still quite pronounced. The southern side was never laid out according to Spanish colonial town-planning regulations, and so the street plan is much more disordered, with narrow, cobbled streets winding between crumbling colonial and nineteenth-century houses of adobe or rough-cut stone, topped with sagging tiled roofs. These are interspersed with more modern but equally ramshackle brick homes that creep up the slope of Cerro Rico, ending with rows of semi-abandoned tin-roofed miners' cottages built by the state in the 1960s and 1970s. Many of the colonial parish **churches** still survive, though they're by no means as spectacular as those in the city centre and their interiors are rarely open to the public – the best time to catch a glimpse inside them is on Saturday evening or Sunday morning between 7.30am and 9am.

From the **Arco de Cobija**, the colonial arch which marks the old border between the indigenous and Spanish cities, Calle Mejillones leads uphill and southwest to a second arch, the **Arco de Mejillones**, and then down to the Plaza Diego Huallpa and the crumbling **Iglesia de San Benito**, which was the parish church for *mitayos* from the Cochabamba region and the Collas of

Orcosuyo. Originally built between 1711 and 1727 and extensively modified since, San Benito is a hulking structure of rough cut stone with nine white-washed domes that give it the appearance of a mosque. On your way back up Mejillones on the right you can see the simple, ochre-painted adobe tower that's all that remains of the **Iglesia de Santa Bárbara**, which dates from the earliest years of the city and was the parish church of the Collas from Omasuyos. If you then turn right and work your way east along Calle Guzmán you'll reach the **Iglesia de Copacabana**, completed in 1685 in honour of the Virgin of Copacabana and notable for the *mudéjar* carved wooden ceiling and the stone retablo behind the altar.

Continue east from here then turn south after three blocks to reach the **Iglesia de San Pedro**, whose simple, whitewashed mestizo-Baroque facade dates from 1725, when the church was rebuilt. A couple of blocks southeast of here is the **Plaza El Minero**, centred on a statue of a revolutionary miner who stands helmeted and bare-chested above an open mine shaft with a drill in one hand and a rifle raised triumphantly above his head in the other. In a city full of monuments to the glory of God, this is one of only two dedicated to the people who actually created the city's wealth. From here you can make your way southeast to **Plaza El Calvario** at the top of Calle Hernandez, where you'll find shops and stalls selling all manner of mining supplies, including essentials such as coca, alcohol and dynamite – tours stop here on their way up to visit the mines at Cerro Rico. For an alternate route back down to the city centre from the Plaza Minero, head down Calle Arenas to the north. A block before you reach the Ingenio San Marcos you'll pass the **Iglesia de San Sebastián**, the parish church for *mitayos* from Canchis in what is now southern Peru. Originally built in 1581, the church lost most of its distinctive mestizo-Baroque features when it was restored in 1854, but still boasts an elegant portico decorated with a distinctive shell motif.

Cerro Rico

There are those who, having entered only out of curiosity to see that horrible labyrinth, have come out totally robbed of colour, grinding their teeth and unable to pronounce a word; they have not known even how to ponder it nor make reference to the horrors that are in there.

Bartolomé Arzans de Orsua,
Historia de la Villa Imperial de Potosí, 1703

Immediately south of Potosí the near-perfect cone of **Cerro Rico** (Sumaj Orko in Quechua) rises above the city, its slopes stained in startling hues of red and yellow by centuries of mining waste, and pockmarked with the entrances to the thousands of mines that lead deep into its entrails. Though Potosí's famous silver is now pretty much exhausted, many of the shafts are still worked by miners who eke out a marginal existence from the ores still to be found there. For many travellers a visit to one of the mines is a highlight of their trip to Potosí, an amazing and disturbing journey into the bowels of the earth that also feels like a trip back in time, so primitive are the working conditions inside. No less fascinating are the customs, rituals and beliefs that sustain the Quechua-speaking miners in their back-breaking labour.

All the agencies listed in the box on p.175 run regular **tours** to the mines. These last half a day and should cost the official rate of $10 per person, though some companies charge less than this, particularly outside the June to September high season. Almost all the guides are former miners themselves and so really know what they're talking about, though few speak more than limited English. Groups should be no bigger than eight people, and you should be provided with rubber boots, a mining jacket or overalls, safety helmet and headlamp. Be warned, though, that this is an unpleasant and highly dangerous environment, where **safety precautions** are largely left to supernatural forces. The mines are dirty, wet, muddy and very claustrophobic. The air inside is fetid with dust and gases, including arsenic, and the chances of being hit by falling rocks or a speeding mine trolley are real. Many of the tunnels are narrow and have low ceilings, and temperatures can reach over 40°C, so walking and crawling through the mines would be exhausting even if the entrances weren't situated at over 4000m above sea level. Of every group of eight or so visitors, one or two usually head for the exit within ten minutes of entering the mine – if you don't like it, your guide will lead you out. Once inside the mine, tours generally involve walking, crawling and clambering through often dirty and narrow tunnels deep underground for two or three hours – you should be reasonably fit and altitude acclimatized, and it's not a good idea to visit if you have heart or respiratory difficulties or are claustrophobic. Some people also question the ethics of making a tourist attraction of a workplace where conditions are so appalling. That said, however, most people who do visit the mines find the experience one of the most unforgettable in Bolivia.

Tours of the mines begin with a visit to the **miners' market** on and around Plaza El Calvario, where you can buy coca, dynamite, black-tobacco cigarettes, pure cane alcohol and fizzy soft drinks – you should take a selection of these as gifts for the miners you'll be visiting. About 7000 miners still work in Cerro Rico, including 1000 children, divided between around 27 different mining cooperatives. The most commonly visited mines include Candelaria, Santa Rita, Santa Rosita and Rosario.

Most of the miners are reworking old colonial silver mines for tin, lead and other less valuable metals, so the **entrances** to the shafts tend to be lined with stone facing dating back to the colonial era. As you descend deeper, though, the passageways become narrower and less well made. When a vein of ore is discovered a dynamite charge is placed to break up the rock, which is then extracted using picks and crowbars and carried up to the main shaft on the backs of men, then taken to the surface on a wheeled wagon running along narrow rails. The miners work in shift teams who divide the profits of what they extract on an equal basis, though some of those working in the mines – particularly the children – are paid a fixed daily wage as employees. The miners are generally proud of their work and the hardship they endure, and are usually happy to talk about their lives with visitors. Many of the miners previously worked in large state-run mines, but were made redundant after the great tin crash of 1985; others are campesinos who come to work in the mines for short periods on a seasonal basis. Few earn more than a marginal living, though stories abound of those who have struck lucky and uncovered a rich silver seam – the dream of making such a discovery sustains many in their labour, though the price of pursuing this dream is invariably an early grave. Life expectancy in the mines is about fifteen years, with most miners falling victim to silicosis, a deadly lung disease caused by inhaling silicon dust. Cave-ins and other accidents claim the lives of many others. Most of the mining cooperatives run limited pension and life-insurance schemes, though these are seldom sufficient to support the family of a miner who loses his life.

Given such terrible working conditions, it's no surprise that the miners turn to stimulants and religion to help them through the day. Few eat when they are underground, even during long shifts, relying for sustenance instead on coca leaves, harsh black-tobacco cigarettes and the occasional swig of neat cane

Sympathy for the Devil: El Tío

In every mine, usually in an alcove just beyond the point from which the last ray of sunlight can be seen, you'll find a statue of a sinister horned and bearded figure complete with erect phallus and leering smile. Known as **El Tío** – Uncle – this demonic character is considered the king of the underworld, to whom sacrifices must be made and homage paid if miners are to find rich mineral deposits and emerge from the mine unscathed. El Tío is given regular libations of alcohol and offerings of coca and lit cigarettes, particularly on Fridays, when the miners spend an hour or more sitting together with their Tío drinking and chewing coca. At certain times of the year, blood sacrifices are also made to the Tío, with llamas being slaughtered outside the mine entrance to assuage a thirst for blood which might otherwise be satisfied only by the death of a miner. Though El Tío is clearly related to pre-Columbian mountain deities and is never referred to as the Devil by name, there's little doubt that he owes much to Christian belief. When the first *mitayos* heard Spanish priests describe heaven and hell, they can only have concluded that the mines were hell itself. If that was so, then they were working in the Devil's domain, and it was to him that they had to look for succour. To this day most miners are Christians when above ground, taking part in fiestas and worshipping Christ and the Virgin. But once inside the mines, it is to the owner of the minerals and the king of the underworld that they pray.

alcohol. Today, as in the colonial era, coca is considered an essential requirement without which work in the mines would be impossible. Miners spend a good hour chewing coca before entering the shaft to begin work, and all agree that it helps them endure the heat, exhaustion and backbreaking labour. Coca, tobacco and alcohol are also taken in as offerings to **El Tío** – the supernatural being who is believed to own the mine's silver and other metals (see box above).

Eating, drinking and nightlife

Potosí's popularity with travellers is reflected in the city's growing variety of **places to eat**, with more and more cafés and restaurants offering vegetarian food and travellers' favourites like pizza and pasta. Don't miss out, though, on the tasty and distinctive local cuisine, particularly the thick, warming, carbohydrate-laden soups and meat dishes cooked in spicy sauces. The **Mercado Central** on Calle Bolívar is the best place to eat if you're on a budget, with coffee, pastries and *apí* – a delicious hot thick maize drink flavoured with cloves and cinnamon – served up from early in the morning, as well as juices, soups and main courses throughout the day. The *salteñas* and *empanadas* sold by street vendors throughout the city also make tasty snacks.

Outside the main fiestas, local **nightlife** is fairly low key. A few of the city's restaurants and cafés double as **bars** where you can escape the night-time cold with a warming *singani* or a beer, and several places stage frequent **live folk music** performances.

Café Cultural Kaypichu Millares 16. Well-prepared vegetarian food including muesli and fruit salads, a good-value set almuerzo, substantial salads and sandwiches, and good pizza and pasta. It's decorated with beautiful local weavings and the mellow atmosphere is spoiled only by the sometimes grumpy service. Closed Mon.

Café Top Matos and Boulevard. Cosy candlelit hideaway serving the closest you'll get to a decent cup of coffee in Potosí, a wide-range of liqueur-laced hot drinks to chase the cold away, and an impressive range of cocktails.

Chaplin Matos and Quijjaro. Friendly little café attracting a young local crowd with a wide range of inexpensive snacks, including burgers and delicious empanadas, as well as juices and decent coffee. Closed Sun.

Cherry's Salón de Té Padilla 8. Refined tearoom which is extremely popular for its very good home-made cakes, biscuits, pastries and pies. Also serves fairly good pasta and other more substantial dishes.

Da Tong Bustillos and Frias. Good-value Chinese restaurant with fast servings of large, straightforward rice and noodle dishes. It's popular with locals, especially on Sunday nights.

Den Danske Café Corner of Quijjaro and Matos. Laid-back gringo café offering a wide range of international snacks and meals, served at a very slow pace. Favourites include good meat and vegetarian lasagne, Danish meatballs, burgers and chicken curry, as well as an extensive selection of herbal teas, listed alongside the maladies they can be used to treat.

Doña Eugenia Opposite the cemetery just off Chayanta. Popular and inexpensive little restaurant on the outskirts of the town which is worth visiting as it's about the only place you can still get *kala phurka*, a thick, spicy maize soup served in earthenware bowls into which a hot stone is plunged just before serving, so it stays piping hot and bubbles like a volcano as you eat it.

La Candelaria Ayacucho 5. Mellow first-floor travellers' café opposite the Casa Real de la Moneda serving up a combination of traditional Bolivian dishes like roast llama and international favourites like pizza and burgers. It opens early for breakfast, and also has tasty cakes and snacks, a good vegetarian set almuerzo ($1.50), as well as a book exchange, tourist information and internet access.

La Manzana Magica Oruro 239. Welcoming hole-in-the-wall vegetarian restaurant serving hearty breakfasts, good-value set almuerzos and a wide variety of salads and snacks, including seven different kinds of veggie-burger. Closed Sun evening.

Le Boulevard Bolívar 853. Upmarket French restaurant serving a mix of French and Bolivian

dishes. It's popular at lunchtime for its good set almuerzo, but less so in the evening, when à la carte dishes go for about $4.

Pizzeria Argentina Padilla just off Plaza 6 de Agosto. Popular with local students, this place dishes up inexpensive and reasonably good pizza – you can order either a full pizza or just a slice. Closed Sun.

Potocchi Millares 13. Small café-restaurant serving reasonable traditional Bolivian and international food – it's worth visiting for the live folkloric music shows it hosts several nights a week, when there's a small cover charge.

Pub La Casona Frias 41. The liveliest nightspot in town, housed in an eighteenth-century mansion whose inside walls are decorated with contemporary graffiti. The atmosphere is friendly, with ice-cold beer and good but expensive food including excellent trout. Live folk music on Thurs nights.

San Marcos Inside the Ingenio San Marcos museum, La Paz with Betanzos. One of the best restaurants in town, with glass tables mounted on restored pieces of nineteenth-century industrial machinery and a menu of hearty Bolivian traditional dishes like llama steak for about $5, plus an excellent set almuerzo for just under $3. You can also have a look round the museum (see p.181) while you're here.

Sumaj Orcko Quijjaro 46. Inexpensive restaurant serving large portions of hearty rural cuisine and good-value set almuerzos. Regional specialities worth trying here include *picante de viscacha* – a large Andean rabbit-like animal cooked in a spicy sauce – and *perdiz* – a partridge-like game bird. Closed Sun.

Tukos Third floor, Junin 9. This self-styled "highest cyber café in the world" serves coffee, juices, beer, snacks, good breakfasts and main courses like pasta and pizza in a warm and friendly atmosphere. There are also internet terminals, a pool table, chess, books and newspapers, and occasional live music.

Shopping

Unsurprisingly, Potosí is home to a fair number of **silversmiths**, though they tend to produce traditional religious ornaments and household items like teaspoons rather than fashionable jewellery. There are several shops selling silverwork on Bolívar and Sucre, but be careful buying silver from street stalls, especially if it seems very cheap, since its purity is often lower than the sellers would have you believe. A wide variety of beautiful **textiles** (*tejidos*) can also be bought – they're hand-woven by different indigenous groups in the region, the most famous weaving communities including Potolo, Chayanta and Calcha. With their complex, multicoloured designs, laden with symbolism, these make excellent souvenirs, though larger pieces, like the ponchos worn by men and the *llijllas* (shawls) worn by women, can cost $50–100 if the quality is good,

Moving on from Potosí

Buses to Cochabamba, La Paz, Oruro, Sucre, Tarija, Tupiza and Villazón depart regularly from the Terminal de Buses on Avenida Universitario. Buses for **Uyuni** leave from the various bus company offices on the corner of Avenida Universitario and Sevilla, two blocks up from the terminal. Most long-distance departures are in the morning or evening for overnight journeys – you can check departure times by calling the **bus information office** (daily 7am–noon & 2–8pm; ☏02/6227354). Ticket offices are on the first floor, and departing passengers must buy a $0.30 ticket to use the terminal before boarding their bus. If you're heading to **Sucre** you can save time by travelling in one of the collective taxis that depart from the back of the bus terminal as soon as they have at least four passengers. These are faster, more comfortable and depart more frequently than the buses, and cost only about $1 more per person. Though Potosí has an **airport**, there are no regular passenger services. The nearest airport with scheduled flights is at Sucre, about three hours away by road. You can buy airline tickets in advance from LAB (☏02/6222492) inside the *Hotel Turista* on Lanza, or from Aerosur (☏02/6228988) on Cobija.

even more if they are antique. If your budget doesn't stretch to this, you can always buy a smaller *chumpi* (a kind of waistband) or a knitted woollen hat for a dollar or two. Textiles are sold from shops on Sucre and in the **Mercado Artesanal** on the corner of Sucre and Omiste, where you can also find a good range of other souvenirs including beautiful hand-crafted **musical instruments** like charangos and many different types of Andean reed pipes and flutes. There's also a cooperative shop selling weavings from Calcha beside the Ingenio San Marcos on La Paz.

Listings

Banks and exchange The Banco Nacional de Bolivia on Bolívar changes cash and travellers' cheques, and several shops along Bolívar change US dollars cash. There are several ATMs where you can withdraw cash on Visa or Mastercard, including the Banco Mercantil, on Padilla and Hoyos, and Banco de Crédito, on Bolívar and Sucre.
Bus information ☏02/6227354.
Doctor Clínica Británica, Oruro 221 ☏02/6225888.

Internet access There are plenty of internet cafés in town: try *Tuko's*, on the third floor at the corner of Junín and Bolívar, or *Candelaria*, on Ayacucho opposite the Casa Real de la Moneda.
Laundry La Veloz, corner of Quijjaro and Matos.
Post office Correo Central, a block south of Plaza 10 de Noviembre on Lanza and Chuquisaca.
Telephone office ENTEL, Av Camacho and Plaza Arce.

Around Potosí

There a couple of good excursions from Potosí. Immediately southeast of the city, the **Cordillera Kari Kari** is a good place for hiking amidst the lakes which provided water for the silver-processing *ingenios*. To the northeast, the natural **hot springs** at Tarapaya make a good place to relax and get the Altiplano cold out of your bones.

Cordillera Kari Kari

The **Cordillera Kari Kari** is home to a network of artificial lakes, dams, aqueducts and dykes which Viceroy Toledo ordered built in the late sixteenth century to ensure the supply of water to the *ingenios* in Potosí. By contemporary standards, the artificial lakes represented a monumental feat of construction, employing 20,000 indigenous forced labourers and taking the best part of half a century to complete. During peak silver production there were 32 lakes, but only a few now survive to supply the city's water. In 1625 the retaining wall supporting San Sebastian lake burst, washing away entire blocks of the city and killing thousands of people.

Set amid arid red-brown mountains, the lakes are easily reached from the city and make a good place for one or two days' **hiking**, albeit at altitudes of up to 5000m. If you're planning to stay overnight you'll need your own food and camping gear, and you'll have to be prepared for sub-zero temperatures. Alternatively, you can go on organized trip with one of the tour companies in Potosí (see box on p.175), who will organize food, camping equipment and transport. To reach the lakes by foot, walk up to Plaza Sucre along Calle Chuquisaca, then follow the road to the southeast that turns into a track leading up into the mountains. The first lake, about 5km from the city centre, is **Laguna San Sebastián**, which is supported by a massive restraining wall, built by hand in the sixteenth century. From here you can head across the ridge to the northeast to **Laguna San Idelfonso**, about 1.5km away, or continue south along the remains of an abandoned aqueduct towards lagunas **Pisco Cocha** and **Chalaviri**. Keep sight of Cerro Rico and you shouldn't have any problems finding your way back to Potosí.

Tinku: ritual combat in the Andes

Of all the traditions practised by indigenous communities in the Bolivian Andes, perhaps none appears so strange to outsiders as the **Tinku**, a form of ritual hand-to-hand combat that still takes place on certain feast days in some small rural towns in the northern areas of Potosí department. During the *Tinku*, young men from two rival communities (*ayllus*) take turns to engage in bloody one-on-one fist fights in the midst of a drunken and raucous fiesta. The young fighters wear leather helmets modelled on those worn by the Spanish conquistadors, and leather breastplates for protection. They bind their fists with woven belts, sometimes adding a stone in the palm of their hand to add extra force to their blows.

The two- or three-day fiestas start with the arrival of the young men from their home villages, marching in close order and playing long pan-pipes known as *suqusu*. The individual clashes take place in a charged atmosphere of music, dancing and drunkenness. Townspeople and sometimes the police oversee proceedings, but as the fiesta goes on things often escalate beyond their control, with pitched battles between rival *ayllus* breaking out, and it's rare for a year to go by without someone being killed in the *Tinku* somewhere in the northern Potosí region. That said, bloodshed is perhaps the most important part of the ritual: as well as serving as a warlike rite of passage for young men, the *Tinku* acts as a fertility rite during which blood must be shed on both sides to satisfy the earth goddess, Pachamama, and ensure a bountiful harvest. The *Tinku* is also an important way of reaffirming indigenous cultural identity, and can help defuse all too real conflicts between communities that can otherwise erupt into more serious violence. Unmarried young women also sometimes fight in the *Tinku*, though their aim is usually to pull hair and rip clothes rather than draw blood. The Bolivian authorities generally disapprove, considering the *Tinku* primitive and atavistic, although anyone who's seen the blood lust of spectators at a boxing match will recognize that such violent rituals are by no means confined to the Andes.

The best known *Tinku* takes place in the community of **Macha**, north of Potosí, in the first week of May, but there are several others in small villages in the region at other times of the year (including Torotoro; see p.252). It is possible to visit these fiestas, and one or two tour companies in Potosí (see p.175) take groups along each year. Be warned, though, that these violent and alcoholic spectacles often get out of hand and it's easy for an outsider to unwittingly provoke trouble. If you do visit, go with a Bolivian guide who knows the area, stay clear of the crowds, don't take photographs without permission and generally exercise maximum cultural sensitivity.

Tarapaya hot springs

For something more relaxing, the *aguas termales* (hot springs) at **Tarapaya**, 25km northeast of Potosí, can be visited as a half-day trip from the city. Known as **El Ojo del Inca** (The Eye of the Inca), the natural hot spring bubbles up into a perfectly circular pool about fifty metres in diameter – it's believed to have curative powers and, according to legend, was visited by Inca Huayna Capac for just this purpose. The greenish waters are pleasantly warm, though as with all hot springs you should check the temperature before jumping in. Locals advise strongly against swimming out into the bubbling centre of the pool, where they say occasional whirlpools can suck unwary bathers to their doom – best be careful and stay close to the edge.

Micros to Tarapaya leave every half-hour or so from Avenida Universitaria. To get to the Ojo del Inca, take a micro to Tarapaya and ask to be dropped off just after the bridge before Tarapaya, from where it's a ten-minute walk up the track that climbs to the left. Alternatively, a return trip by **taxi** (with around an hour's waiting time at the spring) will cost about $8. There are further hot springs beyond Tarapaya in the resort village of **Miraflores**, but these have been channelled into drab concrete swimming pools that are usually busy with local children and lack the natural appeal of the Ojo del Inca.

Uyuni

Set on the bleak southern Altiplano 212km southwest of Potosí, the cold and windswept railway town of **UYUNI** has little to recommend it except its usefulness as a jumping-off point for expeditions into the beautiful and remote landscapes of the far southwest. Founded in 1889 at the junction of the railways that enter Bolivia from Chile and Argentina, in its heyday Uyuni was Bolivia's main gateway to the outside world and a symbol of modernity and industrial progress. Today, by contrast, its streets are lined with a collection of shabby, tin-roofed houses and semi-abandoned railway yards filled with the decaying skeletons of redundant trains. Given the decline in the fortunes of Bolivia's railways, it's surprising Uyuni hasn't become a ghost town like many of the mining settlements whose ore exports once passed through it. That it hasn't is due to the ever-growing number of travellers who come here to visit the spectacular scenery of the **Salar de Uyuni** and the **Reserva de Fauna Andina Eduardo Avaroa**, which are usually visited together on a four-day tour from Uyuni.

Arrival and information

Uyuni is a small town, and everything you might need is concentrated within a few blocks. The **train station** is on Avenida Ferroviaría, right in the centre of town. **Buses** from Potosí, Oruro and Tupiza pull up in front of the various bus company offices (an area optimistically described as "the terminal"), three blocks north of the train station along the partly pedestrianized Avenida Arce.

There are a couple of **tourist information offices** in Uyuni. The most useful is run by the Reserva Eduardo Avaroa and is located inside the nineteenth-century clocktower at the junction of avenidas Arce and Potosí (Mon–Fri 9.30am–12.30pm & 2.30–7.30pm; ✆02/6932400). You can pick up a good free leaflet on the reserve here, and they also sell a nice little Spanish-language illustrated guide to the birds of the reserve and a delightful book (available in English or Spanish) about the Salar de Uyuni. You can also pay the reserve entrance fee here, though it's just as easy to pay when you arrive at Laguna

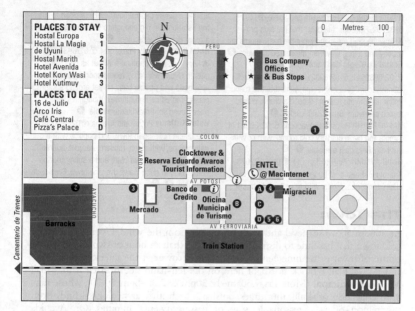

PLACES TO STAY
Hostal Europa	6
Hostal La Magia de Uyuni	1
Hostal Marith	2
Hotel Avenida	5
Hotel Kory Wasi	4
Hotel Kutimuy	3

PLACES TO EAT
16 de Julio	A
Arco Iris	C
Café Central	B
Pizza's Palace	D

UYUNI

Colorada (see p.200). The Oficina Municipal de Turismo is just across the road on the corner of Arce and Potosí, but the opening hours are irregular and even when the staff do turn up they're not much help. It's only really worth coming here if you want to complain about a tour agency. The **tour agencies** themselves, all situated within a few blocks of Avenida Arce, are as a good a source of information as any for planning a trip to the Salar and the reserve, though obviously their main aim is to sell you a trip.

There are several **internet cafés** which open sporadically on and around the clocktower at the intersection of Potosí and Arce – Macinternet is the most reliable. The **ENTEL** office is just south of the clocktower on Avenida Arce. The only **bank** in town is the Banco de Crédito on Potosí between Arce and Bolívar. You can change US dollars here, but they don't cash travellers' cheques or give cash advances on credit cards. Most tour agencies will change dollars and take travellers' cheques as payment, and some occasionally accept payment by credit card and change travellers' cheques for a hefty commission, but it's best not to have to count on it. The **migración** is on Potosí between Arce and Sucre. You'll need to get an exit stamp here if you're heading into Chile by train via Avaroa (see p.193). If you're crossing **into Chile** at Laguna Verde in the Reserva Eduardo Avaroa you can usually get a stamp at the border – check with the tour agency that's taking you or ask at the *migración* just to make sure. If you need extra **warm clothing** for your trip to the Salar you can buy woollen jumpers, hats, gloves, socks and ponchos from the street stalls along Potosí.

Accommodation

There's a limited range of **accommodation** in Uyuni, and most of it is pretty basic, though a couple of more upmarket places now exist where you'll get a warm room and a comfortable bed – most places stay open late for train passengers arriving in the middle of the night. Places can fill up between June and September, when it may be worth booking a room in advance if you're arriving late.

Hostal Europa Av Ferroviaria and Sucre ☎02/ 6932752. Far from "the best" that the sign proclaims: the staff are friendly, but the basic rooms are grubby and a long way from the shared showers. **②**

Hostal La Magia de Uyuni Colón 432 ☎02/6932541, ⓕ02/6932121, ⓔmagia_uyuni@ latinmail.com. Pleasant rooms with attractive rustic decor and private bath set around a warm, plastic-roofed courtyard. Breakfast included. **④**

Hostal Marith Potosí and Ayacucho ☎02/6932174. Simple and clean but very cold rooms, with or without bath. Breakfast available. **②–③**

Hotel Avenida Av Feroviaria 11 ☎02/6932078. The biggest and best budget option in town, with clean, functional rooms with or without bath set around a sunny central courtyard. It's close to the train station and big enough to ensure that getting a room is rarely a problem. **②**

Hotel Kory Wasi Av Potosí 304 ☎02/6932670, ⓔkory_wasi@hotmail.com. About as good as it gets in Uyuni, with cosy rooms sporting comfortable beds and private bath, all set around a sunny, plastic-roofed central hallway, though it's a bit pricey even so. Breakfast available. **④**

Hotel Kutimuy Potosí and Avaroa ☎02/6932391. The tallest building in town, and popular with big tour groups, with clean, modern, parquet-floored rooms (with or without bath) and a sunny rooftop cafeteria with good views over the town. Breakfast available. **②–③**

The Town

At 3668m above sea level and with no shelter from the wind, Uyuni is a bitterly cold town that has little to distract you for more than an hour or two. The effective centre of town is the nineteenth-century **clocktower** at the intersection of Arce and Potosí. Half a block north of here on the left-hand side of Arce is the small **Museo Municipal** (Mon–Fri 9.30am–12.30pm & 2.30–6pm; $0.20), whose random collection of skulls, mummies, potshards and other archeological finds from the region offers a reasonable way of passing twenty minutes. On Avenida Ferroviaria in front of the station are two monuments to the golden age of steam: the first, a **statue** of a railway worker, spanner in hand; the second, a well-maintained **steam locomotive**, made in West Yorkshire in the early twentieth century.

If you've an hour or two to kill, it's worth walking west out of town down Avenida Ferroviaria and along the railway line for about fifteen minutes to the **Cementerio de Trenes** (Train Cemetery). Set on the desolate fringe of the Salar de Uyuni, with good views back towards the town, this graveyard of rusting steam locomotives, passenger carriages and freight wagons that used to carry ore from long-abandoned mines is a sombre monument to the past glory of the age of steam and steel, as well as a popular but dangerous adventure playground for local children.

Eating and drinking

As with accommodation, the range of places **to eat** in Uyuni is pretty limited. There are a few restaurants concentrated around the pedestrianized Plaza Arce, offering generally overpriced and mediocre gringo-oriented food: pizza and American breakfasts are ubiquitous. Otherwise, you can find soups, juices and snacks in the indoor market on Potosí, though it's far from being the most hygienic in Bolivia. If you're heading out to the Salar and beyond for a few days, it's worth taking along some extra food supplies – biscuits, chocolate, fruit and the like – which you can buy from the market and the surrounding shops.

16 de Julio Plaza Arce. Warm, glass-fronted restaurant serving up a good, filling four-course set almuerzo for just over $2, as well as the usual pizza and Bolivian meat dishes.

Arco Iris Plaza Arce. Decent but rather expensive pizza and pasta in a cosy ambience with good background music. Popular with travellers, particularly in the evenings, despite the very slow service.

Café Central Plaza Arce. Tucked away under the bandstand with plenty of outdoor seating where you can soak up the sun's rays while enjoying hot drinks, juices, decent breakfasts and snacks.

Pizza's Palace Plaza Arce. Appropriately named restaurant serving about the best pizza you'll find in Uyuni, though that's not saying much.

If you're heading north to Oruro and beyond, or south to Tupiza and Villazón, you should travel by **train** if possible, as the line passes through stunning scenery – see p.217 for full details of trains and schedules. **Buses** leave from the company offices north of the clocktower. There are several departures to **Potosí** every morning and evening (7–8hr). Buses to **Oruro** (9hr), with connections to **La Paz** (a further 3hr 30min), travel by night only. Buses to **Tupiza** (9hr) operated by Flota 11 de Julio leave twice a week on Wednesdays and Sundays at 10am.

Crossing the Chilean border

There are two ways of **crossing into Chile** from Uyuni. Twice a week, on Mondays at 3am and Thursdays at 2.40pm, a passenger train travels from Uyuni to **Calama** in Chile via the Bolivian border post of **Avaroa**, a spectacular journey along the southern edge of the Salar and through stunning high Andean scenery. If you're travelling this way you'll need to get an exit stamp at the *migración* in Uyuni. A more popular route into Chile is across the border at **Laguna Verde** in the far south of the Reserva Eduardo Avaroa. Most of the tour agencies will happily drop you off here during the tour and arrange transport across the border into Chile and on to the town of **San Pedro de Atacama**. You can get your exit stamp at the border here, though the border officials have been known to charge small unauthorized fees for letting you cross. The best agency to do this with is **Colque Tours**, who have their own transport on the Chilean side and an office in San Pedro de Atacama. Note that by doing this you cross the border only after seeing all the highlights of the standard tour of the Salar de Uyuni and Reserva Eduardo Avaroa, missing out only on the arduous return journey from Laguna Verde to Uyuni.

The far southwest: the Salar de Uyuni and Reserva Eduardo Avaroa

Covering some 9000 square kilometres of the Altiplano west of Uyuni, the **Salar de Uyuni** is by far the biggest salt lake in the world, and one of Bolivia's most extraordinary attractions. The Salar is not a lake in any conventional sense of the word: though below the surface it is largely saturated by water, its uppermost layer consists of a thick, hard crust of salt, easily capable of supporting the weight of a car. Large areas of the surface are covered by water during the rainy season between December and April, but even then it's rarely to a depth of more than a metre, and usually much less. Driving across the perfectly flat white expanse of the Salar, with the unbroken chains of snowcapped mountains lining the far horizon, it's easy to believe you're on another planet, so harsh and inhospitable is the terrain. When dry, the dazzling salt surface shines with such intense whiteness that you'll find yourself reaching down to check that it's not ice or snow, whilst by night the entire landscape is illuminated by the eerie white glow of moonlight reflected in the salt. When it's covered in water after rain, meanwhile, the Salar is turned into an enormous mirror that reflects the surrounding mountain peaks and the sky so perfectly that at times the horizon disappears and the mountains appear like islands floating in the sky.

Covering some 12,000 square kilometres of the Altiplano west of Uyuni, the **Salar de Uyuni** is by far the biggest salt lake in the world, and one of Bolivia's most extraordinary attractions. Set at an altitude of 3653m, its sheer immensity and strangeness are breathtaking, and when driving across the perfectly flat, hard white

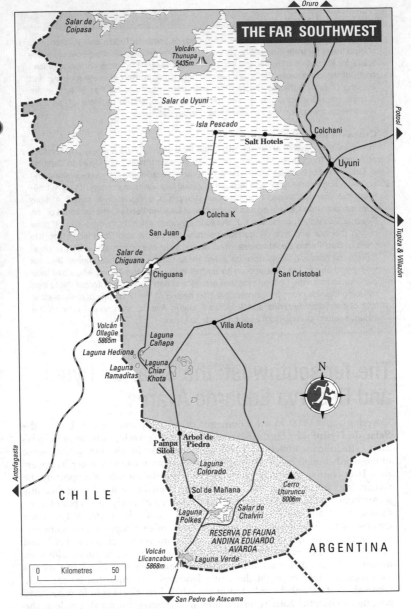

THE FAR SOUTHWEST

Salar de Coipasa

Volcán Thunupa 5435m

Salar de Uyuni

Isla Pescado

Salt Hotels

Colchani

Uyuni

Colcha K

San Juan

Salar de Chiguana

Chiguana

San Cristobal

Volcán Ollagüe 5865m

Laguna Hediona

Laguna Cañapa

Villa Alota

Laguna Chiar Khota

Laguna Ramaditas

Pampa Siloli

Arbol de Piedra

Laguna Colorado

Cerro Uturuncu 6006m

Sol de Mañana

CHILE

Laguna Polkes

Salar de Chalviri

RESERVA DE FAUNA ANDINA EDUARDO AVAROA

ARGENTINA

Volcán Llicancabur 5868m

Laguna Verde

N

0   Kilometres   50

▲ Oruro ▲

Potosí ▶

Tupiza & Villazón ▶

Antofagasta ◀

▼ San Pedro de Atacama

surface of the salt lake, with the unbroken chains of snowcapped mountains lining the far horizon, it's easy to believe you're on another planet, so harsh and inhospitable is the terrain. In addition, the appearance of the Salar changes dramatically depending on whether it's covered in water or not. When dry, the dazzling salt surface of the Salar shines with such intense whiteness that you'll find yourself reaching down to check that it's not ice or snow, whilst by night the entire landscape is illuminated by the eerie white glow of moonlight reflected in the salt. When it's covered in water after rain the Salar is turned into an enormous mirror that reflects the surrounding mountain peaks and the sky so perfectly that at times the horizon disappears and the mountains appear like islands floating in the sky.

No less strange are the tenacious **ecosystems** that survive around the arid and salty margins of the Salar, including colonies of cactuses and other hardy plants, the rabbit-like viscachas that live on the islands in the centre of the lake, and the flamingos that feed and nest here during the rainy season. Equally hardy are the isolated communities of Aymara and Quechua campesinos who eke out a marginal existence on the shores of the Salar, cultivating quinua in the brackish soils and scraping up salt for sale or exchange.

The southwesternmost corner of Bolivia is covered by the **Reserva de Fauna Andina Eduardo Avaroa**, a 7147-square-kilometre wildlife reserve, ranging between 4000m and 6000m in altitude, that encompasses some of the most startling scenery in Bolivia. Like the Salar de Uyuni, the desolate landscapes of this remote region possess a surreal, otherworldly beauty. This is a land of glacial salt lakes whose icy waters are stained bright red or emerald green by micro-organisms or mineral deposits; of snowcapped volcanic peaks and frozen, high-altitude deserts; of rock outcrops scoured by the unremitting wind into strange, Dali-esque formations.

As the name of the reserve suggests, this unforgiving environment supports a wide range of rare **Andean wildlife**, including many species which are rarely seen elsewhere. The algae-rich salt lakes support large colonies of all three South American species of flamingo, including the world's largest population of the rare James flamingo, one of the eighty different bird species found in the reserve. You're almost certain to see large herds of vicuña grazing on the scant vegetation of the high, semi-desert grasslands. Rabbit-like viscachas and even the elusive Andean fox are also frequently spotted.

Visiting the Salar and the reserve

Given their remoteness, pretty much the only way to visit the Salar de Uyuni and Reserva Eduardo Avaroa is on an **organized tour**, which can be easily arranged from Uyuni – you'll usually be able to find space on a tour leaving the next day. Even if you have your own 4WD complete with supplies and navigational aids, you should be very cautious about venturing onto the Salar. It's easy to get lost in the uniform white landscape, while the hard crust on the surface can give way under the weight of vehicles and the consequences of breakdown can be grave. In 2001 a truck carrying a local family home from Uyuni to their village on the other side of the Salar broke down. The passengers tried to walk out but got caught on the Salar after dark; all five froze to death. The Reserva Eduardo Avaroa is equally difficult to visit independently, with a population of only a few hundred people living in isolated llama-herding settlements and mining camps, this remote wilderness has no real roads.

In Uyuni, avenidas Arce, Ferroviaria and Potosí are lined with some two-dozen **tour agencies**, all of which run combined trips to the Salar and the reserve. Some companies run one-day bus excursions out to the Isla de Pescado on the Salar for $20 per person, but if you've come this far it would be crazy not to go for the full circuit. The **standard trip** is a four-day tour by 4WD around a circuit comprising the Salar de Uyuni and Lagunas Colorada and Verde in the reserve. It's difficult to recommend any particular agency: all offer pretty much identical tours, but all are prone to the same problems, and late departures, dangerous drivers, insufficient food, inadequate accommodation and vehi-

△ Arbol de Piedra, Reserva Eduardo Avaroa

cle breakdowns are all possibilities no matter which agency you go with. All the agencies now hand out written contracts detailing exactly what you are paying for; though hardly a cast-iron guarantee, these are at least worth having in case you need to try to get some of your money back if they don't do all they promised. The two most important factors are your vehicle's reliability and your guide's knowledge, but both these are difficult to check before you go and vary over time within individual agencies. As usual, the best advice is to talk to travellers just returned from a tour. Despite all the hassles and potential pitfalls, however, these tours are well worth the trouble, and almost everyone who goes counts them amongst their best experiences in Bolivia.

The **cost** of the standard four-day tour varies between $80 and $110 per person, depending on the time of year. You'll get charged more in peak season (June–Aug) and when the Salar is partly covered in water during the rainy season (Dec–April), since the salt water damages the vehicles – it can sometimes get so deep that parts of the Salar west of the Isla de Pescado become impassable, in which case tours are often rerouted to return to Uyuni from the Salar before going down to Lagunas Colorado and Verde. The agencies all tend to charge about the same price, though if you turn up with a group already formed you may be able to talk your way into a discount. Even if you're travelling alone, though, you should be able to find a group to go with within hours of arriving in Uyuni. The cost includes food, accommodation, transport and Spanish-speaking guide (an English-speaking guide will cost extra). You also have to pay a $4.50 fee to enter the Reserva Eduardo Avaroa, payable in Uyuni or at the rangers' office at Laguna Colorada. Be sure to get a ticket when you pay, as otherwise your money is unlikely to end up funding wildlife protection, as is intended.

The vehicles – almost all of which are Toyota Landcruisers – have room for six or seven passengers plus the driver; if they take seven you should pay a little less. **Accommodation** is in very basic huts or refuges, either on rough bunks or on mats on the floor, unless you pay extra to stay in one of the salt hotels on the Salar de Uyuni (see p.198). **Food** on the trips is usually little more than adequate, so it's worth taking along some extra supplies like chocolate, biscuits and fruit – and maybe a little *singani* to chase away the cold. Bear in mind that this is a wilderness adventure over hundreds of kilometres of very rugged terrain, so that even with the best-maintained vehicle mechanical failures and breakdowns are likely. Drivers from different companies usually help each other out to make sure everyone gets back to Uyuni safely, but don't be too surprised if your four-day trip turns into a six-day odyssey.

Even compared to the rest of the Altiplano, the Reserva Eduardo Avaroa and, especially, the Salar de Uyuni can be extremely **cold**. Though by day the sun can take temperatures as high as 30°C, the high altitude and reflective surface of the Salar mean that little heat is retained, so by night temperatures can drop below –25°C, and as far as –40°C when the wind chill factor is included – one of the widest day–night temperature fluctuations anywhere in the world. Take a good sleeping bag (most agencies will rent you one for the trip for $5) to supplement the blankets which are usually available in the refuges, a warm hat, gloves, a windproof jacket and several layers of clothing including a fleece or woollen jumper and, ideally, thermal underwear. You should also take sun block and sunglasses to counter the fierce glare – snow blindness is a real possibility here.

Uyuni to Colcha K

Tours invariably enter the Salar via **COLCHANI**, a salt-processing village on its eastern shores about 20km north of Uyuni. Here you can see the way locals extract salt, scraping it off the ground into small mounds which are carried off on bicycles or in wheelbarrows for processing. The salt is then dried and has iodine added before being packaged – a legal requirement, as iodine deficiency leads to cretinism and goitre, two ailments once common amongst people who consumed untreated salt from the Salar. Until relatively recently, communities like Colchani exploited the salt primarily as a resource to exchange with other indigenous communities. Every year dozens of pack llamas would set off carrying salt as far away as the department of Tarija, returning with maize, coca and other goods not produced in the Altiplano, though such caravans are a rarity now, and have largely been replaced by trucks. Greyish blocks of salt cut straight from the surface of the Salar are also used as salt licks for cattle, while some villagers carve the salt into ashtrays and other souvenirs which you can buy.

Side by side a few kilometres west of Colchani are two **salt hotels** built from greyish blocks of raw salt cut from the surface of the Salar. It's worth having a look round for the novelty value, and staying out for a night in such unusual buildings is certainly memorable if you can get over the slightly gimmicky feel of both places. Of the two, The **Palacio del Sal** (no phone; ❻) is a larger and more extravagant construction, boasting rooms with domed salt roofs, salt furniture and beds, as well as indoor medicinal salt baths and sauna and a collection of salt sculptures. The **Hotel de Sal Playa Blanca** (☎02/6932772; ❺) is simpler, smaller, cosier and better value than its neighbour. If you want to stay at either as part of your tour of the Salar it's best to book through an agency in Uyuni, Potosí or La Paz – though note that pressure is growing for the hotels to be closed down, amid concern over the impact they may be having on the pristine environment of the Salar. Close to the hotels are several holes in the Salar where water bubbles up from beneath the hard surface crust. Known as **ojos de sal** – salt eyes – these holes are a good place to find beautiful, newly formed salt crystals.

From the salt hotels all tours head 60km or so west across the Salar to the **Isla de Pescado** (Fish Island), one of several small islands in the Salar. More properly known by the traditional name of Inca Wasi – "Inca House" in Quechua. From its peak, a short sharp climb up from the shore on a well-marked trail, the views across the immense white expanse of the Salar are unforgettable. To the north is a series of snow-capped peaks, including the imperious cone of Thunupa, the extinct volcano that is the most powerful *achachila*, or mountain god, in the region. To the west you can just make out a straight line like an old agricultural terrace running along the mountainside that rises from the shore: this is the ancient shoreline of Lago Tauca, 70m above the surface of the Salar. On the island itself, the rocks are covered in **fossilized algae**, another reminder of the prehistoric waters which once covered the entire area.

Marooned in the centre of a lifeless desert of salt, the island manages to support a delicate but extremely tenacious ecosystem despite the harsh climate, low rainfall and thin, brackish soil. Its entire surface is covered by **giant cacti**, some of which are more than ten metres tall and thought to be hundreds of years old. In January and February the cacti produce bright white flowers which attract large numbers of giant hummingbirds to the island from across the Salar, while in March and April they bear an edible fruit called *pasakana* which was until recently harvested by local campesinos. The trunks of these giant cacti are about the only locally available source of wood, and you can see their distinctively pockmarked timber in doors and roofs in villages all around the Salar.

The island gets pretty busy during the June to September high season, with over a dozen different tour groups sometimes visiting on the same day. Some groups **stay overnight** here in one of several basic huts built by an elderly Aymara couple who have come to live on the island since the tourist boom took off. This is well worth doing, as you'll have the island largely to yourself

The Salar de Uyuni in history and legend

According to geologists, the Salar de Uyuni occupies what was once the deepest part of an enormous lake, known as **Lago Tauca**, that covered the southern Altiplano until 12,000 years ago. Reaching depths of up to 70m, Lago Tauca existed for a thousand years and covered the area now occupied by Lago Poopó, the Salar de Coipasa and the Salar de Uyuni – and was itself the successor to an earlier lake, Lago Minchín, that covered the same area to an even greater depth up until 25,000 years ago. The Salar was formed when the last waters of Lago Tauca evaporated, leaving behind salt that had been washed into the lake after being leached by rain from the surrounding mountains, where it had been deposited millions of years ago before the Andes were formed, when what is now Bolivia was beneath the ocean.

Studies of the lake have found that the **salt** extends to depths of up to 120m, packed in layers sandwiched between sedimentary deposits. The top layer, which is about 6m thick, was laid down by the final evaporation of Lago Tauca. In the dry season, the surface of the Salar, up to a depth of 10–20cm, becomes extremely hard and dry. Beneath this crust, though, the salt remains saturated with water. As the top layer dries, it contracts, forming cracks which draw the underlying salt water up by capillary action, thereby forming the strange polygonal lines of raised salt that cover the Salar in the dry season. As well as salt, the Salar is also home to the world's largest deposit of **lithium**, a mineral with a growing number of industrial applications. So far, this has not been exploited, but there are fears that future mining could have disastrous consequences for the fragile ecosystems surrounding the Salar and for the communities that live there.

For the campesinos who live on the shores of the lake, explanations of the Salar's origin are rather different. Legend has it that the mountain goddess **Yana Pollera** – the nearest peak to Uyuni – was amorously involved with both Thunupa, the volcano that rises imperiously on the north shore of the Salar, and a second volcano named Q'osqo. When she gave birth to a child, named Kalikatin, the two male volcanoes fought bitterly over who was the father. Worried for the child's safety, Yana Pollera sent it far away to the west. Then, concerned that her child would not survive alone, she flooded the plain between them with her milk so it could feed. Eventually the milk turned to salt, and the lake – traditionally known as the **Salar de Thunupa** – came into being.

and can enjoy the spectacular sunset from the peak of the island in relative solitude – if you want to do this, you'll have to agree it with the other members of your group and ask your tour company to arrange it before you leave Uyuni. Staying here makes the second day of the circuit a long one, however, and many groups prefer to spend the night in **Colcha K** or one of the other villages on the south shore of the Salar, about ninety minutes' drive away. During the rainy season this part of the Salar is sometimes too deeply flooded to be crossed by car, in which case tours return to Uyuni before continuing down to the Reserva Eduardo Avaroa along the normal return route via San Cristóbal. When it's dry enough, though, they head straight down from Isla de Pescado via Colcha K – this route is described in the following section on the Reserva Eduardo Avaroa.

South from the Salar de Uyuni

From Colcha K, just south of the Salar de Uyuni, it's a 160-kilometre drive down to the **entrance** to the reserve. En route you cross the edge of the smaller Salar de Chiguana and the railway line that runs from Uyuni to the Chilean border – there's also a forlorn military outpost where you may have to show your passport. The rough track then climbs above 4000m and runs past a series of snow-frosted volcanoes straddling the border. One of these, the 5865-metre **Ollagüe**, is Bolivia's only active volcano, and you can usually make out thin plumes of smoke rising from just below its peak – if you have an extra day available, you can actually drive to the summit. The trail south runs through a series of ancient lava fields, with eroded red rock interspersed with stretches of grey dust strewn with black volcanic rocks from past eruptions. It then passes a series of four brackish, blue-white lakes – Cañapa, Hedionda, Ramaditas and Chiar Khota – surrounded by snowy peaks. All four lakes support large colonies of **flamingos** as well as other water birds like ducks and wallata geese, and you're also likely to see herds of vicuña nearby.

The trail then climbs still higher to over 4500m and across the **Pampa Siloli**, a high-altitude desert of volcanic ash and gravel scattered with rock outcrops that have been sand-blasted into surreal shapes by the constant, howling winds. The strangest of these is the **Arbol de Piedra** (Stone Tree), a massive boulder eight metres high which balances on a narrow stem. Even the hardy Andean grasses struggle to survive in this harsh desert environment, but amongst the rock outcroppings you may catch a glimpse of a viscacha or an Andean fox – both are encouraged to provide photo opportunities by passing tour drivers, who leave food for them.

Laguna Colorada to Laguna Verde

Shortly afterwards the trail enters the Reserva Eduardo Avaroa and drops down to the extraordinary blood-red waters of **Laguna Colorada**, the biggest lake in the reserve. The lake owes its bizarre red colour, which changes in intensity during the day, to the natural pigments of the algae that live in its shallow, mineral-laden water – were it not for the presence of the flamingos and other water birds, it would be easy to think the lake's hue was the result of some mining accident, so unnatural is its appearance. These algae are also a rich source of food for flamingos, all three species of which nest here in large numbers – the lake is thought to be the single biggest nesting site of the rare James flamingo in the world. The fringes of the lake are encrusted with bright white deposits of ice and borax, a mineral used in paint, acid and glass manufacture. The **park office**, where you have to pay the $4.50 entrance fee, is beside the lake, and there are several basic huts and refuges where almost all tour groups spend the night. Be warned that it gets bitterly cold here, with temperatures often dropping below −20°C.

You need to set off before dawn the next morning in sub-zero temperatures to enjoy the full spectacle of the **Sol de Mañana geyser**. Set at an altitude of 5000m amid boiling pools of mud and sulphur, the geyser's high-pressure jet of steam shoots out from the earth to a great height, but diminishes in power once the air temperature rises later in the day. After the geyser the trail drops down to **Laguna Polques**, which has a series of **hot springs** on its southern shore. No matter how cold you may feel, don't miss out on the chance to bathe here – the deliciously warm waters are the perfect antidote to the high-altitude chill.

The next stop, about 30km further on, is **Laguna Verde**, a striking green lake set at over 4300m in the southeasternmost corner of the reserve – and, indeed, of Bolivia. Covering about seventeen square kilometres and divided into two sections by a narrow causeway, the lake owes its dramatic green hues to the arsenic and other minerals which are suspended in its waters – the lake's colour ranges from turquoise to deep emerald depending on how much the wind stirs up its sediments. Above the lake rises the perfect snow-covered cone of **Volcán Licancabur**, a 5868-metre dormant volcano straddling the frontier with

Chile, on the peak of which archeologists recently discovered the ruins of an Inca ceremonial site.

There's a small **refuge** beside the lake where you can spend the night, though most groups press on from here. You can cross into **Chile** at the manned border post about 7km away – it's usually possible to get an exit stamp here, though you'd be strongly advised to get one in advance in Uyuni. If you want to continue into Chile you should let the tour company you're travelling with know before leaving Uyuni, as they should be able to arrange onward transport to **San Pedro de Atacama**, 35km away, which otherwise may be hard to come by.

From Laguna Verde, tours make the 360km or so return trip to Uyuni by a more easterly route, stopping overnight at one of the few scattered llamaherding hamlets or mining camps along the way. The route follows the course of the Río de Lípez, passing through desolate high-Andean scenery which is rarely anything less than spectacular. As you head out of the reserve look out for good views of Laguna Colorada below you in the distance to the west, and for the white peak of the highest mountain in the region, the 6006-metre **Cerro Uturuncu**, to the east.

Tupiza and around

Some 200km southwest of Uyuni, the isolated mining town of **TUPIZA** nestles in a narrow, fertile valley that cuts through the harsh desert landscape of the Cordillera de Chichas. Sheltered from the bitter winds of the Altiplano by the jagged mountains that rise steeply on either side of the valley, the town enjoys a comparatively warm climate. while its friendly and laid-back inhabitants are helping to make it an increasingly popular stop for travellers passing through southern Bolivia. The real attraction, though, is the dramatic **desert scenery** that surrounds Tupiza, a landscape of red, eroded rock formations, cactus-strewn mountains and deep canyons that is ideal for hiking, horse-riding or just touring in a jeep. All these activities are easy to arrange in the town, a peaceful and friendly place where a fledgling but well-organized tourist industry has sprung up to cater to the growing number of foreign visitors.

Tupiza was originally founded in 1535 by the conquistador Diego de Almagro, who passed through here at the head of the first Spanish expedition to penetrate into the southern Andes. For most of its history the town's economy has been dominated by mining operations in the surrounding mountains, where silver, lead, tin, antimony and bismuth were once found in abundance. In the late nineteenth and early twentieth centuries this was the home base of Carlos Aramayo, one of the biggest mining barons in Bolivia, and the mine payrolls were rich enough to attract the attentions of the infamous North American gunslingers **Butch Cassidy** and the **Sundance Kid** (see p.206), who are believed to have died in a shoot-out in the town of San Vicente, some 100km to the northwest. Today, though, the mineral deposits are largely exhausted or simply no longer worth mining due to declining metal prices, and Tupiza's economy depends more on its role as a market centre for the agricultural communities of the surrounding region and, increasingly, on tourism.

Arrival and information

Tupiza is a small town and it's easy to find your way around. The **bus terminal** (☎0694/2501) is on Avenida Araya, three blocks south and two blocks east of the main square, Plaza Independencia. The **train station** (☎0694/2529) is three

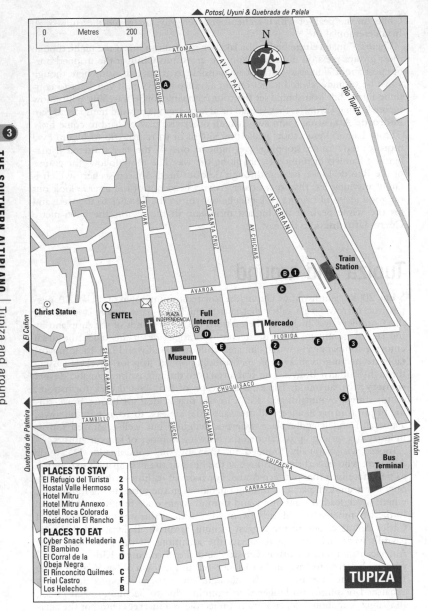

El Cañon

Quebrada de Palmira

Villazón

PLACES TO STAY
El Refugio del Turista	2
Hostal Valle Hermoso	3
Hotel Mitru	4
Hotel Mitru Annexo	1
Hotel Roca Colorada	6
Residencial El Rancho	5

PLACES TO EAT
Cyber Snack Heladeria	A
El Bambino	E
El Corral de la Obeja Negra	D
El Rinconcito Quilmes	C
Frial Castro	F
Los Helechos	B

TUPIZA

blocks east of the main plaza on Avenida Serrudo. **Taxis** wait for arriving passengers at both locations, but everything is so close that you may as well walk. There's no formal **tourist information** office in the town, but the two main tour operators – Tupiza Tours, inside the *Hotel Mitru* on Avenida Chichas, and Valle Hermoso tours, opposite the hotel of the same name – can tell you all you need to know, though obviously with a view to selling you some kind of trip.

Organized tours from Tupiza

Tupiza's three **tour agencies** all offer broadly similar guided excursions into the desert landscapes around the town in 4WDs or on horseback, as well as longer trips to **San Vicente** (see p.207), where Butch Cassidy and the Sundance Kid are thought to have died, and **Huaca Huañusca** (see p.207), where they committed their final robbery. Horse-riding trips cost a uniform $2.70 per person per hour, including mount and guide. Jeep excursions cost about $70 per day for a vehicle seating up to six, while a long day-trip to San Vicente should cost about $100 per vehicle – it's rarely a problem finding people to go with. Tupiza's agencies can also organize trips to the **Reserva de Fauna Andina Eduardo Avaroa** and the **Salar de Uyuni**, entering the reserve via the remote Sur Lípez region, heading north into the Salar and then either dropping you off in Uyuni or returning to Tupiza along the main road. This four-day circuit should cost about $100 per person in a jeep with at least four passengers.

Explore Andina Tours Av Chichas 220, inside the *Hotel Roca Colorada* ☎02/6943016. The smallest and newest of the three agencies, offering the usual local horse and jeep tours as well as the Salar de Uyuni circuit. They also rent self-drive jeeps out for about $70 per day.

Tupiza Tours Av Chichas 187, inside the *Hotel Mitru* ☎02/6943001, ⓦwww.tupizatours.com. This is the oldest and biggest operator in Tupiza, running regular and highly efficient jeep and horse-riding excursions as well as longer trips, including a two-day jeep tour following the last steps of Butch and Sundance to Huaca Huañusca and San Vicente.

Valle Hermoso Tours Av Pedro Araya, opposite the *Hostal Valle Hermoso* ☎02/6942370, Ⓕ02/6942592, ⓦwww.bolivia.freehosting.net. Offer the same local horseback and jeep tours as their rivals, as well as longer horseback camping trips (1–4 days).

Several cambios east of the plaza on Calle Avaroa will change **travellers' cheques**, as well as US dollars and Argentine pesos. Tupiza Tours, inside the *Hotel Mitru*, and the *Hostal Valle Hermoso* also change US dollars, Argentine pesos and travellers' cheques, and may also give cash advances on credit cards. There's expensive **internet access** ($2/hr) at Cyber Snack Heladería, on Chorolque, and at Full Internet on the plaza. The **post office** is just west of Plaza Independencia on Avaroa, while the **ENTEL** office is on the corner of Calle Avaroa and Avenida Aramayo, a block west of the plaza.

Accommodation

There's only a small range of **accommodation** in Tupiza, all of it inexpensive and relatively simple, and aimed specifically at backpackers on limited budgets. Half the places listed are under the management of the *Hotel Mitru* chain, which controls much of Tupiza's incipient tourism boom, but they do a good job of meeting travellers' needs, as do their emerging rivals.

El Refugio del Turista Av Chichas and Florida ☎02/6943003. Next door to the Hotel Mitru and under the same management, but with simpler rooms with shared bath, pleasant outdoor garden seating and the use of a kitchen. ❷

Hostal Valle Hermoso Av Pedro Araya 478 ☎02/6942370, Ⓕ02/6942592, ⓦwww.bolivia.freehosting.net. Welcoming and helpful establishment, with recently refurbished,

clean and sunny rooms, with or without bath. There's also a comfortable common room with TV and a rooftop terrace, and breakfast and laundry service are available. ❷–❸

Hotel Mitru Av Chichas 187 ☎02/6943001, ⓦwww.tupizatours.com. This friendly place has clean, simple rooms with or without bath, set around a sunny central courtyard – its popularity makes it a good place to organize groups for tours.

Breakfast available. ❷–❸

Hotel Mitru Annexo Av Avaroa and Chichas
⊕02/6943002. Just around the corner from the
original Hotel Mitru, with the same facilities and
welcoming atmosphere. ❷–❸

Hotel Roca Colorada Av Chichas and
Chuquisaca ⊕02/6943016. The plushest place in

town, with cosy rooms with or without bath, nice
big beds and feather quilts. Breakfast available.
❷–❸

Residencial El Rancho Av Pedro Araya 86
⊕02/6943116. Basic but good value, with clean,
spacious rooms with bath, plus laundry facilities.
❶

The Town

Though it's a pleasant place to hang out, Tupiza has little in the way of conventional tourist attractions. The main square, the **Plaza de Independencia**,
is filled with tall palm trees under which people sit to warm themselves in
the morning sun whilst reading yesterday's newspapers. At its centre stands a
statue of José Avelino Aramayo, founder of the great mining dynasty of the
same name that was based in Tupiza and long dominated its economy. As in
most Bolivian mining towns, the late nineteenth- and early twentieth-century civic architecture around the square reflects a past age of prosperity now
long gone. The unexceptional Neoclassical church, with two ornate belltowers, on the west side was built in 1897. There's a **museum** of sorts behind
the town hall just south of the plaza on Calle Sucre, but if you want to see
the limited collection of historic photographs and archeological finds you'll
have to ask in the town hall for someone to let you in, as there are no regular opening hours. The hillside to the west is topped by a **statue of Christ**,
from where there are good views over the town's tin rooftops and the narrow valley of the Río Tupiza; to reach the statue just walk a few minutes west
of the plaza along Avaroa, then follow the stations of the cross up the hill.
Another good walk near the town is up the unimaginatively named **El
Cañon**, a deep, narrow canyon lined with spectacularly eroded rock pinnacles. Walk out of town to the west, past the church, and follow the road as it
curves round behind the hill with the Christ statue. From here, turn up the
(usually) dry riverbed that climbs into the mountains on your left – the
canyon gets deeper and narrower as you climb. In all it's a two-hour walk
there and back.

Eating and drinking

There's only a small choice of places **to eat and drink** in Tupiza. As usual, the
cheapest place for food is at the **market**, on the first floor of the corner of
calles Chichas and Florida, where you'll find fruit juices, inexpensive soups and
meals. Alternatively, there are a few restaurants where you can find good-value
set almuerzos and the usual Bolivian meat-based main courses, as well as a
growing number of dishes aimed at travellers, like pizza and pasta. Local specialities include *asado de cordero* (roast lamb), usually served on weekends, and
cangrejitos, soft-shelled freshwater crabs fried with onions.

Cyber Snack Heladeria, Chorolque and Arandía.
Efficient internet café serving reasonable coffee,
juices, ice cream and snacks.

El Bambino, Florida and Santa Cruz. Busy little
restaurant just off the plaza serving good *salteñas*
and other snacks in the morning, a reasonable set
almuerzo, and pizza and meat and chicken dishes
in the evening.

El Corral de la Obeja Negra, Florida and
Cochabamba. Incongruous café-bar with psyche-

delic purple and pink decor and pop music videos,
serving cold beer and tasty tacos and other snacks
from early evening until late at night.

El Rinconcito Quilmes, Avaroa and Chichas. The
best food place in town, popular with locals for its
filling set almuerzos ($1), excellent meat dishes
(including delicious Argentine-style steaks; $2),
and special lamb roasts on the weekend. There's
indoor and outdoor seating, and live music on
Sunday afternoons.

All routes out of Tupiza pass through some fairly spectacular landscapes, so if you can it's worth timing your departure so you travel in daylight. Several **buses** leave every morning and evening for **Potosí**, eight hours away, from where there are connections to Oruro, La Paz and Sucre; there's also usually a direct overnight bus to La Paz each evening. Buses make the three-hour trip to **Villazón** several times a day, and there are usually three buses daily to **Tarija** (8hr), departing in the evening; if you want to travel this beautiful route by day, take an early-morning bus to Villazón and pick up an onward connection from there. Buses make the scenic nine-hour journey to **Uyuni** on Mondays and Thursdays at 11am.

You can also travel north to Uyuni and Oruro and south to Villazón by **train**, which is an altogether more comfortable experience. See the box on p.217 for full details.

Frial Castro, Florida and Araya. Small shop that also prepares tasty and reasonably priced meals, including spaghetti and lasagne. Good for vegetarians, but you'll need to order a couple of hours or so in advance.

Los Helechos, Av Avaroa and Chichas. Popular travellers' hang-out serving all the gringo favourites at gringo prices, from fruit salads and American breakfasts in the morning to pizza, pasta, chicken and a decent salad bar at lunchtime and in the evenings.

Around Tupiza

Around Tupiza stretches the harsh but beautiful **Cordillera de Chichas**, a striking landscape of cactus-strewn badlands, deep gulches and canyons, and strangely shaped rock formations and pinnacles. The easiest way to see the cordillera is take a jeep excursion wih one of Tupiza's tour companies (see p.203), but travelling on foot or horseback offers a much more relaxed way to explore the eerie desert landscapes and enjoy the tranquillity and ever-changing colours of the mountains, as well as offering the chance to indulge any Wild West outlaw fantasies you may harbour. Take plenty of water with you, though, particularly if you're on foot, as the sun can be very intense in these enclosed canyons, and water is scarce. There are plenty of good spots to camp in the cordillera's secluded valleys, but avoid pitching your tent on riverbeds in case of flash floods after rain.

A few kilometres northwest of Tupiza along the road to Uyuni is the mouth of the **Quebrada de Palala**, a ravine formed by a tributary of the Río Tupiza. The riverbed is dry for most of the year, and is used as a highway by vehicles heading to isolated mines up in the wilderness to the northwest. If you drive, ride or walk 6km or so up the gorge you'll come to a series of red rock formations that have been eroded into massive fins. A few kilometres further on you'll reach a high saddle between two peaks known as **El Sillar**, around which stands a stone forest of tall pinnacles of eroded rock.

A few kilometres southwest of Tupiza, the **Quebrada de Palmira** is another deep, cactus-strewn ravine gouged out of the red mountains by a seasonal river, with dramatic rock formations on either side. If you walk, ride or drive about 6km along the *quebrada* you'll reach the **Puerta del Diablo** (Devil's Gate), a gateway formed by two great vertical slabs which look as if they have been deliberately placed there by massive, unseen hands. A few kilometres further along is the **Valle de Los Machos,** a stone forest of rock pinnacles eroded into distinctly phallic shapes. The ravine eventually peters out into a narrow canyon with steep blood-red walls known as the **Canyon del Inca**.

About 10km south of Tupiza, **Quebrada Seca** is another deep and usually dry ravine with dramatic, eroded rock formations. Here, soft conglomerate rock has been worn by wind and seasonal rain into a series of spires, pinnacles and even arches, giving the sides of the valley the appearance of a Gothic cathedral. A few kilometres east of Quebrada Seca, also about 10km south of town, the road and railway to Villazón pass through a narrow defile known as **La Angostura**, where the Río Tupiza has cut a deep gorge through a narrow

The last days of Butch Cassidy and the Sundance Kid

The wilds of Bolivia have always attracted their fair share of renegades and desperadoes, but few have received as much posthumous attention as the North American outlaws **Butch Cassidy and the Sundance Kid**. Made famous by the 1969 Hollywood movie starring Paul Newman and Robert Redford, the two gunslingers started life as Robert LeRoy Parker and Harry Alonso Longabaugh. Born in Utah in 1866, Butch adopted his first name after a stint as a butcher and his surname from a cowboy he admired, while Sundance, who was born a year later in Pennsylvania, adopted his after a spell in jail as a horse thief in Sundance, Wyoming. Together, they belonged to a band of outlaws – known variously as the Hole-in-the-Wall Gang, the Train Robbers' Syndicate and the Wild Bunch – who robbed banks, trains and mines in the Rocky Mountains. In 1901, with the golden age of Wild West gunslingers coming to an end, a price on their heads and the ruthless Pinkerton Detective Agency (the predecessor of the FBI) hot on their trail, Butch and Sundance fled the US by ship to South America.

They settled in Argentina under assumed names, living on a ranch in the Cholilla Valley in Patagonia, where they raised sheep, cattle and horses. But the Pinkerton Agency had not given up the hunt, and in 1905 the two outlaws went on the run after their names were linked with a bank robbery in Río Gallegas, in the far south of Argentina. They fled to Chile, appparently returning to Argentina to rob another bank before showing up in Bolivia in 1906, where they found work at the Concordia Tin Mine – their duties, ironically, included guarding the payroll. A year later they made a trip to Santa Cruz, and Butch returned determined to start life again as a rancher in the Eastern Lowlands. Perhaps in need of capital to finance their retirement, in 1908 they quit their jobs and returned to their old ways, heading to **Tupiza**, where the wealth of the Aramayo mining company offered a tempting prize. Put off from robbing the town bank by the presence of Bolivian troops, on November 3 Butch and Sundance intercepted a convoy of mules carrying a mine payroll at **Huaca Huañusca**, a mountain pass north of Tupiza. Finding only $90,000 rather than the half million they had been led to expect, the outlaws fled south with the loot loaded onto an Aramayo company mule. The alarm was quickly raised against them, however. With military patrols and posses of angry miners (whose pay had been stolen) scouring the countryside, and the Argentine and Chilean border guards alerted by telegram, the bandits stopped at the home of an English friend, the mining engineer A. G. Francis. Francis later reported that Sundance told him of the hold-up, but insisted "he had never hurt or killed a man except in self-defence, and had never stolen from the poor, but only from rich corporations well able to support his requisitions".

Warned that the authorities were on their trail, Butch and Sundance turned north, heading towards Uyuni. On November 6 they stopped for the night in **San Vicente**, a remote mining village about 100km northwest of Tupiza. Unknown to them, however, a four-man military patrol was also spending the night in the village. Informed of the outlaws' presence, they attacked the room where Butch and Sundance were staying. After a brief shootout, all went quiet. In the morning, the two bandits were found dead, Butch having apparently shot his wounded partner before turning his gun on himself. The bodies were buried in an unmarked grave in the cemetery. Or were they? In subsequent decades repeated rumours suggested that the two dead men were not Butch and Sundance. The two outlaws were reported to have returned to the US or to Argentina having assumed new identities; one report even had them finally gunned down in Paris. In 1991 forensic anthropologists exhumed a body from the San Vicente cemetery, but were unable to settle the mystery surrounding the outlaws' fate.

opening – it's usually included in day-long jeep tours of the region around Tupiza, though isn't worth making a special journey to see on its own.

San Vicente and Huaca Huañusca

Tour agencies in Tupiza run two-day trips following the trail of the infamous US outlaws, **Butch Cassidy and the Sundance Kid**, to Huaca Huañusca and San Vicente, the sites respectively of their final robbery and deaths – though there's actually almost nothing related to the gunslingers to see at either site. Located some 100km northwest of Tupiza at an altitude of over 4300m, the bleak mining village of **SAN VICENTE**, where Butch and Sundance are believed to have died in a shootout, is pretty much abandoned. Locals can show you the adobe hut where the outlaws made their last stand – against four Bolivian soldiers rather than the entire regiment shown in the film – and you can also see the grave in the cemetery where they are thought to have been buried. Apart from that, though, there's not much else to look at in this virtual ghost town apart from abandoned tin-roofed mining shacks. There's even less to see at **HUACA HUAÑUSCA**, the mountain pass about 45km north of Tupiza where Butch and Sundance made their last robbery. There's not really much point visiting these places unless you have a real interest in the two dead outlaws. Having said that, quite a few travellers obviously do, and it's usually possible to get a group together for a tour within a day or two.

Villazón and the Argentine border

About 92km south of Tupiza by road or rail, the dusty, ramshackle frontier town of **VILLAZÓN** is the main border crossing between Bolivia and Argentina. Set at an altitude of 3445m, it's a busy little place which bustles with cross-border traffic, though a recent crackdown on smuggling and the burgeoning economic crisis in Argentina has somewhat reduced the flow of goods and people. Most of the people crossing the border here are Bolivian migrants who live and work in Argentina – there are over a million Bolivians in the far richer neighbouring country, though economic slowdown and growing hostility towards migrants means that Buenos Aires doesn't exert the same attraction it did up until the mid-1990s. Unless you get stuck in Villazón overnight, there's really no reason to linger; you're better off pushing on into Bolivia or crossing into Argentina.

Practicalities

The **train station** is about 400m north of the central plaza on Avenida República de Argentina, the main road out of town. The **bus terminal** is just north of the plaza on the same road. From the plaza, Avenida Internacional runs down to the frontier a few hundred metres to the south, lined with shops filled with cheap and rather shoddy consumer goods to sell to cross-border shoppers and Bolivian migrants heading down to Argentina. There are also several **cambios** where you can change dollars and Argentine pesos; some also change travellers' cheques, though only for a steep commission. If you're heading into Argentina, it's best to get rid of your Bolivian pesos before you cross the border. The **ENTEL** office is two blocks north of the plaza on Avenida República de Argentina, and there are several phone booths around town. There's an **internet** café opposite the bus terminal.

The best **place to stay** in Villazón is the clean and comfortable *Hotel Plaza* (℡02/5963535, ℻02/5962026; ❷–❸), on the main square, which has cheap rooms with shared bathroom and slightly more expensive ones with private bath and cable TV. A cheaper alternative is the simpler *Residencial Martinez* (☎02/5963353; ❷), behind the bus terminal, or one of the basic places on Avenida República de Argentina like the *Residencial Mirador* (☎02/5962492; ❷) or the good-value *Residencial Salvador* (no phone; ❷).

The best **place to eat** is the rather expensive *Chifa Jardin*, which serves decent Chinese food 24 hours a day. Also good is the *Charquekan*, behind the bus terminal, where you can find filling set almuerzos and cenas as well as reasonably priced meat and chicken dishes. Otherwise, there are plenty of **food stalls** around the bus terminal and inside the covered market on the east side of the plaza, and a number of cheap fried-chicken restaurants on the way down to the border along Avenida Internacional.

Tarija and around

In the far south of the country, hemmed in by the high Altiplano to the west and by the cactus-choked hills that drop down into the impenetrable forests of the Chaco to the east, the isolated city of **TARIJA** is in many ways a world apart from the rest of Bolivia. Set in a broad, fertile valley at an altitude of 1924m, the city lies at the centre of a rich agricultural region known as the Andalucía of Bolivia on account of its sunny climate, vineyard-filled valley and the arid mountain scenery that surrounds it. Indeed so striking are the similarities with southern Spain that Luis de Fuentes, the conquistador who founded the city, named the river on whose banks it sits the Guadalquivir, after the river which flows past Seville.

Tarija is also famous for its **wine** production, and the valley's rich soils and fecund climate attracted large numbers of Andalucían farmers. The peasant culture they brought with them survived in isolation and is still very evident in the traditional costumes of the Tarijeños, in their folkloric dances and religious fiestas, in their love of food and wine, and in their languid, sing-song accents. Known as **Chapacos**, the Tarijeños take considerable pride in their distinct cultural identity. Largely mestizo rather than indigenous, and closer culturally to northern Argentina, they think of themselves as a people apart from the rest of Bolivia, and though the region has provided two presidents in recent decades – including the hugely influential Victor Paz Estenssoro – it otherwise managed to avoid much of the social and political upheaval of the past century.

Tarija was founded on July 4, 1574 as a frontier outpost on the far southeast edge of Alto Peru to guard against incursions by the indomitable **Chiriguano** tribes of the Chaco. The settlement thrived on the valley's rich agricultural produce, exporting wine, cattle and grain to the mines of the Altiplano, but despite its prosperity, Tarija remained on the front line of missionary and military expeditions against the Chiriguanos – only after the final Chiriguano uprising was crushed in 1892 were outlying settlements finally freed from the threat of tribal raiders. The greatest moment in Tarija's history came during the Independence War on April 15, 1817, when a combined force of Argentine troops and Chapaco guerrilla riders led by a one-armed rebel named Eustaquio "Moto" Mendez defeated a Spanish army outside the city at the battle of **La Tablada**. After this victory Tarija enjoyed eight years of de facto independence before voting to join the newly proclaimed Republic of Bolivia rather than Argentina in 1825.

Fiestas in Tarija

Tarijeños are known throughout Bolivia for their love of music, dance and a good party, so it's no surprise that the city stages some vibrant annual fiestas. Though not as strongly influenced by pre-Christian rites and indigenous cultures as the fiestas elsewhere in the Bolivian Andes, fiestas in Tarija are still deeply rooted in the agricultural cycle and the calendar of Catholic saint's days. The distinctive Chapaco **folk music** features strongly at all the fiestas, played on unusual woodwind instruments typical of the region like the *erque* and *quenilla*, as well as those imported directly from Spain like the violin and small *tambor* drum. This music is accompanied by poetic and often comic traditional folk songs known as *coplas* – usually sung as duets by a young man and woman. The best known and most colourful of the region's folkloric **dances** is the *Chuncho*, in which dancers wear brightly coloured robes, feathered headdresses and masks in ritual portrayal of the Chiriguano tribes of the Chaco, whose determined resistance to conquest provided a constant menace to Tarijeño settlers until the end of the nineteenth century.

Tarija's **Carnaval** celebrations in February or March are amongst the most colourful in Bolivia. On the Thursday before Carnaval, the Dia de Comadres is marked by an exchange of cakes and other gifts, and by a parade of all the women in the city dressed in their finest traditional attire. Carnaval itself is celebrated with a mass parade of folkloric dances and campesinos in elaborate traditional costumes, and several days of water-fighting, dancing, singing, drinking and eating in the main streets and plazas and in outlying villages. The fiesta ends with the ritual burial of the devil, who's blamed for tempting people into the excesses of Carnaval, accompanied by a host of drunken mourners. The end of Carnaval coincides with the **Fiesta de la Uva** (Grape Festival) in La Concepción, 35km south of the city, where grape-growers show off their wares amid further eating, drinking and folkloric dancing.

On August 15 each year Tarijeños celebrate the fiesta of the **Virgen de la Asunción** with a mass pilgrimage to the village of Chaguaya, 70km south of the city; unusually in Bolivia, this fiesta is not accompanied by music and dance. Tarija's patron saint is **San Roque**, whose fiesta is celebrated on the first weekend of September with a religious procession accompanied by troupes of *Chuncho* dancers.

Though its population has mushroomed to over 100,000 people in recent decades, the city itself remains provincial in all the best senses of the word, small enough to get around on foot and culturally self-contained, but open to foreign influences and welcoming to outsiders. Though it doesn't boast much in the way of formal tourist attractions, the laid-back and gregarious Chapacos make Tarija a great place to hang out for a few days and relax, and if you happen to be passing through around **Carnaval** time it's well worth stopping to take part in what's widely considered one of Bolivia's most enjoyable fiestas. The countryside around the city is beautiful without being spectacular, particularly in the spring (Jan–April), when the vineyards come to fruit and the whole valley blooms. Above the valley to the west, the **Reserva Biológica Cordillera del Sama** is home to some striking high Andean scenery, as well as an Inca trail that drops down into the valley, making an excellent hike.

Arrival and information

The **bus terminal** is ten blocks or so southeast of the city centre on Avenida Las Américas – it has a helpful bus information office (daily 6am–noon & 3–8pm; ☎04/6636508), as well as telephones and restaurants. It's about twenty minutes into the city centre on foot from here, or a short **taxi** ride ($0.50). Alternatively, catch one of the frequent **micros** that run along Avenida Las Américas from the stop opposite the terminal. The **airport** (☎04/6642282 or 6631270) is on the outskirts of town a few kilometres further east along Avenida Las Américas. A taxi into the town centre from here should cost about $1, and there are also frequent micros. Unusually for Bolivia, micro stops in Tarija are marked with the destination of the vehicles that stop at them, though other than travelling to the bus terminal or the airport, you're unlikely to use them, as distances within the compact centre are easily walkable. To return to the airport or bus terminal, catch a micro heading east along Calle Domingo Paz.

There are two **tourist information offices** in Tarija, but sadly they compete with each other for the title of worst in the country. The Oficina Departamental de Turismo (Mon–Fri 9.30am–noon & 2.30–6.30pm; ☎04/6631000), on the Plaza Luis de Fuentes, should be able to provide a free map of the city, but is otherwise laughably unhelpful. The Oficina Municipal de Turismo (Mon–Fri 9.30am–noon & 2.30–6.30pm; ☎04/6650144), on the corner of Bolívar and Sucre, is slightly better, with a range of free leaflets and maps and some chance of getting basic questions answered in Spanish. Better sources of information are the city's two **tour operators**: Viva Tours, on Sucre and Madrid, and VTB Tours, inside the *Hostal Carmen* at Ingavi and Ballivián, though the main aim of both is obviously to sell you a trip. For permission to visit the Reserva Biológica Cordillera del Sama (see p.216) and information on it and other protected areas in the department of Tarija, go to the conservation group **PROMETA** at Alejandro del Carpio and O'Connor (☎04/6645865 or 04/6633873, Ⓔsamatja@olivo.tja.entelnet.bo).

Accommodation

Tarija has a good range of **accommodation**, almost all located in the very centre of town – the exceptions are around the bus terminal, though there's no point staying down there unless you're just passing the night before continuing your journey. Some of the city's mid-range hotels are particularly good value, making Tarija a good place to splash out on a little luxury.

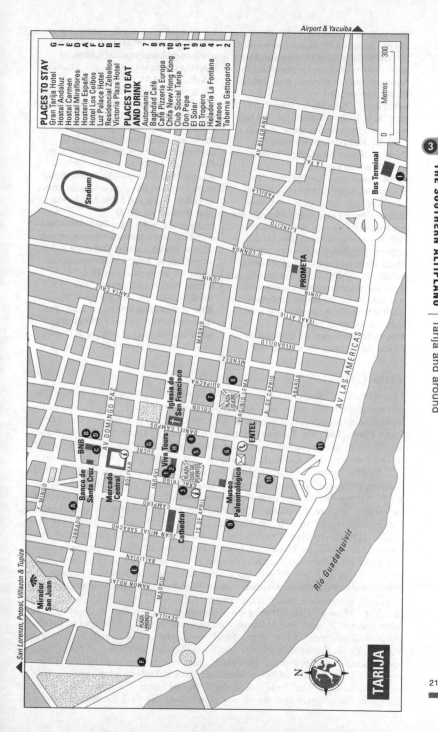

PLACES TO STAY
Gran Tarija Hotel	G
Hostal Andaluz	I
Hostal Carmen	E
Hostal Miraflores	D
Hostería España	A
Hotel Los Ceibos	F
Luz Palace Hotel	C
Residencial Zeballos	B
Victoria Plaza Hotel	H

PLACES TO EAT AND DRINK
Automania	7
Baghdad Café	8
Café Pizzeria Europa	3
Chifa New Hong Kong	10
Club Social Tarija	5
Don Pepe	11
El Solar	9
El Tropero	6
Heladería La Fontana	4
Mateos	1
Taberna Gattopardo	2

Airport & Yacuiba ▲

San Lorenzo, Potosí, Villazón & Tupiza ▲

Stadium

Bus Terminal

PROMETA

Iglesia de San Francisco

Viva Tours

Museo Paleontológico

BNB

Banco de Santa Cruz

Mercado Central

Cathedral

Mirador San Juan

ENTEL

Río Guadalquivir

TARIJA

N

211

3

Gran Tarija Hotel Sucre 770 ☎04/6642893 or 6642684, ⓕ04/6644777. Modern business hotel with comfortable carpeted a/c rooms and all the usual amenities – including a restaurant and bar, sauna and cable TV – though not much character. Breakfast included. ❻

Hostal Andaluz Behind the bus terminal on Av Victor Paz ☎04/6631436. Simple and clean lodgings, despite the unattractive exterior, and with a reasonable steak restaurant downstairs. Convenient if you're just stopping in Tarija overnight to break a journey. ❷

Hostal Carmen Ingavi 784 ☎04/6643372 or 6644341, ⓔvtb@olivo.tja.entelnet.bo. Recently refurbished hostal with warm, well-decorated rooms set around a glass-roofed central patio and boasting plentiful hot water, internet access and cable TV – there's also a small apartment with kitchen for longer stays. Breakfast included. ❹

Hostal Miraflores Sucre 920 ☎04/6643355 or 6644976 ⓕ04/663091. Converted colonial house with a sunny central courtyard, helpful and efficient staff, and a choice between comfortable rooms with cable TV and private bath, or small, spartan rooms without. ❷–❸

Hosteria España Corrado 546 ☎04/6641690. Friendly and welcoming, with small but clean rooms set around a flower-filled courtyard, though the cheaper rooms without private bath are windowless cells. Laundry facilities available. ❸

Hotel Los Ceibos Av Las Américas and Madrid ☎04/6634430, ⓕ04/6642461, ⓔceibohot@cosett.com.bo. Luxurious and relatively good value hotel, with warm, spacious and well-appointed modern rooms with cable TV, all with balconies overlooking a large swimming pool. There's also a bar-restaurant, and breakfast is included. ❻

Luz Palace Hotel Sucre 326 ☎04/6635700 or 6635701, ⓕ04/6644646, ⓔluzpalac@olivo.tja.entelnet.bo. Modern and stylish business hotel, with bright and spacious rooms with cable TV set around a glass-roofed central patio. Breakfast included. ❺

Residencial Zeballos Sucre 966 ☎04/6642068 or 6633313. Rather ramshackle but welcoming little place, offering simple but clean rooms (with or without bath) set around a bright courtyard overflowing with plants and flowers. ❷–❸

Victoria Plaza Hotel Madrid and Sucre ☎04/6642600 or 6635064, ⓕ04/6642700, ⓔhot_vit@olivo.tja.entelnet.bo. Grand but rather old-fashioned hotel overlooking the main plaza, with lavish, well-equipped rooms, cable TV and a bar-café. Breakfast included. ❻

The City

Laid out in the classic grid pattern of Spanish colonial cities, Tarija has few obvious sightseeing attractions – its appeal lies more in the easy charm of its citizens and the warm, balmy climate. The centre of town is the peaceful, palm-lined **Plaza Luis de Fuentes**, named after the city's founder, whose statue stands in the middle, dressed in full conquistador armour, flourishing his sword in front of him. The **Cathedral**, a block west of the plaza, is a dull modern construction whose only redeeming feature is the brightly coloured stained glass depicting local peasants harvesting grapes. It stands on the site once occupied by the Jesuit college, founded in 1690, which was an important base for missionary ventures down into the Chaco before the order was expelled from the Spanish empire in 1767. A block east of the plaza on Calle Madrid is the simple **Iglesia de San Francisco**, the first church in Tarija when it was founded in 1606. The Franciscan college beside the church still houses a massive archive of historical documents from several centuries of Franciscan missionary endeavour, and there's also a small collection of colonial religious art inside, but you'll need to persuade one of the priests to show you around.

A block south of the plaza on the corner of Virginio Lema and Trigo, the outstanding **Museo Paleontológico** (Mon–Fri 8am–noon & 3–6pm, Sat 9am–noon & 3–6pm; free) is worth visiting for its fantastic collection of **fossils** from the Tarija valley. Most of the fossils on display are of mammals from the Pleistocene era, between a million and 250,000 years ago, many of them from species similar to ones that still exist today, such as horses, bears and llamas. There are also a large number of bones from the extinct **Andean elephant**, or mastadon, including several complete skulls with tusks over 1.5 metres long and a complete skeleton, along with photos of its discovery by a Tarijeño family in their backyard on the outskirts of the city. Also on display are an enormous skull and many bones of the **megatherium**, or giant sloth, at five metres long one of the biggest land mammals ever to exist, and said by scientists to be long extinct, though it's rumoured to live on in the depths of the Amazon rainforest. Stranger still is the almost complete fossilized skeleton of a **glyptodon**, an extinct mammal whose thick armoured shell and clublike tail made it look like a distant relative of the armadillo. Upstairs there's also a small collection of archeological finds, featuring the usual ceramics, arrowheads and mummified bodies, though it pales in comparison with the fossils downstairs.

On a hilltop above the city to the west is the **Mirador San Juan**, a pleasant park shaded by palm trees with good views across the red-tiled rooftops of Tarija and the mountains rising above the valley beyond. To get there, walk west along Avenida Domingo Paz then follow the stations of the cross up the hill to your right.

Eating and drinking

Nowhere is Tarija's strong Argentine influence more evident than in its **restaurants**. Good-quality grilled beef features strongly, ideally accompanied by a glass of local wine, while Tarijeños are also justly proud of their distinctive traditional cuisine featuring chicken and meat dishes cooked in delicious spicy sauces – try *ranga-ranga*, *saice* or *chancao de pollo* – meat (or chicken) dishes cooked in delicious spicy sauces. As usual, the best place to sample these is in the **Mercado Central** on the corner of Sucre and Bolívar, where you can also find fresh fruit juices and early-morning breakfasts. A particular local speciality is *sopa la poderosa*, a rich soup made with a bull's penis – unsurprisingly, it's considered a powerful aphrodisiac.

In keeping with the city's laid-back and gregarious Mediterranean flavour, **nightlife** tends to involve sitting around outdoor tables with a bottle or two of wine until late at night. On the weekends, local youngsters tend to congregate on the **Plaza Sucre** to indulge in billiards, pizza and beer.

Automania Plaza Sucre. Trendy bar-nightclub, decorated with motor-racing paraphernalia and drawing a wealthy young crowd who come here to groove the night away to the latest Latin and Western dance music whilst drinking cold beer and cocktails named after famous drivers.

Baghdad Café Plaza Sucre. Cosy little bar-café with a bohemian atmosphere – it attracts a lively young crowd who come here for coffee in the afternoon and wine and hot snacks in the evening.

Café Pizzería Europa Plaza Luis de Fuentes. Pleasant little café serving reasonable breakfasts, juices, pizzas and snacks, and good strong coffee. There's outdoor seating on the plaza, so you can watch the world go by as you eat, and they have internet access too.

Chifa New Hong Kong Sucre and Victor Paz. Complete with laughing Buddhas and fish tanks, the decor in this Chinese restaurant is more authentic than the food, but it still makes an enjoyable change. Main dishes big enough for two people go for about $3.50, and you can get a filling almuerzo or cena for $2. Closed Sun.

Club Social Tarija Plaza Luis de Fuentes. Good-value traditional almuerzos in a rather staid atmosphere favoured by Tarija's business community and older citizens.

Don Pepe Daniel Campos and Las Américas. Spacious open-air restaurant with good-value traditional meat dishes; it gets popular at weekends, when there's live folk music.

El Solar Campero with Virginio Lemo. A welcome vegetarian alternative, this New-Age oasis serves a healthy yet tasty four-course almuerzo for $1.50, as well as a range of salads, snacks, juices and herbal teas. Lunchtime only.

El Tropero Virginio Lema and Daniel Campos. Authentic Argentine steakhouse with outdoor seating serving excellent grilled beef and chicken as well as a filling almuerzo for $2.

Heladería La Fontana Madrid and Daniel Campos. Popular ice-cream parlour that's a good place to cool down in the afternoons; also serves snacks and cold drinks.

Mateos Trigo and Madrid. Superior restaurant with indoor and outdoor seating and a refined ambience, serving a superb four-course almuerzo

Moving on from Tarija

Tarija's isolation is underlined by the fact that Bolivia's two biggest cities, **La Paz** and **Santa Cruz**, are both 24 hours away by road. Both are served by several **buses** a day – via Potosí and Oruro for La Paz and via Villamontes in the Chaco for Santa Cruz. Several buses a day make the trip to **Potosí** (12hr), from where there are connections to Cochabamba, Oruro and Uyuni. There are two or three buses a day to **Tupiza** (9hr), but these leave in the evening and travel overnight. If you don't want to miss the scenic views on this route, get one of the two or three services that leave in the morning to **Villazón**, from where you can catch another bus to make the short journey on to Tupiza in the afternoon. If you're travelling down into the **Chaco** it's worth going by day if you can, as the roads taken by buses to Villamontes (3–4 daily; 10–12hr) and Yacuiba (6–8 daily; 10–12hr) pass through a beautiful and sparsely populated landscape, twisting over a succession of jagged mountain ridges, covered with dense scrubby forest and cacti, that march down into the plains. The closest border crossing into **Argentina** is at Bermejo (5–6 daily; 7hr), a gas- and sugar-producing town just over 200km south of Tarija.

Given the distances involved, it's tempting to move on from Tarija **by air**. LAB and AeroSur between them fly several times a week to Cochabamba, La Paz, Santa Cruz and Sucre, while the military airline TAM flies once a week to La Paz and Santa Cruz.

($3.50), as well as à la carte meat, fish and pasta dishes; there's also a very good salad bar.
Taberna Gattopardo Plaza Luis de Fuentes. Stylish bar-restaurant serving a wide range of well-prepared meals including pizza, pasta, grilled meat and chicken dishes – it's also a popular place to enjoy a cold beer or a glass of wine, and there's a choice between outdoor seating on the plaza and discreet booths inside. It gets pretty lively at weekends, and stays open late.

Listings

Airlines AeroSur, Ingavi and Sucre ⊕04/6630894 or 6645820; LAB, Trigo and Lemo ⊕04/6645706 or 6642195; TAM, Madrid and Trigo ⊕04/6642734.

Banks and exchange The Banco Nacional de Bolivia, opposite the *Hotel Gran Tarija* on Sucre, changes cash and travellers' cheques and has an ATM that takes Visa and Mastercard. There are several other ATMs in town, including at the Banco de Santa Cruz on Trigo and Domingo Paz.

Bus information ⊕04/6636508.

Consulate The Argentine consulate is on Ballivián and Bolívar ⊕04/6644273.

Internet access *Café Pizzeria Europa*, Plaza Luis de Fuentes, and many others on Plaza Sucre.

Laundry Lavamatico, inside the furniture shop on Domingo Paz and Suipachi.

Post office The Correo Central is on Lema and Sucre.

Radio taxis Moto Méndez ⊕44480; Tarija ⊕43478.

Telephone office The ENTEL office is on Lema and Daniel Campos.

Tour operators VTB Tours, inside the *Hostal Carmen* at Ingavi 784 ⊕04/6643372 or 6644341, ⓔvtb@olivo.tja.entelnet.bo, and Viva Tours, just off the Plaza Luis de Fuentes on Sucre ⊕04/6638325, ⓔvivatour@cossett.com.bo, both run one-day tours of the city and around the vineyards and bodegas of the Tarija Valley with experienced English-speaking guides. Both also take groups on the Inca Trail in the Reserva Cordillera del Sama (p.216), while VTB run paleontology tours on which you can find and excavate your own fossil (though you can't keep it).

Around Tarija

There are some worthwhile excursions close to Tarija in the warm and fertile **Tarija valley**, which is notable for its sleepy but welcoming villages and easy pace of life. Just outside the city near the airport are rich **fossil** deposits that attract paleontologists from all over the world, while further afield you can visit the bodegas and lush **vineyards** of the world's highest wine-producing region.

Tarija Valley fossils

About 5km outside Tarija to the northeast, the eroded gulches and badlands around the airport and the gas pipeline on the other side of the main road are a treasure-house for **fossil** hunters. The sedimentary layers of volcanic ash, clays and sand here are full of well-preserved fossilized bones and teeth from Pleistocene megafauna like the mastadon (Andean elephant) and megatherium (giant sloth), as well as distant ancestors of llamas, horses and other contemporary mammals, and every year, rain washes away more of the steep canyon sides to reveal further remains. If you take a micro or taxi out to the airport and wander around for a while, you're likely to come across fossils embedded in the crumbling sides of canyons, though to the untrained eye they can be difficult to recognize. If you find anything major you should report it to the Museo Paleontológico in Tarija, and on no account take away anything you discover. If you've a particular interest in fossils then it's worth hiring a knowledgeable **guide** through one of the tour agencies in Tarija (see p.210), as this way you're likely to see, and understand, far more. VTB Tours run special fossil-hunting trips with university approval in which you're allowed to excavate major fossils under supervision before handing them over to the museum – an opportunity no budding paleontologist should pass up.

Tarija valley vineyards

The **Tarija valley** and surrounding area is Bolivia's prime wine-producing region, and a visit to one of the **bodegas** (wineries) to see how the wines are produced (and sample a few glasses at source) makes an excellent half-day excursion from the city. The first vines were planted by Franciscan monks, who found the soil and climate of the Tarija valley ideal for producing wine, and during the colonial era Tarija produced much of the wine consumed in Potosí, as well as large quantities of **singani**, a fierce, white-grape brandy with a strength of about 40° proof which is still extremely popular throughout Bolivia. Today, Tarija's expanding wine industry produces well over two million litres of wine a year, with a growing number of wines made with fine grape varieties like cabernet, sauvignon, merlot and riesling. Wine consumption within Bolivia is growing and production techniques in the main bodegas have been modernized, with quality improving all the time. The main obstacle to further increases in production is the influx of contraband wine from Chile and Argentina, which is much cheaper than Bolivian wine, since no duty is paid on it.

At up to 2000m above sea level, these are the highest vineyards in the world; they are at their greenest and most beautiful during the February to March grape harvest. On a visit to one of the bodegas you can see all the stages of the production process, including pressing, fermentation, storage and – for *singani* – distillation. The closest bodega to Tarija is **Aranjuez**, on the southern outskirts of the city, while **Kohlberg** and **Casa Real** are in Santa Ana, a small village about 15km further southeast. Generally you can only visit these three bodegas on an organized trip with a Tarija-based agencies (about $6 per person for a half-day tour). Further south, about 35km away from Tarija in the idyllic Valle La Concepción, which runs down into the Tarija valley from the west, the **Concepción-Rugero** bodega (☎04/6118008) is easier to visit independently – and produces arguably the best wine in Bolivia. If you telephone in advance to make an appointment, the staff are usually happy to show you around, though you can't buy any wine on the premises and visits may not be possible during particularly busy periods of the harvest. To get there, take a micro marked "V" from the Plaza Sucre in Tarija. This will drop you in the village of Concepción, from where it's about a twenty-minute walk to the bodega along a track that heads out across a bridge to the right of the main road – ask the micro driver or anyone in the village for directions.

Tomatitas and San Lorenzo

About 5km north of Tarija, the village of **TOMATITAS** is a popular weekend getaway for Tarijeños, who come here to swim in the natural river pools during the warmer, wetter summer months from November to April. You can also picnic in the fragrant eucalyptus woods beside the river, or eat in one of the many inexpensive **restaurants** in the village, where you can sample traditional local specialities like *chicharron* (deep-fried pork) and *cangrejitos* (soft-shelled freshwater crabs fried with onions), ideally accompanied by a glass or two of the local wine.

Another 10km further north, the peaceful farming village of **SAN LOREN-ZO** is still home to many colonial buildings including, on the corner of the palm-lined plaza, the former home of the one-handed independence guerrilla hero, **Eustaquio "Moto" Méndez**, which has been preserved as a shrine-like museum (daily 9am–noon & 2.30–6pm; free) in his honour. The leader of a guerrilla band that played a key role in the Battle of La Tablada, which liberated Tarija from Spanish control in 1817, Moto Méndez is considered the consummate ideal of Chapaco (Tarijeño) manhood. Inside, the whitewashed colonial-era house has been left much as it was when he lived there, complete with rustic furniture and agricultural tools. Also on display are a series of busts and portraits of Méndez, his spurs and stirrups and an arsenal of weapons. **Micros** "A" and "B" to Tomatitas and San Lorenzo depart from Avenida Domingo Paz in Tarija every ten minutes or so.

Reserva Biológica Cordillera del Sama

Starting about 5km west of Tarija, just over a thousand square kilometres of the Altiplano and the deep valleys that drop down into the Tarija valley are protected by the **Reserva Biológica Cordillera del Sama**, a sparsely populated region that is still home to many endangered Andean wildlife species including vicuñas, Andean deer, pumas and a wide variety of birds. Established in 1991, the reserve is administered by the non-governmental organization PROMETA, whose office in Tarija (see p.210) you should contact for permission to visit the region. Most of the reserve is composed of the high-altitude grasslands (*puna*) of the Cordillera de Sama, which rises above the Tarija valley to an altitude of over 4000m and marks the eastern edge of the Altiplano. The three brackish lakes here – the largest is the **Laguna Tajzara** – are home to many different water birds, including all three species of Andean flamingo. The main road from Tarija to Tupiza passes through the reserve close by the lakes, making them easily accessible from the city. You can reach here by getting on any Tupiza- or Villazón-bound bus and asking the driver to drop you at the village of **Pasajes**, about two hours' drive from Tarija. Pasajes is about 2km from Laguna Tajzara, on the shore of which is a PROMETA **visitors' centre**, equipped with a kitchen, hot water and beds, where you can stay overnight (**⑤**) – contact their office in Tarija in advance of you want to do this.

From a high pass about two hours' walk due east of Pasajes (also reachable by 4WD from Pasajes), a well-preserved **Inca Trail** drops down through spectacular scenery to the village of Los Pinos in the Tarija Valley, making for an excellent hike. If you get an early start from Laguna Tajzara (or if you're lucky enough to get a lift up to the pass with PROMETA), at a push you can walk this trail in a day and be back in Tarija the same evening. The trail itself is a good seven- or eight-hour hike, and from its end at the village of Los Pinos it's another 16km – about three hours – along a flat road to the village of San Andrés, where you can get transport back to Tarija. If you have camping equipment, it may be better to break the walk into two days. Alternatively, you can arrange to do the hike with a tour agency in Tarija, which will provide a guide and transport to the pass and back to Tarija from Los Pinos – Viva Tours should be able to arrange an all-inclusive two-day trip for around $100 per person for a group of four to six people; alternatively, you could arrange transport and a guide (or transport alone) independently for considerably less.

The first pass is marked a large *apacheta* or stone cairn, which is visible from Pasajes below; once you've found it, the rest of the trail is easy to follow without a guide. From the pass, the trail zigzags down to the clearly visible village of **Calderillas**, about two hours' walk away. From Calderillas, walk southeast for about thirty minutes to where two rivers meet and enter a narrow gorge. Cross over to the right bank of the river and follow the lower path that runs into the gorge along the river bank. After about 45 minutes the path climbs to the right and over a ridge, opening up spectacular views of the Tarija valley below – it's also an excellent spot to see condors. The path follows the ridge round and then zigzags down to the east to **Los Pinos**, about two hours' walk away. From here, an easy-to-follow road runs 16km to San Andrés, from where there are frequent micros back to Tarija. If you arrive after dark when the last micro has gone, use the public telephone in a shop on the plaza to call a radio taxi from Tarija to come and pick you up – they should charge about $6 for the journey.

Travel details

Buses

Oruro to: Cochabamba (every 20min; 6hr); Iquique, Chile (2–3 daily; 8hr); La Paz (every 30min; 3hr 30min); Potosí (6 daily, 8hr); Santa Cruz (11 daily; 12hr); Sucre (3 daily; 11hr); Uyuni (2–3 daily; 9hr); Villazón (2–3 daily, 15hr).
Patacamaya to: Sajama (1 daily; 3hr 30min).
Potosí to: La Paz (4–6 daily; 11hr); Oruro (6 daily; 8hr); Sucre (every 30min; 3hr); Tarija (3–4 daily; 12hr); Tupiza (3–4 daily; 8hr); Uyuni (4 daily; 7–8hr); Villazón (6–8 daily; 12hr).
Sajama to: Patacamaya (1 daily; 3hr 30min).
Tarija to: La Paz (1–2 daily; 24hr); Potosí (3–4

daily; 12hr); Santa Cruz (1–2 daily; 24hr); Tupiza (2–3 daily; 9hr); Villamontes (3–4 daily; 10–12hr); Villazón (1–2 daily; 8hr); Yacuiba (6–8 daily; 10–12hr).
Tupiza to: Potosí (3–4 daily; 8hr); Tarija (2–3 daily; 9hr); Uyuni (2 weekly; 9hr); Villazón (6–8 daily; 3hr).
Uyuni to: Oruro (2–3 daily; 9hr); Potosí (4 daily; 7–8hr); Tupiza (2 weekly; 9hr).
Villazón to: Oruro (2–3 daily; 15hr); Potosí (6–8 daily; 12hr); Tarija (1–2 daily; 8hr); Tupiza (6–8 daily; 3hr).

Trains

For full timetables, see p.166
Oruro to: Tupiza (4 weekly; 11–13hr); Uyuni (4 weekly; 6–7hr); Villazón (3 weekly; 14–17hr).
Tupiza to: Oruro (4 weekly; 11–13hr); Uyuni (4 weekly; 5–6hr); Villazón (3 weekly; 3hr).

Uyuni to: Oruro (4 weekly; 6–7hr); Tupiza (4 weekly; 5–6hr); Villazón (3 weekly; 8–9hr).
Villazón to: Oruro (3 weekly; 14–17hr); Tupiza (3 weekly; 3hr); Uyuni (3 weekly; 8–9hr).

Planes

Tarija to: Cochabamba (1–2 daily; 50min); La Paz (4 weekly; 1hr); Santa Cruz (5 weekly; 50min);

Sucre (3 weekly; 45min).

Sucre, Cochabamba and the central valleys

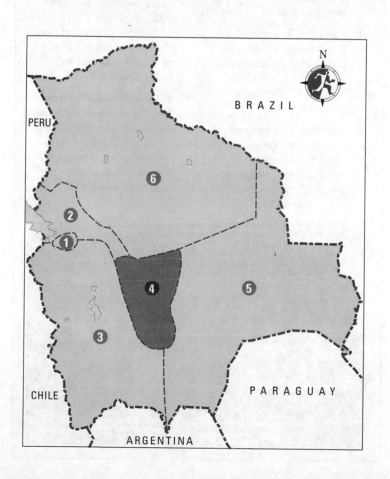

CHAPTER 4

Highlights

✳ **Chicha** The sacred drink of the Incas, this thick, tart and mildly alcoholic maize beer can be found for sale throughout the Cochabamba Valley wherever you see a white flag on a pole – though it's something of an acquired taste. **See p.36**

✳ **Sucre** Known as the White City, Bolivia's official capital combines delightful colonial architecture with the lively atmosphere of a university town. **See p.223**

✳ **Museo de Arte Indigena** Sucre's best museum, dedicated to the remarkable weavings of the indigenous groups of the surrounding region. **See p.230**

✳ **Cal Orko** Visit the world's biggest collection of dinosaur footprints, recently discovered in a cement quarry outside Sucre. **See p.233**

✳ **La Cancha** Cochabamba's vast covered market is the throbbing heart of this commercial city, and of the Quechua-speaking communities of the surrounding valley. **See p.244**

✳ **Parque Nacional Torotoro** Set in a remote mountainous region amidst a landscape of deep canyons and rushing waterfalls, and dotted with dinosaur footprints and pre-Inca ruins. **See p.252**

4

Sucre, Cochabamba and the central valleys

East of the Altiplano, the Andes march gradually down towards the eastern lowlands in a series of rugged north–south mountain ranges, scarred with long narrow valleys formed by rivers draining to the east. Blessed with rich alluvial soils, and midway in climate and altitude between the cold of the Altiplano and the tropical heat of the lowlands, these **central valleys** have historically been among the most fertile and habitable areas in Bolivia. The Incas recognized this, and in the fifteenth century established substantial agricultural colonies in the region, which formed the easternmost frontier of their empire – to this day the majority of the rural population still speak Quechua, the language the Incas introduced. The Spanish were attracted by the same qualities, and added wheat to the maize crops that flourished on the valley floors, which they developed as the main source of food for the mining centres of the Altiplano. The two main cities they founded, Sucre and Cochabamba, remain the most important in the region, though origins aside they could not be more different in character.

The administrative, political and religious centre of all Bolivia during Spanish rule, and still officially the capital of the republic, **Sucre** is a masterpiece of immaculately preserved colonial architecture, filled with elegant churches and mansions, and home to some of Bolivia's finest museums. Now a provincial backwater basking in past glories, it's also the market centre for the deeply traditional Quechua-speaking communities of the surrounding mountains, whose fine weavings are sold at the regional market town of **Tarabuco**.

The charms of **Cochabamba**, on the other hand, are much more prosaic. A bustling market centre for a rich agricultural hinterland, it possesses little in the way of conventional tourist attractions, and for most travellers is no more than a place to break a journey between La Paz and Santa Cruz in the eastern lowlands. Those who do spend some time here, however, find it one of the friendliest cities in Bolivia, and the surrounding Cochabamba Valley's mixture of Inca ruins and lively rural market towns is also worth exploring. It's also the jumping off point for an adventurous journey south into the harsh, arid mountain scenery of the remote Northern Potosí province, where the diverse attractions of the **Parque Nacional Torotoro**, Bolivia's smallest national park, include

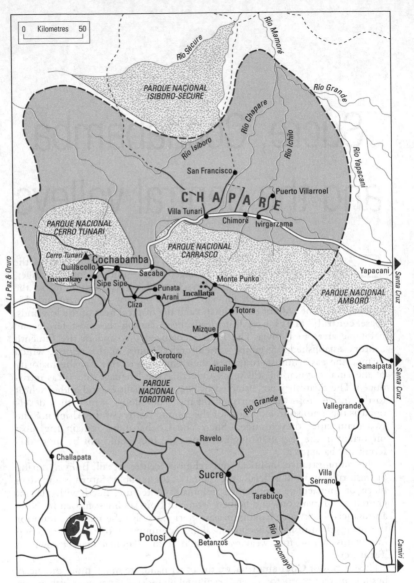

labyrinthine limestone caves, deep canyons and waterfalls, dinosaur footprints and ancient ruins.

East of Cochabamba, meanwhile, the main road to Santa Cruz passes through the **Chapare**, a beautiful region of rushing rivers and dense tropical forests, where the last foothills of the Andes plunge down into the Amazon basin. The area has become notorious in recent decades as the source of most of Bolivia's coca crop, which is used to make a large proportion of the world's illegal cocaine supply, and conflicts continue between government coca-eradication officers and local peasant farmers. As such, it's hardly an ideal area for travellers, but some areas remain safe to visit and provide a frontline insight into the war on drugs, one of the great dramas of contemporary Bolivia.

Sucre and around

Set in a broad highland valley on the eastern edge of altiplano about 162km north of Potosí, **SUCRE** is widely considered the most refined and beautiful city in Bolivia. Known at various times as Chuquisaca, Charcas and La Ciudad de la Plata – and thus also as "The City of Four Names" – it boasts some of the finest Spanish colonial architecture in South America, and enjoys a pleasant, spring-like climate all year round, thanks to its setting at an altitude of 2790m.

Sucre was the centre of Spanish power in Alto Peru throughout the colonial period, and was made **capital of Bolivia** after independence, a status it retains today, in name at least, although all real power has long since passed to La Paz. In many ways this unusual state of affairs suits Sucre very well. Whilst preserving the dignity of capital status, it has avoided many of the disadvantages faced by La Paz: its city centre has not been scarred by modern high-rises or encircled by a sprawl of urban misery, and it has escaped being focus of the constant protests, coups and insurrections that have been a regular feature of life in the de facto capital over the last century. By contrast, Sucre exudes the sense of being frozen in time somewhere back in the late nineteenth century, and the city's incongruous official status as capital gives its citizens a somewhat exaggerated sense of their own importance. But though the courtly manners and conservatism of the old aristocratic families who dominate Sucre can seem stuffy and pompous, it's nicely tempered by the youth and vitality the city enjoys as a major university centre – Sucre's is one of the oldest universities in the Americas, and still attracts thousands of students from all over Bolivia, as well as from neighbouring countries.

In addition, the city is also the administrative and market centre for a mountainous rural hinterland inhabited by Quechua-speaking **indigenous communities**, whose traditional Andean cultures provide a welcome contrast to the sometimes over-refined and Europeanized city. These communities are particularly renowned for their beautiful weavings, considered amongst the finest in all the Andes; they can be seen – and bought – in the city itself or on a daytrip to **Tarabuco**, a rural town about 60km southeast of Sucre that hosts a market every Sunday for the surrounding communities.

Some history

The city now known as Sucre was founded some time between 1538 and 1540 (the exact date is still hotly disputed by Bolivian historians) by the conquistador Pedro de Anzures during the second major Spanish incursion into the Andes south of Lago Titicaca. Initially named **Chuquisaca** (no doubt a Spanish corruption of the original indigenous name Choquechaca, meaning "Golden Bridge"), it was given the official title **Villa de la Plata** (City of Silver) after the discovery of significant quantities of silver nearby. The title proved prescient, as the massive silver deposits of Potosí were discovered soon after, and the city quickly emerged as the administrative headquarters for the mines and the centre of Spanish political, religious and military power in the region. In 1559 the **Audiencia de Charcas** – an independent court, representing the Spanish crown, with judicial and executive power over an area comprising modern-day Bolivia, Argentina and part of Peru – was established

SUCRE

PLACES TO STAY

Alojamiento El Turista	1
Alojamiento La Plata	4
Grand Hotel	9
Hostal Charcas	3
Hostal Colonial	10
Hostal de Su Merced	12
Hostal Libertad	5
Hostal Los Pinos	7
Hostal Recoletadel Sur	6
Hostal San Francisco	2
Hostal Sucre	11
Residencial Bolivia	8

PLACES TO EAT AND DRINK

Arco Iris	M
Bibliocafé	N
El Germén	F
El Huerto	A
El Mirador	R
El Patio	B
Joy Ride Café	L
Kaypichu	E
La Plaza	I
La Taverne	C
Monte Bianco	P
New Hong Kong	H
Paso de los Abuelos	Q
Pastelería Amanecer	K
Penco Penquitos	G
Pizzeria Napolitana	J
Repizza	O
Tertulia	D

Metres 0 200

▲ & Airport
▲ Cochabamba
▲ Potosi
▶ & Tarabuco
▶ Convento-Museo La Recoleta

Parque Bolívar
Corte Suprema de Justicia
Teatro Gran Mariscal
PLAZA DE LA LIBERTAD
Hospital de Santa Bárbara
Santa Mónica
Facultad de Derecho
University
Casa de la Libertad
San Agustín
San Felipe Neri
La Merced
Museo Eclesiastico
Cathedral Basilica
Prefectura
Punto ENTEL
PLAZA 25 DE MAYO
San Miguel Municipal
Alcaldia
Mercado Central
San Francisco
Banco de Santa Cruz
Banco Nacional de Bolivia
Internet 2000
ENTEL
Santo Domingo
Migración
Museo Universitario Charcas
Museo-Convento Santa Clara
Santa Teresa
Museo de Arte Indígena
San Lázaro

N

here. The city become home to the first bishopric in Alto Peru in 1552, and in 1624 the **Universidad de San Francisco Javier** – only the third university in all the Americas – was founded here to train the religious and administrative specialists needed to manage the vast conquered territories.

The first half of the seventeenth century was La Plata's golden age, as the wealth from the Potosí mines funded the construction of lavish churches and monasteries, extravagant palaces and administrative buildings. The city also served as a base for the exploration, evangelization and conquest of territories to the east and south. Its power waned with the flow of silver, however, and in 1776 it was made subject to the rule of the new Spanish Virreinato de la Plata in Buenos Aires, reverting to the name of Chuquisaca to avoid confusion. The university retained its importance, even so, and became a centre in developing the liberal ideas that led to the first qualified declaration of independence from Spain, which was made here on May 25, 1809. After independence in 1825 the city was made the **capital** of the new Republic of Bolivia and renamed **Sucre** in honour of **Antonio José de Sucre**, the Venezuelan general who completed the defeat of the Spanish at the battle of Ayacucho and served as Bolivia's first president. Its economic importance continued to decline, however, and when the seat of both congress and the presidency was moved to La Paz after the civil war between the two cities in 1899, it merely confirmed long-established realities. In a very Bolivian compromise, Sucre remained the seat of the supreme court – the third of the three branches of government – and was allowed to retain the title of official or constitutional capital, an honorary position it still holds today.

Arrival and information

Sucre is a small, compact city with a straightforward grid streetplan that makes it easy to find your way around, and other than the bus terminal and airport everything is within easy walking distance of the historic city centre, which is where all the accommodation is located. The **airport** (T04/6454445) is about 8km northwest of the city; Micros I and F run from there into the centre of town along Avenida Siles (30min); alternatively, a taxi should cost about $3. All long-distance buses arrive and depart from the **bus terminal** (T04/6452029), about 3km northwest of the town centre on Ostria Gutierrez. From here it's a $0.70 taxi ride into the centre of town, or you can catch Micro A, which runs down to the Mercado Central, a block north of the main Plaza 25 de Mayo. **Collective taxis** arriving from Potosí will drop you off outside your hotel or anywhere else in the centre of town.

By Bolivian standards, Sucre is extremely well equipped with tourist information offices. The main municipal **tourist office** (Mon–Fri 8.30am–noon & 2.30–6pm; T04/6455136 or 6451083) is on the first floor of the Casa de Cultura, a block southeast of Plaza 25 de Mayo on Calle Argentina, and there are also information **kiosks** (Mon–Sat 8.30am–noon & 2.30–6pm) at the airport, the bus terminal and on the corner of calles Argentina and Olañeta. The staff at all these offices are helpful and will do their best to answer questions in Spanish; they also usually have a colourful street map of Sucre and a glossy pamphlet on the city's major attractions available for sale, as well as a range of leaflets. There's also an **Oficina Universitaria de Turismo** (Mon–Fri 8.30am–12.30pm & 2.30–6.30pm; T04/6452283) on the southeastern side of Plaza 25 de Mayo, run by enthusiastic university students who are a good source of information and can sometimes provide student guides (free, though a tip is always appreciated) to show you around the major sites – you'll also need to come here if you want to get onto the roof of the Iglesia de San Felipe Neri (see p.228).

Fiestas in Sucre

Sucre's main annual religious celebration is the **Fiesta de la Virgen de Guadeloupe**, on September 8, which is marked by a procession and folkloric dances. In the second half of September each year the city hosts an **International Cultural Festival**, with performances by theatre and dance groups from around Bolivia, Latin America and the rest of the world. The anniversary of the 1809 "Primer Grito Libertario de America", the first declaration of independence in South America, is marked every **May 25** with civic and military parades, and is a public hoiliday throughout the Department of Chuquisaca. The department's most famous annual fiesta, however, is the indigenous celebration of **Pujjlay** (see p.238), staged on the third Sunday of March in Tarabuco, 60km southeast of Sucre.

Accommodation

Sucre has a pretty good range of **accommodation**, almost all of it conveniently located in the heart of the old city centre. There are some particularly beautiful places, set inside converted colonial mansions, which represent very good value in the middle and upper prices ranges: if you're on a tight budget but like to splash out every so often, this is the place to do it.

Budget

Alojamiento El Turista Ravelo 114 ⊕04/6453172. Bright but basic and rather grubby rooms with shared bath and limited hot water. Strictly for those on a tight budget. ❶

Alojamiento La Plata Ravelo 32 ⊕04/6452102. Popular budget option offering small but clean rooms with shared bath around a sunny courtyard. ❷

Hostal Charcas Ravelo 62 ⊕04/6453972, ⑨04/6455764. Modern and efficient establishment, with abundant hot water and helpful, welcoming staff. Rooms are scrupulously clean but rather cramped, and those with private bathrooms lack ventilation. Breakfast available. ❸

Hostal San Francisco Arce 191 ⊕04/6452117, ⑨04/6462693, ⓔ hostalsf@mara.scr.entelnet.bo. Modern, colonial-style building with pleasant rooms opening onto sunny balconies around the usual central patio. Excellent value, and is breakfast available. ❸

Residencial Bolivia San Alberto 42 ⊕04/6454346. Friendly and good-value *residencial*, with spacious, airy rooms (with or without bathroom) set around a bright courtyard with plenty of plants. A modest breakfast is included. ❷–❸

Moderate and expensive

Grand Hotel Arce 61 ⊕04/6452104, ⑨04/6452461. Good-value mid-range option with comfortable and well-decorated rooms set around two peaceful colonial patios, the innermost of which overflows with lush tropical vegetation. Breakfast included. ❹

Hostal Colonial Plaza 25 de Mayo 3 ⊕04/6440309 or 6440310, ⑨04/6440311, ⓔ colonial@mara.scr.entelnet.bo. Excellent location on the main plaza, though it feels less colonial than most of its rivals, despite the name. Rooms are adequate, if a bit musty and gloomy, and only the rather overpriced suites have views over the plaza. Breakfast included. ❺–❻

Hostal de Su Merced Azurduy 16 ⊕04/6442706 or 6445150, ⓦ www.boliviaweb .com/companies/sumerced. Immaculately restored and converted eighteenth-century house with a delightful central patio and rooftop sun terraces with panoramic views of the city. Rooms combine opulent antique furniture with a full range of modern comforts, including cable TV. Breakfast included. ❻

Hostal Libertad Arce with San Alberto ⊕04/6453101/2, ⑨04/6460128. Purpose-built modern hotel which lacks some of the charm of its colonial rivals but makes up for it with spacious, well-appointed and reasonably priced rooms (with cable TV), helpful and efficient staff, and a rooftop restaurant with excellent views. Breakfast included. ❹

Hostal Los Pinos Colón 502 ⊕04/6454403, ⑨04/6455639. Peaceful and secluded family-run hotel with comfortable modern rooms and a delightful flower-filled garden. Breakfast included. ❹

Hostal Recoleta del Sur Ravelo 205 ⊕04/ 6454789 or 6446603, ⓦ www.boliviaturista /contur. Modern, carpeted rooms with cable TV in a converted colonial house with a glass-roofed patio and a classic stone-pillared corner doorway. Breakfast included. **4**

Hostal Sucre Bustillos 113 ⊕04/6451411 or

6461928, Ⓕ04/6452677. Converted colonial mansion with period décor and pleasant if slightly gloomy rooms set around two charming flower-filled courtyards. Breakfast included. **4**

The City

Laid out in the classic grid pattern required by Spanish imperial ordinances, Sucre is a jewel of colonial and nineteenth-century architecture, its splendid churches, monasteries and mansions a reminder of the wealth and power the city once enjoyed. The historic city centre was declared a UNESCO world heritage site in 1991, and strict building codes mean most of it has been preserved much as it was a hundred years ago. Neon signs are banned, and a municipal regulation requires all buildings to be whitewashed once a year, maintaining the characteristic that earned Sucre another of its many grandiose titles: "La Ciudad Blanca de Las Americas" – the White City of the Americas. In the seventeenth century the city boasted a church or chapel for almost every single block, and many of these still stand, while the extravagant sculpture and paintings that filled them are on display in several of the city's museums, in quantities large enough to exhaust even the most dedicated enthusiast. The one museum not to miss, however, is the **Museo de Arte Indigena**, which is dedicated to art of a very different nature – the beautiful weavings of the indigenous groups of the surrounding Department of Chuquisaca.

Plaza 25 de Mayo

The centre of Sucre is the spacious **Plaza 25 de Mayo**, shaded by tall palms and dotted with benches where people of all social classes – from eminent lawyers to humble campesinos – pass the time of day chatting, reading newspapers or greeting passing acquaintances. It's a great place to watch the world go by whilst having your shoes shined or enjoying a hot *salteña* or a cool glass of the orange juice which is sold from handcarts by ever-present street vendors. In the middle of the plaza, flanked by bronze lions, stands a statue of **Mariscal Antonio José de Sucre**, the Venezuelan-born South American independence hero and first president of Bolivia whose name the city bears. The plaza is lined with elegant colonial and republican public and religious buildings, all painted an immaculate white that dazzles in the usually bright sunshine.

On the northwest side of the square is the Neoclassical **Alcaldía Municipal**, the town hall, built in 1888 to replace a colonial *cabildo* dating back to 1610. Beside it stands the simple but well-preserved colonial facade of the original seventeenth-century Jesuit University, with carved wooden balconies overlooking the square and an elegant stone portico bearing the university's coat of arms. Now known as the **Casa de la Libertad** (Mon–Fri 9am–noon & 2.30–6.30pm, Sat 9.30am–noon; $1.50), this was where the Bolivian act of independence was signed on August 6, 1825, and the building now houses a small but interesting museum dedicated to the birth of the republic. Inside, the original signed document proclaiming a sovereign and independent state is on display in the assembly hall where the declaration was made by a constitutional assembly of 48 representatives from across the country; the same hall also housed the Bolivian congress from then until the seat of government was moved to La Paz in 1899. On the walls hang portraits of Sucre and Bolívar – the latter, by the Peruvian painter Gil de Castro, was described by the *libertador* himself as being the best likeness ever made of him. A side room houses portraits of the principal signatories, while another has paintings of pro-independence guerrillas and their royalist foes, plus a collection of captured royalist swords, guns and bloodstained banners. There's also a gallery of portraits of almost all Bolivia's presidents, an impressive number given the youth of the republic, thank to frequent coups and assassinations, most of them looking more dignified in profile than they were in office. Around the corner on the southwest side of the plaza stands the lavish Neoclassical facade of what was to have been the **presidential palace**, a glorious monument to hubris completed shortly before the seat of the presidency was moved to La Paz; it now houses the Prefectura (departmental government) de Chuquisaca.

The Cathedral and Museo Eclesiastico

Next to the Prefectura, facing sideways onto the southwest side of the plaza, stands the **Cathedral**, or Basilica Mayor. Built between 1551 and 1712 and extensively modified since, it combines a variety of architectural styles. The side door facing the plaza and main door looking onto Calle Ortiz are both highly decorative seventeenth-century stone porticos carved in the mestizo-Baroque style, while the square belltower with three balconies decorated with statues of the apostles and evangelists dates from the late eighteenth century; the clock in the tower, which still keeps perfect time, was made in London in 1772.

The décor in the lavish Neoclassical **interior** dates back to 1826, with soaring pillars painted in immaculate white piped with gold, extravagant crystal chandeliers and massive silver candlesticks. A side chapel houses the jewel-encrusted image of the **Virgen de Guadeloupe**, the religious patron of Sucre. Painted in 1601 by Fray Diego de Ocaña, the image quickly developed cult status, and wealthy devotees began sticking gold, diamonds, emeralds and pearls to the picture as an expression of faith or in gratitude for wishes granted and miracles performed. These were arranged in a more orderly fashion when the image was laminated in gold in 1734, and though the popular saying that the value of the jewels would be enough to pay off Bolivia's international debt is probably an exaggeration (as well as being a veiled critique of the wealth of the Church compared to the poverty of many Bolivians), the glittering opulence of the bejewelled Virgin is astonishing nonetheless.

Though it's open most mornings for Mass, the best way to see the cathedral – and the Virgin – is as part of a visit to the **Museo Eclesiastico** (Mon–Fri 10am–noon & 3–5pm, Sat 10am–noon; $1.50), which boasts a fine collection of colonial religious art. The entrance to the museum is beside the cathedral just along Calle Ortiz. Visits are by **guided tour** only, so it's best to turn up shortly after opening, as otherwise you may have to wait a while for the next group to form; tours last about an hour. Amongst the paintings on display are a series of portraits of saints by the Cochabamba-born master of the mestizo-Baroque style, Melchor Pérez de Holguín, and several works in a much more European style by the sixteenth century Italian-born Jesuit Bernardo Bitti, who studied under Raphael. There's also a substantial hoard of finely crafted silver and gold religious paraphernalia such as candelabras, crucifixes and chalices, much of it encrusted with gems, further evidence of the enormous wealth that flowed through Sucre (and the Church) during the colonial silver-mining boom in Potosí.

South of Plaza 25 de Mayo

Two blocks southwest of the plaza along Calle Ortiz stands the formidable Neoclassical bulk of the **Iglesia de San Felipe Neri**, with its two tall belltowers. Built in the last years of the nineteenth century, this is the only building in the city not painted white – its tall brick and stone walls have been left bare, as they have been throughout its existence. The church itself is rarely open to the public, but you can get up onto its **roof** (Mon–Fri 4–6pm; $1) to enjoy the splendid panoramic views across the city – you'll have to arrange in advance to go up with a student guide from the Oficina Universitaria de Turismo on Plaza 25 de Mayo (see p.225); they usually take visitors up onto the roof every weekday afternoon, so you get to enjoy the sunset over the city, but be aware that they're not noted for their punctuality. The adjoining **monastery**, which boasts an elegant colonial courtyard surrounded by arched cloisters on two levels, is now a school. Opposite San Felipe, on the corner of calles Perez and Azurduy, is the unremarkable seventeenth-century **Iglesia de la Merced**. It's usually locked, though if you do find it open for a service, it's worth a look inside for the extravagant Baroque altarpieces smothered in gold leaf, one of which is thought to be the oldest in Bolivia; the elaborately carved wooden pulpit and altar are also very beautiful.

Housed in a delightful seventeenth-century mansion a block east of La Merced on the corner of calles Dalence and Bolívar is the rambling but worthwhile **Museo Universitario Charcas** (Mon–Sat 8.30am–noon & 2.30–6pm; $1.50), which is really four museums in one, combining the university's archeological, anthropological, colonial and modern art collections, all set around a series of colonial patios filled with flowers and surrounded by arched cloisters. Visits are by guided tour only and last at least an hour: you'll be assigned a student guide on arrival. Some of the guides speak a little English, and how long the tour lasts depends on your and their enthusiasm: don't be afraid to hurry the guide through any sections you find unexciting and linger in those you find more interesting.

The **modern art** collection is perhaps the least impressive of the four, comprising works by local artists in derivative styles ranging from surrealism and abstract expressionism to socialist realism, applied to local subjects: romanticized depictions of the indigenous cultures of the region surrounding Sucre predominate. The **colonial religious art** collection is much more substantial and includes some very fine works, though the subject matter – Christ, the Virgin, and assorted saints and bishops – is repetitive, to say the least. Highlights include a whole room full of pictures by the mestizo-Baroque master **Melchor Pérez de Holguín** and a finely detailed bird's eye view of Potosí painted in 1758 by Gaspar Miguel de Berrio. There's also some beautiful colonial furniture on display, including decorative desks richly inlaid or delicately carved with images of flowers and animals, and wooden "portable chapels", taken by priests on expeditions to convert the indigenous populations, which unfold to reveal carved figures of saints and brightly painted biblical scenes.

The **anthropology** section is a mish-mash of indigenous costumes and artefacts from all over Bolivia: Andean musical instruments; woven vegetable-fibre clothes from the Amazon; lurid *diablada* masks from Oruro. Particularly striking are the traditional Tarabuceño costumes, with their bright striped ponchos, leather hats shaped like the helmets of the conquistadors, and thick-soled wooden shoes. The **archeology** section comprises an extensive collection of artefacts – pottery, tools, weapons, some metalwork, textile fragments – from all the major Andean civilizations, ranging from paleolithic arrowheads through to Inca copper axe heads and idols, all displayed chronologically, though with little explanation or background information.

Two blocks northeast along Calle Bolívar on the corner with Calvo stands the rather plain **Iglesia de Santo Domingo**, founded by the Dominican order in 1545 but extensively remodelled in the early eighteenth century. If you still have an appetite for further colonial religious art after visiting the university and cathedral museums, it's worth a trip to the **Museo-Convento Santa Clara** (Mon–Fri 9am–noon & 3–6pm, Sat 9.30am–noon; $0.80), a block southeast on the corner of Calvo and Bolívar. This still-functioning nunnery has a range of fairly standard colonial religious pictures, most of them painted by anonymous indigenous artists in Sucre in the seventeenth and eighteenth century, as well as some antique furniture and religious vestments; you can also see the church's Neoclassical interior, most notable for its seventeenth-century organ.

Two blocks further southeast on Calvo stands the **Iglesia de San Lázaro**, the oldest church in the city and the original cathedral, which was first built around 1538 but extensively remodelled over the following centuries; the building you see today is an unexceptional Renaissance-style structure dating from the late eighteenth century. If you want to look inside you'll have to come at 7am, when it opens for Mass, but the elaborate carved wooden altarpiece has been painted over in white, and other than some colourful statues of saints and a particularly gruesome Christ image, there's little worth seeing.

Museo de Arte Indigena

Housed in an elegant colonial building three blocks southeast from Plaza 25 de Mayo on the corner of calles San Alberto and Potosí, the fascinating **Museo de Arte Indigena** (Mon–Fri 8.30am–noon & 2.30–6pm; $2) is dedicated to the distinctive weavings of two local Quechua-speaking indigenous groups: the **Jalq'a**, who number about 26,000 and live in the mountains west of Sucre, and the **Tarabuceños** (see p.237), a more numerous group who live around the town of Tarabuco to the east. The museum is run by the non-governmental organization ASUR (Antropologos del Sur Andino), which since the mid-1980s has been successfully working with Jalq'a and Tarabuceño communities to revive traditional weaving designs and techniques that had been dying out as older textile pieces were bought by collectors, leaving no examples to inspire younger weavers. This renaissance of indigenous art has seen both the quality and market value of the weavings of both groups rise dramatically, turning the craft into a source of income for hundreds of desperately poor campesino families.

Expertly laid out, with precise text explanations in Spanish, English French or German, the museum introduces the different ethnic groups with maps and colour photos, then explains the weaving techniques (with plenty of examples of looms and other tools) and describes the different plants used to make natural dyes. There's often a Jalq'a or Tarabuceño woman weaving away in the courtyard as you wander around the museum, so you can see the creative process in action. **Archeological finds** on display demonstrate that many of the wood and bone-weaving tools in use today are identical to those used in the Andes more than a thousand years ago, while some beautiful and very well-preserved ancient textile fragments reveal an astonishing continuity of style, technique and aesthetic vision stretching back over many centuries. The central attractions, though, are the weavings themselves: though they're mostly everyday items of clothing, it's hard to deny the museum's central premise that they should be treated as fine art rather than mere *artesania*. Brightly coloured, intricately detailed and laden with a complex symbolism, they're works of great creativity that express a distinctively Andean artistic vision. The textiles are displayed in chronological order, revealing the development and changing style over time – the decline in quality in the 1970s before the renaissance project began is clearly evident. There are also examples of how they are worn in daily dress and in ritual costumes for fiestas.

The difference in style between the weavings of the Jalq'a and Tarabuceños could hardly be more dramatic, even though the two groups live only a short distance apart to the west and east of Sucre. **Tarabuceño ponchos** (*unkus*) are woven with bright stripes of orange, black, red, green and gold, while smaller items like the *chu'spa* bags used to carry coca and *chumpi* waist bands are decorated with finely detailed and usually symmetrical designs depicting scenes from everyday life: wild and domestic animals like condors, horses, llamas and pumas; trees and crops like potatoes and maize; people ploughing, harvesting or dancing at fiestas. The **Jalq'a designs**, on the other hand, are entirely figurative, eschewing symmetry and abstract geometry. Woven into women's shawls known as *aqsus* and almost always only black and red in colour, they depict a kind of primordial chaos filled with a plethora of strange beasts: animals with elongated bodies and multiple heads or eyes sprouting from their tails; birds with puma heads; toads with wings. The few human figures that do appear seem lost in this forest of supernatural animals. This is the *ukchu pacha*, a mythological underworld of extraordinary and untamed creatures, over which rules the *Sax'ra*, a horned devil-like figure with wings who appears in the centre of some of the weavings, part Andean demon and part god of fertility and abundance. Many of the designs are inspired by dreams, and new themes are constantly being incorporated, but though every piece is unique they all fall within a set of artistic norms that makes them instantly recognisable as Jalq'a – both to neighbouring ethnic groups and to international art collectors. Examples of both weaving styles are available to buy in a shop attached to the museum, and though they're far from cheap, particularly the Jalq'a stuff – larger individual pieces can cost well over $100 – the money goes direct to the indigenous artists who made them, and the quality is exquisite.

Convento-Museo La Recoleta

Seven blocks southeast from Plaza 25 de Mayo, Calle Calvo climbs steeply uphill towards **Plaza Pedro de Anzares**, a broad square used as a playground by local schoolchildren which enjoys commanding views across the red-tiled rooftops of Sucre and the surrounding mountains. On the southeast side of the plaza stands the **Convento-Museo La Recoleta** (Mon–Fri 9–11.30am & 2.30–4.30pm; $1.20) a tranquil Franciscan monastery that now houses an interesting little museum of colonial religious art and materials related to the missionary work of the Franciscan order in Bolivia. Visits are by guided tour only, so it's best to turn up shortly after opening so you don't have to wait long for a tour – if you do have to wait, the *Café Mirador* on the other side of the plaza is a good place to pass the time over a drink whilst taking in the views over the city.

Founded in 1538, La Recoleta was for nearly three centuries the headquarters of Franciscan efforts to convert the indigenous peoples of Bolivia. Set around a series of delightful flower-filled colonial patios lined with arched cloisters, the museum is home to a substantial collection of **colonial religious paintings**, though if you've been to Sucre's other museums you may by now have had your fill of pictures of enraptured mystics and agonized saints. More interesting is the display of items relating to Franciscan missionary efforts, including bows and arrows, feather headdresses and plant-fibre clothing given to the missionaries by the different lowland tribes they contacted, and photographs of early twentieth-century missionaries, mounted on horseback in ponchos and sombreros and looking more like desperadoes than priests.

Though it dates back to 1600, the **monastery church** was remodelled in rather anodyne style in the nineteenth century: the one noteworthy feature is the exquisite Baroque wooden choir stalls in the upper choir, beautifully carved in 1674 with gruesome images of a massacre of Franciscan missionaries in Nagasaki, Japan: crucified or stabbed with lances, the monks are shown going to their deaths with the sublime smiles of those who believe their place in paradise is assured. Though it's now back in Franciscan hands, in the early nineteenth century the monastery was briefly requisitioned by the Bolivian authorities and used as a barracks; in the corridor outside the choir a plaque and portrait marks the spot where the Bolivian president Pedro Blanco was murdered during a successful coup in 1829, just five days after taking office. Beside the monastery stands the **Cedro Millenario**, a great, gnarled *cedro* tree over a thousand years old and five metres in diameter – it requires at least eight people hand in hand to encircle its trunk.

Northwest of Plaza 25 de Mayo

Half a block northwest of Plaza 25 de Mayo along Calle Arenales, the modest whitewashed Baroque facade of the **Iglesia de San Miguel** (open for mass early most mornings), completed in 1621, conceals one of the most lavish church interiors in Sucre, with glorious carved Baroque altarpieces covered in gold leaf and an exquisite panelled *mudéjar* ceiling of intricate interlocking geometric shapes. On the corner of the next block, the **Iglesia de Santa Mónica**, founded in 1547, boasts a extravagant stone portico that is the finest example of the mestizo-Baroque style in Sucre, carved with palm trees and floral designs, spiralled columns, and pillars supported by human figures looking like pre-Columbian idols; sadly, the interior is always closed.

Just southwest of Santa Mónica along Junín is the main entrance of the **University** (or the Universidad Mayor Real y Pontificia de San Francisco Xavier, to give it its full title). The university was originally founded by the Jesuits in 1624, predating Harvard in the US, and was a major seat of learning throughout the colonial period as well as an important centre of liberal thought in the early nineteenth century. Ideas developed here, particularly the so-called *Silogismo altoperuano* – the argument that the loyalty of the colonies was owed to the person of the king and not to the Spanish government, and that sovereignty therefore reverted to the colonies once King Fernando VII was forced to abdicate by Napoleon – played a key role in the declaration of independence from Spain in 1809. The university is still central to the city's social, cultural and economic life, and is worth visiting for a look inside the **Facultad de Derecho** at Junín 652, which has the biggest colonial courtyard in Sucre, a beautiful open space flanked on all sides by arched cloisters on two levels.

A block northeast of Plaza 25 de Mayo beside the bustling public market on the corner of Ravelo and Arce, the **Iglesia de San Francisco** (daily 7am–7pm) was built between 1540 and 1581 to minister to the growing indigenous population of the newly founded city, and remains the most popular church with Sucre's Quechua-speaking population – modern signs on the walls warning against the use of holy water in witchcraft and magic reveal that, centuries later, the priests here still face an uphill struggle against deeply entrenched pre-Christian practices. The entrance to the church is flanked by two square towers, one of which houses the **Campana de la Libertad**, the bell that sounded the call to arms at the start of the pro-independence uprising in 1809. The interior boasts splendid gilded Baroque altarpieces and an elaborate panelled *mudéjar* ceiling.

Three blocks northwest of Plaza 25 de Mayo along Calle Arenales is the small **Plaza de la Libertad**, lined with palm trees and centred on an obelisk donated by the city of Buenos Aires to commemorate the 1809 Declaration of

Independence. On the southwest side of the square stands the elegant Renaissance facade of the **Hospital Santa Bárbara**, built between 1554 and 1563 and still functioning as a health centre. On the northwest side is the grandiose facade of the **Teatro Gran Mariscal**, one of several buildings in this part of town built in French Neoclassical style at the start of the twentieth century. The road that runs down the right-hand side of the theatre leads to the **Parque Símon Bolívar**, a peaceful park neatly laid out in French style – there's even a model of the Eiffel Tower at its centre – which is popular with families at weekends. Looking over the park from its south end stands the grandiose **Corte Suprema de Justicia**, completed in 1945 in opulent French Neoclassical style. This is the only branch of government still based in Sucre, and as such the only real justification for the city's continuing status as constitutional capital of Bolivia.

Cal Orko dinosaur footprints

Five kilometres outside Sucre on the road to Cochabamba, the low mountain of **Cal Orko** is home to the world's biggest known collection of **dinosaur footprints**, which were discovered in 1994 by workers at a local cement works and limestone quarry. Approximately 5000 prints from at least 150 different types of dinosaur can be seen here, covering an area of around 30,000 square metres of near-vertical rock face, an astonishing profusion given that the second biggest known site, in Germany, contains just 240 prints from two types of dinosaur. The prints were laid down between 65 and 85 million years ago on a flat bed of mud or sand covered by shallow water, and were then covered by a protective layer of ash from a volcanic explosion. Further layers of ash, silt and other sediments followed, the prints became fossilized, and about 25 million years ago the Andes began to rise, eventually bringing them to where they stand today.

You can only visit the dinosaur tracks on a guided tour in the **Dino-Truck** – a painted pick-up truck – run by the Abbey Path tour agency (☎04/6451863), which leaves daily at 10am and noon (and also at 3.30pm on Sundays) from outside the cathedral. Transport costs $1.50 and the tour an additional $1.50 – there's no need to buy tickets in advance as they lay on extra transport when numbers are high. The guides usually speak English as well as Spanish, and are generally very informative and able to bring the footprints to life, which is crucial if, like most visitors, you know little about paleontology.

As well as a good guide, it requires some imagination to appreciate the footprints. At first sight, they're not even easy to spot: scattered across a long plane of greyish rock about 100m high and set at an incline of about 70°, they look at first like so many pockmarks. Study them for a while, though, and you'll see the clear footprints of many different sizes running in long lines across the surface, and the astonishing fact that you're looking at the trails of animals who lived some seventy million years ago in the Cretaceous Era begins to sink in. It's thought the site may have been the scene of a chase and kill by predators, who were followed by various scavengers. The largest prints are about a metre in diameter – these are thought to have belonged to a brontosaurus. The longest single track (and by far the longest in the world) stretches for over half a kilometre and was laid down by a baby tyrannosaurus rex known to researchers as Johnny Walker. Other species whose footprints have been identified include the three-horned triceratops and the carnivorous alosaurus. The cement plant is still operating, and new prints are constantly being revealed, but ongoing quarrying and natural erosion threaten to destroy the tracks so far uncovered. The site has been declared a national monument, but no serious conservation measures are yet in place, and though there has been talk of establishing a "Cretaceous Park" to protect the tracks, of preserving them with silicon injections into the rock face, or even of moving them to a purpose-built exhibition centre, as yet there's no sign of any organization coming forward with the substantial funds this would require. All the more reason then to visit Cal Orko while the tracks are still there.

Castillo La Glorieta

About 6km outside Sucre on the road south to Potosí is the bizarre shell of the **Castillo La Glorieta** (daily 8.30am–noon & 2–6pm; $1.10), a private palace built at the end of the nineteenth century and a must for lovers of kitsch. Built over seven years from 1890 as a home for the mining baron Francisco Argandoña and his wife Clotilda, the Castillo is probably the most ridiculous construction in Bolivia, and a clear example of how wealth and taste do not always coincide. Now being gradually restored after years of neglect (it was taken over by the military in the 1950s), the extravagant pink sandstone structure combines a surreal mish-mash of different architectural styles, including a minaret, a Gothic clocktower and a Byzantine onion dome, while life-size stucco horses' heads running the length of the roof add a sublime Dali-esque touch. The once-lavish interior still boasts elaborate Neoclassical stucco ceilings, Venetian stained glass and fireplaces of pink Veronese marble, as well as portraits of Francisco and Clotilda in full princely regalia meeting Pope Leo XIII, who pronounced them "Principes de la Glorieta" during their visit to Europe in 1898 in recognition for their work looking after orphans. To reach the Castillo, take **micro #4** from the corner of calles Ravelo and Arce, a thirty-minute trip.

Eating, drinking and nightlife

Perhaps because of its status as official capital and growing international population, Sucre is home to a good variety of **restaurants** where you can get everything from the spicy local cuisine to authentic Chinese, French, Italian and vegetarian food at reasonable prices. Even cheaper, if you're on a budget, is the **Mercado Central**, at the junction of calles Ravelo and Arce, which has filling soups and meals for under $1, a delicious range of fresh fruit juices, and hearty breakfasts from early in the morning.

The **salteñas** in Sucre are rightly considered the best in Bolivia, and locals consume them with a passion – they're available from stalls and handcarts throughout the city, and from specialist *salteñerias*, which open only from midmorning to noon and serve almost nothing else. Another local speciality is **chorizos chuquisaceñas**, spicy pork sausages sold in the market and in restaurants. Sucre is also famous throughout Bolivia for the quality and variety of its **chocolates**, which you'll find on sale at specialist shops in the city centre: try Taboada, on the corner of Plaza 25 de Mayo and Calle Arenales.

Nightlife revolves around the lively student bar and café scene; many places stay open into the early hours, especially at weekends (despite the opposition of the archbishop). For late-night dancing there are also several **discos**, all dominated by the under 20s – *Mitsu Mania*, on Venezuela with Maestro, is about the most popular. In addition, several of town's restaurants host frequent performances of **Andean folk music**, which are popular with locals as well as tourists, and some double as late-night drinking spots. The Casa de Cultura, on Calle Argentina a block from the plaza, also hosts frequent live folk music performances, as well as art exhibitions and other cultural events.

Restaurants and salteñerias

Arco Iris Ortíz 42. Swiss restaurant, popular with tour groups, serving decent pasta dishes for about $2 as well as Swiss classics like fondue and rosti. Evenings only; live folkloric music on Saturdays.

El Germén San Alberto 237. Good German-run vegetarian restaurant offering an imaginative range of main courses ($2–3) as well as excellent cakes and pastries. Closed Sun.

El Huerto Ladislao Cabrera 86. Ask a local for the best restaurant in town, and the chances are they'll direct you here. The menu features excellent meat, chicken and fish dishes cooked to both traditional Bolivian and sophisticated international recipes for about $4–5, served outdoors in a beautiful garden. It's some distance from the city centre, but well worth the taxi fare. Lunchtimes only.

El Patio San Alberto 18. Popular *salteñeria* serving rich, juicy *salteñas* in a beautiful colonial patio filled with bougainvillea and other flowering plants. Mornings only.

Kaypicchu San Alberto 168. Popular vegetarian restaurant offering a wide range of tasty and healthy dishes including muesli, fruit and yoghurt for breakfast, good soups, salads and pastas, and a decent set almuerzo for $1.50. Closed Mon.

La Plaza Plaza 25 de Mayo. First-floor restaurant whose generous $2 four-course set almuerzos are so popular with well-to-do locals that if you don't get here by 12.30pm you may miss out. Sadly, the tables on the balcony overlooking the plaza are almost always reserved, and the service is rather brusque. Live folkloric music on Friday nights.

La Taverne Arce 35. Authentic French restaurant attached to the Alliance Française serving classic dishes like coq au vin, boeuf bourguignon and rabbit for about $4, as well as excellent home-made pâté and delicious chocolate gateaux.

Monte Bianco Colón 149. Wonderful little Italian-owned restaurant with a warm, cosy atmosphere and delicious pasta and pizza for about $3. The *penne a la vodka* is particularly good, and the tiramisu irresistible. Evenings only; closed Sun.

New Hong Kong San Alberto 242. Tasty and authentic Cantonese food at surprisingly low prices given the upmarket decor, with main couses from just $1.50, and a wide choice of filling set lunches for $2.

Paso del Los Abuelos Bustillos 216. Upmarket *salteñeria* where Sucre's wealthier citizens go for their mid-morning snacks: at $0.50 each the *salteñas* are relatively expensive, but worth every cent.

Pizzeria Napolitana Plaza 25 de Mayo 30. Sucre's longest-established Italian restaurant, serving reasonable pizza and pasta, home-made ice cream, strong coffee and a daily choice of six different set lunches for $2–3. Closed Tues.

Repizza N. Ortíz 78. Cosy pizzeria popular for its good-value set almuerzo. Not the best pizza, but they keep serving until the early hours of the morning, and the menu also includes lasagne and several meat dishes. Live folk music at weekends.

Bars and cafés

Bibliocafé N. Ortíz 50. Bohemian bar-cafe attracting a good mix of locals and travellers from early evening until late at night with its mellow music and intimate atmosphere. Also serves snacks and light meals, and there are live rock bands at weekends. Closed Mon.

El Mirador Plaza Anzures. Outdoor café, with fantastic views over the city, serving snacks and light meals throughout the day, along with beer, juices and excellent iced cappuccinos. Profits help fund a museum and educational project for local children. Closed Mon.

Joy Ride Café Ortíz 14. Trendy European-run bar-café serving tasty meals and snacks as well as cocktails and ice-cold beer. It gets particularly lively on Friday and Saturday nights.

Pasteleria Amanacer Junín 810-B. Cosy little café serving delicious cakes and biscuits, run by a social project helping disabled Bolivian children. Open daytime only.

Penco Penquitos Estudiantes 54. Café-bakery serving good strong coffee, decadent cream cakes and excellent *salteñas* and pastries, including delicious hot cheese-filled croissants. There's another branch behind the Mercado Central at Av Hernando Siles 713.

Tertulia Plaza 25 de Mayo 59. Popular night-time drinking hideaway for Sucre's artists and intellectuals, dimly lit and decorated with a bizarre mix of colonial religious and surrealist art; they also serve tasty but expensive food. Closed Wed.

Listings

Airlines Aerosur, Arenales 31 ☎04/6462141; LAB, Bustillos 121 ☎04/6452666; TAM, Junín 742 ☎04/6452213.

Banks and exchange Casa de Cambios Ambar, San Alberto 7, and El Arca, España 134, both change travellers' cheques and cash dollars at

Moving on from Sucre

Buses to Cochabamba, La Paz, Oruro and **Santa Cruz** (via Samaipata) depart from the bus terminal, about 3km northwest of the town centre on Ostria Gutierrez. Most long-distance buses depart in the evening and travel overnight – you can check departure times by calling the terminal on ☏04/6452029. If you're heading **to Potosí, collective taxis** depart from outside the bus terminal as soon as they have at least four passengers. These are faster, more comfortable and more frequent than the buses, and cost only about $1 more per person. When the road is passable, usually only in the dry season, buses also run via Camiri **to Villamontes** and **Yacuiba**, an arduous but exceptionally scenic journey down from the Andes into the Chaco lowlands.

There are daily **flights** from Sucre's airport (☏04/6454445) to La Paz, Santa Cruz and Cochabamba, as well as less frequent (2–3 weekly) services to Tarija. The airport is about 8km northwest of town: micros I and F run there from Avenida Siles with Junín; alternatively, a taxi should cost about $3.

reasonable rates. There are also plenty of ATMs around town where you can withdraw cash on Visa or Mastercard, including at the Banco de Santa Cruz and Banco Nacional de Bolivia, opposite each other at San Alberto with España.

Bus information ☏04/6452029

Car rental Auto Cambio Chuquisaca, Av Mendoza 1106 ☏04/6460984; Imbex, Potosí 499 ☏04/6461222.

Hospital Hospital Santa Bárbara, Plaza de la Libertad ☏04/6451900.

Immigration Pastor Saínz 117 ☏04/6453647.

Internet access There are internet cafés all over the city, most of which charge about $0.60 an hour: try Punto Entel on the plaza, Refugio de los Chateadores a couple of doors down, or Internet 2000 on San Alberto with España.

Language courses Academia Latinoamericana de Español, Dalence 109 with Ortiz (☏04/6460537, ✉latino@sucre.bo.net), part of the international Casa de Lenguas chain, offers weekly programmes of private or group lessons, and can arrange for students to live and eat with Bolivian host families or find voluntary work in Sucre.

Laundry Limpieza La America, Ravelo 50 opposite the Mercado Central; Lavanderia Laundry, Loa with Av Siles.

Post office Correo Central, Junín with Ayacucho.

Telephone office The main ENTEL office is at España 271 with Camargo, and there are smaller Punto ENTEL offices on the northeast side of Plaza 25 de Mayo and on the corner of Ravelo with Junín, plus numerous card-operated phone booths on Plaza 25 de Mayo and at major intersections around the city.

Tour operators SurAndes, Ortíz with Audiencia (☏04/6452632), organize a range of excursions and guided treks to the weaving villages in the Cordillera de los Frailes, the mountain range west of Sucre, lasting from half a day to five days for around $20–30 per person per day all inclusive depending on the size of the group. Tarco Tours, Plaza 25 de Mayo 25 (☏04/6461688), offer half- and one-day tours of the main attractions in the city. For something completely different, the Dutch-run Joy Ride Bolivia, located inside the Joy Ride Café at Ortíz 14 (☏04/6425544, ✇www.joyridebol.com, ✉info@joyridebol.com), offer exciting half- and one-day tours on 400cc motorcycles and quad ATVs in the mountains surrounding Sucre, as well as longer trips further afield – they cost upwards of $60 per person per day, all inclusive. Machines are well maintained and full safety equipment (including helmet, gloves and boots) is provided, as is insurance. You'll need a full driving licence for the ATV, and a motorcycle licence for the bikes.

Tarabuco

By far the most popular excursion from Sucre is to the small rural town of **TARABUCO**, set amid crumpled brown mountains about 60km southeast of the city. The town itself is an unremarkable collection of red-tiled adobe houses and cobbled streets leading to a small plaza with an unexceptional modern church, but its real claim to fame is its **Sunday market**, which acts as a focus for the indigenous communities of the surrounding mountains, the so-called **Tarabuceños** (see box opposite), who come to sell the beautiful weavings for which they're famous throughout Bolivia. The market is actually a bit of a tourist trap – there are usually several busloads of foreign tourists in attendance – but it's still principally geared towards the indigenous campesinos of the surrounding region, and the stalls selling weavings and other handicrafts to tourists are far outnumbered by those selling basic supplies such as dried foodstuffs, agricultural tools, sandals made from tyres, big bundles of coca and pure alcohol in great steel drums. If you walk a few blocks away from the centre of town you can still see campesinos engaging in *trueque*, a traditional Andean system of non-monetary trade in which agricultural products from different ecological zones are exchanged according to standard ratios – potatoes for maize, dried llama meat for oranges, and so on.

You can pick up some nice souvenirs at the market, though it's best to have some idea of quality and price before you arrive (have a look at things on sale on the streets of Sucre), though prices here are generally cheaper, and the choice much wider. Small items like decorative *chuspa* coca bags make good mementoes and are inexpensive and portable; larger items like ponchos and shawls cost a lot more. Be prepared to bargain, but not too hard: remember that many of the sellers are poor campesinos who may be desperate to sell something so they can buy essential goods to take home to their families. Also be aware that photographing people without permission is considered rude and can provoke an angry reaction: ask first, and be prepared to pay a few bolivianos for the privilege.

The Tarabuceños

Though they wear the same traditional costume, speak the same language (Quechua) and share many cultural traditions, strictly speaking it's not correct to refer to the **Tarabuceños** as an ethnic group: the name was simply given by the colonial authorities to all the indigenous communities living around Tarabuco. When the Spanish first arrived, the region had only recently been conquered by the Incas and marked the very limit of their domain. To secure the frontier and defend against raids by the indomitable Chiriguano tribes to the east, the Incas settled the area with different ethnic groups brought from elsewhere in the empire. All these indigenous communities speak Quechua, the lingua franca of the Inca empire, and at some point after the Spanish conquest they also adopted the distinctive costumes that give a semblance of unity today, but they have no collective name for themselves nor any tradition of collective political organization that suggests a common origin.

These distinctive **traditional costumes** make the Tarabuceños difficult to miss: the men wear leather hats, known as *monteros* and shaped like the steel helmets worn by the Spanish conquistadors, along with woollen ponchos woven with bright horizontal stripes of red, yellow, orange and green on a brown background, and three-quarter-length white trousers. In addition, they often use accessories like *chumpi* belts and *chuspa* coca-bags that are finely woven with intricate abstract designs and pictures of people, animals and plants. Though generally more muted in colour, the traditional costumes worn by the women, particularly the woollen shawls known as *llijlas* or *aqsus*, are also decorated with beautiful and complex designs, and the ceremonial hats and headdresses they wear on special occasions match the *monteros* of the men in their unusual shape and design: black pillboxes with a flap covering the neck decorated with sequins and bright woollen pom-poms, or boat-shaped sombreros embroidered with silver thread. More even than their costumes, however, it is Tarabuceño **weavings** (see p.230) that draw travellers to Tarabuco, and selling them has become a major source of income for the Tarabuceños, who otherwise depend on agriculture for their livelihoods and live in great poverty.

Pujllay

Every year on the third Sunday of March, Tarabuco celebrates **Pujllay** (also known as the Carnaval de Tarabuco), one of the best-known indigenous fiestas in Bolivia. Pujllay commemorates the battle of Jumbate on March 12, 1816, during the Independence War, when the Tarabuceños ambushed a battalion of marauding Spanish troops, slaughtering all but the drummer boy and eating their hearts in ritual revenge for abuses committed by the Spanish. During the fiesta, all the surrounding Tarabuceño communities come to town dressed in their finest ceremonial costumes, joined by thousands of Bolivian and foreign tourists. Following a Mass to commemorate the battle, the participants stage folkloric dances and parades whilst knocking back copious amounts of *chicha* (fermented maize beer), beer and pure cane alcohol. The climax of the celebration takes place around a ritual altar known as a *pukara*, raised in honour of the Tarabuceños who died in the battle and formed from a kind of wooden ladder decorated with fruit, vegetables, flowers, bread, bottles of *chicha* and other agricultural produce. Drinking and dancing continues through the night: if you want to sleep, you're better off returning to Sucre.

Practicalities

Buses and trucks to Tarabuco from Sucre (2hr; $1) leave on Sunday mornings (and most weekdays) from Plaza Huallparimachi in the east of the city, returning in the afternoon; however, it's much more convenient and only slightly more expensive to go in one of the **tourist buses** organized by hotels and tour agencies in Sucre, which will pick you up outside the Mercado Central on Calle Ravelo in the morning and bring you back in the afternoon – the *Hostal Charcas* organizes this every Sunday. If you want to stay overnight in Tarabuco, there's rudimentary accommodation in the *Restaurant Florida* (no phone; ❶), just off the plaza on the road in from Sucre. There are several other restaurants on the plaza where you can get basic meals and drinks, though on Sundays it's more fun to do as the locals do and eat soup or *chicharrón* (deep-fried pork) from market stalls.

Sucre to Cochabamba

The road **from Sucre to Cochabamba**, 366km to the northwest, passes through a scenic region of rugged mountains and fertile valleys, but unfortunately all public transport between the two travels overnight (allowing Bolivians to make trips between the two without splashing out on accommodation), so unless you've got your own transport, you're unlikely to see much. The road also passes through what were until recently two of the prettiest colonial villages in Bolivia – **Aiquile**, about 150km north of Sucre, and **Totora**, 75km further north. Sadly, both these villages were devastated by a powerful earthquake that shook the region in 1998. Although substantial funds were raised internationally to pay for their reconstruction, almost none of this money ever reached its intended destination – an instance of corruption so flagrant it shocked even the most cynical Bolivian observers. As a result, both villages remain largely in ruins, and as such are not really worth stopping off to visit, especially as to do so by public transport you'll need to get off a through bus in the middle of the night, then catch another one the next night to continue your journey in either direction.

Cochabamba and around

Set at the geographical centre of Bolivia, midway between the Altiplano and the eastern lowlands, **COCHABAMBA** is one of the country's most welcoming cities, and the commercial hub of the country's richest agricultural region, the Cochabamba Valley. A broad inter-Andean basin set at an altitude of about 2600m and blessed with rich alluvial soils and a warm, spring-like climate, the valley produces abundant harvests of wheat, maize, fruit and vegetables, and also supports large dairy herds – not for nothing is it known as the breadbasket of Bolivia.

The **Incas** were quick to spot this agricultural potential when they conquered the region in the mid-fifteenth century, moving Quechua-speaking agricultural colonists here from across their empire to cultivate the maize they needed to fill the imperial granaries and feed their armies. Inca control of the area was ended by the arrival of the **Spanish**, who founded the city on January 1, 1574, naming it La Villa de Oropeza in honour of the Conde de Oropeza, father of the Viceroy Francisco Toledo, who ordered its settlement. Locals soon reverted to calling it by the indigenous place name Cochabamba, a combination of the Quechua words for lake and plain, though all but one of the shallow, swampy lakes that once stood here have been filled in as the city expanded (the exception, known as Laguna Alalay – Quechua for "Oh how cold!" – lies to the southeast of the city centre). The Spanish established haciendas to produce grain for the silver mines of Potosí, and so important was their agricultural work to the colonial economy that the valley's indigenous population was exempted from having to work in the mines under the *mita* system. When the mines went into decline towards the end of the colonial period and the early republican era, many of the hacienda lands were rented out, and the region saw the emergence of a class of small but independent Quechua-speaking **peasant farmers**, very different in culture and outlook from the rather closed Aymara *ayllus* of the Altiplano. These peasant farmers played a central role in the emergence of Bolivia's radical peasant political organizations in the 1950s and 1960s and, as migrants to the Chapare, have assumed a key role in the coca-growers' movement of recent years.

Despite its tradition of protest, however, Cochabamba is an essentially peaceful and friendly place. With a population of about half a million, it's now a

Cochabamba and the Water War

Referred to by its inhabitants as "La Llacta", the Quechua equivalent of the Spanish word *pueblo*, meaning at once city and people or nation, Cochabamba is the centre of a vigorous regional identity, and throughout Bolivian history has enjoyed a reputation for political independence and rebelliousness, a tradition that continues to this day. In 2000 the city's water system was privatized and sold to a consortium of international companies which immediately doubled or even tripled water rates. In response, Cochabamba erupted in a series of spontaneous protests that became known as **La Guerra del Agua** – "the Water War". Thousands of citizens from all social classes took to the streets to demand rates be lowered, blocking roads in and out of the city. The Banzer government responded in familiar fashion: a state of siege was declared, protest organizers were arrested, armed troops were sent in, and plainclothes snipers opened fire on protesters, killing one and injuring many others. Despite this oppression, the demonstrations continued, and the water consortium eventually backed down – a popular victory which was welcomed by anti-globalization campaigners around the world.

modern, unpretentious and outward-looking commercial city. Named the "City of Eternal Spring", it enjoys a year-round sunny climate that is matched by the warmth and openness of its population – though most travellers who come here are just passing through, those who spend time here find Cochabamba the most welcoming city in Bolivia, and a good base for exploring the understated but rewarding attractions of the surrounding valley. Chief among these, in the eyes of the locals at least, is **chicha**, a thick, lightly alcoholic beer made from fermented maize that was the sacred drink of the Incas and is still the main social lubricant in rural areas. With a tart, yeasty flavour it's definitely an acquired taste, and can play havoc with the digestion, but drinking a few glasses in a roadside *chicheria* is the best way to get talking with the local campesinos; you'll find it on sale from massive earthenware pots from *chicherias* and private homes all over the valley – just look out for a white flag or bunch of flowers raised on a pole outside.

Arrival and information

Almost all long-distance buses – including those from La Paz, Oruro, Sucre and Santa Cruz – arrive and depart from Cochabamba's **bus terminal**, in the south of the city on Avenida Ayacucho just south of Avenida Aroma. The terminal is modern and fairly well organized, with a bus **information kiosk** (daily 6am–11pm; ☎155 or 04/4234600), post office, ENTEL office and plenty of phone booths, a left-luggage store, a 24-hour café-restaurant, and a number of ATMs outside where you can withdraw cash on Visa or Mastercard (though you should be careful using these, especially at night). Many of the city's hotels are within easy walking distance of the terminal; otherwise, a taxi to anywhere in the city centre should cost about $0.50 per person – taxis queue up outside the terminal or can easily be flagged down on the streets. Buses from the **Chapare** region east of Cochabamba arrive around the junction of Avenida Oquendo and Avenida 9 de Abril to the southeast of the city centre. Cochabamba's extremely modern but underused Jorge Wilsterman **airport** (☎04/4222846) is a few kilometres outside town to the southwest; a taxi into the city centre should cost about $2–3; alternatively, take micro B, which goes up Avenida Ayacucho to Plaza 14 de Septiembre, the city's main square.

The regional **tourist office** (Mon–Fri 8.30am-4.30pm, Sat 9am–noon; ☎04/4504103) is in a kiosk on Calle Achá, half a block west of Plaza 14 de Septiembre. The usually helpful and enthusiastic staff speak a little English and can answer most basic inquiries, and usually have free maps of the city and a range of leaflets. Cochabamba's **street numbers** are prefixed N, S, E or O – north, south, east or west – depending on whether they run north or south from Avenida Heroínas, or east or west from Avenida Ayacucho. The first two digits in the street number refer to the block in terms of how far it is from these two major interstices, the second two to the number of the building: thus España N-0349 is on España at no. 49, three blocks north of the intersection with Avenida Heroínas.

Accommodation

Accomodation in Cochabamba reflects the nature of the city: though functional and reasonably priced, it's unexceptional and generally not aimed at tourists (the city sees few). The better places are generally rather dull business hotels, and the budget ones – concentrated around the bus terminal – are mostly doss-houses for poor migrant workers. That said, almost all accommodation is conveniently located in the centre of town, and there are a few really quite pleasant budget places that cater primarily to tourists. The only time accommodation can be difficult to find is in mid-August during the **Fiesta de la Virgen de Urkupiña** in nearby Quillacollo: it's best to book in advance during this period.

Alojamiento Cochabamba Aguirre S-0591 ☏04/4225067. About the best of the many bottom-of-the-range *alojamientos* near the bus terminal, with basic rooms (with shared bathrooms) and hot water in the mornings only. **❶**

Gran Hotel Ambassador España N-0349 ☏04/4259001 or 4256991, ℱ04/4257855, ✉ambassrv@comteco.entelnet.bo. Efficiently run and fairly luxurious – if not particularly stylish – modern multistorey hotel with over a hundred rooms, all with cable TV and fridge. Breakfast included. **❻**

Gran Hotel Cochabamba Plaza Ubaldo Anze E-0415 ☏04/4282551 or 4282552, ℱ04/4282558. Luxurious Art Deco country club-style hotel with spacious, fully equipped and stylishly decorated rooms looking out over a swimming pool and extensive palm-filled garden. There's also a bar and a classy restaurant, and breakfast is included. **❽**

Hostal Americana Arce S-0788 ☏04/4250552 or 4250553, ℱ04/4250484. Good-value modern high-rise hotel with attentive staff and comfortable, well-equipped rooms with good views but rather garish pink décor. **❺**

Hostal Colonial Junín N-0134 ☏04/4221791. Friendly and good-value family-run place offering clean but slightly dilapidated rooms on two floors, overlooking a charming garden overflowing with lush tropical vegetation. Breakfast available. **❷**

Hostal Elisa Lopéz S-0834 ☏04/4254406, ℱ04/4235102, ✉helisa@supernet.com.bo.

Helpful and friendly little place just a block away from the bus terminal. It's much nicer than it appears from outside, with small but clean rooms (with or without bath) around a pleasant central garden with outdoor seating. There's also a cafeteria, and internet access is available. **❸**

Hostal Florida 25 de Mayo S-0583 ☏04/4257911 or 4235617, ✉floridah@elsitio.com. Rightly popular backpackers' favourite halfway between the bus terminal and the city centre. The simple but clean rooms (with or without bath) are set around a sunny central courtyard, and breakfast is available. **❷–❸**

Hostal Jardin Hamiraya N-0248 ☏04/4247844. Small but reasonably comfortable rooms (with or without bath) opening onto a peaceful garden with outdoor seating. Breakfast available. **❸**

Hotel La Fontaine Hamiraya N-0181 ☏04/4252838. Small and comfortable business hotel offering nicely furnished modern rooms equipped with fridge and cable TV and decorated with colonial religious paintings – but beware the hazardously low ceiling beams. Internet access is available, and breakfast is included. **❻**

Hotel Regina Reza with España ☏04/4257382 or 4229163. Good-value mid-range hotel with efficient and helpful staff, plus a bar and restaurant. The large, bright and comfortable rooms have cable TV and kitchenette units, so you can cook for yourself, though they're in need of redecoration. Breakfast available. **❺**

The City

For all its charm, Cochabamba has little to offer in terms of conventional tourist attractions. Other than a few old but unspectacular churches, little remains of the original colonial city centre, though the **Museo Archeológico** is worth a visit, as is the **Cristo de la Concordia**, the Christ statue, accessible by cable car, that overlooks Cochabamba from the east and gives panoramic views over the city. Otherwise, the most interesting areas are the massive, rambling **street markets** that stretch to the south of the city centre, the commercial heart of this market city.

Plaza 14 de Septiembre and around

The centre of Cochabamba is **Plaza 14 de Septiembre** a peaceful and pleasant square with flower-filled ornamental gardens, a colonial stone fountain which (amazingly for Bolivia) actually works, and plenty of benches where Cochabambinos sit under the shade of tall palm trees reading newspapers, having their shoes shined and generally passing the time of day. At its centre stands an obelisk topped by the statue of a condor – a monument to the Cochabambinos who died during the Independence War. The plaza is flanked by nineteenth-century buildings that extend over the pavement and are sup-

PLACES TO STAY

Alojamiento Cochabamba	7
Gran Hotel Ambassador	3
Gran Hotel Cochabamba	1
Hostal Americana	9
Hostal Colonial	6
Hostal Elisa	10
Hostal Florida	8
Hostal Jardin	4
Hotel La Fontaine	5
Hotel Regina	2

Micros to Cliza & Tarata ▼   *Buses to Torotoro &* ▼   *Micros to Arani*

ported by pillars, forming arched arcades that shade pedestrians from the sun. Sideways on to the plaza on the south side stands the **Catedral Metropolitana**, founded in 1571 and thus the oldest church in the city, though almost nothing of the original structure remains. The main entrance, facing out onto Calle Arce, is a fairly straightforward mestizo-Baroque portico decorated with spiralled columns, carvings of flowers and squat angels that look

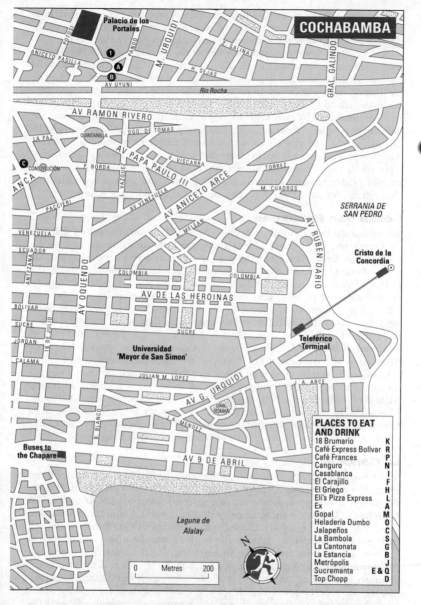

PLACES TO EAT AND DRINK

18 Brumario	K
Café Express Bolívar	R
Café Frances	P
Canguro	N
Casablanca	I
El Carajillo	F
El Griego	H
Eli's Pizza Express	L
Ex	A
Gopal	M
Heladeria Dumbo	O
Jalapeños	C
La Bambola	S
La Cantonata	G
La Estancia	B
Metrópolis	J
Sucremanta	E & Q
Top Chopp	D

rather like pre-Columbian idols. The airy but unexceptional Neoclassical interior is brightly painted with floral designs and images of saints.

A block south of the plaza on the corner of calles Aguirre and Jordán is the interesting and extensive **Museo Archeológico** (Tues–Fri 8.30am–6.30pm, Sat & Sun 9am–noon; $2.20). As in most Bolivian museums, the items on display are poorly explained, but as you peruse the collection a picture of the evolution of pre-Hispanic culture in the Cochabamba region gradually emerges, stretching from the Tiwanaku culture (which influenced the area from about 300 AD), through a number of regional groups to the Incas, who arrived here in the mid-fifteenth century, just a hundred years before the Spanish conquest. Among the most interesting exhibits are a series of small stone idols (thought to represent the earth goddess, Pachamama), along with bronze Inca axeheads, ceremonial knives, star-shaped stone maces and some well-preserved Tiwanaku woven skull caps made specially to fit skulls deformed by ritual trepanation. Also intriguing are the series of items used by early Catholic missionaries in their efforts to convert the indigenous peoples – these include sheepskins painted with bizarre hieroglyph-like ideographs, and clay discs encrusted with fragments of stone and pottery which were used like rosaries to remember sequences of prayer and other mysteries of the faith. There's also a small display of ethnographic material from the peoples of the Amazon lowlands, including bows and arrows, vegetable-fibre clothing, sinister carved wooden ceremonial masks, and feather headdresses.

Colina San Sebastián

Just east of the bus terminal on Avenida Aroma, about 600m south of Plaza 14 de Septiembre, a tree-lined pedestrian avenue leads up to the summit of the **Colina San Sebastián**, a low hill with good views over the city that was the scene of one of the most dramatic events in Cochabamba's history. During the Independence War, Cochabamba was quick to join the rebellion against Spanish rule, but in 1812, after the city's menfolk had gone off to fight else-where, the women of Cochabamba found themselves virtually defenceless against an advancing royalist army. Refusing calls to surrender, the women for-tified the hill where, on May 27, they fought heroically until finally over-whelmed. Known as Las Heroinas de la Coronilla, these women are com-memorated by a **monument** at the top of the hill, a cast-iron statue of Christ surrounded by images of women fighting or sheltering their children. The path up to the monument is lined with busts of independence leaders, including Manuela Gandarillas, the blind woman who led the resistance here. In Bolivia, Mothers' Day is celebrated on May 27 in memory of the Heroinas de la Coronilla, a somewhat surprising example of motherhood to venerate in a country where conventional gender stereotypes generally hold sway.

La Cancha

In the south of the city, about nine blocks south of Plaza 14 de Septiembre, an entire block between calles Tarata and Pulucayo on the east side of Avenida Barrientos is occupied by the massive covered street market known as **La Cancha** (a Quechua word meaning walled enclosure), where campesinos and merchants from all over the Cochabamba department come to buy and sell their produce. Wandering through the market's sprawling labyrinth of stalls is the best way to get a feel for the vibrant commercial culture of the city and the surrounding region: the buzz of Quechua fills the air and the traditional costumes of different campesino groups are very much in evidence, in partic-ular the straw sombreros and bright-coloured *pollera* skirts of the women of the Cochabamba valley. This is effectively one massive clearing-house for agricul-tural produce, and the range of foodstuffs on sale reflects the full diversity of Bolivia's different ecological zones. You'll also find pretty much anything else poor Bolivians might need: sacks, rope, ironmongery, medicinal herbs, ritual items for making offerings to Pachamama and the mountain gods, along with cheap manufactured goods. One consequence of the free-market economic policies pursued by successive Bolivian governments since the mid-1980s has

△ Palacio de los Portales, Cochabamba

been an explosion in the number of people trying to make a living by buying and selling in the market, and La Cancha has since overflowed its original bounds, spreading across Avenida Barrientos onto the disused railway, and northwest to occupy another entire block between Tarata and Punata, an area now known as the **Mercado Inca Llajta** (Inca Town in Quechua).

Palacio de los Portales

About 1km north of the city centre, with its entrance on Avenida Potosí, the **Palacio de los Portales** (visits by guided tour only, Mon–Fri 5–6pm, Sat 11am–noon; $1.50) is the luxurious former house of the Cochabamba-born "King of Tin" **Simón Patiño** (see box on p.162). Built between 1915 and 1922 in a bizarre mix of architectural styles including French Neoclassical and *mudejár*, the palace shows that the mining magnate possessed rather more money than artistic sense. The interior is decorated with astonishing opulence: marble fireplaces and statues of Roman emperors and St Bernard dogs; walls covered in rich damask or panelled in fine wood; Venetian crystal chandeliers and Louis XV furniture. If anything, though, it's the magnificent garden that really impresses, laid out in perfect proportion by Japanese specialists and featuring a beautiful and rare ginko tree. Patiño never actually lived here, as by the time the palace was complete he was based permanently overseas, and the building now houses the Instituto Cultural Simón I. Patiño, a charity set up in his name to promote education and literacy. The basement is home to the **Museo de Arte Contemporáneo** (Mon–Fri 2.30–6.30pm, Sat 10.30am–noon; $0.50), which has a fairly unexciting selection of works by modern Bolivian artists and sometimes hosts good temporary exhibitions.

Cristo de la Concordia

About 1.5km east of the city centre, on the summit of the Serrania de San Pedro, stands the **Cristo de la Concordia**, a monumental statue of Christ with arms outstretched overlooking the city. The statue was modelled on the more famous Christ figure that looms over Río de Janeiro in Brazil but, as Cochabambinos will proudly tell you, it's just that little bit taller, measuring over 34m (40m, if you include the pedestal), and is thus the tallest statue in South America. Towering high above the city and weighing over 2000 tons, by Bolivian standards it's a truly massive monument, and even if this sort of thing doesn't impress you, it's worth going up for the view.

From a station at the eastern end of Avenida Las Heroínas, a modern **cable car** (*teleférico*; Mon–Sat 10am–6.30pm, Sun 9am–8pm; $0.25 each way) makes the five-minute journey to the top (the alternatives are a hard slog up the steps at the end of Avenida Heroinas or a more expensive taxi ride). A visit to the foot of the Cristo is popular with locals, particularly at weekends, but it never gets too crowded and is usually fairly peaceful. The **views** of the city and surrounding valley from the base of the statue are splendid, and on weekends you can climb up the spiral staircase inside the hollow steel figure for an even better panorama (Sat & Sun 10am–6.30pm; $0.15). There's also a small **café** where you can get snacks and cold drinks, and several stalls sell ice cream; others rent binoculars and telescopes if you want to study the view more closely.

Eating, drinking and nightlife

The best places **to eat** if you're on a tight budget are Cochabamba's many **markets**, in particular the Mercado Calatayud, on San Martín with Aroma, where you'll find local Cochabambino specialities like *picante de pollo* (chicken in a spicy sauce) or *silpancho* (a kind of breaded beef schnitzel) for about $1, as well as huge fruit juices, inexpensive breakfasts and delicious *empanadas* and *salteñas*, which in Cochabamba seem about twice as big as elsewhere in Bolivia and are served accompanied by a choice of half a dozen different sauces. Cochabambinos are generally adventurous eaters, and the choice of **restaurants** in the city is broad, with some very good meals available at relatively low prices.

Cafés and restaurants

Café Express Bolívar Bolívar with San Martín. Old-fashioned little café serving good strong espresso and cappuccino (but little else) accompanied by classical music. Look out for the photos on the wall of the elderly owner when she was Miss Cochabamba many decades ago. Closed Sun.

Café Frances Les Temps Modernes España with Colombia. Sophisticated French bar-café serving good coffee, imaginative mixed juices, sweet and savoury crepes, and various other snacks and pastries. Closed Sun.

Canguro Colombia with España. Popular, no-nonsense *salteñeria* serving delicious beef, chicken and pork *fricasé salteñas*, with indoor and outdoor seating.

El Griego España with Venezuela. Inexpensive Greek-style restaurant serving tasty *gyros* (a kind of doner kebab) accompanied by good Greek salads or not-so-Greek spaghetti. Evenings only.

Eli's Pizza Express 25 de Mayo with Ecuador. No-nonsense US-style fast-food outlet with reasonably good pizza and a wide range of inexpensive hot snacks. Good value, though the neon lighting and plastic décor don't encourage a lengthy stay.

Gopal España with Ecuador. Inexpensive Hare Krishna wholefood restaurant serving up cheap and tasty vegetarian meals and snacks, including a filling set almuerzo for just under $1.50.

Heladería Dumbo Heroínas with Arce. Cochabamba branch of the nationwide restaurant chain, serving up good ice cream, inexpensive but unexciting main courses like steak or chicken, pastries, juices and snacks, and excellent value American breakfasts. There's another branch on Av Ballivián near Plaza Colón.

Jalapeños Chuquisaca N-0711. Upmarket Mexican restaurant serving all the usual favorites like tacos and burritos at about $4 a go, as well as more substantial meat and fish dishes. The food's tasty (but far from authentic, despite the music and décor), though the drinks are overpriced.

La Bambola Jordan with Lanza. US-style snack bar serving good cappuccino and espresso, juices, *salteñas*, salads and massive sub sandwiches.

La Cantonata España with Venezuela. Elegant and sophisticated restaurant serving good but rather overpriced Italian food to Cochabamba's wealthiest residents.

La Estancia Boulevard Recoleta. Excellent Argentine barbecue restaurant serving generous portions of delicious grilled beef, chicken or fish

accompanied by a massive salad bar, all for about $5 a head.

Metrópolis España N-0299. Cosy corner café which is extremely popular with students and travellers alike for its savoury German pancakes, massive salads and varied pasta dishes – the latter (about $3.50) are so big they're usually enough for two. They also serve good strong coffee, fruit juices and cocktails in the evening. Closed Sun morning.

Sucremanta Arce. Popular restaurant specializing in traditional pork-based dishes from the Chuquisaca department (Sucre), including delicious *chorizo* (sausage) and *fritanga*, a thick, spicy stew. Open lunchtimes only. There's another branch on Avenida Ballivián.

Drinking and nightlife

Nightlife in Cochabamba is centred on three different districts, each catering to a distinct crowd. The wealthier Cochabambinos head to **Boulevard Recoleta**, just east of Plaza Anza, north of the Río Rocha at the top of Avenida Oquendo, about 1km from Plaza 14 de Septiembre: this pedestrianized street is lined with upmarket restaurants and fairly exclusive bars where jazz and expensive cocktails predominate. More straightforward and popular entertainment – cheap steakhouses, beer palaces with sport on big screen TVs and soundsystems pumping out Latin pop music – can be found along **Avenida Ballivián**, (also known as El Prado), just north of the city centre. Centred on the intersection of **España and Ecuador**, in the city centre, meanwhile, is a laid-back bohemian scene of small bars and cafés which is popular with Cochabamba's large student population. As elsewhere in Bolivia, many restaurants stay open late at weekends and double as bars, and in all three areas places go in and out of fashion very quickly – especially as the municipal authorities have a tendency to close down any nightclub where the city's young people appear to be having too much of a good time.

El Carajillo España with Paccieri. Candlelit bohemian hideaway attracting a slightly older crowd with its groovy 1960s music and sometimes anarchic staff, who serve good coffee, spirits and cold beer until the early hours. Closed Sun.

Casablanca España with Ecuador. Trendy Hollywood-themed bar serving cold beer, good cocktails and pretty much the same food as *Metrópolis* (see above), opposite. The first-floor balcony is great for people-watching, and they also sometimes show classic films in an upstairs movie theatre.

18 Brumario Ecuador with España. Lively bar and

live music venue with frequent performances by local rock, blues and Latin bands. It's an unpretentious hang-out, despite the name (an obscure Marxist reference), and one of many such places in this area. Open till late; small cover charge on weekends.

Ex Recoleta with Padilla. The wildest and most popular nightclub of the moment, deservedly notorious for its foam-filled weekend dance floor.

Top Chopp Av Ballivián with Reza. Raucous lager palace pumping out loud Latin dance music and serving cheap cold beer and straightforward Bolivian food for about $2.50 a dish.

Listings

Airlines Aerosur, Edificio America, Av Ayacucho with Achá ☏04/4228385; LAB, Av Heroínas with Baptista ☏04/4250750; TAM Mercosur, Edificio El Clan, Av Ayacucho ☏04/4251067.

Banks and exchange Casa de Cambio Exprintbol, Plaza 14 de Septiembre, changes cash dollars and travellers' cheques, and there are street moneychangers at all the major intersections in the centre of town. There are also plenty of ATMs in the city centre where you can withdraw cash in dollars or bolivianos on Visa or Mastercard, including the Banco de Santa Cruz, Av Heroínas with Hamiraya, and the Banco Nacional de Bolivia, Jordán with Aguirre.

Bookshop Los Amigos del Libro, Av Ayacucho with Heroínas, has a reasonable selection of books in English, as well as an extensive range in Spanish.

Bus information ☏155 or 04/4234600.

Camping equipment There's a good range on sale at Nanos Sports, Lanza with San Martín.

Car rental J. Barron's, Sucre E-0727 ☏04/4222774; J. R., Ladislao Cabrera 232 Tiquipaya ☏04/4288465.

Doctor Clínica Belga, Antezana N-0457 ☏04/4231404.

Immigration For visa extensions, the *migración* office is at Arce with Jordán ☏04/4225553.

Internet access Internet cafés abound. One of the best is ENTEL internet, Av Ayacucho with Achá (9am–midnight; $1 per hour).

Language classes Escuela Runawasi, Maurice Lefebvre N-0470, Villa Juan XXIII ☏04/4248923, ⓦwww.runawasi.org, offers Spanish and Quechua lessons at all levels, with intensive courses from about $125 a week. They can also arrange for students to stay with local families.

Laundry Superclean, 16 de Julio with Jordán, same-day service.

Post office Correo Central, Av Ayacucho with Av Heroínas.

Taxis America ☏04/4245678; La Rosa ☏04/4241190.

Telephone office ENTEL's main office is at Av Ayacucho with Achá, and there are plenty of card-operated phone booths around town.

Tour operators The excellent and highly respected Fremen agency has its home base in Cochabamba at Tumulsa N-0245 (☏04/4259392, ⓦwww.andes-amazonia.com). They offer a wide range of excellent tailor-made tours throughout Bolivia, including river trips on the Río Mamoré (see p.325) on their own luxury floating hotel, the *Reina de Enín*. In the Cochabamba region, they run trips down into the Chapare (where they own the *Hotel El Puente* in Villa Tunari – see p.258), as well as city tours and visits to the market towns of the Valle Alto, to the Parque Nacional Torotoro, and to the ruins at Incarakay and Incallajta. They also run adventurous camping trips by motorized canoe into the Parque Nacional Isiboro-Sécure (see p.328), starting in the Chapare and ending in Trinidad. Other respected Cochabamba tour operators include Turismo Santa Rita, Buenos Aires 866 ☏04/4280305, ☏04/4280512, and Caxia tours, Arze S-0559 ☏04/4226148, ☏04/4250937, both of which run trips to most of the same regional destinations – city tours, Valle Alto, Incarakay and Incallajta, Torotoro and the Chapare.

Moving on from Cochabamba

Almost all **long-distance buses**, including those **to La Paz**, **Oruro**, **Santa Cruz** and **Sucre**, depart from the bus terminal in the south of the city on Avenida Ayacucho, just south of Avenida Aroma; you can check departure times by calling the bus information kiosk (daily 6am–11pm; ☏155 or 04/4234600). Buses to Sucre travel by night; those to Santa Cruz leave either early in the morning or in the evening and travel along the faster and shorter asphalt-surfaced lowland road through the Chapare (unless the road is blocked by protesting coca-growers). If you want to travel along the slow but scenic highland route via Samaipata, the best way to do so is to take a bus **to Vallegrande** (see p.287), spend the night there, and then get another bus on to Santa Cruz. Expreso Guadelupe run buses to Vallegrande twice a week, usually on Wednesdays and Saturdays. Buses to the **Parque Nacional Torotoro** leave from the corner of Avenida 6 de Agosto and Avenida Republica at about 6am on Thursdays and Sundays, while frequent buses to **Villa Tunari** and other towns in the **Chapare** leave from the around the intersection of Avenida Oquendo and Avenida 9 de Abril.

Cochabamba's **airport** (☏04/4222846) has daily flights to La Paz, Santa Cruz, Tarija and Sucre, and less frequent connections to Cobija, Guayaramerín and Trinidad. The airline TAM Mercosur (not to be confused with the Bolivian military airline TAM) also flies internationally from Cochabamba to Asunción in Paraguay, Buenos Aires in Argentina, and São Paulo in Brazil.

Around Cochabamba

East of Cochabamba stretches the upper Cochabamba Valley – or **Valle Alto** – a densely populated agricultural region whose broad and well-irrigated fields of maize and wheat are amongst the most fertile and productive in the country. This region is dominated by small-scale but independent peasant farmers: though still Quechua-speaking, they're much more outward looking than the communities of the Altiplano, and played a key role in the emergence of radical peasant federations in Bolivia in the 1960s and 1970s.

Easily reached by regular micros from Cochabamba, the rural centres of **Cliza**, **Punata** and **Arani** all make interesting excursions from the city, especially during their weekly **markets**, bustling and strictly local agricultural when peasants from the surrounding districts come to buy supplies, sell produce, meet friends and drink *chicha*. The women wear the characteristic brightly coloured *pollera* skirts and white straw boaters of the Cochabamba Valley, and carry their goods on their backs in luridly striped machine-made shawls. The markets are rather prosaic compared to more tourist-oriented market at Tarabuco (see p.236), and there's almost nothing in the way of handicrafts on sale, but it's still interesting to watch the energetic scenes, as people haggle over great piles of fruit and vegetables, live sheep and cattle, and cheap manufactured clothes. The liveliest markets are on Thursday in Arani, about 55km from Cochabamba, and on Sundays in Cliza, about 40km away. The Tuesday market in Punata, 45km from Cochabamba, is smaller, but the town is famed as home to the best *chicha* in all Bolivia.

Micros to Arani (every 15min; 45min) and Punata (every 30min; 40min) leave from the corner of Avenida Republica and Calle Manuripi in Cochabamba; those for Cliza (every 10–15min; 25min) leave from the corner of Avenida Barrientos and Manuripi.

Parque Nacional Cerro Tunari

Immediately north of Cochabamba, some 3000 square kilometres of the Cordillera Tunari – the mountain range that forms the northern boundary of the Cochabamba Valley – is protected by the **Parque Nacional Cerro Tunari**. Named after the tallest peak in the region, the 5200-metre Cerro Tunari, the park was set up primarily to protect the forested watershed that provides the irrigation water that is vital to the agriculture of the Cochabamba Valley, and to conserve rare high-altitude queñua forests which are home to the Cochabamba mountain finch, which is found nowhere else in the world.

Given its proximity to city and the heavily settled Cochabamba valley, the park's ecosystems are in a far from pristine condition; the lower slopes closest to Cochabamba in particular are affected by illegal building. It's easy to visit from the city, however, and is popular amongst Cochabambinos at weekends. To reach the most accessible section of the park, immediately above Cochabamba, take trufi #103, which heads along Avenida Ayacucho to the park gate, about 7km north of the city centre. From the gate, a track climbs steeply up into the park; an hour or so's walk (or a short drive) will bring you to a series of picnic sites and children's playgrounds under the shade of cool eucalyptus groves where Cochabambinos like to relax around a barbecue, enjoy the views of the city in the valley below, and stroll or ride mountain bikes along the various track and trails. If you continue walking uphill for two to three hours you'll reach a series of small lakes from which the views are even more spectacular.

To get into the higher reaches of the park and climb the 5200-metre peak of **Cerro Tunari** itself, you'll need to take a micro early in the morning to

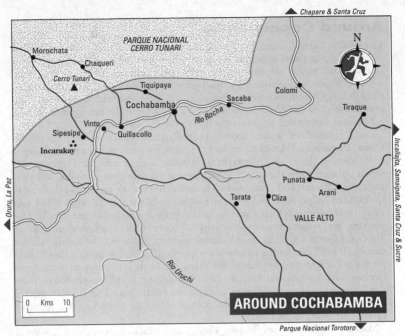
Chapare & Santa Cruz

PARQUE NACIONAL
CERRO TUNARI

N

Morochata
Chaqueri
Cerro Tunari
Tiquipaya
Cochabamba
Sacaba
Colomi
Rio Rocha
Tiraque
Vinto
Sipesipe
Quillacollo
Incarakay
Oruro, La Paz
Punata
Tarata
Cliza
Arani
VALLE ALTO
Incallajta, Samaipata, Santa Cruz & Sucre
Rio Uruchi

0   Kms   10

AROUND COCHABAMBA

Parque Nacional Torotoro

Quillacollo (see below) and then catch another micro from Quillacollo towards
the rural town of Morochata (1 daily at about 7am), which lies north of
Quillacollo on the other side of the Tunari range and the national park. You
alight from the micro at the hamlet of **Chaqueri**, about 25km from Quillacollo
at an altitude of 4200m, from where a path leads to the summit, a fairly straightforward four-to-five-hour ascent, though you may need to ask locals for directions. The views from the peak are magnificent, with Cochabamba and the surrounding valley laid out far below and the shimmering peaks of the Cordillera
Real far to the west visible on a clear day; condors are also a frequent sight.
Transport back to Quillacollo passes by Chaqueri in the afternoon, but given
the timing you'll need to camp overnight if you're doing the ascent independently – alternatively, you can do the trip with a Cochabamba-based tour agency,
which will provide transport, guide and accommodation.

Quillacollo

About 15km west of Cochabamba, and now all but engulfed by the city's urban
sprawl, is the bustling market town of **QUILLACOLLO**, the second biggest settlement in the Cochabamba Valley. Reached by frequent micros from Avenida
Aroma in Cochabamba (every 10min; 25min), it's a lively commercial centre and
transport hub which is famous throughout Bolivia for its **Fiesta de la Virgen de
Urkupiña** (see box opposite), staged in August each year. Outside fiesta time, however, there's nothing much to see other than the reputedly miraculous but rather
ordinary-looking image of the Virgen de Urkupiña herself, inside the modest
Neoclassical Iglesia de San Idelfonsino a few blocks south of the main plaza. The
town is also well known for the spicy food and heady brews available in its raucous
chicherías (traditional restaurants serving *chicha*): the most famous is *Chernobyl*, named
in honour of a particularly potent batch of *chicha* which was brewed shortly after
the Ukrainian nuclear reactor exploded in 1986 – ask locals for directions.

Fiesta de la Virgen de Urkupiña

Every year for three days around August 15, Quillacollo hosts the **Fiesta de la Virgen de Urkupiña**, which attracts up to half a million visitors and involves a massive parade of costumed folkloric dancers from all over Bolivia, as well as the usual copious eating and drinking intertwined with sincere expressions of spiritual faith – many pilgrims walk to Quillacollo by night from Cochabamba as a sign of religious devotion. The fiesta dates back to the early nineteenth century, when a local Quechua-speaking shepherdess had repeated visions of the Virgin Mary on the nearby hill of **Cerro Cota**. When the villagers of Quillacollo investigated they saw a brief glimpse of the Virgin ascending to heaven, and later found a carved image of her hidden among the rocks. This was carried to the parish church of San Idelfonsino, and soon credited with numerous miracles. The name Urkupiña is derived from the Quechua for "on the mountain" – the shepherdess's cry when she pointed out the Virgin to the villagers.

As with most major Bolivian religious fiestas, however, there's little doubt that its true origins lie deep in the pre-Christian past. Significant pre-Hispanic burial sites have been uncovered in the centre of Quillacollo, and the town's name means **"mountain of the moon"** in Quechua – the Incas considered the moon to be a major female deity, and following the Spanish conquest it was often conflated with the Virgin Mary. As well as the procession and dances (themselves a feature of most Inca celebrations), a central feature of the fiesta is a visit to the rocky outcrop where the Virgin appeared, during which tourists and pilgrims alike hack lumps of rock from the sacred mountain to take home with them in the belief that this will ensure health and material prosperity. They also make libations of coca and alcohol and burn candles, offerings associated with the Andean earth goddess Pachamama. As in the fiesta of Alasitas in La Paz (see p.75), pilgrims buy miniature replicas of objects they wish to possess – trucks, houses, university degrees, wads of fake dollars – in the belief that by doing so the real thing will be theirs before the year is out.

The best way **to visit** the fiesta is as a day-trip from Cochabamba, though you'll need to get to Quillacollo early in the morning to ensure a good spot from which to watch the dances. Be warned, too, that accommodation in Cochabamba can hard to find during the fiesta.

Incarakay

Set high on the mountainside overlooking the Cochabamba Valley about 25km west of the city, the ruins of the Inca outpost of **Incarakay** make an excellent if rather strenuous day-trip from the city. To reach the ruins, take a micro from Avenida Aroma in Cochabamba to Quillacollo (every 10min; 25min), then another from Plaza Bolívar in Quillacollo to **Sipe Sipe** (every 15–20min; 20min), a peaceful agricultural town about 8km east of Quillacollo. From Sipe Sipe it's a steep two-to-three-hour climb up to Incarakay; the route is fairly easy to find on your own, though if in doubt you can always ask directions from the locals. From the southwest corner of the plaza in Sipe Sipe, follow the road that heads out of town towards the mountainside. About 1km from the plaza, the road crosses a stream and turns sharply to the left; about 160m further on, just past a gully, a path climbs from the right-hand side of the road up to the ruins. The path is indistinct, but if you keep climbing towards the southwest the ruins will eventually become visible above you.

The **site** itself is fairly small, a collection of a dozen or so buildings made of rough cut stones with the trapezoidal internal niches and doorways and earthquake-resistant inward-leaning walls characteristic of Inca architecture. What really impresses, however, is the setting: perched on the mountainside at an altitude of 3200m, Incarakay enjoys fantastic views over Cochabamba to Cerro

Tunari, which soars imperiously to the north. From up here, the flat expanse of the Cochabamba valley with its neatly irrigated green fields of maize seems a vision of order and fertility in contrast to the harsh, arid mountain ranges on either side.

It's not certain quite what purpose Incarakay served, but it seems likely that it was some kind of imperial administration centre. The Incas invested great energy in the Cochabamba valley after they conquered the region in the mid-fifteenth century, bringing in agricultural settlers from other parts of the empire to cultivate the maize which fed the Inca armies, and this would seem a perfect site from which to calculate how much the imperial share of the harvest should amount to each year. On the return journey it's well worth stopping off in Sipe Sipe to sample some *chicha*, the fermented maize beer that was sacred to the Incas and which is still produced and consumed in large quantities in the Cochabamba valley: served from huge earthenware pots and drunk from gourds, it's particularly refreshing after a long day walking in the sun. You'll find it on sale in a number of private houses, marked by a white flag or bunch of flowers raised on a pole outside.

Incallajta

The other major Inca site in the Cochabamba region is **Incallajta**, a far more substantial complex about 143km east of Cochabamba, which was built as a military outpost to protect the valley from raids by the unconquered Chiriguano tribes of the eastern lowlands. Incallajta is about 15km off the road to Sucre, just south of the point where it joins the old highland road between Cochabamba and Santa Cruz. Unless you rent a 4WD, the easiest way to visit the site is with a Cochabamba-based tour agency – a day-trip should cost about $70 per person for a group of four people. Reaching Incallajta by public transport is very difficult: you'll have to catch a bus from Cochabamba heading to Totora as far as the turn off at the village of **Collpa**, then walk 15km to the ruins and spend the night there before returning the next day. There are good camping spots at the ruins and water is available, but you'll have to take all the food you need with you.

Parque Nacional Torotoro

Some 130km south of Cochabamba, the **PARQUE NACIONAL TORO-TORO** protects a remote and sparsely inhabited stretch of the arid, scrubby landscape which is characteristic of the eastern foothills and valleys of the Andes. Covering just 164 square kilometres around the small town of the same name, Torotoro is Bolivia's smallest national park, but what it lacks in size it makes up for with its powerful scenery and varied attractions. The park encompasses a high, hanging valley and deep eroded canyons, ringed by low mountains whose twisted geological formations are strewn with fossils, dinosaur footprints and labyrinthine limestone cave complexes. In addition, the park's cactus and scrubby woodland supports considerable wildlife – including flocks of parakeets and the rare and beautiful red-fronted macaw, found only in this particular region of Bolivia – while ancient rock paintings and pre-Inca ruins reveal a longstanding human presence. The main attractions are the limestone caves of **Umajallanta**, the beautiful, waterfall-filled **Torotoro Canyon**, and hiking expeditions to the pre-Inca ruined fortress of **Llama Chaqui**.

Though reached from Cochabamba, Parque Nacional Torotoro actually lies within Northern Potosí department, a region famous within Bolivia as a repository of traditional Andean culture and society. Before the Spanish conquest this was the core territory of the **Charcas Confederation**, a powerful collection of different ethnic groups subject to Inca rule. Following the conquest, the different Quechua- and Aymara-speaking groups that made up the confederation retained their distinct identities, each as separate *ayllus* – an Andean term for an extended kinship group, made up of a few thousand members and similar to a clan or tribe. The *ayllus* of Northern Potosí – Laymis, Jukumanis, Machas, Pocoatas, Chayantakas – mostly live in the higher-altitude lands to the west of the region, where they grow potatoes and raise sheep, llamas and other livestock, but they maintain islands of territory in the dry valleys such as Torotoro, where they cultivate maize, wheat and other lower-altitude crops. They travel frequently between the two, and depending on the time of year you may see individuals in their distinctive brightly embroidered shirts coming down to tend the crops or long llama-trains carrying produce from the Torotoro valley up to the highlands. This system of widely dispersed territories ensures that each ethnic group has access to the produce of different altitudes, and represents a distinctly Andean form of organization that has long fascinated anthropologists.

Throughout the colonial era and long after independence, Northern Potosí was the focus of frequent indigenous uprisings as the different *ayllus* resisted attempts by Spanish and Bolivian hacienda owners to occupy their lands. The town of Torotoro itself was only founded in the late colonial period by mestizo migrants from Cochabamba. As recently as 1958, during the upheaval following the revolution of 1952, it was ransacked by armed *ayllu* members, who drove away many of the townspeople and seized the lands of the haciendas that had been established on their traditional valley territories. Torotoro's main annual celebration is the **Fiesta de Tata Santiago**, held on July 25 each year, when the *ayllus* descend on the town to drink, dance and stage ritual Tinku fights (see p.189).

Torotoro village and around

The administrative centre of the park and the only base from which to explore it is the village of **TOROTORO**, a sleepy collection of adobe houses with sagging red-tiled roofs set around a small plaza with an incongruous modern church – the only building in town that enjoys regular electric light (the village has a generator, but rarely enough funds for diesel). Home to just a few hundred people, the village stands beside the river of the same name at the top of a broad hanging valley at an altitude of about 2600m and is the place to find food, accommodation, guides and information (see Practicalities, p.255).

The clearest **dinosaur tracks** in the park are on the lower slopes of Cerro Huayllas, the mountain that rises just east of the village across the Río Torotoro (which is generally little more than a stream in the May–Sept dry season). To reach them, walk back along the road to Cochabamba and cross at the ford, turn right and walk upstream about 100m, then climb about 20m up the rocky slope to your left. The tracks were made by a quadruped herbivore that roamed the region in the Cretaceous era, more than sixty million years ago – they comprise a trail of deep circular prints about 50cm in diameter imprinted in a sloping plane of grey rock; set about 1m apart. A little further upstream there's another trail of smaller prints left by a three-toed carnivore, but these are less distinct and much more difficult to find.

If you follow the river downstream for about twenty minutes you'll reach a stretch where the rushing rainy season waters have carved great stone basins out of the soft bedrock – locals refer to this stretch as **Batea Cocha** ("beating pool"), as they look a bit like basins for pounding laundry. About 7m up the rock face on the left bank, protected by a low adobe wall to stop casual vandalism, but clearly visible nonetheless, is a collection of ancient **rock paintings** (*pinturas rupestres*). Mostly abstract designs painted in red ochre, with several zigzags – including one that looks like a serpent and another that could be the sun or a star – the paintings are all less than a metre long and have already been partly defaced, but they provide a focus for what is anyway a pleasant stroll down the river. A little further downstream there's a small but pretty **waterfall** that forms a good swimming hole; beyond that, the river plunges down into the deep Torotoro canyon and you can walk no further, though you can access the canyon from further downstream (see below).

Torotoro Canyon

Just north of Torotoro village the Río Torotoro plunges through the deep **Torotoro Canyon**, probably the most beautiful section of the park. Enclosed on either side by sheer, 200-metre-high cliffs covered with stunted trees festooned with spiky bromeliads, the river creates a series of waterfalls as it tumbles over a jumble of massive boulders, forming pools that are ideal for swimming. The rock-strewn canyon floor is perfect for scrambling over boulders, and the route down is easy to find without a guide (though you shouldn't go alone in case you hurt yourself and can't get back).

To get down into the canyon, follow the road out of town towards Cochabamba for about 200m. Where the road turns sharply to the right, follow the track heading off to the left, and walk for about twenty minutes until you see some well-made stone steps dropping steeply down the side of the canyon to your left. The most picturesque stretch of the canyon is a few hundred metres downstream from where the steps reach the bottom, where a ten-metre-high waterfall known as **El Vergel** emerges from the side of the canyon on the right in several streams which cover the rock face in slimygreen water weeds – hence it's Quechua name, Waca Senq'a, meaning "the cow's nose".

Caverna de Umajallanta

The most extensive and easiest to visit of the many limestone cave systems in the park is the **Caverna de Umajallanta**, where nearly 5km of underground passages have been explored. The cave makes a great day-trip from Torotoro and is one of the park's most popular attractions. The entrance to the cave is about 8km northwest of Torotoro, a walk of ninety minutes to two hours across the rolling landscape with good views of the dramatic geology of the mountain ridges that surround the Torotoro valley – about halfway you'll pass a trail of **dinosaur footprints**: a series of four-toed tracks about 30cm in length and about a metre apart.

The cave complex was formed by the waters of the Río Umajallanta, which disappears below the surface here and re-emerges as a waterfall high above the Torotoro Canyon, 6km away to the east. It consists of a series of interconnected limestone caverns of varying sizes, one of which contains a lake fed by the river that is home to some blind white fish. Sadly, most of the stalactites and stalagmites have been broken off by visitors in the years before protective measures were established (they should grow back in a few centuries), but a visit to the cave is still very enjoyable, unless you're claustrophobic – trips involve clambering and crawling for a couple of hours through some very tight places up to 800m underground. Take a torch and drinking water, expect to get dirty, and on no account attempt to visit the caves without a guide. For serious cavers and speleologists there are a number of other caves in the area to explore – talk to staff at the park office.

Llama Chaqui

About 16km east of Torotoro stands **Llama Chaqui**, a ruined pre-Inca fortress that energetic hikers can visit in a long day-trip from the village, or less hardy walkers could explore in a more leisurely two-day camping trip. Either way, you'll need a guide to find the route. The walk to the ruins takes you over the mountains to the east of the Río Torotoro, with spectacular views across the deep valley of the Río Caine and the rugged brown mountains that march away to Cerro Tunari, the peak that rises above Cochabamba. The scenery is very beautiful, with steep rocky slopes and narrow hanging valleys patch-worked with maize and barley fields set around the occasional isolated hamlet.

Set on a knife-edge ridge high above the Río Caine, Llama Chaqui itself is an excellent observation point and natural fortress, though other than the walled enclosure (still sometimes used by local campesinos as a cattle pen) lit-tle remains of the ancient settlement, and the entire complex is heavily over-grown with thick vegetation. Even so, you can still make out the foundations of individual houses, and the ground is scattered with pottery fragments and rough cut stones.

Practicalities

Buses to Torotoro leave Cochabamba from the corner of Avenida 6 de Agosto and Avenida Republica at about 6am on Thursdays and Sundays, and return from Torotoro at 6am on Fridays and Mondays, so you can either spend three or four whole days in the park – two days are enough to see the main attrac-tions (the Torotoro Canyon, Caverna de Umajallanta and the dinosaur foot-prints) though it's worth taking four if you want to explore the area more fully. The bus ride lasts about seven hours in the dry season, a rough and dusty trip along unpaved roads and dry riverbeds – in the rainy season it takes much longer and the route can become impassable when rivers are too high to cross.

On arrival you should head to the **tourist office** (daily 8am–noon & 2–5pm), on the main street of the village, where you'll need to pay the $2.50 park admission fee. The office has basic information about the park and can find you a local **guide** for about $7 a day for groups of up to five people (slightly more for larger groups) – the village is so small that forming a group with other travellers is rarely a problem if you want to share the cost. There's usually only one **place to stay**, the *Alojamiento Charcas* (✆04/4133927; ❶), which has plenty of simple but clean rooms with shared toilet and shower, though there's no hot water and rarely any electricity (the only phone in town, an ENTEL public phone, is also here. There are a couple of other similar *alo-jamientos* that open up very occasionally if things get really busy. Torotoro does-n't have any real restaurants, but a couple of women in the village prepare basic **meals** for about $1 if you order a few hours in advance – just ask around to find out who's cooking. Otherwise, there are a handful of basic shops where you can get bread, tins of sardines, crackers, oranges, soft drinks and other sim-ple provisions, as well as tea and coffee, though it's worth bringing some sup-plies with you from Cochabamba to supplement this rather meagre fare, par-ticularly if you're planning a longer stay.

The Chapare

Northeast of Cochabamba, the main road to Santa Cruz crosses the last ridge of the Andes and drops down into the **CHAPARE**, a broad, rainforest-covered plain in the Upper Amazon Basin which has been heavily settled by peasant migrants from the highlands, who over the last few decades have turned the region into the main source in Bolivia of coca grown to manufacture **cocaine** (see box below). For the traveller, the ongoing conflict between local coca farmers and Bolivian government troops trying to eradicate their crops means that despite its great natural beauty the Chapare is not the place for expeditions far off the beaten track – you're likely to be mistaken for a US agent or a narco-trafficker. For all the region's troubles, however, the towns along the main Cochabamba to Santa Cruz road are peaceful and safe to visit – at least

The Chapare: coca, cocaleros and cocaine

The **coca** produced in the Chapare is grown by small peasant farmers, known as **cocaleros**, most of whom migrated to the Chapare from the highlands when this previously inaccessible region was opened up to settlement in the 1970s with the construction of the new Cochabamba to Santa Cruz road – ironically, funded by the US Agency for International Development. Following construction of the road, thousands of poor peasants poured down from the highlands in search of land and new opportunities (followed after 1985 by further thousands of former miners laid off by the state), displacing the region's small populations of indigenous Yuracaré and Yuqui, who moved deeper into the forest to the north. With little experience of farming in the tropics, the migrants found in coca an ideal cash crop – easy to grow even on poor, deforested soils, commanding a high price and attracting buyers who actually collected from the growers' doorstep. Raised in small plantations throughout the region, the coca is harvested and carried along jungle trails to innumerable kitchens to be processed into coca paste, then flown north in light aircraft to rainforest laboratories deep in the Beni or up through the Amazon to Colombia for final processing, before being smuggled into the US.

As demand for cocaine grew and prices rose in the 1980s, the Chapare experienced a coca boom of gold-rush proportions. But though the export of cocaine from the Chapare was of vital importance to the Bolivian economy during the late 1980s and 1990s, at times equalling or exceeding the value of all legal exports combined, in recent years the Bolivian government, under enormous pressure from the US, has been trying to eradicate the coca crop and end exports of cocaine. Initially, growers were paid to eliminate their coca crops, but efforts to find viable alternative products have had little success, and many simply replanted coca after taking the money. Under US pressure the government position has hardened, moving to forcible eradication without compensation, with the Bolivian army and its US Drug Enforcement Agency advisors now uprooting coca crops by hand. Understandably, this has provoked a severe conflict with the thousands of small peasant producers whose livelihoods depend on growing coca, and who have opposed eradication with mass protests and road blockades. The Chapare is now a highly militarized region, and *cocalero* resistance has become more radical. Dozens of *cocaleros* have been killed in clashes with the security forces and hundreds arrested, while several soldiers and police officers have been killed by gunmen or boobytrap bombs left in coca plantations. Much of the coca crop has been eliminated and cocaine exports substantially reduced, but though the government claims it will reach its target of "coca zero" by the end of 2002, the *cocaleros* remain defiant, and the conflict looks set to continue, with plantations and processing labs being moved deeper into the rainforest to the north.

when the road isn't blocked by protesting *cocaleros* – though most are unattractive and economically depressed frontier settlements, serving as functional market centres for a sadly deforested hinterland. The exception is **Villa Tunari**, a one-time narco-traffickers playground which is now at the centre of efforts to promote the Chapare as a tourist destination. The town is a good place to break a journey between Cochabamba and Santa Cruz and also to get a brief introduction to the Amazon lowlands – the well-preserved rainforests of the **Parque Nacional Carrasco** are within easy reach, and the town enjoys a beautiful setting and is a good place to relax. Otherwise, the main point of stopping in the Chapare is to make the exciting river trip from **Puerto Villarroel**, the region's main port, north to Trinidad in the Beni.

Villa Tunari and around

The paved road through the Chapare between Cochabamba and Santa Cruz was completed in the 1970s, replacing the longer highland road via Samaipata (see p.281) as the main route between the two cities. From Cochabamba, it climbs slowly through high-valley scenery, past mountain slopes patchworked with wheat and potato fields and groves of eucalyptus and pine. About 90km from Cochabamba the road passes **Laguna Corani**, a large artificial lake that provides much of Cochabamba's water supply, before crossing the last ridge of the Andes and plunging down into the Chapare. Almost immediately the vegetation closes in on either side of the road as it winds down through dense cloudforest that clings to the steep mountainside, its trees bearded with lichen and covered with spiky bromeliads that thrive on the moisture brought by great banks of cloud that sweep in from the north. On the way down, you'll pass a major road block where soldiers and UMOPAR anti-narcotics police search passing vehicles for cocaine going out and precursor chemicals (ether and sulphuric acid) for its manufacture coming in – you'll be asked to get off the bus and may have to show your passport.

About 160km from Cochabamba, the road reaches the town of **VILLA TUNARI,** the biggest settlement in the Chapare and the centre of efforts to develop the region as a tourist destination. Set beside a broad sweep of the Río San Mateo, with the last forested foothills of the Andes rising behind, Villa Tunari is extremely picturesque, and at an altitude of just 300m enjoys a warm, tropical climate. Its chances of becoming a successful resort or an ecotourism destination like Rurrenabaque, however, are severely limited so long as the current instability continues, and independent travel off the beaten track remains inadvisable. This is a shame, as from Puerto San Francisco, an hour's drive north of Villa Tunari, you could rent a motorized canoe and boatman to take you down the Ríos Chipiriri and Isiboro into the rainforests of the Parque Nacional Isiboro-Sécure (see p.328), but though the Cochabamba-based tour agency Fremen occasionally run trips along this route, doing so independently is not a safe proposition at present.

The main road through the town is lined with large restaurants and overpriced hotels where in better days the movers and shakers of the cocaine industry would come to blow some of their massive earnings, but which now depend for custom on drug enforcement officials, the occasional weekender from Cochabamba and foreign development workers. Away from the main road Villa Tunari is a pleasant, laid-back town which has clearly seen better days. Broad, cobbled streets lined with profuse gardens and houses that are fairly luxurious by Bolivian standards lead off a spacious main square, surrounded by modern public buildings including the offices of the United Nations and other international aid agencies. Municipal efforts to promote tourism as an economic alternative to coca and cocaine have so far resulted in little more than an expensive sign across the main road proclaiming Villa Tunari a "Paraíso Etno-Ecoturistico".

A 250-metre walk east along the main road and across the bridge over the Río Espíritu Santo brings you to the entrance of the **Parque Machia** (Mon–Sat 9.30am–5.30pm; $1, cameras $2, video cameras $3), a small private ecological reserve that also serves as a refuge for Amazonian animals rescued from captivity. The park has four kilometres of trails running through the forest and some lookout points with beautiful views across the Río Chapare and the forest-covered mountains rising to the high peaks of the Andes behind. Along the trails you'll meet most of the semi-tame animal residents, which include several species of monkey, macaws and a puma, many of which roam free but still depend on humans for food. The park and refuge are managed by the Inti Wara Yassi organization (☎04/4134621), which relies largely on volunteers, many of them young foreign travellers who stop here for a month or two. Volunteers must stay for a minimum of two weeks and can sleep in the Casa de Voluntarios dormitory for about $2 a night.

Practicalities

Most services in Villa Tunari are strung out along the Cochabamba–Santa Cruz road; the main plaza is two blocks north of this opposite the *Hotel Las Palmas*. **Buses** from Cochabamba arrive and depart from the office of Trans Tours 7 de Junio on the main road; you can also flag down buses passing through on their way to Cochabamba from elsewhere in the Chapare. Through buses from Santa Cruz will drop you off at the police control *tranca* at the west end of town, and buses heading to Santa Cruz sometimes pick up passengers here if they have room, though most pass through in the middle of the night. To travel to Ivirgarsama and thence to Puerto Villaroel, you'll need first to take a trufi to Shinaota (every 20–30min; 20min), which trawl up and down the main road in search of passengers, then take another trufi from Shinaota to Chimoré, and then a third from Chimoré to Ivirgasama.

The best **place to stay** is the *Hotel El Puente* (book through Fremen in Cochabamba on ☎04/4259392; ❺, including breakfast), about 4km east of town, which has modern comfortable *cabañas* for two people with fans and hot water set amid a patch of rainforest with a swimming pool and several natural river pools close by, and a restaurant. To get there either take a taxi ($2–3) or walk out of town along the main road to the east, then take the track that leads off it to the right after the second bridge. On the south side of the main road are a couple of rather overpriced mid-range country club-style hotels with small swimming pools: the *Hotel Las Palmas* (☎04/4134103; ❺) has comfortable but rather run down rooms with fans and private baths, some with views over the river, and a good restaurant; while the *Hotel San Martín* (☎04/4134115; ❹) has cool modern rooms with fans and private baths around an exuberant garden. The best budget option is the friendly *Hostal San Antonio* (☎04/4134138; ❷) on the west side of the plaza, which offers pleasant rooms with fans and cold water with or without bathroom; also adequate is the *Hotel La Querencia* (no phone; ❷), a block north of the main road on the last turning before the bridge at the east end of town, which has simple but clean rooms with private or shared bathrooms and cold water only; some have views over the river.

The best **restaurant** in town is the *San Silvestre*, on the main road, where for about $4 you can get excellent local river fish including the delicious *surubí* and a range of game dishes including *jochi* (agouti) and *taitetú* (peccary or wild pig), if your ecological conscience allows, as well as cold beer and a range of freshly squeezed exotic fruits. The restaurant in the *Hotel Las Palmas* serves much the same stuff for similar prices, as well as decent coffee and breakfasts. Less expensive food is available from the foodstalls and shacks along the north side of the main road, which cater mostly for passing lorry drivers and bus passengers; here you'll find filling set almuerzos for around $1, as well as inexpensive fried fish and steak, fruit juices and cold drinks.

Parque Nacional Carrasco

A few kilometres south of Villa Tunari on the other side of the Río San Mateo, some 6226 square kilometres of the forested northern slopes of the Andes are protected by the **Parque Nacional Carrasco**, which adjoins the Parque Nacional Amboró (see p.279) to the east. Plunging steeply down from high mountain peaks, the park encompasses a variety of ecosystems from high Andean grasslands and cloudforest to dense tropical rainforest, ranging in altitude from 4000m to just 300m. It also supports a great range of wildlife, including all the major Amazonian mammals, among them jaguar, tapir and peccary, and over 700 species of bird, including several which are endemic to the region. The park is seriously threatened by illegal logging, hunting and forest clearance for agriculture by settlers along both its northern and southern margins, but the mountainous and forest-covered landscape is so impenetrable that the inner regions remain pristine – there are even unconfirmed reports of uncontacted groups of indigenous Yuracaré hunters living deep in the interior of the park.

Close to Villa Tunari on the southern border of the park are the **Cavernas del Repechón** (Sat & Sun 8am–noon & 1.20–4pm; $1.50; to visit during the week contact SERNAP in Cochabamba two days in advance on ☎04/4421056 or 4335660), a group of natural caves that are home to a large population of *guacharós*, or **oil birds**, a large nocturnal fruit-eating bird found in very few other places in South America. To visit the caves you'll need to reach the settlement of **Paractito**, about 10km from Villa Tunari on a side road heading south off the main road just east of town – a taxi should cost about $4–5, twice that if you want the driver to wait around for a few hours and take you back after your visit. At Paractito the park guards will collect your entrance fee and take you across the tumultuous Río San Mateo on primitive cable car. Visits to the cave are by guided tour only, so even at weekends it's best to arrive early to ensure you don't miss the park guards when they set off – ideally it's worth booking in advance by telephone so they know you're coming. From the other side of the river it's a thirty-minute walk through the rainforest to the caves, where you'll be able to see (and hear) the oil birds nesting (except in May and June, when they often migrate to Venezuela). The birds only leave the caves at night to eat fruit, and navigate by echo-location, emitting a strange clicking sound.

East from Villa Tunari to Santa Cruz

From Villa Tunari **the road to Santa Cruz** continues east across a flat, heavily settled and largely deforested landscape punctuated with regular towns strung out along the main road – scruffy, tin-roofed frontier settlements where satellite dishes preceded sanitation, and whose unpaved streets turn to quagmires in the rain. The first of these is **SHINAOTA**, which was the centre of the cocaine trade in the early 1980s and one of the most expensive towns in Bolivia, a place where huge quantities of cocaine and coca paste were bought and sold openly on the streets like so much sugar. Those days are long gone now, however, and little of the money made was reinvested in the town. Whatever trade still goes on is conducted in secrecy deeper in the forest to the north, and Shinaota has the melancholy feeling of a gold-rush town after the gold has run out. Trufis to and from Villa Tunari (every 20–30min; 20min) and Ivergarzama (every 20–30min; 35min) arrive and depart from the main street, where you can also catch buses direct to Cochabamba; there are a few restaurants and a couple of *alojamientos*, but no reason to spend the night.

Just east of Shinaota, 35km from Villa Tunari, the town of **CHIMORÉ** is the headquarters of drug-eradication efforts in the Chapare, and the road passes several major military and police bases, fenced and fortified compounds from which the Bolivian joint task force and US Drug Enforcement Agency helicopters sally forth each day in search of coca plantations to uproot and clandestine cocaine kitchens to raid. Another 29km further east along the Chapare road, the unappealing market centre of **IVIRGARZAMA** has little to distinguish it from other Chapare towns apart from the fact that it's from here that a side road leads north to Puerto Villarroel, from where you can travel by boat to Trinidad in the Beni. Trufis to Shinaota and buses to Cochabamba leave from one end of the main street, trufis to Puerto Villarroel (every 20–30min; 30min) from the other, and there are a handful of places to eat and some basic *alojamientos*, but no reason to stay.

From Ivirgarzama the main road continues east to Santa Cruz, 247km away, passing through **Buena Vista** (141km), the main entrance point to the Parque Nacional Amboró (see p.279). Most buses to Santa Cruz pass through by night, but will usually stop for passengers if they have spare seats.

Puerto Villaroel and the Río Ichilo

From Ivirgarzama, a rough dirt road runs 26km north to **PUERTO VILLARROEL**, a small river port on the **Río Ichilo** from where regular cargo boats travel north to Trinidad (see p.320). This river route is the main transport link between Cochabamba department and the Beni, and was the only route between Trinidad and highland Bolivia until the road from Santa Cruz to Trinidad was completed in the 1970s. With a population of about 2000, Puerto Villarroel is an untidy collection of tin-roofed wooden and concrete houses, many of them raised above the muddy, unpaved streets to protect them from flooding when the river bursts its banks – a not infrequent occurrence in the November-to-March rainy season.

Trufis to Ivirgarzama arrive and depart from the small central plaza, where you'll find an ENTEL telephone office, a few restaurants selling cheap set almuerzos and tasty fried river fish, and a couple of basic **places to stay** – the friendly *Alojamiento Sucre* (no phone; ❶), which has a few rooms off a big dancehall (which gets very noisy on the weekends when boatmen and *cocaleros* come to drink the night away); and the more peaceful *Alojamiento La Pascana* opposite (no phone; ❶). Most activity takes place on the river bank, a couple of blocks away, where there's a naval base, a series of oil storage tanks, and a rudimentary port where ramshackle river boats line up to load and unload cargo – bananas and cattle arriving from downstream, gasoline to take down to Trinidad, basic supplies for the few settlements downriver.

To find a **boat** to take you downstream, ask around amongst the captains or in the Capitanía del Puerto (the naval port authority office). The river journey through the rainforest to Trinidad should cost about $20–30 including food and takes five to seven days, depending on the level of the river, the size and power of the boat, and how many stops it makes to load and unload cargo. In the dry season (May–Sept) river levels can drop so low that the trip downstream becomes impossible. During the rest of the year there are usually several departures to Trinidad each week, though you may have to wait around a day or two – boat captains generally let passengers sleep on board while waiting to load. You'll need your own hammock and mosquito nets (you can buy these in the markets in Cochabamba or Ivirgarzama), insect repellent and drinking water, and fruit and snacks to supplement the basic food supplied on board.

Transport details

Buses

Cochabamba to: La Paz (every 30min; 7–8hr): Oruro (every 20min; 6hr); Santa Cruz (8–12 daily; 10–12hr); Sucre (7–10 daily; 10–12hr); Vallegrande (2 weekly; 10–12hr); Villa Tunari (4–6 daily; 4–5hr).

Sucre to: Cochabamba (7–10 daily; 10–12hr); La Paz (4–5 daily; 15hr), Oruro (3 daily; 11hr); Potosí (every 30min; 3hr); Santa Cruz (5–7 daily; 14hr); Villamontes (daily; 20–25hr); Yacuiba (daily; 21–26hr).

Boats

Puerto Villaroel to: Trinidad (2–3 weekly; 5–7 days).

Planes

Cochabamba to: La Paz (3–5 daily; 45min); Riberalta (1 daily; 1hr 30min); Santa Cruz (5 daily; 45min); Sucre (via La Paz; 1–2 daily; 2hr); Tarija (1–2 daily; 50min); Trinidad (2–3 daily; 40min).

Sucre to: Cochabamba (via La Paz; 1–2 daily; 2hr); La Paz (2–3 daily; 1hr); Santa Cruz (2–3 daily; 40min); Tarija (3 weekly; 45min).

Santa Cruz and the Eastern Lowlands

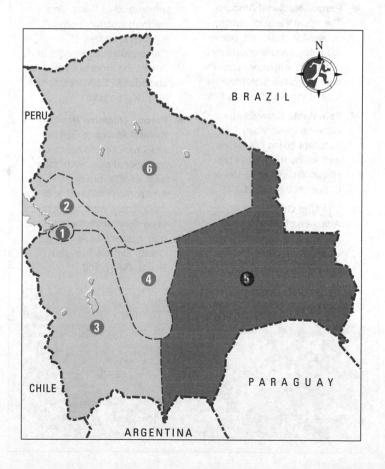

N

BRAZIL

PERU

2

1

6

4

5

3

CHILE

PARAGUAY

ARGENTINA

CHAPTER 5

Highlights

* **Santa Cruz nightlife** It may be short on tourist sights, but when to comes to nightlife, Bolivia's eastern capital is closer in style and spirit to Brazil than to the rest of the country. **See p.274**

* **Parque Nacional Amboró** The country's most easily accessible rainforest, boasting a spectacular abundance of birdlife, with more species than any other protected area in the world. **See p.279**

* **Samaipata** Charming town set in an idyllic valley with excellent hiking nearby, as well as the mysterious pre-Hispanic ceremonial site of El Fuerte. **See p.281**

* **The Che Guevara trail** Admirers of the iconic Argentine revolutionary can visit the site of his recently uncovered grave in Vallegrande, as well as the nearby hamlet of La Higuera, where his ill-fated guerrilla campaign ended in capture and execution. **See p.287**

* **The Jesuit Missions of Chiquitos** Scattered across the sparsely populated forest region east of Santa Cruz, the immaculately restored mission churches of Chiquitos are a reminder of one of the more unusual episodes in Bolivia's colonial history. **See p.291**

* **Parque Nacional Noel Kempff Mercado** Bolivia's most remote and spectacular national park, with abundant wildlife, pristine Amazonian rainforest and magnificent waterfalls tumbling down from the plateau that inspired Sir Arthur Conan Doyle's *The Lost World*. **See p.303**

Santa Cruz and the Eastern Lowlands

S tretching from the last foothills of the Andes east to Brazil and south to Paraguay and Argentina, Bolivia's **Eastern Lowlands** – the Llanos Orientales – were until recently amongst the least-known and least-developed regions in the country. Spread across a vast and sparsely populated plain, the lowlands' varied ecosystems range from Amazonian rainforest in the north, through broad savannahs and tropical dry forest in the centre, to the immense wetlands of the Pantanal in the far east and the arid scrub and thorn brush of the Chaco to the south. Rich in natural resources, in recent decades the region has undergone astonishingly rapid development, while its economy has grown to become the most important in the country, fuelled by oil and gas, cattle-ranching and massive agricultural development.

At the centre of this unprecedented economic boom is the city of **Santa Cruz**, the regional capital, which in the space of a few decades has been transformed from an isolated provincial backwater into a booming modern metropolis with a brash commercial attitude and lively tropical outlook utterly distinct from the reserved cities of the Bolivian highlands. Though Santa Cruz has little to offer in terms of conventional tourist attractions, it is a crucial transport hub and the ideal base for exploring the many attractions of the surrounding area, where much of the region's beautiful natural environment survives, despite the ravages of deforestation and development.

Just an hour and a half's drive west of the city, the pristine and exceptionally biodiverse rainforests that cover the easternmost foothills of the Andes are protected by the **Parque Nacional Amboró**, one of the most easily accessible wilderness areas in Bolivia. The beautiful cloudforest that covers the upper regions of Amboró can be visited from **Samaipata**, an idyllic resort town that is also home to one of Bolivia's most intriguing pre-Inca archeological sites, El Fuerte. From Samaipata, you can also head further southwest through the Andean foothills to the town of **Vallegrande** and the nearby hamlet of **La Higuera**, scene of the last desperate guerrilla campaign of the iconic Argentine revolutionary Ernesto Che Guevara, who was killed here in 1967.

East of Santa Cruz the railway to Brazil passes through the broad forested plains of **Chiquitos**, whose beautiful Jesuit mission churches, built in the

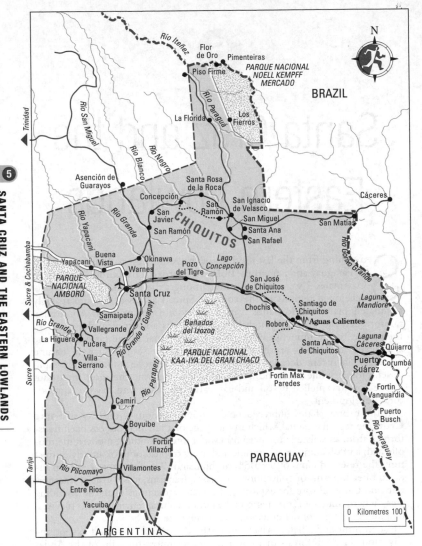

eighteenth century and recently restored, bear witness to one of the most extraordinary episodes in Spanish colonial history, when a handful of priests established a semi-autonomous theocratic state in the midst of the wilderness. In the far north of the region, accessible only by air or by an arduous overland journey, the **Parque Nacional Noel Kempff Mercado** is perhaps the most beautiful and pristine of all Bolivia's protected rainforest areas, combining dramatic scenery with unparalleled wildlife-spotting opportunities. Finally, south of Santa Cruz stretches the vast and inhospitable **Chaco**, an arid wilderness of dense thorn and scrub, stretching south to Argentina and Paraguay.

Santa Cruz

Set among the steamy, tropical lowlands just beyond the last Andean foothills, the city of **SANTA CRUZ** has emerged in recent decades as the economic powerhouse of Bolivia. An isolated frontier town until the middle of the twentieth century, the city has grown in the last fifty years to become the second biggest in the country, a sprawling metropolis that now rivals La Paz for power and influence, with a booming economy based on oil and gas, timber and cattle, and large-scale agro-industry. Largely because most of it is so new, Santa Cruz has little to match the colonial charm of highland cities like Sucre and Potosí, and few conventional tourist sights beyond a few mediocre museums and an architecturally unexciting cathedral. But while some travellers find its brash modernity, commercialism and pseudo-Americanism unappealing, others enjoy its blend of dynamism and tropical insouciance, and the lively optimism of its inhabitants.

The city of Santa Cruz de la Sierra was founded in April 1561 by the Spanish conquistador **Nuflo de Chavez**, who had arrived in the region at the head of a large military expedition accompanied by thousands of indigenous Guaraní, having marched across the desolate plains of the Chaco from the Spanish settlement of Asunción on the Río Paraguay in search of new lands and a route through to the silver of the Andes. The original city stood some 260km east of its present location, close to the site of the later Jesuit mission town of San José de Chiquitos (see p.301). The new settlement proved isolated and precarious, however, surrounded by a hostile indigenous population and far from any other outpost of Spanish power. In 1594 it was moved to its present location, a more easily defended site on the west side of the Río Grande, close to the last foothills of the Andes. For the next three and a half centuries Santa Cruz remained an isolated frontier outpost, all but cut off from the rest of Bolivia and Paraguay by great distances, inhospitable terrain and (at least until the last major Chiriguano uprising was crushed in 1892) unconquered indigenous groups.

Only in the 1950s did things begin to change, with the construction of a railway link to Brazil and a road to Cochabamba, after which Santa Cruz became the main supplier of cotton, rice, sugar, soya and other tropical agricultural produce to the rest of Bolivia (and, increasingly, to foreign markets as well). The economic boom really took off in the 1970s, when Santa Cruz emerged as the centre of the Bolivian **cocaine industry**. Cocaine brought enormous wealth – as well as corruption – to the city, much of which was reinvested in land, agriculture, construction and other legitimate businesses. Growth was further fuelled by oil and gas revenues from the Chaco, and generous government subsidies (often in the form of loans which were never repaid) to large landowners and agro-industrialists, particularly during the regime of General Banzer, himself a Cruceño. The population of Santa Cruz leapt from around 42,000 in 1950 to over a million in 2001, making it the second biggest city in Bolivia after La Paz. Rapid economic growth and the availability of land attracted large numbers of immigrants to Santa Cruz, including Japanese rice farmers, German-speaking Mennonites from Canada and Mexico, and a small but influential group of fugitive Nazis. The Bolivian government actively encouraged immigration to the region: at one stage even offering white farmers from South Africa and Rhodesia "empty" land around Santa Cruz – the fact that these lands were in fact already occupied by the much-depleted indigenous groups who had always lived there was conveniently ignored, but in the end the offer was not taken up.

Most of the new arrivals, however, were poor indigenous migrants from the Andes, who settled in ever-expanding shantytowns around the city, transforming the make-up of the city's population. But for all that, it's still the native Cruceños who dominate the city and its economy. Known as *cambas* by the people of the highlands, the Cruceños are culturally a world apart from the rest of Bolivia (they in their turn refer with mild contempt to the highland immigrants as *collas* – the two terms being old Inca words for lowland and highland peoples respectively). Generally loud, brash and happy-go-lucky, their language, music and outlook are infused with a tropical ease and sensuality which makes the city feel closer in spirit to Brazil or Colombia than to the rest of Bolivia.

Arrival and information

Santa Cruz is divided into concentric rings by successive ringroads – called **anillos** – beginning with the **Primer Anillo**, which encompasses the colonial city centre, and extending outwards to the ninth ring. Other than the airport, you'll find almost everything you're likely to need within the first two *anillos*; when travelling outside this central area you'll need to know which *anillo* you want when giving directions.

Long-distance buses and all **trains** arrive and depart from the recently completed **Terminal Bi-Modal de Transporte**, the combined bus and train terminal (information on ☎03/3463388 or 3463900) located about 2km west of the city centre just outside the Segundo Anillo at the end of Avenida Brasil. There are always plenty of taxis outside (a trip from here to most city hotels won't cost more than about $1); otherwise, you can get into the city centre by catching any micro heading east along Avenida Brasil and marked "Plaza 24 de Septiembre". At the time of writing, all buses and trufis travelling between Santa Cruz and destinations within the department of Santa Cruz were supposed to arrive and depart from the Terminal Bi-Modal as well, but drivers were resisting the move, so you may well be dropped off at the old destinations. Trufis from **Buena Vista** and **Yapacani** arrive and depart from near the old bus terminal, just south of the city centre; trufis from **Samaipata** arrive and depart from two blocks south of the old terminal on Avenida Omar Chavez with Solis de Olguín; and buses from the various former Jesuit mission towns of Chiquitos – **San Javier**, **Concepción** and **San Ignacio** – terminate at three different bus company offices inside the Segundo Anillo: Expreso Misiones (at Avenida Omar Chavez with Solis de Olguín); Linea 131 del Este (at Suàrez Arana with Barrón); and Expreso Jenecheru (at Choferes del Chaco with the Segundo Anillo). For getting around the city, **taxis** can be hailed on all the main streets; they charge a standard rate of just under $1 within the Primer Anillo, plus an additional boliviano for each extra *anillo* you cross.

Santa Cruz's main airport is the modern **Aeropuerto Viru-Viru** (☎03/3852400 or 181), 17km north of the city centre, from where it's a $6 flat-fare taxi ride into the centre of town; alternatively, you can catch a micro (every 20min; 30min) to the corner of avenidas Irala and Cañoto, outside the old bus terminal, though this still leaves you a fair walk from any city-centre accommodation. The city's second airport, the smaller **Aeropuerto El Trompillo**, is used by the military airline, TAM Mercosur, who operate weekly flights to San Ignacio.

Information

Santa Cruz's tourist information office, the **Unidad de Turismo** (Mon–Fri 8am–4pm; ☎03/3368900), is inside the Prefectura building on the north side of Plaza 24 de Septiembre. You can usually get a good free map of the city

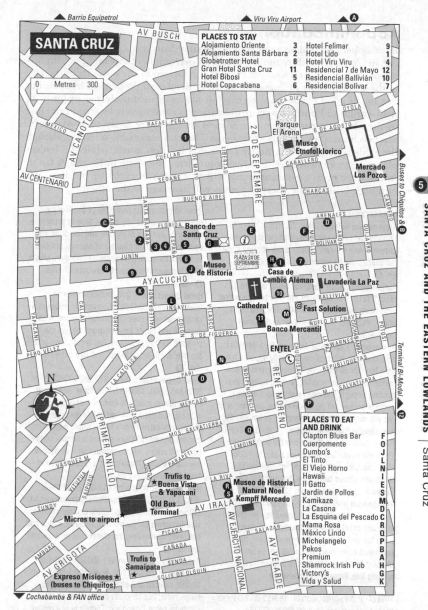

SANTA CRUZ

Metres 300

PLACES TO STAY

Alojamiento Oriente	3	Hotel Felimar	9
Alojamiento Santa Bárbara	2	Hotel Lido	1
Globetrotter Hotel	8	Hotel Viru Viru	4
Gran Hotel Santa Cruz	11	Residencial 7 de Mayo	12
Hotel Bibosi	5	Residencial Ballivián	10
Hotel Copacabana	6	Residencial Bolívar	7

PLACES TO EAT AND DRINK

Clapton Blues Bar	F
Cuerpomente	O
Dumbo's	J
El Tinto	L
El Viejo Horno	N
Hawaii	I
Il Gatto	E
Jardin de Pollos	S
Kamikaze	M
La Casona	D
La Esquina del Pescado	C
Mama Rosa	R
México Lindo	Q
Michelangelo	P
Pekos	B
Premium	A
Shamrock Irish Pub	H
Victory's	G
Vida y Salud	K

SANTA CRUZ AND THE EASTERN LOWLANDS | Santa Cruz

and whatever flyers and brochures are currently available, and the staff will try to answer simple questions in Spanish, though their understanding of what independent foreign tourists might find interesting is limited. For information on the Parque Nacional Noel Kempff Mercado you should contact Saira Duque at the office of the **Fundación Amigos de la Naturaleza** (FAN), 7km out of town on the old road to Cochabamba (☎03/3556800, ⓦwww.fan-bo.org).

269

Accommodation

Possibly because building and running **luxury hotels** is a good way of investing and laundering dirty money, there's an oversupply of top-range accommodation in Santa Cruz. However, most of it is located in the outskirts of the city in the wealthy Barrio Equipetrol, which is useful if you're here on business but not much good if you want to explore the city. Fortunately the majority of **mid-range** and **budget accommodation** is conveniently located in or close to the old city centre, from where most things you're likely to need can be reached on foot or by a short taxi ride. There's a reasonable selection, though the mid-range places are mostly rather dull business hotels, while the budget places are more expensive than their equivalents elsewhere in Bolivia. A fan or (more expensive) air-conditioning is pretty much essential in the heat and humidity – all but the cheapest rooms will have one or the other.

Budget

Alojamiento Oriente Junín 362 ☎03/3321976. Friendly and reasonably priced single-storey *alojamiento* with a sunny central patio, offering clean but pretty spartan rooms with or without bath. ❷–❸

Alojamiento Santa Bárbara Santa Bárbara 181 ☎03/3321817 or 3321928. No-frills budget option with basic but clean rooms with cool tiled floors and shared bath (but no fans) around a small courtyard. ❷

Residencial 7 de Mayo Av Brasil ☎03/3489634. Sparkling new establishment directly opposite the new Terminal Bi-Modal de Transporte, and so convenient if you're arriving late, leaving early or just passing through, The clean and modern rooms come in a variety of prices depending on whether or not you want a private bath and a/c or fan. ❷–❸

Residencial Ballivián Ballivián 71 ☎03/3321960. Rather rundown but always popular budget option. The basic rooms are set around a peaceful flower-filled courtyard and have cool high ceilings, tiled floors and shared bathrooms (but no fans). Che Guevara once stayed in room 17. ❷

Residencial Bolívar Sucre 131 ☎03/3342500. Longstanding backpackers' favourite with helpful staff and small but immaculately clean rooms (with fan and shared bath) around a cool, leafy patio with hammocks. Often fills up, so worth phoning in advance to reserve a room if you're arriving late. Breakfast available. ❸

Mid-range and expensive

Globetrotter Hotel Sara 49 ☎03/3372754. Pleasant and good-value little hotel with spacious but slightly musty a/c rooms – all boasting cable TV, fridge and comfortable beds – set around a cool, peaceful, colonial-style courtyard. The helpful owner speaks English, and breakfast is included. ❺

Gran Hotel Santa Cruz Moreno 269 ☎03/3348811, ℗03/3324194, ⓦwww .granhotelsantacruz.com. One of the few top-range hotels in the city centre, built in grandiose style with lashings of marble and spacious and opulently furnished rooms and suites. Facilities include a swimming pool, sauna and gym, plus a good restaurant and bar. Breakfast included. ❽–❾

Hotel Bibosi, Junín 218 ☎03/3348548 or 3369173, ℗03/3348887. Reasonably priced mid-range hotel with clean, comfortable rooms with cable TV and fan or (more expensive) a/c; the pleasant rooftop restaurant has great views across the city. Breakfast included, and free coffee available. ❺

Hotel Copacabana Junín 217 ☎03/3362770 or 3321843, ℗03/3330757. Functional mid-range hotel catering mainly to commercial travellers, with clean, comfortable but drably decorated rooms with cable TV and fan or (more expensive) a/c, set on several floors around a narrow central courtyard with a slightly prison-hall feel, despite the many plants. There's also a restaurant, and breakfast is included. ❻

Hotel Felimar Ayacucho 445 ☎03/3346667, ℗03/3323232, ✉tramitur@roble.scz.entelnet.bo. Efficient but rather bland business hotel offering well-furnished a/c rooms with cable TV, fridge and balconies overlooking the street, plus a restaurant and bar. ❻

Hotel Lido 21 de Mayo 527 ☎03/3363555 or 3370596, ℗03/3363322, ⓦwww.lido-hotel.com. Stylish, modern and efficiently run upper-mid-range hotel. The spacious rooms have plush furnishings, cable TV and a/c. There's also a restaurant, and breakfast is included. ❼

Hotel Viru-Viru Junín 338 ☎03/3335298 or 3362922, ℗03/3367500. Excellent, centrally located mid-range option boasting comfortable modern a/c rooms with cable TV and balconies overlooking a large central courtyard swimming pool. ❺

The City

Santa Cruz continues to grow at a phenomenal rate, spreading inexorably over the surrounding countryside in a mixture of ragged shantytowns, office developments and exclusive residential districts where oil executives, businessmen and made-good drug-traffickers relax in opulent mansions protected by armed security guards and high spiked walls. But though the ox-drawn carts that were a frequent sight on the city's muddy, unpaved streets until the 1960s have been entirely superseded by imported luxury 4WDs (known locally as "narcocruisers" because of the likely provenance of their owners' wealth), for all its new-found prosperity, Santa Cruz retains some of the feel of the isolated tropical outpost it was for so long. The old colonial **city centre** is still dominated by humble whitewashed houses with tiled roofs that extend over the pavements to provide shade and protection from wet weather, and when everything closes up in the middle of the day for an extended lunch break the city is suffused with a languid tropical indolence that belies its economic dynamism. Santa Cruz's bizarre cosmopolitanism also adds appeal: poor Andean migrants – their traditional costumes utterly out of place in the tropical heat and humidity – rub shoulders with Japanese rice farmers, Chinese businessmen, US oil workers, missionaries, DEA agents, and stern, red-faced Mennonites in denim dungarees.

Plaza 24 de Septiembre and around

At the centre of Santa Cruz is **Plaza 24 de Septiembre**, a spacious square with well-tended gardens shaded by tall trees that are home to a small population of three-toed sloths, whose lethargic nature is reflected in the easy pace of human life below. The plaza is named after the day in 1810 when Santa Cruz declared independence and joined the struggle against Spanish rule. At its centre stands a statue of **Colonel Ignacio Warnes**, a pro-independence Argentine guerrilla leader who was military governor of Santa Cruz from 1813 to 1816, and carried out a great massacre of over a thousand indigenous Chiquitano prisoners captured fighting on the Spanish side before being executed himself along with 900 others when a Spanish army recaptured Santa Cruz – his head was displayed outside the city on a spike.

On the south side of the plaza stands the salmon-pink **Cathedral** (daily 7am–7pm), or Basílica Mayor de San Lorenzo, a hulking brick structure with twin belltowers which was built between 1845 and 1915 on the site of an original church dating back to 1605. The cool, vaulted interior boasts some fine silverwork around the altar, but the best religious art, sculpture and silverware is tucked away in the **Museo de Arte Sacro** (Tues & Thurs 10am–noon & 4–6pm; $0.80), whose entrance is just to the right as you face the altar. Wood and canvas do not survive well in the warm, humid climate of Santa Cruz, and much of the cathedral's colonial religious art collection has been lost, but there are still some beautiful eighteenth-century mestizo-Baroque wood carvings of saints on display, including a magnificent **Santiago Matamoros** (St James the Moor-slayer), patron saint of Spain. Also known in South America as Santiago Mataindios, the Indian killer, Santiago is depicted here on horseback with sword raised aloft at the head of a Spanish army, trampling hordes of fleeing foreign foes. Another room is filled with exquisite silver plate, chalices, candlesticks and other religious ornaments, all decorated in a florid Baroque riot of intertwined leaves, flowers and fruit-laden vines populated by birds with extravagant plumage and angels that look more like satyrs.

Half a block west of the plaza on Calle Junín, the modest **Museo de Historia** (Mon–Fri 8.30am–noon & 3.30–6pm; free) houses an interesting exhibition on the traditional culture of the indigenous Chiquitanos, who live in the lowlands east of Santa Cruz (see box on p.292). The exhibition is illustrated with good photos and a few artefacts – baskets, hunting bows, fishing traps and poisons – from their daily lives, showing in particular the manifold ways they make use of different rainforest plant species. Less interesting is the small archeological collection, comprising a few fairly ordinary pots and ceramic shards, made by ancient lowland cultures, which were uncovered during construction of the natural gas pipeline to Brazil.

Museo Etnofolklórico

Four blocks north and a block east of Plaza 24 de Septiembre inside the Parque Arenal (a little park with an artificial lake), the **Museo Etnofolklórico** (daily 8am–noon & 2.30–6pm; $0.80) houses a small but varied collection of artefacts that gives a good introduction to the different indigenous ethnic groups of the Eastern Lowlands. Exhibits include photos and examples of the traditional dress worn by various groups, including the colourful costumes, wooden masks carved with animal faces, and bright feather headdresses worn by dancers during religious fiestas. Particularly striking are the brightly coloured robes and hoods of the "Gigantes" costumes from San Ignacio de Velasco – these are worn by dancers who use tall stilts and white facemasks to represent mythological giants. (Many of these ritual dances were used by the Jesuits either as a means of incorporating elements of traditional religion into Christian practice or to allegorically represent the triumph of Christianity over pre-Christian deities.) Also on display are some violins and other musical instruments handmade by the Chiquitanos and Guarayos of the former Jesuit missions, along with bows and arrows, plant-fibre hammocks and bags from the simpler material culture of the Ayoreos, a semi-nomadic hunter-gatherer people of the Chaco who were never successfully settled and converted by the Jesuits.

Museo de Historia Natural Noel Kempff Mercado

Eight blocks south of the plaza on Avenida Irala with Avenida Ejército Nacional, the **Museo de Historia Natural Noel Kempff Mercado** (daily 8am–12.30pm & 2.30–6pm; free) houses an extensive collection of dead insects, stuffed birds and pickled snakes, all displayed with good explanations in Spanish of their biology, habitat and lifecycle. Of particular interest is the display of various dangerous insects, such as the *vinchuca* or **assassin bug** (see p.19), with descriptions of the threat they pose. Look out paticularly for the *vibora cuco*, a moth that bears a passing resemblance to a snake's head and which is widely considered extremely dangerous: it's traditionally believed (or at least put about) that someone bitten by one of these faces certain death unless he or (more usually) she has sexual intercourse within hours – in fact, its bite causes nothing more than slight irritation.

Eating

Santa Cruz's relative wealth and cosmopolitanism are fairly well reflected in the city's wide variety of **restaurants**, catering to all budgets. Different kinds of international cuisine and vegetarian food are widely available, though local **camba food** predominates, dominated by good beef simply cooked and accompanied by rice and yucca or plantain. With a few exceptions, the places listed here are all in the **city centre**, though in fact many of the more popular restaurants are outside the city centre on the **Segundo Anillo** (Avenida Cristóbal de Mendoza) between calles Alemania and Beni: massive, open-air places where Cruceños come to eat huge plates of barbequed meat at weekends.

As elsewhere in Bolivia, the public markets are the best places to find cheap eats. The **Mercado Los Pozos**, in the northeast corner of the city centre, is arguably the best food market in Bolivia, with row upon row of stalls serving up inexpensive and delicious local dishes like *locro de gallina* (chicken stew) and *sopa de mani* (peanut soup), while others sell an astonishing variety of tropical fruit juices and excellent *empanadas* and *salteñas*. There's also a whole subsection of Chinese foodstalls where you can get a tasty meal for less than $1.

City centre

Cuerpomente Busy vegetarian restaurant offering a varied self-service buffet priced by weight (good value at around $2.30 a kilo) as well as soups, juices and *empanadas*. The food is tasty and wholesome, as long as the overzealous healthy-living mantras posted on the wall don't put you off.

Dumbo's Ayacucho 247. Painted in lurid shades of pink, yellow and green, and with indoor and outdoor seating around a fake waterfall, the Santa Cruz outlet of the nationwide chain is a veritable ice-cream palace, doling out a huge range of ice creams, snacks and juices as well as good breakfasts and some more substantial meals.

El Tinto Ingavi with España. Stylish café serving a range of sandwiches, snacks and good breakfasts, as well as excellent espresso and cappuccino, and alcoholic drinks in the evening.

El Viejo Horno Velasco with Pari. No-nonsense *colla* restaurant serving up filling set almuerzos for less than $1 as well as La Paz favourites like *fricase* (pork stew) and *riñon al jugo* (kidneys in sauce) to impecunious Altiplano migrants.

Hawaii Sucre with Beni. This bar-café is popular for its good strong coffee, juices, pastries, snacks and ice cream, and also serves more substantial meals. It's reasonably priced, despite the over-opulent décor, and is open from early in the morning till late at night

Il Gatto Calle 24 de Septiembre with Arenales. Popular and moderately priced restaurant offering decent pizza and tasty Brazilian-style self-service food priced by the kilo, as well as live music or comedy on weekend evenings. Closed Mon.

Jardin de Pollos Irala with Av Ejército Nacional. No-nonsense restaurant serving chickens and ducks roasted whole over a wood fire, a cheap set almuerzo, and not a lot else.

La Esquina del Pescado Florida with Sara. Excellent, inexpensive and always popular little fish restaurant in a wooden shack on a corner, serving big plates of delicious freshwater fish like *surubí*, *sabalo* and piranha fried, grilled or baked for around $2; the fish soup with yucca on the side ($1) is a meal in itself.

Mama Rosa Av Ejército Nacional 47. Homely European-run restaurant serving decent pizza and pasta in the evenings, and a good and very filling set

almuerzo for less than $2 at lunchtime. Closed Sun.

México Lindo Independencia with Salvatierra. Far from authentic but nonetheless pretty good Mexican food, with plates of tacos and enchiladas for about $1.30, and more substantial main courses (including an OK chicken in *mole* spicy chocolate sauce) for around $4. Evenings only; closed Mon.

Michelangelo Chuquisaca 502. One of the finest restaurants in Bolivia, offering superb, authentic Italian cuisine and immaculate service in an intimate atmosphere. It's not cheap, with main courses from around $5, but is an excellent place to splash out, especially if you've just hit town after a spell in the wilderness. Closed Sun.

Victory Junín with 21 de Mayo. On the first floor of the Galería Casco Viejo shopping arcade, with outdoor seating, this popular bar-restaurant is a good place to relax and watch the world rush by in the busy streets below. There's a wide range of reasonably priced sandwiches, pizzas and pastas, and more substantial meat and fish main courses, as well as good breakfasts, excellent coffee and juices, cold beer and cocktails until past midnight. Closed Sun.

Vida y Salud Ayacucho with Vallegrande. Popular little vegetarian restaurant whose tasty and filling set almuerzo is such good value at less than $2 that you need to get here before 1pm to be sure of getting served. The a la carte menu in the evening is also good, but a little more expensive. Mon–Fri only.

Segundo Anillo

Casa del Camba Av Cristóbal de Mendoza 569. The best of the many large traditional Cruceño restaurants on this stretch of the Segundo Anillo, and a great place to enjoy reasonably priced *parillada* (barbecued meat) and *pacumutu* (a kind of massive shish kebab), served by straw-sombreroed waiters to the accompaniment of live traditional *camba* music.

Escuela Gastronomica Tatapy Av Santa Cruz 832. Restaurant school run by a Spanish NGO where you can get excellent international cuisine prepared by local trainee chefs: a full meal will set you back about $10 a head. It's out on the Segundo Anillo, so you'll need to take a taxi from the city centre. Mon–Fri evenings only.

Drinking and nightlife

Whether its because of the humid climate (as visiting *collas* assert), the beauty and hot-bloodedness of the Cruceñas (as popular mythology insists), or the combination of large disposable incomes and abundant cocaine (as one can only suspect), many Cruceños love nothing better than to stay up late eating, drinking and dancing the night away. After dark the city moves to a tropical rhythm, and Santa Cruz's nightlife scene is definitely the liveliest in Bolivia. This comes to the fore during Carnaval (late Feb or early March), when as well as the usual frenzy of water-fighting, dancing and carnival queens, the city stages a series of massive and wild masked balls.

The nightlife centre for Santa Cruz's wealthier residents is out in the exclusive **Equipetrol** neighbourhood, about 5km northwest of the city centre, where a stretch of Avenida San Martín between the second and third *anillos* is lined with a series of flashy bars, restaurants and nightclubs. Unless you have your own car (in which case you'll be able to imitate rich Cruceños by cruising between different bars with the stereo on full blast hooting at passers-by), you'll need to take a taxi out here and back from the city centre. You'll also need to bring plenty of cash and dress to impress – drinks are expensive, cover charges standard, and doormen aren't afraid of turning away scruffy gringo backpackers.

Within the **city centre** nightlife is more low-key and dispersed, but there's still a good range of lively bars and restaurants where you can drink till late and enjoy live music and dancing on the weekends.

City centre

Clapton Blues Bar Murillo with Arenales. As the name suggests, this is a dimly lit, smoke-filled blues bar that really only gets going after about 11pm on Thursday to Saturday nights, when live local blues and rock bands perform. Closed Sun & Mon.

Kamikaze Chuquisaca 113. Trendy but rather expensive bar attracting a young, pre-disco crowd on Friday and Saturday nights, when the place fills up and things get a bit wild. Fairly quiet the rest of the week, when it makes a good central late-night drinking venue.

La Casona Arenales 222. Upmarket Bohemian bar-restaurant with rustic décor, mellow music and a relaxed ambience. There's live jazz and blues music on Thursday, Friday and Saturday nights (small cover charge), as well as refined European meals like goulash and sausages ($5–7). Closed Sun.

Pekos Av Suárez Arana 276, between the Primer and Segundo Anillos. Upmarket bar and traditional music venue with rustic décor, attracting a rather arty (for Santa Cruz) crowd with music with a conscience from Latino songsters like Silvio Rodriguez and Pablo Milanes on the stereo, as well as live bands at weekends, when there's a small cover charge. Closed Sun.

Premium Av Cristobal de Mendoza 1205. US-style brew pub, attracting a raucous and largely male crowd, where the (surprisingly good) beer is made

in great steel vats on one side of the bar, and consumed in equally industrial quantities on the other.

Shamrock Irish Pub Plaza 24 de Septiembre. On the first floor of the Bolívar shopping centre, with tables overlooking the plaza, this upmarket Irish-themed bar is a great place to enjoy a beer, cocktail or coffee while watching the world go by outside, and gets very lively in the evenings, especially at weekends. Food is also available, including exotic delights like Irish stew and full Irish breakfasts.

Equipetrol

Automania Av San Martín. Popular motor racing-themed bar-club decorated with racing paraphernalia, serving cocktails named after different drivers and pumping out Latin dance music. Open late; closed Sun.

Discoteca M@d Av San Martín. A block southeast of Automania, this is currently Santa Cruz's wildest and most extravagant nightclub, a state-of-the-art, purpose-built disco with futuristic décor, a high-tech lightshow and a pumping sound system that draws crowds of rich and beautiful Cruceños.

Friend's Pub Av San Martín. Located in the basement of *Automania* (see above), this is currently the drinking venue of choice for young, trendy and rich Cruceños, with pricey drinks and cocktails, and live music – Latin, jazz, blues, rock – from 10pm every night.

Listings

Airlines Aerosur, Colón with Av Irala
☎03/3364446; American Airlines, Beni 167
☎03/3361414; LAB, Warnes with Chuquisaca
☎03/3344159 or 3343998; TAM, Aeropuerto El
Trompillo, ☎03/3532639; TAM Mercosur, 21 de
Mayo with Florida ☎03/3371999; Varig, Celso
Casedo 39 ☎03/3331105.

Banks and exchange You can change US dollars
and travellers' cheques at the Casa de Cambio
Aleman, on the east side of Plaza 24 de
Septiembre, and there are plenty of banks with
ATMs where you can make cash withdrawals on
Visa or Mastercard: try the Banco Mercantil, Av
Moreno with Figueroa, or the Banco de Santa Cruz,
just west of Plaza 24 de Septiembre on Junín.

Bookshop Los Amigos del Libro, Ingavi with
Moreno, has a reasonable collection of English-
language books and magazines.

Car rental Barron's, Av Cristobal Mendoza 286
☎03/3338823; Localiza, Carretera al Norte 3km
☎03/3433939, ⊛www.localiza.com.bo.

Hospital The Clinica Lourdes, Moreno with Pari
(☎03/3325518), is a good place to go if you need
a doctor. For emergencies, head to the Hospital
San Juan de Dios Cuéllar with España
(☎03/3332222), or the Hospital Japonés, 3rd
Anillo, close to junction with Conavi
(☎03/3462031).

Internet access There are numerous internet
cafés around the city centre: Fast Solution,
Chuquisaca with Ballivián, has good, fast
machines, opens early till late and charges under
$1 an hour.

Laundry Lavandería La Paz, La Paz 42 with
Chuquisaca, offers an efficient same-day service
for about $2 a kilo.

Outdoor equipment Caza y Pesca El Aventurero,
at Arenales 150, has a comprehensive range of
quality imported equipment.

Pharmacy Farmacia Gutierrez, just off Plaza 24 de
Septiembre at 21 de Mayo 76 (open 24hr).

Post office Correo Central, just northwest of Plaza
24 de Septiembre on Junín.

Taxis El Cristo ☎03/3622828 or 3538585;
Exclusivo ☎03/3572323 or 3577471; Flecha
Camba ☎03/3520770 or 3526282.

Telephone office The main ENTEL office is on
Warnes with Av Moreno, and there are plenty of
ENTEL phone booths on the city's main streets,
most of them with brightly coloured moulded plastic covers shaped like macaws, toucans and other
birds and animals. For local calls and calls within
Santa Cruz department, you're better off using the
cheaper COTAS co-operative telephone boxes
(yellow, and not shaped like birds or animals);
COTAS phonecards are sold by street vendors
throughout the city.

Tour operators Most tour agencies in Santa Cruz
are in the business of selling holidays in Florida to
wealthy Cruceños, but several operators do offer
guided excursions to the main attractions of the
Eastern Lowlands, including half-day tours of
Santa Cruz, overnight trips to the Parque Nacional
Amboró and the Jesuit Mission towns of Chiquitos,
and longer trips to the Parque Nacional Noel
Kempff Mercado or the Patanal. The following
companies are all well established and have good
reputations: Camba Tours, Sucre 8 ☎03/3349999,
℻03/3349998, ✉cambatour@cotas.com.bo;
Fremen, Av Cañoto with 21 de Mayo
☎03/3338535, ℻03/3360265, ⊛www.andes
-amazonia.com; Rosario Tours, Arenales 193
☎03/3369656 or 3369977, ℻03/3369656,
✉aventura@tucan.cnb.net.

Moving on from Santa Cruz

Santa Cruz is the transportation hub for the whole of eastern Bolivia, and
exploring the region inevitably involves several trips in and out of the city by
bus, trufi (long-distance collective taxi), train or plane. The city is also well
connected to the rest of Bolivia by road and air, and to neighbouring
Argentina, Brazil and Paraguay by railway, road and air.

By bus

Most long-distance buses depart from the modern **Terminal Bi-Modal de
Transportes**, the combined bus terminal and train station (information on
☎03/3463388 or 3463900), about 2km west of the city centre just outside the
Segundo Anillo at the end of Avenida Brasil. Most **long-distance buses** –
including those to Camiri, Sucre, Trinidad, Villamontes and Yacuiba – depart in
the evening and travel overnight. Those to **La Paz** leave either early in the
morning or in the evening, while to **Cochabamba** there are departures

throughout the day – if in doubt, phone the information office to check departure times and frequency. For the major routes – Cochabamba, La Paz, Trinidad – there's generally no need to buy a ticket in advance, but for other destinations it's a good idea to buy a ticket a day in advance (or on the morning before for overnight departures). From the terminal there are also daily buses to **Asunción** in Paraguay, a tough journey across the vast wilderness expanse of the Gran Chaco which takes 24 hours when conditions are good, and perhaps twice that in the November–April rainy season.

Buses to the Jesuit mission towns of **Chiquitos** still leave from outside the offices of three different bus companies, located in various parts of the city, though it's possible they'll be moved to the Terminal Bi-Modal during the lifetime of this book. The three companies are Linea 131 del Este, Suárez Arana with Barrón; Expreso Misiones, Av Omar Chavez with Solis de Olguín; and Expreso Jenecheru, Choferes del Chaco with the Segundo Anillo – all have buses leaving every evening to San Ignacio. Linea 131 del Este also has four departures daily to San Javier and three departures daily to Concepción.

To reach **Buena Vista**, the main entrance point for the Parque Nacional Amboró, catch a trufi headed to the town of **Yapacani** from Calle Izozog with La Riva, just north of the old bus terminal, these leave throughout the day as soon as they have enough passengers. To **Samaipata**, several micros leave daily each afternoon from the Terminal Bi-Modal, but unless you're on a very tight budget you're better off getting a trufi from the Expreso Samaipata office two blocks south of the old bus terminal on Avenida Omar Chavez with Solis de Olguín. These are faster, more comfortable and more convenient than the buses, and only slightly more expensive. They leave as soon as they have five passengers, but most people travel in the morning, so the earlier you turn up, the less time you're likely to have to wait.

By train

Santa Cruz is the hub of the **Ferrocarril Oriental**, Bolivia's eastern railway, which runs east to the Brazilian border at Quijjaro, via San José de Chiquitos, and south to the Argentine border at Yacuiba in the Chaco, via Villamontes. Trains run from the Terminal Bi-Modal **to Quijjaro** (18–24hr) on Monday and Saturday at 3.30pm, and on Tuesday, Wednesday and Thursday at 7pm, while those **to Yacuiba** (12–16hr) leave on Monday, Wednesday and Friday at 5pm. Trains have three different classes: first and second class are both fairly basic and almost always crowded, with first class costing a little more and having slightly better seats; **Pullman** costs twice as much but is still reasonably good value, and has comfortable reclining seats that are well worth the extra expense. Both lines are also served by a **Ferrobus**, a much faster and more expensive two-carriage train that stops at few intermediate stations and is equipped with semi- or fully-reclining sleeping seats, air-conditioning, piped music, video screen and revolting airline-style food. The Ferrobus to Quijjaro (14hr) leaves on Tuesday, Thursday and Sunday at 7pm; the Ferrobus to Yacuiba (10–12hr) on Tuesday and Saturday at 8pm. Tickets for all trains usually go on sale at the **ticket office** (Mon–Fri 8am–12.30pm & 2.30–6pm, Sat 8am–12.30pm & 1.30–3.30pm) the day before, or on the morning of the same day for evening departures. To get seats in the cheaper carriages, you may need to turn up before the ticket office opens and queue to be sure of getting a ticket, especially on the Santa Cruz to Quijarro line, and especially during public holiday periods. Getting a seat at intermediate stations along the Santa Cruz–Quijarro line can be a real problem, though fortunately the practice of ticket touting has largely been eliminated by the requirement that passengers present their identity card or **passport** when buying tickets and boarding trains – the passenger's name and document number is then written on the ticket to stop anyone else to use it.

Other than the Ferrobuses, trains on both these long routes are slow and unreliable. Snacks, drinks and full meals are sold through the windows at intermediate stations, and vendors often board the train with empanadas, coffee and the like, but it's worth bringing something to eat with you, as well as plenty of water, insect repellent and a blanket or sleeping bag. Trains travel largely by night, and the lowlands scenery is fairly monotonous anyway – the Santa Cruz to Quijarro route is known as the "Train of Death", not because it's dangerous but because it's such a boring ride.

By plane

Moving on from Santa Cruz by **plane** is a good way of saving time and avoiding arduous overland journeys, especially in the November–April rainy season when road conditions deteriorate. From **Viru-Viru airport** (for flight information call ☎03/3852400 or ☎181), there are several flights daily to Cochabamba, La Paz, Sucre and Trinidad, as well as less frequent flights to Cobija, Puerto Suarez and Tarija. In addition, American Airlines, LAB, TAM Mercosur and Varig all have several **international flights** weekly to destinations including Asunción, Buenos Aires, Salta, Tucuman, Manaus, Río de Janeiro, São Paulo, Montevideo, Panamá City and Miami. The military airline TAM also flies once a week to San Ignacio de Velasco (see p.297) from the smaller **El Trompillo airport**, just south of the city centre.

Buena Vista

Some 100km northwest of Santa Cruz along the main road to Cochabamba lies the picturesque and peaceful little town of **BUENA VISTA**, the northern gateway to the Parque Nacional Amboró. Raised slightly above the plains, and with a somewhat fresher climate, the town is aptly named, enjoying good views to the densely forested mountain slopes of Amboró. Buena Vista is now an emerging ecotourism centre and a popular retreat for weekenders from Santa Cruz, though during the week it remains a sleepy place with a population of just a few thousand.

The town was originally founded in 1694 as a **Jesuit mission** from which it was hoped to convert the Chiriguanos, the region's Guaraní-speaking indigenous inhabitants who proved the staunchest opponents to Spanish (and later Bolivian) rule in the Eastern Lowlands. Sadly, the eighteenth century Jesuit church, the Iglesia de los Santos Desposorios – similar in style to those of Chiquitos, but with a central stone belltower – was demolished in the 1960s and replaced by the unattractive modern brick structure that stands today.

Practicalities

Micros and **trufis** from Santa Cruz drop passengers off in the main plaza before continuing to Yapacani. To return to Santa Cruz, either wait around on the plaza for one of the infrequent micros, or go to the 10 de Febrero trufi company office just off the plaza next to the *Residencial Nadia*: they'll phone Yapacani and reserve you a space in the next trufi for Santa Cruz. If you're planning to visit the Parque Nacional Amboró, you should first go to the **park office** (Mon–Fri 8am–noon & 2–5pm; no phone), a block southwest from the

BUENA VISTA

0   Metres   200

★ Trufis to Santa Cruz

Park Office

Mercado

Main Road & Santa Cruz

ACCOMMODATION
Cabañas Guaitu   3
Cabañas Quimorí   4
Hotel Flora y Fauna   5
Hotel Sumuqué   1
Residencial Nadia   2

EATING AND DRINKING
Café Buena Vista   D
La Tapera   C
La Tranquera   B
Los Franceses   A

▼ ❸,❹,❺, *Huaytú & Parque Nacional Amboró*

plaza. You need to register here to enter the park (though there's no charge as yet), and the busy but usually helpful staff can give you information on how to get there, and can also arrange for you to stay overnight at one of the refuges inside the park. If the office is closed you can also get information on the park from the tour companies around the plaza (see p.281), though obviously their main aim will be to sell you one of their tours.

Accommodation

Although Buena Vista is beginning to take off as a weekend destination for Cruceños, **accommodation** is still fairly limited, with a dearth of budget options. There are also a number of luxury country club-style places with air-conditioning and swimming pools several kilometres from town on the main Cochabamba–Santa Cruz road, but these are expensive and inconvenient if you want to visit Amboró.

Cabañas Guaitu About 300m outside town on the road south towards Huaytú ☎01942529 (mobile). Large, self-contained cabins that sleep up to six people, with cooking facilities and private bath ($30–40). There's also a shady camping area ($3, plus $1 per person).

Cabañas Quimorí About 400m outside town on the road south towards Huaytú ☎03/9322081. Clean, well-appointed *cabañas* with private bath set amid a spacious and secluded forest garden, with good views of Amboró. ❹

Hotel Flora y Fauna 4km from town on the road south towards Huaytú, then another 1km up the marked drive off to the left – a $1.50 or so motor-

bike taxi ride from town ☎01943706 (mobile). Owned by the renowned British ornithologist Robin Clark, this delightful place is strictly for serious nature lovers, with simple but comfortable *cabañas* with fan and private bath, set amidst well-preserved, wildlife-rich rainforest – there's a bird observation tower and expert guides can be arranged. Guests are required to stay for a minimum of two nights, and all-inclusive packages with English-style food are available for $50 per person per night. ❼

Hotel Sumuqué 250m northwest of the plaza ☎03/9322080. Reasonably comfortable family-style *cabañas* with fan and private bath that sleep up to five people, set in a large, peaceful garden.

③
Residencial Nadia Just off the north corner of the plaza ☎03/9322049. The only real budget option in town, and the lack of competition shows, with grubby, basic, noisy and overpriced rooms. **②**

Eating and drinking

As usual the cheapest place **to eat** is the **market**, a block northeast of the plaza, where stalls serve up coffee, juices, *empanadas* and more substantial meals like soup from early in the morning; this is also the place to buy food and other supplies if you're heading into the Parque Nacional Amboró. By far the best **restaurant** in town is the French-run *Los Franceses*, a block southwest of the plaza opposite the park office, which has substantial and delicious main courses like pork in white wine sauce or exquisite *surubí a la provençale* ($4–5), as well as excellent home-made pâtés and home-cured ham. Alternatively, the *La Tranquera* and *La Tapera* restaurants side by side on the northwest side of the plaza: both serve up good, reasonably priced Bolivian standards like beef *churrascos* and fried chicken, as well as coffee, cold drinks, juices, pizzas, sandwiches and other snacks. In a kiosk in the middle of the plaza with outdoor seating, the friendly *Café Buena Vista* serves excellent locally grown coffee, as well as cold drinks, juices, cakes and other snacks.

Parque Nacional Amboró

Forty kilometres east of Santa Cruz, the **Parque Nacional Amboró** covers some 4300 square kilometres of a great forest-covered spur of the Andes that juts out into the eastern plains. Situated at the confluence of three major biogeographic regions – the Andes, the Amazon rainforest and the Northern Chaco – and ranging in altitude from 3300m to just 300m above sea level, Amboró's steep, densely forested slopes support an astonishing biodiversity, including over 830 different types of **bird** – the highest confirmed bird count for any protected area in the world – among them a large number of endemic species and such rarities as the cock-of-the-rock, red-fronted and military macaws, and the blue-horned curassow or unicorn bird, which was thought to have been extinct until it was rediscovered here. The park is also home to pretty much the full range of rainforest **mammals**, including jaguars, giant anteaters, tapirs and several species of monkey, while its enormous range of plant and insect species is still largely unexplored.

This biological wealth is all the more amazing given that Amboró is so close to Santa Cruz, and accessible from both the old and new roads between that city and Cochabamba, which run along the southern and northern boundaries of the park. However, though it makes life easier for scientists and ecotourists eager to explore the park, this ready accessibility and proximity to a major city has made Amboró particularly vulnerable, placing in on the front line in the battle between conservationists and impoverished peasant farmers. The national park was first established in 1984, and was expanded in 1990 to encompass some 6300 square kilometres. However, by this time the fringes of the park were already under huge pressure from thousands of poor peasant farmers, most of them migrants from Potosí and Cochabamba departments, who began clearing the forest for agriculture, as well as hunting and logging inside the park boundaries. Amid rising tension between peasant colonists and conservation groups, in 1995 the Bolivian government gave in to political pressure from the colonists and reduced the park by 2000 square kilometres, creating a "Multiple-Use Zone" around the borders of the park. In theory, this is a sort of buffer zone where the land claims of already established peasant farmers are recognized but where sustainable development practices are supposed to be implemented. In practice, with no previous experience of tropical agriculture and little technical support, the Andean migrants have already largely deforested this buffer zone and exhausted its fragile soils, and are beginning to encroach on the remaining park area, despite the efforts of a dedicated but under-resourced team of park guards.

For the visitor, this means that the parts of the park that are easiest to reach are also those most likely to have been affected by colonist incursions, while the pristine interior regions of the park are deliberately kept relatively inaccessible. Nonetheless, the park refuges reached from Amboró are set amid splendid and largely intact rainforest, and the chances of seeing some wildlife on even a short visit are fairly high. The higher-altitude southern section of the park, which includes some beautiful cloudforest, can only be visited from Samaipata (see opposite).

The park: Buena Vista section

From Buena Vista, a rough road runs southeast along the borders of the Multiple-Use Zone (marked by the rushing waters of the Río Surutú), passing through a series of colonist settlements from where side trails cross the river and head into the park. The landscape around the settlements is heavily deforested, with large clearings where meagre crops of maize and rice grow in overgrown fields dotted with the blackened stumps of felled trees, but on the west side of the river the steep, densely forested mountains of Amboró loom inviolate.

Some 20km from Buena Vista, the road reaches **Huaytú**, from where a rough track crosses the river and leads 14km to **La Chonta**, a park guards' station just across the "red line" between the Multiple-Use Zone and the national park itself. Local colonists have constructed a **refuge** here: rustic but adequate, it can accommodate up to eight people, with bunks, mosquito screening, solar-powered lights, cooking facilities, toilet and shower. The price of staying here hadn't been fixed at the time of writing, but is unlikely to be more than a few dollars per person. There are plenty of trails through the surrounding forest from here, and good swimming in the nearby Río Saguayo – either one of the park guards or a local campesino will act as a guide for around $10 a day. About four hours' walk from here in the interior of the park is a site where the extremely rare blue-horned currasow can be seen, while a tough day's walk downstream along the Río Saguayo brings you to another park guards' station, Saguayo, from where it's another day or so back to Buena Vista.

Continuing along the main track beyond Huaytú for a further 15km brings you to the settlement of **Santa Rosa**. From here, a rough ten-kilometre track crosses the river and heads to the park guards' refuge at **Macuñuco**, inside the Multiple-Use Zone. There are plenty of trails into the forest here, one of which leads to a delightful waterfall. A few kilometres before you reach Macuñuco on this track, you pass the village of **Villa Amboró**, where there's another basic **refuge** with cooking facilities and a series of forest trails – locals act as guides and rent out horses. You can book a stay here through the NGO Probioma in Santa Cruz (Calle Cordoba 7 Este 29, Equipetrol ☎03/3432098, ⓦwww-.probioecotur.es.vg). Accommodation with all meals and guided walks through the jungle costs around $35 per person per day, but if you just turn up and have your own food you can negotiate a price for accommodation alone. Alternatively, you could just come for the day, and hire a guide to lead you along the forest trails.

Practicalities

There are two ways to visit the park from Buena Vista. The easiest is to go on an organized trip with one of the **tour operators** in Buena Vista. For about $30 per person they offer two-day trips into the park, camping overnight or staying in one of the refuges, usually at either La Chonta or Macuñuco, with all meals, a guide, camping equipment and transport included. They can also arrange longer trips and treks deeper into the park. Amboró Tours (℡03/9322093, ✉amborotours@yahoo.com), opposite the church just off the plaza in Buena Vista, are the most professional outfit; Puertas del Amboró (℡03/9322059), on the plaza, are also good.

You can also visit the park **independently**, camping or staying overnight at the refuges in La Chonta or Macuñuco, though you'll need to bring a sleeping bag and your own food, and make arrangements with the park office in advance. A **micro** from the plaza in Buena Vista runs daily along the boundary of the park via Huaytú and Santa Rosa, returning the next day – times vary so ask around in Buena Vista to see when the micro passes through, and check the return time with the driver so you don't get stuck on the way out. From the road you'll still have to cross the Río Saguayo (which can be impassable in the Nov–April rainy season) and walk over 10km to reach either La Chonta or Macuñuco. A good alternative therefore is to **rent a jeep** to take you into the park and return later to collect you – you can arrange this through the park office in Buena Vista or through one of the tour operators.

Samaipata

Some 120km west of Santa Cruz on the old mountain road to Cochabamba, the peaceful little town of **SAMAIPATA** is enjoying growing popularity as a tourist destination amongst Bolivians and foreign travellers alike. Nestled in an idyllic valley surrounded by rugged, forest-covered mountains, the town enjoys a cool, fresh climate compared to the sweltering eastern plains, and has emerged as a popular weekend resort for people from Santa Cruz – appropriately enough, since its Quechua name means "rest in the highlands". Innumerable good walking trails run through the surrounding countryside, the beautiful cloudforests of the Parque Nacional Amboró are within easy reach, and just 9km outside town stands one of Bolivia's most intriguing archeological sites: the mysterious, ruined pre-Hispanic ceremonial complex known as **El Fuerte**. All this makes Samaipata the kind of place many travellers arrive in planning to stay a couple of days and end up staying a week or longer – indeed, a growing number of European residents have settled here permanently, setting up hotels, restaurants and tour agencies. They've also helped establish Samaipata as the flagship of modern organic agricultural techniques in Bolivia, and the surrounding farms produce many of the non-tropical vegetables consumed in Santa Cruz.

Arrival, information and accommodation

Micros from Santa Cruz arrive in the Plaza Principal, the central square. **Trufis** from Santa Cruz also stop here, but should drop you off wherever you want – convenient if you want to stay in one of the out-of-town places. For **information** on Samaipata and the surrounding area, the best place to go is the helpful

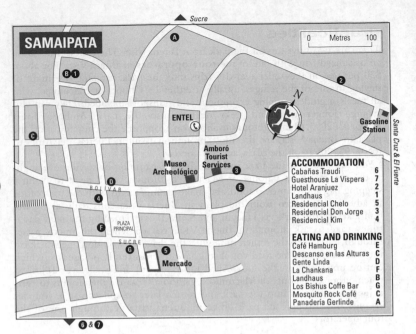

▲ Sucre

SAMAIPATA

0   Metres   100

ENTEL

Gasoline
Station

N

Santa Cruz & El Fuerte

Amboró
Tourist
Services

Museo
Archeológico

B O L Í V A R

PLAZA
PRINCIPAL

S U C R E

Mercado

ACCOMMODATION
Cabañas Traudi   6
Guesthouse La Víspera   7
Hotel Aranjuez   2
Landhaus   1
Residencial Chelo   5
Residencial Don Jorge   3
Residencial Kim   4

EATING AND DRINKING
Café Hamburg   E
Descanso en las Alturas   C
Gente Linda   D
La Chankana   F
Landhaus   B
Los Bishus Coffe Bar   G
Mosquito Rock Café   C
Panadería Gerlinde   A

and enthusiastic English-, German- and Spanish-speaking Roadrunners
(☎03/9446193), in the *Café Hamburg* on Calle Bolívar. Amboró Tourist Services
(☎03/9446293), on the same street, is also helpful, while if you're staying at the
Guesthouse La Vispera (☎03/9446082), the owners Pieter and Margarita will
happily share their immense knowledge of the region with you.

There are no **banks** in Samaipata, but Roadrunners will sometimes change
dollars and travellers' cheques for a small commission. The **ENTEL** office is two
blocks north of the Museo Archeológico, and there's also a card-operated phone
booth on the Plaza Principal. **Internet access** is available (evenings only) at the
Café Hamburg and at Amboró Tourist Services opposite (both charge about $2 per
hour). **Taxis** can be found at the taxi office (☎03/9446129 or 9446133) on
Bolívar, a block north of the Plaza Principal.

Accommodation

Accommodation in Samaipata comes in two categories: simple budget *alojamientos* in the centre of town where you can get a basic double room for less
than $10, and more expensive rustic chalet-style *cabañas* on the outskirts of
town, many of them family-size, with a kitchen and fireplace. Everything fills
up (and prices go up) at weekends and public holidays, particularly between
October and April, when the heat and humidity in Santa Cruz drive many
people to seek relief in Samaipata's cooler climate.

Cabañas Traudi Outside town, 800m south of the
plaza ☎03/9446094. A wide range of quirkily
designed *cabañas* sleeping between two and eight
people, with kitchen, private bathroom and fireplace,
set amid spacious grounds with a large swimming
pool and sauna. There are also smaller, cheaper
double rooms with shared bathroom. ②–③

Guesthouse La Víspera Outside town, 1km
south of the plaza ☎03/9446082, ⊕www
.travelxs.com/agents/boliviajes. Delightful Dutch-
run place set amid a beautiful organic herb garden and fields with great views across the valley.
Accommodation is either in two comfortable, simply decorated two-person *cabañas* with

kitchenette and shared bath, or two much larger *cabañas* that sleep up to ten people; there's also a campsite ($4 per person) with full bathroom and kitchen facilities. The friendly owners, Pieter and Margarita, are a mine of advice, and also run the Boliviajes tour agency. ❸–❹

Hotel Aranjuez At the entrance to town on the main road from Santa Cruz ☎03/9446223. Simple hotel offering clean, carpeted rooms with private bath. It's a bit out of the way, but good value, and breakfast is included. ❷

Landhaus A block west and four blocks north of the plaza ☎03/9446033, ⓔlandhaus@cotas.com.bo. Cosy, nicely decorated cabins sleeping between two and seven people, with fireplace, bathroom and kitchen ($35 for two rising to $70 for seven), and smaller double

rooms with private bath around a pleasant garden with outdoor seating, a small swimming pool and sauna, and a café. ❹–❺

Residencial Chelo Half a block east of the plaza ☎03/9446014. Good-value little place with pleasant modern rooms (with private bath) around a plant-filled courtyard. ❷

Residencial Don Jorge Bolívar, three blocks east of the plaza ☎03/9446086. Straightforward budget place with small, basic but clean rooms with or without bath around a shady central courtyard. ❷

Residencial Kim Half a block east of the plaza ☎03/9446161. A good budget option, with clean and modern rooms (with or without bath), friendly staff, and kitchen and laundry facilities. ❷

The Town

The centre of Samaipata is the small **Plaza Principal**, about 800m southwest of the main road from Santa Cruz to Cochabamba and at the centre of the town's small grid of tranquil, unpaved streets, lined with pretty whitewashed houses under red-tiled roofs. Although generally quiet and peaceful, things can get busy (and noisy) with visiting Cruceños at weekends. A block north and two blocks east of the plaza on Bolívar, the **Museo Archeológico** (Mon–Sat 8.30am–12.30pm & 2.30–6.30pm, Sun 8.30am–4.30pm; $0.80, free if you

Tour agencies in Samaipata

Samaipata's **tour agencies** make it easy to visit the surrounding area's less accessible attractions (some also offer English-speaking guides). Prices vary according to the number of people going on the trip: generally, for groups of three or more you'll pay under $20 per person for a day-trip to La Yunga or La Pajcha; for longer treks, expect to pay around $25 per person per day, with food and camping equipment included.

Amboró Tourist Service Bolívar ☎03/9446293. Local agency running tours of El Fuerte and treks in the Parque Nacional Amboró. They also hire out horses and have mountain bikes and camping equipment to rent.

Boliviajes *Guesthouse La Vispera* ☎03/9446082, ⓦwww.travelxs.com/agents/boliviajes. Long-established Dutch-run agency with expert knowledge of the region and multilingual guides, specializing in trekking in the Parque Nacional Amboró and the mountains south of Samaipata. Treks range from a five-hour walk to El Fuerte to an eighteen-day trans-Amboró trek to Buena Vista – a hardcore wilderness expedition. They also organize trips throughout

Bolivia for international clients, and hire horses and rent camping equipment.

Don Gilberto Aguilera Sucre ☎03/9446050. Samaipata's most experienced trekking guide, Don Gilberto is the man to go with if you want an off-the-beaten-track adventure in the cloudforest north of Samaipata.

Roadrunners Inside the *Café Hamburg* on Bolívar ☎03/9446193, ⓔDustyRoad99@hotmail.com. Friendly, enthusiastic and efficient European-run agency with English-speaking guides leading frequent trips to La Yunga in the Parque Nacional Amboró, El Fuerte and La Pajcha. They also organize longer trips into Amboró or following the footsteps of Che Guevara.

have a ticket to El Fuerte) has a small collection of archeological finds from all over Bolivia, including some beautiful Inca carved wooden ceremonial *chicha*-drinking cups known as *kerus*; Inca stone axes and mace heads; and a range of pottery from various different cultures. Disappointingly, however, there's very little on display related to El Fuerte other than some wooden pillars, a scale model of the site and a few old plans.

Eating

Samaipata's status as a resort town and its significant international community ensure a varied range of **restaurants and cafés**, though some only open at weekends. As usual, the cheapest place to eat is the **market**, a block south of the Plaza Principal, where you can get coffee, juices and cheese *empanadas* from early in the morning and hearty basic soups and meals until mid-afternoon. This is also the place to come for fruit, vegetables and other picnic provisions; alternatively, try the *Panadería Gerlinde*, a German **bakery** at the north end of town on the main road, where you can get excellent fresh bread, biscuits and pasta as well as home-made jam and good cheeses and sausages.

Café Hamburg A block north and three blocks east of the plaza on Bolívar. The liveliest bar in town and a good place to meet other travellers, with friendly, helpful staff, ice-cold beer, good coffee and tasty food, including very good pasta and a fiery *pique a lo macho* (about $4).

Descanso en las Alturas Two blocks north and three blocks west of the plaza. Argentine restaurant (also known as the *Chancho Rengo*), offering large pizzas with tasty, imaginative toppings ($5), and big, juicy *churrascos* ($3).

Gente Linda A block north of the plaza on Bolívar. Straightforward restaurant serving good, simple Bolivian food like chicken and steak, as well as inexpensive set almuerzos.

La Chankana, Plaza Principal. Small European-run café serving good but rather expensive coffee, juices and snacks; the vegetarian set almuerzo is better value at around $2.50.

Landhaus A block west and four blocks north of the plaza. Excellent German restaurant with attractive rustic décor serving delicious and mainly European food, including very good steak, lasagne and pork dishes ($5–6). There's also a raucous late-night disco on Saturdays. Open Thurs–Sun only.

Los Bishus Coffe Bar Plaza Principal. Cosy little bar that's popular with locals, and a good place to enjoy a beer sitting out on the plaza; also serves inexpensive Bolivian mainstays like *milanesa de pollo* and beef steaks.

Mosquito Rock Café Two blocks north and three blocks west uphill from the plaza, above *Descanso en las Alturas*. Incongruous German-owned bar lovingly decorated with heavy rock and motor-racing memorabilia – there's even a car on the roof. It's a good place for a cold beer or cocktail from early evening until late at night, and gets lively at weekends.

Moving on from Samaipata

Moving on from Samaipata, **micros to Santa Cruz** leave early each morning from the Plaza Principal, while faster, more regular and slightly more expensive trufis leave throughout the day when full from the gasoline station (*surtidor*) at the entrance to town. If you're heading to Vallegrande or Sucre, you can flag down a through bus from the main road opposite the gasoline station. Those for **Vallegrande** pass through in the afternoon and always stop for passengers; those for **Sucre** pass through in the evening but are often full and don't always stop. You've a better chance of getting on one if you take a taxi to Mairana, 16km west, where the buses stop for dinner; alternatively, for a small fee Roadrunners tour agency will buy a ticket for you in advance from Santa Cruz. There's no regular transport between Santa Cruz and **Cochabamba** along this road: you'll either have to try to find a truck to take you, or catch a bus to Vallegrande and get another bus from there – either way, it's almost certainly quicker to return to Santa Cruz.

Around Samaipata

Other than a visit to **El Fuerte** (see below), the main attraction of Samaipata is the opportunity to explore the surrounding countryside, a beautiful region of rugged, forested mountains divided by lush valleys whose lower slopes are covered by rich farmland, where hummingbirds, condors and flocks of green parakeets are a frequent sight. The low mountains surrounding Samaipata make for excellent hiking – just follow any of the paths or tracks leading out of town. The southern border of the **Parque Nacional Amboró** (see p.279) lies just a dozen kilometres from the town on the other side of the mountain ridge that rises to the north, and is easy to visit with one of the town's tour agencies (see box on p.283). This section of Amboró is much higher in altitude than the areas close to Buena Vista (see p.277), and is therefore ecologically very different, comprising beautiful cloudforest with gnarled trees covered in lichen and epiphytes. Most one-day trips to Amboró head along a rough track to the hamlet of **La Yunga**, from where a short walk takes you into the cloudforest. Although you'll see large numbers of rare and strangely prehistoric-looking tree ferns up to ten metres high, this region lies in the Multiple-Use Zone close to areas of human settlement, so the chances of seeing much in the way of birds or other wildlife are slim. To get into pristine cloudforest you'll need to trek further into the park and camp overnight – a good place to head for is **Río Barrientos**, reached via the Abra de los Toros.

About 40km south of Samaipata on the road towards the village of Postrer Valle, a path leads 6km or so to **La Pajcha**, a beautiful triple-tiered waterfall that plunges thirty metres into a cool pool which is excellent for swimming. There's no public transport, so you'll either have to come by taxi and arrange to be picked up later, or go on an organized trip with one of the Samaipata tour agencies.

El Fuerte

About 9km east of Samaipata, the archeological complex known as **El Fuerte** (daily 9am–5pm; $3) is amongst the most striking and enigmatic ancient sites in the Andes. At the centre of the complex lies a great sandstone rock carved with a fantastic variety of abstract and figurative designs, including animals and geometric shapes. The rock is surrounded by the remains of more than fifty Inca buildings (and more are being discovered in ongoing archeological investigations), but the carvings predate Inca occupation of the region by over two thousand years. The site's original indigenous name has been lost – the Spanish name El Fuerte, meaning "the fort", reveals more about the military obsession of the Spanish conquistadors than it does about the primary purpose of the site, which was clearly religious and ceremonial.

It's thought the first carvings were made before 1000 BC by an ancient lowland people who were perhaps driven from the region by the **Chiriguanos**, who arrived here in force in the fifteenth century after migrating across the Chaco from the lands east of the Río Paraguay, and for whom this may have also been an important ceremonial centre. The **Incas** arrived here around the same time, occupying the site, which served as an administrative and military outpost at the easternmost fringes of their empire. They altered and embellished the rock itself, suggesting that they too considered it a sacred site – though, like the Spanish, they had a habit of appropriating the religious centres of conquered peoples as a means of reinforcing their domination. Archeological evidence shows the Inca occupation occurred in two distinct periods, suggesting the outpost may have been overrun and destroyed by Chiriguano raiders before being re-established. The site was then occupied by the Spanish and their indigenous allies in the 1570s during their border war with the Chiriguanos, and eventually abandoned when the town of Samaipata was founded in the early seventeenth century.

The site

The easiest way to reach El Fuerte is to take a **taxi** from Samaipata (about $5 one way, or $8 return with an hour's waiting time) or go on a **guided tour** with one of the Samaipata tour agencies. Otherwise, you can walk to the ruins in about two hours – just follow the road out of Samaipata towards Santa Cruz for a few kilometres, then turn right up the marked side road that climbs to the site. Most visitors find that an hour is enough time to appreciate the ruins, though others linger much longer.

Set on a hilltop at just under 2000m above sea level, with commanding views of the surrounding mountains and the valley below, **the rock** itself is a huge lump of reddish sandstone measuring 160m long and up to 40m wide. Its entire surface has been sculpted and carved with all manner of figurative and abstract designs, including pumas, serpents, birds, spirals, zigzags, lines, steps and niches. Sadly, past vandalism and the inevitable wear and tear mean that visitors are no longer allowed to walk on the rock and examine the carvings close up, and the designs are in any case being gradually eroded by wind and rain. Even so, by following the path that runs around the outside you can get a reasonable look at the carvings.

On the **westernmost end** of the rock you can still make out two circular carvings, two metres in diameter, of pumas or jaguars, and one of a coiled serpent. Beyond this are a series of square indentations and a low Inca wall with numerous niches, behind which are two long, parallel slots running exactly west to east with zigzags down either side and in the centre: the controversial New Age amateur archeologist Erich von Daniken has suggested this was a launching ramp for extra-terrestrial spacecraft, but in fact it's more likely to have been used for ritual libations of *chicha* or blood – similar carvings are found on sacred rocks throughout the Andes, while the Incas' use of them for ceremonial purposes was documented by the first Spanish chroniclers.

A path runs along the **south side** of the rock, which is carved with stone steps, platforms, seats and niches of all shapes and sizes, including classic Inca trapezoids two metres high, all facing due south: these probably once held idols and the mummified bodies of long-dead Inca priests and officials. On your right as you walk round are the foundations of several Inca stone buildings that may have housed priests and other attendants, and the remains of a small sixteenth-century Spanish building. Walking round to the **north face** of rock you'll find a low Inca wall, five massive north-facing niches cut out of the rock face, and a good view of the surface of the rock, here carved with recesses and channels. **East of the rock** a path leads down to the ruins of a building with commanding views of the valley below, then on to the foundations of a classic Inca *cancha* (living compound), where archeologists have also found post holes from wooden houses and ceramic fragments suggesting an earlier, possibly Chiriguano occupation of the site.

From the rock's east end, a path runs downhill to the south, reaching a broad terrace. From here, the path continues 200m to **La Chinkana**, a deep well that has inspired improbable myths of underground tunnels leading to far away Inca sites. Returning to the terrace and turning right bring you to the site's main complex of Inca buildings. Passing the foundations of several ruined Inca buildings, you emerge on a broad plaza measuring about 100m by 150m and flanked on three sides by partially overgrown Inca ruins of which only low walls or foundations now remain. The biggest of these is on the south side, a long hall with eight doors opening onto the plaza. This was the **Kallanka**, the principal Inca public building in the complex, which would have been used for civic, military and religious ceremonies. The building on the west side of the plaza is thought to have been the **Allkahuasi**, the house of the "Virgins of the Sun", women specially selected as temple attendants. From here, the path climbs uphill past more ruins (currently being excavated) and takes you back to the mirador overlooking the west end of the rock.

Vallegrande

Some 68km west of Samaipata on the old road from Santa Cruz to Cochabamba, a side road leads 53km south to **VALLEGRANDE**, a pleasant market town set in a broad valley at an altitude of just over 2000m. A peaceful backwater founded as a Spanish outpost in 1612, Vallegrande leapt briefly to the world's attention in 1967, when the arid region of low mountains and broken hills to the south of the town became the scene of a doomed guerrilla campaign led by the famous Argentine communist and hero of the Cuban revolution, **Ernesto "Che" Guevara**. Vallegrande served as the headquarters of the Bolivian army's successful counter-insurgency campaign; after Che was captured and executed on October 9 in the hamlet of La Higuera, about 50km to the south, his body was flown here strapped to the skids of a helicopter and put on display in the town hospital.

What happened next remained a closely guarded secret for the next 28 years, until the Bolivian general Mario Vargas Salinas revealed that **Che's body** – minus his hands, which were amputated for identification purposes – had been buried by night in an unmarked pit near the airstrip on the edge of town, to prevent his grave from becoming a place of pilgrimage. After a year and a half of investigation, in 1997 his remains, along with those of several of his guerrilla comrades, were found by a team of Cuban and Argentine forensic scientists and flown to Cuba, where they were re-interred in a specially built mausoleum on the outskirts of the city of Santa Clara, the scene of his greatest victory in the Cuban revolutionary war. Today, Che's erstwhile grave and the hamlet of La Higuera, where his dreams of leading a continent-wide revolution ended in defeat and death, attract a steady trickle of pilgrims but, unless you share their veneration of the charismatic revolutionary icon, there's little reason to come here.

The Town

The centre of Vallegrande is the peaceful and spacious Plaza 26 de Enero, on the southeast side of which the municipal Casa de Cultura houses a small **museum** (Mon–Fri 10am–noon, 3–5pm & 7–9pm, Sat & Sun 10am–noon; $0.80), which has an unexciting collection of local archeological finds. There's also an upstairs room dedicated to Che Guevara, with plenty of photographs of him and his guerrilla comrades in camp; of Bolivian soldiers hunting them down; of their bullet-ridden corpses; and of the emotional ceremonies held in La Higuera to mark the thirtieth anniversary of Che's death. Three blocks south of the plaza on Calle Señor de Malta, you should be able to persuade staff at the hospital of the same name to let you have a look at the laundry room where Che's body was put on gruesome display to the world's press, though

The life and death of Ernesto "Che" Guevara

Of all the romantics and adventurers to pass through Bolivia, none have matched the iconic status of **Che Guevara**, the Argentine-born hero of the Cuban Revolution who was killed in the backwoods southwest of Santa Cruz while attempting to launch a continent-wide guerrilla war. Born in the Argentine town of Rosario to upper middle class parents on May 14, 1928 (though his birth was registered a month later to conceal the fact that he was conceived before his parents were married), Ernesto Guevara de la Serna studied medicine at the University of Buenos Aires and qualified in 1953, but never practised as a doctor in his homeland: he preferred life on the road as a self-styled vagabond and adventurer, travelling virtually penniless throughout Latin America both during and after his studies, including a brief period in Bolivia during the revolutionary upheaval of the early 1950s.

By 1954 his travels brought him to **Guatemala**, where he witnessed the CIA-backed military overthrow of the progressive Arbenz regime, an event that confirmed both his growing commitment to revolutionary Marxism and his fervent opposition to US imperialism. It was also here that he was given the nickname **Che**, after his typically Argentine habit of peppering his speech with the Guaraní-derived word, used to mean "hey you" or "mate". From Guatemala he headed to Mexico City, where he met **Fidel Castro**, an exiled Cuban rebel planning to return to his country to launch a guerrilla campaign to overthrow the dictator Fulgencio Batista. Che was signed up as the expedition's doctor. Within days of landing on Cuba's southern coast, the rebels walked into an ambush, which proved an epiphany for Che. Under heavy fire, with comrades falling dead and wounded around him, he faced a split-second decision over whether to rescue a medicine box or an ammunition case. He chose the latter, his instincts as a fighter overcoming his training as a doctor. Over the next two years of fighting, Che proved himself amongst the most ruthless, determined, fearless, politically radical and tactically astute of the guerrilla commanders. By the time Fidel Castro took power in January 1959, Che was one of his closest associates. For several years he served Cuba as president of the National Bank, roving ambassador and Minister of Industry. His mixture of good looks, incendiary rhetoric and self-sacrifice made him appear the living embodiment of the revolutionary "New Man".

However, his radicalism and his continued insistence on promoting revolution in other countries proved a liability to Castro's Soviet allies, who feared being drawn into a war with the US and were suspicious of Che's Maoist leanings. Che saw the Cuban revolution as the first step in a continent-wide revolution against US imperial control, and believed the guerrilla strategy used in Cuba – whereby a small rural *foco* or nucleus of determined fighters could radicalize the peasantry and create the conditions for revolution, as detailed in his book *Guerra de Guerrillas* – was a scientific model that could be exported all over the world. In 1965 he formally resigned his Cuban citizenship, ministerial position and rank of *commandante*, left his family behind and set off to spread revolution. After an unsuccessful stint leading a Cuban guerrilla contingent supporting rebels in the **Congo**, he turned his attention to

there's nothing to see today – at the time, word that he bore a striking resemblance to Jesus Christ spread quickly, and local women cut locks from his hair as good-luck charms.

Che's former grave is on the edge of the airstrip on the outskirts of town, a short taxi ride or a ten-minute walk from the plaza: head northeast up Calle Montes Claros, then turn right when you reach the "La Tradición" fiesta venue and head east until you reach the airstrip and a fork in the road. Take the left fork that runs alongside the airstrip and you'll see a sign just before the cemetery with a silhouette of Che's head and an arrow pointing to the left: 100 metres away behind the cemetery (and thus not on consecrated ground) you'll find the grave from which his remains and those of six other

Bolivia, where he hoped to start a guerrilla conflagration that would spread into neighbouring countries (including his native Argentina) and draw the US into a "second Vietnam", culminating in a continent-wide revolution. Bolivia's rugged terrain, strategic position in the centre of the continent and proximity to Argentina made it an attractive location, though in fact the choice was to prove a fatal mistake – in all South America, Bolivia was the only country where radical land reform had already been carried out, and so the revolutionary potential of the peasantry was low.

In 1966, Che set off to Bolivia with a few chosen Cuban companions and set up his base at Ñancahuasu, a farm on the fringes of the Chaco in the Andean foothills, 260km southwest of Santa Cruz. With hindsight, Che's Bolivian venture was doomed from the start. Opposed to Che's guerrilla strategy and anxious to run things on its own territory, the Bolivian Communist party quickly withdrew its support. The few Bolivian recruits he did manage to enlist proved unreliable and squabbled with the Cubans, and the guerrillas' presence was betrayed by deserters even before initial preparations were complete. Unable to attract a single recruit from the local peasantry, Che's small band (they never numbered more than fifty) quickly found itself on the run, divided into two groups blundering through harsh terrain with little food or water while the Bolivian army, backed by US military trainers and CIA advisers, closed in from all sides. Without sufficient medicine, Che himself was crippled by the asthma that had plagued him all his life, and reduced to travelling by donkey. On September 26, 1967, Che's ragged fighters marched through the hamlet of **La Higuera**, straight into an army ambush in which three guerrillas were instantly killed. Che and the sixteen other survivors retreated into a canyon, the **Quebrada del Churo**, where they were quickly surrounded. On October 8 they were captured by a company of elite US-trained Bolivian Army Rangers. In the ensuing shootout, Che was hit in the calf; another bullet destroyed his carbine, and he was captured. Filthy and emaciated, he was taken to La Higuera and held in the schoolhouse for interrogation by Bolivian army officers and a Cuban-born CIA agent. The next day, the order to execute Che came through from the Bolivian high command. His dreams of a continent-wide revolution were ended by two bursts from a semi-automatic rifle fired by a sergeant who volunteered for the task. According to legend, Che's last words were: "Shoot, coward, you are only going to kill a man."

His body was flown to **Vallegrande** and displayed to the press before being secretly buried, as if his enemies feared him more in death than in life. In many ways, they were right to do so, as Che's example inspired thousands of young men and women across Latin America. In his last public message, recorded before he left Cuba, Che appeared to predict this: "Wherever death may surprise us", he said, "let it be welcome, provided that this, our battle cry, may have reached some receptive ears and another hand may be extended to wield our weapon and other men may be ready to intone the funeral dirge with the staccato singing of machine guns and new battle cries of war and victory."

guerrillas were exhumed in 1997. The pit has been left open and is now covered with an unfinished red-tiled brick and concrete mausoleum, decorated with cheap plastic wreaths and scribbled on with tributes left by visitors; a simple wooden cross at one end bears the slogan "Por la Solidaridad, la Libertad y la Justicia" – for solidarity, liberty and justice. If you return to the fork in the road and walk up the right side you'll reach a house on the right with an unused swimming pool, behind which are four pits where the bodies of many of Che's mostly Cuban and Bolivian guerrilla comrades were buried after being killed in combat or executed after capture, each now marked by a stone plaque listing the names of those once buried there and the date and place of their deaths.

Practicalities

Daily **buses** from Santa Cruz via Samaipata arrive and depart from the offices of two different bus companies: Trans Vallegrande on Santa Cruz with Florida, two blocks southeast of Plaza 26 de Enero, and Trans Señor de los Milagros, a block further southeast on Florida. Twice-weekly buses to and from Cochabamba (leaving Mon at 6pm and Fri at 7.30am, and returning from Cochabamba on Wed at 6.30pm and Sat at 6.30pm) arrive and depart from the office of Expreso Guadelupe, also on Santa Cruz with Florida. The best **place to stay** is the good value *Sede Residencial Ganadera* (☎03/9422003; ❷), a block northeast of the plaza on Bolívar, which has clean, spacious modern rooms with private bath and breakfast included. Cheaper and more basic rooms with shared bath can be found at the *Residencial Vallegrande* (☎03/9422112; ❷) and *Alojamiento Teresita* (☎03/9422151; ❷), both just off the plaza on calles Sucre and Escalante y Mendoza respectively.

The best **place to eat** is the German-run *El Mirador* (evenings only; closed Sun), overlooking the town from the top of Escalante y Mendoza, which offers a daily changing selection of tasty beef, pork chicken and trout dishes for about $2–3; also good is the *Churasqueria El Gaucho*, just off the plaza on Señor de Malta, where massive slabs of Argentine-style steak with all the trimmings go for about $3. There are plenty of other simple and inexpensive places to eat on Calle Chaco near the covered **market**, which as usual is good for fresh fruit juices, coffee and *empanandas* from early in the morning. The **ENTEL** office is just off the plaza on Bolívar, and there's **internet access** at Comunicación Digital Vallegrande, near the market on Chaco. Several shops on Chaco change cash dollars, but not travellers' cheques.

La Higuera

LA HIGUERA, the hamlet where Che Guevara met his end, lies about 50km south of Vallegrande, a two- to three-hour drive drive along a rough dirt road via the slightly larger village of Pucará. Set in a region of low, crumpled mountains covered in scrubby vegetation broken by occasional maize and potato fields, La Higuera is a miserable collection of simple adobe houses with tiled roofs, many of them scrawled with revolutionary slogans. Two **monuments** commemorate the fallen guerrilla leader. The most recent is a large, well-made bronze bust of Che, erected in 1997 on the thirtieth anniversary of his death. The other is a small, roughly fashioned plaster bust which has been destroyed three times by the Bolivian army over the years, and replaced each time by local sympathizers. The schoolhouse where Che was executed is now a medical post: ask around and you should be able to find someone with a key, though there's nothing to see inside. Most locals are happy to share their reminiscences of events in 1967, even those far too young to have been there; if you ask around you'll probably find someone willing to guide you to the **Quebrada del Chura**, the ravine a few kilometres away where Che was captured.

There's also a one-room **Museo Historico del Che** (Thurs & Sun; $0.80, free if you're travelling in the curator's truck), which has the atmosphere of a shrine, complete with relics including Che's machete; the wooden chair where he sat for the last time; bullets, ammo clips and a rifle used by the other guerrillas or their military pursuers. There's also a map of the campaign; plenty of photos and newspaper cuttings; and lots of leaflets and pamphlets donated by Che sympathizers.

The museum is run by Rene Villegas, who drives a truck between Vallegrande and La Higuera on Thursdays and Sundays and can tell you a great deal about the failed guerrilla campaign. On October 8–9 each year there's a small gathering of revolutionaries and other sympathizers who come to commemorate Che's death.

Practicalities

To reach La Higuera from Vallegrande you can either take a **taxi**, which should cost around $25 round trip, or go by **lorry** ($3 return) – these leave most days from Calle Señor de Malta early in the morning, returning the next day. On Thursdays and Sundays, Rene Villegas drives his lorry there and returns the same day; he also runs the museum, which only opens when he's in town, so this is really the best way to visit – trips can be arranged by calling him on ☎03/9422003. There's no formal **accommodation** in La Higuera, but you can camp, or you may be able to persuade one of the locals to put you up; a basic shop sells soft drinks, tinned food and biscuits, but there are no restaurants. From the village of Pucará between Vallegrande and La Higuera, irregular pick-up trucks carry passengers to the town of **Villa Serrano**, 100km or so further south, where there's basic accommodation and buses most days west to Sucre (7–8hr), making a scenic alternative route out for more adventurous travellers.

Chiquitos: the Jesuit missions

East of Santa Cruz stretches a vast, sparsely populated plain broken by occasional low rocky ridges and covered in scrub and fast-disappearing dry tropical forest, which gradually gives way to swamp as it approaches the border with Brazil. Named **Chiquitos** by the Spanish (apparently because the original indigenous inhabitants lived in houses with low doorways – *chiquito* means small), in the eighteenth century this region was the scene of one of the most extraordinary episodes in Spanish colonial history, as a handful of Jesuit priests established a series of flourishing **mission towns** where the previously hostile indigenous inhabitants of the region, known as Chiquitanos, converted to Catholicism and settled in their thousands, adopting European agricultural techniques and building some of the most magnificent colonial churches in South America. This theocratic socialist utopia ended in 1767, when the Spanish crown expelled the Jesuit order from the Americas, allowing their indigenous charges to be exploited by settlers from Santa Cruz, who seized the Chiquitanos's lands and took many of them into forced servitude; the region has been in a state of economic decline ever since. Six of the ten Jesuit **mission churches** still survive, however, and have now been restored to their original magnificence and recognized as UNESCO World Heritage Sites – their incongruous splendour in the midst of the wilderness is one of the most remarkable sights in Bolivia.

The six missions can be visited in a five-to-seven-day loop by road and rail from Santa Cruz. From the city a rough road runs northeast to **San Javier** and **Concepción**, then continues to **San Ignacio** (from where the churches of San Miguel, San Rafael and Santa Ana can all be visited by taxi in a day). From San Ignacio, the road heads south to **San José**, the easternmost of the surviving missions, which is on the railway line between Santa Cruz and the Brazilian border at Quijjaro. Buses connect all these mission towns as far as San José, from where you can get the train back to Santa Cruz or continue east to the Brazilian border. Alternatively you could travel the loop counter-clockwise, starting from San José and returning to Santa Cruz by road via the other mission towns – indeed, transport links are slightly more convenient going in this direction, as you avoid having to catch a bus in the middle of the night from Concepción to San Ignacio, as well as the hassle of getting a seat on the train back to Santa Cruz from San José.

The utopian kingdom of the Jesuits in Chiquitos

When the Spanish first arrived in what is now eastern Bolivia, the vast, forest-covered plains between the Río Grande and the Río Paraguay were densely populated by up to fifty different indigenous groups, each speaking a distinct language. To the Spaniards this was a strategically vital region, providing a link between the silver of the Andes and the settlements in Paraguay and the Río de la Plata. Even so, a century of constant military expeditions across the region failed to subdue the indigenous population – known collectively as the **Chiquitanos** – who proved themselves amongst the fiercest enemies the conquistadors had yet encountered.

In exasperation, at the end of the seventeenth century the colonial authorities in Santa Cruz turned to the **Jesuits** to pacify the region and secure the empire's frontier. By this time the Jesuits had more than a century of missionary experience in South America, and were quick to implement the missionary strategy that had proved successful elsewhere. Small groups of dedicated priests set out to convert the indigenous peoples and persuade them to settle in missions known as *reducciones*, places where they could be brought together and "reduced" to European "civilization", which including being converted to Catholicism. Though many missionaries met gruesome deaths at the hands of those they sought to convert, the different tribal groups of Chiquitania quickly flocked to join the new settlements, which offered them many advantages. After a century of war, many had anyway been seeking a peaceful accommodation with the colonial regime, and under the aegis of the Jesuits they were protected from the rapacious slave raids of the Spaniards in Santa Cruz and the Portuguese in Brazil, as well as from their own tribal enemies.

Ten **missions** flourished under the Jesuit regime. European livestock and crops were successfully introduced, producing great food surpluses; the Chiquitanos had limited autonomy under their own councils or *cabildos*, and were taught in their own languages (one of these, Chiquitano, was eventually adopted as the main language in all the missions); indigenous craftsmen were trained in European techniques and built huge churches whose sheer magnificence served as an effective tool in the conversion of other tribes; European musical instruments were introduced and quickly mastered by the Chiquitanos, establishing a musical tradition that survives to this day. Admittedly, the missions were not quite the autonomous socialist utopia Jesuit sympathizers have since tried to make out – many indigenous people were brought in by force, using methods little different from those of the slavers of Santa Cruz, and the political and ideological control exercised by the fathers was pretty much absolute – but in general the missions provided a far more benign regime that anything else on offer under Spanish rule.

In the end, though, for all their self-sufficiency and autonomy, the Jesuit missions were utterly dependent on the Spanish colonial authorities. When in 1767 political developments in far off Europe led the Spanish king to order the Jesuits out of the Americas, the fathers meekly concurred, and the Chiquitanos were quickly subjected to forced labour and the seizure of their best lands by the settlers of Santa Cruz. Within a few decades the missions were a shadow of their former selves, and this decline has continued pretty much ever since, leaving only the beautiful mission **churches**, now restored to their full glory with European aid money, to testify to the missions' former prosperity.

San Javier

Some 220km northeast of Santa Cruz, **SAN JAVIER** is the westernmost of the Chiquitos Jesuit mission towns and was the first to be established in the region, having been founded in 1691 by Father José de Arce. A collection of low, whitewashed houses strung out along the dusty main road, San Javier is now a quiet cattle-ranching centre with a pleasant enough setting but no real attractions other than the mission church itself, the **Iglesia de San Javier** (daily 8am–7pm; $0.30), which stands on the plaza, a block north of the road. Completed in 1752 under the direction of Martin Schmidt, the formidable Swiss Jesuit priest, musician and architect who was responsible for several of the Chiquitos mission churches (and immaculately restored between 1987 and 1993 under the guidance of the equally dedicated Swiss Jesuit architect Hans Roth), the church is a massive, barn-like structure with a squat, sloping roof supported by huge spiralled wooden pillars hewn from single tree trunks, with a simple Baroque plaster facade painted in muted shades of light brown and barley-sugar orange. Above the doorway a Latin inscription common to most Jesuit mission churches in Bolivia reads *Domus Dei et Porta Coeli* (House of God and Gateway to Heaven); above this a wooden beam is carved with a dedication to Saint Francis Xavier in Chiquitano.

On the right side of the church as you face it a doorway leads into a cloistered **courtyard**, inside which is the free-standing belltower, again supported by four massive carved tree trunks, with a spiral stairway up the middle. At the far end of the courtyard are the parish offices (*secretaria*), where you can find someone to open the church for you if necessary, and pay the entrance fee. **Inside**, the church roof is supported by sixteen great spiralled pillars, painted with simple Baroque floral patterns in muted shades of brown and orange and decorated with wooden statues of angels. Carved and painted by local craftsmen, the exquisite modern wooden retablo behind the altar features beautiful carved scenes from the Bible and of the Jesuit missionaries at work in Chiquitos. In the bottom left panel an image of St Peter crucified upside down is surrounded by scenes of black-robed Jesuits being gruesomely martyred by indigenous warriors, their names held aloft by worried-looking cherubs, while other tribesmen are led off in chains from a burning mission by armed European slavers; the bottom right panel shows the missionaries Martin Schmidt and Juan Messner playing piano and violin alongside a Chiquitano choir and accompanied by angels with trumpet and mandolin, while the Jesuit linguist Ignacio Chomé teaches other Chiquitanos to write in the sand. The IHS inside the flaming sun at the top of the retablo stands for "Jesus Saviour of Man" in Latin: combined with three nails and a crucifix, this is the symbol of the Jesuit order, and you'll see it painted and engraved on mission buildings throughout Chiquitos.

The church is now run by the Franciscan order, which works closely with the Chiquitano communities of the surrounding region and has re-introduced the indigenous *cabildo*, or semi-autonomous local council; the masses every weekday evening at 6.30pm and on Sunday mornings are usually well attended. Postcards, leaflets and several books by the parish priest – including a Chiquitano–Spanish dictionary – are on sale in the parish office.

Practicalities

Buses to and from Santa Cruz arrive and depart from the offices of Linea 131 del Este on the main road through town; through buses travelling in either direction pick up and drop off passengers here. If you just want to visit the church you could easily come here on the first bus in the morning from

Concepción or Santa Cruz, spend an hour or two looking around, then catch another bus onwards. If you want **to stay** the night, there are a couple of good budget options: the *Alojamiento San Javier* (☎03/9635038; ❷), on the main road, has simple but clean rooms with shared bath around a peaceful garden; the equally pleasant *Alojamiento Amé Tauna* (☎03/9635018; ❷–❸), on the plaza facing the church, offers a choice of shared or private bath. The best **places to eat** are the reasonably priced *Restaurante El Turista* and *Restaurante Ganadero*, both on the plaza – the later does very good steaks – and there are several other inexpensive restaurants on the main road through town, where you'll also find the ENTEL telephone office.

Concepción

About 68km to the east, the former mission town of **CONCEPCIÓN** is slightly larger than San Javier, but in all other respects a similarly sleepy agricultural backwater dominated by cattle ranching. The mission was founded in 1709 by Father Lucas Caballero, a Jesuit missionary who was killed two years later by the Puyzocas tribe, which latter settled here. At the centre of town is a broad plaza lined with single-storey whitewashed adobe houses with tiled roofs that extend over the pavement, a colonial architectural style introduced after the expulsion of the Jesuits, when the town was taken over by mestizos from Santa Cruz and the long communal houses built for the Chiquitanos were gradually replaced. In the middle of the square stands a simple wooden cross, surrounded by four palm trees – originally a feature of all the mission compounds.

N

Linea 131 del Este
(Bus company)

Flota Misiones
del Oriente
(Bus company)

ENTEL **Museo**
Misional

SUBTENIENTE ROCA LADO

LUCAS CABALLERO

Catedral de
Concepción

Mission
Workshops

Flota Jenecheru
(Bus company)

ACCOMMODATION
Alojamiento Tarija   1
Apart Hotel Las Misiones 4
Gran Hotel Concepción   5
Hotel Colonial   3
Posada El Viajero   2

EATING AND DRINKING
Alpina   D
Buen Gusto   B
Club Social Ñuflo de Chavez   C
Posada El Viajero   A

CONCEPCIÓN

0   Metres   200

The Chiquitos musical renaissance

Of all the European arts and crafts introduced to Chiquitos by the Jesuits in the eighteenth century, the one that gained most rapid acceptance amongst the indigenous tribes was music. Organs, trumpets violins and other instruments imported by the fathers were enthusiastically adopted by the Chiquitanos, who quickly learned to manufacture their own instruments, while the choirs and orchestras of the mission settlements were said by contemporaries to have matched anything in Spanish America at the time. Father Martin Schmidt, the Swiss Jesuit who designed the churches of San Javier, San Raphael and Concepción, was a keen composer who taught music and brought the first church organs to the region, while the missions also benefited from the presence of an Italian named Zipoli, who had been a well-known composer in Rome before coming to South America.

Like all the cultural accomplishments of the missions, their musical tradition all but disappeared in the centuries following the expulsion of the Jesuits, though its influence remained in the folk music of the Chiquitanos themselves. When the restoration of the mission churches began in the 1970s, however, researchers in Concepción discovered a substantial archive of liturgical and orchestral Renaissance Baroque musical scores, including works by Schmidt and other Jesuit composers. The rediscovery of this lost music inspired a musical revival in Chiquitos, and throughout the mission towns and outlying settlements you'll come across children and young adults playing violins and other instruments with the same skill for which their ancestors were famous in the mission era.

In 1996 this revival inspired a group of music lovers to organize the first **Chiquitos Missions Music Festival**, featuring performances of the music recovered from the lost archives. Since then, the festival has grown into a major biennial event, attracting dozens of orchestras and musical groups from around the world, and involving performances in all the mission towns of Chiquitos as well as in Santa Cruz. For information on future festivals, check out the festival's website at ⓦwww .festivalesapac.com.

Catedral de Concepción

The town's mission church, now the **Catedral de Concepción** (daily 7am–8pm; free), stands on the east side of the plaza: a massive barn-like structure with an overhanging roof supported by 121 colossal tree-trunk columns, and with a separate, similarly supported belltower. Originally designed by Martin Schmidt and completed in 1756, it was the first Jesuit church in Chiquitos to be restored, and is the most extravagantly decorated of them all, with a lavishly painted facade decorated with golden Baroque floral designs, angels, and two images of the Virgin Mary on either side of the door. The **interior** is so smothered with gold leaf it's almost garish, but this extreme opulence is a powerful reminder of the vast wealth the missions once possessed, and of the dramatic decline Chiquitos has undergone since then. Amidst the beautifully carved altarpieces, confessionals and statues of saints, the most interesting detail is the modern **Via Crucis**, a depiction of the Easter story that runs around the top of the walls, carved and painted in a bright, naif style similar to that of the original eighteenth-century carvings, but with a distictly modern theme. Christ is shown living in present-day Chiquitos, surrounded by lush tropical forest inhabited by parrots and tortoises, and his betrayal and death is imbued with contemporary political and ecological metaphor. Christ is flogged by a sombrero-wearing landowner with a machete and revolver in his belt; yellow bulldozers destroy humble homes and hunters carry off wild animals as he suffers under the weight of the cross; police officers and loggers play dice for his robe while others work with chainsaws in the background and timber trucks rumble through a desolate landscape; the forest burns behind him as he's nailed to the cross.

The workshops and Museo Misional

Concepción is the centre for efforts to reconstruct the Jesuit mission churches of Chiquitos (which may explain why restoration work on the church here has gone so over the top) and the main **workshops** for woodcarving and painting are behind the church a block east of the plaza; the staff here are usually happy to show visitors around at 10.30am and 3.30pm each day.

On the south side of the plaza, an old colonial house that was the childhood home of the former military dictator and later elected president Hugo Banzer now houses the **Museo Misional** (Mon–Fri 7.30am–noon & 1.30–5.30pm, Sat & Sun 8am–noon & 2–5.45pm; $0.80), dedicated to the restoration of the mission churches of Chiquitos. On display are some good pictures of the different churches before, during and after reconstruction; examples of the crumbling original wooden pillars and statues which were replaced; and a small workshop where a local craftsman demonstrates the laborious task of restoring the original statues. There are also photographs of letters written and musical scores composed by Father Martin Schmidt which were discovered in the 1970s, and an irreverent totem pole-like statue of Hans Roth, the architect who led the reconstruction effort for 27 years until his death in 1999. The museum shop sells beautiful miniature carved wooden angels and other souvenirs made by local craftsmen involved in the restoration work, as well as CDs of Baroque music written by Martin Schmidt and others which was played in the missions; there are several other handicrafts shops selling similar stuff around the plaza.

Practicalities

For a small town, Concepción offers a reasonable range of **accommodation**: the cheapest places are the very basic *Posada El Viajero* (no phone; ❶) and *Alojamiento Tarija* (no phone; ❶), both opposite the Linea 131 del Este office a block north of the plaza; much better and only slightly more expensive is the friendly and pleasant *Hotel Colonial* (☎03/9643050; ❷), half a block north of the plaza on Calle Subteniente Roca Lado, which offers clean modern rooms with private bath and hammocks strung outside in the shade. The *Apart Hotel Las Misiones* (☎03/9643021; ❹), just off the plaza to the north on Calle Lucas Caballero, offers a considerable step up in price and comfort, with comfortable, well-furnished rooms with cool tiled floors around a flower-filled garden and a good breakfast included. At the top of the range is the incongruously luxurious *Gran Hotel Concepción* (☎03/9643031 or 9643033, ℱ03/9643032; ❺), on the west side of the plaza, popular with visiting dignitaries and tour groups, which has immaculate rooms around a beautiful courtyard garden with a swimming pool, hammocks, sun loungers and an outdoor restaurant.

By far the best **place to eat** is *Buen Gusto*, on the north side of the plaza, which offers delicious beef and chicken main courses (about $2) and hearty set almuerzos ($1.50) in a shaded, plant-filled courtyard; you can also eat decent almuerzos and steak at the *Club Social Ñuflo de Chavez* on the west side of the plaza. *Alpina*, on the southwest corner, serves cold drinks, snacks and ice cream, while the *Posada El Viajero*, opposite the Trans 131 del Este office a block north of the plaza, is good for early-morning coffee and *empanadas*.

Moving on from Concepción

Moving on from Concepción, **buses** to Santa Cruz depart three times daily (at 7.30am, 2pm and 5pm) from the Linea 131 del Este office a block north of the plaza. To reach San Ignacio de Velasco, you'll need to catch a through bus from Santa Cruz, which pass through in the middle of the night. Of the bus companies that serve this route, two have offices in town where you can buy a ticket in advance and be picked up sometime after midnight: these are Flota Misiones del Oriente, on the north side of the plaza; and Flota Jenecheru, two blocks south of the plaza on Calle Lucas Caballero.

San Ignacio de Velasco

SAN IGNACIO DE VELASCO, 178km east of Concepción, was founded in 1748, just nineteen years before the expulsion of the Jesuits from South America, but quickly grew to become one of the largest and most developed of the mission towns. It's now the largest settlement in Chiquitos, a bustling market centre for an extensive frontier hinterland of large cattle ranches and isolated indigenous Chiquitano communities. At its centre lies the broad **Plaza 31 de Julio**, which is graced by numerous massive swollen-bellied Toboroche trees, whose tangled branches blossom into brilliant pink and white during

SAN IGNACIO DE VELASCO

ACCOMMODATION
Casa Suiza	4
Hotel 31 de Julio	1
Hotel Guapamó	5
Hotel La Misión	3
Hotel Plaza	2

EATING AND DRINKING
Pizzeria Pauline	B
Restaurante Barquito	C
Snack Marcelito	A

Laguna Guapamó

Catedral de San Ignacio

PLAZA 31 DE JULIO

Parque Nacional Noel Kempff Mercado Office

Mercado

ENTEL

Airstrip

0   Metres   200

June and July. The **Catedral de San Ignacio** (daily 4–6pm; free) stands on the north side of the plaza. The town magnificent original church collapsed in 1948 – the attempt to rebuild it in the style of the original is spoiled by the ugly modern concrete belltower but otherwise well executed, though the painted facade decorated with statues of saints, each accompanied by an animal, is if anything too neat and symmetrical. The **interior** still houses many of the original statues of saints and magnificent carved Baroque altarpieces that graced the old mission church.

The town's wide, unpaved streets fan out from the plaza, covered in red dust that turns to mud in the rain and lined with low houses whose tiled roofs extend over the pavement, supported by wooden beams. A short distance behind the church to the north on the outskirts of town the streets run down to **Laguna Guapamó**, an artificial lake created by the Jesuits to provide water and fish for the mission, where locals like to come swimming and fishing on sultry afternoons.

Practicalities

San Ignacio has no bus terminal, so **buses** to and from Santa Cruz, San José and San Matías on the Brazilian border arrive and depart from the offices of the various different bus companies, most of which are located on and around Calle 24 de Septiembre in the market area, a block east and a few blocks south of the central plaza.

Accommodation

There's a fair range of **accommodation** in San Ignacio, though most of the budget places are fairly insalubrious dives used mainly by people involved in cross-border traffic with Brazil.

Casa Suiza A block north and six blocks west of the plaza on Sucre (no phone). Welcoming Swiss-run guesthouse with a homely European feel, and full or half board available, with good European home cooking. The simple but clean rooms come with good beds and shared bath (with excellent showers), while the helpful and friendly owners Horst and Cristina are a fount of information. There's also a book exchange. ❸

Hotel 31 de Julio Plaza 31 de Julio (no phone). Basic accommodation in simple, cell-like rooms with shared bath and no fan – strictly for those on a tight budget. ❶

Hotel Guapamó 24 de Septiembre with Sucre ☎03/9622095. Set around a big garden shaded by the sprawling tree that gives the hotel its name,

with small, simple rooms varying in price depending on whether you want a shared or private bath, a fan or a/c. ❷–❹

Hotel La Misión Plaza 31 de Julio ☎03/9622333, ℻03/9622460, ⊕www.hotel-lamision.com. Incongruously opulent modern hotel built in neo-colonial style, with carved wooden pillars outside and a cool courtyard with a fountain and small swimming pool within. The stylish and comfortable rooms come with a/c, and there's also a good but expensive restaurant. ❻

Hotel Plaza Plaza 31 de Julio ☎03/9622035. Good-value Church-owned hotel with cool, spotlessly clean rooms with fan and private bath around a pleasant garden courtyard. ❸

Eating

There's a limited choice when it comes to **places to eat** in San Ignacio. *Snack Marcelito*, on the southwest corner of the plaza, serves good coffee and fresh fruit juices; snacks like burgers, *empanadas* and *sonso* (fried balls of cheese and manioc flour), as well as main courses like steak and *milanesa*. *Pizzeria Pauline*, also on the south side of the plaza, serves reasonable pizza, filling set almuerzos and main courses like steak and chicken for $3–4, while *Restaurante Barquito*, a block west of the plaza on Calle 24 de Septiembre, offers a tasty and plentiful Brazilian-style buffet including barbecued beef for about $2 a head. Cheaper meals, snacks and juices can be found at a series of food stalls in the market area along Calle 24 de Septiembre.

Buses to **Santa Cruz** travel mostly by night, departing in the evening from one of the half a dozen or so bus company offices on Calle 24 de Septiembre and around the market area; if you're heading to **Concepción** or **San Javier** you need to get on one of these. Several buses leave every day to **San Matías** on the Brazilian border, from where you can enter **Brazil** and continue to the city of Cáceres in the northern Pantanal. To **San José de Chiquitos**, Trans Carreton on Calle 24 de Septiembre have buses on Tuesday, Thursday and Sunday at 8am, while Trans Universal have buses on Monday, Wednesday, Friday and Saturday at 2pm. From the market, several micros go daily to **San Miguel**, but visiting the other mission towns south of San Ignacio by public transport is more difficult. Trans Bolivia, on Calle 24 de Septiembre, have one micro a day to **San Rafael** via **Santa Ana**, but this leaves at 4pm and returns the next morning, so going there on a day-trip this way is impossible.

If you're heading to the **Parque Nacional Noel Kempff Mercado**, you'll first need to go to the office of the Fundación Amigos de la Naturaleza (FAN; Mon–Fri 8.30am–noon & 2–5pm; ☎03/6922194), the organization that administers the park, which is half a block south of the plaza on Calle 31 de Julio. The staff here can give you permission to enter the park and have plenty of information. They can also arrange for the park rangers to pick you up from La Florida, on the edge of the park, and take you to *Campamento Los Fierros*, or arrange the hire of a pick-up truck to take you all the way from San Ignacio to the park and back ($250–300). To reach the park by public transport, your only option is to take the once-weekly bus run by Trans Carreton which heads to La Florida on Friday, returning on Sunday.

The military airline TAM has one **flight** a week between Santa Cruz and San Ignacio (currently on Wed) – to buy a ticket ask around at the airstrip, which is just south of town about five blocks away from the main plaza.

South of San Ignacio

South of San Ignacio, the three former Jesuit mission towns of **San Miguel**, **Santa Ana** and **San Rafael** all have beautiful eighteenth-century mission churches and – if you hire a taxi – can be visited together in a one-day trip. San Miguel is about 40km south of San Ignacio on the main road to San José de Chiquitos, and San Rafael is another 35km or so further southeast on the same road. From San Rafael another road runs back to San Ignacio via Santa Ana, 20km away, so the three churches can be visited in a loop of about 145km. A taxi should cost $20–30; you can find them on the main plaza, and most drivers are happy to do this trip. San Miguel can easily be visited in a half day using one of the **micros** which depart from around the market area (every 1–2hr; 45min). Visiting Santa Ana and San Rafael by public transport involves an overnight stay in San Rafael: you'll need to take the once-daily micro to San Rafael that leaves in the afternoon from the market area in San Ignacio (stopping in Santa Ana long enough for a look at the church), and return the next morning.

San Miguel

Set amid scrubby forest broken by patches of cattle pasture, **SAN MIGUEL** is a sleepy collection of whitewashed houses, many of them built using a traditional technique known as *tabique*, by which walls are made of a framework of durable forest vines plastered with mud. These humble structures make the first sight of the splendid **Iglesia de San Miguel** even more astounding: set on a small rise overlooking the grassy central plaza and dominating the town, the church has been immaculately restored and is perhaps the most beautiful of all the Chiquitos mission churches. Founded in 1721 and built in the same barn-like style as most of the others (though not designed by Martin Schmidt), the church facade is beautifully painted with Baroque floral designs in muted shades of natural ochre, yellow and white, with pictures of St Peter and St Paul on either side of the main door.

To get inside, you'll need to enter the walled **cloister** to the right – part of the original mission compound or Jesuit college which is now used by the parish priest: go under the freestanding white adobe belltower and ask in the parish offices for someone to let you in – there are no fixed opening hours and no entrance fee, but by day it shouldn't take long to find whoever has the key. Inside, the soaring roof is supported by massive tree trunks carved in spirals, while the walls are lined with metre-high wooden statues of angels, all carved and painted by local craftsmen during the restoration under the direction of foreign specialists – much as the originals would have been. The walls are painted with simple patterns, but the main altarpiece is smothered in gold leaf and beautifully carved with intertwined flowers and vines, with alcoves filled by statues of angels and saints including (in the centre) the Archangel Michael, in a golden helmet and shield, holding a three-pronged sword aloft as he tramples the devil underfoot.

Other than the church, there's nothing much to see in San Miguel. You can get basic **meals** and a Spartan **room** (❶) for the night at the *Restaurante La Pascana* on the opposite side of the plaza, which is also where you'll find **micros** heading back to San Ignacio (every 1–2hr; 45min); through buses from San Ignacio to San José also stop here to pick up passengers.

San Rafael

The second Jesuit mission in Chiquitos when it was founded in 1696, the town of **SAN RAFAEL** boasts the biggest of all the region's Jesuit churches, the **Iglesia de San Rafael**, a cavernous, barn-like structure with a free-standing belltower supported by four spiralled wooden pillars, built under the direction of Martin Schmidt between 1747 and 1749. The magnificent interior features beautiful frescoes of angels playing trumpets, violins and other musical instruments, and some beautifully carved statues of saints in the alcoves of the golden altarpiece, including the central figure of San Rafael, depicted here with a fish in one hand – the Chiquitanos are said to associate the saint with a pre-Christian forest spirit considered the keeper of fish and the patron of those who collect wild honey. The church is usually open during the daytime; if not, asking around the plaza will soon turn up someone with a key.

By the time of the Jesuits' expulsion in 1767, San Rafael was home to over seven thousand people, but its population is now only about a thousand, and the gilded opulence of the church contrasts sharply with the poverty and decline of the town, whose failing economy is now based on cattle ranching and logging, though the once-rich surrounding forests are now reduced to scrub and secondary growth. There are a couple of basic **restaurants** around the plaza and a simple **alojamiento** (❶) where you can find a room for the night. The one **micro** a day to San Ignacio leaves from the plaza in the morning, returning in the afternoon; you can also flag down the once-daily through bus from San Ignacio to San José.

Santa Ana

About 20km north of San Rafael on a different road back to San Ignacio, the small village of **SANTA ANA** is home to the least dramatic of the six mission churches of Chiquitos. Occupying one side of a large grassy plaza where donkeys graze and schoolchildren play football, the **Iglesia de Santa Ana** has not yet been fully restored and as such retains an intimate, rustic charm more in keeping with the sleepy atmosphere of its surroundings than the grandiose edifices of San Rafael or Concepción. Indeed, there's some speculation as to whether this is the original Jesuit church at all – built entirely of wood, it has none of the usual IHS signs and may have been rebuilt shortly after the order was expelled in 1767. Inside, there are some beautiful but decaying wooden statues, and local children often use the interior to practise the violins and other musical instruments which were introduced with so much success by the original missionaries and are now enjoying a resurgence in popularity. There's a small **restaurant** to the left of the church where you can get coffee, soft drinks and simple meals, but no other facilities in the village.

San José de Chiquitos

About 130km south of San Rafael, the sleepy town of **SAN JOSÉ DE CHIQUITOS** is home to the westernmost of the six mission churches, and also stands on the railway line that runs east from Santa Cruz to Puerto Suarez, Quijjaro and the Brazilian border. Despite this (for Chiquitos) abundance of transport connections, like the other mission towns San José has the torpid feel of a place that has been in gradual decline for two and a half centuries – it's now nothing more than a dusty frontier market town and supply centre for the cattle ranches and Mennonite colonies of the surrounding hinterland.

The mission of San José was founded in 1696, close to the original site of the city of Santa Cruz de la Sierra, which had been abandoned over a century before. The **mission complex** (7am–7pm; free) was built in the last decades before the Jesuits' expulsion from the Americas in 1767. Occupying one side of the town's grassy central plaza, it's utterly distinct from the other churches of Chiquitos, being closer in design to those of the Paraguayan missions, with an elegant Baroque facade built entirely of stone. The complex consists of four buildings linked by a three-metre-high wall that forms a defensive compound. From right to left, these four buildings are the Casa de los Muertos (chapel of the dead), where bodies where once stored before being buried; the church itself; the four-tiered stone belltower that would also have served as a lookout post; and the Jesuit college, a long hall with the date 1750 and the IHS insignia inscribed above the doorway. That these elegant structures have survived in the midst of the wilderness for two and a half centuries is all the more impressive given the fact that they were built by indigenous masons with no previous experience of stonework (they may never have seen a stone building before) in a region where stone itself was hard to come by – even the original Spanish settlement of Santa Cruz La Vieja had been built of wood and adobe. Behind this facade, however, the main body of the church is built of wood, with a roof supported by tree-trunk pillars: this may have been completed by the Chiquitanos after the Jesuits had departed, perhaps in the hope that if the fathers could no longer protect them, God would. The interior itself is in a poor state of repair but is currently undergoing restoration, and there are beautiful but dilapidated religious statues and other ornaments lying around awaiting repair.

Other than the church there's nothing to see in San José, though if you've got an afternoon to kill while waiting for a train you could walk down to the site of **Santa Cruz La Vieja**, the original site of the city of Santa Cruz, founded by Nuflo de Chavez in 1561 but abandoned in 1594 in the face of persistent indigenous attack and moved to its current site 260km to the west. From the plaza, turn right as you face the church and head south out of town for about 4km and you'll reach a sign to the Parque Nacional Histórico Santa Cruz La Vieja, a grandiose title for what is in fact simply a series of overgrown mounds set amid dense scrub and giant cactus trees, all that remains of the Spanish settlement.

Practicalities

Buses to and from San Ignacio arrive and depart from the offices of the two bus companies that serve the route: Trans Carreton, a block east of the plaza; and Trans Universal, four blocks north of the plaza beyond the gasoline station on the road out of town. The **train station** is two blocks north and four blocks east of the plaza. Trains in both directions pass through late at night, and it's worth buying tickets in advance, especially if you're travelling west to Santa Cruz, though this can involve a long time queuing – it's best to turn up before 8am on the morning of the day you want to travel. There are two basic **places to stay**: the clean and comfortable *Hotel Raquelita* on the west side of the plaza opposite the church (☏03/9372037; ❷–❸) is the best bet, and offers a choice between simple rooms with fans or more expensive rooms with private bath and air-conditioning; the *Hotel San Silvestre* (☏03/9372141; ❷), opposite the station, is less attractive, but convenient if you're leaving or arriving on a late-night train.

The Mennonites

San José's most unlikely sight is the bizarre spectacle of tall white people with flaxen hair and ruddy cheeks – the men dressed in denim dungarees and straw hats, the women in full-length dresses and headscarves – walking around town or driving horse-drawn buggies. These are the **Mennonites**, members of a radical Protestant sect founded in the Netherlands by Menno Simmons in the sixteenth century. For the next four centuries the Mennonites found themselves driven from country to country as they attempted to escape religious persecution and conscription, and to find land on which to pursue their dreams of an agrarian utopia. After migrating to Germany, they moved in succession to Russia, the US and Canada, Mexico and Belize, until finally arriving in Bolivia and neighbouring Paraguay in the twentieth century, attracted by the availability of cheap land, guarantees of religious freedom, and exemption from military service. Perhaps 20,000 Mennonites now live in communities across the Eastern Lowlands, successfully farming maize, soya and sorghum, and raising cattle in self-contained agricultural communities.

The central tenets of the Mennonites are the refusal to take oaths or bear arms (they are exempt from military service in Bolivia); the baptism only of believers; simplicity of dress and personal habits; and an unwillingness to marry outside the faith. They also to varying degrees reject most modern technology, including cars and computers, though faced with the difficult agricultural conditions of Chiquitos, many Bolivian Mennonites allow the use of tractors – though not, bizarrely, of rubber tyres, so their wheels are covered with steel spikes. Though some speak Spanish, and a few of the older ones who grew up in North America also have some English, amongst themselves they speak Plattdeutsch, an archaic German dialect. If you can bridge the language barrier, many Mennonite men are happy to talk about their unusual lives, and are often just as curious about your own lifestyle, which to them is equally bizarre. The irony is that, two and a half centuries after the Jesuits were expelled, religiously inspired utopian dreams are still being pursued in the plains of Chiquitos, albeit by white Protestants instead of indigenous Catholics. This isn't, however, an irony that would have been appreciated by the Jesuits themselves – their order was set up precisely to combat Protestant sects like the Mennonites, who they would have regarded as dangerous heretics.

There are a few basic **restaurants** serving simple almuerzos, steaks and fried chicken on and around the plaza; a few shops serving coffee and *empanadas* on the street that runs north along its east side; and plenty of food stalls along the railway line. The most popular restaurant is *Choza de Don Pedro*, out beyond the railway line on the road north to San Ignacio, which serves filling and inexpensive set almuerzos and steaks. The **ENTEL** telephone office is half a block east of the plaza on the south side of the church complex.

Parque Nacional Noel Kempff Mercado

Occupying 16,000 square kilometres of Bolivia's far northeast, on the border with Brazil, the **PARQUE NACIONAL NOEL KEMPFF MERCADO** is the most isolated, pristine and spectacular national park in the country, and one of the most remote wilderness regions in all South America. Encompassing a range of different ecosystems including different types of Amazon rainforest, dry and seasonally inundated savannah, and scrubby Brazilian *cerrado*, the park supports an astonishing range and abundance of wildlife, including over 630 species of birds (among them twenty different types of parrot and seven of macaw), as well as multicoloured tanagers and toucans, and such rarities as the mighty harpy eagle. In addition, eleven species of monkey inhabit the park, and all the major Amazonian mammals – including jaguar, tapir, peccary, deer, giant anteater and armadillo – roam its forests and savannahs, while its rivers and lakes are home to abundant pink freshwater dolphins and the highly endangered giant river otter. Of course, most of these species are also present in many of Bolivia's other national parks; the difference is that Noel Kempff Mercado is so comparatively undisturbed by human activity that your chances of actually seeing all these different animals are much higher here than anywhere else in the country.

The park's most remarkable natural feature is the **Huanchaca Plateau** (also known as the Caparú Plateau), a vast sandstone *meseta* which rises five hundred metres above the surrounding rainforest to an elevated plain of grasslands and dry *cerrado* woodlands, from where spectacular waterfalls plunge down the sheer escarpment into the park's rivers. This isolated plateau covers over seven thousand square kilometres, or a bit under half the park, and provided the inspiration for Sir Arthur Conan Doyle's novel *The Lost World* – at least according to Colonel Percy Harrison Faucett, the legendary British explorer who was the first European explorer to see the plateau when he came here in 1910 while demarcating Bolivia's borders, and who later described the landscape to Conan Doyle in London. The park was first established in 1979 as the Parque Nacional Huanchaca, but was renamed in 1988 (when it was also expanded) in honour of the pioneering Bolivian biologist and conservationist Noel Kempff Mercado, who was murdered here by drug traffickers after stumbling across a secret cocaine laboratory high on the Huanchaca plateau.

The park was expanded again in 1997 under a pioneering "carbon credit" scheme, whereby two US energy corporations and the oil giant BP paid around $10 million to buy out loggers operating in an adjacent forest area of 6340 square kilometres, which was then added to the park – this allows the corporations to claim credits for the carbon dioxide which the rescued trees will absorb towards their targets for reducing emissions under the international Kyoto treaty on global warming. As yet this is the biggest such carbon-

△ Capybaras

credit project in the world, but the fact that the US government has since withdrawn its support for the treaty means that for the moment further such agreements are unlikely.

Visiting the park

The park's remote location inevitably means that it's expensive and difficult to visit. The southern border of the park is over 200km from the nearest town, San Ignacio de Velasco in Chiquitos, which is itself another 400km by road from Santa Cruz. The park is administered by the Santa Cruz-based conservation organization, Fundación Amigos de la Naturaleza (FAN), whose main office is 7km out of town on the old road to Cochabamba (℡03/3556800, Ⓦwww.fan-bo.org). They also have an office in San Ignacio (℡ 03/6922194), just off the plaza on Calle 31 de Julio. If you want to visit the park you must contact them first for information and permission to enter, which costs $30, irrespective of how long you stay. FAN maintain two "camps" (*campamentos*) with accommodation for visitors in the park: **Los Fierros**, towards the southern end, which can be reached by light aircraft or overland along a rough logging trail that runs along the park's western boundary from San Ignacio; and the more luxurious **Flor de Oro**, on the banks of the Río Iténez (which marks the park's northern boundary and the Bolivian border with Brazil), which can be reached either by light aircraft or by a circuitous overland route via Brazil. Both camps are close to pretty much the full range of the park's different ecosystems, with ample opportunities to see wildlife, and both also offer the chance to climb up onto the Huanchaca plateau. Los Fierros is considered the best place for spotting large mammals, particularly jaguars, while Flor de Oro is close to the park's two most spectacular waterfalls, though these can only be visited during the rainy season (Nov–May).

Only a few hundred people visit the park each year, and almost all of those arrive by chartered light aircraft from Santa Cruz, a spectacular flight across hundreds of kilometres of virtually uninhabited rainforest, which can be arranged either by FAN or by a handful of tour agencies in Santa Cruz (see p.275). A return flight to Flor de Oro costs several hundred dollars per person depending on the size of the plane, whether or not all the seats are full, and how long you spend at the park; flights to Los Fierros cost slightly less. A typical five-day all-inclusive package with a Santa Cruz-based tour agency visiting both camps by plane should cost about $1000 – a high price for Bolivia, but one which few visitors regret paying.

Los Fierros

Los Fierros lies at the southern end of the park, within easy hiking distance of the Huanchaca plateau, and with many trails leading through the surrounding rainforest and savannahs with excellent wildlife-spotting possibilities – jaguars are regularly spotted here, and other mammals like monkeys are abundant, as is a kaleidoscopic variety of birds. The park guards based here are usually happy to act as guides. The most popular excursion is to **El Encanto**, a narrow but spectacular waterfall that plunges eighty metres off the sheer sides of the plateau. The waterfall is a one-day walk from the camp along a fairly clear track, and there's a basic shelter close by where you can camp out if you have you own equipment, but otherwise you're better off hiring the park guards' pick-up truck to take you there and back in a day. Other day hikes lead up onto the plateau via the "Subida de los Españoles" and to the Laguna Chaplín, which is home to abundant aquatic bird life.

Accommodation in Los Fierros is in rustic dormitories (each sleeping up to fourteen people) with foam mattresses and shared bathrooms; the cost is about $25 per person per night with simple meals included, less if you prepare your own food using the basic cooking facilities available. You can also camp out here if you have your own equipment. To reach Los Fierros overland you can either hire a **pick-up truck** in San Ignacio ($250–300 round trip), which the FAN office there can organize, or catch the once-weekly bus to **La Florida**, which lies on the western margin of the park some 200km north of San Ignacio. The bus leaves on Friday and returns on Sunday and takes twelve to fourteen hours in good conditions, so going this way you'll end up spending over a week in the park. Once in La Florida, it's still another 35km to Los Fierros along a track through the rainforest; if you're arriving by bus you can arrange for the rangers at Los Fierros to pick you up and take you back again at a cost of $120, including an excursion to the El Encanto waterfall.

Flor de Oro

Based in a former ranch which once belonged to one of the suspected drug traffickers implicated in the murder of Noel Kempff Mercado, **Flor de Oro** enjoys a beautiful setting on the banks of a broad sweep of the Río Iteñez, which marks the border with Brazil. Numerous trails lead through the surrounding wildlife-rich rainforest and semi-inundated termite savannahs around the camp, and the park guards based here act as guides. You can also take boat trips out on the river and into the tranquil lakes along its length, which are excellent places for spotting pink freshwater dolphins, playful giant river otters and all manner of waterbirds. The real attraction of Flor de Oro, though, is the opportunity to visit the Ahlfeld and Arco Iris **waterfalls**, which tumble down the steep escarpment of the Huanchaca Plateau. If you arrived by plane, you'll already have seen these falls from the air; reaching them on the ground involves a four-hour motorboat trip with one of the park guards down the Río Iteñez and up the smaller Río Paucana to the smaller and more rustic **Campamento Ahlfeld**, a trip which is only possible when rivers are high enough in the rainy season, roughly between November and May. The **Ahlfeld** waterfall, twenty minutes' walk from the camp, is a stunning multiple waterfall forty metres high and twice as wide terminating in a deep pool of cool emerald water which is excellent for swimming. You can also climb to the top of the falls, from where the view is equally dramatic.

It's a lengthy hike (4–5hr return) to the **Arco Iris** waterfall from Campamento Ahlfeld, including a steep climb up the escarpment onto the top of the Huanchaca Plateau, but well worth the effort. The vegetation on the top of the plateau is very different from the rainforest below, consisting of dry and thorny scrub and low forest known by the Brazilian word *cerrado*. Utterly unaltered by human action and surrounded by a seemingly endless sea of rainforest below, it's easy to see why this landscape inspired Arthur Conan Doyle's fantasy of a Lost World inhabited by strange prehistoric beasts. Viewed from above, the Arco Iris waterfall is an overwhelming sight: a vertical cascade plunging a hundred metres down through virgin rainforest and throwing up great clouds of spray, which refract the sunlight, creating the innumerable rainbows that give the falls their name.

Practicalities

Almost everyone who comes to Flor de Oro does so by **plane** from Santa Cruz, but you can also get here **overland via Brazil**. To do this you'll need to cross the border at San Matías, a day's bus journey east of San Ignacio, then work your way north using the fairly regular buses which run via Cáceres and

Vilhena to the town of Pimenteiras, on the north bank of the Río Iteñez, from where you can hire a boat to make the thirty-minute journey upstream to Flor de Oro. This journey takes two to three days, and you should inform FAN of your plans and book accommodation in Flor de Oro before you set off.

Accommodation in Flor de Oro costs around $65 per person per day, with all meals included. Visitors sleep in spacious, fully furnished and immaculately clean private rooms with solar-powered lights and fans, plus private bathrooms, with hammocks strung up in a mosquito-screened patio overlooking the river outside. The meals are very good, with a distinctly Brazilian flavour, and are served in a fully screened dining room.

East from Santa Cruz to the Brazilian border

From Santa Cruz, the railway line runs some 680km east to the Brazilian border across a seemingly endless expanse of forest and tangled scrub, gradually giving way to the vast swamplands of the **Pantanal** as the border draws near – it's known as the Train of Death, not because of any danger, but because the interminably slow journey across the hot, monotonous plain can become so boring. Travellers today should think themselves lucky, however: until well into the twentieth century the trip across this vast wilderness took up to a month

The Pantanal

Much of Bolivia's far east along the border with Brazil is covered by the **Pantanal**, the vast floodplain on either side of the Río Paraguay that forms the biggest freshwater wetland system in the world. Stretching over 200,000 square kilometres, this immense inland river delta is a mosaic of different ecosystems, including swamp, lakes, seasonally flooded grasslands and different kinds of forest, most of which is turned into an immense inland freshwater sea when the waters of the Río Paraguay rise in the rainy season between November and March. This largely pristine wilderness supports possibly the densest concentration of wildlife in the Americas, including an astonishing variety of birds, reptiles like anacondas and caimans, and large mammals including swamp deer, giant otter, jaguar, capybara and tapir, all of which can be seen with greater frequency here than anywhere in the Amazon.

About eighty percent of the Pantanal lies in Brazil, but the fifteen or so percent that lies within Bolivia's borders (the rest is in Paraguay) is arguably more pristine, largely because the Bolivian side of the border is virtually uninhabited. The Bolivian side is also better protected, on paper at least – north and south of Puerto Suárez, huge areas of the Pantanal are covered by the **Area Natural San Matías** and the **Parque Nacional Otuquis**, which together cover almost 40,000 square kilometres. However, the isolation and lack of development that have allowed the Bolivian Pantanal to survive in largely pristine condition also mean that it's very difficult to visit. Almost no organized ecotourism facilities exist on the Bolivian side, and (particularly since the devaluation of the Brazilian currency against the dollar in the late 1990s) it's cheaper and much easier to organize an expedition into the Pantanal from Corumbá in Brazil. Other than hiring a fisherman in Puerto Suárez to take you out across Lago Cáceres, the only real ecotourism operator on the Bolivian side is El Tumbador (☎01628699), situated on a turn-off from the main road midway between Puerto Suárez and Arroyo Concepción, who can arrange half- and one-day excursions into the Pantanal, though at a higher price than operators on the Brazilian side.

by ox-cart, while the possibility of attack by nomadic tribes remained a genuine possibility. The dream of a railway line across Chiquitos to the Río Paraguay and Brazil was a Bolivian national aspiration for over a century, and when the line was completed in the late 1950s it provided a huge boost for the economic development of Santa Cruz and the Eastern Lowlands. Even so, human settlements along the line remain few and far between. After San José de Chiquitos, roughly halfway along, there are no major towns until you reach the border, and such settlements as there are – Roboré, Aguas Calientes, Candelaria, El Carmen – are forlorn villages or military outposts where the arrival of the train is the most exciting event of the day. The region's main towns are both close to the Brazilian border: **Puerto Suárez**, a half-forgotten lakeside outpost that was once the focus of Bolivian dreams of access to the Atlantic via the Río Paraguay, but which has now been commercially overshadowed by the dismal border trading settlement of **Quijarro**, the train's last stop before the frontier.

Puerto Suárez

Just before reaching the Brazilian border at Quijarro, the railway line passes through the much older and more agreeable town of **PUERTO SUÁREZ**, situated on the shores of Lago Cáceres, a large freshwater lake linked to the waters of the mighty Río Paraguay. Founded in 1875, Puerto Suárez has long been the focus of Bolivian ambitions to gain access to the Atlantic Ocean via the Ríos Paraguay and Paraná, but the lake has always been too shallow and choked with weeds to take anything but small, shallow-bottomed lakes. In the 1980s Bolivia, together with Brazil, Paraguay and Argentina, began discussing proposals for the construction of a Paraguay-to-Paraná "**Hidrovia**", or waterway, which would have involved straightening and deepening the channel of the upper Río Paraguay to make it navigable to large vessels all year round. However, the project's cost, possible environmental consequences, and the fact that the harvest and shipment of soya beans, the region's main export, takes place in June and July when water levels are naturally high enough for large vessels to use the river, led to the project being shelved.

Until recently Puerto Suárez enjoyed a modest flow of tourists and duty-free shoppers from Brazil, and benefited from a considerable cross-border smuggling industry. All this dried up, however, following the devaluation of the Brazilian currency in the late 1990s, and the town has yet to get its act together and tap into the growing number of ecotourists who visit the region to visit the wildlife-rich wetlands of the Pantanal (see box on p.307). This is a shame, as it's a peaceful and dignified place, beautifully set on a bluff overlooking the calm blue waters of the lake, and with the white city of Corumbá in Brazil visible in the distance. Plans are underway too build a tourist pier out over the lake, and if you ask around by the shore it's fairly easy to find a boatman willing to take you out fishing or wildlife spotting, but for a lengthier trip into the Pantanal you're better off going from Corumbá in Brazil, where ecotourism is better organized and less expensive.

Practicalities

The **train station** is a couple of kilometres from town, a short ride in one of the collective taxis that meet every train. There's no great reason **to stay** unless you're waiting for a train or plane to Santa Cruz; if you do, the best place is the *Hotel Sucre* on the main plaza (☎03/9762069; ❹), which offers small but comfortable air-conditioned rooms around a pleasant courtyard garden, and also has a decent restaurant. A cheaper option is the basic *Hotel Beby* (☎03/9762700; ❷–❸), a few blocks northwest of the plaza along Avenida Bolívar, which has simple, box-like rooms with fan or air-conditioning. There are several cheap **restaurants** and snack bars strung out along Avenida Bolívar, but the best place for lunch is the outdoor *El Mirador*, on the bluff overlooking the lake two blocks southeast of the plaza, where you can get big plates of delicious fried river fish or even – if your ecological conscience allows – *jacaré*, the small caimans with which the lake waters teem. If you need a visa, the **Brazilian consulate** (Mon–Fri 8am–2pm) is two blocks southeast of the plaza on the waterfront.

If you're **moving on** from Puerto Suárez to Santa Cruz by train, you'll need to buy a ticket in advance from the station. The airport, from where there are flights three or four times weekly to Santa Cruz, is about 6km away, a $1 taxi ride from the plaza. You can buy airline tickets from the LAB and Aerosur offices on the plaza. To get to Quijarro, you need first to take a collective taxi from the plaza to the border at Arroyo Concepción ($0.80), and catch another one from there.

Quijarro

The last stop on the railway line in Bolivia is **QUIJARRO**, a dismal collection of shacks and dosshouses surrounding the station – if you're heading on to Brazil, you're better off pushing on to the border at Arroyo Concepción. If you end up having to spend the night here, the best budget option is the basic but clean *Residencial Ariane* (☎03/9782129; ❶–❷), directly opposite the station; a more upmarket option is the *Hotel Bibosi* (☎03/9782113; ❹–❺), two blocks east of the station, which offers comfortable rooms with TV and air-conditioning, has a swimming pool and can organize rather expensive tours into the Pantanal, though really you're better off doing this from Brazil. The *Bibosi* also has the best restaurant in town, though that's not saying much – otherwise, there's a series of cheap and unsalubrious-looking restaurants strung out opposite the station.

Moving on from Quijarro

Collective taxis wait outside the station to take passengers to the Brazilian border at **Arroyo Concepción** ($0.50 per person, though they often try to overcharge), a couple of kilometres away, where there are several moneychangers as well as collective taxis on to Puerto Suárez if you want to kill some time while waiting for a train. To **cross the border**, get your passport stamped at the Bolivian *migración* office (Mon–Sat 8am–noon & 2.30–6pm, Sun 9am–noon), then walk across into Brazil, where taxis, motorcycle taxis and regular buses wait to take passengers across the bridge over the Río Paraguay and on into the delightful city of Corumbá, where you'll need to get an entry stamp from the Federal police office.

If you're arriving from Brazil, you should go straight to the train station to get a ticket – these go on sale the day before departures or the same morning for evening departures. You may have to queue for some time to get a ticket, and the cheaper ones often sell out quickly, particularly during public holidays, though this is rarely a problem for Pullman and Ferrobus tickets. Trains currently leave at about 3pm on Monday, Tuesday and Thursdays, and at noon on Saturday, while the faster but more expensive Ferrobus leaves at 7pm on Monday, Wednesday and Friday.

The Chaco

South of the Santa Cruz–Quijarro railway line, the tropical dry forest gradually gives way to **the Chaco**, a vast and arid landscape of dense scrub and virtually impenetrable thornbrush which stretches south to the Paraguayan border and far beyond, inhabited only by isolated cattle ranchers and occasional
communities of Guaraní and semi-nomadic Ayoreo. The Chaco is one of the
last great wildernesses of South America and supports plenty of wildlife,
including jaguar, peccary and deer – much of it now protected by the **Parque
Nacional Kaa-Iya del Gran Chaco**, the biggest protected area in all South
America, which covers over 34,000 square kilometres southeast of Santa Cruz
adjacent to the Paraguayan border. However, your chances of seeing any of this
wildlife are slim. There are no organized tourist facilities in the Chaco, so unless
you have your own 4WD and are prepared to organize a wilderness adventure,
your view of the region will be limited to what you can see from the window
of a bus or train: a wall of dense, scrubby vegetation broken only occasionally
where farms or ranches have been hacked out of the bush.

There are two routes through the Bolivian Chaco, both starting from Santa
Cruz. The first and less taxing is the route by road or railway down the region's
western edge to the towns of **Villamontes**, the biggest settlement in the Bolivian
Chaco, and **Yacuiba** on the Argentine border. The second and more strenuous is
along the rough **trans-Chaco road**, which splits off from the road and rail route
to Yacuiba at Boyuibe, heading east to the Paraguayan border at Hito Villazón,
from where it runs across the heart of this great wilderness to the Paraguayan capital, Asunción, an arduous and adventurous journey (served by daily buses from
Santa Cruz) that takes 24 hours in the May-to-September dry season when conditions are good, and much longer after rain, when the road turns to mud.

South from Santa Cruz to Villamontes

From Santa Cruz a rough road and single-track railway run south into the
Chaco, following the eastern foothills of the Andes down towards the
Argentine border. About 285km south of Santa Cruz the road (but not the rail

> ### The Guaraní
>
> The western Bolivian Chaco is home to the **Guaraní** people – known historically as
> the Chiriguanos – the largest indigenous group in the Bolivian lowlands, with a pop-
> ulation of about 75,000. The Guaraní originally migrated across the Chaco from east
> of the Río Paraguay in search of a mythical "Land Without Evil" (the abode of the
> gods, believed to lie in the west), occupying the southwestern fringes of the Andes
> in the fifteenth and sixteenth centuries just as the Inca empire was expanding into
> the same region. Despite this, the Guaraní successfully resisted conquest by the
> Incas, and subsequently proved amongst the fiercest and most tenacious indige-
> nous opponents of the Spanish. Not until well into the Republican era were they
> completely subjugated, when the last great Guaraní uprising was brutally crushed in
> 1892, after which their remaining lands were seized by the Bolivian state and divid-
> ed into large private ranches defended by army forts. In recent decades, the Guaraní
> have been struggling to regain control of their ancestral territories using land reform
> and indigenous rights legislation, and in spite of obstructive bureaucracy have now
> recovered large areas, where they farm maize, cotton, peanuts and other crops.
> Despite this, hundreds if not thousands of Guaraní still work on large cattle ranches
> under conditions of debt servitude which are little different from slavery.

way) passes through **Camiri**, a grim and functional oil-producing town and military garrison from where a rough road (served by daily buses in the dry season) leads up though the highlands to Sucre, 450km away. Camiri has a small range of basic places to stay and eat, but unless you're in the oil industry there's no earthly reason why you should want to come here, never mind spend the night. About 60km south of Camiri the road and railway meet again at **Boyuibe**, a forlorn military outpost at the edge of the Chaco from where a poor side road heads 135km east to **Hito Villazón** and the beginning of the great trans-Chaco road across Paraguay.

From Boyuibe, the main road and railway continue 90km south to **VILLA-MONTES**, the main town in the Bolivian Chaco. A hot and dusty but welcoming frontier town with a mostly Guaraní population, Villamontes was the scene of one of Bolivia's few military victories during the disastrous **Chaco War** with Paraguay. In 1935–36 the town was successfully defended against Paraguayan attack, reversing the Paraguayan thrust towards Bolivia's oilfields and leading eventually to a peace agreement. Today, Villamontes remains very much dominated by the Bolivian army, and indeed the military provide the only real tourist sight in town: from the central Plaza 6 de Agosto a diagonal road leads two blocks northeast to Plaza 15 de Abril, where a large white mansion houses the **Museo Historico Militar Heroes del Chaco** (daily 6am–9pm; free), which is full of military paraphernalia from the war with Paraguay, though there's little to suggest that Bolivia lost. The garden of the house is filled with trenches, dugouts and bunkers with machine guns, mortars and artillery pieces, while the walls are painted with maps justifying Bolivia's territorial claims in the Chaco. Inside, there are plenty of photos of the terrible conditions endured by troops on both sides in a war where thirst was as big a killer as the enemy, and in which Bolivia sustained casualties proportionally comparable to those of European countries involved in World War I. One particularly poignant shot shows a priest blessing fresh-faced Andean conscripts about to go over the top: the caption reads: "There go those who will never return."

Practicalities

The centre of Villamontes is the broad **Plaza 6 de Agosto**, from where the town's main street, Avenida Mendez, runs north eight blocks to the small **bus teminal**, where daily buses to and from Tarija and Santa Cruz arrive and depart. The **train station** is another two blocks north on the same street; a taxi from either into town should cost about $0.40. The best place to stay is the popular and good-value *Residencial Raldes* (☎04/6722088; ❷–❸), a block east of the plaza, which has clean modern rooms with fan or (more expensively) air-conditioning around a pleasant central courtyard; for those on a tight budget, the friendly *Residencial Miraflores* (☎04/6722991; ❶), on Avenida Mendez midway between the plaza and the bus terminal, offers grubby, basic rooms with shared bath. Inexpensive **meals**, coffee and juices can be found in the covered public market a few blocks north of the plaza on Avenida Mendez; alternatively, the excellent *Restaurant El Arriero*, one of several on the plaza, dishes up exquisite Argentine-style grilled steaks (about $5), as well as good fish and pizza. On the road out of town towards Yacuiba a series of foodstalls serve delicious fried *surubí* fish from the nearby Río Pilcomayo, considered one of the finest fishing rivers in all Bolivia. The **ENTEL** telephone office is just off the plaza to the west.

Moving on from Villamontes, buses and trains **to Santa Cruz** both leave in the evening – they take about the same time but the trains are more comfortable – while buses **to Tarija** from Santa Cruz stop here on their way through in the early hours of the morning and pick up passengers if they have room, though there's no guarantee they will; if you're travelling to Tarija you've a better chance of getting a seat on a bus from Yacuiba. Micros and collective taxis **to Yacuiba** leave every half-hour or so from three blocks north of the plaza on Avenida Mendez.

Yacuiba and the Argentine border

The small and modern border town of **YACUIBA** lies about 90km south of Villamontes by road and rail. Yacuiba sprang up following the construction of the railway and oil pipeline to Argentina in the 1960s, and retains a distinctly Argentine flavour, dominated by restaurants and duty-free shops catering to tourists from across the border. However, following Argentina's protracted economic crisis of the late 1990s – and above all since the devaluation of the Argentine currency in 2002 – this cross-border flow of tourists and shoppers in one direction and smuggled goods in the other has virtually dried-up, giving Yacuiba a mournful feel, like a tourist resort that's permanently out of season. As such, there's no reason to linger unless you arrive at night and have to wait for a bus or train out.

The **train station** is two blocks south and a block west of the central plaza, while the **bus terminal**, from where there are morning and evening departures to Tarija and Santa Cruz, lies about 1km south of the plaza. Micros and trufis to and from Villamontes arrive and depart from offices just off the plaza on the road to the bus terminal. There are plenty of **places to stay** in Yacuiba, aimed primarily at Argentine tourists, truck drivers, and Bolivian migrants. Budget options are concentrated around the bus terminal – try the *Residencial Urkupiña* (☏04/6822320; ❷), which offers basic rooms with fans and a choice of shared or private bath. The more upmarket places are in the streets that run north from the plaza: of these, the best is the stylish *Hotel Paris* (☏04/6822182; ❹), on Calle Comercio, which has comfortable modern rooms with air-conditioning and cable TV. There are plenty of good **restaurants** on and around the plaza serving delicious Argentine beef, chicken and pizza – the *Parillada Ricardo* is particularly popular. Also on the plaza are the **ENTEL** telephone office and Cybernet café, which has **internet** access. There are plenty of **cambios** along Calle Comercio, where you can change cash but not travellers' cheques, as well as a Banco de Credito with an ATM (Visa and Mastercard). The **border crossing** with Argentina is at Pocitos, 4km south of town: to get there, take a collective taxi ($1 per person) from the main plaza.

Travel details

Buses and trufis

Buena Vista to: Santa Cruz (8–10 daily; 1hr 30min).
Concepción to: Santa Cruz (3 daily; 6–7hr).
Samaipata to: Santa Cruz (6–8 daily; 3–4hr).
San Ignacio to: La Florida (1 weekly; 12–16hr); San José (1 daily; 5–6hr); San Matías (4–6 daily; 10–12hr); Santa Cruz (3–4 daily; 10–12hr).
San Javier to: Santa Cruz (4 daily; 4–5hr).
San José to San Ignacio (1 daily; 5–6hr).
Santa Cruz to: Buena Vista (8–10 daily; 1hr

30min); Cochabamba (8–12 daily; 10–12hr); Concepción (3 daily; 6–7hr); La Paz (15–20 daily; 16–18hr); Oruro (11 daily; 12–14hr); Samaipata (6–8 daily; 3–4hr); San Ignacio (3–4 daily; 10–12hr); San Javier (4 daily; 4–5hr); Sucre (5–7 daily; 14hr); Tarija (1–2 daily; 24hr); Trinidad (12 daily; 10–12hr); Vallegrande (3–4 daily; 6–7hr); Villamontes (5–7 daily; 10–12hr); Yacuiba (5–7 daily; 12–14hr).
Vallegrande to: Cochabamba (2 weekly;

5

10–12hr); Santa Cruz (3–4 daily; 6–7hr).
Villamontes to: Santa Cruz (5–7 daily; 10–12hr); Yacuiba (hourly; 2hr).

Yacuiba to: Santa Cruz (5–7 daily; 12–14hr); Tarija (3–4 daily; 12hr); Villamontes (hourly; 2hr).

Trains
Quijarro to: Santa Cruz (1 daily; 20–24hr; Ferrobus 14–16hr).
Santa Cruz to: Quijarro (1 daily; 20–24hr; Ferrobus 14–16hr); Villamontes (5 weekly; 12–14hr; Ferrobus 8–10hr); Yacuiba (5 weekly;

14–16hr; Ferrobus 10–12hr).
Villamontes to: Santa Cruz (5 weekly; 12–14hr; Ferrobus 8–10hr).
Yacuiba to: Santa Cruz (5 weekly; 14–16hr; Ferrobus 10–12hr).

Planes
Santa Cruz to: Cobija (5 weekly; 2hr); Cochabamba (5 daily; 45min); La Paz (6–8 daily; 1hr 30min); Puerto Suárez (3–4 weekly; 1hr);

San Ignacio (1 weekly; 35min); Sucre (2–3 daily; 40min); Tarija (5 weekly; 50min); Trinidad (1–2 daily; 1hr).

The Amazon

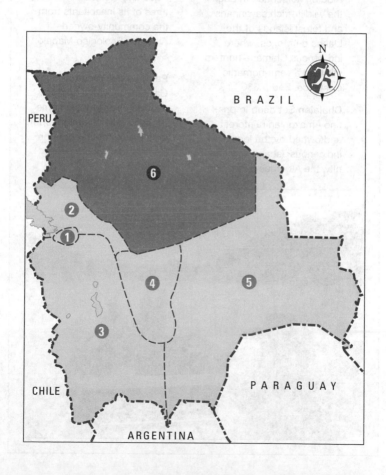

BRAZIL

PERU

6

2

1

4

5

3

CHILE

PARAGUAY

ARGENTINA

N

CHAPTER 6

Highlights

* **Río Mamoré** Sling your hammock and relax on a slow boat down this mighty wilderness river between Trinidad and the Brazilian frontier. **See p.325**

* **Reserva Biosfera del Beni** Ride on horseback through the wildlife-rich savannahs and forest islands of the Llanos de Moxos, where indigenous Chimane hunters still lead a semi-nomadic existence. **See p.330**

* **Chalalán** Set deep in pristine Amazonian rainforest and owned by the local indigenous Tacana community, the Albergue Ecologico Chalalán is the ideal place to explore the Parque Nacional Madidi, and a model of how ecotourism ought to be. **See p.338**

* **Mapajo** Explore the rainforests of the Reserva Pilon Lajas and the traditional cultures of its inhabitants from the community-owned Albergue Ecologico Mapajo. **See p.339**

* **Pampas del Yacuma** Caiman, capybara and pink river dolphins are just some of the wildlife you might spot on a canoe trip through the Pampas del Yacuma. **See p.340**

The Amazon

About a third of Bolivia lies within the **Amazon basin**, a vast, sparsely populated and largely untamed lowland region of swamp, savanna and tropical rainforest (known as *selva*) which supports a bewildering diversity of plant and animal life. Often known as the **Beni**, after one of the rivers that are its dominant geographical feature, the Bolivian Amazon lies more than a thousand kilometres from the mainstream of the mighty River Amazon itself and occupies just a fraction of the total basin. Generally much less developed than the Brazilian Amazon – and consequently boasting a much better preserved natural environment – this is one of the most biodiverse regions in the world, and though in recent decades the rate of forest destruction has accelerated to worrying levels, large areas remain relatively untouched and virtually unexplored. Here, jaguars, tapirs and giant anteaters roam beneath the towering forest canopy; monstrous anacondas slither through the swamps; and the skies are filled by a kaleidoscopic variety of birds. Turtles and caymans bask in the sun on the banks of the mighty rivers, which support a great variety of fish, including the much-maligned piranha, as well as playful pink freshwater dolphins.

Contrary to what you might expect, not all the region is covered by rainforest. Though the last foothills of the Andes are fringed with dense and humid **premontane forest**, the great watery plains that open up beyond are partially covered by a seemingly endless sea of savannah, dotted with islands of forest. Known as the **Llanos de Moxos** (and similar in size to the whole of Great Britain), these plains are flooded each year when the mighty rivers that meander slowly across them – the Beni, Mamoré, Guaporé and their tributaries – are swollen by the innumerable streams that rush down from the Andes and burst their banks, turning the whole area into a vast swamp. This entire wilderness region remains sparsely populated, apart from the great herds of semi-wild cattle which were first introduced by the Jesuit missionaries in the sixteenth century. Though not as spectacular or as biodiverse as the rainforest, the Llanos de Moxos are also home to abundant wildlife – and, given the more open nature of the vegetation, it's often easier to spot. Further north, around the city of Riberalta towards the Brazilian border, the savanna gradually gives way to the high-canopied **Amazonian rainforest** more characteristic of the Amazon region as a whole, where logging and the collection of wild rubber and Brazil nuts are the only industries of any size. Though generally hot and humid all year round, the region is subject to occasional cold snaps, known as *surazos*, when weather fronts sweep in from Patagonia and the temperature drops suddenly and dramatically. Roads in the region are poor in the best of conditions and in the rainy season between November and April are often completely impassable; even in the dry season sudden downpours can quickly turn roads to quagmires.

Linked by road to Santa Cruz, the capital of the Beni is **Trinidad,** a bustling frontier city with few obvious attractions, though for the adventurous it's the starting point for slow boat journeys down the Río Mamoré to the Brazilian border or south into the Chapare. From Trinidad, a long and rough road heads east across the **Llanos de Moxos**, passing through the **Reserva del Biosfera del Beni**, which is an excellent place to get close to the wildlife of the savanna, before joining the main road down into the region from La Paz at Yucumo. Just north of Yucumo, the small town of **Rurrenabaque**, on the banks of the Río Beni, is the obvious destination for anyone wanting a taste of the Amazon, given its proximity to the pristine forests of the **Parque Nacional Madidi**, one of Bolivia's most stunning protected areas, and the savannas of the Llanos de Moxos along the wildlife-rich **Río Yacuma**. From Rurrenabaque the road continues north to the city of **Riberalta**, a centre for rubber and Brazil nut collection, and on to the Brazilian border and the remote, forest-covered department of **Pando**.

Some history

Recent archeological evidence suggests that the pre-Columbian Bolivian Amazon supported a populous and sophisticated society (see p.326), but by the time the Spanish arrived it had already collapsed. In the sixteenth century, inspired by the myth of a fabulously rich empire hidden somewhere in the rainforest – known as

El Dorado or **Paititi** – the conquistadors sent several expeditions down from the Andes in a vain search for new conquests to match the incredible wealth seized from the Incas. But although the indigenous population had already been devastated by epidemics of diseases introduced from Europe, the region resisted major colonization. Most incursions ended in disaster, defeated by the ferocity of the local tribes, the dangers of the rivers, climate and wild animals, and the overwhelming immensity of the alien rainforest environment itself. Realizing there was little worth conquering in a region they referred to as *El Infierno Verde* – the "Green Hell" – the Spanish turned the region over to the religious orders, above all the Jesuits, in the hope that they might have more success in subjugating the forest tribes and securing the northeastern border with Brazil.

In the late seventeenth century a handful of **Jesuit missionaries** did just that, accomplishing in 25 years what the civil and military authorities had been unable to do in over a century. In a precursor of the theocratic society they were later to establish in Chiquitos (see box on p.292), the Jesuits founded a series of mission communities where the various indigenous tribes adopted Christianity and a settled, agricultural existence, raising cattle and growing crops. These missions flourished, and by the mid-eighteenth century were home to over 31,000 converts, supervised by just 45 European priests. But with expulsion of the Jesuits from the Spanish Empire in 1767, the mission inhabitants were left at the mercy of Spanish landowners, with many being forced into slavery.

Worse was to come in the nineteenth century as a result of the growing international demand for rubber, a material derived from trees which were particularly abundant in the Bolivian Amazon. An unprecedented economic boom ensued, and the industry was quickly dominated by a small group of ruthless **rubber barons** who made overnight fortunes and subjected the indigenous population to a brutal regime of forced labour. The most famous of these was **Nicolás Suaréz** (see p.345), who ruled over a vast rainforest empire and remains a legendary figure in the Beni.

The region remained beyond the control of the Bolivian state, a savage frontier where the only law was "article 44 of the legal code", meaning rule by the gun (the reference is to the .44 Winchester rifle). The richest rubber-producing area, the Acre, was largely settled by rubber collectors from Brazil. When the Bolivian government sought to tax rubber exports, these Brazilian rebelled and declared independence. A short conflict – **the Acre War** – ensued, ending with Bolivian defeat, and in 1903 the Acre was annexed by Brazil. In the early twentieth century, the rubber boom collapsed after the English smuggled rubber seedlings out of the Amazon and established plantations in Asia, rendering wild rubber collection uncompetitive.

By the middle of the twentieth century the economy began to recover as large landowners began exporting **cattle** (the wild descendants of those originally introduced by the Jesuits), transporting them by river to the growing markets in Brazil and in military surplus aircraft to the Altiplano. Some landowners also made great fortunes during the **cocaine** boom of the 1980s and 1990s. Strategically positioned between the coca-growing Chapare and the markets to the north, the isolated ranches of the Beni provided the perfect location for clandestine drug laboratories, and their private airstrips were ideal bases for the light aircraft that used to smuggle the cocaine north, leapfrogging through the Amazon to Colombia. Meanwhile, new roads linking the region with the rest of Bolivia opened up its natural resources for exploitation and settlement from the highlands, with disastrous consequences for the environment. The struggle between conservationists, coca-growers, loggers and the region's indigenous inhabitants continues to this day – see the boxes on p.320 and p.327.

Although the forests of the Beni can appear endless when you fly over them by plane or pass through by bus or boat, in fact, they're disappearing at an alarming rate. Every year towards the end of the dry season the skies above Bolivia are obscured by thick smoke from thousands of fires set to clear the forest for agriculture and cattle pasture, a process known as *chaqueo*. In such a vast area no one can tell exactly how fast the forests are disappearing, even with satellite monitoring, but latest estimates suggest that Bolivia is losing about two thousand square kilometres of forest a year, most of it in the Beni, with catastrophic consequences for the region's unique ecosystems.

The causes of this deforestation are various. The most obvious culprits are **timber companies**, ranging from small gangs with chainsaws to major commercial operations. Rather than clear-cutting the forest, they concentrate on valuable hardwood species such as mahogany and Spanish cedar. But for every tree they extract several others are damaged, and the trails they cut into even the most remote areas open the way for **colonists** who are responsible for even greater destruction. Successive Bolivian governments have seen the comparatively empty lands of the Amazon as a solution to poverty and land shortage in the highlands, encouraging the migration of poor farmers from the Andes, who have moved down into the lowlands, clearing the forest to plant food and cash crops. But the exuberance of the Amazonian vegetation belies the relative infertility of the soil beneath it. Most of the nutrients in the rainforest are locked in living matter, and the ecosystem survives by rapidly recycling nutrients from dead organisms before they enter the soil. When the forest cover is slashed and burned on a wide scale, these nutrients are quickly leached away by rain, and within a few years soil fertility declines so much that the land becomes useless for agriculture. Locked into a cycle of diminishing returns, the colonists are forced to move on to clear new areas of forest, and after a few years most find they have abandoned their Andean villages only to encounter a new kind of misery in the tropics. In addition, **cattle ranchers** are increasingly extending their grazing lands by clearing forested areas, further threatening the ecological balance.

Having finally recognized the potential biological value of the country's rainforests, the government has now established extensive national parks and other protected areas in the Amazon, as well as recognizing large areas as indigenous territory (arguably the most effective way of protecting the rainforest) and introducing new laws to limit logging and forest clearance. But the immense scale and remoteness of the region makes enforcing these laws almost impossible, and many of the protected areas exist only on paper. Much of the Amazon is still beyond effective government control, and the powerful local interest groups that dominate the timber industry continue to operate illegally.

Trinidad and around

Close to the Río Mamoré, some 500km northwest of Santa Cruz, the city of **TRINIDAD** is the capital of the Beni and the commercial and administrative centre of a vast wilderness hinterland of swamp, forest and savanna where rivers remain the main means of transport and cattle-ranching is the biggest industry. Like most towns in the region, Trinidad was originally a Jesuit mission, but few signs of that past remain, and it's now a modern commercial city that's dominated by a vigorous cattle-ranching culture and economy. Hot and humid, with few real attractions, Trinidad doesn't really merit a visit in its own right, and though you can organize excursions into the surrounding rainforest, it's more difficult and expensive than in Rurrenabaque, where the forests are also more spectacular and better preserved. It is, however, the jumping-off point for an adventurous trip by slow boat **down the Río Mamoré** to Guayaramerín on the Brazilian border.

Trinidad was founded in 1686 by **Father Cipriano Barace**, a pioneering Jesuit missionary who introduced the first cattle herds to the region and was later martyred while attempting to convert the indigenous tribes on the Río Baures to the northeast. The town prospered under the Jesuits, but fell into rapid decline after their expulsion in 1767, with many of its indigenous inhabitants – drawn from several different tribes from the surrounding area but known collectively as the **Mojeños** – being dragged off to work as virtual slaves on plantations near Santa Cruz. The Mojeños were still strong enough to play an important role in the wars of independence, when an indigenous government led by Pedro Ignacio Muiba was briefly established in Trinidad in 1810, before being ruthlessly crushed by a royalist army which also stripped the town of the last valuable ornaments of the Jesuits.

With the advent of the **rubber boom** the town's population fell dramatically as thousands were forcibly recruited to work as rubber collectors in the forests to the north, while many others fled rather than face the same fate. In 1887, at the height of the rubber boom, the Mojeños launched their last uprising, a non-violent religious movement led by a messianic chief called Andrés Guayocho, who was said to be a great sorcerer and excellent ventriloquist. But the rebellion was swiftly and brutally put down by the Bolivian authorities, many of the survivors fled, and the town was left in the hands of non-indigenous merchants and landowners.

The region's **cattle economy** really developed in the second half of the twentieth century, when enterprising ranchers began cross-breeding the semi-wild cattle descended from the herds brought in by the Jesuits with sleek Xebu cattle brought in from Brazil. Until the road down from Santa Cruz was built in the 1970s, Trinidad was effectively cut off from the rest of Bolivia, and it remains an isolated and somewhat inward-looking place. The ranchers – known as *ganaderos* – see themselves as rugged, self-reliant pioneers who have tamed a wild region and created prosperity with almost no help from central government.

Arrival and information

Buses from Santa Cruz, Guayaramerín and Rurrenabaque arrive at the **terminal** on Avenida Mendoza on the corner with Calle Viador Pinto Sucedo, about eight blocks east from the centre of town. Buses from San Borja arrive just behind the terminal on Avenida Beni. Almost all buses for Santa Cruz depart in the evening between 5pm and 7pm; departures to San Borja, and to Guayaramerín via Rurrenabaque and Riberalta, leave in the morning. **Trucks and buses** from San Ignacio de Moxos arrive at the ticket office on the corner of Calle La Paz and Avenida 18 de Noviembre. The **airport**, on the outskirts of town to the northeast, is served by LAB, TAM and Aero Sur, with frequent flights from La Paz, Santa Cruz and elsewhere in the Beni. The easiest way to get around is by **motorcycle taxi**: they charge about $0.30 for journeys in the town centre, and about $1.50 to or from the airport. If you're arriving by **boat** along the Río Mamoré from Guayaramerín to the north or Puerto Villaroel in the Chapare to the south (see p.260) you'll dock at **Puerto Barador**, Trinidad's river port, about 13km west of town. Frequent trucks run between the port and the intersection of Avenida Pedro Ignacio Muiba with the ring road on the outskirts of town, from where you can get a motorbike taxi into the centre.

There's a **tourist information office** (Mon–Fri 7.30am–3.30pm; ☎03/4620665) of sorts in the Prefectura building just south of the plaza on Avenida Ignacio Muiba; the staff are friendly and try to be helpful but have only limited information about Trinidad and the surrounding area.

Accommodation

There's a good range of **accommodation** in Trinidad, most of it a short distance from the Plaza Ballivián. All the hotels listed here have fans in the rooms, but if the heat is still too much you can splash out on a room with air conditioning.

Hotel Beni Av 6 de Agosto ☎03/4622788. Clean and pleasant, with well-furnished rooms; those with a/c cost twice as much as those without. ❹

Hotel Gran Moxos Corner of Av Santa Cruz and Av 6 de Agosto ☎03/4622240. Slightly overpriced establishment, popular with businessmen and offering spacious, elegant rooms with cool tiled

floors, a/c, cable TV and fridge. Buffet breakfast included; credit cards accepted. ❼

Hotel Mi Residencia M. Limpiaz ☎03/4621529 or 4621376, ℻03/4622464. Trinidad's best upmarket option, with quiet, well-decorated rooms equipped with a/c, cable TV and fridge. The hotel's annex, a few blocks away on Calle Felix Pinto Saucedo, is similar and has a swimming pool. ❼

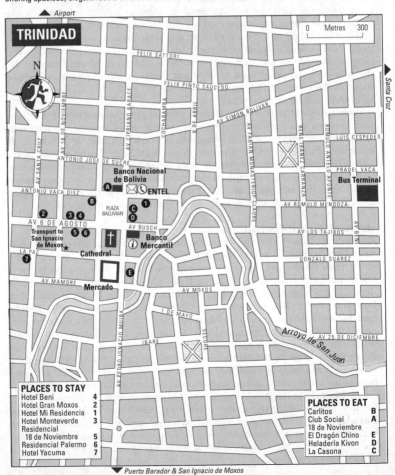

▲ Airport

TRINIDAD

0 Metres 300

▶ Santa Cruz

FELIX SATTORI
FELIX PINTO SAUCEDO
ANTONIO JOSE DE SUCRE
Banco Nacional de Bolivia Ⓐ ✉ ☎ENTEL
ANTONIO VACA DIEZ Ⓑ
PLAZA BALLIVIAN Ⓒ ❶ Ⓓ
AV 6 DE AGOSTO ❷ ❸ ❹
Transport to San Ignacio de Moxos ❺ ❻ AV BUSCH
LA PAZ ❼
Cathedral ✝ Banco ⓘ Mercantil
AV MAMORE Ⓔ
Mercado
AV MOXOS
1 DE MAYO
IBARE
SECURE
Arroyo de San Juan AV 25 DE DICIEMBRE

AV 18 DE NOVIEMBRE
AV SANTA CRUZ
AV CIPRIANO BARACE
COCHABAMBA
9 DE ABRIL
AV SIMON BOLIVAR
AV FABIAN MONASTERIO CLAURE
HENE IBAÑEZ CARRANZA
ROMULO ANTELO AFUNTE
LUIS CESPEDES
PRADEL VACA
Bus Terminal
AV ROMULO MENDOZA
AV LOS TAJIBOS
AV BENI
GONZALO SUAREZ
AV PEDRO IGNACIO MUIBA

PLACES TO STAY
Hotel Beni	4
Hotel Gran Moxos	2
Hotel Mi Residencia	1
Hotel Monteverde	3
Residencial 18 de Noviembre	5
Residencial Palermo	6
Hotel Yacuma	7

PLACES TO EAT
Carlitos	B
Club Social	A
18 de Noviembre	D
El Dragón Chino	E
Heladería Kivon	D
La Casona	C

▼ Puerto Barador & San Ignacio de Moxos

Hotel Monteverde Av 6 de Agosto
☎03/4622750. Cool, bright and modern hotel
offering comfortable rooms with TV, a/c and fridge,
plus a few cheaper rooms without a/c. **④**–**⑤**
Hotel Yacuma Corner of Av Santa Cruz and La
Paz ☎03/4622249. The first hotel in the Beni
when it was built in 1948, and though it's now
run-down and crumbling, it still retains a certain
dilapidated charm, with a cool central patio and
underground cisterns that store rainwater. Cheaper

rooms with shared bath available. **②**
Residencial 18 de Noviembre, Av 6 de Agosto,
two blocks west of the plaza ☎03/4621272. Basic
but good value and friendly place, with a small
snack bar and patio with hammocks. Cheaper
rooms with shared bathroom available. **②**
Residencial Palermo Av 6 de Agosto, two blocks
west of the plaza ☎03/4620472. Small, basic
rooms around a cool, shaded patio; cheaper rooms
with shared bathroom are also available. **②**

The Town

Though most of its buildings are modern, Trinidad maintains the classic layout
of a Spanish colonial town, its streets set out in a neat grid pattern around a
central square, the **Plaza Ballivián**, which the locals proudly insist is the
biggest in Bolivia. Shaded by tall trees and with well-maintained gardens, the
plaza is the most popular hang-out in town and the focus of the weekend
evening ritual of motorcycle courtship, when what seems like half the youth
of Trinidad ride round in endless circles on motorbikes, chatting and flirting.
At the centre of the plaza is an extravagant fountain decorated with herons,
dolphins, a Mojeño warrior armed with a bow and several frolicking cherubs.
If you look closely up to the tree-tops you may catch a glimpse of the rather
miserable-looking three-toed sloths brought here by local campesinos. On the
south side of the plaza, the **Cathedral** is an unexceptional modern structure
built between 1916 and 1931 on the site of the earlier Jesuit church.

The buildings around the plaza and the surrounding streets are all built with
eaves overhanging the pavement designed to protect pedestrians from the harsh
tropical sun and torrential Amazonian rain, while the pavements are raised up
to two feet above the ground to escape flooding in the rainy season. In addition, the streets are lined with open sewers which, while they may be necessary for drainage, emit a horrible stench, provide an ideal breeding ground for
the mosquitoes that plague the town, and represent a dangerous obstacle for
unwary pedestrians.

Eating

There are some pretty good **restaurants** on and around Plaza Ballivián. If
you're on a tight budget try the **market**, two blocks south of the plaza, where
you can get cheap filling meals, fresh fruit juices, delicious fried cheese
empanadas and *masaco*, a deep-fried mixture of mashed plantain or yucca and
dried meat. The beef in Trinidad is excellent and very good value; the local speciality is *pacumutu*, great chunks of meat and chicken marinated and grilled on
a skewer.

Carlitos Plaza Ballivián. The best restaurant in
town, serving up surprisingly sophisticated Bolivian
and international meat, fish and pasta dishes for
$4–5.
Club Social 18 de Noviembre Plaza Ballivián. A
vast, elegant dining hall with a rather old-fashioned
feel, serving up good-value almuerzos and standard Bolivian dishes like *milanesa* and *pique a lo
macho*.
El Dragón Chino Av Muiba opposite the market, a
couple of blocks south of the plaza. Pretty good
Bolivian-style Chinese food, which makes a

change from endless steaks. Don't be put off by
the prices on the menu: each dish serves two people, and you can order a half portion.
Heladeria Kivon Plaza Ballivián. Ice-cream parlour with tables looking out onto the plaza – a
great place to cool down with a sundae and
watch the world go by. Also serves good cakes,
sandwiches, main dishes and disappointing
breakfasts.
La Casona Plaza Ballivián. Lively and popular
place with good almuerzos, pizza and pasta, as
well as steak and fried river fish.

Rainforest trips from Trinidad

A couple of **tour operators** run trips into the wilderness around Trinidad. **Turismo Moxos**, Avenida 6 de Agosto 114 (℡03/4621141, ℻03/4622189, ✉turmoxos@sauce .ben.entelnet.bo) organize various one- to three-day trips into the rainforest by motorized canoe along the Río Ibare, a tributary of the Mamoré, with plenty of opportunity for seeing wildlife and visiting indigenous communities. One of their trips involves staying on a privately owned ranch where the extremely rare blue-throated macaw can be seen – a must for serious birders. Trips cost around $50 per person per day.

The highly professional **Fremen** agency, Av 6 de Agosto 140 (℡03/4622276, ⓦwww.andes-amazonia.com) operate similar excursions, as well as four- to six-day cruises on the Mamoré aboard the luxury floating hotel the *Reina de Enin*. They also offer more adventurous eight-day trips into the enormous Parque Nacional y Territorio Indigena Isiboro-Sécure (see p.328).

In addition to the trips detailed in the "Around Trinidad" section below, you could also try heading out to some of the isolated former **mission towns** north and east of Trinidad, either by boat (ask around at the port) or by catching a ride on a light aircraft from the airport. The towns of **Magdelena** and **Bella Vista**, to the northeast, are set amid some beautiful rainforest and have some basic tourist facilities, though the emphasis is still on expensive hunting and fishing trips rather than ecotourism. They can also be reached by a precarious road, though even in the dry season this is often impassable; trucks and buses to Magdelena and Bella Vista leave from the intersection of Avenida Ciprián Barace and the ring road, close to the airport.

Listings

Airlines LAB, Av Santa Cruz 234 ℡03/4620595; AeroSur, Cipriano Barace opposite the post office ℡03/4652119; TAM at the airport ℡03/4622363.

Banks and exchange The Banco Naciónal de Bolivia (Mon–Fri 8.30–noon & 2.30–5.30pm), on the plaza, and the Banco Mercantil (Mon–Fri 8.30am–12.30pm & 2.30–6.30pm), just off the plaza on Av Pedro Ignacio Muiba, both change cash and travellers' cheques; the latter also gives cash advances on credit cards. Otherwise, there are plenty of street moneychangers on Av 6 de Agosto.

Hospital Hospital German Busch, Bolívar with Lopez ℡118.

Internet access *Café Camb@net* (daily 9am–midnight), inside the shopping arcade on the west side of the plaza.

Laundry Lavanderia Pro Vida, Felix Sattori just off Av Nicolás Suárez.

Motorbike hire Bikes are available all over town; the easiest place to find one is on the plaza, where there's always a group of people waiting to rent out their machines. A basic moped will cost about $1.60 an hour; a 125cc dirt bike about $2 an hour; daily rates are negotiable. You'll need to leave your passport as a deposit. If you're heading out of town or carrying a passenger it's worth paying slightly extra for a more powerful bike.

Post office Just off the plaza on Av Ciprian Barace (Mon–Sat 8am–noon, 2.30–6pm).

Telephone office The ENTEL office (Mon–Fri 7.30am–11pm, Sat & Sun 8am–10pm) is in the same building as the post office, just off the plaza on Av Cipriano Barace.

Around Trinidad

The area immediately around Trinidad is dominated by the **Río Mamoré**, which runs through a landscape of forest, swamp and lakes, dotted with the artificial mounds left by the mysterious pre-Columbian Moxos civilization. About 13km west of the city, **PUERTO BARADOR** is Trinidad's main river port and makes a worthwhile and easy excursion. There are several ramshackle riverside restaurants where you can eat fresh fried fish and watch the boats that ply the length of the Río Mamoré carrying cattle and other cargo being slowly loaded and unloaded – you may also catch a glimpse of pink river dolphins frolicking in the water. Frequent trucks run to the port from the intersection of Avenida Pedro Ignacio Muiba with the ring road on the outskirts of Trinidad, and it's also easy to reach by motorbike. The journey out there involves a short river crossing by ferry at **Puerto Almacen**, a smaller port on the Río Ibare, a tributary river that flows into the Mamoré just north of Trinidad.

Loma Suárez and Loma Chuchuni

Another dirt road runs about 10km northeast of Trinidad to **Loma Suárez**, an artificial mound on the banks of the Río Ibare that's believed to have been built by the ancient Moxos civilization (see box on p.327). Once the local headquarters of the Suárez rubber empire, the mound is now covered by buildings belonging to the navy, and you may have to show your passport on arrival. There are good views from the top of the mound and you'll see plenty of birdlife.

From Loma Suárez, the road continues another 5km or so to **Loma Chuchuni**, another ancient mound that's now the centre of a small private ecological reserve and visitors' centre. It makes an interesting day-trip from Trinidad, though there's no public transport so you'll have to come by motorbike, and sadly the Hinojosa family who run it charge a rather excessive $10 per person to visit. There's also a small **museum** housing a collection of potshards and other minor artefacts from the Moxos culture that were found during excavations on the mound. Few of the Moxos's material possessions have survived, so the museum isn't exactly overwhelming, but it is as yet the only place in the Beni where such artefacts can be seen.

Less inspiring are the many **caged animals** on display, including pumas, jaguars and ocelots – a fairly depressing spectacle. The family also offers **guided tours** on foot and by canoe through the surrounding forest and swamp, which are relatively undisturbed and home to a great variety of wildlife. Food and drink are available, and there are a few comfortable but overpriced **cabins** where you can stay the night – it's $210 per person for a three-day package including collection from Trinidad. Contact the Hinojosa family in Trinidad on ☏03/4624744.

Down the Río Mamoré

From Puerto Barador you can get a ride on the regular cargo boats which ply the waters of the **Río Mamoré**, either downstream to Guayaramerín on the Brazilian border or upstream as far as Puerto Villarroel in the Chapare (see p.260). In places more than three kilometres wide, the mighty Mamoré – its name means "Great Mother" in Moxeño – was once one of the great waterways of the Bolivian Amazon and still sees a good deal of traffic. Canoes, barges and double-decker river boats ply its silt-laden waters, carrying supplies to the isolated communities along the river bank, collecting cargos of timber or bananas, and carrying cattle downstream to markets in Brazil.

Travelling this way is one of the classic Amazon experiences, and an excellent way to get a feel for the immense scale of the forest and the lifestyle of its inhabitants. The river boats glide through the forest at a languid pace, with plenty of opportunities for spotting wildlife along the way, particularly cayman, pink river dolphins, and innumerable birds. Every so often the dense vegetation of the river bank breaks to reveal a riverside settlement, usually no more than a cluster of thatched houses on stilts. For the villagers, isolated in the midst of this immense wilderness, the arrival of a boat can be the main event of the day, and if yours stops to load or unload cargo it's likely to be besieged by locals selling bananas or fish, or simply seeking the latest news and gossip from upriver.

Moundbuilders of the Amazon

Long before the Spaniards first arrived in the Americas, the Incas told stories of a mighty civilization in the watery plains to the east of the Andes. In the fifteenth century the Inca Yupanqui sent a great army down one of the rivers of the Upper Amazon in search of this kingdom. After a long and perilous journey the depleted Inca force eventually came across a numerous and warlike nation known as the Musu, or **Moxos**. Heavily outnumbered, the Incas were in no position to conquer the Moxos, but instead offered them an alliance. The Moxos accepted, and allowed the surviving Inca warriors to settle amongst them. This story suggests that in the Moxos, the Incas had found their equals, and when the Spanish heard this tale, it fuelled the growing legend of **El Dorado** – the belief that hidden somewhere in the depths of the Amazon there existed a wealthy and powerful kingdom. In the sixteenth-century numerous Spanish expeditions went down into the Amazon in search of this mythical realm, which was also known as **Paitití**, the land of the celestial jaguar. Nothing was ever found, however, to match their dreams of wealth and conquest, and most explorers encountered only despair and an untimely death in the hostile rainforest environment.

Until about thirty years ago archeologists doubted that any large, settled population could ever have survived in the Amazon Basin. The accepted wisdom was that the region's thin, acidic soils made intensive agriculture impossible, and that the area could support only small, scattered communities practising slash-and-burn agriculture along with hunting and gathering. But subsequent research has suggested that the forests and savannas of the Llanos de Moxos were in fact once densely populated by well-organized societies who, some time between 3000 BC and 1000 BC, modified the environment on a massive scale to allow intensive agriculture and large urban settlements. The region is dotted with hundreds of raised earth mounds, known as **lomas**, most of which are covered by forest. Seen from the ground, these mounds are hardly impressive, and were long thought to be merely the remnants of natural levees left by rivers as they meandered across the plain. But when archaeologists looked at these mounds from the air, they realized they were far too extensive and regular to be natural. Instead, they concluded that they were the remnants of a massive system of earthworks – including raised fields, canals, causeways, reservoirs, dykes and mounds stretching over hundreds of square kilometres – that could only have been built by a large and well-organized society.

Excavations on some of the mounds revealed that they had been built up over many centuries. By cultivating these raised mounds, researchers believe the ancient inhabitants of the Moxos were able to overcome the problems of poor soil and seasonal flooding and drought, producing enough food to support a population density much greater than was previously believed possible in the Amazon. The network of canals, weirs and causeways, meanwhile, is thought to have provided a sophisticated water management system that converted the seasonally flooded plains into a huge fish farm, overcoming the protein scarcity that is considered the main limitation on population growth in the Amazon. That the Spanish never found this civilization is due to the fact that – perhaps as a result of European introduced epidemics or sustained drought – the whole social network collapsed shortly before they reached the region, and the abandoned raised field systems were colonized by forest.

These recent discoveries have enormous implications for both conservation and development in the Amazon. They suggest that, far from being a fragile natural environment, large areas of the Amazon are in fact **anthropogenic**, or man-made, ecosystems, modified by centuries of human activity and capable of supporting far larger populations than is currently the case. Not surprisingly, these interpretations remain controversial, with some researchers continuing to claim that the mounds and causeways of the Moxos are in fact natural. But as more and more evidence is uncovered, the argument that the Llanos de Moxos were once home to a large and sophisticated civilization becomes ever more compelling.

Boats depart up- and down-river two or three times a week, though when river levels fall in the dry season the route south to Puerto Villaroel can be impassable. The trip downstream to Guayaramerín takes between three days and a week, depending on the level of the river, the size and power of the boat, whether it's equipped to travel by night, and how many stops it makes to load and unload cargo; upstream to Puerto Villaroel takes five to seven days. Both trips should cost between $20 and $30 including meals, but be prepared to bargain. The **food** served on board the boats is usually pretty bland, consisting mainly of rice, plantains and *charque*, so it's worth taking along fresh fruit and maybe some tinned food. You should also take drinking **water** or purifiers. Accommodation on board is fairly basic; you'll need your own hammock to string up on deck as well as a mosquito net if the boat is likely to moor at night. Comfort varies considerably and you should take some care when choosing which boat to travel in and securing your hammock space; sleeping beside an unsilenced diesel engine for a week is not much fun, for example, while stringing your hammock above a cargo of steaming cattle has obvious disadvantages.

The **Distrito Naval** (navy headquarters) on Avenida 6 de Agosto in Trinidad usually has information on departures, but you're better off heading to Puerto Barador to talk with officials at the **Capitanía del Puerto** (port authority) office and the boat captains to check departure dates and arrange passage. You may have to wait around a few days before getting a ride; some captains will let you sleep on board while awaiting departure.

Indigenous peoples of the Bolivian Amazon

The Bolivian Amazon is home to more than twenty indigenous peoples, each with their own distinct language and culture, ranging in size from the **Moxeños**, who number around 40,000, to groups like the **Araona**, now reduced to no more than about a hundred people. Between them, the populations of these indigenous tribes now number in the region of 100,000, a mere fraction of the population which lived here before the arrival of European diseases and the near-genocidal impact of the rubber boom, when huge numbers were enslaved and forced to work in appalling conditions. After centuries of external contact – with conquistadors, missionaries, rubber barons, soldiers, drug traffickers, anthropologists and now tourists – many of the indigenous people of the Amazon now speak Spanish and have adopted a fairly conventional Bolivian lifestyle, engaging in the market economy as workers and consumers and preferring rubber boots and football shirts to their traditional handmade costumes. However, many others still survive by hunting, fishing and cultivating manioc and other crops in small clearings in the forest, much as they have done for thousands of years, and relying for medicine on the powers of traditional healers and their encyclopedic knowledge of thousands of different rainforest plants. The most traditional indigenous groups are the uncontacted tribes – known as the **Nahuas** and **Toromonas** – small nomadic bands thought to be living deep in the rainforest who eschew all contact with Bolivian society.

Largely dependent on the rainforest for their livelihoods, the indigenous peoples of the Bolivian Amazon were amongst the first to recognize the danger posed by the gathering pace of deforestation. In 1990 they staged the first of several "**Marches for Territory and Dignity**", walking 650km from Trinidad to La Paz to demand the recognition of their right to land and self-determination. This campaign drew international attention to their plight and led to new legislation and the recognition of large areas of the Beni as indigenous territorial reserves. Though huge areas of territory still remain to be titled, and the bureaucratic process is obstructed at every turn by cattle ranchers and logging companies, the indigenous peoples of Bolivia are gradually regaining control of their own lands.

Parque Nacional y Territorio Indígena Isiboro-Sécure

Starting some 80km southeast of Trinidad, some 12,000 square kilometres of rainforest are protected (on paper at least) by the **Parque Nacional y Reserva Indígena Isiboro–Sécure**, a beautiful wilderness region between the Ríos Isiboro and Sécure, which rush down from the rugged, forest-covered Cordillera de Mosetenes, the last ridge of the Andes north of Cochabamba. As its name states, Isiboro–Sécure is both a national park and the semi-autonomous territory of the indigenous Moxeño, Yuyucare and T'simane peoples, who live here in fifty or so small and isolated communties, mostly on the banks of the two rivers. Unfortunately, the park lies just north of the coca-growing Chapare region (see p.256), and in recent decades has been used for smuggling and as a hiding place for cocaine laboratories. It's also faced a continual invasion by loggers and settlers from the Andes, many of them displaced from the Chapare and looking for somewhere to grow coca away from the prying eyes of the security forces.

All of this has provoked a bitter conflict with the indigenous population, who are understandably anxious to defend their territory. Given the present situation, independent travel to Isiboro-Sécure is dangerous and shouldn't currently be attempted – a shame, as otherwise the park would make an exciting back-door route by boat between the Chapare and Trinidad. If you're still keen, the tour operator **Fremen**, which has offices in Cochabamba, La Paz, Santa Cruz and Trinidad (see under organized tours sections in each city), sometimes runs visits to the park, starting in Cochabamba and ending in Trinidad.

The Llanos de Moxos

East of Trinidad stretches the vast, watery plain known as the **Llanos de Moxos** (or Mojos). Spanning the area between the Ríos Mamoré and Beni, the region is largely covered by seasonally flooded savanna or natural grassland interspersed with swamp and patches of forest. During the November to April rainy season, the whole area is flooded for months at a time and the road becomes impassable, while during the dry season between May and September the grasslands become very dry, resembling the savannas of Africa much more than the lush greenery usually associated with the Amazon basin.

This is **cowboy country**, and the economy of the plains is dominated by enormous ranches, stocked with the semi-wild descendants of the cattle first introduced by the Jesuits in the seventeenth century. Some individual ranchers have herds numbering tens of thousands, and travelling by road you'll often find the way blocked by cattle being led to market over hundreds of kilometres by mounted men little different in appearance and lifestyle from the iconic cowboys of the nineteenth-century North American West. To complete the illusion, the Llanos are also home to semi-nomadic indigenous groups such as the T'simane (or Chimane), for whom hunting is still an important source of food, though shotguns have now largely replaced bows and arrows as the weapon of choice.

Away from the former mission towns of **San Ignacio de Moxos** and **San Borja**, the Llanos remain a sparsely populated wilderness where most of the wild animal species of the Amazon still thrive, and because of the open vegetation they can be easier to spot than in the forest. Even from the road, the

Savanna ecology

The **origin of the savannas** of the Llanos de Moxos is debatable. Certainly much of the open vegetation is of natural origin. Rainfall levels in the region are lower than elsewhere in Amazonia, and many tree species cannot tolerate the extreme alternation between flooding in the rainy season and severe desiccation in the unusually long dry season. But the region has also been grazed by cattle and burned by ranchers – and indigenous tribes before them – for hundreds of years. It may be that the existing vegetation is the result of a shifting ecological balance between nature and human activity known as **fire climax**, and that the boundary between forest and grassland has always been variable. Indeed, some ecologists believe such fluctuations may have been a prime cause of the exceptional biodiversity in Amazonia today. During the Pleistocene era, they argue, changes in climate and rainfall over thousands of years meant the forest cover in the region was periodically reduced to small isolated tracts, where species evolved in isolation. When the forest cover expanded again, these species would be mixed with others that had evolved separately to fill the same ecological niches, thus increasing species diversity. However, there's growing concern that the expansion of cattle-ranching in recent decades, with larger areas being burned and the introduction of new grass species, is increasing the extent of the savanna at the expense of the rainforest, disturbing the delicate equilibrium established between humans and nature over many centuries.

birdlife you'll see here is spectacular and abundant, with water species like storks and herons being particularly evident. Jaguars also abound, despite the efforts of ranchers to protect their herds, and you may also spot species not found in the forest, like the maned wolf, a long-legged, solitary hunter that moves through the high grasses with a loping stride, or the rhea, a large flightless bird similar to the ostrich. A few hours west of San Ignacio, a large area of this distinctive environment is protected by the **Reserva de la Biosfera del Beni**, Bolivia's longest established protected area, which has excellent facilities.

San Ignacio de Moxos

About a hundred kilometres west of Trinidad lies **SAN IGNACIO DE MOXOS**, the only town of any size between San Borja and Trinidad – the journey here involves three river crossings by barge, where there's a good chance of spotting pink dolphins playing in the water. Originally founded by Jesuit missionaries in 1689, San Ignacio is a poor town, where horse- or ox-drawn carts are as common as motor vehicles, and with a largely indigenous population that retains more of the traditions of the Jesuit era than any other town in the Beni. For most of the year it's a sleepy backwater except from July 28 to 31, when it rouses itself from its tropical torpor to celebrate its patron saint's day with processions, dancing and drinking in what's considered the greatest **folkloric festival** in the Bolivian Amazon. The highlights of the fiesta are the elaborate costumed dances performed by the area's indigenous Moxeño population. Dressed in crowns of feathers, long cotton robes and carved wooden masks, they dance to the music of metre-long woodwind instruments and violins which bear a striking resemblance to those the Jesuits taught their ancestors to make. The most famous dance, known as the *Machetero*, is a thinly veiled portrayal of the struggles of the Moxos against Spanish rule. Similar celebrations are held during Holy Week, though these tend to attract fewer visitors.

The Town

There's not much to do in San Ignacio outside fiesta times, but it's a friendly, laid-back place where time seems to stand still. Many of the houses are simple palm-thatched cane structures, but the main **plaza** is lined with stone houses with tiled roofs which extend over the pavement to provide shelter from the harsh tropical sun and frequent rain. In its centre stands a **statue** of an indigenous warrior in the same costume as that worn by the *Machetero* dancers during the fiesta, while on the east side stands the **Iglesia de San Ignacio**, the town's physical and spiritual centre. Built in the barn-like style favoured by the Jesuits, its interior is brightly painted in a beautiful naïve style with scenes from the life of Ignacio Loyola, the mercenary soldier turned saint who founded the Jesuit order. His statue stands behind the altar where you would normally expect to see Christ. The church is run by Spanish Jesuit priests, who are once again heavily involved in defending the rights of the indigenous population against logging companies and large landowners, and who continue to inspire a deep faith in their congregation. Thousands of people attend mass on Sundays, when religious singing inside the church is sometimes accompanied by music and ritual dancing outside.

Practicalities

Buses to and from Trinidad arrive and depart from one of two transport syndicate offices, either on the main square or a block away on Calle Santisteban, the road that heads out of town to the east. There are three **places to stay** on the main square, all of them fairly simple but clean, with fans and a choice between shared or private bathrooms. The *Residencial Don Joaquin* (℡03/4822112; ❷) has a pleasant courtyard garden with hammocks; the *Hotel San Ignacio* (℡03/4822063; ❷) has cool rooms with high ceilings; while the *Hotel Plaza* (℡03/4822032; ❷) is a little more basic. Prices tend to double at fiesta times, when beds are very difficult to find.

There are several basic **restaurants** on Calle Santisteban, all of which open late and close early: the most popular is the *Cherlis*, where through buses usually stop for lunch. The only upmarket alternative is the *Pescadería San Francisco*, a block from the plaza on the road that runs beside the church. For an early breakfast, head for the small covered **market** on Calle Santisteban. **Moving on**, if you're heading east, buses to Trinidad leave early in the morning – there's usually only one departure a day, so it's worth buying a ticket the night before. Through buses between Trinidad and San Borja and beyond usually stop here for lunch: if you're heading west, these are your best bet.

Reserva de la Biosfera del Beni

Covering some 1350 square kilometres of savanna and rainforest to the east of San Borja, the **Reserva de la Biosfera del Beni** (Beni Biosphere Reserve) was one of the first protected areas to be established in Bolivia. Standing at the intersection of two important bio-geographical zones, the reserve is exceptionally biodiverse, hosting some 500 species of birds and 100 species of mammals – these include almost half the protected species in Bolivia, among them many that are in danger of extinction.

Unusually for Bolivia, the reserve also has very well-organized facilities for visitors, based at the **Beni Biological Station** at El Porvenir, a former ranch about 100km west of San Ignacio on the road to San Borja. Though most of the reserve is actually rainforest, the area immediately around El Porvenir is largely savanna, a seemingly endless sea of natural grasses up to two metres high, dotted with islands of forest. The reserve is open all year round, but during the rainy season the whole area becomes flooded and the road is impassable, so you can really only visit between May and October.

Exploring the reserve

As well as organizing food and accommodation, the park rangers (see below) can arrange for villagers from the nearby community of Totaizal to take you on tours in the reserve on foot or on **horseback** (prices for walking tours are given below; horseback tours cost around an extra $7.50 per day). Walking through the savanna is arduous, particularly in the heat of the day, but riding is less taxing and also raises you above the savanna grasses. The most popular tour is the half-day trip through the savanna to **Laguna Normandia** ($8 per person), a large lake which you can cruise around in canoes in search of the abundant but elusive black cayman that patrol the dark waters. The lake is also home to an astonishing variety and number of herons and other wading birds, as well as a great number of snail kites. Another good half-day excursion is the **Sabana** tour ($12 per person), which involves visiting some of the **forest islands** that dot the savanna – these range from small copses to patches of forest several kilometres across. Much of the research conducted at the reserve is aimed at understanding these islands and the shifting balance between them and the surrounding grasslands. The islands support much the same wildlife as the rainforest proper, including red howler monkeys, whose eerie dawn chorus is one of the Amazon's most unforgettable sounds, and several different species of macaw.

A good day- or overnight trip is the **Torres** ($20 per person including a horse and food), which involves riding through swamp and high grassland to three different observation towers, from where panoramic views bring home the sheer scale of the savanna and reveal the gradual transition between grassland and forest. The last tower is on the fringes of the forests to the north of the reserve, where you can camp overnight in a basic shelter – with a little luck you may see a rare swamp deer or armadillo.

Other overnight and more extended trips, for which you'll need your own camping gear, include **El Trapiche** ($20 per person, $27 with food), a two-day trip which takes you to an abandoned sugar mill further into the reserve, with correspondingly better chances of seeing wildlife. For the more adventurous, the three-day **La Pascana** circuit ($33 per person, $48 with food), takes you deep into the forests in the north of the reserve and offers good chances of spotting larger mammals such as deer or even jaguars. This trip also takes you into part of the 300 square kilometres of the reserve that has been recognized as the territory of the semi-nomadic indigenous T'simane, part of a much larger indigenous territorial reserve which stretches south of El Porvenir – this area is sometimes off limits when the T'simane are hunting in the area. Finally, for those looking for a more serious wilderness experience it's also possible to accompany the park rangers on their regular four-day **patrols** ($80 per person including food) to guard against loggers.

Practicalities

If you're travelling in a big group it's probably worth phoning the reserve office in San Borja (☏03/8953898) a day in advance to let them know you're coming, but otherwise it's fine to arrive at El Porvenir unannounced. To reach the biological station take any bus or truck heading east from San Borja or west from San Ignacio and ask the driver to let you off at El Porvenir. **Admission** to the reserve costs $5 per person and **accommodation** in basic but clean barrack-like rooms with shared bathrooms costs $12 per person, including three meals a day, or $9 a day if you bring your own equipment and **camp**.

They also have an extensive scientific library which visitors can use and a small exhibition of T'simane crafts; in addition, local T'simane sometimes bring bows and woven baskets to sell to visitors. **Moving on** from El Porvenir can be tricky: your only option is to try to flag down one of the few passing vehicles.

San Borja

About 140km east of San Ignaco de Moxos and 40km east of El Porvenir, **SAN BORJA** is an uneventful former mission town with a surprisingly prosperous feel, reflecting the wealth of the big cattle ranchers who dominate the surrounding region, as well as the possible involvement of some of its residents in the even more lucrative cocaine business. That said, though, it's a peaceful place with a pleasant central square that serves as a market and supply centre for outlying ranches.

There's no reason to stop here, but if you're heading for the Beni Biosphere Reserve from the west you might have to **spend the night** before catching the regular morning bus east to Trinidad; the driver is usually happy to take passengers to the reserve entrance at Porvenir. If you do, the *Hotel San Borja* (☎03/8483133 or 8483291; ❷–❻) on the central plaza is the best place in town, with a range of rooms to suit all budgets; the *Hotel Tropical* (❶) a couple of blocks away, is a little more basic.

There are a few simple **restaurants** on and around the plaza which serve cheap almuerzos and occasionally set up outdoor barbecues on the street, roasting juicy slabs of local beef over charcoal fires. The FFP Prodem bank a block from the square on Calle Selim Majluf will **change US dollars**, as will the Comercial El Chiman hardware store opposite. Daily **buses** to Trinidad, Guayaramerín and La Paz leave early in the morning from the bus terminal, a \$0.50 motorcycle taxi ride away on the outskirts of town. For transport to Yucumo head down to the *paradero* on the main road, from where trucks leave when there are enough passengers – your chances are best early in the morning.

Yucumo

About 50km southwest of San Borja the road across the Llanos de Moxos from Trinidad joins the road down from La Paz into the Beni at the scruffy settlement of **YUCUMO**, populated largely by Aymara migrants. The entire road down here from Caranavi in the Yungas (see p.143) has been heavily settled by poor migrants from the highlands, with devastating environmental consequences: the landscape is now dominated by scrubby cattle pasture and secondary forest growth, and the migrants are not much better off than they were in the highland villages they abandoned to seek a new life in the tropical lowlands.

From Yucumo it's another 100km or so north to Rurrenabaque; there's no scheduled bus service but traffic's fairly regular and truck drivers often stop here for meals, so if you're heading to Rurrenabaque you can just flag down anything that's moving in that direction. Heading west, several trucks and pick-ups carry passengers daily between Yucumo and San Borja. If you get stuck overnight you can find a **room** at the basic *Hotel Tropical* (no phone; ❷), which also has a reasonable restaurant.

Rurrenabaque

Set on the banks of the Río Beni some 430km by road north of La Paz, the small town of **RURRENABAQUE** has emerged in recent years as by far the most popular ecotourism destination in the Bolivian Amazon, and with good reason. Standing between the last forest-covered foothills of the Andes and the great lowland plains, Rurrenabaque is close to some of the best-preserved and most accessible wilderness areas in the region, including the spectacular rainforests of the **Parque Nacional Madidi** and the **Reserva de Biosfera y Territorio Indígena Pilon Lajas**, as well as the wildlife-rich pampas along the **Río Yacuma**, all of which are easily visited with one of Rurrenabaque's numerous tour agencies. It's also the easiest Amazon town to reach from La Paz, though that's not saying much. By air it's a short and spectacular flight across the cordillera, but by road the trip down through the Yungas is a gruelling adventure that takes at least eighteen hours, though it can be broken with a stop off in Coroico (see p.138).

Rurrenabaque first came to prominence during the **rubber boom** in the late nineteenth century, serving as the gateway to the Amazon region from the highlands. Until recently, the extraction and processing of **timber** from the surrounding rainforest was Rurrenabaque's main industry, but this has been curtailed somewhat by the exhaustion of valuable timber species and the establishment of the Parque Nacional Madidi and other protected areas. The developing **ecotourism industry** has emerged as one of the few economic alternatives to this highly destructive and largely illegal activity.

Arrival and accommodation

The military airline TAM has five weekly **flights** to Rurrenabaque from La Paz. These arrive at the airstrip a short distance north of the town, and are met by a shuttle bus which will take you to the TAM office in the centre of town. **Buses** arrive at the Terminal Terrestre a few blocks away from the centre of town on the corner of Calle Guachalla and Calle 18 de Noviembre; you can

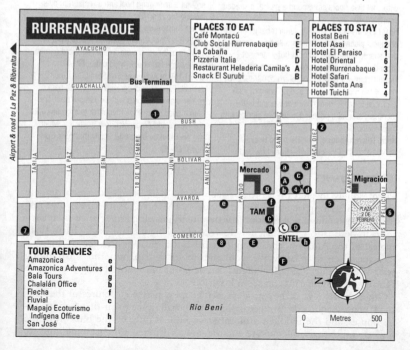

get a motorbike taxi into the centre for about $0.25. When the road is closed in the rainy season, **motorized canoes** occasionally carry passengers between Rurrenabaque and Guanay (see p.144) and Riberalta (see p.341); they moor on the beach at the end of Calle Santa Cruz. In general, though, the Río Beni is rarely used for long-distance transport, as moving goods and passengers by road is far cheaper, although it's still fairly busy with local traffic.

There are no banks in Rurrenabaque. Some tour agencies accept payment with **travellers' cheques** and credit cards, and may change cheques or advance cash on credit cards, though only for a large commission: try Bala Tours or Amazonia Adventures.

Accommodation

For a small town, Rurrenabaque has an impressive number of places **to stay**, though rooms can still be difficult to find in high season (May–Aug), particularly if you arrive in the evening after the flights from La Paz have come in; if you're going on a tour it's a good idea to book a room for your return (all places will store luggage when you're out on a tour). Unless otherwise mentioned, everywhere listed has hot water and fans, though the water and electricity supply is less reliable in the cheaper places, and the electricity supply for the whole town is cut off daily between 3am and 7am.

Hostal Beni Comercio with Pando ℡03/8922408. Clean and modern rooms with cool, tiled floors (some also have a/c); travellers' cheques accepted. ❷, ❹ with a/c.

Hotel Asai Vaca Diez with Bush ℡03/8922439. A touch classier and more expensive than Rurre's other budget places, with clean, spacious, rooms with cool tiled floors set around a peaceful shaded courtyard. ❸

Hotel El Paraiso Bush with Junin (no phone). The cheapest place in town, with small, basic rooms and shared bathrooms without hot water, set around a scruffy, hen-pecked courtyard. ❶

Hotel Oriental Plaza 2 de Febrero ℡03/8922401. One of the most appealing budget options, with cool, comfortable rooms (with or without bathroom) set around a peaceful courtyard garden with hammocks. ❸

Hotel Rurrenabaque Vaca Diez and Bolivar ℡03/8922481. Pleasant two-storey hotel with basic but clean rooms, with or without bathroom, some with balconies overlooking the street. ❸

Hotel Safari Comerico and Tarija ℡03/8922210 or 8922410. Ten minutes' walk from the town centre, this is Rurrenabaque's only upmarket option, and popular with wealthy weekenders from La Paz, with comfortable and spacious cabins set around a swimming pool and a restaurant overlooking the river. ❺

Hotel Santa Ana Corner of Avaroa and Vaca Diez ℡03/8922399. Clean, pleasant rooms (with or without bath) set around a cool courtyard garden and a large hammock-filled patio. ❷–❸

Hotel Tuichi Avaroa and Av Santa Cruz (no phone). Popular backpackers' hotel with basic, rather cramped rooms with or without bath. It's also a good place to put together tour groups with the Fluvial and Amazonica tour agencies, which are operated by the same family that runs the hotel. ❷–❸

The Town

Picturesquely located on a broad sweep of the Río Beni, with steep, densely forested hills rising behind, Rurrenabaque – or "Rurre", as it's know to its residents – maintains a real frontier feel, despite its growing importance as an eco-tourism destination. It's a friendly town, with a languid, laid-back charm that's typical of the Amazon, and though there's not a great deal to see or do, it's a pleasant place to relax while you prepare for a trip into the surrounding wilderness, while after a few nights camping out in the forest or pampas, even Rurre's modest charms can seem luxurious.

Other than a few shabby modern brick and concrete structures in the centre, Rurrenabaque's dirt streets are lined with traditional palm-thatched wooden houses, and the indolent atmosphere is broken only by the buzz from the few sawmills that still operate on the town's fringes. Official buildings are clustered around the pleasant **Plaza 2 de Febrero** at the south end of town, but most commercial activity is concentrated along the first few blocks of **Calles Avaroa** and **Comerico**, which run north from the plaza parallel to the river, lined with ramshackle stores selling hammocks, rubber boots, machetes, chainsaws, tinned food and other supplies for people living in the surrounding area. The riverside itself is an interesting place to while away the time watching canoes arriving along the Beni and unloading cargoes of bananas or freshly caught fish. It's particularly lively during the small Sunday-morning **market**, when indigenous people from the hinterlands of the surrounding rainforest come to town to pick up supplies and sell fish, agricultural produce, and (for tourists) handicrafts like woven baskets and wooden bows.

If you've got some time on your hands you can take the **ferry** (every 10min; $0.15) across the river to the small village of **San Buenaventura** on the opposite bank; this is inside the department of La Paz, so for bureaucratic reasons several public buildings are located here rather than in Rurrenabaque, including the Parque Nacional Madidi administration office.

Eating and drinking

A large number of **restaurants** have sprung up in Rurrenabaque to cater to the ecotourism boom, with most serving Bolivian dishes along with gringo favourites like pizza and pasta. Local river fish is particularly delicious, especially the succulent *surubi*. Several local places on Calle Comercio serve cheap almuerzos and fried chicken, and there's a good variety of fresh fruit juices available in the **market** on Calle Avaroa.

Café Montacú Av Santa Cruz next to the TAM office. Imaginative vegetarian meals and snacks, along with home-made cakes, fruit salads and excellent coffee (open 8.30am–noon & 5.50–8.30pm; closed Sun & Tues).
Club Social Rurrenabaque Comercio with Av Santa Cruz. Upmarket but good-value establishment, popular among locals, with a massive open-air patio overlooking the river where uniformed waiters serve big portions of meat and fish, as well as several vegetarian options.
La Cabaña Bottom of Av Santa Cruz by the river-bank. Large meat and fish dishes and filling

almuerzos; it's also a great place to drink a cold beer and watch the sunset over the Río Beni.
Pizzeria Italia Comercio with Av Santa Cruz. Imaginative range of pizza, good pasta dishes and plenty of vegetarian options.
Restaurant Heladeria Camila's Av Santa Cruz with Avaroa. Friendly and popular place serving steaks, fish and pizza, as well as good ice cream.
Snack El Surubi Avaroa with Av Santa Cruz. Friendly and good-value little place serving large portions of standard mainstays – beef, fish, pasta and pizza – as well as filling breakfasts and strong coffee.

Around Rurrenabaque

Rurrenabaque is the best place in the Bolivian Amazon to organize a trip into the wilderness, either to the **rainforests** of the Parque Nacional Madidi and the Reserva de Biosfera y Territorio Indígena Pilon Lajas, or into the **pampas** along the Río Yacuma to the north. Deciding which region to visit is tricky, and ideally it's worth visiting both types of terrain. The rainforest comprises by far the richest ecosystem and is undoubtedly more spectacular: few experiences can compare to travelling by motorized canoe up the fast-flowing rivers of the upper Amazon or walking under the emerald vault of the forest canopy. But, though abundant, rainforest wildlife can be elusive, and to see larger animals requires patience, time and a little luck. The pampas, by contrast, are much less scenic, but in the dry season are a much easier place to see animals, particularly cayman, capybaras and pink river dolphins.

Tour agencies in Rurrenabaque

Amazonica Next to the *Hotel Tuichi* on Avaroa. Run by the same family as the Fluvial agency (see below), and offering pretty much the same tours.

Amazonia Adventures Avaroa with Santa Cruz ☏03/8922036. Standard three- to four-day pampas and selva tours, and also good for longer specialist expeditions into Parque Nacional Madidi.

Bala Tours Av Santa Cruz with Comercio ☏03/8922527. Specializes in longer tours into Parque Nacional Madidi.

Flecha Corner of Avaroa and Santa Cruz ☏03/8922476. Popular agency offering standard three- to four-day tours of the pampas and rainforest, as well as longer trips into Parque Nacional Madidi.

Fluvial Next to the *Hotel Tuichi* on Avaroa. The oldest tour operator in Rurrenabaque, with experienced guides and frequent departures to the pampas and selva.

San José Santa Cruz with Avaroa. La Paz-based company now operating trips from Rurrenabaque with very experienced guides, excellent food and the most comfortable campsite on the Río Yacuma.

A growing number of **tour agencies** in Rurrenabaque offer trips to the rainforest and the pampas, generally lasting three nights – this is long enough to see the pampas properly, though to really appreciate the rainforest it's worth taking a longer trip. The tour agencies listed in the box above all have good reputations and offer pretty similar packages, but standards vary over time and guides move between different operators – the best way to choose an agency is to talk to other travellers returning from trips. It's also worth discussing the details before you sign up so you know exactly what you should be getting. Most guides only speak Spanish, but agencies can usually arrange an English-speaking interpreter for larger groups. Prices for all-inclusive trips are fixed by the local authorities at $30 per person per day for the selva, and $35 per person per day for the pampas. **Security** is also an issue. Several sexual assaults on travellers by a guide working with one of the major companies not listed above have been reported and, though the culprit is said to have been jailed, you should still be careful and avoid going on a trip alone or with freelance guides who don't hold an official licence issued by the municipal authorities.

Parque Nacional Madidi

Covering nearly 19,000 square kilometres, **Parque Nacional Madidi** is home to some of the more diverse plant and animal life in South America. In altitude it ranges from less than 300m to over 5500m above sea level , encompassing a variety of Andean and Amazonian ecosystems which ranges from dense tropical rainforests and seasonally flooded savannas to pristine cloudforest and glacial mountain peaks. Virtually undisturbed by permanent human settlement, the park is home to an astonishing variety of wildlife: more than 700 species of animal have been recorded, along with 620 species of bird, although the total may be more like 1000 – more than in the whole of North America; there are also more than 5000 species of flowering plant. Madidi was recognized as a national park in 1995 and, together with the neighbouring Pilon Lajas reserve and Parque Nacional Tambopata-Candamo across the border in Peru, forms a corridor of biodiversity that is generally considered to be one of the twenty-five most critical conservation areas in the world.

The establishment of the national park was bitterly contested by local **logging** companies, and much of the area was illegally stripped of mahogany before demarcation. As well as the direct damage they continue to cause, loggers usually hunt for their supper, with devastating consequences for wildlife; animal populations in the more accessible areas are just beginning to recover. The latest threat to Madidi is the proposal to build a **hydroelectric dam** on the Río Beni, just north of Rurrenabaque, where it bursts through the last ridge of the Andes in a narrow defile. The proposed dam, known as Bala, would flood a huge area of rainforest and displace hundreds of forest dwellers. The dam's electricity output will far exceed Bolivia's future needs and would mainly be exported to Brazil. Critics say the income from export sales would be scant compensation for the resulting loss of biodiversity, and have also raised doubts over the technical viability of the project.

The real wonder of the park is its spectacular scenery and the bewildering complexity of the rainforest ecosystem, and you should treat viewing **wildlife** as a bonus rather than the main purpose of a visit to the park. Having said that, on a standard three- or four-day trip you should see a fair amount of wildlife, including several species of monkey, capybaras, cayman and a kaleidoscopic variety of birds, including brightly coloured toucans, macaws and parrots. If you're lucky you may also see larger animals like the mighty jaguar or the lumbering tapir. Be warned, though, that many species are rare, nocturnal and shy, and the areas of the park most easily accessible by river were logged and hunted until a few years ago.

Practicalities

As yet, you don't have to pay to visit Madidi, but an entrance fee is likely to be introduced to help cover the cost of managing and protecting the park. The park **administration office** is in San Buenaventura, on the opposite bank of the Río Beni from Rurrenabaque. The easiest way to visit Madidi is by taking a tour with an agency from Rurrenabaque. Most run fairly similar trips, travelling up the Río Beni by motorized canoe, camping on the banks of the rivers Tuichi or Hondo, and following trails into the forest. Campsites are pretty basic, with makeshift plastic shelters and mosquito nets, and food (which should be included) is cooked over campfires; the only washing facility is likely to be the river. **Independent travel** to the park is not recommended unless you have plenty of experience of rainforest survival techniques, and even then shouldn't be undertaken lightly – Rurrenabaque's tourist boom was in part inspired by the adventures of **Yossi Ginsberg**, an Israeli traveller who in 1981 tried to reach Rurrenabaque independently from the highlands with his two companions, trekking down through what's now the Parque Nacional Madidi. Lost in the forest and running out of food, the group split up. Ginsberg continued and eventually reached the Río Tuichi, where he was rescued and taken to Rurrenabaque. His two companions were never seen again. Ginsberg's account of the ill-fated expedition, *Back from Tuichi*, became a bestseller in Israel, inspiring many Israeli backpackers to visit the region, while his rescuer founded Rurrenabaque's first rainforest tour company.

If you want to get into the park's really pristine areas you'll need to go on a trip of about a week, travelling on foot or horseback into the more remote regions of the forest around the headwaters of the Río Madidi. Extended trips can be arranged through some of the tour agencies in Rurrenabaque – the daily rate should be less or about the same as for shorter trips – though if you don't already have a group formed it may take some time to get one together. The upper regions of the park can only be reached from the highlands north of La Paz, and even from there are pretty much inaccessible unless you organize a serious expedition.

△ Parrots, the Amazon

Albergue Ecologico Chalalán

The only alternative to an agency tour is to stay at the **Albergue Ecologico Chalalán**, a beautiful ecolodge in the heart of the park beside the Río Tuichi, four to five hours by boat from Rurrenabaque. Chalalán was established with support from international conservation groups in a bid to demonstrate how rainforest conservation can provide sustainable livelihoods for local people who might otherwise turn to logging or other destructive activities, and is owned and managed by the Quechua-Tacana community of **San José de Uchupiamonas**, 25km further up the Tuichi, which is the only settlement of any size inside the park. The lodge overlooks a large lake, teeming with cayman and all manner of water birds (a boat trip with a guide is included in the price of your accommodation), and the surrounding forest is covered by a 25-kilometre network of **trails** which you can explore with local guides from San José. Most speak a little English, and all are knowledgeable about the forest in the way that only those who grew up in it can be, highlighting the many plant species that can be used for food, medicine or building materials.

Accommodation at Chalalán is in comfortable thatched wooden cabins built in a traditional Tacana style, with mosquito netting, comfortable beds and solar-powered lighting, and shared bathrooms with solar-heated showers (further cabins with private bathrooms are under construction). A four-day stay including transport to and from Rurrenabaque costs about $280 per person. The lodge has an office in Rurrenabaque on Calle Avaroa, but it's best to book in advance through America Tours in La Paz (see p.88).

Reserva de Biosfera y Territorio Indígena Pilon Lajas

Just south of Rurrenabaque some four thousand square kilometres of rainforest between the Río Beni and the road south to La Paz are now protected by the **Reserva de Biosfera y Territorio Indígena Pilon Lajas**. Though threatened by loggers and migrant settlers along the road that marks its eastern boundary, the rainforests of Pilon Lajas, like those of Parque Nacional Madidi, are exceptionally biodiverse and survive in a largely pristine state. Pilon Lajas is also home to a small population of indigenous Mosetén, T'simane and Tacana communities, spread out along the length the Río Quiquibey, which runs through the centre of the reserve. In 2001 several of these communities opened the **Albergue Ecologico Mapajo** on the Río Quiquibey, three hours by motorized canoe from Rurrenabaque. Similar in ethos to the Albergue Ecologico Chalalán (see opposite) – but established at a fraction of the cost and with a greater degree of community autonomy – the lodge is administered by Mapajo Ecoturismo Indigena, a company wholly owned by the indigenous communities of the Río Quiquibuey. A two- to four-day visit to the lodge offers excellent opportunities

The mysterious Colonel Fawcett

The forests of the Bolivian Amazon have long attracted adventurers, eccentrics and explorers, but few have matched the exploits of **Colonel Percy Harrison Fawcett**. An officer in the British Indian Army, Fawcett first came to Bolivia in 1906 to survey the unmarked and largely unexplored wilderness frontiers between Bolivia and Peru and Brazil. Over the next nineteen years, he travelled the length and the breath of the Beni, keeping a diary in which he painted a vivid picture of life in the Amazon at the peak of the rubber boom. This was a time when "slavery, vice and bloodshed ruled supreme on the rivers", and during which the indigenous inhabitants – considered "wild and hostile savages" – were "as a rule . . . either shot on sight like dangerous animals or ruthlessly hunted down to be sent as slaves to rubber estates". Meanwhile, in the region's few towns and settlements, a motley cast of renegade Europeans existed "surrounded by brutality and bestial passions, living in unbelievable squalor, isolated by vast distances and impassable swamps". Colonel Fawcett's gift for hyperbole was matched by a penchant for exaggeration. His own adventures involved frequent close encounters with twenty-metre-long anacondas, ferocious cannibal tribes, virulent tropical diseases and brutal and corrupt officials. On one occasion he and a small exploration party found their canoe marooned on a sandbar in the Río Heath and surrounded by heavily armed Guarayos warriors. Realizing that to fight was to be hopeless, Fawcett says he ordered his companions to sing, accompanied by an accordion. After a few verses of "A Bicycle Made for Two", the previously hostile tribesmen were completely pacified.

In other respects a typical product of the British Empire, the longer Fawcett spent in the Amazon, the more he came to love the wilderness and sympathize with its inhabitants. Over the years he became convinced that somewhere hidden deep in the forest stood a magnificent city inhabited by an ancient and highly advanced race of white Indians. Condemned by many of his contemporaries as a mystic and dreamer, in 1925 he set off to find this mythical city in the wilds of the Brazilian Amazon, and was never seen again. Since then, several expeditions have gone in search of the colonel, while rumours concerning his possible end abound – some say he was eaten by cannibals, others that he found his lost city and stayed there, fathering his own tribe of white Indians. The truth behind his disappearance has never been established, however, and his own fate has now become the kind of mystery that so entranced him when he was alive.

for exploring the rainforest and spotting wildlife, as well as the chance to visit the local indigenous communities and see at first hand their unique lifestyle, and the skills that enable them to survive in the rainforest.

With a beautiful setting on a high bluff overlooking the river, the lodge features six comfortable cabins built in traditional indigenous style, with the added luxury of mosquito-screening, balconies with hammocks, and shared bathrooms and showers; there's also an interpretation centre with books and other information. Deeper in the forest are some more rustic **campsites** where you can stay overnight on longer excursions. Inclusive visits to Mapajo with accommodation, food, transport, boat excursions, guided walks and visits to indigenous communities can be arranged through the Mapajo Ecoturismo Indígena office in Rurrenabaque on Calle Comercio with Vaca Diez (☎03/8922317, Ⓦwww.mapajo.com). Prices for these all-inclusive trips had not been set at time of writing, but they're likely to compare very favourably with the Albergue Ecologico Chalalán, and to be competitive with rainforest trips offered by tour companies in Rurrenabaque.

Pampas del Yacuma

Northeast of Rurrenabaque, the dense forests of the Andean foothills quickly give way to the **pampas**: the vast, swampy grasslands that dominate much of the Beni. Though they have been grazed by cattle for hundreds of years, the pampas still support a great deal of wildlife, particularly along the forested banks of the great rivers that meander across them. Tours with the agencies listed in the box on p.336 head into the pampas by motorized canoe along the Río Yacuma from **Santa Rosa**, a small cattle-ranching town about four hours north on the road to Riberalta and Guayaramerín. In the rainy season, the Yacuma bursts its banks and floods great expanses of the surrounding grasslands, causing wildlife to become more dispersed, but in the dry season it's reduced to a narrow river which attracts an amazing abundance of fauna. Sinister black and white **cayman** – some over two metres long – lounge on the muddy banks, slipping quietly into the water as you pass; turtles queue up to sun themselves on logs protruding from the water; groups of **capybara**, the world's largest rodent, watch with apparent indifference as canoes pass right in front of their noses. Most spectacular of all, though, are the **pink freshwater dolphins**, known as *bufeos*, that fish and play in the wide bends of the river. All the wildlife seems largely unconcerned by the passage of motorized canoes, even though the river can get pretty crowded with tour groups. In addition, all manner of **birds** live on the banks of the river, including herons, three different species of kingfisher, elegant roseate spoonbills, massive storks and the clumsy hoatzin.

Away from the river, the pampas itself is not that impressive: a great expanse of swamp and tangled cattle pasture with the occasional lake where your guide will inevitably try to find an anaconda – these can allegedly grow to lengths of up to ten metres and have been known to attack and swallow whole calves and even people. Trudging through a mosquito-infested swamp searching for reptiles isn't everyone's idea of fun, but a trip to the pampas is worth it just for the amount of wildlife you will see on the river. The agencies all have makeshift camps of varying quality along the river, usually with plastic shelters and mosquito nets. In the rainy season (roughly Nov–April) the whole area is flooded and wildlife becomes much more dispersed, while the ferocious mosquitoes offer an additional disincentive, though you can always find someone willing to take you if you're still keen.

Riberalta and around

Now a remote economic backwater, just over a hundred years ago Bolivia's **northern Amazon** frontier was one of the most commercially desirable stretches of territory on earth. The region supports some of the richest natural rubber forests in the whole of the Amazon, and in the late nineteenth century a surge in international demand for rubber generated an unprecedented economic boom. Great fortunes were made by the so-called "rubber barons" who controlled production, but for the indigenous peoples of the Amazon the rubber boom was an unmitigated disaster. They were recruited by force to work in the collection of wild rubber under conditions of appalling brutality, and their population declined catastrophically. Little of the money made was reinvested, and when the boom ended in the early twentieth century with the establishment of rubber plantations in Asia, the region slipped back into the economic torpor which characterizes it today, with collection of wild Brazil nuts – known as *castañas* – the main export industry.

From Rurrenabaque a dirt road continues north across a wide savanna-covered plain towards the Brazilian frontier, more than 500km away. After the cattle-ranching towns of **Reyes** and **Santa Rosa**, settlements are few and far between. The road passes through a sparsely populated and virtually untamed landscape of seasonally flooded grassland dotted with patches of forest and interspersed with swamps. As the road draws near to **Riberalta**, the biggest city in the northern frontier region, the savanna gradually gives way to dense Amazonian rainforest, a carpet of green that stretches almost unbroken across Brazil to the Atlantic ocean. Riberalta itself is the communications hub of the frontier region, a river port at the confluence of the Beni and Madre de Dios rivers – it's at least twelve hours by road from Rurrenabaque when conditions are good in the dry season. East of Riberalta the road continues 100km to the town of **Guayaramerín**, on the banks of the Río Mamoré, which is the main border crossing point if you're heading north into Brazil (see p.342). Just north of Guayaramerín, the settlement of **Cachuela Esperanza** provides a reminder of the wealth and importance this remote region once enjoyed: formerly the headquarters of the biggest of all the Bolivian rubber barons, it's now a semi-abandoned ruin all but swallowed by the forest.

Riberalta

Set on a bluff above a great sweep of the Río Madre de Dios just after its silt-laden waters are joined by those of the Beni, **RIBERALTA** is the second biggest town in the Amazon lowlands, with a population of about 40,000, largely employed in the processing and export of Brazil nuts. Riberalta's economic fortunes never really recovered from the collapse of the rubber boom, and it now has the sleepy feel of a place basking in the memory of past glories – most people like nothing better than to escape the heat of the day by whiling away the hours in a hammock. There's no great reason to stop unless you're heading for Cobija (see p.346) and want to break your journey.

The centre of town the pleasant, tree-lined **Plaza Principal**, surrounded by cafés and ice-cream parlours that are a good place to sit out the heat with a cold drink. Otherwise, it's worth walking down to the riverfront Parque Costanera, where the first and last steamboat to navigate the rivers of the Bolivian Amazon, the *Tahuamanu*, stands mounted in concrete as a monument. Built in Scotland, it entered service in 1899 in time to see action in the Acre War with Brazil.

Practicalities

Buses arrive and depart from the offices of various transport companies scattered around town. Services from La Paz, Trinidad and Rurrenabaque arrive at Flota Guayara (on the corner of Calle Nicolas Suárez and Avenida Republica de Brasil) or Flota Yungueña (a few blocks further east on Republica de Brasil); buses from Guayaramerín terminate at Flota Guayara; and those from Cobija at Flota Guayara or Trans Pando (on Calle Moreno a block west of Avenida Martinez) – all three companies are close to the centre of town, though you can always flag down one of the many **motorbike taxis**, which charge about \$0.50 for short rides. The **airport** is about ten minutes' walk away from the town centre along Avenida Ochoa. LAB and AeroSur both have regular flights to La Paz, Santa Cruz and other towns in the Beni. The AeroSur office (℡03/8522798) is on the Plaza Principal; LAB (℡03/8523129) is a block south along Avenida Martinez. The completion of the road from La Paz has reduced Riberalta's importance as a river port, but you can still find occasional **boats** heading up the Madre de Dios to Puerto Maldonado in Peru: departures are posted on a noticeboard outside the Capitanía del Puerto office on the riverfront. Boats also travel up the Beni to Rurrenabaque when the road is closed during the rainy season (Nov–March).

The **post office** is on the Plaza Principal and the **ENTEL** office is next door. The Banco Mercantil, also on the plaza, will **change dollars** but not travellers' cheques, and nowhere in town will advance cash against a credit card. **Motorcycle hire** is available a block south of the plaza on Avenida Nicolas Suárez for about \$1.60 an hour: hiring a bike and heading off along any of the tracks running out of town into the hinterlands of the surrounding rainforest is one of the few active ways to pass the time here.

The best **place to stay** is the *Hotel Colonial* (℡03/8523018; ❸), just off the plaza on Calle Placido Mendez, which has pleasant rooms set around a cool courtyard garden. The *Hotel Bahia* (℡03/8522606; ❸), on the riverfront three blocks east of Calle Nicolas Suárez, is also comfortable and commands great views over the river. The best budget option is the basic but clean *Hotel Lazo* (℡03/8522352; ❷), a couple of blocks from the plaza on Calle Nicolas Salvatierra, which has cheaper rooms with shared bathrooms. The *Residencial El Pauro* (℡03/8522452; ❷–❸), on the same street a block east of the plaza, is also pretty good, despite its ramshackle exterior. The best value lodgings are at the welcoming *Residencial Reyes* (℡03/8522615; ❷) close to the airport on Avenida Sucre, but it's quite a long way from the centre of town.

There are plenty of **places to eat** on the Plaza Principal: *Snack Tom*, on the southeast corner of the plaza, has decent almuerzos as well as the two Beni stalwarts: beef steaks and river fish. The inevitable *Club Social*, next door, is less popular but also pretty good. There are also a couple of *heladerías* serving ice cream, snacks and juices, and a small pizzeria on the plaza. Away from the plaza on the riverfront Parque Costanera, the *Club Social Nautico* serves good Bolivian food and cheap almuerzos; you can also cool off in the **swimming pool** for \$1.50.

Guayaramerín

Set on the banks of the Río Mamoré some 86km east of Riberalta, **GUA-YARAMERÍN** is the main crossing point on Bolivia's northern border with Brazil, a modern and prosperous frontier town with a distinctly Brazilian flavour and a thriving economy based on duty-free sales. Many of the streets are lined with shops and boutiques selling perfume, electronic goods and designer clothes to the thousands of Brazilian bargain-hunters who flock over the border on shopping trips, though the devaluation of the Brazilian currency in the late 1990s has seen this flow decrease substantially. Most people who make it to Guayaramerín only come here to cross the border to or from Brazil, but even if you're just passing through, a trip out to the semi-abandoned rubber settlement at **Cachuela Esperanza** is a worthwhile diversion.

Practicalities

Buses from Riberalta and beyond arrive at the Terminal de Buses, about 3km from the centre of town along Calle Beni: a **motorbike taxi** from here should cost about $0.50. Everything you might need is concentrated around the Plaza Principal, a few blocks south of the river. The **airport** is just four blocks east of the plaza along Calle 25 de Mayo. For ticket sales, the AeroSur office is on the plaza, and the LAB office is two blocks east on Avenida 25 de Mayo. You can **hire motorcycles** for $1.80 an hour on the plaza – essential if you want to head out to Cachuela Esperanza.

The *Hotel San Carlos*, a block north and east from the Plaza on Avenida 6 de Agosto, changes **travellers' cheques** – the only place in town that does – and also changes dollars and Brazilian *reais*. You can also change cash at the Casa de Cambio on the plaza or with the many street-changers around the port. There are no ATMs in town, but many shops accept credit cards and you may be able to persuade them to give you a cash advance, though don't count on it. The **post office** is on Calle Oruro, three blocks south of the plaza. The **ENTEL** office is on Calle Mamoré, near the corner with Calle Oruro, two blocks north of the plaza.

The railway to nowhere

Guayaramerín is the last navigable point on the **Río Mamoré**, the most important waterway in the Bolivian Amazon. Downstream from Guayaramerín a series of nineteen cataracts and rapids, stretching for over 400km down the ríos Mamoré and Madeira, cuts off the Bolivian river network from Brazil and access to the Atlantic Ocean. During the rubber boom, Bolivians and foreign speculators dreamed of bypassing these rapids and opening up the Bolivian Amazon to trade with the world. In 1872 the US journalist and speculator **George Church** formed a company to build a railway circumventing the rapids. The crews sent to begin the work met with immediate disaster, however. Their boats sank, and ravaged by fever and Indian attacks the workforce abandoned their equipment and fled through the forest. Church's company went bankrupt and the contractors concluded that the region was "a welter of putrefaction where men die like flies. Even with all the money in the world and half its population it is impossible to finish this railway."

Church himself was undeterred, and by 1878 had raised enough financial support to launch another attempt, with equally disastrous consequences. By the time the project was abandoned three years later, five hundred workers had died but only six kilometres of track had been laid. But the dream of a railway around the rapids would not die. In 1903 Brazil promised to complete the project in compensation for the annexation of the Acre territory from Bolivia. Work began again in 1908, and three years later the Madeira–Mamoré Railway – or the **Devil's Railway**, as it had become known – was finally completed. More than six thousand workers are thought to have died in its construction, a sacrifice that was quickly shown to have been made in vain, since the railway opened for business just as the Amazon rubber boom collapsed. The Brazilian government kept it running until 1972, when it was finally abandoned, its rusting rails, swallowed by encroaching jungle, providing an eloquent testimony to a failed dream of progress in the Amazon.

There are several good **accommodation** options in town. The cheapest is the *Hotel Central* (℡03/8553911; ❷) on Avenida Santa Cruz, a block north of the plaza, which has small, basic rooms with shared bathrooms. The *Hotel Litoral* (℡03/8553895; ❷), just east of the plaza on Avenida 25 de Mayo, is a bit more spacious and comfortable. Directly opposite is the similar *Hotel Santa Ana* (℡03/8553900; ❷), with a cool courtyard garden. The most upmarket place is the plush *Hotel San Carlos*, a block north and east from the Plaza on Avenida 6 de Agosto (℡03/8553555 or 8552419; ❺), which has comfortable, air-conditioned rooms and caters mainly to business people. The best **places to eat** are on and around the plaza; the two *heladerías* are good for ice cream, coffee, juices and snacks. The *Club Social* serves reasonably good almuerzos and the Beni staples of steak and river fish, while the *Restaurant Karla Breta*, on Calle Federico Roman, serves fairly good Brazilian food and is popular with Brazilian day-trippers.

Crossing the Brazilian border: Guajará-Mirim

From the port at the bottom of Avenida Federico Roman, regular passenger **boats** (every 15min; $1; $1.40 to return) make the ten-minute crossing to **Guajará-Mirim** in Brazil. The Bolivian **migración** (Mon–Fri 8am–4pm, Sat 8am–noon) is to the right of the port as you face the river: you should get an exit stamp here if you're continuing into Brazil but it's not necessary if you're just making a day-trip across the river. If you need a visa, the **Brazilian Consulate** (Mon–Fri 9am–1pm, 3–5pm) is on the corner of calles Beni and 24 de Septiembre, a block east of the plaza. Note that to enter Brazil here you need to have an international certificate of **yellow fever vaccination**; if you don't there's a clinic beside the immigration office in Guajará-Mirim where you can get vaccinated. From Guajará-Mirim there are frequent buses to Puerto Velho, from where there are connections to other destinations in Brazil.

Cachuela Esperanza

From Guayaramerín a rough dirt road runs 42km northwest to the small town of **CACHUELA ESPERANZA**. Founded in the heart of the wilderness in 1882, Cachuela Esperanza was once the headquarters of **Nicolás Suárez** (see box opposite) and most advanced town in the Bolivian Amazon, with modern offices and homes, state-of-the-art medical facilities, a theatre which attracted international stars, its own narrow gauge railway and a network of roads to accommodate Suárez's fleet of imported limousines. Today Cachuela Esperanza is a dilapidated ghost town, all but swallowed by the encroaching vegetation, but though little remains of the once thriving settlement, there's still enough here to give you an idea of what the place was like in its heyday, and as a monument to failed dreams of progress it has few equals.

The Town

With a spectacular setting overlooking a broad sweep of the Río Madre de Dios, Cachuela Esperanza is nowadays a sleepy little backwater with a population of just a few hundred, but enough buildings remain to give an idea of its former grandeur. Though run down, the sturdy wooden and brick houses built in the early twentieth century are as well put together as anything you'll see in the region today, and are in remarkably good condition given their age and the ravages of heat and humidity – they were built from Canadian pine which was specially imported for its resistance to the insects that otherwise devour wooden structures in the Amazon. Some are now deserted, but other still serve as homes to the few people who continue to live here.

Nicolás Suárez: rubber baron

At the peak of his powers, **Nicolás Suárez** was the absolute ruler over more than six million hectares of rainforest where rubber was collected by a massive workforce of Caripuña Indians who were slaves in all but name. He also controlled the rapids that separated the Bolivian river system from the Amazon proper (charging huge tolls for the transport of cargo around them) and even raised a private army to fight the separatist rebellion of Brazilian settlers in the northern territory of Acre 1899. With the annexation of Acre by Brazil, however, he lost many of his rubber holdings, and after the collapse of the rubber boom a few years later his empire gradually disintegrated. He died in Cachuela Esperanza in 1940, and though virtually forgotten elsewhere in Bolivia, in the Beni and Pando he is still revered by some as a heroic pioneer who brought progress and civilization to the wilderness. Ironically, decades later his great-nephew, **Roberto Suárez**, came to control a similarly powerful empire based on the export of another Amazonian product for which the industrialized world had developed an insatiable appetite – cocaine – amassing in the process a personal fortune so vast that in the 1980s he reputedly offered to pay off Bolivia's entire national debt.

Coming into town along the road from Guayaramerín you pass a small **wooden church** built in 1909 that would look more at home in New England than here in the Amazon. Close by stands the modest stone **tomb of Suárez**, with an inscription praising him as a "heroic patriot and eminent industrial progressive". Just beyond the church on your left is the well-preserved **cinema-theatre** built in the 1930s to entertain Suárez and his army of foreign technicians. On the riverfront a **bust of Suárez** looks out over a fierce set of rapids known as Hell's Cauldron, the first in the series of riverine obstacles that effectively cuts Bolivia off from the Amazon mainstream; close by to the right a broken **monument** commemorates the men who died trying to negotiate these rapids, while along to the left stands a small **steam locomotive** that served the railway Suárez built to circumvent them. Suárez's mansion, known as **Villa Luta** – the "House of Mourning" – occupies the highest point in town, a crumbling shell overgrown with vegetation.

Practicalities

On most days a **truck** runs from to Cachuela Esperanza –ask a motorbike taxi to take you to the *paradero* (truck stop) on the edge of town to catch it – but it's difficult to get there and back on the same day this way. The best plan is to hire a **motorbike**: it's an easy one-hour ride. As this is a border area, you're supposed to carry your passport, and there's a police roadblock on the way out of Guayaramerín where you'll have to register. If you've hired a motorbike and left your passport as a deposit, be sure to bring a photocopy with you. You can stay overnight in Cachuela Esperanza at the pleasant *Hotel Esperanza* (☎03/8552201; ➎) which occupies a restored old building on the riverfront. There are some good **swimming** spots along the river just outside town: the local children can show you where they are.

Cobija and the Pando

The northwestern-most tip of the Bolivia is covered by the department of **Pando**, a remote and sparsely populated rainforest region where logging and the collection of wild rubber and Brazil nuts are the main economic activities. Until recently the Pando was accessible only by boat along the Madre de Dios, Tahuamanu and Orthon rivers, which flow into the region from Peru, but now a rough road cut through the rainforest runs from just south of Riberalta to **Cobija**, the departmental capital, on the Brazilian border. The exciting and unpredictable journey along this road takes you through exuberant rainforest broken only by occasional settlements where the first signs of forest clearance can be seen, with blackened stumps of trees protruding like broken teeth from pale green pasture and scrubby secondary growth. The journey also involves three major river crossings by ferry and takes at least twelve hours when the road is in good condition; in the rainy season (Nov–March) it's often completely impassable.

The forests of this wild frontier region are hotly disputed. The businessmen who control the collection of rubber and Brazil nuts, some of whom are descended from the nineteenth-century rubber barons, claim ownership rights over some 30,000 square kilometres of forest – nearly half the department. But these claims are contested by the indigenous and campesino communities who collect the nuts and rubber – often working under a system of permanent debt so severe it amounts to a disguised form of slavery. These communities are now using land-rights legislation to demand that the forest be recognized as theirs. To complicate things further, a large area of forest is now covered by the recently established **Reserva Nacional Amazónica Manuripi Heath**, which on paper at least has severely restricted the activities of the logging companies. Though it has almost no infrastructure as yet, this reserve can now be visited from Cobija.

The Bolivian government has invested a lot of money in the Pando, building infrastructure to encourage economic development and attract settlers from other parts of Bolivia. This policy is in part aimed at establishing a human frontier to prevent a repeat of what happened across the border in the Brazilian State of Acre (see pp.319 & 363).

Cobija

With a population of just 15,000, **COBIJA** is the smallest departmental capital in Bolivia, an isolated border town with a distinctly Brazilian flavour. Founded in the early twentieth century as a rubber collection centre, the town's economic fortunes now depend more on duty-free sales to Brazil and central government investment in infrastructure. Most of the streets are well paved and the town boasts a modern airport out of all proportion to its needs, but for all that it retains the indolent charm of a half-forgotten tropical outpost. With few obvious attractions and the highest rainfall in Bolivia, it's no surprise that few travellers make it here. But if you do it does offer an adventurous back route into Brazil and even Peru, and the chance to explore a rainforest region where organized tourism has yet to make an impact. Note that, because of its isolation, everything in Cobija is more expensive than elsewhere in the Bolivian Amazon.

Built on hilly ground, the town has an irregular street layout rather than the conventional grid plan of most Bolivian cities. The town's busiest area is around the **central plaza**, close to the **Río Acre**, which forms the border with Brazil. From the plaza the main thoroughfare, **Calle 9 de Febrero**, heads east towards the airport and an intersection with Avenida Internacional, which runs across the river into Brazil.

Practicalities

Buses from Riberalta and beyond arrive at the offices of the three transport companies, Trans Pando, Flota Guayara and Flota Yunqueña, all of which are on Calle 9 de Febrero. If you're arriving from Brazil and heading overland into

Bolivia, you'll have to go first to Riberalta and then get another bus from there, unless you can face the direct bus with Yungueña to La Paz every Sunday, a harrowing 72-hour journey. The modern **airport**, served by LAB, AeroSur and TAM flights from La Paz, Santa Cruz and Trinidad (often via Riberalta and Guayaramerín), is on the outskirts of town to the southeast: a taxi from here to the centre should cost around $2. For ticket sales, the AeroSur office is just off the plaza on Avenida Molina, while LAB is at the far end of the same avenue, and TAM is on Calle 9 de Febrero. The **post office** is on the plaza, while the **ENTEL** office is a couple of blocks away on Calle Sucre. There's **internet** access (Mon–Fri 8am–10pm, Sat & Sun 8am–noon; $1.20 per hour) in the small university building, a block south of the plaza on Calle Cornejo.

There are several **places to stay** in Cobija, though all are relatively expensive compared to elsewhere in the Amazon. The best budget option is the small, basic *Residencial Cobija* (℡03/8422375; **❷**), a block away from the plaza on Calle Ayacucho. The *Residencial Frontera* (℡03/8422740; **❷**), a few doors down, is similar but a bit overpriced; alternatively, try the friendly, family-run *Residencial Cocodrilo* (℡03/8422215; **❸**), around the corner on Avenida Molina – both also have cheaper rooms with shared bathroom. The only decent upmarket option is the *Hotel Avenida* (℡03/8422108; **❸**), on the way out to the airport on Calle 9 de Febrero, which is clean and comfortable, and also has more expensive rooms with air-conditioning.

For a small, remote town, Cobija has some good **places to eat**. The most popular is *El Rincón de la Abuela*, a block away from the plaza on Avenida Molina, which has excellent meat and fish dishes. *Chifa Hong Kong*, opposite, serves reasonable Chinese food, while *El Mesón de la Pascana*, on Calle Ayacucho, offers moderately priced Altiplano favourites like *sajta*. For good breakfasts, strong coffee and delicious Brazilian cakes and pastries try *Panaderia y Confiteria Cobija*, two blocks from the plaza just off Cornejo. *Heladeria Nishi*, on the plaza, is good for ice cream, ice cold fruit juices and ferocious Brazilian *caipirinhas*.

Crossing the Brazilian border: Brasiléia

The Bolivian **immigration office** (open daily 24hr) is on the main border crossing, the international bridge over the Río Acre at the end of Avenida Internacional. A **taxi** from the town centre across the bridge to the federal police office (where you'll need to clear immigration) in the Brazilian town of **Brasiléia** should cost about $4; otherwise it's a twenty-minute walk. You need an international yellow-fever vaccination certificate to enter Brazil here. If you need a visa, the **Brazilian Consulate** (Mon–Fri 8am–1pm) is just off the plaza on Calle Ayacucho. From Brasiléia there are regular buses to **Río Branco**, from where you can get onward connections.

There's also an adventurous route into the Peruvian department of **Madre de Dios** from here. From Brasiléia you can get a bus to Asis Brazil, 95km west on the border with Peru, and cross over to the Peruvian settlement of Iñapari, from where a marginal road heads south to Puerto Maldonado, served by occasional trucks. Alternatively, light aircraft connect Iñapari with Puerto Maldonado when the road is closed. Puerto Maldonado is linked by road and regular flights to Cuzco.

Reserva Nacional Amazónica Manuripi Heath

South of Cobija between the ríos Tahuamanu and Madre de Dios, some 850,000 hectares of lowland Amazon rainforest are now protected, at least on paper, as the

Reserva Nacional Amazónica Manuripi Heath. There's no real tourist infrastructure in the reserve, so you'll need to take all your own food and bedding, but you can get there by truck and stay with the park guards in **San Silvestre**, a small settlement on the Río Manuripi about 111km south of Cobija. There are plenty of trails through the rainforest from here which are used by the *castañeros* during the Brazil nut collecting season (Nov–Feb), and the guards also have canoes with which they patrol the river in search of illegal loggers.

Visiting the park is an adventurous trip through a wilderness area that is also frequently used to smuggle cocaine from Peru to Brazil. Before setting off you need authorization from the **park office** (☎03/8423399) in Cobija, which is on a side street near the football stadium on Calle 9 de Febrero: take the first right after the stadium as you head east, then second left. The staff there will let the park guards know you're coming, and may be able to help you find transport. Trucks head down to San Silvestre (3–4hr; $6) several times a week. From San Silvestre, irregular trucks continue south along the road through the reserve to Chivé on the Río Madre de Dios, where you may be able to catch a lift on a boat heading upstream into Peru or downstream to Riberalta.

Travel details

Buses

Times given are for good road conditions during the dry season; journeys can take twice as long or more after rain, if they're possible at all.

Cobija to: La Paz (1 weekly; 48hr); Riberalta (1–2 daily; 12hr).

Guayaramerín to: La Paz (4–5 weekly; 32hr); Riberalta (6 daily; 2hr); Trinidad (1–2 daily; 30hr).

La Paz to: Cobija (1 weekly; 2 days); Guayaramerín (4–5 weekly; 32hr); Riberalta (1–2 daily; 30hr); Rurrenabaque (1–2 daily; 20hr); San Borja (1 daily; 20hr).

Riberalta to: Cobija (1–2 daily; 12hr); La Paz (1–2 daily; 30hr); Trinidad (5 weekly; 28hr).

Rurrenabaque to: La Paz (1–2 daily; 20hr); Trinidad (4 weekly; 20hr).

San Borja to: La Paz (1 daily; 20hr); Trinidad (daily; 10–12hr); Yucumo (3–4 daily; 2hr).

Santa Cruz to: Trinidad (12 daily; 10–12hr).

San Ignacio de Moxos to: Trinidad (1–2 daily; 3–4hr).

Trinidad to: Guayaramerín (1–2 daily; 30hr); Rurrenabaque (4 weekly; 20hr); San Borja (daily; 10–12hr); San Ignacio de Moxos (1–2 daily; 3–4hr); Santa Cruz (12 daily; 10–12hr).

Boats

Guayaramerín to: Trinidad (2–3 weekly; 5–8 days).

Puerto Villaroel to: Trinidad (2–3 weekly; 5–7 days).

Trinidad to: Guayaramerín (2–3 weekly; 3–7 days); Puerto Villaroel 2–3 weekly; 7 days).

Planes

Cobija to: La Paz (1–2 daily; 1hr 40min); Santa Cruz (5 weekly; 2hr); Trinidad (3 weekly; 1hr 40min).

Guayaramerín to: La Paz (1–2 daily; 1hr); Santa Cruz (1 daily; 2hr); Trinidad (5 weekly; 1hr).

La Paz to: Cobija (1–2 daily; 1hr 40min); Guayaramerín (1–2 daily; 1hr); Riberalta (1–2 daily; 1hr); Rurrenabaque (5 weekly; 40min); Trinidad (1–3 daily; 1hr).

Riberalta to: La Paz (1–2 daily; 1hr); Santa Cruz (5 weekly; 1hr 30min); Trinidad (5 weekly; 1hr).

Rurrenabaque to: La Paz (5 weekly; 40min).

Santa Cruz to: Cobija (5 weekly; 2hr); Guayaramerín (1 daily; 2hr); Trinidad (1–2 daily; 1hr).

Trinidad to: Cobija (3 weekly; 1hr 40min); Guayaramerín (5 weekly; 1hr); La Paz (1–3 daily; 1hr); Riberalta (5 weekly; 1hr); Santa Cruz (1–2 daily; 1hr).

contexts

contexts

A brief history of Bolivia

Bolivia's first inhabitants were descendants of the nomadic hunting groups that migrated into the Americas from Asia during the last Ice Age, between 20,000 and 40,000 years ago. Having crossed the Bering Strait between Siberia and Alaska, when sea levels were lower and a bridge of land and ice linked the two continents, successive generations gradually migrated throughout the Americas, reaching the Andes at least 20,000 years ago, where they lived in semi-nomadic tribes, hunting prehistoric animals like mastodons and giant sloths.

At the end of the Ice Age (around 10,000 years ago) these species became extinct as a result of rapid climate change – though hunting pressure may also have played a part. During the same period, humans began the long, slow transition to an agricultural society based around settled villages, domesticating plants, including maize and potatoes, as well as animals such as llamas and alpacas. By about 2500 BC, agriculture and herding had become the main form of subsistence in the highlands and along the Pacific coast, though in the forested lowlands a semi-nomadic lifestyle combining hunting and fishing with limited cultivation remained the norm. As population density increased and agricultural techniques developed, social organizations grew gradually more complex and governments and ceremonial religious centres began to emerge, along with a specialist class of priests and chiefs. By about 1800 BC, pottery was in widespread use throughout the region, and primitive metal smelting developed soon after – two key technological advances.

Tiwanaku

The first major civilization to develop on the Bolivian Altiplano was the **Tiwanaku** (also spelt Tiahuanaco) culture, centred on the city of the same name which was located on the southern shores of Lago Titicaca. First founded around 1000 BC, by 100 BC Tiwanaku had become an important religious and urban centre with distinct classes of peasants, priests, warriors, artisans and aristocrats, and an economy based on mining, llama and alpaca herding and, above all, the cultivation of potatoes and other crops along the shores of Lago Titicaca, using a sophisticated and highly productive system of raised fields known as **sukakullos** (see p.93). This system produced huge food surpluses, which offered security against poor harvests, freed labour for the construction of monumental religious-ceremonial centres, allowed trade with other societies, and fuelled a dramatic imperial expansion.

From around 700 AD Tiwanaku's influence – as revealed by the presence throughout the region of characteristic pottery and textile styles, decorated with distinctive abstract designs and often featuring serpents and pumas – spread across the Andes, dominating an area comprising much of modern

Bolivia, southern Peru, northeast Argentina and northern Chile. Quite how the influence of Tiwanaku culture spread remains unclear: some experts say it was the result of trade and religious influence; others, that it was through conquest, particularly in the later centuries, when the more militaristic regional centre of Wari–Tiwanaku in the southern Peruvian Andes played a greater role in imperial expansion. The truth probably lies somewhere in between: like all Andean societies, Tiwanaku needed access to products from different ecological zones – potatoes, meat and metal from the Altiplano, maize and peppers from the temperate valleys, coca and hardwoods from the tropical lowlands – so that, as its power grew, direct control of other regions through conquest or colonization probably came to replace trade.

At the height of its power, the city of Tiwanaku was a sophisticated urban-ceremonial complex with a population of over 50,000, lying at the centre of a vast empire of colonies and religious centres linked by paved stone roads served by huge llama caravans. Some time after 1000 AD, however, the Tiwanaku empire collapsed as dramatically as it had risen, its population dispersed and its great cities of stone were abandoned and fell into ruin. The reasons for the empire's sudden downfall remain unclear: possible explanations include a cataclysmic earthquake or foreign invasion, though the most likely is climate change – scientists studying ice cores from Andean glaciers have discovered that, from about 1000 AD, the region suffered a long-term decline in rainfall, suggesting that a prolonged drought may have wiped out the intensive agriculture on which Tiwanaku depended.

The Aymara

The Tiwanaku empire was suceeded by a large number of much smaller regional states. The Altiplano around the shores of Lago Titicaca fell under the control of the **Aymara**, who probably migrated to the region from the highlands to the east sometime after the collapse of Tiwanaku – Aymara territory was subdivided into at least seven militaristic kingdoms, of which the **Lupaca** and **Colla** were probably the largest and most powerful. Aymara society was radically different from that of Tiwanaku: they lived in fortified settlements (*pucaras*) some distance from the lakeshore, relied on large-scale llama and alpaca herding rather than intensive cultivation, and followed a much more localized religion, building few ceremonial sites other than the stone tombs (*chulpas*) where important individuals were buried.

The basic unit of Aymara society was the **ayllu** – an extended kinship group, rather like a clan, each of which was divided into two halves – above which were powerful regional nobles, or **kurakas**, who held land independently from the ayllus over which they ruled; the *kurakas* were in turn subject to a warrior chief or king. Though centred overwhelmingly on the Altiplano, the Aymara maintained colonies in different ecological regions to ensure access to a wider range of produce: in return for meat, wool and potatoes from the highlands these colonies provided fish and salt from the Pacific coast; maize and other crops from the inter-Andean valleys; and coca, fruit and hardwood from the Yungas. As well as major livestock herders, the Aymara were also important producers of gold and silver, which were found in abundance on the Altiplano, making it one of the wealthiest regions in the Andes.

The Incas

By the mid-fifteenth century the Aymara kingdoms found themselves in growing competition with the **Incas**, an expansionist, Quechua-speaking people with their capital at Cusco in southern Peru. Despite their military power, the Aymara kingdoms proved incapable of uniting against this common threat and were gradually incorporated into the Inca empire. Initially, this was a fairly peaceful process: the Incas left the conquered kingdoms intact and did little to alter Aymara society, contenting themselves with extracting tribute. In 1470, however, the main Aymara kingdoms around Lago Titicaca rose in revolt, prompting the Incas to despatch a great army from Cusco to crush the rebellion.

Thereafter, the Incas moved swiftly to reinforce their control of the Altiplano, building roads, storehouses and fortresses, and incorporating the region into their domains as the **Collasuyo**, one of the richest and most populous of the empire's four quarters, or *suyus*. The Aymara rulers were permitted to remain in place, though with a limited degree of autonomy; they were also required to send their young nobles to Cusco both to serve as hostages and to be indoctrinated with the imperial Inca ideology. A different system of government was used in the fertile inter-Andean valleys east of the Altiplano, particularly around Cochabamba, where the Incas established military–agricultural colonies of loyal Quechua-speakers, known as **mitamaqs**. These guaranteed Inca control of this rich and temperate region and protected the southeastern frontier of the empire against raids by semi-nomadic peoples from the Eastern Lowlands, whom they never managed to conquer. Broadly speaking, the ethno-linguistic boundaries established in this period survive to this day. The inter-Andean valleys remain largely Quechua speaking, while Aymara remains dominant in the Altiplano – it's one of few Andean languages to have survived both Inca and Spanish rule, an indication of the strength and resilience of Aymara ethnic identity.

With the conquest of the *Collasuyo* the Incas confirmed their status as the most powerful Andean empire since Tiwanaku, with whom they consciously sought to associate themselves, claiming that their founding ancestor, Manco Capac, had been brought into being on the Isla del Sol in Lago Titicaca, the sacred centre of the Andean world where the sun itself had been created. In the space of a century, the Incas had progressed from being just one of a number of regional groups to becoming masters of the greatest empire yet seen in the Americas – an empire which stretched over five thousand kilometres from southern Colombia to northern Chile, boasted a population of perhaps twenty million, and which was ruled by a god-emperor who claimed direct descent from the sun.

The Inca empire combined authoritarian government with rational and egalitarian social and economic organizations, a unique system that has been described as **theocratic communism**. Though the powerful Inca armies played a key role in the expansion of the empire, many regional groups submitted voluntarily, such were the advantages of Inca rule (and the futility of resistance). Conquered peoples were required to accept the official state religion – which held the sun god Inti to be the supreme deity, and saw the Inca ruler as his direct representative – but beyond that they were allowed to maintain their own religious and cultural practices. Local rulers who surrendered voluntarily were often allowed to remain in place, while the Andean peasantry was left to work the land in return for supplying tribute either in the form of produce (whether food, textiles or other goods) or labour service (*mita*). The enormous food surplus created by this system was stored in a system of imperial warehouses and used to feed standing armies and the ruling Inca elite of priests, administrators and nobles, as well as providing insurance against crop failure and famine for the peasantry themselves. The labour service was used to construct a massive network of roads, to build the monumental palaces and temples that graced Cusco and other major Inca sites, and to construct sophisticated agricultural terracing and irrigation systems that greatly increased food production.

As well as this civil engineering, the genius of the Incas lay in their administrative bureaucracy, which succeeded in controlling the movements of goods and people to an astonishing degree despite having no written language, creating a level of prosperity, well-being and security that the people of the Andes have probably never seen matched before or since. Quite how this great empire would have developed, however, will never be known. Within eighty years of their conquest of the Altiplano, the Inca empire was brought to a catastrophic end by a small band of Spaniards led by Francisco Pizarro, who landed on the coast of northern Peru and set about a war of conquest that would change the Andean world forever.

The Spanish conquest

From the Incas' point of view, the arrival of the first conquistadors in 1532 could not have come at a worse time. Just five years before, the empire had been swept by a devastating epidemic – probably smallpox, introduced from Europe by the Spaniards, which had worked its way down overland from Mexico. Amongst the innumerable victims – almost a third of the population are thought to have died – had been the ruling Inca, **Huayna Capac**. Huayna Capac left his empire divided between two of his sons: his favourite, **Atahualpa**, who had established himself at Quito in the empire's far north, where he commanded the armies that had recently conquered what is now Ecuador, and **Huascar**, the legitimate heir to the throne, who was based in the capital at Cusco. A bloody civil war broke out between the two, from which Atahualpa emerged victorious.

Atahualpa retired to the thermal baths at Cajamarca in northern Peru to savour his victory. It was here that messengers brought him news of the arrival of strange bearded foreigners on the coast nearby. At the first decisive encounter between the two, Pizarro and his 170 followers kidnapped Atahualpa and massacred thousands of his men, demonstrating for the first time their overwhelming military superiority: mounted on horseback (an animal never previously seen in South America), with steel weapons and armour, and backed by terrifying cannon, the Spanish conquistadors were virtually invincible, and even small bands proved capable of defeating massive indigenous armies. Atahualpa was ransomed for a fabulous hoard of gold and silver and then treacherously killed, though not before sending orders for Huascar to be executed. Huascar's faction in Cusco initially welcomed the Spaniards, if not quite as liberators then at least as useful mercenaries who had defeated their enemy just as all seemed lost. With large areas of the Inca Empire only recently conquered and not yet fully assimilated, the Spaniards also found indigenous allies amongst the subject tribes. They occupied Cusco without a fight and installed **Manco Inca** as a puppet emperor.

Following this military success, **Diego de Almagro** led the first Spanish expedition south into the Altiplano, accompanied by Inca allies and reaching as far as present-day Chile. However, in 1537, Spanish abuses in Cusco and the realization that they were bent on permanent conquest prompted a massive

Inca rebellion led by Manco Inca himself, forcing the various Aymara groups of the Altiplano to choose sides. The Colla backed the Spanish, causing them to be attacked by Inca armies and the neighbouring Lupaca. A year later, with the Inca siege of Cusco broken and Manco all but defeated, Pizarro sent a force led by his brothers south to aid the Colla. After a series of bloody battles, the military conquest of the *Collasuyo* – which the Spanish referred to variously as Charcas, the Collao or, most commonly, **Alto Peru** – was swiftly completed.

The first Spanish city founded in Alto Peru was **La Plata** (or Chuquisaca, now Sucre), strategically located in a temperate valley southeast of the Altiplano. With its dense indigenous population and rich mineral wealth – the two resources that the conquistadors were keenest to exploit – Alto Peru offered a rich prize, though initial efforts to consolidate control of the region were delayed by an outbreak of fighting between rival Spanish factions, an episode in which more Spaniards were killed than in all the fighting with the Incas. The full extent of the region's potential became apparent in 1545, when the continent's richest deposit of silver was discovered southwest of La Plata at what became known as **Cerro Rico** (Rich Mountain). The mining city of **Potosí** that sprung up at the foot of this mountain of silver quickly became the centre of the colonial economy and the source from which vast wealth flowed out of South America to the Spanish crown. A second city, **La Paz**, was founded in 1548 just east of Lago Titicaca to reinforce control of the densely populated northern Altiplano and to secure the route between Potosí and Lima, the centre of Spanish power on the Pacific coast of Peru. Further cities at **Cochabamba** and **Tarija** (both 1574) followed, strategically located in the well-populated, fertile and temperate inter-Andean valleys, where maize and crops introduced from Europe, like wheat, could be grown to supply food to the mines of Potosí. La Plata was confirmed as the **capital of Alto Peru** in 1558, when it was made the seat of an independent royal court and administration – the Audiencia de Charcas – with judicial and executive power over the entire region. This status was enhanced by the creation of an archbishopric in 1609, while in 1624 a Jesuit university was established in order to train the religious and administrative specialists needed to govern the conquered territories.

Like the Incas before them, the Spanish were initially only able to establish control over the settled peasant populations of the highlands; the semi-nomadic peoples of the Amazon lowlands and eastern plains remained unconquered despite numerous military expeditions. In 1561 the city of **Santa Cruz de la Sierra** was founded in the midst of the Eastern Lowlands by a group of conquistadors who had marched across from Paraguay, the centre of Spanish power on the Atlantic side of South America, with the aim of reaching the silver of the Andes and establishing a strategic link across the continent, but the new settlement remained an isolated and precarious outpost surrounded by hostile indigenous groups. The most resilient of these were the Guaraní-speaking **Chiriguano** tribes of the Chaco, who posed a constant menace to the Spanish, and were only finally conquered in the late nineteenth century.

Colonial society

Initially, the Spanish sought to continue the Inca pattern of control through indirect rule. Colonial society was conceived of as consisting of two separate communities, the Spanish and the *Republica de Indios*, with the latter clearly subject to the former. A class of indigenous nobles – known as *kurakas* or *caciques* – was left in place to act as intermediaries between the Spanish and the mass of Aymara and Quechua-speaking peasants, who were permitted to remain in control of their land in return for tribute in the form of crops, animals, textiles and labour service. These peasants were administered through the exploitative **encomienda** system, whereby individual conquistadors were granted control of the tribute paid by large indigenous groups in return for taking charge of converting them to Catholicism and generally "civilizing" them – the standard moral justification for the Spanish conquest.

Though most Spanish *encomenderos* were more concerned with extracting as much wealth as they could from their indigenous subjects than with saving their souls, the need for a spiritual conquest to reinforce the already achieved military conquest was taken seriously by the Spanish crown, which sponsored all the major religious orders – above all the Franciscans, Dominicans and Jesuits – to undertake the conversion of the Aymara and Quechua masses. Inca religious ceremonies, pilgrimages and public rituals were banned, and a great number of idols and ceremonial sites destroyed in a campaign known as the **extirpation of idolatory**. Beneath the surface, however, their mystical and magical appeal endured and, while publicly accepting Christianity, the indigenous population preserved its own deep-rooted pre-Inca cults. With time, elements of Catholicism and traditional indigenous beliefs intermingled, as the Aymara and Quechua appropriated the symbolism of the Christian faith, turning it into a vehicle for their own religious expression.

The religious orders were also employed as a cheap means of pacifying the tribes of the **northern and eastern lowlands**, who had resisted conquest despite repeated military incursions. Small groups of dedicated missionaries had considerable success in drawing semi-nomadic groups into settled agricultural communities, where they were converted to Catholicism and enjoyed the mixed benefits of Spanish civilization – as well as, most importantly, being protected from the ravages of the conquistadors. However, the regime of forced labour and the constant epidemics that swept the settlements meant that many groups later abandoned or rebelled against the mission regimes, and many missionary priests met violent deaths. Missionary efforts reached their apogee in the seventeenth and eighteenth centuries in the **Jesuit missions** of Moxos and Chiquitos, where a handful of priests established a utopian and semi-autonomous society – a kind of theocratic socialism where thousands of indigenous people successfully adopted European agricultural techniques and built flourishing mission communities graced by some of the finest churches in all the Americas.

In the highlands, it didn't take long for the strict boundaries the Spaniards erected between themselves and the indigenous majority to break down. The conquistadors were overwhelmingly men, and most quickly took indigenous wives and concubines, so that within a few decades they were surrounded by an ever-increasing number of mixed-race children – known as **mestizos** or **cholos**. A complex system of class and caste developed, with Spanish-born **peninsulares** at the top, followed by Spaniards born in the Americas, the so-called **criollos**. The middle orders comprised a range of different mestizo classes, while at the bottom were to be found the oppressed indigenous majority.

The initial colonial settlement was undermined by the catastrophic decline in the indigenous population caused by European epidemics and diseases, as well as by the harsh burden of the *encomienda* system. With the indigenous tribute base falling each year and the supply of labour for the mines in decline, and fearing that the *encomenderos* were becoming over-powerful, in the 1570s the representative of the Spanish king in Peru, the Viceroy **Francisco Toledo**, launched a major reform of the empire's social and economic structures. The *encomiendas* were gradually phased out, and the indigenous peasant population was moved into large communities and towns known as *reducciones*, where tribute payments direct to the crown could be more easily assessed and collected. To solve the problem of labour shortage in the mines of Potosí, Toledo revived and adapted the Inca system of labour service, the **mita**. Under this regime, an area stretching from Cusco to northern Argentina was divided into sixteen districts, each of which was obliged to send one-seventh of its male population to the mines each year, providing an annual workforce of about 13,500 men – known as *mitayos* – at almost no cost to the mine owners. A series of other reforms introduced by Toledo further boosted silver output, while he also established a royal mint in which all silver mined in Potosí was turned into coins or ingots, thereby ensuring the Crown received its share of mining revenues. These reforms launched a century-long boom that turned Potosí into one of the biggest cities in the world and the single most important source of wealth in the Spanish empire. The regional economy revolved around supplying the needs of Potosí, while the city's silver also had a global impact, funding Spanish wars, fuelling long-term inflation and economic growth in Europe, and even financing emerging trade relations between Europe and Asia.

For the indigenous population, however, the *mita* labour system was a disaster. Of the thousands of *mitayos* who went to the mines each year only a few ever returned to their home communities: during three centuries of colonial rule, up to nine million indigenous workers and African slaves are thought to have died working in the mines – a major factor in the demographic collapse of the Andean indigenous populations. As only original members of landowning indigenous communities were subject to *mita* service and tribute payment, many left the communities to become landless wage labourers in other mining areas or on **haciendas**, the large, Spanish-owned farms that gradually took over much of the declining indigenous communities' agricultural lands.

The Great Rebellion

Unsurprisingly, indigenous discontent with Spanish rule remained strong throughout the colonial period, manifesting itself in frequent uprisings. Generally, these revolts tended to be local in nature and in response to specific abuses by particular officials, rather than wide-scale rebellions against colonial rule, and were usually crushed by the authorities with ease. In 1780–82, however, the Andes were swept by a massive indigenous rebellion that shook the Spanish colonial regime to its foundations. Encompassing the southern Peruvian highlands and all of Alto Peru, this so-called **Great Rebellion** was in part provoked by the **Bourbon reforms**, a tightening of the tribute system aimed at centralizing administration and boosting royal revenues, which had declined substantially during a long period of economic depression (caused by a decline in silver production) in the late seventeenth and early eighteenth centuries. A particular grievance was the hated *reparto de mercancías*, implemented in 1754, whereby the *corregidores* (royal officials responsible for tax collection) were able to force indigenous subjects to buy shoddy manufactured goods at inflated prices.

Above all, though, the rebellion was inspired by the messianic Andean belief that a reincarnated **Inca king** would return to drive the Spanish from the Andes and re-establish a just and equitable society. The leading figure in the uprising was José Gabriel Condorcanqui, an indigenous *kuraka* from the mountains south of Cusco who in November 1780 declared himself the direct descendant of the last ruling Inca (Túpac Amaru, who had been executed by Viceroy Toledo in 1572) and rightful Inca king of Peru, adopting the name **Túpac Amaru II**. Raising a large indigenous army and slaughtering a Spanish force sent to arrest them, Túpac Amaru and his supporters seized control of most of the southern Peruvian highlands and laid siege to the city of Cusco for several months. Though Túpac Amaru himself was captured and killed by royal forces after the siege was broken, his nephews – all of whom also took the name Túpac Amaru – continued the rebellion in the south around Lago Titicaca. Here, they formed an uneasy alliance with Aymara forces led by the radical Julian Apaza, a commoner rather than a *kuraka*, who adopted the name **Túpac Katari** (*amaru* and *katari* are the Quechua and Aymara words meaning serpent – a symbolic reference to the mythic underworld where the Inca king was believed to be waiting to return).

Though they joined forces to lay siege to La Paz, however, the two movements were deeply suspicious of each other, and fatally divided by ideology and factionalism. While the moderate Túpac Amarus sought to form a broad-based, multi-ethnic rebel coalition – including mestizos and even white *criollos* – Túpac Katari and the *Katarista* leaders were extreme Aymara nationalists intent on killing all whites and erasing all aspects of Spanish rule. So confused was the mix of messianic ideologies behind the rebellion that some leaders claimed the Catholic church and the king of Spain himself had ordered them to kill all the Spaniards in Peru. Several powerful indigenous *kurakas* rejected the revolutionary message altogether and sided against the rebels, leading large indigenous forces to fight on the Spanish side. The war was characterized throughout by great brutality on both sides, with massive destruction of property and loss of life: in two years of fighting about 100,000 people were killed – perhaps a twelfth of the total population.

In October 1781, La Paz was relieved by a royalist army which had marched up from Argentina. The Túpac Amaru leaders surrendered to the Spanish in return for pardons or exile, while Túpac Katari – perhaps betrayed by his erstwhile allies – was captured and executed, his body torn to pieces by horses. By early 1782, the rebellion had been comprehensively crushed, while the remaining *kurakas* were removed from office and their property confiscated, completing the destruction of the indigenous nobility. Thus ended the last major indigenous uprising against Spanish rule in the Andes. The next great rebellion, when it came, was motivated by very different ideas and led by white *criollos* rather than would-be Inca kings.

The Independence War

By the early nineteenth century, growing discontent with Spanish rule had spread amongst the white *criollo* and mestizo population of Alto Peru, the result of severe economic depression, their exclusion from high-level administrative jobs (which were reserved for Spanish-born immigrants), and regulations preventing trade with any country other than Spain. At the same time the powerful ideas of the French Revolution and the Enlightenment, as well as the example of the successful revolt in North America, made independence from Spain seem a much more realistic prospect. However, the traumatic experience of the Great Rebellion had left whites and mestizos alike with an abiding fear of disorder and indigenous revolt, and the Spanish imperial bureaucracy was more than capable of putting down any local pro-independence revolts, so it wasn't until the sudden collapse of the government in Spain following Napoleon's invasion in 1808 that the impetus for revolutionary change arrived.

With Napoleon's brother Joseph crowned king, a radical "Junta Central" claiming to rule on in the name of the abdicated Fernando VII, and others supporting the claim to the throne of Fernando's sister Carlota, the elite classes throughout the Spanish empire were confronted with conflicting loyalties. Surprisingly, it was in Alto Peru that the first moves towards open revolt against Spanish rule took place. On May 25, 1809, the judges of the Audiencia de Charcas in La Plata rejected the demands of the president of Audiencia that they recognize the authority of the Junta Central, arguing that the colonies owed loyalty to the person of the king (now abdicated) rather than to Spain. In July, the citizens of La Paz went a step further, declaring an independent government – the first declaration of independence by a Spanish colony in America. These revolts were quickly crushed by armies sent by the viceroys in Lima and Buenos Aires, but this only fuelled the growing *criollo* enthusiasm for independence. Though Spain controlled the main cities, pro-independence guerrilla forces quickly established control of six rural areas that became known as **Republiquetas** – little republics.

In May 1810, the citizens of Buenos Aires successfully rebelled against Spain, and the same year sent an army to drive the Spanish from Alto Peru. Supported by the *Republiquetas* and revolts in several cities, the Argentine army liberated the whole region before being routed by a Spanish army sent from Cusco. Over the next seven years three further Argentine armies were sent to Alto Peru, but each failed to drive Spanish forces permanently from the region. Most major cities changed hands and were sacked several times, with the retreating Argentine armies showing the same contempt for local citizens as the Spanish. The forces unleashed by the independence struggle proved difficult to control, as both sides came to rely more and more on arming the indigenous population to provide troops, which led to growing violence and social conflict in rural areas.

Though it was the first region in South America to declare independence from Spain, Alto Peru was the last to achieve it. From 1817 until 1823 it remained relatively quiescent under Spanish control while the great events of the independence war took place elsewhere. In 1817 the Argentine General **José de San Martín** crossed the Andes to liberate Chile, and by 1821 the great Venezuelan independence leader **Simón Bolívar** – known as *El Libertador*, "The Liberator" – was advancing south through Ecuador having finally liberated Venezuela and Colombia. The two forces converged on Peru, the last major centre of Spanish power. Lima was occupied and, in 1824, Bolívar's most brilliant general, **Antonio José de Sucre**, destroyed the last Spanish army at the battle of Ayacucho in the southern Peruvian Andes, securing Alto Peru's freedom early the following year.

Despite its new freedom, the fate of Alto Peru remained uncertain. Bolívar himself initially opposed the creation of an independent state there, and handed control of the region over to Sucre. In 1825, Sucre called a constituent assembly in the city that would later be renamed in his honour. The delegates unanimously rejected union with either Peru or Argentina, and on August 6 adopted a **declaration of independence**. Five days later they resolved to name the new republic **Bolivia**, rightly guessing that Bolívar would be less likely to obstruct the independence of a country named in his own honour.

The early republic

The new **Republic of Bolivia** faced enormous problems from the outset. Sixteen years of war had devastated the country's infrastructure and severely disrupted the economy, while the mining industry in particular was in sharp decline thanks to scarcity of labour and the destruction, flooding, and abandonment of mines that had taken place during the Independence War. Nor did independence change much for the vast majority of the population – the indigenous Aymara and Quechua campesinos of the highlands – who remained excluded from power, which was exercised by a narrow ruling elite of mostly white *criollo* soldiers, merchants and landowners. Though the *mita* system had been abolished by Bolívar (and no subsequent government dared reintroduce it), the head tax levied on indigenous community members was maintained, generating over half of all government income.

The country's first president, General Sucre, sought to organize the Bolivian state along classic liberal lines, but his efforts to introduce a modern tax system were frustrated by the lack of a trained bureaucracy, while his attempts to attract foreign capital to revitalize the mining industry remained largely ineffective. His one major success was his radical attack on the Catholic Church, which had largely sided with the royalist cause during the Independence War – Sucre's response was to confiscate most of its wealth and property, a revolutionary act from which the Bolivian church never really recovered. After surviving a coup and assassination attempt by former comrades in arms, he left office in 1829 and went into voluntary exile (and was assassinated a year later in Ecuador).

Sucre's liberal and reformist policies were maintained by his successor, the La Paz-born **General Andrés de Santa Cruz**, who had also served with distinction under Bolívar in the Independence War. An able administrator, during his ten-year rule Santa Cruz created a relatively stable political and economic order, systemizing local administration and introducing modern law codes. Though he ruled as a dictator, he kept bloodshed to a minimum by contemporary standards, and remained widely popular amongst the *criollo* elites, despite being unable to revitalize the economy. His downfall followed his involvement in politics in neighbouring Peru, where he had served Bolívar briefly as president in 1826–27. In 1835 he intervened decisively in a civil war in Peru, defeating his arch rival, Peruvian General **Agustín Gamarra**, and naming himself protector. He then sought to join Bolivia and Peru together in a confederation, a move seen as a threat by Chile, which sent aid to rebels and then an entire army to Peru. In 1839, Santa Cruz was finally defeated at the battle of Yunguyo and went into exile, and the Peru–Bolivia confederation was dissolved.

The honour in which Santa Cruz is still held in Bolivia owes much to the nature of the presidents who followed him. For the next forty years the country was characterized by political chaos, presided over by a series of military strongmen, or *caudillos*, many of whom lasted less than a year before being ousted by an equally ruthless and ambitious colleague. General **José Ballivián** (1841–47) defeated General Gamarra at the battle of Ingavi, ending the entanglement of Peru and Bolivia's affairs. He also reduced the size of the army (though it still consumed over half the national budget) and established the department of the Beni, sending military colonies to the Amazon lowland region where *Cinchona* bark – from which the malaria medicine quinine is extracted – emerged as a major export. General **Manuel Isidoro Belzu** (1848–55), who took power a year after Ballivián was overthrown, was a populist demagogue who appealed to the indigenous masses with his fierce attacks on the land-owning elites and protectionist economic policies. After surviving over forty coup attempts in just seven years, he had the dignity to hand over power peacefully in 1855 in Bolivia's first legal elections (although only 13,000 people were allowed to vote in them) and went into exile, though he later conspired unsuccessfully to return to power.

Bolivia's first civilian president was **José María Linares** (1857–61), though even he assumed dictatorial powers. Linares changed the course of economic policy, reducing tariffs and opening the country to free trade and foreign investment, but was unable to control the military and was ousted within four years and replaced by **General José María Achá** (1861–64). In terms of its repression of opponents, Achá's regime was the most violent of all Bolivia's nineteenth-century governments: in one notorious incident in 1861, some seventy supporters of the exiled former president Belzu were massacred in La Paz. However, even Achá's notoriety was exceeded by that of his successor, **General Mariano Melgarejo** (1864–71), the archetypal Bolivian *caudillo*, famous for his violence, drunkenness, womanizing and corruption – as well as for signing away a vast area of the Amazon lowlands and Pacific coast to Brazil and Chile. Melgarejo also launched a sustained attack on the land holdings of free indigenous communities in the highlands, demanding that they purchase individual titles for land they already owned collectively or have it confiscated by the state. This scheme was largely blocked by massive and violent protests across the highlands – throughout this period indigenous political participation was largely limited to defending their lands and resisting new taxes – but the same approach was used later in the century to break the power of the indigenous communities. Though his hold on power proved resilient – in 1865 he defeated a coup attempt by Belzu by personally shooting the former president dead – he was overthrown in 1871 and died a year later in Lima, murdered by the brother of his mistress.

Surprisingly, the endless succession of military coups, plots and revolts that characterized the early decades of the republic caused little disruption to the social and economic life of Bolivia: politics was an elite pursuit, and the conflicts were usually limited to a few hundred men on either side. During the middle of the century, the nation's economy actually began to improve thanks to a revival in the **silver-mining** industry, the result of the availability of cheaper mercury, more effective steam-powered machinery and fresh investment by a wealthy new class of merchants and *hacienda*-owners. From 1870 onwards the growth of Bolivian silver production was phenomenal, and an influential new class of mine owners emerged, though initially their power was not reflected on the political stage.

The War of the Pacific and the age of silver

As well as silver exports, economic growth in the second half of the nineteenth century was also spurred by the export of guano and nitrates (both used as fertilizer) found on Bolivia's desert coastal strip. This lucrative industry was controlled by British and Chilean companies – desperate for revenue, Bolivia had sold off the rights to the nitrates cheaply and guaranteed freedom from tax increases. In 1878, president Hilarión Daza, the latest military *caudillo*, increased export taxes, ignoring protests by Chilean and British companies and offering Chile the excuse it had been waiting for to pursue longstanding expansionist aims. Early the next year Chilean forces began the **War of the Pacific**, occupying the entire Bolivian coastline – where the population was in any case already two-thirds Chilean – and then invading Peru, which was allied to Bolivia. Bolivian forces sent to fight alongside the Peruvians were easily defeated, and Bolivia watched helplessly as its coastline was annexed and its ally Peru defeated and occupied. Though Bolivia officially ceded the territory to Chile in 1904, the loss of the coast – and with it direct access to the outside world – was seen as a national tragedy. Ever since, Bolivian politicians of all hues have invoked the loss of the sea as a means of cementing national identity – even today, government radio adverts (read against a backdrop of crashing waves) solemnly announce: "Bolivian, the sea is yours, to recover it is your duty."

The War of the Pacific proved a turning point in Bolivian history. Having witnessed an incompetent military regime stumble into a conflict that disrupted their exports and damaged relations with Chilean investors, the new silver-mining elite realized that a stable and financially sound government was vital to their long-term interests. The mining entrepreneurs formed a new party, the **Partido Conservador**, to pursue their aims of a civilian presidency and a powerful congress. For the next nineteen years the silver-mining conservative oligarchy ruled Bolivia through the Partido Conservador. They were opposed by the **Partido Liberal**, initially formed by those opposed to an early settlement with Chile, but otherwise differing little in ideology. Between 1880 and 1936, the parliamentary system worked fairly well, despite the limited nature of the electorate (a tiny handful of men of sufficient income and literacy) and the fact that neither party was ever prepared to relinquish the presidency when voted out of office, ensuring that limited violence remained a feature of Bolivian political life.

The highpoint of conservative rule came during the presidency of **Aniceto Arce** (1888–92), one of the country's biggest silver-mine owners, who carried out a massive road-construction programme and completed the railway from La Paz to the Chilean port of Antofagasta, Bolivia's first rail link to the sea and thus a vital route for mining exports. The expansion of the mining industry and transport infrastructure had a strong impact on rural Bolivia. The growing demand for food in the mining centres of Potosí and Oruro stimulated the expansion of the **hacienda system** at the expense of the free indigenous communities, with *hacienda*-owners acquiring indigenous land through purchase, fraud or outright force – often leading to local uprisings which had to be put down by the army. Though some communities maintained their traditional social and political structure as *hacienda ayllus*, working as serfs on the *haciendas* in return for small plots which they were allowed to cultivate independently, many others broke down, and migration to the cities and mining centres increased.

The late nineteenth century also saw the explosion of the **rubber boom** in the Amazon lowlands. The massive increase in the international demand for rubber – used to make car tyres, and in hundreds of other industrial applications – transformed the remote rainforests of northern Bolivia into some of the most valuable real estate in the world, and the region was quickly overrun by **rubber barons**, who gained control over huge areas of the rainforest, making immense fortunes and forcing the previously unconquered tribes of the region to work as virtual slaves collecting wild rubber. The indigenous population declined catastrophically and was saved from total destruction only by the end of the Bolivian rubber boom in the early twentieth century, after rubber plantations had been successfully established by the British and Dutch in their Asian colonies, where production costs were much lower. One consequence of the rubber boom was the occupation of the richest rubber-producing area along the Río Acre by Brazilian rubber-tappers. When the Bolivian government sought to tax their production they rebelled, declaring the Acre an independent state in 1900. After three years of sporadic fighting – the **Acre War** – the region was annexed by Brazil, an act later recognized by Bolivia in return for compensation.

The Federal Revolution and the rise of tin

The dependence on mining exports made Bolivia increasingly subject to international economic forces, and towards the end of the nineteenth century the international price of silver collapsed, breaking the power of the conservative silver-mining oligarchy. Fortunately for Bolivia, this collapse coincided with a growing global demand for **tin**, a formerly unimportant by-product of the country's silver mines. A tin boom ensued, centred on the mines around Oruro and led by a new class of Bolivian entrepreneurs who replaced the traditional silver-mining elite.

This change in the focus of economic power was soon reflected in Bolivian politics. The new tin-mining elite and the growing urban professional classes of La Paz (the main service centre for the tin mines) increasingly backed the Partido Liberal. Frustrated by the impossibility of taking power through peaceful means – election results were always rigged – they moved to overthrow the conservative regime. In 1898 a revolt broke out after the conservative government in Sucre rejected the demands of liberals in La Paz for local federalist rule, whilst a major Aymara uprising erupted simultaneously in the Altiplano against the continued despoliation of indigenous lands. Breaking the traditional rules of elite politics, the liberal leader **José Manuel Pando** sought an alliance with the Aymara rebel leader **Pablo Zárate Willka**, no doubt promising to protect indigenous lands in exchange for support against the conservatives. With the help of thousands of Aymara, Pando defeated the conservatives in bloody fighting in 1899 and took power in what became known as the **Federal Revolution**. No sooner was this achieved, however, than Pando reneged on his promises and turned against his Aymara allies, crushing the uprising and executing or imprisoning its leaders. Nor did Pando's federalism last: once in power, the Liberals simply made La Paz the seat of an equally centralized government (though Sucre remained the capital in name).

The Federal Revolution ensured the political supremacy of the new tin-mining elite, but rather than govern themselves they chose to rule indirectly through a class of professional politicians (most of them lawyers), a system that became known as **La Rosca** – The Screw. Their dominance was such that, between 1899 and 1920, there was not a single coup attempt. In other respects, however, politics remained much the same as under conservative rule: voting was restricted to a small elite of whites and wealthy mestizos, with the indigenous majority completely excluded; a liberal economic policy with low taxes was maintained for the benefit of the tin-mining entrepreneurs and major landowners; and the assault on indigenous landholdings continued.

Perhaps surprisingly, given that there were no restrictions on foreign investment in the mines, tin-mining came to be dominated by home-grown capitalists, above all by three **tin barons** – Simón I. Patiño, Mauricio Hochschild and Carlos Aramayo – who between them owned most of Bolivia's mines. But when world demand for tin slumped in 1913–14, opposition within the Partido Liberal grew, leading to the formation of a splinter **Partido Republicano**. In 1920 the Republicans, led by **Daniel Salamanca** and **Bautista Saavedra**, seized power. Their new government quickly found itself under pressure, however: a major Aymara uprising erupted on the Altiplano, while the mostly indigenous miners had begun to organize trade unions to push for better conditions. The first **general strike** was staged in 1922, and a year later the army carried out the first of many massacres of striking miners at the Uncía mine near Oruro.

As the 1920s progressed, the increasingly factional Republicans faced economic decline and growing social unrest in both the mines and the countryside. The international price of tin fell, and the government found it difficult to make payments on its huge foreign loans. Tin production peaked in 1929, and then plummeted as the **Great Depression** struck Bolivia's economy with a vengeance. Massive job losses further fuelled labour unrest, while strikes and military intervention in the mines became ever more frequent.

The Chaco War

By 1931 the government, led by Salamanca, was confronted by widespread opposition and deepening economic crisis, a situation to which it responded by stepping up its oppression of trade unions and the opposition and increasing its military spending. At the same time, the Bolivian army began aggressively probing the disputed frontier with Paraguay in the thorny wilderness of the Chaco. Border clashes escalated and, by July 1932, the **Chaco War** had broken out. Though many Bolivians afterwards came to believe the conflict had been provoked by foreign oil companies anxious to exploit deposits in the Chaco (they later turned out not to exist), in fact it's now clear that Salamanca himself deliberately started the war despite the opposition of his generals, perhaps thinking that a quick victory would improve his political standing.

It was a disastrous mistake. Over the next two years the Bolivian army was smashed and driven out of all the disputed territory with terrible loss of life. Late in 1934 the army arrested Salamanca and forced him to resign; early the next year Major **Germán Busch** successfully defended Villamontes, ending the Paraguayan advance, and both sides sued for peace. For Bolivia, the war was an unparalleled tragedy. Some 65,000 soldiers, mostly indigenous conscripts, had died out of a population of around two million – losses equivalent to those suffered by the European nations in World War I. Known as the "Chaco Generation", many Bolivians of all classes emerged from the war appalled by the corruption and incompetence of the high command and deeply critical of the traditional political system. The country became increasingly open to radical left-wing ideas, and the old political parties faded in importance.

These ideas also affected the army. In 1936 a group of young officers who had served in the Chaco, led by David Toro and Germán Busch, seized power, establishing a radical "military socialist" regime clearly influenced by European fascism. In an unprecedented step, the next year the government nationalized without compensation the holdings of the US Standard Oil company, which had illegally sold Bolivian oil to Paraguay via Argentina during the war while claiming it couldn't produce enough for Bolivia. In alliance with a range of left-wing parties, the military regime drew up a new constitution committing the state to much greater social and economic intervention, but these radical initiatives ended in 1939 when Busch committed suicide. A more conservative military regime close to the tin barons followed, but the growth of radical ideas in the post-war period meant that any return to the pre-war consensus was increasingly impossible.

The road to revolution

The most important of the many new political parties that emerged in the period following the Chaco War was the **Movimiento Nacionalista Revolucionario** (MNR), which advocated nationalization of the mines, though its pro-Nazi stance led to some of its leaders being jailed on accusations of plotting a fascist coup (using fabricated evidence supplied by the US, whose war effort depended on Bolivian tin exports). Together with other left-wing groups, it quickly came to dominate the national congress, as the middle-class electorate grew increasingly radicalized. Meanwhile, the trade union movement was also growing more extreme in its demands and began to stage frequent strikes: one of these, at the massive Patiño-owned **Catavi** tin-mining complex, was brutally put down by the army in 1942, a notorious massacre that became a rallying cry for the left.

In 1943, in alliance with a small cabal of radical army officers known as **Razon de Patria**, the MNR seized power. The new regime, with the previously unknown **Major Gualberto Villaroel** as president, supported the labour movement and sought to involve the indigenous masses more fully in national politics. In 1944 the mineworkers formed the **Federación Sindical de Trabajadores Mineros de Bolivia** (FSTMB; Federated Union of Mineworkers of Bolivia), which immediately took over leadership of the labour movement and gave important support to the MNR – over the following decades it proved one of the most powerful and revolutionary political forces in the country. In 1945 the government sponsored the first National Indigenous Congress and also banned the hated labour service obligation (known as *pongueaje*) required of indigenous communities on *hacienda* lands (though this decree was never enforced). These populist measures were accompanied by the vicious suppression of any opposition, however – when the Marxist Partido de la Izquierda Revolucionaria did well in elections in 1944, the government assassinated its leaders and jailed its members, while the same happened to the traditional parties in 1945. The use of violence against middle-class politicians outraged public opinion, and in 1946 Villaroel was hanged by a civilian mob from a lamp-post outside the presidential palace in La Paz, while the army stood by and watched.

For the next six years Bolivia was ruled by an alliance of the traditional parties known as the **Concordancia**, which struggled to cope with growing popular unrest and the economic downturn which followed World War II. During this period the MNR distanced itself from its fascist roots and re-created itself as a radical populist party closely allied to the labour movement. In 1949, it launched a major civilian revolt that saw fighting in all the major provincial cities; though crushed by the army, this revolt moved the MNR closer to the FSTMB, led by **Juan Lechín**, which had adopted a revolutionary communist agenda and turned the mining camps into bastions of radical activism. Though its leaders remained in exile, in 1951 the MNR contested general elections and won outright, only for the army to intervene, making the party believe that a popular armed uprising was the only way it would return to power.

The National Revolution

The uprising which the MNR had been hoping for – the **National Revolution** – began in La Paz on April 9, 1952. MNR activists distributed arms to civilians, while the miners marched on the city and stopped army reinforcements from reaching it. After three days of fighting in which over six hundred people died, the army surrendered, and the MNR's leader, **Víctor Paz Estenssoro**, took power. However, by arming the general population and involving the workers, the MNR effectively found itself committed to a massive social revolution far beyond its original programme. The first step was the introduction of **universal suffrage** – increasing the electorate at a stroke from 200,000 to almost a million, as the indigenous majority gained the right to vote for the first time – followed by a drastic reduction in the size of the army, with hundreds of officers cashiered and the military academy closed down. In addition, the government supported the organization of a powerful national workers' confederation, the **Central Obrera Boliviana** (COB), which was controlled by the powerful miners' union and headed by its leader, Juan Lechín. The COB, which represented the MNR's most important support base, immediately pressed for further revolutionary measures. In October, the government nationalized the holdings of the three big mining companies of Patiño, Aramayo and Hochschild, bringing two-thirds of the tin-mining industry under state control. The mines were managed by a new state mining company, **COMIBOL**, which, like the mines, was to be partly administered by the workers themselves. Despite these radical measures, the MNR was wary of offending the US by appearing communist, and so promised compensation to the tin barons, as well as leaving medium-sized mines – including those owned by US companies – in private hands.

In the countryside, events quickly spiralled out of the new government's control. With no army or police to restrain them, the indigenous Aymara and Quechua campesinos began taking over *haciendas*, killing or driving out landowners and overseers, and organizing peasant syndicates and militias. Though it had never been part of their policy, the MNR was forced by events to issue a radical **Reforma Agraria** (agrarian reform) decree, under which *hacienda* lands in the highlands were given back to the indigenous peasants to be managed collectively through community organizations – the resulting indigenous federations emerged as a powerful force, and have played a major role in national politics ever since.

With the support of the newly enfranchised peasants and workers, the MNR easily won subsequent elections in 1956, with **Hernán Siles** taking over as president from Paz Estenssoro. But with the economy in crisis, the MNR leadership shied away from further revolutionary measures and turned to the US for financial aid. The US responded with loans and food aid, hoping that this support would stop Bolivia from turning towards communism, though the aid also came with strings attached, including open access for US oil corporations, an end to workers' control of the mines, a wage freeze and many other limits to government expenditure and action.

These harsh measures stabilized the economy to a degree and helped attract foreign investment, while the US loans were used to build an extensive road system, invest in health and education and drive development in the Santa Cruz region – all key aims of moderates within the MNR. Despite this, a bitter factional rift opened within the party, so that Lechín, Siles and the trade unions were eventually driven into opposition. To counterbalance this, Paz Estenssoro began rebuilding and rearming the army in an attempt to shift the balance of military power away from the workers' militias. This move was quickly to prove a terrible mistake. In 1964, Paz Estenssoro was elected for a third term with an army officer, **General René Barrientos**, as his vice-president. Within months of the vote, a military junta led by Barrientos had turned on Paz Estenssoro and ousted him from power.

Military rule

At first it was thought that the coup would be only a temporary break from civilian rule, but in fact the army was to remain in government for the next eighteen years, inspired by a self-serving belief that military rule was the only way to ensure economic development and avoid communism. Barrientos immediately moved against the left: the leaders of workers' organizations were sent into exile, wages were slashed and thousands of miners sacked; the army also occupied the mining camps to crush strike action, resulting in a major massacre of miners and their families in the Siglo XX–Catavi mine in 1967. A charismatic orator and fluent Quechua speaker, Barrientos simultaneously maintained the support of the peasant federations (who, having secured their rights to land, had become relatively conservative) by promising not to reverse the Agrarian Reform in return for their continuing loyalty – an agreement formalized in 1964 as the Pacto Militar-Campesino. This relationship underlay the failure of Argentine revolutionary **Ernesto "Che" Guevara**'s attempt to launch a continent-wide guerrilla war in Bolivia, which was crushed by Barrientos (with substantial US support) in 1967 without gaining a single peasant recruit.

Barrientos remained in control of the country until his death in a helicopter crash three years later. After a brief civilian interregnum he was replaced by General Alfredo Ovando, who was ousted just over a year later by **General Juan José Torres**. Torres sought to move military government to the left, even turning to the Soviet Union for financial aid, but was ousted within a year by right-wing army colleagues backed by the US. This latest coup brought to power **Colonel Hugo Banzer**, whose regime lasted for the next seven years – the longest presidency in more than a century. Initially, Banzer ruled in coalition with the conservative Falange Socialista Boliviana and the rump of the MNR led by Paz Estenssoro, before seizing absolute power, after which he banned all political parties and established an entirely military regime. In this he was clearly influenced by events in neighbouring Chile and Brazil, where similar military regimes had taken power (Argentina followed soon after). Like his regional counterparts – though not on the same scale – Banzer employed ruthless violence to enforce his rule, including torture, mass detention without trial and the murder of hundreds of political opponents. Even exile was no escape, as in the case of former president Juan José Torres, murdered by a death squad in Buenos Aires in 1976.

Banzer's regime coincided with unprecedented economic growth, fuelled by a long-term rise in mining production and mineral prices, and underwritten by the legacy of the MNR's investments in public education, roads and other infrastructure. Foreign investment poured into the privately owned mining sector and also into the **Santa Cruz region**, where vast areas of land remained concentrated in private hands. The region's subsequent agricultural boom, together with the exploitation of local oil and gas deposits, produced massive economic growth in the Eastern Lowlands, transforming the city of Santa Cruz into the second biggest city in the country.

Despite the success of the economy and the brutality of his regime, Banzer was unable to prevent opposition to his rule. Although he maintained land grants under the Agrarian Reform and further encouraged the colonization of lowland areas by peasants from the highlands, Banzer alienated the peasant federations by ignoring their growing demands for price controls, credit and government assistance. The Pacto Militar–Campesino ended in 1974 with the **Massacre del Valle** in the Cochabamba Valley, when the army machine-gunned protesting peasants, while the labour movement regained its strength and launched a series of strikes despite the military presence at the mines – even Banzer's traditional middle-class nationalist support was eroded by his failure to negotiate a Bolivian outlet to the sea with his Chilean counterpart General Pinochet. Under pressure from the new US president Jimmy Carter, Banzer promised to hold democratic elections, but popular discontent with his regime was by now boiling over, and in 1977, amid widening protests and strikes, Banzer prepared to step down.

The next four years saw dramatic political turmoil. In 1978 elections were held then annulled after massive fraud by Banzer's chosen successor, General Juan Pereda, who was set to lose to a left–centre alliance led by Hernán Siles. Pereda seized power, but was then overthrown by younger officers who, sensing the depth of popular opposition to military rule, promised fresh elections with no military candidate. Two elections, two brief presidencies (including that of Lidia Gueiler, the first woman president) and a further bloody coup followed, as new political groupings formed and attempted to gain electoral majorities. Finally, in elections in 1980, the centre-left coalition led by Hernán Siles emerged victorious.

Before Siles could take office, however, hardline officers launched yet another military coup, bringing to power General **Luis Garcia Meza**. Backed by a fearsome conspiracy involving the Argentine military, the Italian fascist lodge P-2, drug barons and wanted Nazi war criminals (including Klaus Barbie, the infamous "Butcher of Lyon", who conducted interrogations for the new regime), Garcia Meza presided over the most brutal and corrupt military regime in modern Bolivian history, enforced by paramilitary death squads who were used ruthlessly against opponents of the regime and funded by his government's direct involvement in the emerging international cocaine trade. But, despite its repressive measures, the extent of popular hatred against the military government, together with growing economic chaos and international disapproval, was such that it could not to survive long.

The return to democracy

Garcia Meza was deposed in an army revolt in 1981 and two years later the last military junta was forced to resign following massive protests. The recalled congress elected Hernán Siles as president, marking a **return to democratic rule** that has lasted ever since, though few would have guessed it at the time. Siles quickly fell out with his coalition partners and was unable to control the economy, which had entered a sharp decline after years of military mismanagement. With hyperinflation rampant, Siles stepped down in 1985. The largest share of the vote in the subsequent election was won by none other than Hugo Banzer, standing as head of a new right-wing party, the ADN (Alianza Democratic Nacional). This wasn't enough to secure him the presidency, however: instead, the centre-left parties allied with the MNR and elected the 77-year-old Víctor Paz Estenssoro, the central figure of the National Revolution thirty-three years before, for his fourth presidential term.

To the surprise of all, Paz Estenssoro turned his back on the traditional MNR approach and adopted the **New Economic Plan** – a raft of orthodox liberal shock policies designed to rescue the economy and combat hyperinflation. The currency was devalued, price and wage controls scrapped and government expenditure slashed, while steps were taken to dismantle the state mining corporation COMIBOL, which had become a massive drain on government finances. The inevitable strikes and protests by the miners' union followed, until in 1985 the international price of tin crashed completely and the state-run industry effectively collapsed. The government was able to sack most of the miners and the power of their union on the national political stage was broken irrevocably.

The New Economic Policy was backed by the three main parties – the MNR, Banzer's ADN and the centre-left MIR led by Jaime Paz Zamora – and maintained by subsequent governments. Although it succeeded in ending hyperinflation, its immediate effect was to plunge Bolivia into a recession which was eased only by a growing trade in the production and export of **cocaine**. Starting in the 1970s in response to rising demand in the US, highland migrants in the Yungas and in the Chapare had begun growing coca, which was then processed in secret laboratories in the Beni and flown north to Colombia and on to the US. By the 1980s, coca had become a boom industry, generating good incomes for the peasant growers (whose numbers were swelled by thousands of laid-off miners after 1985) and huge fortunes for the traffickers. Much of the money made was reinvested in legitimate businesses in Santa Cruz, fuelling economic growth in the Eastern Lowlands – at the peak of the boom, cocaine exports were estimated to exceed all Bolivia's legal exports combined, and at one stage the leading Bolivian cocaine baron, Roberto Suárez, even offered to pay off the entire national debt in return for immunity from prosecution.

The enormous wealth generated by the cocaine industry created enormous corruption at every level of Bolivian society, however, with all the major political parties having links with drug traffickers. Elections in 1989 saw the MNR win a majority of votes, but horse trading in the congress led to the third-placed candidate, MIR leader **Jaime Paz Zamora**, becoming president with the backing of the ADN. Dubbed the Patriotic Accord, this cynical alliance between two former enemies shocked many Bolivians, although it also highlighted the growing consensus between the main parties and their common belief in the need to share power and rally behind the free-market economic programme launched in 1985.

However, new political forces outside the party system were making themselves heard. By the end of the 1970s, a new generation of radical Aymara leaders had formed a powerful new national peasant union, the **CSUTCB**, which played a major role in the protests that drove Banzer, and subsequent military regimes, from power. Inspired by a new ideology of Aymara resurgence known as **Katarismo** (after the nineteenth-century rebel Tupac Katari), these peasant leaders demanded recompense for the unequal treatment meted out to indigenous peasants by successive governments and the redefining of Bolivia's national identity to reflect its indigenous majority. When the MNR returned to power in 1993, president **Gonzalo Sánchez de Lozada** recognized Bolivia multicultural society and introduced a series of far-reaching reforms, as well as inviting the moderate Katarista leader **Víctor Hugo Cárdenas** to serve as vice-president, the first time an Aymara had occupied so high an official position.

In 1997, Hugo Banzer was elected president, in coalition with the MIR and several minor parties. Under pressure from the US, Banzer made the eradication of illegal coca, the so-called **Coca Zero** campaign, a priority – a particular irony given the known links of most of his government to drug traffickers. The campaign provoked massive resistance from the well-organized campesino syndicates and an escalating death toll as the Bolivian army was sent in to clear road-blocks and tear up coca plantations. By the end of 2001 the regime was claiming Coca Zero a success, though it remains to be seen if coca production has been eliminated or just temporarily cut back. As well as the human cost, the loss of coca dollars had a knock-on effect on the Bolivian economy, which in the late 1990s slid into recession following financial crises in Brazil and Argentina. With the economy in crisis, Banzer approached the end of his democratic term in familiar style, declaring a state of emergency in 2000 and sending troops in to clear roads blocked in a combined national protest by coca-growers, Aymara peasants, and residents of Cochabamba outraged at the sale of their water supplies to foreign corporations. The following year, with protests escalating, Banzer was diagnosed with cancer (he died in 2002) and forced to retire, leaving his successor, the technocrat **Jorge Quiroga**, to serve out the rest of his party's term. Thus, Bolivians approached the elections of 2002 facing a familiar choice of political parties with little hope that any of them can solve the country's fundamental social and economic problems – though they can at least be reasonably confident that their choice will be respected by the military.

Books

There are few books published exclusively about Bolivia, and even fewer Bolivian writers ever make it into English. That said, the works listed below offer a good range of background material on Bolivian history, culture, society and the natural world. If you read Spanish, Bolivian novelists to look out for include Alcides Arguedas, Oscar Cerruto, Renato Prada Oropeza and Juan Recacochea. A fairly good range of books in English – and many more in Spanish – is available from the excellent Los Amigos del Libro chain, which has bookshops in La Paz, Cochabamba and Santa Cruz. Titles marked ⊠ are especially recommended. In most of the following reviews, publishers in the UK and US are listed (where they differ) in the form "UK publisher/US publisher"; "o/p" signifies out of print.

History and society

⭐ **Jon Lee Anderson** *Che Guevara: a Revolutionary Life* (Bantam/Grove Press). Absorbing and exhaustively researched account of Latin America's most famous guerrilla, by the journalist whose investigations led to the discovery of Che's secret grave in Vallegrande.

Brian S. Bauer and Charles Stanish *Ritual and Pilgrimage in the Ancient Andes: The Islands of the Sun and the Moon* (University of Texas Press). Richly detailed description of the archeology of the two sacred islands in Lago Titicaca and their role as a major pilgrimage centre in the Inca and pre-Inca world.

Domitila Barrios de Chungara *Let Me Speak* (o/p). Harrowing autobiographical testimony of one of the miners' wives who took part in the hunger strikes that brought an end to the Banzer military regime.

James Dunkerley *Rebellion in the Veins: Political Struggle in Bolivia 1952–82* (Verso/Schocken Books). Dense but readable academic account of the National Revolution that transformed Bolivia in 1952, and of the bitter cycles of dictatorship, repression and popular resistance that followed. Particularly good on the labyrinthine politics of the labour movement and the left.

Claire Hargreaves *Snowfields: The War on Cocaine in the Andes* (Zed/Holmes & Meier). Detailed journalistic account from the frontline of the war on drugs during the coca boom of the 1980s, based on interviews with all the main protagonists, including coca-growers, traffickers, drugs barons, politicians, police and DEA agents.

Olivia Harris *To Make the Earth Bear Fruit: Ethnographic Essays on Fertility, Work and Gender in Highland Bolivia* (ILAS). Collection of ethnographic essays exploring the culture and everyday lives of the deeply traditional *ayllus* of the northern Potosí department.

Kevin Healy *Llamas, Weavings and Organic Chocolate: Multicultural Grassroots Development in the Andes and Amazon of Bolivia* (Kellogg Institute). Intriguing portrait of nine different rural development projects – including the one which led to the renaissance of traditional weaving techniques in Sucre – which have used imaginative and culturally appropriate approaches to tackle poverty in Bolivia.

John Hemming *The Conquest of the Incas* (Papermac/Harvest Books). The authoritative account of the Spanish conquest, combining academic attention to detail and excellent use of contemporary sources with a compelling narrative style.

★ **Herbert S. Klein** *Bolivia, the Evolution of a Multi-Ethnic Society* (Oxford). The best standard English-language history of Bolivia from the arrival of early man to the present day: concise, detailed and clearly written, if a little dry.

Alan Kolata *Valley of the Spirits: a Journey into the Lost Realm of the Aymara* (Wiley). Lively account of the rise and fall of Tiwanaku by the archeologist who has done most to reveal its secrets, linking the ancient empire of the Altiplano with the culture and traditions of the contemporary Aymara.

Paul Van Lindert and Otto Verkoren *Bolivia in Focus* (Latin American Bureau). Clearly written introduction to the people, politics and culture of Bolivia, with particular emphasis on ordinary Bolivians and their struggle against poverty.

Anne Meadows *Digging Up Butch and Sundance* (Nebraska). Lively account of an adventurous quest to solve the mystery of what really happened to the infamous North American outlaws – were they really killed by police in Bolivia and buried in the bleak mining camp of San Vicente?

June Nash *We Eat the Mines and the Mines Eat Us* (Columbia). Fascinating and sensitive anthropological study of the daily lives of the miners of Potosí and the deeply rooted customs and beliefs that help them survive the tremendous hardship of the mines.

Leo Spitzer *Hotel Bolivia: The Culture of Memory in a Refuge from Nazism* (Hill & Wang). Thoughtful account of the little-known history of the thousands of Jews who fled to Bolivia with the rise of the Nazis in Europe, forming a refugee community that never felt quite at home in Bolivia, and which has since largely migrated to Israel.

★ **Steve J. Stern (ed)** *Resistance, Rebellion, and Consciousness in the Andean Peasant World* (Wisconsin). Absorbing collection of richly detailed historical essays on Quechua and Aymara insurrections and uprisings, ranging from the Great Rebellion of the late eighteenth century to the radical peasant politics of today.

Chris Taylor *The Beautiful Game: A Journey through Latin American Football* (Victor Gollanz). Entertaining account of the history of the continent's sporting obsession. The chapter on Bolivia focuses on the country's struggle to defend its right to play international fixtures at high altitude, and on the Tahuichi youth football academy in Santa Cruz, which turns street kids into major stars.

Travel

Yossi Brain *Trekking in Bolivia: A Traveller's Guide* (Cordee). Specialist trekking guide covering a good range of routes throughout Bolivia, with clear descriptions, sketch maps and useful background information and advice for anyone planning independent treks.

Yossi Brain *Bolivia: A Climbing Guide* (Cordee). A must for all serious climbers, with expert route descriptions and excellent logistical advice and information by the man

was the leading climbing guide in Bolivia.

Mark Cramer *Culture Shock! Bolivia* (Kuperard). Light-hearted and sometimes witty introduction to Bolivian culture, customs and etiquette from a US expatriate living in La Paz.

Percy Harrison Fawcett *Exploration Fawcett* (o/p). Rip-roaring account of the adventures of the eccentric British explorer who surveyed the borders of Bolivia at the height of the rubber boom in the early twentieth century. The book was published posthumously after the author disappeared looking for the mysterious civilization which he believed lay hidden somewhere deep in the Amazon.

Yossi Ginsberg *Back from Tuichi: the Harrowing Life and Death Story of Survival in the Amazon Rainforest* (Random House). First-hand account by the only survivor of a disastrous expedition by three young travellers who tried to reach Rurrenabaque overland through the forests of the Alto Madidi – this is the book that launched Rurrenabaque as a back-packer destination.

★ **Richard Gott** *Land Without Evil: Utopian Journeys in the South American Watershed* (Verso). Wonderful account of a journey through the former Jesuit mission towns of Brazil and Eastern Bolivia, interspersed with finely researched histories of the many fruitless jour-

neys and forgotten expeditions across the same region of swamp and track-less scrub made by travellers through the centuries.

Ernesto "Che" Guevara *Bolivian Diary* (Pimlico/Pathfinder Press). Published posthumously after being smuggled out of Bolivia to Cuba by a defecting general, the iconic Argentine revolutionary's description of his disastrous attempt to launch a continent-wide guerrilla war from the backwoods of Bolivia reads like the chronicle of a death foretold.

Ernesto "Che" Guevara *The Motorcycle Diaries* (Verso). Amusing account of Che's motorcycle trip through South America in the 1950s, providing an intimate portrait of a young beatnik traveller and romantic idealist undergoing some of the experiences – particularly in revolutionary Bolivia – that would later transform him into a ruthless guerrilla leader.

Wildlife and the environment

Michael Bright *Andes to Amazon: A Guide to Wild South America* (BBC). Good general introduction to the astonishing range of ecosystems and wildlife in South America, lavishly illustrated with colour photographs.

L. H. Emmons *Neotropical Rainforest Mammals: A Field Guide* (Chicago). Excellent paperback with authoritative descriptions and beautiful illustrations of over 200 species, ideal for identifying animals in the wild.

Susannah Hecht and Alexander Cockburn *The Fate of the Forest: Developers, Destroyers and Defenders of the Amazon* (Harper Collins). Comprehensive and highly readable account of the threat to the Amazon rainforest, with detailed description of the political and social conflicts that underlie the destruction of the rainforest and a heartfelt and well-argued plea for its survival.

John Kricher *A Neotropical*

Companion (Princeton University Press). Enjoyable general introduction to the flora, fauna and ecology of the tropical lowlands of South and Central America, well written and packed with detail.

Norman Myers *The Primary Source: Tropical Forests and our Future* (Norton). Compelling account by a leading expert of the most diverse and complex ecosystem in the world, the manifold ways in which humans benefit from it, and the dangers arising from its destruction.

Martin de la Pena *Illustrated Checklist: Birds of Southern South America and Antarctica* (Collins/Princeton University Press). Comprehensive field guide with descriptions and illustrations of over a thousand bird species, many of which are found in Bolivia, the serious bird-watcher's best bet given the lack of a Bolivia-specific bird book.

Bolivian music

Bolivia's music is as vibrant and as various as the myriad colours of its weaving. Much of it has a similar flavour to that of neighbouring Andean countries, evidence of the continuity of musical traditions amongst the indigenous peoples of the Andes, and there's a multitude of popular musics connected either with the various festivals which dot the year, or to key events in the agricultural calendar, from cleaning village irrigation channels to potato planting. Throughout the country, music is performed by groups ranging from exuberant bands of villagers playing panpipes of all shapes and sizes to the exuberant brass bands which march through the streets during the country's major festivals. And, inevitably, much of this music is inextricably involved with dance: if you're lucky you might see the unforgettable sight of a full squad of young women *comparsas* swirling their *pollera* skirts, with manta shawls tied around their shoulders and bowler hats on their heads

Andean traditions

The persistence of Bolivia's agricultural traditions means that musical life in most rural areas has enjoyed enormous continuity, and traditional music, bearing a direct relationship to that played in pre-Inca times, still thrives today at every kind of celebration and ritual. Because all the country's musical traditions are oral and bound to local events, music varies from one village to another – all over the Andes, villages have different ways of making and tuning instruments and composing tunes, just as each has distinctive weaving designs, ways of dressing or wearing their hats.

Panpipes and quenas

Many of Bolivia's distinctive musical **instruments** date back to pre-Hispanic times and can still be found throughout the Andean region. Perhaps the most haunting and memorable are the breathy-sounding hand-made sets of bamboo panpipes and *quena* flutes which are played by local musicians across the Altiplano. In addition, other pre-conquest Andean instruments – conch shell trumpets, shakers (using nuts for rattles), ocarinas, wind instruments and drums – are still used by groups all over the country.

Panpipes (*siku* in Aymara, *antara* in Quechua, and *zampoña* in Spanish) are ancient instruments, and archeologists have unearthed panpipes tuned to a variety of scales. While modern panpipes – played in the city or in groups with other instruments – may offer a complete scale, allowing solo performance, traditional models are played in pairs, as described by sixteenth-century Spanish chroniclers. The pipes share the melody, each playing alternate notes of the scale, so that two or more players are needed to pick out a single tune using a hocket technique. Usually one player leads and the other follows. Symbolically this demonstrates reciprocity and exchange within the community; in practice it enables players to play for a long time without getting too dizzy from over-breathing.

Played by blowing (or breathing out hard) across the top of a tube, panpipes come in various sizes. Several tubes made of bamboo reed of different length are bound together to produce a sound that can be jaunty, but also has a melancholic edge depending on tune and playing style. Many tunes have a minor, descending shape to them, and panpipe players traditionally favour dense overlapping textures and syncopated rhythms. Playing is often described as "breathy", as overblowing to produce harmonics is popular (interestingly, modern city-based groups often evoke this breathiness using special microphone techniques).

Simple **notched-end flutes**, or **quenas** (which do not have an proper mouthpiece to blow through, just a cut in the open bamboo end) are another characteristic Andean instrument found in both rural and urban areas. The most important pre-Hispanic instrument, *quenas* were traditionally made of fragile bamboo (though these days they're sometimes made from plumbers' PVC water pipes) and played in the dry season, with **tarkas** (stocky vertical flutes, like a shrill recorder made from the wood of a taco tree) taking over in the wet season – they're played solo or in groups and remain tremendously popular today. Another small Andean flute with a span of three octaves is called the **pinquillo**, also made of bamboo, and made for the main part in the Patacamaya area between Oruro and La Paz. The **moseño** is a long thin bamboo flute probably modelled on the European tranverse flute and played from the side.

Charangos

The **charango** is another characteristic Andean instrument. This small indigenous variant of the lute or mandolin was created in Bolivia in imitation of early string instruments brought by the Spanish colonizers, which indigenous musicians were taught to play in the churches. Its characteristically zingy sound was the result of the natural Andean preference for high pitches, and because its size was restricted by the fact that it was traditionally made from the shell of an armadillo (although modern charangos are now generally made of wood, as the armadillo has become increasingly rare). There are many varieties of charango: from flat-backed instruments with strident metal strings to larger instruments with round backs which are capable of deeper and richer sounds – though all are small enough to be easily carried from place to place. The charango usually has five pairs of strings, though tunings vary from place to place and from musician to musician (British ethnomusicologist Henry Stobart once identified up to twelve tunings in a single Bolivian village). Some players prefer metal strings, others nylon, to suit a variety of strumming and plucking techniques. The charango may have acquired its name from the Quechua word *ch'ajranku*, from the verb *ch'ajray*, meaning to scratch, since in early colonial times indigenous Bolivians used to refer to the way Spanish musicians played their plucked instruments as *sumaj ch'ajranku*, meaning "rich scratch".

The charango is used to play a host of different types of music and dances. In many rural areas different instruments are played in different seasons: the charango is usually played during the winter months of June and July, when its shrill sound is thought to attract the frosts essential for freezing potatoes to make *chuño* (according to Henry Stobart, in the village of Macha in northern Potosí the older farmers now complain that in places where traditions are disappearing and the young men play the charangos at the "wrong" time of the year, the weather has become mixed and the harvests poor). Elsewhere, it seems campesinos still observe the instrument's traditional seasonal use, though those in small towns and urban areas often play it all year round. In some areas, different tunings and melodies are used for different seasons.

Charangos, courtship and mermaids

In rural areas, particularly around Lago Titicaca, the charango is used by young, single men to woo and court the female of their choice, often involving the figure of a mermaid (*la sirena*), who offers supernatural aid to young men embarking on a musical pursuit of their chosen one. The ethnomusicologist Tom Turino records that most towns and villages around Titicaca claim that a mermaid lives in a nearby spring, river, lake or waterfall, and notes that new charangos are often left overnight in such places – wrapped in a piece of woven cloth, along with gifts – to be tuned and played overnight by the mermaid. Some villagers even construct the sound box in the shape of a mermaid to invest their charango with supernatural power.

When young men go courting at the weekly markets in larger villages they not only dress in their finest clothes, but also decorate their charangos in elaborate coloured ribbons. These represent the number of women their charango has supposedly conquered, thus demonstrating their manliness and the power of their instrument. At times a group of young people will get together for the ancient **circle dance** called the *Punchay kashwa* where the men form a half circle playing their charangos, facing a half circle of young women. Both groups dance and sing in bantering fashion, participants using a set syllabic and rhyming pattern so that they can quickly improvise. "Let's go walking", one might call, to a riposte such as "A devil like you makes me suspicious", or an insult like "In the back of your house there are three rotten eggs".

Fiestas

Major fiestas and other significant social events call for musical performance on a more extended scale, including large **marching bands** of brass instruments, drums or panpipes, whose predecessors captivated the Spanish in the 1500s. The drums are deep-sounding, double-headed instruments known as *bombos* or *wankaras*, originally made out of the hollowed-out trunk of a tree with the skins of a llama or goat. These marching bands exist for parades at fiestas, weddings and dances in the Altiplano and around Lago Titicaca – there's nothing more memorable than being in a village and hearing the sound of a fifty-man panpipe band approaching, especially after they've been playing for a few hours and have had a few well-earned drinks. It is perfectly normal for a whole village to come together to play as an orchestra for important events and fiestas – music is an integral part of all communal celebrations and symbolically represents the sharing and inter-dependence of Andean rural life.

Andean fusions: Los Jairas and after

The political events of the 1950s and 1960s are crucial to an understanding of recent Bolivian folk music. The 1952 Revolution led to a period of social and economic reform which accorded more rights to Bolivia's indigenous inhabitants, introducing laws which favoured Aymara and Quechua peasants, initiating agricultural reform and giving everyone the right to vote. Such reforms conferred new respect on Andean traditions, and were enthusiastically supported by many Latin American intellectuals, some of whom began wearing woven ponchos (which had previously been shunned as peasant wear) and taking a keen interest in Amerindian artefacts and culture. At the same time, rural people migrated to urban areas, bringing their languages and traditions with them. The new Bolivian administration created a division of folklore in the Ministry of Education, one of whose functions was the organization and sponsorship of traditional music festivals. Radio stations started to broadcast in Aymara and Quechua and began playing the music of these communities, often with musicians performing live in the studio, with recordings following.

Around 1965, an influential new form of Andean music emerged with **Los Jairas**, founded by Edgar "Yayo" Jofré. Jofré established the group to play at the Peña Naira in La Paz – one of a string of new urban venues where people could hear what became know as *música folklorica*. The idea was to form a quartet of charango, guitar, *quena* and *bombo* (drum): instruments that had never been played together before, having had their own traditions and seasons in the mountain villages. The quartet arranged the music to show off each of the instruments both individually and together, adapting Aymara and Quechua tunes and restructuring Andean melodies to suit an urban and European aesthetic. In addition, the group's *quena* player, the Swiss–French flautist Gilbert Favre, brought to his playing approaches learnt for the European flute, including the use of vibrato, dynamics and swooping glissandos, all of which were completely novel to the traditional Amerindian aesthetics. It was this style which became standard for urban folk music groups.

Los K'jarkas

Innumerable groups have followed the Los Jairas model. While some continue to deliver inspired arrangements of traditional tunes, others play foreign music on traditional instruments in an attempt to demonstrate these instruments' virtuosity. There are also those who use both instruments and music as the basis for new compositions. As a result, the same tune can appear in different guises under different titles in various styles. **Los K'jarkas**, from the city of Cochabamba, are one of the country's most influential and successful groups. Like many such bands, they formed around a family – the three Hermosa brothers, all bilingual in Quechua and Spanish, and all composers. In common with other Bolivian bands they retain a strong sense of national identity: the name "K'jarkas" refers to a pre-Spanish fortress, while the group's logo – a stylized anthropomorphic condor and carving from the archeological site of Tiwanaku – appeals to a pre-Columbian past and millenary culture at the heart of the Andes. Astute composition and arrangements, which take into account the multiple audiences within Bolivia itself, earned Los K'jarkas an enormous following. In 1992, when one of the brothers died, fifty thousand mourners followed his funeral procession.

K'jarkas songs are largely sentimental, conjuring up a bucolic, rural vision of beautiful maidens, alongside evocations of Pachamama (Mother Earth). Where they score at home is in large part due to their incorporation of traditional urban dance forms. They mainly use the **huayno** dance form, but also employ the hugely popular **sayas** – a dance that originated with African slaves brought to Bolivia during the seventeenth and eighteenth centuries. *Sayas* are especially popular during fiestas, when they're popularly played by the brass bands, as well as *música folklorica* groups – the K'jarkas song "Llorando se fué" is a classic example (indeed it was this song, in the version by the Paris-based group Kaoma, that launched into the global lambada craze of the 1980s).

Canto nuevo

The sound of Andean panpipes and *quenas* was also at the heart of early Chilean **nueva canción** through groups like Los Curacas, Inti Illimani and Quilapayún. Influenced by Los Jairas and the work of Chilean folklorist and composer Violeta Parra, they adopted Andean instruments and music in the 1960s and 1970s, adding extra Latin percussion, guitars and other instruments. The move neatly combined music and politics: the Andean roots asserting collective values and an unmistakable ancient indigenous identity. Their styles have fed back to Bolivia, where they have been adapted into an even richer blend of harmonized singing, with alternating solo and chorus patterns. In Bolivia, *nueva canción* was reinterpreted in the 1980s as **canto nuevo**, whose top exponent is the folk singer **Emma Junaro**, who has performed politically inspired music as well as the subtle and graceful songs of Bolivian poetess and singer, **Matilde Casazola**.

Other dances

Salsa, **cumbia**, **merengue** have come down from Central America and the Caribbean to enjoy great popularity among young Bolivians, who are now making tropical hybrids with their own dance genre. Likewise samba has come

Panpipes and ponchos in Europe and back home again

Wander round the centre of any European town from Dublin to Budapest in the summer months and you're likely to find a band of musicians clad in ponchos and busking on *quenas*, panpipes and charangos. Their music ranges from the mestizo traditions of the towns and the roots music of the villages to the more international Andean tunes. Andean music in this popular form found its way to Europe sometime in the 1950s and by the mid-1960s it had acquired a following amongst the intellectuals of Paris through the work of groups like Los Calchakis. In Paris in the 1970s Bolivia Manta, a co-operative community of Andean migrants, kept the flame alive. In the 1980s and 1990s the most familiar groups to bring this highly professional, well-arranged and extremely beautiful music to Europe were Rumillajta (City of Stone) and Awatiñas (Shepherds) – both groups continue to tour Europe, Japan and Australia. In the 1990s, a new band, Kallawaya, emerged in La Paz, its line up including ex-members of Rumillajta.

Awatiñas were brought up as Aymara speakers and a good half of their performance consists of traditional Aymara music, including festive and circle dances that form part of the regular rituals associated with the land. Awatiñas often appear with a banner saying "awatkipasipxananakasataki" (let our integrity shine) and are keen ambassadors for their culture. They compose much of their other repertoire themselves in the style of urban mestizo music.

Rumillajta perform mainly mestizo songs in beautiful arrangements, often on instruments they make themselves, although more recently they have included songs from other countries in Latin America, including some *nueva canción*. Their album *Hoja de coca* (Coca Leaf) is a good example of their music's rich textures. This is typical of overseas Andean groups – a style of playing developed to evoke the wind, rain and animals of the Andes – which you won't find in the music played back home. Rumillajta's successor group **Kallawaya** offer a superb array of original compositions, covering a gamut of moods and calling on styles which, while rooted in Bolivian traditions, are also in tune with modern folk movements in the rest of the Americas and Spain.

Awatiñas *Kullakita* (Awatiñas Records, France). Most tracks are new compositions in traditional style, arranged with this band's characteristic taste and skill.

Emma Junaro *Canta a Matilde Casazola "Mi corazón en la ciudad"* (Riverboat, UK). Junaro's beautiful voice here brings to life the mestizo songs of the great poetess, singer, guitarist and painter Matilde Casazola – sultry and nostalgic, with subtle and evocative arrangements played by an ensemble which blends piano, violin, percussion with guitars and Andean instruments.

Emma Junaro *Si De Amor Se Trata* (Tumi, UK). A passionate set of Latin American songs from Cuban to Bolivian composers showing the full range of Junaro's political committment.

Kallawaya *Shaman (Medicine Man)* (Tumi, UK). A magnificent disc by a relatively new group (four of whom were founder members of Rumillajta), with superb ensemble performances of the group's own compositions which draw on styles and traditions from the whole of the Americas.

K'jarkas *Canto a la mujer de mi pueblo* (Tumi, UK). While this tribute to Bolivian women in true male Latin fashion idealises women and their lives it contains superb examples of the genre with texts which blend the lives of women and nature. Also includes their own original song "Llorando se fue" which became the notorious Brazilian lambada.

K'jarkas *El Amor y La Libertad* (Tumi, UK). Another set of beautiful songs sung in the rich style of this group who epitomize modern folkloric styles. Vibrant harmony and vocal arrangements for passionate lyrics which tell of the experiences and dreams of today's rural Bolivians.

Mallku de los Andes *On the Wings of the Condor* (Tumi, UK). One of the most popular Andean albums ever, but none the worse for that, with the engaging sound of its panpipes and charangos smoothly and beautifully arranged.

Rumillajta *Hoja de coca* (Tumi, UK). Beautifully produced and arranged album of Bolivian music displaying a full range of styles and delivered by a fine group of musicians, many of them playing instruments they've made themselves.

Various *Bolivia Calendar Music of the Central Valley* (Chant du Monde, France). Contemporary recordings of music dating back to pre-Colombian times, including music for panpipes, flutes and drums used for Quechua rituals and ceremonies. Excellent notes, with explanations of how different instruments are used with the seasons.

Various *Charangos et guitarillas du Norte Potosí* (VDE-Gallo/AIMP, Switzerland). Spirited local recordings from north Potosí department of songs in Quechua, often sung by a woman in high tones with a man contributing a lower second part, accompanied by charango, *vihuela*, guitar or *guitarilla*. The intriguing notes explain the use of special tunings for different times of the year and explain each piece, from potato planting songs to those used in fiestas.

Various *Peru and Bolivia, The Sounds of Evolving Traditions: Central Andean Music and Festivals* (Multicultural Media, US). Lively and accessible introduction to today's sounds from both Peru and Bolivia, ranging from music performed in settings as various as private homes, clubs, fiestas and on the street, with harps, violins, drums, panpipes, and much more. Moving from Cuzco to Ayacucho, La Paz to Lima, Lago Titicaca and back to Marcapata village near Cuzco. Good notes as well.

Various *The Rough Guide to the Music of the Andes* (World Music Network, UK). A vigorous and broad range of Andean music from contemporary urban based groups – including key 1960s musicians Los K'jarkas and Ernesto Cavou, and their 1980s European travelling brethren Awatiñas and Rumillajta; soloists Emma Junaro, Jenny Cardenas and Susana Baca; seminal Chilean group Inti Illimani and new song singer Victor Jara. Plus saxes and clarinets from Picaflor de los Andes.

C

CONTEXTS | Bolivian music

from Brazil. Older dances which remain popular include the **huayño** which involves swirling partners and can be done processionally, like European country dances. Other dances include *taquiraris, tarqueada, sayas, chovena, machetero*, all of which come from ancient rituals influenced by Spanish tradition. The most popular couple dances which have persisted from those that emerged from Spanish and European folk and ballroom traditions are the waltz and notably the **cueca** (which remains the national dance in Chile), which imitates the amorous adventures and conquest of a farmyard cock and hen, with complex choreographic figures and footwork.

Jan Fairley
With thanks to Gilka Wara Céspedes in Bolivia and Henry Stobart in the UK

language

language

Language

Although **Spanish** is the language of government and commerce, nearly sixty percent of Bolivians speak one or more of the country's thirty or so indigenous languages as their mother tongue, and over ten percent speak no Spanish at all. English and some other European languages are spoken in tourist centres and well-to-do hotels and agencies, but otherwise you'll need to know a bit of Spanish to get around the country and conduct day-to-day business. The most widely spoken indigenous language is **Quechua** – the language of the Inca Empire, spoken above all in the highlands of Cochabamba, Potosí and Chuquisaca – followed by **Aymara**, which is spoken mainly in the Altiplano. Most of the country's other thirty languages are spoken by minority groups in the Amazon and the Eastern Lowlands, ranging in size from tens of thousands to just a few hundred speakers.

Technically Spanish, Quechua, Aymara and **Guaraní** (the largest of the lowland languages) are all official languages. In practice, however, unless you're trekking in particularly remote regions, you're unlikely to come across communities where you can't get by with Spanish – although learning just a few phrases of Quechua or Aymara is a good way of making a favourable impression.

f you already speak Spanish you'll have little trouble adjusting to the way the language is spoken in Bolivia, which pretty much conforms to standard textbook **Castellano**, spoken without the lisped "c" and "z". That said, it does, of course, have its own idiomatic peculiarities, one of which is the tendency to add the ending *-ito* or *-cito* to words. Technically this is a diminutive, but in fact asking for a *cervezita* won't get you a smaller beer – it's more often used to express familiarity and affection, and failing to add it onto the ends of words can seem abrupt or impolite amongst the indigenous peoples of the highlands. Bolivian Spanish is also peppered with indigenous expressions, particularly **Quechua** and **Aymara** words such as *wawa* (baby), *pampa* (plain) and *soroche* (altitude sickness); the indigenous languages also influence the somewhat unorthodox grammar and sentence structure used by many highland Bolivians when speaking Spanish. Bolivian Spanish also readily borrows from **English**, resulting in a slew of words which are regarded with horror by the Spanish themselves, such as *chequear* (to check), *parquear* (to park), *rentar* (to rent), *mitín* (meeting) and *líder* (leader) – this tendency is particularly evident in mining regions where a host of nineteenth-century English technical terms are still in use.

The fact that Spanish is a second language for most Bolivians means that they're generally patient with foreigners' attempts to speak the language and not too precious about the finer points of grammar. The slow, clear pronunciation of Bolivian Spanish (in the highlands at least) also makes it a good place to learn Spanish, and a number of Spanish (and, for that matter, Quechua and Aymara) language schools catering to foreign travellers have now opened in La Paz, Cochabamba and Sucre. In the Eastern Lowlands around Santa Cruz, Spanish is spoken with a much more relaxed, tropical drawl in which consonants often disappear at the end of words: thus *"arroz con pescado"*, for example, becomes *"arro' con pe'ca'o"*. Here, the diminutive *-ingo* is used instead of *-ito*.

Pronunciation

The rules of Spanish **pronunciation** are pretty straightforward and, once you get to know them, strictly observed. Unless there's an accent, words ending in d, l, r, and z are **stressed** on the last syllable, all others on the second last. All **vowels** are pure and short.

A somewhere between the "a" sound of back and that of father
E as in get
I as in police
O as in hot
U as in rule
C is soft before E and I, hard otherwise: *cerca* is pronounced "serka".
G works the same way, a guttural "h" sound (like the ch in loch) before E or I, a hard G elsewhere – *gigante* becomes "higante".
H is always silent.
J is the same sound as a guttural G: *jamón* is pronounced "hamon".
LL sounds like an English Y: *llama* is pronounced *"yama"*.
N is as in English unless it has a tilde over it, as with *mañana*, when it's pronounced like the "n" in onion or menu.
QU is pronounced like an English "K".
R is rolled, RR doubly so.
V sounds more like B, *vino* becoming "beano".
X is slightly softer than in English – sometimes almost SH – except between vowels in place names where it has an "H" sound – for example México (Meh-hee-ko).
Z is the same as a soft "C", so *cerveza* becomes "servesa".

On the following pages we've listed a few essential words and phrases, though if you're travelling for any length of time a dictionary or phrase book is obviously a worthwhile investment. If you're using a **dictionary**, bear in mind that in Spanish CH, LL, and Ñ count as separate letters and are listed after the Cs, Ls, and Ns respectively.

Words and phrases

Basics

Yes, No - Sí, No
Please, Thank you - Por favor, Gracias
Where, When - Dónde, Cuando
What, How much - Qué, Cuanto
Here, There - Aquí, Allí
This, That - Este, Eso
Now, Later - Ahora, Más tarde
Open, Closed - Abierto/a, Cerrado/a

With, Without - Con, Sin
Good, Bad - Buen(o)/a, Mal(o)/a
Big - Gran(de)
Small - Pequeño/a, Chico
More, Less - Más, Menos
Today, Tomorrow - Hoy, Mañana
Yesterday - Ayer

Greetings and responses

Hello, Goodbye - Hola, Adiós
Good morning - Buenos días
Good afternoon/night - Buenas
tardes/noches
See you later - Hasta luego
Sorry - Lo siento/discúlpeme
Excuse me - Con permiso/perdón
How are you? - ¿Como está (usted)?
I (don't) understand - (No) Entiendo
Not at all/You're welcome - De nada
Do you speak English? - ¿Habla (usted)
inglés?

I don't speak Spanish - (No) Hablo español
My name is . . . - Me llamo . . .
What's your name? - ¿Como se llama usted?
I am English - Soy inglés(a)
. . . American - americano(a)
. . . Australian - australiano(a)
. . . Canadian - canadiense(a)
. . . Irish - irlandés(a)
. . . Scottish - escosés(a)
. . . Welsh - galés(a)
. . . New Zealander - neozelandés(a)

Hotels and restaurants

Twin room - Una habitación doble
Room with double bed - Una habitación
matrimonial
Single room - Una habitación sencilla/simple
Private bathroom - Baño privado
Shared bathroom - Baño compartido
Hot water (all day) - Agua caliente (todo el
día)
Cold water - Agua fría
Fan - Ventilador
Air-conditioned - Aire-acondicionado
Tax - Impuesto
Mosquito net - mosquitero
Key - Llave
Check-out time - Hora de salida
Do you know. . .? - ¿Sabe. . .?
I don't know - No sé
There is (is there)? - ¿(¿)Hay(?)
Give me. . . - Deme. . .
(one like that) - (uno así)
Do you have. . .? - ¿Tiene . . .?
. . . a room - . . . una habitación

. . . with two beds/double bed - . . . con dos
camas/cama matriomonial
It's for one person - es para una persona
(two people) - (dos personas)
. . . for one night - . . . para una noche
(one week) - (una semana)
It's fine, how much is it? - ¿Está bien, cuán-
to es?
It's too expensive - Es demasiado caro
Don't you have anything cheaper? - ¿No
tiene algo más barato?
Can one. . . ? - ¿Se puede. . . ?
. . . camp (near) here? - ¿. . . acampar aqui
(cerca)?
Is there a hotel nearby? - ¿Hay un hotel aquí
cerca?
I want - Quiero
I'd like - Querría
What is there to eat? - ¿Qué hay para comer?
What's that? - ¿Qué es eso?
What's this called in Spanish? - ¿Como se
llama este en español?

Directions and transport

Bus terminal - Terminal terrestre, Terminal
de buses
Bus - Bus, flota, movilidad
Ticket - Pasaje
Seat - Asiento
Aisle - Pasillo
Window - Ventana
Luggage - Equipaje
How do I get to. . .? - Como se llega
a. . .?
Left, right, straight on - Izquierda, derecha,
derecho
Where is. . .? - ¿Dondé está. . .?

. . . the bus station - . . . el terminal de buses
. . . the train station - . . . la estación de
ferrocarriles
. . . the nearest bank - . . . el banco más
cercano
. . . the post office - . . . el correo
. . . the toilet - . . . el baño
Where does the bus to. . . leave from? -
¿De dónde sale el bus para. . .?
What time does the bus leave? - ¿A qué
hora sale el bus?
What time does the bus arrive? - ¿A qué
hora llega el bus?

How long does the journey take? – ¿Cuánto tiempo demora el viaje?
Is this the train for . . . ? – ¿Es éste el tren para . . . ?

I'd like a (return) ticket to. . . – Querría pasaje (de ida y vuelta) para. . .
What time does it leave (arrive at. . .)? – ¿A qué hora sale (llega a. . .)?

Numbers and days

1 – un/uno/una
2 – dos
3 – tres
4 – cuatro
5 – cinco
6 – seis
7 – siete
8 – ocho
9 – nueve
10 – diez
11 – once
12 – doce
13 – trece
14 – catorce
15 – quince
16 – dieciséis
20 – veinte
21 – veitiuno
30 – treinta
40 – cuarenta
50 – cincuenta
60 – sesenta

70 – setenta
80 – ochenta
90 – noventa
100 – cien(to)
101 – ciento uno
200 – doscientos
201 – doscientos uno
500 – quinientos
1000 – mil
2000 – dos mil

first – primero/a
second – segundo/a
third – tercero/a

Monday – lunes
Tuesday – martes
Wednesday – miércoles
Thursday – jueves
Friday – viernes
Saturday – sábado
Sunday – domingo

Food and drink

Basics

Aceite – Oil
Ají – Chilli
Ajo – Garlic
Almuerzo – (Set) lunch
Arroz – Rice
Azúcar – Sugar
La carta – Menu
Cena – (Set) dinner
Comida típica – Traditional food
Cuchara – Spoon
Cuchillo – Knife
La cuenta – The bill
Desayuno – Breakfast
Ensalada – Salad
Galletas – Biscuits
Harina – Flour

Hielo – Ice
Huevos – Eggs
Llajua – Chilli sauce
Mantequilla – Butter
Mermelada – Jam
Miel de Abeja – Honey
Mostaza – Mustard
Pan (integral) – (Wholemeal) bread
Pimienta negra – Black pepper
Plato – Dish
Queso – Cheese
Sal – Salt
Salsa – Sauce
Tenedeor – Fork
Vegetariano – Vegetarian

Cooking terms

A la parilla – Barbequed
A la plancha – Griddled

Ahumado – Smoked
Al ajillo – In garlic

Al horno – Oven baked	Frito – Fried
Asado – Roast	Picante – Spicy
Crudo – Raw	Relleno – Stuffed
Duro – Hard boiled	Revuelto – Scrambled
Frío – Cold	Sancochado – Boiled

Soup (*sopa*), meat (*carne*), poultry (*aves*) and fish (*pescado*)

Anticuchos – Skewered heart	Higado – Liver
Atún – Tuna (tinned)	Jamón – Ham
Bistec – Beefsteak	Lechón – Roast pork
Cangrejo – Crab	Lomo – Filet steak
Carne de cerdo/chanco – Pork	Milanesa – Breaded escalope
Carne de res – Beef	Parillada – Barbequed meat
Charque – Dried meat (usually llama)	Pato – Duck
Chicharron – Deep-fried pork	Pavo – Turkey
Chicharron de Pollo – Deep-fried	Pejerrey – Kingfish
chicken	Pollo (a la brasa) – (Spit-roasted)
Chuleta – T-bone steak	chicken
Chuleta de Cerdo – Pork chop	Riñon – Kidney
Churrasco – Minute steak	Surubí – Catfish
Conejo – Rabbit	Tocino – Bacon
Cordero – Mutton	Trucha – Trout

Vegetables (*verduras*)

Arvejas – Peas	Locoto – Chilli pepper
Camote – Sweet potato	Maíz – Maize, corn
Castaña – Brazil nut	Maní – Peanut
Cebolla – Onion	Palmito – Palm heart
Champiñon – Mushroom	Palta – Avocado
Choclo – Corn on the cob	Papa – Potato
Espinaca – Spinach	Tomate – Tomato
Frijoles – Beans	Yuca – Manioc
Habas – Broad beans	Zanahoria – Carrot
Lechuga – Lettuce	Zapallo – Pumpkin

Fruit (*frutas*)

Banano/Guineo/Plátano – Banana (the latter is also plantain)	Mango – Mango
	Manzana – Apple
Carambola – Star fruit	Maracuyá – Passionfruit
Chirimoya – Custard apple	Naranja – Orange
Durazno – Peach	Papaya – Papaya
Frutilla – Strawberry	Piña – Pineapple
Limón – Lemon	Toronja – Grapefruit
Mandarina – Mandarin	Uvas – Grapes

Snacks

Cuñapes – Yucca and cheese pastry	Salteña – Juicy meat, chicken and vegetable
Empanada – Cheese or meat pasty	pasty
Hamburguesa – Hamburger	Tostados – Toast
Humintas – Maize, cheese and raisin porridge	Tucumana – Fried meat and vegetable
wrapped in leaves	pasty
Papas fritas – Potato chips/French fries	

L

LANGUAGE | Food and drink

387

Desserts (*postres*)

Arroz con leche - Rice pudding
Ensalada de frutas - Fruit salad
Flan - Crème caramel
Gelatina - Jelly
Helado - Ice cream
Torta - Cake

Drinks (*bebidas*)

Agua - Water
Agua hervida - Boiled water
Agua mineral - Mineral water
(con gas/sin gas) - (fizzy/still)
Api - Hot, thick, sweet maize drink
Café - Coffee
Café con leche - White coffee
Cerveza - Beer
Chicha - Fermented maize beer
Chocolate - Hot chocolate

Chopp - Draft beer
Chufflay - Singani and Sprite
Jugo (de naranja) - Orange juice
Limonada - (Real) lemonade
Leche - Milk
Mate - Herbal tea
Mate de coca - Coca tea
Mate de manzanilla - Camomile tea
Refresco - Soft drink
Té - Tea

Glossary

Achachila/Apu - Powerful mountain gods or spirits believed to inhabit high Andean peaks
Adobe - Sun-dried mud brick
Aguas termales - Thermal baths, hot springs
Apacheta - Stone cairn marking mountain passes, created by travellers carrying stones on the climb up as penance and as an offering to the mountain gods
Artesanía - Traditional handicraft
Ayllu - Andean extended kinship group, roughly equivalent to a clan or tribe
Barrio - Neighbourhood, quarter, or suburb
Cabaña - Cabin
Calle - Street
Camba - Old Inca term for lowland tribes, now used as slang term for people from the Eastern Lowlands.
Camion - Lorry
Camioneta - Pick-up truck
Campesino - Peasant, literally: from the countryside.
Canoa - Dugout canoe
Caudillo - Chief, military strongman
Chaco - Cultivated clearing in the forest, also the verb for creating such clearings through slash and burn.
Challa - Ritual offering of alcohol and sweets to the mountain spirits, often carried out as a blessing for a new house or car.
Chicha - Fermented maize beer
Cholo - Mixed race or urbanized indigenous person.
Colectivo - Collective taxi

Colla - Ancient Aymara nation, now a slang term for people from the Altiplano
Cordillera - Mountain range
Criollo - "Creole": used historically to refer to a person of Spanish blood born in the American colonies.
Curandero - Healer
Encomienda - A grant of indigenous labourers to landowners during early colonial times
ENTEL - Bolivia's national telephone company
Finca - Small farm
Flota - Bus (company)
Gringo - Originally someone from the United States, now a non-derogatory term used for all white foreigners
Guardaparque - Park guard
Hacienda - Large private farm or estate
Huaca - Sacred place or object
Indígena - Used adjectivally to mean "indigenous", or as a noun to refer to an indigenous person
Junta - A ruling council; usually used to describe small groups who've staged a coup d'état
Kuraka - Indigenous nobleman in the colonial era
Lejía - Alkaline reagent used when chewing coca
Mestizo - Person of mixed Spanish and indigenous blood
Mirador - Viewpoint
Nevado - Snowcapped mountain
Pampa - Plain

Peña - Nightclub where live music is performed, often folk music

Plata - Silver; slang for money

Puna - High-altitude grassland, starting around 3000m.

Quebrada - Ravine, dried-out stream

Sala - Room or hall

Salar - Saltpan or lake.

Selva - Jungle or tropical rainforest

S/n - Used in addresses to indicate "*sin número*", or without a number.

Soroche - Altitude sickness

Tinku - Andean ritual combat

Tranca - Police road block

Wiphala - Rainbow-chequered flag used as a symbol of indigenous Andean identity

index

and small print

Index

Map entries are in **colour**

INDEX

I

Twenty years of Rough Guides

In the summer of 1981, Mark Ellingham, Rough Guides' founder, knocked out the first guide on a typewriter, with a group of friends. Mark had been travelling in Greece after university, and couldn't find a guidebook that really answered his needs.There were heavyweight cultural guides on the one hand – good on museums and classical sites but not on beaches and tavernas – and on the other hand student manuals that were so caught up with how to save money that they lost sight of the country's significance beyond its role as a place for a cool vacation. None of the guides began to address Greece as a country, with its natural and human environment, its politics and its contemporary life.

Having no urgent reason to return home, Mark decided to write his own guide. It was a guide to Greece that tried to combine some erudition and insight with a thoroughly practical approach to travellers' needs. Scrupulously researched listings of places to stay, eat and drink were matched by careful attention to detail on everything from Homer to Greek music, from classical sites to national parks and from nude beaches to monasteries. Back in London, Mark and his friends got their Rough Guide accepted by a farsighted commissioning editor at the publisher Routledge and it came out in 1982.

The Rough Guide to Greece was a student scheme that became a publishing phenomenon. The immediate success of the book – shortlisted for the Thomas Cook award – spawned a series that rapidly covered dozens of countries. The Rough Guides found a ready market among backpackers and budget travellers, but soon acquired a much broader readership that included older and less impecunious visitors. Readers relished the guides' wit and inquisitiveness as much as the enthusiastic, critical approach that acknowledges everyone wants value for money – but not at any price.

Rough Guides soon began supplementing the "rougher" information – the hostel and low-budget listings – with the kind of detail that independent-minded travellers on any budget might expect. These days, the guides – distributed worldwide by the Penguin group – include recommendations spanning the range from shoestring to luxury, and cover more than 200 destinations around the globe. Our growing team of authors, many of whom come to Rough Guides initially as outstandingly good letter-writers telling us about their travels, are spread all over the world, particularly in Europe, the USA and Australia. As well as the travel guides, Rough Guides publishes a series of dictionary phrasebooks covering two dozen major languages, an acclaimed series of music guides running the gamut from Classical to World Music, a series of music CDs in association with World Music Network, and a range of reference books on topics as diverse as the internet, pregnancy and unexplained phenomena. Visit **www.roughguides.com** to see what's cooking.

Rough Guide credits

Text editor: Gavin Thomas
Series editor: Mark Ellingham
Editorial: Martin Dunford, Jonathan Buckley, Kate Berens, Ann-Marie Shaw, Helena Smith, Judith Bamber, Orla Duane, Olivia Swift, Ruth Blackmore, Geoff Howard, Claire Saunders, Alexander Mark Rogers, Polly Thomas, Joe Staines, Richard Lim, Duncan Clark, Peter Buckley, Lucy Ratcliffe, Clifton Wilkinson, Alison Murchie, Matthew Teller, Andrew Dickson, Fran Sandham (UK); Andrew Rosenberg, Stephen Timblin, Yuki Takagaki, Richard Koss, Hunter Slaton, Julie Feiner (US)
Production: Susanne Hillen, Andy Hilliard, Link Hall, Helen Prior, Julia Bovis, Michelle Draycott, Katie Pringle, Zoë Nobes,

Rachel Holmes, Andy Turner, Michelle Bhatia
Cartography: Melissa Baker, Maxine Repath, Ed Wright, Katie Lloyd-Jones
Cover art direction: Louise Boulton
Picture research: Sharon Martins, Mark Thomas
Online: Kelly Cross, Anja Mutic-Blessing, Jennifer Gold, Audra Epstein, Suzanne Welles, Cree Lawson (US)
Finance: John Fisher, Gary Singh, Edward Downey, Mark Hall, Tim Bill
Marketing & Publicity: Richard Trillo, Niki Smith, David Wearn, Chloë Roberts, Demelza Dallow, Claire Southern (UK); Simon Carloss, David Wechsler, Kathleen Rushforth (US)
Administration: Tania Hummel, Julie Sanderson

Publishing information

This first edition published August 2002 by
Rough Guides Ltd,
62–70 Shorts Gardens, London WC2H 9AH
Penguin Putnam, Inc., 375 Hudson Street, NY 10014, USA
Distributed by the Penguin Group
Penguin Books Ltd,
80 Strand, London WC2R ORL
Penguin Putnam, Inc.,
375 Hudson Street, NY 10014, USA
Penguin Books Australia Ltd,
487 Maroondah Highway, PO Box 257,
Ringwood, Victoria 3134, Australia
Penguin Books Canada Ltd,
10 Alcorn Avenue, Toronto, Ontario,
Canada M4V 1E4
Penguin Books (NZ) Ltd,
182–190 Wairau Road, Auckland 10,
New Zealand
Typeset in Bembo and Helvetica to an original design by Henry Iles.

Printed in Italy by LegoPrint S.p.A.

© James Read 2002

No part of this book may be reproduced in any form without permission from the publisher except for the quotation of brief passages in reviews.

440pp, includes index
A catalogue record for this book is available from the British Library.

ISBN 1-85828-847-9

The publishers and authors have done their best to ensure the accuracy and currency of all the information in **The Rough Guide to Bolivia**, however, they can accept no responsibility for any loss, injury, or inconvenience sustained by any traveller as a result of information or advice contained in the guide.

Help us update

We've gone to a lot of effort to ensure that the first edition of **The Rough Guide to Bolivia** is accurate and up to date. However, things change – places get "discovered", opening hours are notoriously fickle, restaurants and rooms raise prices or lower standards. If you feel we've got it wrong or left something out, we'd like to know, and if you can remember the address, the price, the time, the phone number, so much the better.

We'll credit all contributions, and send a copy of the next edition (or any other Rough Guide if you prefer) for the best letters. Everyone who writes to us and isn't already a subscriber will receive a copy of our full-colour thrice-yearly newsletter. Please mark letters: "**Rough Guide Bolivia Update**" and send to: Rough Guides, 62–70 Shorts Gardens, London WC2H 9AH, or Rough Guides, 4th Floor, 345 Hudson St, New York, NY 10014. Or send an email to
mail@roughguides.com
Have your questions answered and tell others about your trip at
www.roughguides.atinfopop.com

Acknowledgements

James Read would like to thank Till Bruckner for writing the Takesi and Yunga Cruz trail descriptions, Jan Fairley for the section on Bolivian music, and Polly Rodger Brown for additional basics research. Thanks to all those who provided help, encouragement and support along the way including Vice-Minister of Tourism Edgar Torres Saravia, Roberto Calzadilla Sarmiento at the Bolivian Embassy in London, Sergio Ballivián, Isabel Bastos, Jazmín Caballero, David Campfens, Freddy Cespedes, Mariska de Boer, Saira Duque, Margarita Herrera, Pablo and Alejandra Montenegro, Frank Reinkens, Jorge Schmidt, Gert Van der Meijden, and the staff of all the regional tourist offices in Bolivia who provided information and advice.

Special thanks to Alistair Matthew, Richard Beckett, Sarah Shields, Stone Slade and Daniela Mercado, all of whom provided a home from home for a weary traveller as well as invaluable expertise, companionship and support. At Rough Guides, thanks to Gavin Thomas for his hard work and great patience in editing this guide and to Kate Berens for backing the project from the start. Finally, but most importantly, thanks to Emma Pearce for her support, advice and inspiration, without which this book would have been impossible.

The **editor** would also like to thank Stratigraphics for maps; Sharon Martins for the superb pictures; Susannah Wight for proofreading; Link Hall for layout; and especially Maxine, Julia and Link (again) for their supreme forbearance during the preparation of this book.

SMALL PRINT

Photo Credits

Cover
Main front picture, Salar de Uyuni © Jerry
 Callow
Front (small top image) Llama © Trip
Front (small bottom image) Tiwanaku ©
 Jamie Marshall
Back (top) Potosí © Trip
Back (lower) Devil's Molar, near La Paz ©
 Jamie Marshall

Colour introduction
Two men on bench, Tarabuco © Eric Lawrie
Reserva Eduardo Avaroa © Eric Lawrie
Market, Sorata © Jerry Callow
Drinks stall, Copacabana © Eric Lawrie
Altiplano © C. Bowman/Robert Harding
Llamas, Cordillera Real © Kimball
 Morrison/South America Pictures
Isla del Pescado, Salar de Uyuni © Eric
 Lawrie
Pampas © Robert Harding
Day of the Dead amongst the Chipaya © Eric
 Lawrie
Street coca-vendor © Victor
 Englebert/Robert Harding
Ski lodge, Chacaltaya © Tony
 Morrison/South America Pictures

Things not to miss
1. Morenadas, Oruro Carnaval © Eric Lawrie
2. Mercado de Hechicería © Eric Lawrie
3. La Paz © Robert Frerck/Robert Harding
4. Slow boat on the Río Mamoré © Jerry
 Callow
5. Tiwanaku © Eric Lawrie
6. Ritual combat at the *tinku* at Macha © Eric
 Lawrie
7. Hamlet near Charazani, Cordillera
 Apolobamba © Eric Lawrie
8. Goat herd, near Tupiza © Eric Lawrie
9. Pots of *chicha cochabambina*, Cotoca
 market © Tony Morrison/South America
 Pictures
10. Dinosaur footprints at Cal Orka © Kathy
 Jarvis/South America Pictures
11. Huayna Potosí and the Cordillera Real ©
 Eric Lawrie
12. Pink river dolphin © Todd Pusser/BBC
 Wild
13. Fiesta de San Felipe, Amarete © Eric
 Lawrie

14. Isla del Sol © Fiona Good/South America
 Pictures
15. Sorata © Jerry Callow
16. Buying *salteñas* from *Chola's* trolley ©
 Tony Morrison/South America Pictures
17. Rooftops, Potosí © Jerry Callow
18. Condor © Tony Morrison/South America
 Pictures
19. Choro Trail near La Cumbre © Tony
 Morrison/South America Pictures
20. Aymara New Year © Jerry Callow
21. Cha'lla © Jerry Callow/PANOS
22. Andean textiles © Eric Lawrie
23. The Coroico highway © Kimball
 Morrison/South America Pictures
24. Ekeko figure, Feria de Alasitas © Tony
 Morrison/South America Pictures
25. Miners at work, Cerro Rico © Jerry
 Callow
26. Laguna Colorada, Reserva de Fauna
 Andina Eduardo Avaroa © Eric Lawrie
27. Catedral de Concepción, Concepción ©
 Tony Morrison/South America Pictures
28. Colonial architecture, Sucre © Jerry
 Callow
29. Salt shapes, Salar de Uyuni © Eric Lawrie
30. Parque Nacional Noel Kempff Mercado ©
 Jerry Callow

Black and white photos
La Paz © Jerry Callow (p.54)
Market scene, La Paz © Eric Lawrie (p.72)
Totora reed boats, Huatahata © Tony
 Morrison/South America Pictures (p.102)
Cathedral, Copacabana © Christopher
 Rennie/Robert Harding (p.107)
Church at Lagunillas, with Volcán Payachata
 behind © Eric Lawrie (p.150)
Arbol de Piedra, Reserva Eduardo Avaroa ©
 Eric Lawrie (p.196)
Plaza 25 de Mayo, Sucre © Robert Harding
 (p.220)
Palacio de los Portales, Cochabamba © Tony
 Morrison/South America Pictures (p.245)
Two-toed sloth © Tony Morrison/South
 America Pictures (p.264)
Capybara © Jerry Callow (p.304)
Sailing down the Río Orton © Tony
 Morrison/South America Pictures (p.316)
Parrots in flight © Jerry Callow/PANOS
 (p.338)

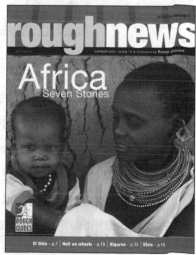

Visit us online
roughguides.com

Information on over 25,000 destinations around the world

- **Read** Rough Guides' trusted travel info
- **Share** journals, photos and travel advice with other readers
- Get exclusive Rough Guide **discounts** and travel **deals**
- Earn membership points every time you contribute to the
  Rough Guide **community** and get **free** books, flights and trips
- Browse thousands of CD reviews and artists in our **music** area

around the world

Alaska ★ Algarve ★ Amsterdam ★ Andalucía ★ Antigua & Barbuda ★ Argentina ★ Auckland Restaurants ★ Australia ★ Austria ★ Bahamas ★ Bali & Lombok ★ Bangkok ★ Barbados ★ Barcelona ★ Beijing ★ Belgium & Luxembourg ★ Belize ★ Berlin ★ Big Island of Hawaii ★ Bolivia ★ Boston ★ Brazil ★ Britain ★ Brittany & Normandy ★ Bruges & Ghent ★ Brussels ★ Budapest ★ Bulgaria ★ California ★ Cambodia ★ Canada ★ Cape Town ★ The Caribbean ★ Central America ★ Chile ★ China ★ Copenhagen ★ Corsica ★ Costa Brava ★ Costa Rica ★ Crete ★ Croatia ★ Cuba ★ Cyprus ★ Czech & Slovak Republics ★ Devon & Cornwall ★ Dodecanese & East Aegean ★ Dominican Republic ★ The Dordogne & the Lot ★ Dublin ★ Ecuador ★ Edinburgh ★ Egypt ★ England ★ Europe ★ First-time Asia ★ First-time Europe ★ Florence ★ Florida ★ France ★ French Hotels & Restaurants ★ Gay & Lesbian Australia ★ Germany ★ Goa ★ Greece ★ Greek Islands ★ Guatemala ★ Hawaii ★ Holland ★ Hong Kong & Macau ★ Honolulu ★ Hungary ★ Ibiza & Formentera ★ Iceland ★ India ★ Indonesia ★ Ionian Islands ★ Ireland ★ Israel & the Palestinian Territories ★ Italy ★ Jamaica ★ Japan ★ Jerusalem ★ Jordan ★ Kenya ★ The Lake District ★ Languedoc & Roussillon ★ Laos ★ Las Vegas ★ Lisbon ★ London ★

in twenty years

London Mini Guide ★ London Restaurants ★ Los Angeles ★ Madeira ★ Madrid ★ Malaysia, Singapore & Brunei ★ Mallorca ★ Malta & Gozo ★ Maui ★ Maya World ★ Melbourne ★ Menorca ★ Mexico ★ Miami & the Florida Keys ★ Montréal ★ Morocco ★ Moscow ★ Nepal ★ New England ★ New Orleans ★ New York City ★ New York Mini Guide ★ New York Restaurants ★ New Zealand ★ Norway ★ Pacific Northwest ★ Paris ★ Paris Mini Guide ★ Peru ★ Poland ★ Portugal ★ Prague ★ Provence & the Côte d'Azur ★ Pyrenees ★ The Rocky Mountains ★ Romania ★ Rome ★ San Francisco ★ San Francisco Restaurants ★ Sardinia ★ Scandinavia ★ Scotland ★ Scottish Highlands & Islands ★ Seattle ★ Sicily ★ Singapore ★ South Africa, Lesotho & Swaziland ★ South India ★ Southeast Asia ★ Southwest USA ★ Spain ★ St Lucia ★ St Petersburg ★ Sweden ★ Switzerland ★ Sydney ★ Syria ★ Tanzania ★ Tenerife and La Gomera ★ Thailand ★ Thailand's Beaches & Islands ★ Tokyo ★ Toronto ★ Travel Health ★ Trinidad & Tobago ★ Tunisia ★ Turkey ★ Tuscany & Umbria ★ USA ★ Vancouver ★ Venice & the Veneto ★ Vienna ★ Vietnam ★ Wales ★ Washington DC ★ West Africa ★ Women Travel ★ Yosemite ★ Zanzibar ★ Zimbabwe

also look out for our maps, phrasebooks, music guides and reference books

The ideas expressed in this code were developed by and for independent travellers.

Learn About The Country You're Visiting

Start enjoying your travels before you leave by tapping into as many sources of information as you can.

The Cost Of Your Holiday

Think about where your money goes - be fair and realistic about how cheaply you travel. Try and put money into local peoples' hands; drink local beer or fruit juice rather than imported brands and stay in locally owned accommodation. Haggle with humour and not aggressively. Pay what something is worth to you and remember how wealthy you are compared to local people.

Embrace The Local Culture

Open your mind to new cultures and traditions - it will transform your experience. Think carefully about what's appropriate in terms of your clothes and the way you behave. You'll earn respect and be more readily welcomed by local people. Respect local laws and attitudes towards drugs and alcohol that vary in different countries and communities. Think about the impact you could have on them.

Exploring The World – The Travellers' Code

Being sensitive to these ideas means getting more out of your travels - and giving more back to the people you meet and the places you visit.

Minimise Your Environmental Impact

Think about what happens to your rubbish - take biodegradable products and a water filter bottle. Be sensitive to limited resources like water, fuel and electricity. Help preserve local wildlife and habitats by respecting local rules and regulations, such as sticking to footpaths and not standing on coral.

Don't Rely On Guidebooks

Use your guidebook as a starting point, not the only source of information. Talk to local people, then discover your own adventure!

Be Discreet With Photography

Don't treat people as part of the landscape, they may not want their picture taken. Ask first and respect their wishes.

We work with people the world over to promote tourism that benefits their communities, but we can only carry on our work with the support of people like you. For membership details or to find out how to make your travels work for local people and the environment, visit our website.

www.tourismconcern.org.uk

TourismConcer

Campaigning for Ethical and Fairly Traded Tou

HOMESICK?

Image courtesy of Jamie Marshall - www.tribaleye.co.uk

Floods in Mozambique, earthquake in India, war in Afghanistan....
every day people are forced to leave their homes due to war or disaster.

Medair, specialising in emergency humanitarian aid, has helped thousands
of people in crisis situations rebuild their homes and their lives,
regardless of race, sex, religion or age.

But with Medair it's life that counts, not statistics.

We're committed to making our assistance as personal as possible.
That's why our programmes are made to suit individual needs, from
reconstruction, food-distribution and improving water supplies to
healthcare, health education and trauma counselling.

Join us on the frontline
and see how you can help
by visiting www.medair.org
or e-mailing info@medair.org.uk

Medair UK, Willow House, 17-23 Willow Place
London SW1P 7JH

Tel: +44 (0) 20 7802 5533
Fax: +44 (0) 20 7802 5501

With thanks to Rough Guides for sponsoring this advertisement.